Understanding Social Welfare

──── Fifth Edition ────

Ralph Dolgoff
University of Maryland, Baltimore

Donald Feldstein
Council of Jewish Federations

Allyn and Bacon

BOSTON ■ LONDON ■ TORONTO ■ SYDNEY ■ TOKYO ■ SINGAPORE

Editor-in-Chief, Social Sciences: Karen Hansen
Senior Series Editor: Judy Fifer
Marketing Manager: Jackie Aaron
Full Service Production Manager: Patti Brecht
Project Coordination, Text Design, and Electronic Page Makeup: UG / GGS Information Services, Inc.

and AB

Library of Congress Cataloging-in-Publication Data

Dolgoff, Ralph.
    Understanding social welfare / Ralph Dolgoff, Donald Feldstein.—
5th ed.
        p.   cm
    Includes bibliographical references and index.
    ISBN 0-8013-3036-X
    1. Public welfare—United States.   2. Social service—United States.
3. United States—Social policy.   I. Feldstein, Donald.   II. Title.
HV95.D64   1999
361.973—dc21   99-18226
                                                                CIP

Printed in the United States of America

10 9 8 7 6 5 4 3 2 1   DOH   03 02 01 00 99

C O N T E N T S

CHAPTER THREE

Social Values and Social Welfare: England From the Middle Ages Onward   37

CHAPTER FOUR

Social Values and Social Welfare: The American Experience I   61

CHAPTER FIVE

America, Poverty, Two Paths: The American Experience II   88

CHAPTER SIX

Concepts for Social Welfare   111

CHAPTER SEVEN

Examining a Social Welfare Program: Structural Components, Alternative Program Characteristics, and Evaluation   136

CHAPTER EIGHT

The Welfare Society and Its Clients   160

CHAPTER NINE

Current Social Welfare Programs—Economic Security   191

CHAPTER TEN

Social Welfare Programs: Sustaining the Quality of Life   232

CHAPTER ELEVEN

Nonprofit and Private Social Welfare   279

CHAPTER TWELVE

Social Work: The Emergence of a Profession   301

CHAPTER THIRTEEN

Social Work: Functions, Context, and Issues   323

CHAPTER FOURTEEN

Social Trends Affecting Social Welfare   343

CHAPTER FIFTEEN

Alternative Programs to Meet Social Welfare Needs   367

APPENDIX

Sources of Information   401

P R E F A C E

This electronically connected world is turbulent and full of conflicting forces, all of which impact on economic growth, employment, financial stability, taxation, and, ultimately, social welfare. In the United States, the political scene is uncertain, and a struggle continues to determine the respective roles and responsibilities of government, individuals, and families. Social policies and programs developed over generations are being debated at every level of government. The decisions that have to be made will be made in the context of this changing and agitated world. Government is viewed by many people as *the* problem. Others suggest Americans want people to pull themselves "up by their bootstraps" but need government's help. All these and additional factors influence the shape social welfare will take as we move into the 21st century. American social welfare must be understood in this dynamic context.

We have attempted in this book to achieve two sometimes mutually exclusive objectives. First, we have written a book with a point of view—one that examines social welfare issues critically, focuses on concepts, and invites challenge and alternative interpretations. Second, we have tried to produce a usable textbook, covering detail and fact in an organized manner, useful for all those concerned with social welfare and human services in our society.

The success of our work can only be judged by individual readers, whom we hope will be challenged to reach their own conclusions about the issues discussed. We will have succeeded if readers attain knowledge and understanding to aid them in decision making both as professionals and as informed and participating citizens.

We are grateful to a number of persons whose reactions and advice have helped us to improve the book: Ana Alvarez, Aaron Dolgoff, Eliana Dolgoff, William Jackson Jr., Heejung Koh, Richard Larson, Margie Simon, and Dr. Raju Varghese. We also want to express our appreciation to Bernetta Hux and Tammy Derry for their assistance and to Pam Rand and Beverly Bowles, librarians, as well as to the Health

Sciences Library of the University of Maryland, Baltimore, and the Milton S. Eisenhower Library of the Johns Hopkins University.

This revised edition reflects change in the social welfare system through the publishing process. In addition to a complete updating, we have tried to anticipate the issues and proposed solutions to various social problems. We have maintained the main theme and focus on the impact of societal structure and change on the nature of peoples' needs and problems. In this edition we have added or augmented material on the following:

- The changed old/new social policy environment;
- An updated review of social welfare policies and programs;
- Managed care and its impact on social welfare and social work;
- Welfare reform and initial findings for the Temporary Assistance for Needy Families program (TANF);
- The future options for Social Security;
- Up-to-date income, poverty, and wealth data;
- Immigration and social work;
- Technology, advocacy, and social action;
- The aging and long-term home health care; and
- Structural-functional and conflict theories.

In addition, we have

- Expanded sources of electronic information;
- Expanded information on Latinos and Native Americans, as well as gays and lesbians;
- Contrasted evolutions of public assistance and social security; and
- Described socio-economic alternative futures.

To communicate with the authors, contact Ralph Dolgoff at rdolgoff@ssw. umaryland.edu. We will respond to your comments as soon as possible.

We are appreciative of the support our families have provided. Special thanks is due to Sylvia Dolgoff, who at various stages has contributed in many ways.

Finally, we want to express our deep appreciation to our students, whom we have taught and from whom we have learned.

Many people have contributed to the development of this book, including our reviewers: Dr. Patricia Brownell, Fordham University; Dr. Anne Botsford, Marist College; Dr. Margaret G. Wilkerson, Arkansas Tech University; Dr. Mark Hanna, California State University, Fresno; Prof. Stewart Epstein, Keuka College; Prof. Carol M. Boyd, Delta State University; Dr. Patricia A.Washington, Florida Gulf Coast University. Nonetheless, the book is ours and we are responsible for its limitations. On each rereading we, as do all authors, become aware of things we should have written or written better. But we hope we have come close to the expression of the aims with which we started and that our readers find this book stimulating and helpful.

CHAPTER ONE

Socio-Economic Structure, Human Needs, and Mutual Responsibility

Competition . . . is a law of nature. . . . if we try to amend it, there is only one way in which we can do it. We can take from the better and give to the worse. We can deflect the penalties of those who have done ill and throw them on those who have done better. We can take the rewards from those who have done better and give them to those who have done worse. We shall thus lessen the inequalities. We shall favor the survival of the unfittest, and we shall accomplish this by destroying liberty. Let it be understood that we cannot go outside of this alternative: liberty, inequality, survival of the fittest, not-liberty, equality, survival of the unfittest.
—*William Graham Sumner*[1]

OVERVIEW

Embedded in Sumner's statement is a deep American belief: Those who have done well materially are better than those who have done not so well. Those who have prospered have done so because of their own individual talents and efforts. The corollary is that those who have not done well have done so because of some personal defect. They are immoral, lazy, unmotivated, or not so bright. Poor people, for example, are individually responsible for their poverty. According to this perspective, each person is responsible for whatever situation in which he or she finds him- or herself. The most important values are self-reliance and the avoidance of dependence. One should not be a burden to family, others, or—especially—society. Essentially, those who are disadvantaged, victimized, poor, or disabled somehow are responsible for their condition; if they were better or more adequate people, they would not be in a dependent position.

We begin this book by noting this perspective because it has had a profound and continuing impact on the nature of social welfare in the United States and reemerged as a widespread force during the 1980s and 1990s. However, this emphasis on individual responsibility is not the only driving force in U.S. social welfare,

1

which is influenced by a mixture of motives rather than one unified, impelling force. Altruism, a refusal to ignore the suffering of others, a sense of fairness, and a concern for mutual aid are also viable American values. Social welfare also functions to meet the maintenance needs of society by preventing instability and providing for social continuity. In part, one's views of the functions of social welfare depend on one's personal perspective, but in reality the U.S. social welfare scene is marked by ambivalent motivations rather than one pure and straightforward intention.

The values of a society, even implicit values, can influence the nature of its social welfare system. What are the roots and several manifestations of social welfare in U.S. society? What are the components of American tendencies to focus on individual responsibility as a major influence on social welfare? How are these and other values expressed in social welfare? And what are the biases of the authors that will inform this volume?

THE IMPACT OF SOCIAL AND ECONOMIC STRUCTURES

Many Americans and most students and practitioners in the helping professions have been socialized to think in a certain way—primarily to understand case situations in individual, family, and group terms, often minimizing the effects of the multiple factors and levels of the social environment on human behaviors and lives.

In this book, in addition to individual responsibility and effort, we want to consider the impact of social and economic structures on us all. Although this approach is not completely explanatory, it does provide a contrasting view and offers other ways of understanding what happens to people.

One way of understanding the difference between individual and structural causes is provided by C. Wright Mills, who defined "private troubles" and "public issues":

> _Troubles_ occur within the character of the individual and within the range of his immediate relations with others; they have to do with his self and with those limited areas of social life of which he is directly and personally aware.

Whereas troubles refer to one's immediate milieu and, to some extent, to one's willful activity, they are essentially private matters. On the other hand, _issues_

> have to do with matters that transcend these local environments of the individual and the range of his inner life. They have to do with the organization of many milieux into the institutions of an historical society as a whole, with the ways in which various milieux overlap and interpenetrate to form the larger structure of social and historical life.

A public issue is a public matter, an economic and political crisis in institutional arrangements. If a few people are unemployed because they resent authority and have difficulty with supervisors, it is a private matter. However, if thousands or millions are unemployed because of the nature of the structure of employment opportunities, their difficulties have origins far beyond their personal, individual control, despite their strenuous efforts.[2]

The following studies illustrate that many social problems are associated with, influenced by, even caused by social and economic structural factors:

1. The stress and strain of the 1989–1990 recession had important health and other consequences: more fatal heart attacks and strokes, more homicides, more suicides, increased cirrhosis deaths, mental illness, arrests, and imprisonments. There were loss of income, increased unemployment, and accelerated business failures, all of which can produce family stress, job anxiety, and altered behavior. Economic policy decisions can be assumed to have profound effects on health and social behaviors.[3]

2. Infant mortality is a sensitive indicator of children's health and measures the capacity to ensure healthy births and adequate health care during the first year of life. In 1995, twenty-two industrialized nations had lower infant mortality rates than the United States. Other health problems affecting American children include provision of prenatal care, births to teenaged mothers, AIDS among children, outbreaks of preventable childhood diseases, oral health problems, and sexually transmitted diseases.[4]

3. Income is an important predictor of mortality. Persistent low income is a powerful predictor of mortality risk, and health disadvantage is particularly pronounced at lower income levels.[5]

4. Studies have shown that those who are laid off when plants close become vulnerable to health and psychological difficulties, as well as family tensions and conflict. Beyond the loss of income, benefits are lost that helped to sustain good nutrition and health care, and there are also social losses such as meaningful work, self-esteem, social ties, and an expected routine of getting up and going to work.[6]

5. Studies have found large percentages of child-abusing fathers and stepfathers were unemployed during the year and/or at the time they were abusers. Reports show that both the number and severity of child-abuse cases increase during recessions, with the greatest number of abuse problems found in counties with the highest unemployment rates. Family service agencies found that family violence increased during a recession, and case studies document an upsurge in the use of child welfare services following the closing of industrial plants. Recessions are stressful for those maintaining continuous employment *and* for those who lose their jobs.[7]

Unemployment and poverty are inextricably tied to the structure of the economy. Among these structural factors are a shift from a goods-producing, manufacturing economy to service-producing industries; the polarization of the labor market into low-wage and high-wage sectors; increasing technology; and the dispersal of manufacturing and other jobs to suburban and overseas locations. Although these structural factors—such as the nature of the job market, the job preparation of potential workers, geographic factors, and racial and other discriminations—affect everyone in our society, they impact differentially on different groups, as we shall see in more detail in chapter 8.[8] For example, the structure of jobs and wages has changed. Many industries require more able and highly skilled workers. Such workers are generally in short supply, bidding up their wages and increasing the gap between their incomes and those of workers with lower educational levels and skills.[9]

One result of these changes, especially the decline in the work options of low-skilled workers, is a decrease of work in many inner-city neighborhoods. Wage inequality affects both men and women, but declining employment opportunities have been concentrated among low-skilled men. The proportion of men who dropped out of the labor force was more than twice as high in the late 1980s as it had been in the late 1960s. A sharp drop in real wages (earnings adjusted for inflation) accompanied increases in unemployment among low-income workers.

Opportunities for job advancement by low-skilled workers have decreased. Nonetheless, there is a paradox. Unemployment overall has decreased, and many workers hold more than one job. Yet, men well below retirement age are working less than they did two decades ago. The proportion of male workers (ages 22 to 58) who worked in a given decade full-time, year-round in at least eight of the ten years decreased almost 10 percent from the 1970s to the 1980s. Those who face the most difficulty are those poorly educated, school dropouts, and minorities.[10]

Finally, there is a concern that inflation be kept under control. However, doing so has accompanying costs. Productive output is lost, jobs are lost, business opportunities are bypassed, and tax receipts are lost. Incomes end up lower than they would have been without these efforts to forestall or ameliorate inflationary threats in the economy.

We will return to these issues and concepts in later chapters. For now we need to recognize the impact of structural factors such as business cycles; the shifts in the number, types, and degrees of skilled labor required by various industries; international trade and competition; and technological change. Additional significant factors are discrimination, immigration, changes in the age and educational composition of the work force, and unionization and the lack of it, as well as changes in the political climate.[11]

DEFINING SOCIAL WELFARE AND SOCIAL WORK

Social welfare is referred to throughout this book. What is social welfare, and what do we mean by this term? The definition is not simple and is discussed at some length at the beginning of chapter 6. But the reader is entitled to a brief definition early on. For reasons explained in chapter 6, we define *social welfare* as follows: *all social interventions intended to enhance or maintain the social functioning of human beings*. We limit our consideration, however, to those parts of the broadest social welfare system that are not clearly the domain or territory of other fields or disciplines such as education, police, and fire services.

Social work is discussed in chapters 12 and 13, where the emergence of the profession, its current functions, the context within which it operates, and other selected issues are examined. At this point, however, it is important that the reader understand that *social work* is a *professional occupation that delivers social welfare services*.[12] Although social work serves preponderantly in the social welfare societal institution, social workers also deliver services in a large number of societal institutions that are not the social welfare institution per se, including business and industry, military defense, and criminal justice, as well as educational, health, and religious institutions, among others. The reader should keep this distinction in mind, differentiating the societal institution of social welfare from the profession of social work.

Our aim in this book is to examine U.S. social welfare and social work. We are mindful of the interconnections and interdependence of U.S. society, in all its aspects, with other parts of the world. The United States in contemporary times is affected by developments in many nations and regions far from our shores. Although the world is a series of societal and ecological interconnections, and these systemic relationships impact on the U.S. economy and general culture—including social welfare, both directly and indirectly—our priority focus will be social welfare and social work within the U.S. context.

THE AMERICAN MYTH OF THE HERO

For more than five centuries people have come to America: the secular Zion, the golden nation, the land of possibilities. Leaving behind families, traditions, and the familiar, people set out for America. Although we note these migrations to a land of dangers and dreams, there was—of course—a major exception. In the case of African Americans, they were forcibly taken to this land.

From the Puritans seeking religious freedom in Massachusetts, to the debtors escaping imprisonment in Georgia, the earliest American settlers were a mixture of indentured persons, craft workers, paupers, businesspeople, sailors, artisans, and adventurers. They were seeking to escape, and they were searching for new horizons beyond the ocean and beyond the constraints of more developed societies.

The pioneers were seen as rugged individualists, self-reliant and independent. The reality was quite different from the myth. A communitarian spirit was needed in frontier territories and pioneering times. Settlements developed, and people became interdependent. In *The Americans*, Daniel Boorstin described the reality this way:

> But, of all the American myths, none is stronger than that of the loner moving West across the land. Without having thought much about why, we have taken for granted that, on landing, the colonial traveler no longer needed his community. The pioneering spirit, we are often told, is a synonym for "individualism." The courage to move to new places and to try new things is supposed to be the same as the courage to go it alone, to focus exclusively and intensively and enterprisingly on oneself. . . . There was, of course, the occasional lone traveler and individual explorer. . . . In history, even the great explorer has been the man who drew others to a common purpose, in the face of unpredictable hardships. . . . To cross the wild continent safely, one had to travel with a group . . . When American ways were taking shape, many, perhaps most, of the people who were the first to settle at a distance from the protected boundaries of the Atlantic seaboard, traveled in groups.[13]

Even the early U.S. government aided the individual with mechanisms similar to those used today. Puritan communities paid a salaried town doctor in a sort of community-supported medicine. New Englanders attempted to regulate wages, prices, and interest rates. Laws were passed to ensure the quality of workmanship and goods. Public officials scrutinized the regulation of weights and measures, as well as ferries, mills, and inns.[14] In fact, the government during early U.S. history played an affirmative role in the economy in regard to credit, a national bank, currency and coinage, public lands, and other matters. During Jefferson's first administration, the Cumberland National Road linked the eastern seaboard with the Ohio Valley. The government also owned stock in the Chesapeake and Delaware Canal Co., as well as in the Dismal Swamp Co. of Virginia and the Chesapeake and Ohio Canal Co. These governmental interventions had many purposes, chief among them the encouragement of travel and trade.[15]

The complexity and specialization of modern society makes interdependence greater and more necessary than ever. Each of us can perform only a small fraction of the functions necessary to help ourselves and society to survive. The astronauts are heroic figures even while they are excellent symbols of the necessary interdependence of "heroes." They need each other's skills; they are dependent on teams of scientists and technicians. Even so, we are left with Americans still idealizing images of self-sufficient persons.

The American idealized myth includes the following:

1. The best people are rugged individualists who are physically strong, psychologically independent, and able to flourish without help.
2. "Making it" is what counts and is to be respected and admired.
3. Everything is possible. Those who try hard enough, no matter how humble their beginnings, can "make it."
4. Humans strive for material gain. If it were not for the carrot of material gain or the stick of hunger and deprivation, motivation for work might disappear. Other motives are shadowy, unreal, or idealistic.
5. The corollary of all the above is that those who fail to "make it" are at least incompetent, and perhaps even lazy and immoral (synonyms).

Although the entire mythology has created some of the strains in American life, it is this final corollary that places personal responsibility and independence at the heart of American values. Somehow, if things do not go well or if one fails, then one is to blame. Other cultures have extolled ambition and progress. It is the combination of this striving philosophy with the corollary that people determine both their successes and failures that makes American society particularly unusual. Not all Americans accept the mythology. At different periods it is stronger or weaker. For example, during the Great Depression of the 1930s people felt simultaneously that they were inadequate and that the social system had failed them.[16] As Americans experience a tension between individualistic and communitarian values, there are trends away from and toward this American mythology. These trends are discussed in chapter 14, because these views continue to have profound effects on life in the United States, particularly regarding social welfare.

This mythology needed nurturing to grow and develop, and the United States supplied it. The United States has been a land of opportunity to a degree unmatched by other societies. There was and continues to be more physical and social mobility in the United States than elsewhere. One price of that mobility has been the assumption that the nonmobile are inadequate.

According to the historian Frederick Jackson Turner, the idea of a constant frontier is central to the American spirit, and it was only in the last decade of the nineteenth century that the frontier was officially declared closed. Illustrative of this idea was the young and vigorous Kennedy national administration that in 1960 named its program "The New Frontier." The idea of a constant frontier stays before the United States in several forms: the reach to fulfill the American dream, to fulfill the potential of the nation and all its citizens, to explore space, to develop the contributions of science and technology for human betterment, and to create throughout our urban centers, suburbs, and rural areas "user-friendly" habitats for all citizens. However, even where agreement exists as to the goals, as we shall see later, there is much and intense disagreement about how to achieve these goals.

Intellectual, scientific, and religious currents all fed the mythology. In chapter 2 we discuss the relationship between the views of human nature in any society and its welfare approach and programs, but it should be noted here that the ideology of industrialism, the development of the Protestant ethic (particularly the Calvinist strain), and social Darwinism each contributed to our placing priority on individual responsibility.

Industrialism drove people from their traditional homes and pursuits to cities and encouraged mobility, material gain, and competition. Industrialism resulted in the amassing of capital, something frowned on in more traditional Christian theology. Industrialism demanded a large pool of low-paid working people. Religion and science generated a rationale and justification for these developments. The element of Calvinist philosophy that concerns us here is that the successful and wealthy are seen as God's elect, whom God has chosen to reward. We need not, therefore, overly pity the poor for receiving their just desserts at the hand of God, nor should we hate the rich, who are God's elect.

Additional support came from economics and evolutionary theory. The theories of laissez-faire capitalism suggested that society functions best and that the common good is furthered most when there is constrained governmental interference in the affairs of the market. The market is a grand anonymous stage in which each commodity finds its own value. If labor is underpaid, this reflects its market value. Any attempt to interfere by regulation lessens the ultimate good to society.[17] Social scientists went further. They took the ideas of natural selection developed by Charles Darwin and created a social equivalent. The theory of natural selection, most simply stated, is that in nature the most fit survive and the least fit die. Similarly, according to this view, in society, in the free market (nature), there is a natural tendency for the best (most fit) to succeed, and any attempt to interfere with this "natural selection" only perpetuates and gives favor to those who can contribute least.

According to these views, social welfare measures, which help the weak, only weaken society. The kindest approach, in the long run, is to let the weak fall. Laissez-faire philosophers acknowledged the value of charity, but more to foster uplifting the soul of the philanthropist than for aiding the victim. President Herbert Hoover claimed that enterprise builds society while charity builds character.

All of these ideas and forces had their impact in shaping the American myth. They were particularly functional to a young, vigorous, and expanding country in which there were many casualties of that expansion, from the indigenous Native Americans to the enslaved African Americans, the working poor, small shopkeepers, and the waves of immigrants in each generation.

It is not our intent here to try to counter the arguments of these philosophies. They are discussed further in chapters 2 and 3. Many Americans reject them on face value, but many others believe them. It is suggested that we live in a welfare society, and "they" are expected to be able to do something about our social problems. Most Americans believe the destitute should be helped. But so deep and pervasive in the American psyche is the philosophy of individual responsibility and competition[18] that we still find ourselves, in many overt and subtle ways, repeating the patterns that belong to ideologies many have long since rejected. Many others believe these ideologies are true and best for each of us and for the nation. We will discuss important ways in which this American myth is still active and particularly how it affects social welfare in the United States.

New Forms of Blaming the Victim

There are consequences of the overemphasis on individual responsibility. In *Blaming the Victim*, William Ryan points out that some persons no longer say of those who have not "made it" that they are evil or responsible for their situations.[19] We may even sympathize with them. But we say that because someone has been oppressed, because of all the injustices that have been done, he or she is now in such a poor state of social functioning that nothing can be done to make things better until the person changes. In other words, the focus of our concern and our change efforts continues to be on the individual rather than on the society's shortcomings.

In welfare planning, policy, and service delivery, this point of view can take many forms. Ryan discusses the "knowledge" that the poor are incapable of deferring gratification, that they can't plan ahead or invest resources. One "proof" of this is the experiment in which the researcher offers young children a choice of one candy bar immediately or two candy bars at school dismissal several hours later. Most middle-class children will opt for the two candy bars later. In a classroom in a poor neighborhood, most children will opt for the one candy bar now. However, Ryan points out that this may not result from an inability to defer gratification so much as from a realistic response to prior experience. A skeptic conducted a study using the candy bar example but added another element: The researcher gave the children an experience in which the promise of delayed gratification (two candy bars next week rather than one right now) was either kept or not kept. When the experiment was repeated, this was the only factor that differentiated between those who chose immediate gratification and those who chose to delay. Class and race were not related to delay. Those who had experienced a broken promise were the ones—not surprisingly—who were not willing to delay and thereby risk another disappointment.[20]

But our thinking continues to be that the problem somehow is in the psyche or the culture of the poor themselves rather than in the social conditions that continue to deny them opportunity. The children's attitudes have to change, we say, rather than the available opportunities. Thus do we shift responsibility.

As the United States has become even more of a multiethnic and multiracial society, "responsibility" is sometimes applied to an entire group—immigrants—especially when the economy is less than robust or in recession. Some persons make the case that the societal tensions and problems of the United States, including recessions and the loss of jobs, are due to the recent immigrants, and if not caused by them are undoubtedly exacerbated by their being here. In chapter 15, we will examine immigration in greater detail and in relation to social welfare.

An overemphasis on individual causation is a clear and present danger in social welfare; refusing to recognize "public issues" that must be dealt with can be equally destructive. Nonetheless, an emphasis on individual responsibility for one's situation regardless of the context and structural factors in society is very much alive and very much with us. In fact, this deeply ingrained value judgment and perception is rather ubiquitous and is found often where one might least expect it. For example, Peggy Say, the sister of Terry A. Anderson, who had been snatched off the streets of Beirut and held captive in Lebanon for many years, reported, "I won't tell him of the accusation that 'he shouldn't have been there in the first place. . . . ' "[21] Every important social problem—crime, mental illness, civil disorder, unemployment, child abuse, health care, slum housing—has been analyzed within the framework of the responsibility of the individual. Those who experience the problem are poorly motivated, lack information, have the wrong characteristics, have poor judgment, or are not acculturated.

What are some of the reasons we shift responsibility from community and society entirely to the individual? To do so serves certain purposes. It makes us feel superior; it allows us to express our hostilities toward relatively safe objects. It also separates and distances us from those in need and allows us subtly to defend the status quo in regard to the poor.

When we consider Mills's differentiation between "private troubles" and "public issues," we can see, in the latter case, that the solution does not lie within the range of opportunities available to a few people. Even divorce, commonly viewed as a personal matter, becomes a "public issue" or structural issue involving the institutions of marriage, the family, and other societal institutions. As we saw earlier, public issues such as unemployment and wages may result in "personal problems" of various types, in which people "carry" the public issue.

To define all personal problems as private troubles is to suggest that individuals can control their fates. However, to understand and accept the point of view implied by "structural" explanations of public issues suggests that something should be done to alter the structure that affects us all, a structure that affects some more positively and others more negatively.

To understand the personal milieu and "private troubles" of people, we often have to look beyond the immediate to the societal context. The sector of the economy, the degree of unionization, the geographic part of the country one resides in— all these and other factors, as we shall see in greater detail in chapter 8, impact on one's well-being. Events in distant locations can have enormous implications for persons and families, events over which, in this interdependent world, we often have little, if any, control.

THE AUTHORS' PERSPECTIVE

The reader deserves to know something more about the biases of the authors. We move from multiple perspectives:

1. Many problems of people in our society are largely caused by the institutional structure of society and not by their own inadequacies or actions.
2. Although societal structures impact on individuals, people ultimately are responsible for their actions and behavior, if not for their fates. There is free will within the boundaries of the opportunities available, boundaries that are defined by both objective and subjective realities.
3. Social policies and programs can have a profoundly positive influence on society.
4. Private troubles and public issues are interrelated. Private troubles are embedded in public issues, and public issues are embedded in private troubles.

All of these perspectives are important. People may be oppressed and be irresponsible or even criminal. That may be society's fault, and it may be society's responsibility to restructure itself so that such people will be less likely to make such destructive choices. Nonetheless, there are those persons who choose to harm others. Because of the circumstances in which people are born and raised, there are different obstacles and opportunities confronting each individual. There are unequal capacities among people, and there are oppressive social forces. We do not deny these factors as part of the reality that confronts each individual in relation to his or her own responsibility. Moreover, people are sometimes so incapacitated that their impairment makes it impossible for them to control their own actions; therefore, they do not have a full measure of responsibility. These exceptions and external forces create dilemmas for human beings, but, it seems to us, we must hold people responsible for their actions precisely because such a claim upon them maintains their very humanity and dignity. The question is this: To what extent are people really human without assuming responsibility for their actions?

Persons who kill other persons must ultimately be considered responsible, or we deprive them of their very humanity. The public official who engages in corruption because he goes along with the others, the Nazi who obeyed orders, and the mugger who must support a heroin habit—all are finally responsible for the acts they commit. There is a song in the musical *West Side Story* in which the juvenile delinquents are addressing their tormentor, Officer Krupke. After several humorous verses in which they mock society's shuttling them from judge to psychiatrist to social worker, the delinquents insist that it is not environment or upbringing that caused their plight but, "Deep down inside us, we're no good."

To make this claim is their way of insisting that they be recognized as individuals in their own right, that there is a certain kind of sociological jargon that is dehumanizing. If one is human, one is deserving of faith in ultimate worth, in capacity to grow. But being human implies being responsible for one's acts in spite of adversity. There is a patronizing element in portraying vandals as social revolutionaries, and there is racism in suggesting that any group cannot be expected to live up to standards for responsible behavior.

At the same time, we believe that poverty and other social problems derive largely from the institutional arrangements of the society in which we live. These arrangements result from an interplay between philosophical beliefs, such as those that have been reviewed here, and the demands of our society. These factors are structural in the society and not simply the by-play of individuals with equal opportunity making their demands felt in a free-market economy. From the tax structure, which is much less progressive than it was in the 1960s, to the availability of social services and supports, to the punishments meted out by the penal system, we observe vast inequalities in how people are treated by society. There is a kind of "welfare" for the wealthy and for large industries not available to the poor. It is our point of view, therefore, that solutions to social problems must be sought mainly in institutional and structural arrangements rather than in the rehabilitation of vast numbers of sick, disturbed, or uncultured people. Although we believe that individuals may need and deserve individual services, the greatest help will come to the most people through institutional change such as jobs, improved housing, and health services.

Recent rhetoric from the highest levels of the U.S. government portrays government as the enemy of social progress, ignoring the impact of societal structure. That rhetoric suggests that government programs can only make problems worse; only the voluntary efforts of people in local communities can really make a difference. There have been poor government programs and exciting local voluntary programs, but this basic proposition is essentially false. Major and massive social problems have, throughout our history, been amenable to amelioration only through major government efforts, including the application of fiscal resources. From the Social Security system to Medicare to any number of other significant programs, changes and improvements in the social system have come about only through such major public efforts, most often national—not local.

We live in a highly complex postindustrial society in which we are all very interdependent. We are not the mythological self-reliant, autonomous, and independent beings we are led to believe are the highest order; we are, in fact, integrally dependent on others. We cannot all assemble automobiles, build roads, grow corn, and teach ourselves, and we are deeply dependent on others who are, in turn, dependent on our own specialized skills and knowledge.

We also believe there is an alternative reading of the information on evolution, which leads us to cooperation and survival. In nature there is competition, but there is also cooperation. There is selfishness, but there is also mutual aid and self-sacrifice. Ashley Montagu, the noted anthropologist, suggested:

> Clearly, the degree of sociality, of co-operativeness, prevailing in any group will constitute an important factor in influencing its fertility rate as well as its survival rate. It cannot be too often repeated that all animals

are members of social groups, and that there is no such thing as a solitary animal, even though some groups are much less integrated than others. Social life is, among other things, a means of ensuring reproduction. To the extent, therefore, that any group is less social, less fully integrated, than another, it is likely to be differentially less fertile. All other factors being equal, with the exception of the degree of social integration, it should be obvious that the group in which its members are closely integrated, are often together, is the group that is likely to leave a greater surviving progeny than the group whose members are less integratedly social.[22]

Contrary to the argument put forth by the social Darwinists with which we began this chapter:

> animals . . . are strikingly unselfish, particularly with their own species—giving warning of predators, sharing food, grooming others to remove parasites, adopting orphans, fighting without killing or even injuring their adversaries. They work dutifully for their communities instead of being hard-bitten, self-seeking individualists.[23]

However, the fact that altruism is natural does not mean it is inevitable. Altruism is in keen competition with other values, is fragile, and has not been socially nurtured in recent U.S. history. Altruistic behavior depends on social structures within which we live. It is neither essential nor a universal characteristic of human nature, and the structural choices our society makes either support or undermine altrusitic behaviors.[24]

We see the poor as the outcome of imperfect systems. We believe this is not the only choice in society and that other options are available. Finally, we suggest that the middle class is also injured by structural factors. Although economically less disadvantaged, the middle class, too, is caught in a snare of individualism run rampant, in which blame for one's situation and mishaps is self-directed. Members of the middle class, often ineligible for public welfare programs and unable to pay for private ones, frequently believe that their problems, too, are the result of individual failure: "If we were really equal to the task, all things would be possible. Whatever our difficulties, they are the result of our failures." The overreaction to this belief system, the other side of the coin, is the tendency among some contemporary groups to deny their own humanity, to disclaim responsibility for their behavior, to despair of achieving progress when "they" don't respond immediately to a political campaign, or to retreat to utopias and inactivity. This is a kind of self-victimization.

It is clear U.S. society has several predominant values in regard to social welfare, sometimes conflicting and always interdependent. An emphasis on self-reliance, individual responsibility, and social Darwinism are strong currents in American thought. However, U.S. society is also influenced by the value of mutual aid, the ideal of equal opportunity, and the "second chance" philosophy. Our social welfare system, as we will see, has been profoundly affected by the English Poor Laws. Even so, when the pain is distributed broadly enough in our society, Americans begin to think more in terms of improving society than of "we" and "them."

There are several strong themes in social welfare. For example, Americans suspend their judgmental values about persons with problems on the basis of human tragedies, especially widespread disasters that affect persons across the board and also in regard to special categories of persons, such as war veterans. We do suggest, however, that an emphasis on individual responsibility is a crucial perspective that is unduly influential in U.S. society. A major thesis of this book is that values inform social welfare, and this theme will be explored as we proceed.

Even though we believe that all persons in the United States are entitled to the inalienable rights provided by the Constitution, they are entitled not on the basis of their problematic situations, but simply because they are human. We do not believe individuals should have to demonstrate how beaten down they are before government intervention helps them out. Similarly, we do not believe that groups should have to contest with each other over how persecuted they have been in order to qualify for necessary benefits and resources. The basic question is: How can U.S. society ensure equal rights and equal opportunities for all? Thus, we see societal values as having profoundly affected the social structure in the United States, particularly in social welfare. We see humans, however imperfectly, as being capable of adopting more humane values and of structuring a more humane society.

Summary

In chapter 1, we introduced the ideas of self-reliance and individual responsibility as driving forces in U.S. social welfare and suggested the importance of societal structures as they impact on our lives. We briefly defined social welfare and social work; explored the American myth of the hero; and introduced intellectual, scientific, religious, and socioeconomic factors contributing to the state of U.S. social welfare. Finally, we introduced the authors' perspectives. Students and readers are entitled to know our perspectives because of the importance we assign to values as determinants of each person's and our society's views regarding social welfare. We hope readers will be encouraged to consider how values play a part in determining how our society deals with social welfare.

We turn now to chapter 2, in which we review the relationship of perspectives on human nature in any society and the approach the society takes to welfare. Early history and examples of social welfare practices over time will be explored.

Electronic information sources are growing in importance. In appendix A, you will find sources of information that you can use to enrich your learning. Among these sources are Web sites on the Internet, encyclopedias and handbooks, indexes and abstracts, serial publications, other sources, and government documents.

Questions for Consideration

1. Can you identify problems and issues that seem to be caused more by societal structures than by individual responsibility?

2. Can you identify in your community and perhaps in your own life experience a "blaming the victim" psychology?
3. Before you have read further in this book, what do you believe social welfare is?
4. What are your reactions to the values expressed in the authors' perspective?

NOTES

1. William G. Sumner, "The Challenge of Facts," in *The Challenge of Facts & Other Essays*, Albert G. Keller, ed., New Haven, Conn.: Yale University Press, 1914, p. 25.
2. C. Wright Mills, *The Sociological Imagination*, New York: Oxford University Press, 1959, pp. 8–9.
3. Mary Merva and Richard Fowles, "Effects of Diminished Economic Opportunities on Social Stress," Washington, D.C.: Economic Policy Institute, 1992.
4. Sara Rosenbaum, "Child Health and Poor Children," *American Behavioral Scientist*, Vol. 35, No. 3, January/February 1992, pp. 275–289; Organization for Economic Co-operation and Development, *OECD in Figures: Statistics on the Member Nations*, 1997 Edition (June/July, 1997), Washington, D.C.: OECD, 1997. For extensive examination of the relationship of poverty to young peoples' development, see Greg J. Duncan and Jeanne Brooks-Gunn, eds. *Consequences of Growing Up Poor*, New York: Russell Sage Foundation, 1997.
5. Peggy McDonough, Greg J. Duncan, David Williams, and James House, "Income Dynamics and Adult Mortality in the United States, 1972 through 1989," *American Journal of Public Health*, Vol. 87, No. 9, September 1997, pp. 1476–1483.
6. Carolyn C. Perrucci, Robert Perrucci, Dena B. Targ, and Harry R. Targ, *Plant Closings: International Context and Social Costs*, New York: Aldine de Gruyter, 1988.
7. Loring Jones, "Unemployment and Child Abuse," *Families in Society: The Journal of Contemporary Human Services*, Vol. 71, No. 10, December 1990, pp. 579–588.
8. William J. Wilson, *The Truly Disadvantaged: The Inner City, the Underclass, and Public Policy*, Chicago: University of Chicago Press, 1987, p. 39.
9. Gary Burtless, "Introduction and Summary," *A Future of Lousy Jobs? The Changing Structure of U.S. Wages*, Gary Burtless, ed., Washington, D.C.: The Brookings Institution, 1990, p. 30.
10. William J. Wilson, *When Work Disappears: The World of the New Urban Poor*, New York: Alfred A. Knopf, 1996, pp. 25–26.
11. Norman S. Fieleke, "Is Global Competition Making the Poor Even Poorer?" *New England Economic Review*, November/December 1994, pp. 3–16.
12. The purpose of social work is to promote or restore a mutually beneficial interaction between individuals and society in order to improve the quality of life for everyone. To achieve these aims, contemporary social work practice focuses on the transactions among individuals, families, groups, organizations, and communities and their respective social environments, as well as the problems and opportunities that grow out of these interactions. This perspective seeks helping strategies predicated on such an interactional view; by broadening the bases for comprehending a problematic situation, social work tends to avoid focusing exclusively on either individuals or their environments.
13. Daniel J. Boorstin, *The Americans*, New York: Vintage, 1967, pp. 51–52.
14. William B. Scott, *In Pursuit of Happiness: American Conceptions of Property from the Seventeenth to the Twentieth Century*, Bloomington, Ind.: Indiana University Press, 1977, p. 11.

15. Frank Bourgin, *The Great Challenge: The Myth of Laissez-Faire in the Early Republic*, New York: George Braziller, 1989, pp. 24–25, 142, 171; Walter I. Trattner, "The Federal Government and Social Welfare in Early Nineteenth-Century America," *Social Service Review*, Vol. 50, No. 2, June 1976, pp. 243–255.
16. "Everybody . . . blamed himself. . . . There was an acceptance that it was your own fault, your own indolence, your lack of ability. . . . We all had an understanding that it wasn't our fault. It was something that happened to the machinery." These contradictory excerpts are from an oral history of the Great Depression. Studs Terkel, *Hard Times*, New York: Pantheon, 1970, pp. 52, 90.
17. Adam Smith's free-market ideas have been invoked by conservatives to support laissez-faire philosophy to an extreme. However, Smith supported labor unions, believed in public works, was suspicious of businessmen, and was not opposed to redistribution of income to the poor. Sylvia Nasar, "Adam Smith Was No Gordon Gekko," *New York Times* (January 23, 1994), p. E6.
18. An educational psychologist, when asked about cooperative learning (a movement to reduce student rivalry and encourage students to help each other), said it is "doomed to failure" because "it goes against the American grain, the individualism that creates the entrepreneurship we as a people have historically espoused. In a Utopia it would be wonderful. But education should prepare kids for life in a particular culture. In reality the name of the game is dog eat dog. Kids have to learn that you get something through your own smarts." William J. Warren, "New Movement Seeks to Replace Rivalry in Class with Team Spirit," *New York Times* (January 4, 1989), p. B11.
19. William Ryan, *Blaming the Victim*, New York: Vintage, 1976.
20. Ibid., pp. 112, 127–128.
21. Peggy Say, "Free At Last," *New York Times* (December 5, 1991), p. A33.
22. Ashley Montagu, *Darwin, Competition, and Conflict*, New York: Henry Schuman, 1952, pp. 102–103.
23. Helena Cronin, *The Ant and the Peacock: Altruism and Sexual Selection from Darwin to Today*, Cambridge: Cambridge University Press, 1992, p. 254.
24. Jerome C. Wakefield, "Is Altruism Part of Human Nature? Toward a Theoretical Foundation for the Helping Professions," *Social Service Review*, Vol. 67, No. 3, September 1993, p. 454.

Social Values and Social Welfare

*Economic life is deeply embedded in social life, and it cannot be
understood apart from the customs, morals, and habits of the society in
which it occurs. In short, it cannot be divorced from culture.*
—Francis Fukuyama[1]

*How selfish soever man may be supposed, there are evidently some
principles in his nature, which interest him in the fortune of others, and
render their happiness necessary to him, though he derives nothing from it
except the pleasure of seeing it.*
—Adam Smith[2]

Overview

In the first chapter we described several ways of understanding the situation of the
poor. There will be critical differences in the social welfare institutions of a society,
depending on where, and to what degree, it places responsibility for poverty. If poor
people are responsible for their plights, then, at worst, society will set up rather
punitive, or very limited, social welfare services. At best, social welfare services will
be directed to improving the poor person. On the other hand, if society assumes that
its own deficient institutions are responsible for poverty, then the efforts of the social welfare system may be directed toward correcting and improving those institutions. The social welfare systems a society constructs and operates are direct outcomes of its inherent social values. Often these values are implicit. They are
understood as such obvious and commonsense truths that they may not even be
stated. And yet they inform the entire approach to social welfare.

In this chapter and the next, we examine how various societies base their social welfare systems on predominant views of human nature. Although this chapter

16

cannot be inclusive, covering all social welfare history, we explore the legacy of the past, taking special cognizance of those social institutions and values that continue to be influential in the U.S. social welfare structure. Primarily, we hope to draw out the relationship between societal values and the organization of social welfare, so that in examining the latter the student will always look to the former for greater understanding.

MODERN VIEWS OF HUMANITY

Some people believe humans are inherently good, and others believe humans are inherently evil. A classic statement about the evil nature of humans was made by the seventeenth-century philosopher Thomas Hobbes, who pictured human nature so "that during the time men live without a common power to keep them all in awe, they are in that condition which is called war; and such a war, as is of every man, against every man . . . continual fear, and danger of violent death, and the life of man, solitary, poor, nasty, brutish, and short."[3] No person is to be trusted, and one should anticipate the evil acts of humans rather than expect their cooperation and goodness.

More recently, exponents of the fundamental, biological nature of human aggression and self-seeking behavior have suggested that "the aggression drive is a true, primarily species-preserving instinct [that] enables us to recognize its full danger; it is the spontaneity of the instinct that makes it so dangerous."[4]

Thus, on both philosophical and scientific grounds, some claim that humans are untrustworthy, evil, aggressive, and dangerous. Counter to this view of human nature is the view expounded, for example, by Jean-Jacques Rousseau, an eighteenth-century philosopher. He suggested that people are naturally good and that evil does not originate in human nature but has its source in the external world. (We have contrasted "evil" and "good" for simplicity. People who believe in the capacity of the environment to influence behavior include those who would substitute "neutral" for "good," with the ability to be influenced either way.) Rousseau suggested that we "lay down as an incontrovertible maxim that nature's first movements are always right; there is no original perversity in the human heart: there is not a single vice in it, of which I cannot say how and where it came in."[5] Arguing that humans are born good and that evil derives from institutional arrangements, Rousseau, unlike the novelist Joseph Conrad, looked into the heart of humankind and saw not darkness but light.

In regard to social welfare, if society believes humans are fundamentally evil, then it must guard against evil, which can be defined to include all unacceptable behavior. Thus poverty, mental illness, out-of-wedlock pregnancies, and hyperactive children are attributed not to external forces but to the evil nature of people. Because one cannot trust statements of need or portrayals of plight, barriers are placed in front of people, and those in need are demeaned.

Rousseau's view of people as basically good fosters the idea that the societal arrangements that create evil and human problems should be altered to allow for the well-being of people. For instance, people should escape from the evil influences of cities and live in the natural countryside environment.

In summary, if people are considered evil, societies can explain away their needs and problems as having been created by evil individuals. Societies may use that argument as a rationale to avoid altering the status quo, except to force the evil to do good, to protect the good against those who would do harm, and to punish those who are judged evil as a result of acts of commission (crimes of action) and acts of omission (laziness and being unproductive). On the other hand, if people are considered good, then one can approach social welfare as a means—in Jane Addams's memorable phrase, "to raising life to its highest value." People's lives can be improved and arrangements in society can be altered to reach higher goals for all citizens.

SELF-ACTUALIZATION VERSUS IRRITATION RESPONSE THEORIES

Just as human nature can be categorized as good or evil, theories about the motivations of humans can be classified into two categories: self-actualization and response to irritation. The belief that people are inherently self-actualizing or that they only respond to irritation and goading has significant consequences on how we think. Abraham Maslow, for example, was a major proponent of the view that humans are self-actualizing and not driven solely by instincts. In his view each person has a hierarchy of needs, including basic physiological needs and the needs for safety, belongingness, love, self-esteem, and self-actualization. Each person tries to satisfy these needs in ascending order so that the basic needs are cared for first, leaving the person free to work on the next "higher-level" need. Fundamental to this point of view is the idea that there is a universal set of basic impulses found in each person to satisfy ascending sets of needs.[6]

Needs also can be seen as arising from the values of a particular culture, much as in American culture we pass on, through values, the need for individualism and achievement. In other cultures, values determine other ways of living and viewing the world. The Arapesh, for instance, "plant their trees in someone else's hamlet, they rear pigs owned by someone else, they eat yams planted by someone else."[7] This example suggests that human behavior and needs themselves are defined by basic societal values. Given this point of view, society could just as easily be arranged in such a manner that people will work without being forced. If one believes in an inherent drive for self-actualization, one can then trust that those in need do not require irritation and goading so much as the opportunities and social structures to enable them to achieve their aims.

Karl Polanyi made a similar point about the importance of basic social values as determinants of social arrangements. He stressed the relationship of noneconomic motives to the economic system, suggesting that the outstanding discovery of recent historical and anthropological research is that the economy, as a rule, is submerged in social relationships. One does not act so as to safeguard his or her individual interest in the possession of material goods; one acts so as to safeguard one's social standing, social claims, and social assets. Material goods have value insofar as they serve this end. The economic system is run on noneconomic motives.[8] The essential point of Polanyi's argument is that the economic motivation of people and society is subsumed in the social texture of life. Economic factors are real, but the suggestion is also made that humans and societies can be motivated by other, equally real motivations.

The irritation philosophy, on the other hand, demands that poor people live uncomfortable lives based on the perspective that this will motivate them to stronger efforts to succeed. John Romanyshyn suggested that to regard people as evil and naturally lazy, driven to useful work only through hunger and fear of starvation, is to suggest that societies characterized by scarcity require an image of people that will justify social discipline. This discipline is required to get necessary but distasteful toil accomplished. Affluent societies can afford wider freedom of choice and can facilitate the development of new views of people more consistent, perhaps, with their true nature.[9]

So it may not be inherent in people that they need goading and irritation to be productive; it may be that such a "reading" of people derives from scarcity in societies or from societies that do not choose to share sufficiently with those in poverty. Or it may be that such views derive from the need in a particular society to accomplish something in the future. Punitive, irritant behavior has been typical in our society when dealing with those in poverty. Payments beneath the acknowledged level of subsistence, disrespectful behavior toward the poor, and various forms of harassment are all ostensibly aimed at restoring the poor to productive lives.

ECONOMICS AND HUMAN MOTIVATION

The irritation response theme implicitly runs from Adam Smith to Milton Friedman and from Karl Marx to Mao Tse-tung: A human is an economic being who works for economic gain and whose behavior is economically determined. In this respect, capitalism, communism, and socialism are triplets, in that they all view people in economic terms.[10] To accept as fact the view that a human being works only for economic gain supports a punitive approach to poverty. This view makes *"less eligibility"* inevitable (no one on welfare can be paid as much as the lowest paid employed person in the community). Although we know in practice there are specific exceptional cases, our societal theory views less eligibility as a necessity. Persons in poverty, it is thought, can be encouraged to rise from their impoverished state only through the discomforts of a life without enough to live on. Thus, if one believes in the economic human being, then less eligibility seems to be almost inevitable, because people would otherwise not work.

Closely related to the view of humans as economic beings is the belief that a market mentality is the central and inevitable reality. This theme suggests that reality is based on economic human beings. The organization of society and the motivations of people are dictated by the market mentality, and other motives are relatively insignificant.

As Polanyi suggests, and as history and the world make abundantly clear, economic relationships are subsumed in social relations. Societies have the ability to create any kind of mechanism to motivate human activity. Economic activity is certainly necessary for the survival of society, but it can be pursued from a multitude of motives, including social ones. Polanyi is critical of the split reflected in the market mentality that humans have two selves: the economic or market self and the other self, which is ideal and spiritual. With such a human-created dichotomy, economic determinism holds sway and inhibits other ways of viewing people and society. Those societies trapped in economic theories of motivation alone make it less probable that fundamental changes in the way we view those in poverty can be attained.[11]

From Polanyi's multimotivational point of view, social motives serve as the engine for society and individuals, not just economic motives. Thus, assistance to poor people could just as well be based on our social responsibility to them. In addition, the motivation of the poor can be stronger as a result of the realization that society holds them as valued citizens and will not let them starve or be punished. Subliminal messages in this case would resound through society: Poor people are to be trusted, cared for, and helped because of our higher social goals.

In our post-industrialized society strong relationships have been established between technology and an emphasis on monetary motivation. Focusing economic effort on production for profit has repercussions on all other aspects of life. Among the results are technological unemployment and the business cycle. This makes it difficult for some people to obtain the fundamental necessities of life. In all nonliterate societies, resources may be meager, and subsistence difficult to obtain, but where there is not enough to go around all go hungry, as all participate when seasons of plenty provide abundance. "No one ever went hungry [among the Baganda of East Africa,] because everyone was welcome to go and sit down and share a meal with his equals," is an expression of the tradition, universal among nonliterate folk, that none must be allowed to want in the face of plenty.[12]

AN OVERVIEW OF HISTORY

Altruism and Mutual Aid

Recent discoveries have led to the conclusion that Neanderthals who resembled modern humans in body movement, use of hands, and language lived with elevated levels of risk and yet had a respect for the living. Life was frequently dangerous; nevertheless, injured individuals were apparently cared for by other members of their social groups. There is extensive evidence of the healing of injuries. Some injured persons lived for many years with considerably disabling conditions that would have prevented their actively contributing to the subsistence of the local group. Some fossil skeletons with evidence of trauma, age-related health deterioration, or disability suggest that persons otherwise normal were cared for by the group, as well as children who lost their parents, most of whom did not live beyond 35 years of age. The skeleton of a young male dwarf whose physical impairments would handicap his participation in a nomadic hunting and gathering society is evidence of the tolerance of and care for a severely deformed individual during the Paleolithic era. Even more recently, the body of a four-year-old with a disability and believed to be dead for 800 years was found in Alaska. Her body was located in a secure area and adorned with protective covers, indicating a great deal of care had been taken. Because of her disabilities, she had to have required extra attention throughout her life.[13]

Peter Kropotkin described mutual-aid mechanisms in all types of societies throughout history, including medieval city life and today's unions and business, political, and remarkably diverse voluntary associations. Kropotkin argues that "the practice of mutual aid and its successive developments have created the very conditions of society life in which man was enabled to develop his arts, knowledge, and intelligence; and that the periods when institutions based on the mutual-aid tendency took their greatest development were also the periods of the greatest progress in arts, industry, and science."[14]

Despite the fact that industrial societies clearly require mutual aid and cooperation, the common perception is that the motivations of people are dictated by the market (supply and demand) and the necessity of competition. In the following section we examine briefly nonliterate societies, other past cultures, and nations, focusing on elements of particular interest to our understanding of human nature, on alternative societal arrangements, and on precedents that influence current social welfare theory. As we will see, modern themes have very ancient parallels.

Robert Trivers reports that reciprocal altruism (mutual aid) exists in all known cultures. People help each other in times of danger, sharing food and helping the sick, the wounded, the very young, and the old. They also share implements and knowledge. Although hunter-gatherer groups make adaptations to regulate group size near optimum, there is no evidence that altruistic gestures are curtailed when groups are above what they consider optimum size.[15]

Our complex and specialized society requires even more, not less, complicated mutual aid and cooperation because we don't do many things ourselves and are dependent on many others during every ordinary day. Nevertheless, we foster the myth of individual responsibility and independence, and the "survival of the fittest" is more or less an accepted societal value.

Altruism grows out of a sociocultural reality, as does an overvaluation of individual responsibility. Every culture develops altruistic components required for the survival of the group. The essential factor to recognize is that the degree of cooperation and altruism, or the emphasis placed on individual responsibility, and the role of social welfare are determined by predominant views of human motivation in any society. The point has been made that "the frequency of behavior that we might regard as altruistic is likely to depend more on the social structures within which people live than on any essential and universal characteristics of human nature. . . . All the features of society that make egoism ring true are human creations—creations that could be different, that indeed are different in different cultures, and may have once been different in our own."[16]

As another aid to our sense of perspective, here is a quotation from a pre-colonial letter written by Amerigo Vespucci describing his experience with Native Americans: "They are so liberal in giving that it is the exception when they deny you anything; and, on the other hand, they are free in begging, when they show themselves to be your friends."[17]

In 1493, Columbus in a letter to King Ferdinand and Queen Isabella described the Native Americans he encountered this way: "After they have shaken off their fear of us, they display a frankness and liberality in their behavior which no one would believe without witnessing it. No request of anything from them was ever refused, but they rather invite acceptance of what ever they possess, and manifest such generosity that they would give away their own hearts."[18] Their society functioned effectively and with a complex social system, using mutual aid and without an all-encompassing market mentality.

In the following brief review of ancient cultures, we focus on elements of particular interest to our understanding of certain influences on social welfare today.

ANCIENT CULTURES

Egypt

Peasants in Egypt during the fourth through sixth dynasties (2700–2200 B.C.) planted and reaped their masters' crops. Before the first autumn crops were gathered, it was likely that peasants were close to starvation. Their lives were described as similar to the lives of animals. They were the property of the lords, beasts of burden themselves, and completely dependent on the yield of the land and the whims of the landowner.[19]

The yield of the land was erratic. One result was that as early as the twenty-eighth century B.C. the tradition of seven lean years was known. The prosperity of Egypt depends on the satisfactory flow of the Nile, and Egyptian texts make frequent references to hunger ("years of misery," "a year of low Nile").

> When the entire Upper Egypt was dying because of hunger, with every man eating his (own) children, I never allowed death to occur from hunger in this nome. I gave a loan of grain to Upper Egypt.[20]

Because of the importance of the grain harvest, the state through the king's commissioners paid special attention to planning, production, and distribution. Grain was stored for two seasons and had to be sufficient for those who were building public works, including canal and dike workers, stonemasons, and the builders of pyramids, tombs, and temples. Thus, centralized planning and coordination are not inventions of the modern age, and specifically, careful provision of food supplies was a fundamental social welfare effort directly tied to national intentions and needs.

However, problems arose when there was a breakdown of the economy. For example, an uprising took place in the twelfth century B.C. in which a group in the state labor corps complained: "We have been hungry for 18 days in this month. We have come here by reason of hunger and thirst, we have no clothes, we have no ointment, we have no fish, we have no vegetables. Send word to Pharoah, our good lord, and write to the vizir, our superior, in order that the means of living be provided for us."[21]

Thus we can see workers were accustomed to receiving various supplies, centrally controlled. But in times of trouble, apparently, local self-interest quickly came into play when supplies became limited, and this self-interest became the sole means of defense in the struggle for existence. One lord was quoted as saying, "When Upper Egypt was in a bad state . . . I closed the frontiers."[22] The frontiers were closed so the available harvest and supplies would suffice for the local population, an early version of residency laws and the forerunner of clashes between national and local political necessities.

At a later time (seventh–sixth century B.C.), Egyptian culture expressed some obligations even toward strangers who were in need. The Egyptians believed God was a protector of the poor against the rich. Around this time, the following instruction was set forth:

> Do not find a widow if thou catchest
> her in the fields (i.e., gleaning the fields).
> Nor fail to be indulgent to her reply.
> Do not neglect a stranger (with) thy oil-jar,
> That it be doubled before thy brethren.
> God desires respect for the poor
> More than the honoring of the exalted.[23]

We can see in ancient Egypt relationships between social welfare and societal goals, conflicts between local self-interest and other levels of government, efforts to feed the hungry, as well as residency requirements. We can observe that centralized planning and services are techniques used early in recorded history by a national government for its own purposes: to support projects, to maintain a workforce, and for social control.

Sumer and Babylonia

As early as the second millennium (2000 B.C.), the Sumerians, an ancient culture that settled in the Euphrates river valley, placed a positive value on the protection of widows, orphans, and the poor. Nanshe, a goddess mentioned in Sumerian mythology, cared for the defenseless:

> Who knows the orphan, who knows the widow,
> Knows the oppression of man over man, is the orphan's mother,

Nanshe, who cares for the widow

> Who seeks out justice for the poorest.
> The queen brings the refugee to her lap,
> Finds shelter for the weak.[24]

Nanshe was also referred to as Truth, Justice, and Mercy.

In the early development of Babylonia, peasants worked the land for the temples. Later they held land either as private property or as rentals. When they assumed the relatively freer state, they then had to brave the onslaught of catastrophes—floods, droughts, blights, and sickness—on their own. Before this the temple had been the owner of everything, including both land and people. Formerly when difficulties had arisen, rations were distributed from the temple granaries to sustain the community through times of trouble.

When peasants were freer they were forced to borrow from the temple at interest, a fact that led to many peasants becoming seriously indebted. This resulted in friction, and there are indications some kings enacted moratoriums on debts, remission of debts, and fixed wages and prices.

During the first millennium (1000 B.C.), several types of persons were dedicated to the temples, in fact entrusted to the care of the temples. Among these were prisoners of war, slaves donated or bequeathed, and persons of free birth including children of poor families handed over in times of famine to save their lives.[25]

There are three noteworthy points to observe about this ancient culture: temples were important economic forces; governmental action was taken to relieve economic burdens and pressures, probably to avoid serious conflicts; and temples served as "social welfare" agencies, anticipating major religious institutional functions to follow in later centuries.

Hebrew and Judaic Societies

Judaic culture developed out of a desert existence in which each person had a responsibility not only to him- or herself but also to the group and the community. This tension between self-interest and group interest was neatly summed up by Rabbi Hillel: "If I am not for myself, who will be? If I am only for myself, what am I? If not now, when?"[26] Judaism established within its own sociocultural reality a God-ordered altruism. When Abraham greets and serves three strangers who approach his tent in the desert, he establishes the principles of hospitality and caring for the stranger.

The Hebrew Bible makes clear provision for the poor based on the agrarian society at the time. Through a series of commandments Judaism established a system of individual responsibility for providing assistance. Several illustrations demonstrate what is in essence a developed system of social welfare, both as an ideal and in fact. For example, Leviticus 19:9–10 states: "And when ye reap the harvest of your land, thou shalt not wholly reap the corner of thy field, neither shalt thou gather the gleaning of thy harvest. And thou shalt not glean thy vineyard, neither shalt thou gather the fallen fruit of thy vineyard; thou shalt leave them for the poor and for the stranger: I am the Lord your God." Gleanings, forgotten produce, and the corners of the field were available for poor people who were free to take food for their own use. Strangers, aliens in the land, were also free to take produce, and apparently there was no such thing as a special amount of time one had to live in the land in order to receive charity. Starvation also was prevented by another commandment:

> When thou comest into thy neighbour's vineyard, then thou mayest eat grapes until thou have enough at thine own pleasure; but thou shalt not put any in thy vessel. When thou comest into thy neighbour's standing corn, then thou mayest pluck ears with thy hand; but thou shalt not move a sickle unto thy neighbor's standing corn. [Deut. 23:25–26]

Public opinion, apparently, enforced this commandment, and there is no record of actual starvation in peaceful times.[27]

These commandments are essentially a tax on producers for the benefit of the poor: the stranger, the fatherless, and the widow (see Deuteronomy 24:19–22). Many centuries later the English poor laws utilized a poor rate as a public tax for the care of the poor.

A tithe was required to be given to the poor. Further, all financial debts still owing by the sabbatical year were canceled. The emphasis on charity of many kinds in the Hebrew Bible did not in itself produce a redistribution of wealth or correct economic inequalities.

Among the Judaic commandments, one series of laws introduced a radical and revolutionary concept: the Jubilee year. Every fiftieth year, slaves were emancipated, and property—with the exception of house property in a walled city—was to be restored to its original owners. This series of laws created a counterbalance to the possible gradual accumulation by a few of most of the property and goods. According to the Talmud and other sources, the observance of the Jubilee was a reality for centuries.

Finally, Deuteronomy introduced the legal requirement for neighborly love. For instance, in Deuteronomy 25:35 the law states: "And if thy brother be waxen poor, and his means fail with thee; then thou shalt uphold him: as a stranger and a settler shall he live with thee." The manner in which charity was given added to its value so that *gemilut hasadim* (acts of loving kindness) is considered one of the three pillars upon which the continued existence of the world depends (*Ethics of the Fathers*, 1:2).

The prophets later stressed the importance of charity and taking care of those in need. Isaiah (58:5–7), in a statement read every year on Yom Kippur, excoriates Jews because fasting and the wearing of a sackcloth and ashes are in themselves not an acceptable offering to the Lord. According to the prophet, an acceptable offering would be giving bread to the hungry, housing the poor, and clothing the naked.

Throughout later rabbinic and other Jewish literature, the performance of charitable deeds is stressed both in spirit and in the giving of things for those who need them. All human possessions belong to God (*Ethics of the Fathers*, 3:8). One interesting device in early times was a community charity box, designed so others would not know whether people were depositing or removing money.

An early social welfare stance of the Jewish community is reflected in an enumeration of some post-biblical communal institutions. These functions are not far removed from some basic social welfare functions: clothing the naked, educating the poor, providing poor girls with a dowry, providing food for Passover, caring for orphans, visiting the sick, caring for the aged, ransoming captives, and providing burials.

Judaism bases its requirements for altruism on essentially two concepts: Tzedakah, a mixture of charity and justice, and Chesed, loving kindness. In the Jewish community, historically, the giver and the recipient both needed each other. Every person has inherent dignity and should strive to live a life in the image of God. Even the poor must perform charitable acts. In regard to its basic view of humans, Judaism postulates both a force for good and a force for evil in every person. Because of these simultaneous drives, humans need the restriction, direction, and support of the commandments that enable people to choose life and avoid death, to be supportive of humanity and justice, and not to become numb either to one's own needs or those of all other humans.

From our perspective today, several important themes appear in the Hebrew and Judaic culture. Social welfare became institutionalized in two important respects: in regard to expected behavior and in provision for the poor in essentially nonstigmatizing ways. Attempts were made to redistribute wealth to offset long-term poverty through diminishing inherited wealth. There appears early to have been provision for the poor as a right or entitlement from individuals and later in an organized fashion. Perhaps these achievements were possible because of the small size of the society. Essentially, a culture developed that valued enterprise but without categorizing the poor as evil or idle. On the contrary, the society and individuals in it would be judged on the degree to which they provided for the poor without demeaning them.

Greece and Rome

In Greece, the beggars scorned by Plato could expect to be sent away from cities. They were viewed by the Greeks as being lazy and not willing to work rather than as lacking opportunity. One Spartan was quoted by Plutarch as saying: "But if I gave to you, you would proceed to beg all the more; it was the man who gave to you in the first place who made you idle and so is responsible for your disgraceful state." Similarly, Plautus made clear the Grecian attitude: "To give to a beggar is to do him an ill service."

Aristotle, in his theoretical State, thought he could avoid the need for charity by making part of the land completely public, thus defraying the costs of providing common meals. Several options were available for the poor and landless. They could move to new colonies, could become mercenaries, could use contraception or abortion, or (with a high incidence of poverty) could resort to infanticide.[28]

Although according to some sources the Grecian poor could only hope for better conditions by starting anew somewhere else, there is also evidence that throughout Greece there were inns or resting places for strangers. Located near or at temples, these places were centers for medical relief and for the poor. Associations for the support of those in need reportedly also existed.[29]

The rejection of beggars illustrates a strong theme in Western culture—actually, it is more a concern with pauperism than with poverty. A *pauper* is a person without means of support, especially someone who depends on aid from tax-based public welfare funds. In modern terms, the issue is how to keep people from getting paid from tax funds when they are not working rather than how to alleviate poverty. This attitude pervades U.S. society and is fundamental, as we see later, to the concept of less eligibility. Harassment of those on welfare continues for reasons probably close to those that motivated the exile of beggars from Greek cities. It is not the desire to alleviate poverty that encourages harassment of the poor; instead, demeaning treatment is used against pauperism and to reduce the extent to which public funds are used to support those in need. The focus on pauperism is one that returns at a later stage as an important ingredient in Western treatment of the poor. The emphasis on preventing funds from being given to those who are not working is a common American aim, a crucial factor in society in general and in social welfare in particular.

Whereas the Egyptians and Hebrews gave the poor special consideration, in Greece hospitality for the stranger was a relationship between nobles or merchants, and the Romans were obliged to give hospitality "only in the case of foreigners of the same standing as the host and [this] was seen as a means of obtaining good relations with them."[30] Nonetheless, by the third century A.D., 175,000 Romans were receiving free food distributions. This was in addition to the system of patrons, in which everyone felt bound to someone more powerful and superior. Patrons distributed both food and money to those who were connected to them in the patronage system. During the second century, there are estimates that almost one half of Rome's population lived on public charity. Of 1.2 million people, all but 150,000 heads of families needed to draw on public resources.[31]

There began the development of huge country manors, and concurrently, there arose a new aristocracy. Fortified manors offered security and refuge to ruined freeholders, poor urban workers, uprooted persons from outlying regions, vagabonds, army deserters, and escaping slaves. All of these became tenants of the large landowners. Where a person had land, it might be placed under complete or partial control of the large landowners in exchange for protection, for which he would pay a part of his crop.

In late Roman times the wages of serfs were set according to those of slave laborers, their competitors. In addition, tenants were forbidden to move from place to place. By the fourth century people were officially tied to the land. Such ties were more easily established in Grecian lands, where hereditary service had been an institution. This relieved landowners of labor worries. Such a system, which tied people to the land in exchange for support from large landowners, as we will see, took on great importance at a later historical point and profoundly influenced our attitudes and welfare philosophy.

CHRISTIANITY

The development of Christianity introduced an important new variable on the scene, with profound implications for social welfare. Two themes were introduced that influenced social welfare for more than 1,500 years and remain with us even today. Charity and the near sanctification of the poor assumed great importance in societies influenced by Christian thought. A second theme derived from Christian thought was the denigration of conspicuous consumption. Until the Protestant revolution, these themes were fundamental to Western social welfare practices.

Jesus, who had been a wandering preacher in Galilee, was a healer of body and soul who cured the sick and cast out demons. He taught that service to people was service to God. So it became the responsibility of Christians to take care of the poor, widows, and orphans. "Therefore love is the fulfilling of the law" (Romans 13:10).

According to Christianity, there are three abiding gifts: faith, hope, and love, but of these love is the greatest (I Corinthians 13:13). Jesus made it clear that the outcasts of society, such as prostitutes, were worthy of special care. The Christian themes of (1) charity and a sanctification of the poor and (2) a denigration of conspicuous consumption brought with them several significant social welfare themes. Very early Christians in Jerusalem pooled their possessions for relief of the poor. "They sold their possessions and their means of livelihood, so as to distribute to all as each had need" (Acts 2:44, 4:34).[32] In Jerusalem there was a daily distribution of food to widows and perhaps to others.[33] The concept of hospitality also became institutionalized when early Christians met in the homes of church members—the house church—and traveling Christians assumed they would receive hospitality, a concrete expression of Christian love.[34]

Early Christians held an ethic of poverty based on scriptural statements such as, "It is easier for a camel to go through the eye of a needle than for a rich man to enter the kingdom of God" (Mark 10:25) and "Blessed are you poor for yours is the kingdom of God" (Luke 6:20). Early believers came primarily from poor groups and were rewarded with a promise that poverty, not wealth, held the key to the kingdom.[35]

Both love of Jesus and love of people were necessary for the Christian life. Judgment was to be on the basis of how one treated those who were hungry, thirsty, strangers, unclothed, sick, or in prison because Jesus was considered present in all such people. By the late first and early second centuries, Christians placed an increased emphasis on giving alms: "Almsgiving is as good as repentance from sin; fasting is better than prayer; almsgiving is better than either." By the middle of the second century, Christian charity had become organized. Voluntary offerings were collected once a week and deposited with the "president" or bishop, whose responsibility it was to protect orphans, widows, those in distress, prisoners, and strangers—all who were in need.[36]

Although charity and relief of the poor were Christian requisites, early Christians also held strong beliefs about the necessity of work. Three motives for work were held: (1) Christians should not be a burden to others; (2) one should obtain resources with which to help the needy; and (3) non-Christians should be favorably impressed so as to commend the faith to them. By contrast, Greeks thought work a servile activity, and Romans felt work was beneath the dignity of a citizen.[37]

By the fourth century, Christians (encouraged to engage in good works) had built hospitals for the sick and established systematic charitable efforts. State, church, and voluntary social welfare functions overlapped, particularly in regard to the Roman grain dole for Roman citizens, such a widespread practice that a "steward over the grain" was appointed. Privately endowed foundations, especially in Italy, invested capital in real estate mortgages. Interest was paid to towns or to state administrators for charitable uses. By the third century, oil was added to the ration of grain and eligibility for the dole was extended to noncitizens. Bread was substituted for grain by the early fourth century.

Byzantium: Christianity in the East

In the East during the third century A.D., 80,000 people received free food at Constantinople. Requisitions and taxes supported large parts of the population. Constantine thought the poor should be maintained by the wealth of the churches and that the rich should support the needs of this world.[38]

By the fourth century A.D., the period often referred to as the Dark Ages began with the advancing disintegration of Roman imperial government in the West. From the fourth century, when official state protection made possible the open accumulation of ecclesiastical wealth, church leaders developed lists of people in need whom the Christian community assisted. There is evidence that widows, young women, as well as men were fed daily, along with prisoners, the ill in hospitals, the mutilated, and the shipwrecked. People traveling through also were dependent upon church resources.

Christian charity was also administered through institutions that assisted the very old, the very young, the poor, and the blind. Many hostels provided shelter for travelers, pilgrims, the diseased, and suffering aging persons. Also formed were leprosariums, old people's homes, and hospitals. These organizations were typically attached to a church or monastery that was supported by donations and ecclesiastical revenues such as income from properties. In part these institutions were intended to redistribute resources of the wealthy to the needy poor.

In the fifth-century eastern monasteries, the underemployed of the towns were hired for service in the Christian church. However, imperial (state) assistance dominated in the development of Byzantine charity. The imperial treasury and public funds frequently ensured the survival of religious-sponsored institutions for the poor. Funding often included a combination of private, imperial, and ecclesiastical funding.[39]

In Alexandria in the early seventh century, a Byzantine welfare state was developed. There were maternity hospitals, medical facilities, and food rationing, all of which were provided from the revenues of the patriarch.[40]

These developments reflect the ubiquitous creation of social welfare institutions, regardless of time, culture, or society. But developments were not always as completely charitable as one might imagine. As early as the first century A.D., the Christian principle of assisting all those in need was modified in practice by a reluctance to support strangers. Apparently, there were abuses of hospitality by visitors extending their stays more than two nights. True Christians were expected not to stay longer. There are examples of putting travelers to work after a week's stay.[41]

It is important to note that Constantine in the East eased the position of women, children, debt-ridden farmers (a theme that arises frequently), prisoners, and slaves. While the western Roman Empire collapsed, the eastern Byzantine Empire survived, and until the thirteenth century Constantinople was the most prosperous place in Europe.[42] A mixed system of voluntary, religious, and state-supported social welfare was implemented. State funds were administered by a private voluntary group for the benefit of both public and private spheres, thus anticipating a modern funding and administrative device.

HOLY POVERTY AND EXPECTATIONS OF THE WEALTHY

Later saints, such as Saint Francis of Assisi, and ordinary Christians in some cases renounced material goods and family ties and led lives of poverty, an expression of being one with the wretched of the Earth and a desire to be of help to them. Such acts were viewed as imitations of the life of Jesus. Christianity expected its adherents to emulate the life of Jesus and to help those who were in need:

> For I was hungry, and you fed me,
> I was thirsty and you gave me drink,
> I was a stranger and you welcomed me,
> I was without clothes and you clothed me,
> I was in prison and you visited me.
> [Matt. 25:31–46]

Beyond helping those who were needy, early Christianity demanded that those who had excess worldly goods should share these with the underprivileged. The gift of one's property, received from God through God's beneficence, was a sign that one was imitating the life of Jesus. Church officials and Christians could distinguish between holy poverty, which was chosen by the person, and involuntary poverty. To an extent during early Christianity it was important for Christians of means to divest themselves of property to support those in need in order to show signs of one's religious commitment. As we will see when we examine the early Middle Ages, these Christian values influenced social welfare in important ways and had long-term effects on western European antecedents of U.S. social welfare.

Eastern Cultures

Although not directly linked to early U.S. social welfare, several additional social welfare histories have in recent years begun to affect the U.S. scene and may play more prominent roles in the future.

China

As early as the eighth century B.C., China developed a political system of monarchy with various subordinate groupings organized into fiefdoms. Peasants worked the land to support their superiors, were attached to the land, and were bestowed along with the land. It is probable that peasants were assigned a piece of land to cultivate for their particular superiors and another for the use of their own families. One contemporary saying was that "dukes live on tribute, ministers on their estates, shih (a group between the power group and the ruled) on the land, and peasants on their own toil." Peasants working for their lords were the source of labor and food for the self-sufficient manorial communities but had few rights, opportunities, or pleasures. A passage in Mencius suggests the state of affairs: "If a common man is called on to perform any service, he goes and performs it."[43]

Later, during the sixth century B.C., taxes were instituted based on the amount of land one possessed. Slowly the former responsibility of the lords to feed, house, and clothe their subordinates fell on the peasants themselves. Emancipation from the status of manorial dependent upgraded the peasants' status and afforded them greater freedom; it also relieved the lord from many of his former responsibilities. The peasants then had only themselves to look after for livelihood. Poverty or prosperity became their own responsibility.[44]

By the fourth century B.C., Mencius expressed the Confucian ideal of the humane and righteous king and suggested that the ruler must pay attention to the people's welfare. People need the necessities of life before they can be expected to concentrate on being good. Mencius, like Maslow, hypothesized a hierarchy of needs that must be met in ascending order so higher-level needs can be met. He advised the king to avoid extravagance at court and to open parks and other state lands so people could gather wood and herbs. He also urged that public funds be used for the care of the aged, the poor, and orphans and for public assistance when natural disasters struck.[45]

By the first century B.C., in times of natural disasters such as floods or famines, the government took several steps. Government granaries were opened. Grain was distributed free to those who were unable to pay for it and sold to those who could afford to pay. The rich were called on to give or lend grain from their personal supplies. Gifts from the imperial treasury were sent to establish relief work for the poor. Court commissioners were sent out to encourage the planting of grain for a new harvest. Finally, if necessary, the poor were taken from the ravaged areas and resettled on new lands.[45]

The Sung Dynasty (960–1279 A.D.) reportedly exceeded the benevolence of earlier dynasties. Emergency relief was provided in times of catastrophe such as floods, drought, fire, and warfare when displaced persons lacked food and shelter. Local authorities with permission of the government distributed grain from granaries and cash. The amount distributed depended on the seriousness of the emergency and stopped when the emergency was over. Normal relief was also provided for the general mass of poor people who were unable to sustain themselves, including the aged, widowers, widows, orphans, and the childless old. There were definite periods of operation of normal relief, special administrative officials, and regulating laws. The ancient guiding principle suggested that it is the responsibility of the government to see to it that the living are given sustenance; the sick, medical care; and the dead, burial.

Charity homes were established all over the empire. Cases were checked for veracity and lodging was provided in the homes of those who died without heirs. If such lodging was unavailable, the indigent were lodged in government buildings. Expenses with no time limit were paid out of the property of the heirless.

Medical relief institutions were established, as were public cemeteries for those who could not pay for their own burials or died while traveling away from home. Other welfare measures included distribution of grain in times of bad harvests. The wealthy were asked to contribute money or grain in return for official posts or ranks. If this was insufficient, the palace storehouses would contribute. When winter weather became too severe or commodity prices rose too high, the government would pour its stocks of rice or fuel into the market and sell at low prices. In addition, maternity clinics were instituted for needy women, children abandoned during a flood were cared for, and famine victims were employed to work on dikes so workers profited from wages and the area gained from the irrigation.[46]

Several themes should be noted from these examples from ancient China. With the breakup of a feudal pattern, the peasant was freed from semi-bondage on the manor but was forced to rely on his or her own resources. One can see a trade-off was made between security on the one hand and mobility and greater freedom on the other. Furthermore, government provided help when people could not care for themselves, particularly in the case of a natural disaster. Moving from place to place to find sustenance must have been done at the expense of the government—an early governmental resettlement program. Perhaps there were additional motives, but specifically the move was made possible through governmental resources when those of the people failed. But Mencius's views reflect a government that had a responsibility for the people's welfare in order to promote the "good" at all times and not just in times of disaster.

India

Aspects of social welfare have been identified in India at least as far back as Buddha (sixth century B.C.). During very early times (fourth and third centuries B.C.), construction projects provided work for the public good. Villagers jointly provided for the care of boys and old or diseased men where they had no guardians or protectors.[47] It was the duty of the village elders to look after the property of minors who lacked a natural guardian until they reached the age of majority, when their property would be returned to them with any accumulated profits.

There also was collective charity. A family would give alms, the residents of a street would give voluntary offerings, or all the inhabitants of a town would do so. Charity (food, clothing, money) was collected especially during times of famine. Gifts supportive of education were highly meritorious. Reportedly, even the poorest person gave something to hungry students. Temples sheltered the homeless. In villages, extended families cared for their aged members, those with physical and other disabilities, and the chronically ill. Caste organizations, guilds, and the *panchayat* (village government in later times) took care of the poor, the aged, the ill, and the disabled and provided housing and food for travelers.

From ancient times all Indian religions have emphasized charity. The responsibility for those needing assistance was shared by the rulers, by the rich, and also by individual members of the general community. Temples and monasteries served as centers for extensive social services and were left endowments for their maintenance; for construction of residences for monks; and as support for the supply of food, cloth, and oil for religious individuals and institutions.[48]

From the medieval period on (thirteenth century A.D.), Indian Muslims provided help to less fortunate persons through payment of the *zakat*, a poor tax, by every Muslim. They also provided endowments for religious and educational institutions, constructed temples and mosques, and established rest houses and *dharamshalas*, a public place of provision for those in need, including travelers, who were given free food and lodging.

Islam

Among the fundamental tenets or requirements of Islam, accepted by all branches, is the obligation to give charity. The Koran contains numerous references to almsgiving to the poor and needy and to those who work for them:

> O ye believers, give in alms of the good things
> that ye have earned, and of what we have brought forth
> for you out of the earth.
> Ye cannot attain to righteousness until ye expend
> in alms of what ye love. But what ye expend in alms,
> that God knoweth.

One was expected to give at least 2.5 percent of what one possessed.[49]

One form of charity is *zakah*, the giving of alms on an obligatory basis. This type of charity requires that one give up a portion of one's wealth in excess of what is personally needed in order to "purify" what one retains. This charity can be paid directly to the poor, to travelers, or to the state. Among others to be assisted were Muslims in debt through pressing circumstances, enslaved persons to buy themselves out of bondage, and for benevolent works. *Sadaqah*, righteousness, was another form of charity that included distribution of a quantity of grain to the poor or its monetary equivalent for every member of a household at the end of Ramadan. A *waqf* is another form of charity in which property is given by will or as a gift in perpetuity to the Islamic state for pious works or for the public good, such as payment for the upkeep of charities and mosques. Those who collected any charity tax were allowed to take their own livelihood from the funds collected.[50]

SUMMARY: EVOLVING VALUES AND SOCIAL WELFARE

This brief excursion enables us to draw several conclusions. From earliest times, all societies, in varying forms, have created social welfare systems for the poor and needy. Motives differ from society to society and situation to situation. Social welfare systems have been based on social, religious, political, economic, and other motives. It is also clear that sometimes social welfare and mutual aid were altruistically and benevolently motivated; at other times, social welfare was used as a social control. Mutual aid mechanisms are universal human inventions that can serve a number of functions; there does not seem to be any historical era or place without them. The availability of a workforce with sufficient energy, aid for victims of disasters, the preservation of life, group morale, the doing of God's will, social justice, the avoidance of violence against the established order—all are reasons for social welfare.

Sometimes there was state and governmental provision; at other times there was religious or private, group or individual responsibility. In some places, strangers were not welcome; in others, strangers were helped, but under certain ground rules. Feudal systems developed in which peasants were owed certain responsibilities by landowners. When the feudal system broke down, peasants had greater independence but also additional problems. Over time a great variety of social welfare institutions were created.

With the spread of Christianity, religious commandments and institutions played the major part in supporting the poor, sometimes at the insistence of the state. We turn now in chapter 3 to developments during the Middle Ages in western Europe, particularly in England, that have influenced most profoundly U.S. social welfare.

QUESTIONS FOR CONSIDERATION

1. Can you identify some ways in which values in your community affect social welfare services or the lack of social welfare services?
2. Are there mutual aid organizations in your community? How many and of what kinds can you identify?
3. Do you see any ways in which the ancient social welfare ideas you read about in this chapter are reflected in today's United States?
4. Religion has always had a major impact on social welfare. Do you think it still does? If so, in what ways?

NOTES

1. Francis Fukuyama, *Trust: The Social Virtues and the Creation of Prosperity*, New York: Free Press, 1995, p. 13.
2. Adam Smith, *The Theory of Moral Sentiments: Of the Sense of Propriety*, eds. D.D. Raphael and A.L. Macfie, Indianapolis: Liberty Classics, 1982, p. 1.
3. Thomas Hobbes, *Leviathan*, Michael Oakeshott, ed., Oxford: Basil Blackwell, 1946, p. 82.
4. Konrad Lorenz, *On Aggression*, London: Methuen, 1967, p. 40; Richard Wrangham and Dale Peterson, *Demonic Males: Apes and the Origins of Human Violence*, New York: Houghton Mifflin Co., 1996; and Richard Dawkins, *The Selfish Gene*, New York: Oxford University Press, 1976.
5. Ronald Grimsley, *The Philosophy of Rousseau*, Oxford: Oxford University Press, 1973, p. 45.
6. Abraham H. Maslow, *Motivation and Personality*, New York: Harper & Row, 1970, pp. 35-58.
7. Dorothy Lee, "Are Basic Needs Ultimate?" in *Personality in Nature, Society, and Culture*, Clyde Kluckhohn and Henry A. Murray, eds., New York: Knopf, 1956, p. 340.
8. Karl Polanyi, *The Great Transformation*, Boston: Beacon Press, 1957, p. 46.
9. John Romanyshyn, *Social Welfare: Charity to Justice*, New York: Random House, 1971, p. 309.
10. Karl Marx, "Capital," *The Communist Manifesto and Other Writings*, Max Eastman, ed., New York: Modern Library, 1932; Milton Friedman, *Capitalism and Freedom*, Chicago: University of Chicago Press, 1962.
11. Polanyi, pp. 163-164.
12. Melville J. Herskovits, *Man and His Works*, New York: Knopf, 1960, p. 267.

13. Erik Trinkhaus, *The Shanidar Neanderthals*, New York: Academic Press, 1983, pp. 422-423. Also see David W. Fryer, William A. Horton, Robert Macchiarelli, and Margharita Mussi, "Dwarfism in an Adolescent from the Italian Late Upper Paleolithic," *Nature*, Vol. 330, No. 6143, November 5-11, 1987, pp. 60-62; Christopher Stringer and Clive Gamble, *In Search of the Neanderthals: Solving the Puzzle of Human Origins*, New York: Thames and Hudson, 1993, pp. 94-95. "Girl of 8, Going on 800," *The Sun*, February 8, 1995, p. 2A.

14. Peter Kropotkin, *Mutual Aid*, Boston: Extending Horizons Books, 1914, p. 296.

15. Robert L. Trivers, "The Evolution of Reciprocal Altruism," *Quarterly Review of Biology*, Vol. 46, No. 1, March 1971, pp. 45-47.

16. Barry Schwartz, "Why Altruism Is Impossible . . . and Ubiquitous," *Social Service Review*, Vol. 67, No. 3, pp. 314-343.

17. Wilcomb E. Washburn, *The Indian and the White Man*, Garden City, N.J.: Anchor Books, 1964, p. 8.

18. Jennings C. Wise, *The Red Man in the New World Drama*, Vine Deloria Jr., ed., New York: Macmillan, 1971, p. 27.

19. John A. Wilson, *The Culture of Ancient Egypt*, Chicago: University of Chicago Press, 1951, p. 74.

20. James B. Pritchard, ed., *The Ancient Near East*, trans. John A. Wilson, Vol. 1, Princeton, N.J.: Princeton University Press, 1973, p. 24.

21. Herman Kees, *Ancient Egypt*, Chicago: University of Chicago Press, 1961, p. 277.

22. Ibid., p. 58.

23. James B. Pritchard, ed., "The Instruction of Amen-em-opet," chap. 28 in *Ancient Near Eastern Texts*, trans. John A. Wilson, Princeton, N.J.: Princeton University Press, 1969, p. 424.

24. Samuel N. Kramer, *History Begins at Sumer*, Philadelphia: University of Pennsylvania Press, 1981, p. 102.

25. H. W. F. Saggs, *The Greatness That Was Babylon*, London: Sidgewick and Jackson, 1966, pp. 171-172, 198.

26. Phillip Blackman, ed., *Ethics of the Fathers*, New York: Judaica Press, 1964, p. 44.

27. Salo W. Baron, *A Social and Religious History of the Jews*, Vol. 1, *To the Beginning of the Christian Era*, New York: Columbia University Press, 1962, p. 86.

28. A. R. Hands, *Charities and Social Aid in Greece and Rome*, London: Thames and Hudson, 1968, pp. 65-69.

29. "Philanthropy," *Encyclopedia Britannica*, Vol. 17, 1970, p. 823.

30. Noel T. Timms, *Social Work*, London: Routledge and Kegan Paul, 1973, pp. 17-18.

31. Jerome Carcopino, *Daily Life in Ancient Rome*, New Haven, Conn.: Yale University Press, 1963, pp. 16, 65.

32. Jean Danielou and Henri Marrou, *The First Six Hundred Years*, New York: McGraw-Hill, 1964, pp. 14-15.

33. Robert M. Grant, *Early Christianity and Society*, San Francisco: Harper & Row, 1977, p. 127.

34. Abraham J. Malherbe, *Social Aspects of Early Christianity*, Baton Rouge, La.: Louisiana State University Press, 1977, pp. 67-68.

35. John G. Gager, *Kingdom and Community: The Social World of Early Christianity*, Englewood Cliffs, N.J.: Prentice Hall, 1975, p. 24.

36. Michael Grant, *The Climax of Rome*, London: Weidenfeld and Nicolson, 1968, pp. 126, 128, 131.

37. John G. Davies, *The Early Christian Church*, New York: Holt, Rinehart and Winston, 1965, p. 66.

38. Grant, p. 60.
39. Judith Herrin, "Ideals of Charity, Realities of Welfare: The Philanthropic Activity of the Byzantine Church," *Church and People in Byzantium*, Rosemary Morris, ed., Birmingham, Eng.: University of Birmingham, 1990, pp. 153–158.
40. Peter Brown, *The World of Late Antiquity*, London: Thames and Hudson, 1971, p. 185.
41. Herrin, p. 159.
42. Grant, pp. 83, 99.
43. Cho-yun Hsu, *Ancient China in Transition*, Palo Alto, Calif.: Stanford University Press, 1965, p. 11.
44. Ibid., pp. 109–110.
45. Nancy Lee Swan, trans., *Food and Money in Ancient China*, Princeton, N.J.: Princeton University Press, 1950, pp. 60–61.
46. I-T'Ang Hsu, "Social Relief During the Sung Dynasty," *Chinese Social History*, E-Tu Zen Sun and John De Francis, eds., New York: Octagon Books, 1972, pp. 207, 208, 214.
47. It is unclear how girls were cared for. In Indian languages there are words that are inclusive of both genders, and inattention may be a function of translation lapses. Or the omission in the sources may reflect a historical attitude toward younger women. Because some castes followed matriarchal systems and others were patriarchal, some ambiguity exists on this point.
48. Gurumukh Ram Madan, *Indian Social Problems*, Bombay: Allied Publishers, 1967, p. 15; R. C. Majumdar, "Social Work in Ancient and Medieval India," *History and Philosophy of Social Work in India*, A. R. Wadia, ed., New York: Allied Publishers, 1968, pp. 16–19.
49. Robert Roberts, *The Social Laws of the Qoran*, Atlantic Highlands, N.J.: Humanities Press, 1990, pp. 71–72.
50. Cyril Glasse, *The Concise Encyclopedia of Islam*, New York: Harper & Row, 1989, pp. 132, 341, 417, 430.

Social Values and Social Welfare: England from the Middle Ages Onward

For the poor shall never cease out of the land; therefore I command thee,
saying: "Thou shalt surely open thy hand unto thy poor and needy brother
in thy land."
—*Deuteronomy 15:11*

OVERVIEW

In this chapter we examine the chief trends and major social welfare events, primarily in England, from the Middle Ages to the development of the Poor Laws, Speenhamland, the workhouses, and the Poor Law of 1834. We undertake this review to demonstrate that events following the Middle Ages represented a significant departure from the earlier ways in which poor people were perceived. We also do this because U.S. social welfare has been influenced in so many ways by historical developments in England and English perspectives on the poor.

THE EARLY MIDDLE AGES

The Middle Ages have been divided into three separate phases. The first stage was the feudalization of western European society, roughly from the sixth to the tenth centuries, when "barbarian" successor states replaced a collapsed Roman Empire. From the king down, a hierarchy was created in which each person knew his or her place and responsibilities. The manorial system of vassalage (vassals were granted feudal land in return for homage and military service) was a system for control of society and included the lord, his vassals, and serfs (peasants bound to the land). The serf owed work and portions of agricultural produce to the lord, and the lord ostensibly owed protection and support to the serfs who worked his land.

The 1066 Norman conquest of Anglo-Saxon England by William the Conqueror established political feudalism on the basis that all the land belonged to this king, who then granted portions of it to barons (the tenants-in-chief) in return for certain services, generally for military purposes such as guard, escort, and provisioning of troops. The barons granted lands to knights, who became their vassals, and, in turn, the knights could grant lands to others. The land grants included the tenants with their obligations to the lords of the manors. Still relatively few people controlled most of England's land.

Peasants were tied to the manor and owed work and taxes. They had to mill their grain at the lord's mill; bake their bread in the lord's oven; pay a fine at the marriage of a daughter; give the lord their best beast at their death; and answer in the lord's court for failure to perform any required services.[1]

The serf's life was hard. Housing was poor, food was short, and starvation loomed during famines. The lord owned the land; he controlled the meadow and the woods. The serfs owed rents, gave labor service and gifts, and also paid fines to the lords. Each household was expected to give tithes to the church and charity to the local poor. The lord's rulings were final and the serf's status was servile. The lords, on their side, gave protection. Welfare benefits did exist for the serfs tied to the manors on which they were born. They could be released from the year-round work for up to 30 days, if sick. If they died, their wives did not have to serve for the following 30 days. Even so, boon work (additional work at ploughing time and harvest) had to be done or a substitute found and paid.[2]

This agrarian economy produced very little surplus; production for market was low. Rents were paid in labor or in-kind because there was little money in circulation. Upper-class incomes were measured in produce rather than cash. There was little effective demand for luxuries. Town populations were small, with the lords and peasants constituting the overwhelming majority of the population.[3] Life was hard for both landlords and tenants, and famines were common. Between the tenth and fifteenth centuries, there were—excluding local outbreaks—49 general famines.[4]

But it was not just famine and wars that threatened stability. Orders prevented people from withdrawing or avoiding services such as threshing and other manual work.[5] Periodically the demands upon the peasantry would become increasingly burdensome. There might be a demand for higher farm rents, restrictions on the freedom of the tenants on lords' estates, or labor obligations added to the rent. Naturally this increased existing tensions among landholders, serfs, and tenants.[6]

The poor were not without certain protections. Canon law demanded that each parish, the ecclesiastic subdivision on the local level, provide for the poor. Poverty was not a crime. Brian Tierney contrasted the attitude of the English in the early Middle Ages with their views during the early twentieth century, when as late as 1909 an English royal commission assumed that every poor person was poor because of a "defect in the citizen character."[7]

In thirteenth-century society, an individual whose wealth exceeded his needs consistent with his status was obligated to assist the poor. The following canonical directives confirm this: "Feed the poor. If you do not feed them, you kill them." "Our superfluities belong to the poor." "Whatever you have beyond what suffices for your needs belongs to others." "A man who keeps for himself more than he needs is guilty of theft."[8]

It was the responsibility of the clergy of each parish to provide "hospitality" for travelers and other guests, and to take care of the poor. Even St. Francis of Assisi made a distinction between holy poverty and other kinds of poverty. He wrote in his last testament: "I have worked with my hands and I choose to work, and I firmly wish that all my brothers should work at some honorable trade. And if they do not know how, let them learn."[9]

The only grounds for refusing to provide charity was the belief that it would encourage idleness. The "willfully idle" should not be assisted. Every able-bodied person was expected to earn his keep after a few days. Several centuries later, distinguishing between the *deserving* and *undeserving* poor became crucial in determining aid. In the early Middle Ages, however, such distinctions apparently were not clearly defined.

As prescribed by canon law parishes and monasteries practiced charitable acts and provided relief. These efforts may have been somewhat haphazard and were clearly insufficient, but they must be viewed within the broader context of scarcity and want. Consider, for example, the general plight of many peasants:

> They all lived in unsanitary conditions; they had no doctors, and at times pestilence swept away whole communities. Few families could store grain; a year of flood or drought created terrible famines. The peasants could not defend themselves against heavy-armed feudal cavalry, and if their lord became involved in a war they were almost sure to see their fields ravaged and their houses burned. It is not surprising that the span of life was short, that a man of forty was considered old.[10]

THE MIDDLE MIDDLE AGES

The second phase of the Middle Ages—from the eleventh to the early fourteenth centuries—brought a growth of the population, an expansion of cultivated areas, some technical progress, and market-oriented production. A surplus appeared owing to three factors: (1) increased technical efficiency; (2) improved administration; and (3) increased pressure to transfer more of the surplus from producers to lords.

The quickened pace of economic activity generally benefitted the urban areas, which became a focus for the efforts of artisans, retail traders, industrial entrepreneurs, unskilled laborers, servants, and other poor people. The movement into the towns also was the consequence of rural overpopulation, which became acute by the end of the thirteenth century. Despite these positive signs, persistent demands for rents, tithes, and taxes by landowners, the church, and the state continued to produce social upheavals and uncertainty.

For example, a village revolt in 1261 at Mears Ashby, Northhamptonshire, was followed by another in 1278 in Harmondsworth, Middlesex. Sometimes these conflicts related to rent collections; at other times they were connected with the collective refusal to provide services for the landlords.[11] Serfdom was degrading, and people were forced into hierarchical relationships. There was confusion regarding individual rights and restraints. But the line between liberty and servitude could never be forgotten. Serfdom meant subordination and arbitrariness, which people feared and resented. At the same time they lacked mobility and freedom.[12]

Still, in the context of U.S. social welfare and our ideas about the poor, one must consider Tierney's view about how the poor were treated in the Middle Ages. He concluded that "in this particular matter, I am inclined to think that, taken all in all, the poor were better looked after in England in the thirteenth century than in any subsequent century until the present one. The only reservation we need make is that perhaps that is not saying much."[13]

Whatever Tierney's judgment as to the treatment of the poor, one has to keep in mind that

> the lord's household could be both a terror and a benefit to the villagers. When a peasant defaulted on payments or revolted, it was the lord's household that would be the ultimate source of discipline.
>
> Members of the household could enter a tenant's house, take his goods, and imprison him with impunity. On the other hand, if the lord wished to look after the interests of his peasants, he would use his household to punish their enemies.[14]

Thus, the relationships of the lords and the peasantry were complicated, reflecting both their need for each other and the tensions relating to their conflicting needs and status differences.

→ THE LATE MIDDLE AGES TO ELIZABETHAN POOR LAWS

In the late Middle Ages, new towns arose, colonization of new lands began, and the growth of international trade spurred the formation of money economies. The feudal system gave way to wage-based relationships, and the serf and the lord severed their allegiances and responsibilities. There was a loss of what economic security existed. By the thirteenth century, many English peasants had become small landholders. Poverty persisted but there also were indications of prosperity: cathedral building and the production of metal, cloth, gold, and other substances. With the rise of wage labor, serfdom declined and those on the land experienced new freedom and independence. The retreat of feudal society was also accompanied by the appearance of vagrants, transients, and migrants. A rooted society was giving way to one in which mobility was becoming more the norm. From a life defined by *status*—the relationship of lord and serf—a new relationship was evolving determined by *contracts* between parties. Power had become a negotiable commodity.

Those needing a steady and dependable labor supply did not appreciate a state of affairs in which people could escape from the traditional roles and places. Nor were they prepared to deal with marauders. Begging became widespread and gained a degree of acceptance, especially because the act of giving charity to care for the poor was a religious obligation and both begging and giving had long been practiced with the blessings of the Church.[15]

In addition to individual acts of charity, more than 8,000 parishes did charitable work in medieval England. Religious monastic orders served both the local poor and strangers passing through.[16] It is of interest, however, that during the Middle Ages, the percentage of monastic income actually devoted to charity varied widely. Estimates ranged from 1 percent to more than 22 percent; however, the national average did not reach 2.5 percent.[17] Strangers were to be helped without discrimination, as well as infidels and excommunicants. Thus, in the thirteenth century, there was little if any discrimination based on eligibility categories or residence.

Other institutions served important roles for the poor. The guilds, which were voluntary commercial and social associations of merchants and artisans, functioned as mutual aid societies and charitable organizations for their own members. They built and maintained hospitals,[18] fed the needy on feast days, distributed corn and barley annually, provided free lodgings for poor travelers, and gave other incidental help.[19]

In addition, the guilds provided disaster insurance, specifying assistance for poverty, sickness, old age, blindness, loss of limb, loss of cattle, fall of a house, false imprisonment, and temporary financial problems, as well as losses by fire, flood, robbery, or shipwreck. There were eligibility limitations, and a member could be helped only three times in a lifetime and then only when the crisis was not of his doing.

Another pillar of social welfare was the private foundation, created by the bequests and gifts of individual philanthropists. At the time of the Reformation there were in England at least 460 charitable foundations. As much a part of medieval life as they are today, foundations established almshouses, hospitals, and other institutions; provided money for funerals; and disbursed funds on the anniversaries of the benefactor.[20]

Hospitals of various types were established during the Middle Ages, including leper houses, orphanages, maternity homes, and institutions for the aged and the infirm. In fact, in mid–fourteenth-century England there were 600 hospitals.[21] But for the most part, peasants would not have had access to hospitals or monasteries for retirement and terminal illness. They formed voluntary organizations on their own that provided some benefits to the aged and the helpless. Of 507 guilds that returned descriptions of their charters in 1389, about one third (154) provided their members with benefits during disaster or old age.[22]

It is estimated that there were some 500 to 700 hospitals in late medieval England, but only a few specialized in caring for the aged, poor women in childbirth, maimed soldiers, and the "deserving poor." Mostly, they provided temporary shelter, taking persons in for only one night. Furthermore, most were small, serving perhaps a dozen persons. A comment by Henry VII in 1509 suggests concern over this situation:

There be fewe or non such commune Hospitalls within our Reame, and
that for lack of them, infinite nombre of pouer nedie people miserably
dailly die, no man putting hand of help or remedie.[23]

Tithing was a feature of life in the Middle Ages, and in England church funds secured from parishioners were divided: one third for the maintenance of the church,
one third for the poor, and one third for the priests.[24] Individuals at every level of society were expected to give to the poor. During the thirteenth century, King John—
in debt himself—continued to give alms to the poor from his revenues.[25]

Several important factors combined to force upon the English of the late Middle Ages a very different attitude toward the poor. The movement from rural to urban settings was stimulated by the introduction of woolen manufacturing. Within a
relatively short period of time the manufacture of woolen goods became in England
so extensive that an export trade was established.

With the growth of cities, trade, money economies, and international relations,
the expiring feudal system forced large numbers of people into social chaos. Wars
created a pool of wanderers who were not eager to stay in one place and who were
skilled thieves. People were also displaced from their former positions, physically
and psychologically. The old truths were no longer valid. With the necessity for
sheep grazing in order to grow wool for the textile industry, land was "enclosed,"
and peasants were forced from the land, dislocated, unattached, and without means
of support.

The fourteenth and fifteenth centuries have been characterized as the third or
last phase of the Middle Ages. Prior to the first part of the fourteenth century, the
population of England had grown. Severe cold weather throughout Europe from
1200 to 1400 A.D. contributed to erratic eras of drought and flood, abundance and
famine. Commencing with flood and famine from 1315 to 1317, the population began to decline. About the middle of the fourteenth century, ensuing events intensified a rapid diminution of the population.[26]

Much starvation and disease followed the first wave of the Black Death
(bubonic plague) in 1348. The plague continued through the fifteenth century,
which saw the demise of serfdom. The plague revisited England in 1361, 1368, and
1375 and was not completely eliminated until the seventeenth century. Not only was
there population loss in England, but also a series of plagues decimated the European
population during this time. Although there is a dispute as to the exact dimensions of
the population loss, the estimates range from 20 to 50 percent of the population.

Even before the middle of the fourteenth century there were difficulties finding
tenants for numerous landholdings. A poor climate for agriculture, famines, continuous wars in northern Europe, as well as plagues decimated many parts of Europe, including England. It was the Plague of 1348, however, that initiated a scarcity of labor
of great proportions, and a new value was awarded to the available labor because of
this scarcity.

Other changes resulted from these devastating events. In England, per capita
bequests were much higher in the 1350s than they had been earlier in the fourteenth
century. Prior to the onset of the plague in London, only about 5 percent of all per-

sons registering their wills in the Hustings Court provided fi
tween 1350 and 1360, this figure tripled and the amount of th
by almost 40 percent. Charity funded institutions helped p
moted the good works that counted toward salvation.[27]

The loss of population undermined the manorial systen
teenth century, and migration to towns created a pronoun
tural workers. In England, more than 1,300 villages were de;
1500, almost all in marginal farming lands. The emancipation of the ..
halt, and landlords tried desperately to retain the traditional services of their tenants.
Free laborers, of course, used the shortage of labor as leverage to demand higher
wages.[28]

There was a general breakdown of law and order as the economic and military
power of the landholders, as well as their social prestige, declined. Local landholders
operated the police and the courts because law enforcement was a local prerogative.
This breakdown is reflected by the increased incidence of homicide, which from
1349 to 1369 was about double that of the period from 1320 to 1340.[29]

Because of the shift in power from landholders to workers, the late Middle
Ages has been referred to as the "Golden Age of Laborers," and it is believed that real
wages were higher in the fifteenth century than at any time in history until the twentieth century. From the beginning of the thirteenth century to the beginning of the
fifteenth century, agricultural prices fell by 10 percent, real wages multiplied 2.5
times, and cash wages nearly doubled.[30]

Because of their scarcity, laborers were in a position to seek higher wages and
to make demands where historically demands had all come from lords and landholders. Illustrative of this trend is the pay scale for ploughmen:

> A ploughman who was paid 2 shillings a week in 1347 received 7
> shillings in 1349 and 10 shillings 6 pence by 1350. . . . Day laborers not
> only received higher wages, but asked for and got lunches of meat pies
> and golden ale.[31]

To deal with the new freedom of the serfs and a scarcity of labor, and to assure
a supply of agricultural workers, a series of laws was enacted. In 1349, the *Statute of
Labourers* was passed to force those who were able-bodied and without other
means of support to work for an employer in their own parish *at rates prevailing
before the plague*. This statute is the first of poor law legislation that evolved over
the next four centuries.

A national system of enforcement was established that made it illegal to demand or offer higher wages than had been the standard in 1346. Laborers were expected to contract to stay with an employer for a year or another appropriate period,
and there was to be no daily hiring. Laborers had to swear an oath that they would
obey the provisions of the statute or be placed in the stocks. Those with sufficient
land to keep them occupied were exempt from the obligation to work for wages. In
some areas, during the first ten years following the statute's enforcement, laborers
paid, through fines, as much as one third or one half of the tax burden that the

ier formerly had paid. But, ultimately, such measures were not successful and ted in a sense of grievance as all efforts to control the workers failed. The landlords discovered the only way to retain laborers was to pay the going rate.[32]

The effects of the bubonic plague not only were problematic in the countryside but affected urban centers and commercial activity as well. The wealthy of the cities also tried to retain what they had, and restrictive guild regulations and city ordinances were enacted. In the twelfth century, any industrious young apprentice might become a master after completion of the appropriate training.[33] By the latter part of the fourteenth century, eligibility for becoming apprenticed in many guilds was limited to the sons of masters or to those who married their daughters. A large group of urban laborers lived at the beck and call of their masters and were forbidden to organize to foster their own interests. Not surprisingly, there was much resentment among these laborers and frequent riots among the peasants, including the French Jacquerie (1358), the English Peasant's Rebellion (1381), and the town revolts by artisans in Bruges (1302), Ghent (1381), and Rouen (1382)—all of which were quickly crushed. One exception occurred in Florence (1378), where workers held control of the city for three years.[34]

The Statute of Labourers denounced not only those who sought higher wages but also, more emphatically, those who chose to beg rather than earn their bread. In an effort to maintain the traditional system, the statute provided that all *able-bodied* persons under 60 years without means of subsistence must work, that alms could not be given to able-bodied beggars, and that runaway serfs could be made to work for anyone who claimed them. In medieval society, work was expected of all; idleness was a crime.

In 1352, in England, workers demanded, and some employers paid, wages two and three times the pay rate before the plague. During the 1350s and 1360s, fugitive laborers were declared outlaws; if caught they were branded on the forehead with an "F," for "fugitive" or "falsity"; stocks were set up for punishment; and imprisonment was often used as a penalty. Those who were wandering and unemployed outside their own parishes were whipped, branded, sent to toil in the royal galleys, or set into stocks for three days.[35]

Begging was permissible for the *impotent* poor, that is, those who could not possibly work. By the last years of the fifteenth century, pregnant women and extremely sick men and women were considered among the impotent. Shortly after, those poor over the age of 60 years were added to the list of the impotent. The categorization of those in need was established, and the beginnings of differentiation between the "*deserving*" and the "*undeserving*" poor were initiated. Thus continued a series of punitive laws that culminated in the Elizabethan Poor Laws in the latter part of the sixteenth century.

WORK AND RELIGION

Martin Luther in 1517 presaged still other changes with his momentous posting of the 95 Theses on the door of Castle Church in Wittenberg, the initiator and focal point of a religious revolution. As a result, the foundations of Roman Catholicism were challenged, especially the notion of papal authority, and the Protestant Reformation followed. With this one act a theological conflagration was lit and a political revolution began that weakened the Holy Roman Empire and fostered the development of the modern nation-state.

Luther defined *vocation* as a calling to do God's work in all things; a vocation was an

> exaltation of the common occupations as the appropriate spheres in which to serve God acceptably. The term vocation was transferred by Luther from the cloister to the workshop. . . . [T]he farmer, the doctor, the school teacher, the minister, the magistrate, the house-mother, the maidservant and the manservant were all of them religious callings, vocations in which one was bound to render no lip service but to work diligently at serving not merely an earthly but also a heavenly master.[36]

Luther's teachings improved the morale of laborers, giving them a sense of duty in doing an honest day's toil; his beliefs also resulted in an elevation of the family, and of individuals as well, in the sense that all callings were important.

During the sixteenth century, Calvinism also began to make its mark. The distinction between the cloister and the marketplace was broken down even more; one could serve God as well in the marketplace as in any other place. Work was a divine vocation and thus a religious activity. Idleness and the temptations of the world distract us from the pursuit of righteous living; work was for the glory of God. Max Weber describes Calvinism in this way: It was "not leisure and enjoyment, but only activity [which] serves to increase the glory of God. . . . Waste of time is thus the first and in principle the deadliest of sins." Loss of time through sociability, idle talk, luxury, even more sleep than is necessary for health (six to at most eight hours) is worthy of absolute moral condemnation. Work could be viewed as a chief end for life and, as St. Paul suggested, "He who will not work shall not eat."[37]

Paradoxically, the "elevation" of the individual enhanced by the "calling" of an occupation was a double-edged sword. According to Calvinist doctrine, a calling reduced uncertainty—the reality of life—by limiting mobility. For the sake of order, each person had an obligation to remain within his or her calling:

> The best way, therefore, to maintain a peaceful life is when each one is intent on the duties of his own calling, carries out the commands that the Lord has given, and devotes himself to these tasks; when the farmer is busy with the work in cultivation, the workman carries on his trade, and in this way each keeps within his proper limits. As soon as men turn aside from this, everything is thrown into confusion and disorder.[38]

The values of Calvinism very much affected our ideas on social welfare through the centuries. The Calvinism of England in particular stressed personal responsibility and discipline and an intense individualism in social affairs. Pauperism was viewed as a question of character. Calvin himself condemned indiscriminant almsgiving and urged ecclesiastical authorities to visit families regularly to see if they were idle, drunken, or otherwise undesirable. Idleness was a sin against God and a social evil; not to work meant to refuse to listen to God's word. For the glory of God, society must be served. Those who were dependent were somehow "marred."[39] The impulse to work was sacred. Upright character, integrity, and work were the products of faith. If one's economic state was improved as a result of industry, sobriety, honesty, and frugality, this was only a by-product of doing God's work.[40] Conspicuous consumption was still frowned on, so wealth tended to be reinvested, to become capital.

A new system was being created, both economic and social; people were being separated from the land and moving to the cities. Towns and cities were being enlarged for manufacture and commerce, including international commerce. Poor people were not just the victims of famines and war; new forces came into play that victimized them in new ways. Employment became variable, with cycles influenced not only by local events but also by unseen international occurrences.

Serfdom provided some insurance against sickness and old age; now poverty of a new kind developed. During the Middle Ages people were poor, but those who had the greatest difficulty surviving were those we would now refer to as *case poverty* (widows, orphans, the old, the blind, the mutilated, and those infirm from long illnesses) in the sense that they resulted from *individual* tragedies. But from the fourteenth century, English poverty was also of the *structural* type and developed from the changed *economic structure* of society. When living on feudal manors, a person disabled by injury could be assisted at the local level. However, when entire industries located in cities were affected by their international markets and people were thrown out of work, the resources available for those affected were far more limited. People could not fall back on the farmland. Previously famine could cause widespread danger, but now industry and commerce could cruelly cause poverty and do so in complex ways beyond the control of individuals.

Laborers gathered into the crowded towns and cities. The extent of exemptions from taxation on the grounds of poverty suggest at least one-third of the population lived marginally in most cities, and in some cities the percentage was more than one half. Those who migrated into towns were mainly unskilled and found only intermittent work.[41]

The expansion of markets and the creation of new technologies in combination with many other factors gave impetus to the Industrial Revolution. According to one interpreter, many factors contributed to that revolution, including the rise of "factory towns, the emergence of slums, the long working hours of children, the low wages of certain categories of workers, the rise in the rate of population increase . . . [and] the concentration of industries." All these in the view of Polanyi "were merely incidental to one basic change, the establishment of market economy." But the rise of a market economy demanded certain costs. Polanyi continues, "Machine production in a commercial society involves, in effect, no less a transformation than that of the natural and human substance of society into commodities."[42]

When people are needed to strive in the "satanic mills," to produce for markets within industrializing and urbanizing societies, they become essential parts, as labor, of the grinding wheels. When this role is viewed within the context that productivity is a sign of the elect standing in the world, the burden of poverty falls squarely on the shoulders of individuals, regardless of the more complicated causation that actually creates their impoverished conditions. The message communicated was that individuals demonstrate their spiritual condition through the signs that God has provided. Poverty, then, means unworthiness, and in fact, poor people can be viewed as undeserving.

In 1531 in an attempt to deal with the phenomenon of beggars and vagabonds, the government of England introduced for the first time the principle of governmental responsibility and provision. Evolving out of great concern about the numbers of persons who were idle, or committing thefts and murders, this initial act first provided for those in genuine need such as aged and disabled poor persons. Local authorities were authorized to certify these people by letter indicating they were eligible to beg, the first legal assumption by government of responsibility for care of the poor.

The able-bodied poor, however, were treated much differently. Fines were imposed on those who would give "any harboring, money, or lodging to any beggars being strong and able in their bodies to work." An idle man was whipped and after the punishment was forced to return to the place of his birth or last dwelling place and there to "put himself to labour like as a true man oweth to do."[43]

In 1536, Henry VIII, under the Dissolution of the Monasteries Act, expropriated all monasteries with an annual income of less than 200 English pounds. The property and wealth of the monasteries were given to the King's followers. By 1540 all monasteries and their wealth were taken with few exceptions. These actions effectively did away with one of the pillars of social welfare and also minimized the ascetic ideal. The people most adversely affected were those monks who had to rely on rather meager pensions; nuns who had still smaller pensions, who remained unmarried, and were not otherwise employed; domestic servants who found it difficult to obtain alternative employment; and an unknown number of poor persons who relied on the monasteries for charity. Those less wealthy persons who donated livestock or other in-kind resources to the monasteries in exchange for permanent food and shelter were protected by the Dissolution Act and paid in cash rather than in-kind.[44]

Also in 1536, a statute was passed creating a comprehensive English system of relief. The statute provided that those returned after punishment to their former places of residence were entitled to food and lodging every ten miles for one night from the parish constable. Further loitering would be punished by whipping, cutting off the right ear, or even death. Children aged 5 to 14 could be apprenticed out. Church collections were to be used to care for "the poor, impotent, lame, feeble, sick, and diseased people, being not able to work." Where parishes had a surplus it was to be used to provide support for the poorer parishes. The collectors were to be paid "good and reasonable" wages and thus became the first paid public welfare personnel. In addition to registration of need, licensed begging was replaced by funds derived from contributions stimulated through the force of the state and the clergy. Those who were "strong enough to labor" were given employment. Although this responsibility for providing jobs was not spelled out, the important principle of public responsibility to provide work when work could not be found was laid down for the first time in England. Thus work relief was born in the welfare system.[45]

Idlers were detested in English society and by 1547 a V could be marked on their breast with a hot iron and they could be enslaved for two years. If idlers ran away when captured a letter S could be burned on their foreheads or cheeks and they could be enslaved forever. If there was a repetition of this behavior, the sentence was death. These laws proved to be too severe and were repealed in 1550. Concurrently, licensed begging was revived.

When the nation-state developed as a full-blown institution in society, there was a simultaneous reevaluation of the role of the monolithic church. Where there had been parallel bodies of binding law, the state began to take on many of the responsibilities that previously rested more fully with the church.

As early as 1526 in Spain, Juan Luis Vives set forth a plan for communal care of the poor in his *De Subventione Pauperum (On the Supervision of the Poor)*. According to his plan, two senators with a secretary were to visit each institution where paupers were housed and investigate the living conditions, meanwhile counting and listing names. Those living in private homes were to be similarly registered. Those who were of a certain age and without a trade were to be taught one. Irksome tasks were to be assigned to those who dissipated their "fortunes in riotous living." Those unable to find work, including the blind, were to be assigned such work. This plan included a communal duty to care for the poor, local-level inquiry into the situations of the poor so as to prioritize them, and the registration and development of different categories of the poor, particularly based on moral grounds. Similar plans were developed in Germany in the early 1520s, in the southern Netherlands in 1524–1525, in Venice in 1528–1529, in France in the 1530s, and in Spain after 1540.

It is instructive to review the Venetian plan for the sake of comparison and to acknowledge the international nature of the problems of poverty and the similar approaches to dealing with those problems. Venice established machinery for discriminating between the worthy and the unworthy poor, developed a system of priorities for giving relief so as to eliminate "social parasites," and distinguished among paupers who were physically handicapped, able-bodied but not employed, and physically whole but ill equipped by upbringing to do manual labor. The Venetians encouraged the greatest number of applicants to be self-supporting: They gave the able-bodied opportunities to work, and they forced those able-bodied who did not want to work to do so through corporal punishment or threat of expulsion from Venice. Beggar children were educated so as to enable them to work and be absorbed into the economic system. The impotent poor, the aged, the crippled, and others were helped through accommodation in hospitals and through distribution of charity to their homes. As a last resort, they were given licenses to beg, which signified their worthiness to be given charity. Paupers were the responsibility of their native communities. Native paupers had priority over strangers, and there was a municipal organization to supervise and administer poor relief.[46]

THE POOR LAWS

During the sixteenth century, a series of laws called the *Poor Laws* were enacted in England. The result of centuries of periodic social unrest—famines, epidemics, wars, enclosures, urbanization, unemployment and labor supply problems, rising prices, and increases in the number of persons seeking poor relief—the laws consisted of experiments with methods of alleviating distress, preventing vagrancy, and maintaining social stability.

In 1572 the aged, poor, disabled, and other persons born within each county or those who had resided there for three years or more were to be "sought out, registered and assigned for their habitations and abidings." Justices of the peace were to determine weekly charges to maintain them; to tax and assess all inhabitants of every city, town, and village; and to use the proceeds for the relief of the poor. Collectors were appointed as well as overseers of the poor and work relief. Thus was started the first legislation for taxes for poor relief and the institution of overseers of the poor who were to put the able-bodied to work. Those who refused to work were sent to the Houses of Correction. Severe punishments were to be taken against "idlers, beggars, rogues, and vagabonds." These latter types were to receive funds only after the worthy poor had their needs met, and the able-bodied were to be helped only in return for their labor.[47]

The Poor Law Compilation of 1601

Following a period of near famine from 1594 on, there were unusual destitution and periodic disturbances, including small rebellions and an increase in vagrancy. Legislation was enacted in 1597 (39 Eliz. c3) and in 1601 (43 Eliz. c2; see Chart 3.1) that systematized earlier laws and became the basis for the English Poor Law system.

These laws provided for the implementation of a national system. This plan placed greater emphasis on civil power, which now made it compulsory for every parish to provide for the poor by levying a tax on all occupiers of property within its bounds. Relief was to be locally financed and locally administered for local residents. An unpaid parish officer—the overseer of the poor—was appointed whose duties were to collect the tax and see that it was spent on relief, to apprentice the children of paupers to a trade, and to assign work to the able-bodied poor. Piecework was to be arranged for persons in their own homes to repay the charity of the local community. It was the responsibility of the overseers and of the church wardens to take care

CHART 3.1   The Chief Provisions of the 1601 Poor Laws

1. A central administration was formed to ensure implementation of the laws throughout England.
2. Each parish was responsible to provide for the poor by levying a tax on occupiers of property.
3. Unpaid officers—overseers of the poor and church wardens—were appointed to collect taxes, spend the funds on poor relief, assign work to the able-bodied, and apprentice the children of paupers.
4. Parents were responsible for their children and grandchildren, as were the grandchildren and children for the grandparents.
5. Justices of the peace were to send to jail those who did not pay their poor taxes or refused to work.
6. Parishes could call upon other parishes when they were unable to provide relief for their poor.

of the various categories of poor people: able-bodied, disabled, children, aged, blind, or those who for other reasons were impoverished. Direct grants were available for the unemployable and a work policy existed for those who were able-bodied. Parents with means were liable for their children and grandchildren. Children with means were responsible for parents and grandparents who were unable to work for their own sustenance.

Justices of the peace could send to jail those who refused to work or send to prison those who did not pay their poor tax. If a parish was unable to support its own poor, it could levy other parishes for additional funds. Beyond this, a central administration was formed to ensure the execution of the laws in all parts of England. Locally financed and locally administered poor relief was for local residents. Although repression did not work, government reluctantly assumed a responsibility to help people who could not provide for themselves.[48]

One emphatic and important alteration in the basic poor laws was the *Act of Settlement of 1662*. This statute "empowered the justices to return to his former residence any person, coming to occupy a property renting for less than ten pounds a year, who in the opinion of the overseers might at some future time become in need."[49] It was expected by the various parishes that they would be protected from the poor who belonged elsewhere—at least back in their own parishes.

The Act of Settlement was passed, in part, to remedy a problem created by masses of disbanded soldiers seeking work. Reportedly, this law was never rigidly enforced because a high degree of labor mobility was needed in an economically expanded society. However, such legislation strengthened the local basis of the poor law, and a strong trend toward residency requirements was united with local responsibility, a theme that has continued to our day. It was only three centuries later, in *Shapiro v. Thompson* (U.S. Supreme Court, April 1969), that residency laws as a factor determining eligibility for public assistance were held to be unconstitutional in the United States. This decision finally recognized the reality that local events, at least in regard to employment, poverty, and rights to freedom of movement, were truly reflective of structural problems on a national scale.

During the eighteenth century, there was a growing tendency to deal stringently with able-bodied poor persons, including granting them relief only within an institution (indoor relief) in which they would be required to work. After this strategy failed, *Gilbert's Act* (1782) required that work be found outside the workhouse for the able-bodied (and subsidized out of the poor tax). The poorhouse became an institution for the aged and infirm.

The poor relief system was a ready means for disciplining potentially disorderly persons and the laboring poor. In the closing decades of the seventeenth century and throughout the eighteenth, it is estimated that one third of the population, despite work and good health, were unlikely to be able to support themselves on a regular basis without assistance. This led to people trying by whatever means possible to support themselves and their families. The Poor Laws were seen as a more agreeable means of controlling the poor than dealing with frequent criminal charges and frequent executions.[50]

Problems of poverty on a national scale were thus met in particular ways through governmental legislation. The statute enacted in 1601 is a summary codification of what has come to be called the Elizabethan Poor Laws, incorporating the attitudes and provisions discussed in the preceding pages.

The responsibility for poor relief had been shifted from voluntary charities sponsored by the church, monasteries, foundations, guilds, and private citizens to local governments, which provided orphanages, hospitals, and almshouses for the old. These legal responsibilities were defined by national legislation with accompanying punishments for noncompliance. The control the Poor Laws exerted on individuals was related to productivity and the scarcity of manufactured goods.

> To make them available, it was necessary to have not only land and capital but also human labor. If every human being in society could somehow be converted into an operating unit and induced to work, more manufactured goods would become available. It thus became important to emphasize the virtues of work and the evils of idleness.[51]

What began in the fourteenth century as a means of dealing with a shortage of labor for agricultural work developed by the sixteenth and seventeenth centuries into an entire philosophy that demanded that the undeserving poor (the able-bodied) be controlled and dealt with punitively while deserving poor were treated differently. This change was a result of alterations in the economic, religious, social, and governmental aspects of society. The Poor Laws then stood for almost 300 years as the basis for English and U.S. social welfare.

SPEENHAMLAND

The issue of subsidies to individuals and families has often focused upon the Speenhamland experiment. The specific context in which the justices at Speenhamland decided to create a subsidy is significant. In 1794 and 1795 (including the severe winter of 1794–1795), there had been short harvests. Imports were sparse because the Baltic Sea was frozen well into spring, thus delaying food shipments from Poland and southern Prussia. England also was at war with France, which was seizing English vessels, and the armed forces needed grain. These factors led to a steep rise in the price of bread, a staple food, and there were increases in destitution, starvation, discontent, and bread riots.

In 1795, meeting at the Pelican Inn at Speenhamland, Berkshire, England, the justices of the peace decided to pay subsidies to currently employed individuals and families when the cost of bread rose to 1 shilling. The justices chose to provide the subsidy rather than regulate wages. They urged farmers and others to raise laborers' wages, recommended that a few areas be set aside for the poor to grow potatoes for their own use and sale, and suggested that fuel be collected in the summer for cheap sale in the winter. The subsidy, called the "bread scale," received much publicity. The pension list previously consisted of women, many widows, children, invalids, and old men. Suddenly, with the enactment of the Speenhamland system, the majority of new names were of men.

The supplementation of low and inadequate wages was not a new development at Speenhamland. Outdoor relief was widespread from 1760 to 1795, preceding Speenhamland's subsidy. Parishes adopted outdoor relief policies as a response to two major changes in the southern and eastern parts of England: There was a decline in allotments of land for agricultural laborers and a decline in cottage industries. Parishes responded to these forces and the losses of incomes by guaranteeing seasonally unemployed laborers a minimum weekly poor relief income. These subsidies were not intended to cover maintenance needs but were supplementary to low and inadequate wages. There are definite instances where allowances were provided for men with families too large to be supported by their wages. This practice was well established at the close of the seventeenth century.[52] Farmers were thus subsidized by other parish taxpayers because rural areas were dominated by labor-hiring farmers.

There were other results of the subsidy. According to one view, the subsidy led to ambiguity in the distinction between pauperism and independence. The fear was that the Speenhamland subsidy system was undermining the independence of agricultural laborers. Such fears strengthened the idea that no outdoor relief should be given to the able-bodied poor and suggested they should be maintained in a workhouse. Further, their lives should be regulated and made less comfortable than those outside and fending for themselves, that is, they should be *"less eligible."*

A confusion was institutionalized among wage supplements, providing cash to employed workers to supplement their earnings, and providing family allowances directly to families to assist them. Able-bodied persons became regular recipients of relief, and employers took advantage of the system to maintain wages at a low level.[53]

A prior history and tradition existed for supplementing inadequate wages in the parishes. The poor were put to work on the land where they were needed in a process called "going the rounds" and were given relief at what was considered an appropriate level. Such a system was open to abuse by employers and acted to depress wages.

The *roundsman* system provided for the pauper-laborer to go from house to house seeking work. If work was provided, then he received food for the day and a small wage, while the parish paid a supplemental sum. In some places the Poor Law administrator contracted with employers who would pay a fixed sum for a certain number of poor laborers; the workers' wages were supplemented by relief funds. Another method used was the labor rate. A parish tax was levied to cover the support of the able-bodied unemployed, and a price was set for their services. Taxpayers could employ a number of paupers at the appropriate wage or pay the tax. In all cases allowances were used to restore order by enforcing work at very low wage levels.[54]

Following the implementation of the Speenhamland system in many parts of England, criticism was voiced that has a familiar ring. It was surmised allowances would undermine individual responsibility, lead people to produce children recklessly, and deplete productivity. Furthermore, such allowances, it was thought, would alter fundamentally the basic psychology of "necessary" goading and encourage freedom of choice in regard to work. Moreover, it would cost too much. Essentially this argument derives from the belief that people must be forced to produce. From another point of view, at times subsidies are needed even by the working poor, to prevent starvation and to provide a healthier family life in order to best support productivity and society in general.

After the beginning of the nineteenth century the birthrate did not rise dramatically, and historians differ as to whether productivity actually fell or rose under the

Speenhamland system.[55] One of the lessons of Speenhamland is that such subsidies do not necessarily result in less productive workers or increased birthrates.

Debates on wage supplementation continue in our age, following the basic arguments established when Speenhamland was in operation. This is an issue today. So long as we operate on the theory of the economic being, wage supplementation may demean the labor market, in the sense that employers may lower wages by taking the supplementation into account. The basic problem is that of *less eligibility*: the belief that no person on relief should be paid as much as the lowest wage earner in the community for fear such a wage will impair the labor market. For those who accept the economic view of human beings, such wages will prove counterproductive by diminishing the motivations of those at the poverty level and those just above it.

THE WORKHOUSE

By 1662, urban poverty was an increasing problem. As we saw earlier, destitute individuals were the responsibility of their parish of birth. When sent to their parish of origin, they often took dependent children with them. These children were strangers to the parish, a factor that was even more problematic for those orphaned or abandoned children who were completely unfamiliar to the parish residents. Children whose parents died or disappeared seemed to have no real connection to the parish to which they were removed. This led to great resentment. Sometimes they were apprenticed at the rate (tax) payers expense and sometimes placed in a workhouse.

In 1723 the English Parliament authorized any parish to establish a workhouse. The poor were to produce goods that would earn money for the state. Typically, notice would be given to the poor that their weekly pensions were to be discontinued. Those who were unable to support themselves could apply for admission to the workhouse.

According to one contemporary quotation, "A workhouse is a name that carries along with it an idea of correction and punishment and many of our poor have taken such an aversion to living in it, as all the reason and argument in the world can never overcome."[56] All categories of the poor were housed under one roof, including "fallen" women, the insane, the old, children, paupers, the sick, the disabled, and vagrants. The problems of the workhouses were so bad that in 1762 the Act for Keeping Poor Children Alive was passed. This law required parishes to maintain records of all children admitted to the workhouses so death rates for institutions and their caretakers could be ascertained.

Infant death in the workhouses took place within a particular historical context. With the rise of the propertyless as a proportion of the population, abandonment and infanticide were stimulated. During the eighteenth century, many abandoned infants were sent to parish workhouses, where they died from starvation, beatings, and disease. Overseers of the poor sometimes received lump sum payments from the father or putative father if the infant was born out of wedlock. These children were sometimes murdered by their caretakers and a profit was made from the lump sum payment upon the early death of a child. At London's Foundling Hospital during its first four years of existence (1741-1745), of the 15,000 children placed there, approximately 10,000 died. In Dublin from 1790 to 1796, of 12,600 children placed in a hospital, almost 10,000 died. Some abandoned children were born out of wedlock. Others, a majority, were from couples unable to support them. There are estimates that in eighteenth-century Europe anywhere from 10 percent to 40 percent of urban children were abandoned.[57]

By the nineteenth century, 4,000 workhouses existed in England with approximately 100,000 residents. Despite the widespread use of the workhouse, relief of the poor in their own homes (*outdoor relief*) was the predominant mode of subsidy, utilizing both in-kind and monetary payments.[58]

Workhouses fell short of their goals. The major aim of the workhouses was the profitable employment of the poor; however, they failed. Workhouse labor had to be inefficient: The laborers were either incapable or unwilling. Workhouses were not capable of providing work in spinning and weaving, precisely those tasks more and more performed by machines. The training some children received proved to be obsolete. In other cases, the use of the workhouse as a punitive deterrent, as a house of correction, was contradictory to the aim of production. Thus, the principles of deterrence and of profitable employment conflicted.

The evidence suggests that workhouses gave only temporary relief to the tax rates. The harshness of the workhouses encountered growing criticism, while many institutions became "unsupervised asylums for a mixed population of the impotent and the vicious, and (unfortunately) children."[59]

THE POOR LAW OF 1834

At the beginning of the nineteenth century, the tax to be paid for the poor rose rapidly, as did per capita expenditures for the poor in the latter part of the eighteenth century. Following the defeat of Napoleon, unemployment increased, food prices fell, many small farmers faced bankruptcy, and starvation forced people to apply for relief. Parishes drove paupers out of their territories, and the enactment of the Corn Law of 1815 increased the price of bread while wages remained low.

In 1832, a royal commission was established to review the Poor Laws. The commission was biased against the poor from the start and was supported by several ideological strands: Adam Smith, Thomas Malthus, and Jeremy Bentham. Adam Smith, a theoretician of laissez-faire capitalism, believed that the private interests of individuals in the market were led by an "invisible hand" toward the interest of the whole society. Government should passively police the market and has only three duties: (1) protect society from invasion and violence by other societies; (2) protect, as far as possible, members of society from injustice and oppression of every other member of it; and (3) develop and maintain public works and institutions that can never be the interest of any individual or small group to create and maintain. He believed in the liberty of the individual and free trade among nations.

Thomas Malthus suggested that the human species would breed itself into starvation and ruin. The geometric increase in population would be greater than the ability of people to produce the subsistence needed because food would be harvested only arithmetically. As a result, Malthus concluded pessimistically that misery and vice would spread. Further, the increase in population would decrease demand for labor and result in lowered wages, which would lead to suffering. The poor could only achieve prosperity by abstaining from reproduction (an impossible task). The resources given to undeserving and unproductive paupers can only be given at the expense of deserving laborers because to do so raises the price of food and reduces real wages. Relief leads to increased poverty. The more severe the attitude toward the poor, the greater the true benevolence.[60]

Jeremy Bentham was an exponent of utilitarianism. The "good" equals adding to the sum total of pleasures or diminishing the sum total of pain for a community. In social and economic matters, government should have a hands-off policy. Yet in certain cases, the pursuit of self-interest by individuals, he believed, might not work to the best interest of all individuals. If the pains endured by the many exceeded the pleasures enjoyed by the few, then the state should step in and do something about it.

In 1834, the Reform Poor Law (the New Poor Law) was enacted. Outdoor relief would be available for the sick and the aged, but not for the able-bodied. No relief would be given to able-bodied persons unless they were residents of the workhouse, a highly stigmatized institution. There would be a three-member central Poor Law commission with the power to group parishes into unions for Poor Law administration and to supervise the work of local authorities. Poor Law guardians elected by local taxpayers would be in charge of the disbursement of local relief. The principle of less eligibility and punitive stigmatization of relief recipients were basic principles of the new law.

The 1834 law was a compromise enactment in that strict Malthusians, laissez-faire economists, and others wanted a law that completely put an end to Poor Law relief. In reality, one of the motivations for the revised law was to reduce poor taxes. This did in fact occur following the enactment of the 1834 law. Good harvests and the building of railways undoubtedly had some effect on this drop. However, the trend reversed itself and taxes began to climb once again, although more modestly than in the past. It is likely that voluntary charity played some part in minimizing the need for more rapidly expanding public assistance. But the intent of the 1834 law was primarily to do away with outdoor relief. Some 15 years after the enactment of the New Law of 1834, five times as many people were relieved outside the workhouses as were being given relief inside them.[61]

Still more complex motivations impelled the attempt to abolish outdoor relief. Farming communities were actually in favor of retaining subsidies such as Speenhamland's. However, Parliament was dominated by large landowners who were convinced that outdoor relief was a threat to their rental incomes. On the other hand, grain farmers developed such subsidies as an inexpensive means to provide income for seasonally unemployed workers. So the original abolishment of subsidies was not because it had disastrous effects on the rural economy. Instead it was because landowners who controlled Parliament feared such future consequences.[62]

PRINCIPLES OF THE POOR LAWS

As we have seen, the principles by which treatment of the poor was determined changed dramatically after the thirteenth century. The Poor Laws evolved as a result of changing features of society, including the dissolution of the feudal system, the alteration of the churches, the emphasis on individual responsibility, and the growth of international money and trade economies. All these factors combined to ensure a market in which labor was simply another resource to be maintained. The series of Poor Laws was created to maintain a motivated workforce available for productive employment as well as to minimize the number of shiftless vagrants who might commit violent acts and the number of those dependent upon the community.

The Poor Laws themselves were based on and slowly evolved several principles for dealing with the poor. These principles have remained with us, sometimes in disguised form and often explicitly. Secularism was established as the basic direction of social welfare, despite the existence of a religious social welfare subsystem. Whereas during the Middle Ages there existed both a governmental and an ecclesiastic system, along with other voluntary systems, gradually social welfare became a public responsibility—that is, a secular task for the entire body politic. This development is part of the rise of nation-states, with their need to care for their citizens in order to maintain morale and build the nation. It is also a result of the secularization trend that has evolved over centuries, by which certain church functions and controls have been shifted to the public and governmental bodies. The powers of the ecclesiastical system and the demands it could make on people diminished, while the demands of the nation-state on its citizens increased. Although recent U.S. history has seen a shift away from federal responsibility and toward state, local, and voluntary welfare efforts, overall the provision of social welfare for the masses remains the responsibility of the taxing authority: the secular state. (This topic will be explored in greater detail in chapters 5, 9, 10, and 11.)

The concept of risk or categories also developed as a principle. For example, not only were the poor divided into categories—aged, children, lame, ill, and so forth—but also these categories were further defined in moral terms: the worthy and the unworthy poor. Such definitions led to *means-testing*, or establishing need on the basis of one's income (which has to be below the level required to purchase necessary goods or services). These definitions were congenial to the view that the poor had caused their own poverty, were morally at fault, and could by sufficient motivation and willpower alter their life circumstances. As we saw in chapter 1, such views of the poor remain with us, accompanied by the idea that poverty should be punished, a remnant of philosophies centuries old. Whereas in the Middle Ages all poor were given assistance without consideration of the "category" they were in, now one differentiates between those who are worthy or unworthy of receiving assistance.

Another principle was the establishment of the distinction between *indoor* and *outdoor* relief. Work was demanded from the poor (a demand present in the early monasteries as well); that is, some poor would have to take shelter in a public house or hospital (indoor), whereas others "more deserving" would be supported in their own homes (outdoor). The outdoor/indoor controversy, of which the workhouse is the prime example, continues today in terms of community care for those with chronic mental illness, persons with developmental disabilities, juvenile delinquents, and others.

Although it almost always costs more to have indoor relief, countermoves are typically resisted with vigor, such as the debate on whether to establish foster homes for persons with disabilities or to place the poor in middle-class neighborhoods. Beneath such resistance can be found fear of differences and also the idea that the unworthy should be shunned and out of sight.

Residency laws, as a principle, required that laborers be tied to their lords and employers and then to their home parishes or place of birth. Binding people to places (a throwback to serfdom) served to minimize their bargaining power through restrictions on their freedom to move and thus set limits on what employers had to pay as wages. Thus, residency laws served important economic purposes and had the intention of maintaining a pool of available labor for production accompanied by control over wages.

The principles of less eligibility and wage supplementation are hotly debated even today. The question of *less eligibility* (the poor must not be supported at a level as high as that of the lowest employed person in the community) is one of the most intractable problems facing social welfare. With the establishment of less eligibility, a problem of great difficulty was identified and a solution was suggested that assumed that humans are economic beings.

The solution, however, has proved problematic. Although the original intent for less eligibility assumed that the poor could be motivated only in this way, the results of following such a principle are open to question. As we saw in the case of Speenhamland, the "payoff" was really not for the employees, but actually was a use of public means to subsidize the employers: The main effect of the allowance system was to depress wages below the subsistence level. Methods need to be found to deal with this problem, especially ways that recognize the structural nature of high unemployment and poverty in a multinational, technological economy.

Finally, the fact that the social problems of the needy were approached by and large on a *case-by-case* basis has supported the assumption that the problem rests with the individual or family. Such views are still subtly expressed in current social work when insufficient attention is paid to the structural determinants of social need and too much emphasis is placed on the responsibility of individuals and families. Such views have far-reaching implications for social welfare.

SUMMARY

In this chapter, we have surveyed the major trends and social welfare events from the Middle Ages to the early nineteenth century in England. We have also examined some of the moral, religious, philosophical, and economic theories and principles behind the practices, institutions, and laws developed to deal with the poor. We will turn in chapter 4 to the U.S. experience, which is based primarily upon the preceding English history and carries over the values of the Poor Laws. We will examine major themes and significant social welfare exemplars from colonial times to today, keeping in mind the relationship of underlying values to the social welfare choices made historically by U.S. society.

QUESTIONS FOR CONSIDERATION

1. What were the benefits and limitations for individuals and families in a *status* relationship and what are they in a *contract* relationship?
2. What relationships can you identify between the Poor Laws and people's ideas about social welfare today?
3. Have any states or the Congress recently attempted to make residency laws regarding social welfare? Does anything stand in their way? For some groups? For all groups?
4. Did Speenhamland provide a family allowance, a wage supplementation, or a subsidy for employers? Do any of these exist in the United States today?

NOTES

1. Clayton Roberts and David Roberts, *A History of England: Prehistory to 1714*, 2nd ed., Vol. 1, Englewood Cliffs, N.J.: Prentice Hall, 1985, pp. 75–81.
2. L. C. B. Seaman, *A New History of England, 410–1975*, Totowa, N.J.: Barnes and Noble, 1982, pp. 114–120.
3. Rodney Hilton, *Bond Men Made Free: Medieval Peasant Movements and the English Rising of 1381*, New York: Viking, 1973, pp. 14–15.
4. Fernand Braudel, *The Structures of Everyday Life*, New York: Harper & Row, 1979, p. 74.
5. Hilton, p. 65.
6. Ibid., p. 86.
7. Brian Tierney, *Medieval Poor Law*, Berkeley: University of California Press, 1959, p. 12.
8. Ibid., p. 37.
9. Ibid., p. 11.
10. Joseph R. Strayer and Dana C. Munro, *The Middle Ages, 395–1500*, New York: Appleton-Century-Crofts, 1970, p. 130.
11. Hilton, pp. 15–16, 86, 88.
12. Richard W. Southern, *The Making of the Middle Ages*, New Haven, Conn.: Yale University Press, 1970, pp. 106–107.
13. Tierney, p. 109.
14. Barbara A. Hanawalt, *Crime and Conflict in English Communities, 1300–1348*, Cambridge, Mass.: Harvard University Press, 1979, p. 31.
15. Karl de Schweinitz, *England's Road to Social Security*, New York: A. A. Barnes and Co., 1975, p. 14.
16. Tierney, p. 61.
17. J. Gilchrist, *The Church and Economic Activity in the Middle Ages*, New York: Macmillan, 1969, p. 79. According to Gilchrist, the income expended on charity never exceeded 5 percent. However, Pound suggests the percentage of monastic income devoted to charity ranged from less than 1 percent to more than 22 percent. But even Pound finds that the generosity of some houses was insufficient to raise the national average to 2.5 percent. See John Pound, *Poverty and Vagrancy in Tudor England*, London: Longman, 1975, pp. 21–22.
18. Roland Bainton, *The Penguin History of Christianity*, Vol. 2, Harmondsworth, Eng.: Penguin, 1967, p. 9.
19. de Schweinitz, p. 15.

20. Barbara A. Hanawalt, *The Ties That Bound: Peasant Families in Medieval England*, New York: Oxford University Press, 1986, p. 264.
21. Gilchrist, p. 79.
22. Hanawalt, p. 235.
23. Ibid., p. 253.
24. de Schweinitz, p. 17.
25. Gilchrist, p. 79.
26. Roberts and Roberts, p. 170.
27. Robert S. Gottfried, *The Black Death: Natural and Human Disaster in Medieval Europe*, New York: Free Press, 1983, pp. xii, xvi, 86.
28. Ibid., p. 135.
29. Ibid., pp. 97–98.
30. Ibid., p. 98.
31. Ibid., p. 94.
32. Hilton, p. 155.
33. Barbara W. Tuchman, *A Distant Mirror: The Calamitous 14th Century*, New York: Knopf, 1978, p. 124. One historian suggests about this period that "if it was a golden age, it was the golden age of bacteria." Sylvia L. Thrupp, "The Problem of Replacement-Rates in Medieval English Population," *Society and History*, Raymond Grew and Nicholas H. Steneck, eds., Ann Arbor, Mich.: University of Michigan Press, 1977, p. 186.
34. Brian Tierney and Sidney Painter, *Western Europe in the Middle Ages, 300–1475*, New York: Knopf, 1978, pp. 511–512.
35. Tuchman, pp. 125–126.
36. Roland Bainton, *The Reformation of the Sixteenth Century*, Boston: Beacon Press, 1964, p. 246.
37. Max Weber, *The Protestant Ethic and the Spirit of Capitalism*, New York: Charles Scribner's Sons, 1958, pp. 157–158.
38. William J. Bouwsma, *John Calvin: A Sixteenth-Century Portrait*, New York: Oxford University Press, 1988, p. 74.
39. See Bainton; Georgia Harkness, *John Calvin: The Man and the Ethics*, New York: Abingdon Press, 1958; R. H. Tawney, *Religion and the Rise of Capitalism*, New York: Mentor Books, 1950.
40. The distinction must be made between the original writings of Calvin and Calvinism as it developed. Weber and Tawney suggest that Calvinism equates amassing wealth with a sign of individual grace and election. Their view is that Calvinism thus contributed to the development of capitalism. Calvin himself, however, did not regard prosperity in this life as associated with election. See John T. McNeill, ed., *Calvin: Institutes of the Christian Religion*, Philadelphia: Westminster Press, 1960, in particular p. 438.
41. David Nicholas, *The Evolution of the Medieval World: Society, Government and Thought in Europe, 312–1500*, New York: Longman, 1992, p. 410.
42. Karl Polanyi, *The Great Transformation*, Boston: Beacon Press, 1957, pp. 40, 42.
43. de Schweinitz, pp. 20–22.
44. Pound, pp.16–24 and David Loades, *Revolution in Religion: The English Reformation, 1530–1570*, Cardiff: University of Wales, 1992, p. 90.
45. de Schweinitz, pp. 22–23.
46. Brian Pullan, *Rich and Poor in Renaissance Venice*, Cambridge, Mass.: Harvard University Press, 1971, pp. 239–240.
47. Sidney and Beatrice Webb, *English Poor Law History*, Part 1, *The Old Poor Law*, London: Frank Case, 1963, pp. 52–66.

48. Ibid., pp. 52–66.

49. de Schweinitz, p. 40.

50. J. A. Sharpe, *Crime in Early Modern England*, London: Longman, 1984, pp. 91, 184.

51. Robert Boguslaw, *The New Utopians*, Englewood Cliffs, N.J.: Prentice Hall, 1965, pp. 132, 134.

52. George R. Boyer, *An Economic History of the English Poor Law 1750–1850*, New York: Cambridge University Press, 1990, pp. 265–267; Dorothy Marshall, "The Old Poor Law, 1662–1795," *Essays in Economic History*, Eleanora Mary Carus-Wilson, ed., London: Edward Arnold Publishers, 1954, p. 304.

53. Geoffrey W. Oxley, *Poor Relief in England and Wales, 1601–1834*, London: David and Charles, 1974, p. 113; Michael Rose, *The Relief of Poverty, 1834–1914*, London: Macmillan Press, 1981, p. 8.

54. Catherina Lis and Hugo Soly, *Poverty and Capitalism in Pre-Industrial Europe*, Atlantic Highlands, N.J.: Humanities Press, 1979, p. 199.

55. According to Marcus, a fall in production accompanied a rise in the poor rates (taxes) (Steven Marcus, "Their Brothers' Keepers: An Episode from English History," *Doing Good*, W. Gaylin, Ira Glasser, Steven Marcus, and David J. Rothman, eds., New York: Pantheon, 1978, p. 49). According to Blaug, however, the allowances did not encourage people to "breed recklessly" and did not devitalize the working class; furthermore, after the turn of the century, there was an increase in production. Blaug suggests that the allowance systems were almost entirely a rural problem in particular parts of the country. The device was chosen to deal with surplus labor in a lagging sector of an expanding but underdeveloped economy; it was a method for dealing with problems of structural unemployment and substandard wages. According to this view, the allowance system contributed to economic expansion (Mark Blaug, "The Myth of the Old Poor Law and the Making of the New," *Journal of Economic History*, Vol. 23, No. 2, June 1963, pp. 151–184, and "The Poor Law Report Reexamined," *Journal of Economic History*, Vol. 24, No. 2, June 1964, pp. 229–245).

56. Frank Crompton, *Workhouse Children*, Phoenix Mill, England: Sutton Publishing Limited, 1997, p. 3.
Norman Longmate, *The Workhouse*, London: Temple Smith, 1974, p. 24.

57. See Lawrence Stone, *The Family, Sex and Marriage in England 1500–1800*, New York: Harper & Row, 1977, pp. 473–478; John Boswell, *The Kindness of Strangers: The Abandonment of Children in Western Europe from Late Antiquity to the Renaissance*, New York: Pantheon, 1988, p. 40.

58. Blanche D. Coll, *Perspectives in Public Welfare*, Washington, D.C.: U.S. Government Printing Office, 1969, p. 8.

59. John R. Poynter, *Society and Pauperism*, London: Routledge and Kegan Paul, pp. 14–17.

60. Robert Pinker, *Social Theory and Social Policy*, London: Heinemann Educational Books, 1973, pp. 55–61.

61. Robert H. Bremner, "The Rediscovery of Pauperism," *Current Issues in Social Work Seen in Historical Perspective*, New York: Council on Social Work Education, 1962, p. 16.

62. George R. Boyer, *An Economic History of the English Poor Law 1750–1850*, New York: Cambridge University Press, 1990, p. 267.

Social Values and Social Welfare: The American Experience I

*The welfare or happiness of mankind consists entirely in the freedom to
exercise the natural faculties. . . . The problem therefore manifestly is how
to secure to the members of society the maximum power of exercising
their natural faculties. . . . Abundant nourishment for the body is therefore
the first condition of liberty.*
—*Lester F. Ward*[1]

OVERVIEW

In the preceding chapter, we described the evolution of the English Poor Law system. In this chapter, we turn to consider factors that influenced social welfare developments in the United States, ranging from the impact of the English system on U.S. social welfare choices; the differential experiences of African Americans, Latinos, and Native Americans; the importance of voluntary mutual aid among all groups; and the impact of the frontier myth. In addition, we review the federal role in social welfare, including the Freedmen's Bureau, the suspension of the ethic for veterans and their families, as well as the important impact of social Darwinism on American values, and the initiation of social insurances in Germany and Great Britain.

AMERICAN POOR LAW MENTALITY

Eight years after the compilation of the Elizabethan Poor Laws, settlements began to be established by colonists along the eastern seaboard of what was later to become the United States of America. During the early stages of settlement, clashes between ideologies took place. When Jamestown was settled, the Virginia Company required all employees to contribute "the fruits of their labor" to a common storehouse. The food was then distributed to each person according to their needs. This plan was later abandoned and the owners turned to settlers to support themselves with individual gardens.[2]

The first years of the Plymouth colony were based on a common sharing of all property. An emphasis on mutual aid and communal organization reflective of early Christian social organization clashed with the Protestant work ethic reflected in the Poor Laws. For the pious, ownership could never be simply a means for personal fulfillment or gain. It must also contribute to communal well-being, and one was a steward of God's property, which was to be used to serve God and society.[3]

Given the need for work and workers, the Protestant ethic in the form of the Poor Laws was used by the early settlers because that was the natural thing for them to do, in the sense that the laws reflected the traditions of the English founding settlers. The English Poor Laws and their underlying attitudes were implanted early in the Atlantic coast colonies: secularism, the concept of risks and categories, indoor and outdoor relief, residency laws, less eligibility, and approaching the poor on a case-by-case basis. But, also, in these ways, American ambivalence toward the poor began; there is community caring but also an inheritance of the Poor Law mentality.

Settlements, Labor, and Imported "Poor Laws"

European events pushed some to America; others were attracted by opportunities; and some were forced to the colonies. For example, the English made efforts to divert to the colonies some part of a mobile labor force during the seventeenth century. The only way poor persons could practically get to the colonies in the seventeenth century was through some form of *indentured service* (a contract to work for someone for a designated period of time). Of the 155,000 English emigrants during that century, the majority fit into this category. The principal labor supply for early settlements was indentured servants until this supply was superseded by enslaved Africans, when, beginning in the 1680s, the mainland colonies underwent a massive shift from indentured to enslaved labor. Adults were indentured and children were apprenticed. But indentured service for some (those at the margin) turned into multiple terms of indenture. Thus, England's need to deal with its labor force and the colonies' need to recruit emigrants for labor combined to foster indentured service and found both emigrants and those who preceded them in the mainland colonies acutely aware of the Poor Laws and their provisions.[4]

Many immigrants came as indentured servants, apprentices, tenants, "all agreeing to the status of a person who, lacking the means, accepts free transportation as the price of four to seven years of unrelenting servitude to an unknown master."[5] This is how indenture worked. Shippers took whatever money individuals or families could pay to transport them to the colonies. Emigrants were then given fourteen days to come up with the balance of the cost due the shipper. If the required amount could not be produced, they were "sold" into indentured servitude for an amount sufficient to repay their debt. This legal contract tied immigrants to their local place of settlement in exchange for transportation to the colony, food, drink, clothing, and shelter during the term of service, which depended upon the amount of the debt owed.[6]

By 1633, the following provision was made for one of the colonists:

> Thomas Higgins having lived an extravagant life, was placed with John Jenny for eight years, to serve him as an apprentice, during which time the said John competently to provide for him; and at the end thereof to give him double apell [apple], 12 bushels of corn and 20 acres of land.[7]

In Massachusetts, as in other parts of America, poor relief was a local responsibility. The smallest unit of government became the instrument for implementing the readily imported English Poor Law system. By 1642, Plymouth had enacted the following law:

> ... that every township shall make competent provision for the maintenance of their poor according as they shall find most convenient and suitable for themselves by an order and general agreement in a public town meeting. And notwithstanding the promise that all such persons as are now resident and inhabitant and within the said town shall be maintained and provided for by them.[8]

Selectmen administered aid to the poor. Almshouse care was not common until approximately the late eighteenth century. Cases were dealt with individually and were presented to the town at a public town meeting. Settlement laws were also enacted to keep strangers out if there was an incompatibility of religious belief or likelihood of early public dependency.

According to town records in Fairfield, Connecticut, during the seventeenth century, the deserving poor were maintained by the town. However, vagrant and idle persons were warned to leave town, and they and persons who harbored them were subject to prosecution. Thus two categories were again established, the worthy and unworthy poor, with the unworthy poor being made to leave town.[9]

Children were viewed as economic assets rather than liabilities, much as in other agricultural societies. In social welfare terms, however, children were placed with various parties by indenture; parents were forced into service to avoid public expense. If parents with children were aided by the town, they were required to set the children out to work. The poor also were boarded in private homes. Outdoor relief was given as well. Sometimes there were local work-relief programs, especially on projects needed by the community.

Settlement laws also played a part in colonial social welfare, as can be seen in the following example:

> December 11, 1634. One Abigail Gifford, widow, being kept at the charge of the parish of Wilsden in Middlesex, near London, was sent by Mr. Ball's ship into this country, and being found to be somewhat distracted, and a very burdensome woman, the governor and assistants returned her back by warrant, 18, to the same parish, in the ship Rebecca.[10]

In the early scattered American communities (primarily rural with subsistence farming), the local community could indeed handle the few cases that were its responsibility. It was familiar with the people involved and made what it considered appropriate provision.

As early as the seventeenth century, when America was newly settled by Euro-pean colonists and was primarily an agricultural society, private and voluntary phil-anthropy and mutual aid developed, on both an individual and cooperative basis. This aid was founded on religious and civic principles and traditions brought from Europe, on the views of the proper role of government, and on the limitations of re-sources available to governmental jurisdictions. For example, several private bene-factors left bequests to Boston that, when combined, enabled the town to build an almshouse. As Pumphrey and Pumphrey pointed out, this "pattern of making individ-ual gifts or bequests to the town, rather than setting up isolated foundations, was re-garded as natural. Private benevolence thus provided the capital, but the public was expected to maintain the donated facility."[11]

It was natural that early colonial social welfare should fashion itself on the model set in seventeenth-century Europe. This era was a great period of European philanthropy, one characterized by missionary enterprises, interest in charitable works, tax-supported poor relief, as well as philanthropic associations. There were efforts at colonization and motivation for converting the natives to Christianity, for poor men to be provided with work and land, and for a wilderness to be supplied with institutions of civilization.[12]

Cotton Mather proposed in 1710 that men and women should engage as indi-viduals or as members of voluntary associations in "a perpetual endeavor to do good in the world." Good works were viewed as an obligation owed to God and a reward in themselves. To help the unfortunate was deemed an honor, and sound policy called for effective social control through pious example, moral leadership, volun-tary effort, and private charity. These were the means by which competing and con-flicting interests could be brought into harmony.[13]

During the colonial period, the line between public and private responsibility was not sharply drawn. A cooperative approach existed. Overseers of the poor called on the churches for special collections. As noted earlier, the bequeathing of property to public authorities during the colonial period was a popular form of phil-anthropy. In many instances, national, occupational, and religious groups relieved the public sector of the necessity for charitable support.[14]

In American port towns during the 1690s, life compared favorably with the con-ditions in English, Irish, and Scottish towns. Although lower-level workers labored long hours in unpleasant and unhealthy conditions and, at the ends of their lives, had little to show for their strenuous labors, they did not starve or go unclothed or un-housed. Meanwhile, in English towns, there was much unemployment and acute poverty. In the colonial cities, workhouses had a dual purpose: to deal with the job-less poor and if possible to reduce tax rates through their labor. The incidence of poverty was confined mainly to the widowed, disabled, and the orphaned, who were viewed as wards of the community. There was little stigma attached to being poor, as this was viewed as being generally due to circumstances beyond one's control. Per-sons in need remained in their homes or in the homes of others and were given out-door relief such as clothes, firewood, bread, and a small weekly cash payment.

Boston in the 1730s illustrates what happens when poor relief rises. The select-men and overseers of the poor sought new solutions to a rise in pauperism. They wished to care for the poor while also caring for their constituents' resources. In 1735, Boston enacted a new Poor Law under which the selectmen could eject strangers without first appealing to the county court for a warrant. The law also authorized the erection of a separate workhouse on Boston Common where able-bodied poor would be put to work. This workhouse was specifically for those who were unable to find work. The almshouse was where the aged, ill, and disabled could receive care.

Those in the workhouse were expected to support themselves by picking oakum, weaving cloth, and making shoes. By 1741, 55 persons were living in the workhouse. The expenses exceeded the income. Nevertheless, an inspection committee judged the experiment to be a success since support of this number of persons on outdoor relief would have been far costlier.[15]

THE EARLY SPANISH INFLUENCE, THE MEXICANS, AND OTHER LATINOS

Social welfare was not only being developed in the English colonies. It is important to remember that Juan Ponce de Leon explored Florida in 1513 and that Hernando Cortes, the Spanish conquistador, invaded Mexico and conquered the Aztecs in 1519, prior to developed settlements on the eastern seaboard. During the sixteenth and seventeenth centuries, Florida was an outpost of the Spanish empire consisting of a fortified garrison at St. Augustine and a string of missions along the Atlantic coast and across the peninsula, mainly used to convert and control the Native Americans. The province was strategically important but was never self-supporting and experienced a series of disasters.

In what is now the southwestern United States, the Spanish established in 1609 Santa Fe de San Francisco and colonized what is now New Mexico and parts of Arizona, Colorado, Texas, Nebraska, and Oklahoma. In the sixteenth century the transplanted Catholic church built missions, convents, monasteries, churches, hospitals, and schools. By the seventeenth century, there were 3,000 missionaries in New Spain, converting nonbelievers but also providing some social welfare services, such as caring for the sick and the poor in almshouses, serving and burying the poor, as well as payment of tithes by non-Native persons and encouraging the giving of charity, especially on feast days.[16]

By the 18th century, there were 21 missions in these territories. Early settlers were given *encomiendas* or grants, which gave them ownership and control over Native American lands, labor, and produce. The *encomienda*, a feudal lord and serf system, was part of colonization since Spanish land grants included the perpetual service of the natives who lived on the land. Initially colonizers sought gold, later silver.

Members of the clergy objected strongly to the encomiendas, and there were Native American revolts in 1541 and 1680. Native Americans were sometimes hired labor and traders but sometimes forced to labor without pay. Although enslavement of pueblo Native Americans was rare, this usually was punishment for certain crimes. Sometimes written permission was given to soldiers to seize Native American orphans as house servants with the assumption the soldier would be the guardian of the seized orphans, teach and indoctrinate them, and in return for protection the master had a claim on the orphan's services. It is unclear how general this practice was. However, captured Apache boys and girls were commonly used as house servants.

Catholic friars had use of both cultivatable and range lands. They defended their use of these lands on three grounds: (1) all their food had to be raised on the spot and they had a right to a certain amount of land; (2) in case of famine they frequently fed large numbers of Native Americans and Spaniards from their food and livestock reserves; and (3) they had to export cattle and other livestock to obtain funds needed for church purposes not supplied by the Crown.[17]

Latinos are among both the oldest and newest immigrants to the United States. As we have seen, Spaniards arrived even before colonizers arrived on the east coast and Latinos have come from many different places. Mexico because of its proximity has had a shared complex history with the United States. Mexican lands were fought over and the annexation of Texas in 1845 began a war that ended officially in 1848 with the signing of the Treaty of Guadalupe Hidalgo. This treaty left Mexicans who chose to stay in the United States with cultural autonomy but in marginal and discriminated situations. Many lost their lands and as a result became agricultural laborers. Discriminatory rules affected voting rights, economic opportunities, education, and the use of the Spanish language. Texans, many of whom originated in the American South, transferred their attitudes to Mexican-Americans who, nevertheless, were citizens, albeit treated—for the most part—poorly.

The Mexican Revolution displaced millions of peasants after 1910 and American railroads recruited many of those who came to the United States into track gangs and dispersed them to where they built urban *barrios*.[18] The Spanish influence was intensified by the Spanish-American War, which entangled the United States further into Latino affairs in Cuba and the Phillipines. After World War I, Mexicans immigrated to the United States legally because the restrictive legislation of the 1920s did not apply to western hemisphere nations. During the Great Depression of the 1930s, as many as half a million Mexican persons were deported or "encouraged" to return. In 1942, during World War II and from 1948 to 1965, federal legislation encouraged the importation of *braceros* (temporary farm workers) to help with wartime shortages. Others came illegally, slipping across the Rio Grande border. Workers were poorly housed, underpaid, and discriminated against.

During the 1960s as part of the general civil rights era, the Chicano movement began in the southwest, demanding better schools, easier access to higher education, and fostering cultural pride. One group, Alianza, led by Reies Lopez Tijerna, failed in its effort to secede from New Mexico. Probably the persons with the widest influence were Cesar Chavez and Delores Huerta, who organized farm workers into unions and founded the United Farm Workers Organizing Committee. His leadership of a grape pickers strike became a nationwide effort as he enlisted the support of church leaders, organized sit ins, marched on the California State capitol, and initiated a nationwide consumer boycott of grapes. These union organizing efforts and demands for equal treatment did not lead to separatism but, instead, opted for economic and political inclusion.

Puerto Rican migrations mainly took place post–World War II and during the 1950s. Later migrations came following the Cuban revolution 1959 and as a result of civil wars in Nicaragua, Guatemala, El Salvador, and other political upheavals. In chapter 8, the economic situation of Latinos will be introduced, and in chapter 14 we will discuss the impact of Latino groups on the current U.S. political situation. Latinos are also discussed in chapter 15 in relation to immigration.

In summary, Latinos settled early on in what became the United States and provided a social welfare system, mainly through the Catholic Church and its missions, and have enriched American society, the economy, and culture for many centuries, despite loss of lands, cultural clashes, and persistent discrimination.

Voluntary Mutual Aid Efforts

Other voluntary mutual aid efforts were also being organized. The Scots' Charitable Society, first among many such nationality-based groups, was formed in 1657 as a mutual aid society for those of Scottish origin.[19]

Voluntary organizations were formed to aid special groups, for example, the Philadelphia Society for Alleviating the Miseries of Public Prisoners (1787), the Massachusetts Charitable Fire Society (1794), and the New York Society for the Relief of Poor Widows with Small Children (1798). Church charities, another form of voluntary social welfare, were financed by collections and gave relief to members of particular congregations. For example, in 1729 the Ursuline Sisters in New Orleans established a private home for mothers and children left homeless by the Native American massacres.

Mutual Aid among African Americans

Mutual aid among African Americans was based on their cultural heritage from western African society and expressed the positive functions of "Africanity," the heritage of the African ethos: the importance of family, survival of the tribe, the oneness of all being, unity, cooperative effort, and mutual responsibility and aid. In Africa, most black people lived within the context of "tribal socialism," in which patterns of mutual concern and sharing even in times of abundance were highly developed. The entire tribe is an interdependent entity. Existence, including the provision of food, shelter, clothing, protection, and a sense of belonging depends on every member of the tribe, living, dead, and yet to be.[20] W.E.B. DuBois observed that "of charity as such there was no need among Africans, since all shared the common fund of land and food."[21]

Blyden, a nineteenth-century Africanist, described African life and culture in this way: "We, and not I, is the law of African life." African social philosophy could be summarized in a folk saying: "I am, because we are; and since we are, therefore I am." Furthermore, no matter how much wealth or power a man attained, he could not place his individual interests above those of the group. This rule applied as well to chiefs, priests, and others of high authority who could not hoard while others were unsheltered or hungry.[22]

In the United States, even during slavery, enslaved persons created mutual aid and burial societies, although usually not openly. In every city of any size in Virginia, organizations operated surreptitiously to care for the sick and to bury the dead. As soon as enslaved persons were emancipated, these mutual aid societies began to be openly formed as fraternal, mutual aid societies and churches.[23] One of the earliest of these organizations was the African Methodist Church (1787). Groups such as the African Union Society, the Free African Society, the Black Masons, and the Negro Oddfellows supplied medical, educational, and burial services, in addition to helping to resolve disputes. In Boston a Masonic Lodge was formed by free African Americans in 1784,[24] and in 1787 they formed the Philadelphia Free African Society. The latter society was formed, according to its mission statement, without regard to religious tenets. Persons should live "an orderly and sober life, in order to support one another in sickness, and for the benefit of their widows and fatherless children." The members of the society made insurance payments, and benefits were paid provided this necessity was "not brought on by their own imprudence." If a member became sick, he or she was exempt from payments and eligible for benefits. In addition, there were benefits for widows and children's benefits, including schooling and apprenticeship.[25] Soon after the Philadelphia Society was formed, similar associations were formed in Newport, Boston, New York, and Charleston.[26] The intention of these mutual aid societies often was to lessen the need for benefits from public funds.

There were almost 500,000 free African Americans in the United States at the outbreak of the Civil War, approximately half in the South and many "well to do." The free African-American community created churches, literary debating societies, fraternal organizations, and other mutual aid groups.[27] But even in slavery there was a system of social obligation among enslaved people for other enslaved persons, and there are many examples of extravagant giving in relation to available resources. Among formerly enslaved people, the indigent or helpless were supported by relatives, parents, friends, and relief associations.[28] In fact, it has been suggested that similar altruistic behavior by freed people over the entire South is an important reason why over the full lifetime of the Freedmen's Bureau it materially assisted only 0.5 percent of the 4 million freed people.[29] Obligations to kin were transformed into larger social and communal obligations such as setting aside a piece of land for a community purpose or supporting free schooling for poor children. The following comments of an African American regarding a school in South Carolina illustrates the mutual aid values of the freed African-American community: ". . . they were all poor, and each could do but little, but this was a work for many. . . . Should each man regard only his own children, and forget all the others? Should they leave that poor neighbor widow with her whole gang of children, and give them no chance for a free schooling?"[30] In addition to the development of cemeteries and educational facilities, in the latter part of the nineteenth century, hospitals, homes, and orphanages were organized, out of which later developed cooperative businesses and insurance societies.

Constitutional conventions following 1865 in the southern states were dominated by old Confederate leaders at a time when 4 million African-American enslaved

people were freed and insufficient industry existed in which they could be employed. It was at this time that southern state legislatures passed the Black Codes,
which relegated African Americans to a status somewhere between slave and free.
These codes were intended to restore forced labor conditions on plantations, that is,
controlled labor for agricultural production.

The Black Codes fixed a legal place for formerly enslaved persons in the postwar South, restricted African Americans' occupations and property ownership,
slowed mobility, reduced bargaining power, and limited access to the judicial system, making appeals difficult. Any freed person who refused to work at the prevailing wage could be defined as a "vagrant" or "loiterer," or, lacking employment, could
be forced to labor. Such forced labor could also be imposed on children whose parents were unable to support them. Employers could control wages in collusive
arrangements, and every African American had to show a license from the police or a
written labor contract to prove employment. Any African American quitting a job
could be arrested. There is some evidence that these Black Codes successfully oppressed African Americans until their repeal by the constitutional conventions of
1868 and the new Reconstruction legislatures.[31]

Harsh vagrancy laws and the Black Codes, particularly where nonagricultural
employment was restricted, were attempts to stem the tide of freed persons to the
cities and to maintain them as landless laborers for agriculture. The purpose of these
laws was to keep these persons working as laborers for white employers—not as an
enslaved person and yet not as a completely free person either. Although there are
no exact parallels, the Black Codes share certain characteristics and purposes with
the vagrancy acts of the Poor Laws of the fourteenth through sixteenth centuries in
Europe. Essentially, both sets of acts attempted to control a labor supply for the benefit of the employing class and set harsh measures to maintain legal restrictions on
mobility, work conditions, and the relationships among communities, employers,
and those recently freed.[32]

The vagrancy laws, as Leon Litwack points out, were more harshly enforced in
regard to African Americans than to whites:

> Enforcement of the vagrancy laws revealed an all too familiar double stan-
> dard. If a white man was out of work, as many were in 1865, that was
> simply unemployment, but if a black man had no job, that was vagrancy.
> If a planter refused to till the fields himself, that was understandable, but
> if a former slave declined to work for him, that was idleness if not inso-
> lence.[33]

Consistently throughout American history there were voluntary, private social
welfare efforts. In New York City, prior to the Civil War, the New York Association
for Improving the Condition of the Poor and the Society for the Prevention of Pauperism in the City of New York were organized. Both perceived poverty and antiso-
cial behavior as results of alcoholism and idleness. There also were numerous groups
concerned with utopianism, political reform, women's rights, economic reform,
land reform, education, abolition of slavery, temperance, and other social issues and
problems.

Following the Civil War, state boards of charities were formed in Massachusetts, Connecticut, New York, Wisconsin, Rhode Island, Pennsylvania, Michigan, Kansas, and Illinois. Representatives from the first four states met in New York in 1874 and formed the Conference of Boards and Public Charities, an important beginning for the development of a communication network among social agencies, both public and private. It was only eleven years earlier that the first state board was created in Massachusetts to supervise charitable, medical, and penal institutions.

The development of both public and private agencies was a result of societal forces. Six percent of the American population lived in cities in 1800; by 1870 this number had risen to 25 percent. The problems of rapidly industrializing cities and the hordes of people moving into them for employment had to be handled in new ways. Social agencies developed on the local and state level to meet the needs of a changing society.

The long-term trend toward public assumption of major responsibility for social welfare in England and the United States always was joined by a continuous involvement of private, religious, and other organizations in the social welfare arena. According to one major early study of social welfare, by the early part of the twentieth century, in the United States private and public social welfare seemed to be assigned different functions:

> The advantages of private charities over public ones are that they afford on the average a somewhat larger share of personal sympathy, that their benefits cannot logically be claimed as a right (although they often are), that they do not oppress the poor by increasing taxation, and that they are supposed to bring a somewhat smaller degree of degradation to the recipient of relief.
>
> The probable lines of demarcation between the field of public and private charity seem to lie between those dependents requiring some degree of control, and those that may be allowed their freedom; between measures for chronic dependents and those looking to prevention; between institutional care on a large scale and private aid to the needy in their homes. Generally speaking, private charity is best fitted to conditions where much personal, individual sympathy is required; public charity, to problems requiring large funds, equipment and control. Finally, private charity, under the stimulus of some individual enthusiast, will mark out new paths which when proven may be adopted by the State.[34]

As we shall see later, the Great Depression of the 1930s confronted the United States with problems on a scale that could only be dealt with by public action at the federal level. But as we can see from the preceding paragraphs, some relief functions shifted to the public sphere long before the cataclysmic social upheaval of the 1930s.

From rural, colonial, agrarian America to the modern, industrial, and urbanized United States, private voluntary welfare, formal and informal, played an important part in meeting human needs. Informal, natural helping systems always played a significant role in social welfare. Extended families, friendship circles, churches, and neighborhood, ethnic, and religious groups have all contributed to individual and family welfare. Although the long-term trend in American society has been toward formalization of social welfare functions, one should not forget that informal, spontaneous helping outside formal channels has been and remains a significant portion of American social welfare.

THE AMERICAN FRONTIER: THE MYTH AND VALUES

America existed as a physical frontier and also as a psychological frontier. It was a place where a new life was possible, where dreams of freedom or sustenance or success could be fulfilled.

The fact that America was a frontier land in which the horizons always beckoned influenced how people viewed themselves and how they viewed others. The frontier myth declared all things possible; the land was open for the benefit of those who were hardy and brave enough to venture forward. Beyond the next hill, beyond the next river, or beyond the next mountain range, life would be better. One part of this frontier philosophy was the belief that riches belonged to those who dared to seek them and who were strong enough to earn their way. The other side of this frontier myth and the frontier people was that those who did not or could not venture forth or "make it" financially were suspect.

Into the frontier land of America came waves of immigrants. At first, during the colonial period, immigrants to America were English, German, and Scottish, with small numbers of French Huguenots, as well as indentured servants and enslaved people exploited for the development of a new country. Later Irish, Swiss, Swedish, Danish, Italian, Portuguese, Spanish, and West Indian immigrants came to America, to be followed by yet other groups.

Immigrants to the colonies came for political, religious, and social reasons. Later immigrants came to the United States primarily for economic reasons in order to make a living. As the various immigrant waves reached America, the earlier settlers would accuse the later settlers of depressing wages and of causing various social problems. Cultural conflicts abounded between the various groups and within ethnic groups. Religious differences caused some conflicts. Within some groups there were conflicts over whether the culture and language of the "home country" should be preserved. And there were differences of race. In addition, many immigrants came from rural homes and had to deal with urban problems in America. The experiences of the waves of immigrants coming to America created a strong "we–they" feeling and attitude. For example, Chinese immigrants who came to the western United States during pioneer days and during the gold rush were viewed as economic competitors; by 1882 Chinese laborers had been excluded from immigration on the basis of race alone.

Of course, immigrant groups found ways to help each other and carried into American society their own unique mutual aid efforts. Chinese were among the servants of Spaniards, sailing between the Philippines and Mexico after 1565. From Mexico, Chinese moved north to Los Angeles and Monterey. The first documented arrival of a Chinese person on the east coast occurred in 1785. From 1850 to 1882, when the Chinese Exclusion Act went into effect, more than 322,000 Chinese entered the United States and worked as merchants, artisans, and mainly as unskilled laborers in railroad construction and mining.

Chinese immigrant organizations derived their structure from loyalty to clan, dialect, or region and were called the "company." They banded together for social and charitable purposes during the nineteenth century to greet new immigrants, help find places to live and eat, borrow and lend money, find work, patronize stores owned by persons from their native locality, provide protection, care for the sick, adjudicate disputes, and help return the dead to China for burial. Subsidiary organizations maintained the cemetery. As early as the 1850s, guilds modeled on organizations for artisans and merchants in China served mutual aid functions.[35]

The Mexicans, or Chicanos, were the first large ethnic group incorporated by annexation following the separation of Texas from Mexico. Between 1845 and 1854, the United States acquired about half the territory belonging to the Republic of Mexico, including all or part of Arizona, California, Colorado, Nevada, New Mexico, Texas, Utah, and Wyoming. Most *sociedades mutualistas* (mutual aid societies) were formed in the late nineteenth or early twentieth century as local organizations or as chapters of regional or national Chicano organizations. These organizations were the focus of social life and provided assistance to families in need, emergency loans, legal services, mediation of disputes, as well as medical, life, and burial insurance.[36]

Italians, too, had their mutual benefit societies, which provided insurance and helped newly arrived immigrants to deal with sickness, loneliness, and death. The hat was passed for members in trouble, guaranteeing help at minimal expense for all concerned. These organizations also provided for attendance at funerals, proper burials, and stipends in the event of sickness or disability. Later such organizations added recreational and social functions.[37]

A similar mutual aid ethic assisted immigrants whether they came to the United States from the South, East, or West; whether over land or over the Atlantic or Pacific oceans or over the Caribbean; whether enslaved, indentured, or free. Norwegians had their *bydelag* societies; Jews, *landsmanschaften*; Japanese, *kenjinkai*; Greeks, *topikas*; Koreans, *kei*; Ukranians, Hungarians, Finns, Czechs and Slovaks, West Indians, and all other groups banded together for social and mutual aid purposes.

The existence of a "we-they" attitude was strengthened by economic competition. However, the attitude that one person was better than another on the basis of some ethnic difference also played a part in how Americans viewed those who were different from themselves, including those who were in need of help, financial or otherwise: They somehow did not fit in. In addition, as the different waves of immigrants came to America, it was always "they" who needed help. Mutual aid may have been retarded and racism and rugged individualism advanced by the notion that it was always some other ethnic group, not one's brothers and sisters, who needed help in America.

As we noted in chapter 1, the myth of individualism, particularly "rugged individualism" as a part of the American frontier tradition, needs to be modified in our understanding of American culture by the influences of mutual aid and social control, even in the evolving West. Ray Allen Billington casts a different light on the idea of American "rugged individualism":

> Actually, the legend of frontier individualism rested on what people
> thought should be true, rather than on what was true. The West was in

truth an area where cooperation was just as essential as in the more thickly settled East. The danger of Indian attack, the joint efforts to clear the forests or break the prairie sod, the community of labor required for the variety of enterprises necessary in establishing a settlement, all decreed that new communities be occupied by groups, and never by solitary individuals.[38]

Billington points out that common perils served as a cohesive force among those who were homesteading the Great Plains "no less than among earlier pioneers, for these grass fires, grasshopper invasions, and cattle wars banded the people together to combat mutual enemies."[39] Communities and individuals benefited from cooperative enterprises that built churches and schools. Laws were also adopted to regulate economic behavior, including the regulation of trade—the price of bread was sometimes fixed, fees were regulated, weights and measures were checked for accuracy.[40]

For one group immigration was not voluntary. In 1619, one year prior to the arrival of the Mayflower, twenty Africans who had been captured by a Dutch vessel from a Spanish vessel en route to the West Indies were traded for food into indentured servitude at Jamestown, Virginia. For forty years or more the first African-American settlers accumulated land, voted, were able to testify in court, mingled on an equal basis with whites, and owned other black servants, some of whom they imported and paid for.[41] From such a relatively small event at Jamestown, however, a tangled web of black–white relationships and problems developed that has confronted American society continually throughout its history.

Some colonial communities made the indenture of African-American paupers harsher than that of whites. Special rules were sometimes established making slavery the punishment for African Americans who became paupers.[42] In 1641, Massachusetts became the first colony to legally recognize slavery, thus institutionalizing different treatment for African Americans and whites. After the middle of the seventeenth century, all African Americans—and only African Americans—came as enslaved persons.[43] In the 1680s, there was a massive shift from indentured to enslaved labor. Until the onset of the Civil War and the promulgation of the Emancipation Proclamation (1862) most African Americans were enslaved by whites, with their only security being the best interests of the slaveholders as the slaveholders saw them. This reality and the fact that the United States was settled at the expense of nonwhite Native Americans has produced a backdrop of racism and oppression of minorities of color throughout U.S. history.

NATIVE AMERICANS AND U.S. HISTORY

One ethnic group preceded European immigration, and its fate at the hands of the immigrant majority was particularly cruel. The early generosity of Native Americans stands in marked contrast to the values of the early American colonists. It is a trait remarked on by the earliest colonists both in the East and the area that has become the southwestern part of the United States. The Native Americans have been described as people who "at times . . . even gave their possessions away for nothing to those who asked for them."[44] The kind and caring quality of Native Americans was noted by Christopher Columbus in a letter to the king and queen of Spain: "So tractable, so peaceful are these people that I swear to your majesties, there is not in the world a better nation. They love their neighbors as themselves and their discourse is ever sweet and gentle, and accompanied with a smile; and though it is true that they are naked, yet their manners are decorous and praiseworthy."[45]

Later, the Native Americans almost universally greeted the British settlers with friendship and assistance. Interestingly, this overt friendliness was viewed by the colonists with suspicion. A contemporary observer reported:

> All accounts agree that for some reason the Indians did daily relieve them for some weeks with corn and flesh. The supplies brought from England had been nearly exhausted, the colonists had been too sick to attend to their gardens properly, and this act of the Indians was regarded as a divine providence at the time. . . . What was the real motive for the kindly acts of the Indians may not be certainly known, but it probably boded the little colony a future harm.[46]

Early American legal commitments to Native Americans were respectful. A much-violated document, the Northwest Ordinance (1787) states:

> The utmost good faith shall always be observed towards the Indians; their lands and property shall never be taken from them without their consent; and, in their property, rights, and liberty, they shall never be invaded or disturbed, unless in just and lawful wars authorized by Congress; but laws founded in justice and humanity shall from time to time be made for preventing wrongs being done to them, and for preserving peace and friendship with them.[47]

Following the Revolutionary War, through a series of treaties the United States acquired lands and assumed legal responsibilities for Native Americans. Tribes ceded their lands and the federal government made commitments in return. From 1830 to 1850, Native-American land east of the Mississippi was "exchanged" for land west of the boundary. Almost the entire Native-American population in the southeastern United States was coerced and removed—in a trek described by the Cherokees as a "trail of tears"—to the west, where they were placed on reservations and promised material and political assistance.

The European colonists and later Americans took Native-American lands by theft, fraud, deceit, purchase, and military force, pushing the Native Americans before them, removing them from the land, decimating them as they moved westward. By the end of the nineteenth century, a policy of assimilation developed in which Native Americans were forced by the Bureau of Indian Affairs to forsake their religious, social, and cultural practices through control of everything from hairstyles to language. Children were separated from their Native-American environments and forced to adopt white ways. Treated as wards of the state, they were not allowed to make decisions about their own lives and were forced into the "melting pot," dependent on rations and assistance.

Although the United States' public policy was creating a dependent group— the Native Americans—it was also creating many social problems among them as immigrant Americans destroyed the fabric of Native-American life. By contrast, there is evidence, for example, that in the 1820s, left to their own social welfare devices, "there were no paupers in New Mexico at that time, nor could there be any."[48] This observation, made by a Mexican lawyer in 1827, only confirmed earlier evidence. In the southwestern culture a poor person would go to a rich livestock and land owner and offer to assist him by herding sheep. The shepherd would give of the future increase, and wool would be contracted at the current market price. Materials from the sheep would be used to construct housing; milk and meat were used as food; and the wool was marketed as blankets, stockings, and the like. Thus the necessities of life were supplied.

With passage of the General Allotment Act (1887), known as the Dawes Act, the United States intervened to break up tribal communal landholdings and distribute them into individual 40-, 80-, and 160-acre shares for agricultural and grazing purposes. (A blood code that assigns one's racial or other status on the basis of familial descent patterns was used to legally define who was a Native American.) The Native American would become a voting citizen if his residence was maintained separate from the tribe and if he became a farmer. This was contrary to the tribal and communal property traditions and values of the Native Americans. The result was that many lost their land. From 1887 to 1934 Native-American landholdings were cut down from 138 million acres to 47 million acres, a two-thirds' loss. Entire tribes became landless. Today, Native-American tribes retain only about 5 percent of their original land.[49]

By 1934, the Indian Reorganization Act permitted tribes to reorganize their own institutions and to handle many of their own concerns. Nevertheless, the Bureau of Indian Affairs sustained for itself a veto power over most tribal decisions. In the 1950s the U.S. government terminated control over certain tribes over which it was thought federal responsibility was unnecessary, and jurisdiction was shifted to state governments. Native Americans were also physically relocated from reservations to urban areas.

In the 1960s, as part of a general claiming of ethnic identities and as part of the Civil Rights movement, Native Americans expressed vigorously their rights to their cultures and civil rights within American society. Although it was quite late and much damage had been done, groups of Native Americans set out to lay claim to their languages, general culture, and a rectification of the history of broken white promises and treaties. As a result, a series of court cases was instituted holding the United States liable for lands belonging to the tribes.

Treaties recognized Native-American tribes as sovereign nations since the eighteenth century, when the government pledged to provide public services such as education and health to the Native-American nations in exchange for land, other resources, and peace. Despite the independent status of the tribes, the U.S. federal government maintained tight management of these public services until 1974.

A movement began to expand and make permanent a restoration of independence to Native-American nations. In 1974, the federal government made a fundamental change in its policy regarding Native Americans when it passed the Self-Determination and Education Assistance Act (amended 1988). The act granted 554 tribes greater autonomy and authority over federal programs designed for their benefit and affirmed their right to be self-governing.

During the 1980s, Native-American programs, like other federal programs, were cut or eliminated despite the trust and treaty relationship. The total privatization of reservation economic development and the application of market forces to Native-American policy was fostered, except where states wished to retain control, such as tribal gaming. There also have been complaints that the federal government has stalled in carrying out the self-determination act.[50]

From 1980 to 1990, the census counted an increase of approximately 33 percent in the Native American population, a result of Americans with Native American heritages increasingly identifying with the group and an improved count by the Census Bureau. Almost 2 million Americans say their race is Native American and there are estimates that as many as one in every thirty-five persons claim some Native American ancestry.

The number of Native American–owned businesses increased 64 percent between 1982 and 1987, as tribes attempted to create sustainable, self-reliant economies, in part to provide jobs and offset unemployment and the problems that accompany it. There are both legal and political efforts to reduce the sovereignty of Native American tribes at the same time the number of Native American lawyers increased substantially. Among these efforts are those challenging the tax status of the tribes and efforts to prevent tribes from taxing businesses on their territories. There are proposals in Congress to limit the expansion of Native American sovereignty, holdings, and jurisdictions. Gambling casinos and tourism, which have enriched some tribes, have also attracted criticism from those who maintain that businesses within a state should be taxed and regulated by the states. The law that legalized the opening of gambling casinos by Native Americans on reservations allowed this as long as the states agreed in a contract (called a compact) that is renegotiable. These businesses, especially the casinos, increase revenues, which in turn create new political power. Critics include those who want more tax revenue for the states, those businesses that compete with the casinos, and those who oppose the extra-territoriality of the tribal territories where a complex set of legal arrangements exist with states, localities, and the federal government. Still others challenge the success of the tribes on other grounds. An example of the intensity of these conflicts is the decision in Utah by the Skull Valley Band of Goshutes (with barely 100 members) to lease part of their reservation as the temporary storage ground for high-level civilian nuclear waste. The governor and the congressional delegation tried to block this lease arrangement. Tensions about these matters have become intense and the challenges of many kinds have created stronger cooperative arrangements by the tribes in defense of their rights. Important factors that affect these conflicts and challenges include (1) the Supreme Court's shrinking of the concept of Native American country and giving states more power to limit Native American gambling and (2) the trend in Congress to move power and decision making from the Federal to the state level.[51]

THE FEDERAL ROLE IN SOCIAL WELFARE

As in the English Poor Law tradition, the U.S. system provided social welfare services at the local level with certain limited supports provided at the state level. Federal governmental intervention in economic matters began during the early years of the republic and included tariff legislation; disposition of the public domain; creation of a banking system; and canal, road, and railroad construction. The active role of the federal government in social welfare has been traced to two early forms of assistance—cash and other types of assistance to victims of floods, fires, earthquakes, and other disasters, and aid provided to two charitable institutions: the Connecticut Asylum for the Deaf and Dumb (a private institution, in 1819) and the Kentucky Deaf and Dumb Asylum (a public institution, in 1826). But these were isolated events and set no pattern of federal intervention in the social welfare domain.[52]

In 1854, Dorothea Dix, who worked strenuously for better treatment of the indigent insane, managed to get the Indigent Insane Bill passed by Congress to provide funds to improve the care of such people. The bill would have granted 10 million acres of public lands to the states, in proportion to their congressional representation. The states could then sell the land and use the proceeds for the perpetual care of the indigent insane. The bill was a popular one because it provided "payoffs" for both land speculators and philanthropists. However, President Franklin Pierce vetoed the bill, and his veto was sustained by Congress, thus halting a landmark advance in U.S. governmental philosophy concerning social welfare.

Pierce used several arguments, including one that President James Madison earlier presented in an 1811 veto: that the federal government could not give legal sanction to charitable governmental acts. Furthermore, if help was to be given to the indigent insane, he suggested that all the needy would have to be helped eventually. Pierce also used President Andrew Jackson's argument that lands given to the states must be used for the common good. In addition, financial expediency played a part: Pierce claimed the lands were security for the Mexican War debt.

However, Pierce intimated he would approve land grants to railroads. The purpose of granting lands to the railroads, as Pierce viewed it, was to enhance the value of the whole nation. The crucial assumption, however, is that property owners need help through governmental assistance while people do not. Interestingly, Pierce previously gave land to soldiers and to railroads but would not do so for the benefit of disabled and ill persons. One editorial interpretation at the time suggested the veto halted an erosion of states' rights. Another argument used by Pierce was based on a strict construction of the U.S. Constitution: If the Founding Fathers had wanted such programs, they would have made it explicit in the Constitution. Essentially, Pierce refused to make "the Federal government the great almoner of public charity throughout the United States."[53] And yet the federal government, so reluctant to assume a welfare role, did so in several instances.

THE FREEDMEN'S BUREAU

Following the Civil War and during the period of Reconstruction, the Freedmen's Bureau (Bureau of Refugees, Freedmen, and Abandoned lands) was created as part of the War Department. The Freedmen's Bureau was an experiment in social policy. Among its responsibilities was the introduction of a workable system of free labor in the South, finding employment for formerly enslaved people, supervising labor contracts affecting freedmen, establishing freedmen on homestead lands, fixing wages and terms of employment, providing transportation to newfound homes, and forming settlements of African Americans.

The Freedmen's Bureau had other daunting responsibilities. There was an expectation the bureau would adjudicate disputes among African Americans and between the races, attempt to secure equal justice from state and local governments, and provide aid for the destitute, aged, ill, and insane. One of its important functions was the arrangement of family reunions. As part of that effort, prior marriages of enslaved persons were formally, religiously recognized and made official, and the children of the deceased were adopted by relatives and friends. By 1870, a large majority of African Americans lived in two-parent family households.

The bureau had a role in health care as well and assumed the operation of hospitals that had been established by the army in larger cities during the war. It also established dispensaries in other less-populated areas. Although the bureau was hampered by limited resources (most of its budget was spent on relief and hospitals) and did not itself establish schools, it did coordinate the activities of northern societies and groups involved in establishing schools. By 1869, there were almost 3,000 schools, which served more than 150,000 African-American pupils in the South. In addition, there were evening, Sunday, and private schools run by missionary groups and by African Americans themselves in which adults, children, and sometimes whole families learned. These schools were influential in establishing a foundation for public education in the South.[54]

True to American experience and values, the administrator of the bureau, Commissioner General Oliver Otis Howard (for whom Howard University is named) stated proudly that the bureau had not been "a pauperizing agency."[55] By the end of 1868, the Freedmen's Bureau ceased most of its activities and was officially abolished in 1872.[56]

Important legacies were established by Reconstruction and the Freedmen's Bureau. But when Reconstruction ended, most energies were directed toward separate public institutions for African Americans and whites with the inferior services designated for African Americans. This pattern culminated in the "separate but equal" Supreme Court ruling in 1896 (*Plessy v. Ferguson*), which gave legal sanction to segregated facilities. Nevertheless, the suggestion has been made that a number of positive accomplishments rose out of public welfare efforts in the South during the period 1865–1880: Universal public education was established, attention was paid to children, agencies were created to improve health conditions, and poor relief was implemented at the local level more than at the state level.[57]

The importance of the Freedmen's Bureau for our discussion lies in its example of governmental intervention during a time of stress to assist people with their problems rather than to leave them entirely at the mercy of events. Thus there was a commitment by the federal government to meet the fundamental welfare needs of people, despite the earlier Pierce veto. Furthermore, governmental programs of a diverse nature provided a comprehensive series of services to deal constructively with serious social upheaval and foreshadowed across-the-board, comprehensive programs like those of the Great Depression and the War on Poverty in the 1960s.[58]

Veterans and a Suspension of the Ethic

The federal government, when motivated by political and pragmatic reasons, established and administered social welfare programs. Welfare services for one group are based on the suspension of the Protestant ethic. Considering the veteran's sacrifice (and our collective guilt?), the veteran is viewed as entitled to help even if he or she is personally unworthy. Following the Revolutionary War, veterans were recipients of generous grants to western lands.[59] An anonymous quote from the period following the War of 1812 makes a straightforward argument: "Who but the Soldier and his family should eat the bread from the Soil his own blood has enriched?"[60]

Although most social welfare efforts during the late eighteenth century were local, beginning in 1776 there was a series of pension acts that generally provided assistance to disabled veterans. But other types of aid were also given. In 1818, the Revolutionary War Pension Act was passed. This federal poor law

> assumed, prima facie, that every Continental soldier was worthy of aid, so the only question to be asked was whether he needed it. Once judged in need of aid, the claimant was not granted relief rated to his need but rather awarded a lifetime pension at a rate higher for officers than for ordinary soldiers. By passing the War Department's means test, the veteran was transformed from an alms seeker into an honored pensioner with a guaranteed annual income for life.[61]

Most social welfare during the nineteenth century was provided by state and local governments, but there was a federally funded pension system for Civil War veterans who fought in the Union army. The costs of these pensions for disabled soldiers and the widows and dependents of deceased soldiers became the largest single item of federal expenditure, except for debt service, in every year from 1885 to 1897, and reached 34 percent of the federal budget in 1890. Following 1890, veterans no longer had to claim a relationship between their disabilities and Civil War military activities, a liberalization that affected three-quarters of a million former soldiers, their widows, and dependents.[62]

Other federal social welfare supports emerged during the nineteenth century. The Homestead Act (1862) made it possible for any American citizen to obtain 160 acres of unoccupied government land if he or she lived on it for five years. By 1870, special privileges were given to soldiers who fought in the Union army. Such soldiers could count their time of military service toward the five-year prerequisite homesteading period. Widows could count the full term of their husband's enlistment.[63] Following every war, various techniques were found to provide resources for veterans and their families.

Although in many cases benefits were specifically meant for those who have been disabled, at other times these benefits were more universally available for all veterans. Following World War II, 10 million veterans had to be reintegrated into civilian life. The Servicemen's Readjustment Act (1944, the "GI Bill") guaranteed loans to buy a home, farm, or business, and provided 52 weeks of unemployment insurance at $20 per week to any unemployed veteran. Among the benefits were job placement services and up to four years of federal aid for learning or training at any level, including tuition and monthly allowances. These benefits were available to each veteran whether or not the veteran had been disabled and, more importantly, whether or not the veteran had actually been engaged in battle. The GI Bills were extended to veterans of the Korean and Vietnam conflicts. These benefits are examples of a type of universal program, which is more the exception than the rule.[64]

The federal government enacted such legislation out of complex motivations. In addition to rewarding veterans, one important factor was the idea that giving benefits to veterans and their families would have a long-term beneficial effect on the total society, raise the average educational and skill level, provide needed technical and other training to be used by society, and enhance social and governmental future income from the improved earnings of the veterans and their families. The GI Bill after World War II is also credited with helping to avoid a postwar depression. Historically, investments in veterans have been viewed as exceptions to the Protestant ethic. Therefore, the eligibility rules do not in general call for rigorous "means testing" (a financial test of one's level of income).

For our purposes, treatment of veterans may be seen as an example of what might be possible were we able to free ourselves from the values of Calvinism, dependency, and our terror of idleness. The veterans who received GI benefits included the majority who used the time to prepare for or to seek work. Some might have used this "dole" to postpone entry into the workforce. Still, the net effect of these programs was (1) to avoid a major economic depression as millions of soldiers were rapidly demobilized and thrown into a civilian economy, and (2) to upgrade the quality and earning power of the American work force for a generation.

In the case of the GI Bills, by forgetting about who was worthy and unworthy, about means tests and the like, a dignified welfare program benefited the whole economy. In fact, if one takes the cost of the GI program following World War II and balances it against the tax revenues gained from a better-educated workforce, the treasury has come out ahead. The avoidance of depression, crime, and the like also must be considered. Thus a shift in values makes possible a shift in types of welfare programs. What might result if all U.S. citizens were deemed as worthy as veterans?

Social Darwinism

In 1859, Charles Darwin published *The Origin of Species*, a book that had a remarkable impact on the world. Essentially a biological study, it postulated the concepts of natural selection and evolution. To this scientific interpretation of biological phenomena, social Darwinism added social, philosophical, and theological elements. From the point of view of a social Darwinist, those who become wealthy in the struggle for existence do so because they are superior people.

Admittedly, the nineteenth-century capitalist economy was the scene of struggle and competition in which morality as such had limits. Almost anything and any action was permitted by some in the capitalist struggle. Beyond this, however, social Darwinism viewed the struggle and competition as justifiable and glorifying the natural order and even God's will.

These ideas were justification for those who had enriched themselves through ruthless competition. In this way, predatory competition in business and industry was provided a philosophical rationale. Herbert Spencer (1820–1903), an English philosopher, sociologist, and coiner of the phrase "survival of the fittest," defended the moral aspects of individualism and laissez-faire economics. He asserted the poor "were unfit . . . and should be eliminated. The whole effort of nature is to get rid of such, to clear the world of them, and make room for better."[65]

Given these perspectives, some people were "elected" to survive and prosper. Logically then, the poor, ill, and disadvantaged were responsible for their limitations and their poverty, perhaps through lack of God's grace but surely through their being unfit. This tangle of interrelated concepts led directly to the assignment of responsibility for one's personal situation. The impoverished were all responsible in some way for their own plights. The way of the world was just as it should be. The status quo reflected not only human achievements and limitations but also God's will. Furthermore, social welfare efforts, however well meant, interfered with the process of natural selection and, in the long run, injured society.

THE COMING OF SOCIAL INSURANCE

Just as the early American social welfare system was influenced by the English Poor Laws, later American developments were influenced by the coming of social insurance in Europe, a forerunner of the U.S. Social Security Act of 1935.

In a Germany recently united during the 1870s, Social Democrats were urging the workers of a rapidly industrializing nation to demand a republican form of government, a bill of rights, and support for the international socialist movement. In the political and industrial ferment of middle Europe, the socialists were gaining strength. As a result, in 1879 antisocialist laws were enacted that forbade parties aimed at "overthrowing the established state or social order."[66] Otto von Bismarck (chancellor of the German empire) shifted from laissez-faire economics and free trade to protectionism, as indicated by the institution of tariffs in 1879.[67]

Since the antisocialist laws created enemies among the workers, Bismarck decided something needed to be done that would assure more contented workers in a period of great industrialization. In 1881, all workers in mines and factories whose earnings did not exceed 2,000 marks per year were insured against accidents. There followed in 1883 the enactment of a Sickness Insurance Law; in 1884 an Accident Insurance Law; and in 1887 an Old Age and Invalidity Law.

Bismarck presented a remarkable argument in his 1881 speech to the Reichstag in which he proposed social insurance: "I am not of the opinion that laissez faire, laissez aller, 'pure Manchester policy,' 'everybody takes care of himself,' 'the weakest must go to the wall,' . . . can be practiced in a monarchically, patriarchically governed state."[68] As his arguments were presented in favor of social insurance and of governmental intervention, Bismarck amalgamated several themes into one: The state has a responsibility to intervene when it assumes that industry cannot handle the problem. These themes are noted in Bismarck's comment that an appropriate title for our enterprise would be "Practical Christianity," but we do not want to feed poor people with figures of speech, but with something solid. Death costs nothing; but unless you will put your hands in your pockets and into the state Exchequer, you will not do much good. To saddle our industry with the whole affair—well, I don't know that it could bear the burden. All manufacturers are having hard times.[69]

By 1889, the method of financing these social insurances included contributions from employers, employees, and the government. Social legislation did not halt the rise of the Social Democratic party because German workers did not trust the government's motivation and workers really wanted improved working conditions and higher wages.

Bismarck, who, however contradictory it might appear, had taken a liberal stance in regard to the creation of social insurances, stubbornly refused legislation on working hours, woman and child labor, factory inspection, or changes in government policy regarding labor unions, which were carefully controlled. He emphasized that the social insurances were intended to bind workers to the state, not only through loyalty but also through self-interest. For the state was all-important, and Bismarck had given all his energies to the creation of Germany under Prussian leadership. Social welfare was a tool directed toward turning the sense of loyalty away from the locality toward the nation. When it suited his purposes, he reverted to Manchester laissez-faire arguments. But the historic principle of contributory social insurance was institutionalized in a modern nation-state for the first time. The reverberations of this event have been felt in every modern society, and the principle of various forms of "social security" continue to be developed and refined.

For a sense of perspective, one can note that social insurance instituted in Germany was soon followed by the United Kingdom and a number of European and South American nations, as well as Australia, Canada, and New Zealand decades earlier than the United States.[70] In the United Kingdom, the Old Age Pensions Act (1908) took a step away from the traditional Poor Law but used a means test: Only deserving persons and those with annual incomes below a certain point were entitled to the benefit. According to the act, the undeserving were those who had habitually failed to work according to their ability and personal need, those who had not saved money regularly over a period of years, and those who had been convicted of habitual drunkenness. Interestingly those dependent on the head of household were also perceived as undeserving. In 1911 the National Insurance Act (Part 1, Health Insurance; Part 2, Unemployment Insurance) was instituted. Precedents existed in cooperative friendly societies and trade unions and the program was based on contributions by employers, employees, and the state.[71]

Society, Social Values, and Modern Views of Human Nature

In preindustrial societies those who were dependent often were deemed worthy of assistance. In times of catastrophe, as we have seen, the larger community had the duty of providing the essentials for survival. Assistance was provided in many ways.

Problems developed in the fourteenth century when "able-bodied" poor, the "sturdy beggars," became visible. As a result of their increased numbers and threat, there began the regulation and differential treatment of beggars.

In general, with the development of industrial society, it was hoped the able-bodied would gain employment through economic expansion. For the rest, self-help, mutual aid, charity, and ad hoc emergency measures would be used. Public assistance would be only for those least able to cope and for those caught up in catastrophes.

In the latter part of the nineteenth century, it became clear that the "invisible hand" (Adam Smith's idea that each individual promoting his or her own self-interest in the marketplace is led by an invisible hand frequently to promote society's best interest more effectively than when the person consciously intends to promote it) of the self-regulating capitalist economy just might not be an invisible hand. The capitalist economy might not be self-regulating. Furthermore, it left many by the wayside, a seemingly natural concomitant of the "self-regulating" mechanisms.

The growing influence of the working classes, of the nearly poor and the poor, resulted in the evolution of economies in which (as in Germany in the 1880s) it became important to create welfare for the vast majority of persons for the sake of productivity and for the cohesion of the society. Dealing with pauperism became a part of the problem of minimum standards for all citizens.

In the early stages of industrialization, it could be argued that punitive welfare laws were necessary to maintain a pool of motivated workers. In this sense, the Poor Laws were functional in that they supported the industrialization of society and thus the creation of more wealth. As welfare systems evolved, especially after the creation of social insurances, support systems for more and more people were indeed built into Western societies.

The historic disjunction that occurred in the late Middle Ages and created 500 years of punitive social welfare legislation was undoubtedly connected with the many trends, ideas, and technical developments we have reviewed. But if changes of such tremendous importance could take place, there is a suggestion that the future also could be different. On the basis of prudence, societies could decide to treat those in need humanely, to avoid clashes, make human relations more peaceful, and assure that all citizens are treated with respect and are sustained.

SUMMARY

In this chapter we reviewed the major developments and themes in U.S. social welfare including the impact of the imported Poor Law mentality, differential experiences of African Americans, Latinos, and Native Americans, mutual aid, federal roles and American ambivalence about them, social Darwinism, and the creation of social insurances. In chapter 5, we turn to periods in U.S. history when poverty was highlighted as a social problem, an exploration of the two divergent social policies and programs resulting from different philosophies and values, a brief history of later American events, a look at the Poor Laws today, modern views of human nature, and human nature and the American dream.

QUESTIONS FOR CONSIDERATION

1. What support can you find for either the American myth of the individual hero or the role of mutual aid and cooperation in American life?
2. Do you believe President Pierce was correct in his interpretation of the U.S. Constitution? If yes, what are your arguments? If not, what are your arguments?
3. What did Bismarck mean by "death costs nothing"?
4. Is social Darwinism alive and well in the United States today?

NOTES

1. Lester F. Ward, *Applied Sociology*, New York: Ginn & Co., 1906, pp. 25, 327.
2. William B. Scott, *In Pursuit of Happiness: American Conceptions of Property from the Seventeenth to the Twentieth Century*, Bloomington: Indiana University Press, 1977, p. 6.
3. Ibid., pp. 8, 10.
4. Bernard Bailyn, *The Peopling of British North America*, New York: Knopf, 1986, p. 60, and Peter Kolchin, *American Slavery 1619-1877*, New York: Hill and Wang, 1993, pp. 10-11.
5. John Van der Zee, *Bound Over: Indentured Servitude and American Conscience*, New York: Simon & Schuster, 1985, p. 11.
6. Abbott E. Smith, *Colonists in Bondage: White Servitude and Convict Labor in America 1607-1776*, Chapel Hill, N.C.: University of North Carolina Press, 1947, pp. 20-21.
7. Robert W. Kelso, *The History of Public Poor Relief in Massachusetts, 1620-1920*, Montclair, N.J.: Patterson Smith, 1969, p. 95.
8. Ibid., p. 92.
9. Ralph E. Pumphrey and Muriel W. Pumphrey, *The Heritage of American Social Work*, New York: Columbia University Press, 1961, p. 24. Colonial society stigmatized unmarried females. In addition, from one third to one half of a town's paupers were likely to be female. See Mimi Abramovitz, "The Family Ethic: The Female Pauper and Public Aid, Pre-1900," *Social Service Review*, Vol. 59, No. 1, March 1985, p. 124.
10. Pumphrey and Pumphrey, p. 20.
11. Ibid., p. 27.
12. Robert H. Bremner, "Private Philanthropy and Public Needs: Historical Perspective," *Research Papers: The Commission on Private Philanthropy and Public Needs*, Vol. 1, *History, Trends, and Current Magnitudes*, Washington, D.C.: Department of the Treasury, 1977, p. 90.
13. Ibid., pp. 91-92.
14. Ibid., p. 103.
15. Gary B. Nash, *The Urban Crucible: Social Change, Political Consciousness, and the Origins of the American Revolution*, Cambridge, Mass.: Harvard University Press, 1979, pp. 21, 125-126.
16. Bernard L. Fontana, *Entrada: The Legacy of Spain and Mexico in the United States*, Albuquerque, N.M.: University of New Mexico Press, 1994, p. 37; Elizabeth A. Foster, ed., *The Motolinia's History of the Indians of New Spain*, The Cortes Society; University of New Mexico, 1950, pp. 143, 154-155; Bonnie G. McEwan, ed., *The Spanish Missions of Florida*, Gainesville, Fla.: University Press of Florida, 1993, pp. 89, 91; Albert Prago, *Strangers in Their Own Land*, New York: Four Winds Press, 1973, p. 33; Engel Sluiter,

The Florida Situado: Quantifying the First Eighty Years, 1571-1651, Gainesville, Fla.: University of Florida Libraries, 1985, p. 1.

17. Himilce Novas, *Everything You Need to Know about Latino History*, New York: Penguin Books, Inc., 1994, pp. xiii, 38, 56, 58; France V. Scholes, "Civil Government and Society in New Mexico in the Seventeenth Century," in Vol.1, *Historical Themes and Identity*, Antoinette Sedello Lopez, ed., New York: Garland Publishing, Inc., 1995, pp. 27-67.

18. Roberto Suro, *Strangers among Us*, New York: Alfred A. Knopf, 1998, p.20.

19. Pumphrey and Pumphrey, p. 30.

20. Wade Nobles, "Africanity: Its Role in Black Families," *The Black Scholar*, Vol. 5, No. 9, June 1974, pp. 11-17.

21. Andrew Billingsley and Jeanne M. Giovannoni, *Children of the Storm*, New York: Harcourt Brace Jovanovich, 1972, p. 46.

22. Joanne M. Martin and Elmer P. Martin, *The Helping Tradition in the Black Family and Community*, Silver Spring, Md.: National Association of Social Workers, 1985, pp. 12-13.

23. W. E. B. DuBois, *Economic Cooperation among Negro Americans*, Atlanta, Ga.: Atlanta University Press, 1907, pp. 20-21.

24. E. Franklin Frazier, *The Free Negro Family*, Nashville, Tenn.: Fisk University Press, 1932, p. 16.

25. Herbert Aptheker, ed., *A Documentary History of the Negro People in the United States*, New York: The Citadel Press, 1951, pp. 17-18; James S. Olson, *The Ethnic Dimension in American History*, New York: St. Martin's Press, 1979, p. 152.

26. E. Horace Fitchett, "The Tradition of the Free Negro in Charleston, South Carolina," *The Making of Black America*, August Meier and Elliott Rudwick, eds., New York: Atheneum, 1969, pp. 206-215.

27. Frazier, p. 16.

28. Herbert G. Gutman, *The Black Family in Slavery and Freedom, 1750-1925*, New York: Pantheon, 1976, pp. 224-225.

29. Ibid., pp. 224-229.

30. Ibid., p. 229.

31. James S. Allen, *Reconstruction, 1865-1876*, New York: International Publishers, 1966, pp. 57-59; Peter Kolchin, *American Slavery 1619-1877*, New York: Hill and Wang, 1993, pp. 209-210.

32. Leon F. Litwack, *Been in the Storm So Long: The Aftermath of Slavery*, New York: Knopf, 1979, pp. 366-371 and passim.

33. Ibid., p. 321.

34. Amos G. Warner, *American Charities*, New York: Thomas Y. Crowell, 1908, pp. 393, 395.

35. H. M. Lai, "Chinese," *Harvard Encyclopedia of American Ethnic Groups*, Stephan Thernstrom, ed., Cambridge, Mass.: Harvard University Press, 1980, pp. 218-219, 221, 222.

36. Carlos E. Cortes, "Mexicans," *Harvard Encyclopedia of American Ethnic Groups*, Stephan Thernstrom, ed., Cambridge, Mass.: Harvard University Press, 1980, pp. 698-699, 709.

37. Humbert S. Nelli, "Italians," *Harvard Encyclopedia of American Ethnic Groups*, Stephan Thernstrom, ed., Cambridge, Mass.: Harvard University Press, 1980, p. 552.

38. Ray Allen Billington, *America's Frontier Heritage*, New York: Holt, Rinehart and Winston, 1966, p. 143. Also see Mody C. Boatright, "The Myth of Frontier Individualism," *Turner and the Sociology of the Frontier*, Richard Hofstadter and Seymour M. Lipset, eds., New York: Basic Books, 1968, pp. 43-64.

39. Billington, p. 145.

40. Ibid., pp. 145-147.
41. Lerone Bennett Jr., *Before the Mayflower: A History of Black America*, New York: Penguin, 1984, pp. 29, 35. Also see Madeleine Burnside, *Spirits of the Passage: The TransAtlantic Slave Trade in the Seventeenth Century*, New York: Simon & Schuster Edition, 1997.
42. Billingsley and Giovannoni, p. 26.
43. Thomas R. Frazier, ed., *Afro-American History: Primary Sources*, New York: Harcourt Brace Jovanovich, 1970, p. 29. An African-American pilgrim, Abraham Pearce, settled in the Plymouth Colony in 1623. Pearce owned land, voted, and had equal standing with others in the community. "Plymouth Historian Says a Black Settled at Pilgrims' Colony," *New York Times*, August 20, 1981, p. A28. Peter Kolchin, *American Slavery: 1619-1877*, New York: Hill and Wang, 1993, pp. 10-11.
44. Lewis Hanke, *The First Social Experiments in America*, Cambridge, Mass.: Harvard University Press, 1935, p. 30.
45. Quoted in Dee Brown, *Bury My Heart at Wounded Knee*, New York: Holt, Rinehart and Winston, 1974, p. xiii.
46. Fremont J. Lyden and Lyman H. Legters, eds., *Native Americans and Public Policy*, Pittsburgh, Penn.: University of Pittsburgh Press, 1992, pp. 14-15.
47. Ibid., p. 15.
48. David J. Weber, ed., *Foreigners in Their Native Land*, Albuquerque: University of New Mexico Press, 1973, p. 38.
49. Ward Churchill and Glenn T. Morris, "Key Indian Laws and Cases," *The State of Native America: Genocide, Colonization, and Resistance*, M. Annette Jaimes, ed., Boston: South End Press, 1992, p. 14; Peter Nabokov, ed., *Native American Testimony: A Chronicle of Indian-White Relations from Prophecy to the Present, 1492-1992*, New York: Viking Publishers, 1991, p. 306; Fremont J. Lyden and Lyman H. Legters, eds., *Native Americans and Public Policy*, Pittsburgh, Penn.: University of Pittsburgh Press, 1992, pp. 18-24, 69.
50. Paul Nyhan, "Senate Clears Bill Giving Tribes More Authority Over Programs," *Congressional Quarterly Weekly Review*, Vol. 52, No. 40, p. 2961.
51. Timothy Egan, "New Prosperity Brings New Conflict to Indian Country," *New York Times*, March 8, 1998, pp. 1, 24. Timothy Egan, "Backlash Growing as Indians Make a Stand for Sovereignty," *New York Times*, March 9, 1998, pp. 1, A16.
52. Walter I. Trattner, "The Federal Government and Social Welfare in Early Nineteenth-Century America," *Social Service Review*, Vol. 50, June 1976, pp. 243-255.
53. Carlton Jackson, *Presidential Vetoes: 1792-1945*, Athens, Ga.: University of Georgia, 1967, pp. 100-102.
54. Eric Foner, *Reconstruction: America's Unfinished Revolution: 1863-1877*, New York: Harper & Row, 1988, pp. 142-151; Peter Kolchin, *American Slavery: 1619-1877*, New York: Hill and Wang, 1993, pp. 208-210, 221-222.
55. Foner, p. 152.
56. Ibid., pp. 84, 142-144, 151. Also see Victoria Olds, *The Freedmen's Bureau as a Social Agency*, unpublished doctoral dissertation, New York: Columbia University, 1966.
57. Howard N. Rabinowitz, "From Exclusion to Segregation: Health and Welfare Services for Southern Blacks, 1865-1890," *Social Service Review*, Vol. 48, No. 3, September 1974, pp. 327-354.
58. Victoria Olds, "The Freedmen's Bureau: A Nineteenth-Century Federal Welfare Agency," *Social Casework*, Vol. 44, No. 5, May 1963, pp. 247-254.
59. Cortez A. M. Ewing, *American National Government*, Norman, Okla.: University of Oklahoma, 1958, p. 583.

60. Marcus Cunliffe, *Soldiers and Civilians*, New York: Free Press, 1973, p. 81.

61. John P. Resch, "Federal Welfare for Revolutionary War Veterans," *Social Service Review*, Vol. 56, No. 2, June 1982, p. 191.

62. Theda Skocpol and John Ikenberry, "The Political Formation of the American Welfare State in Historical and Comparative Perspective," *Comparative Social Research*, Vol. 6, 1983, pp. 95–97.

63. John D. Hicks, George E. Mowery, and Robert E. Burke, *The American Nation*, Boston: Houghton Mifflin, 1963, p. 96.

64. *Those Who Served: Report of the Twentieth Century Fund Task Force on Policies toward Veterans*, New York: The Twentieth Century Fund, 1974.

65. Richard Hofstadter, *Social Darwinism in American Thought*, Boston: Beacon Press, 1967, p. 41.

66. Louis L. Snyder, *Documents of German History*, New Brunswick, N.J.: Rutgers University Press, 1958, p. 234.

67. Ibid., p. 234.

68. Ibid., p. 245.

69. Hajo Halborn, *A History of Modern Germany*, New York: Knopf, 1969, p. 292; Daniel Levine, *Poverty and Society: The Growth of the American Welfare State in International Comparison*, New Brunswick, N.J.: Rutgers University Press, 1988, pp. 51, 52, 55.

70. Social Security Administration, *Social Security Programs throughout the World—1997*, Washington, D.C.: U.S. Government Printing Office, August, 1997.

71. M. Penelope Hall, *The Social Services of Modern England*, London: Routledge and Kegan Paul, 1959.

America, Poverty, Two Paths: The American Experience II

Every modern industrial society is a welfare society. None permits natural or social contingencies fully to determine the life chances of its members. All have programs whose explicit purpose is to protect adults and children from the degradation and insecurity of ignorance, illness, disability, unemployment and poverty.
—Gutmann[1]

THREE DISCOVERIES OF POVERTY

In part the programs that exist today in the United States result from three "discoveries of poverty" and the ways in which American society focuses on poverty. The divergent social welfare paths for dealing with the issue result from different societal values and views of human nature.

Social Darwinism did not go unchallenged during the latter part of the nineteenth century. Among those groups that countered the arguments of the social Darwinists were the Grangers, Single Taxers, trade unionists, populists, and socialists who challenged the existing pattern of free enterprise, demanded reforms by state action, or insisted upon a thorough remodeling of the social order.[2] As early as a century earlier, Thomas Paine argued that the United States had the potential for abolishing poverty and that security could be provided for the aged through the use of inheritance taxes and ground rents.[3]

Social Darwinism was a fatalist, status quo philosophy, useful for those who controlled industry and business. Paradoxically, this conservative philosophy took hold when—because of science and technology—it was thought that human beings could achieve whatever they chose, including modifying society.

Lester Ward, a sociology pioneer, argued against social Darwinism and suggested that restraining power is needed to regulate the conduct of individuals toward one another and to prevent the wholesale exploitation of the weak by the strong. Without constraints, liberty and happiness would be impossible. The highest aim of true individualism is to maximize individual liberty; accomplishing this requires some governmental restraints. From this perspective, the doctrine of laissez faire *at the extreme* is incoherent and futile.[4]

Prior to the 1890s, the predominant attitude in the United States was that society and the community had no real obligation to the poor. Until the last decades of the nineteenth century, reform movements in the United States did not focus on the problem of poverty or on its elimination. During these decades one response of churches to slums and poverty was to preach the *Social Gospel*. Walter Rauschenbusch was a prime proponent of the Social Gospel, which was "the application of the teaching of Jesus and the total message of the Christian salvation to society, the economic life, and social institutions . . . as well as its individuals." Socially conscious ministers suggested that Jesus came to establish a new environment and that all Christians should work to change the world by acting to reform wages, housing, and working conditions. Some defended the demands of labor unions and preached against the economic doctrine based on social Darwinism. Although these ministers argued there are Christian solutions for all social problems, their influence did not reach the mass of churchgoers.[5]

Furthermore, the laissez faire philosophy that prevailed during the intense rush to industrialize America was modified. In 1887, the federal Interstate Commerce Commission was formed, although limited in power, and helped to uncover business and political corruption. This action affirmed the right of the federal government to regulate interstate business, a key ingredient for effective regulation yet to be built. There was a growing interest in improving the living conditions of the poor, illustrated by numerous exposés of dangerous and unhealthy work and home environments. Another force leading to reform were the "muckrakers," journalists who were active in exposing social ills, including corruption in business, city governments, child labor, food packing, and other spheres of life.

First Discovery

The progressive era that spanned the first decade and a half of the twentieth century marked the *first discovery* of poverty in America: Progressives, during this period, had an intense belief in the possibility of social progress and a deep concern for reform in politics and business. They were committed as utopian thinkers to the idea that progress toward social justice was possible and necessary, and they viewed poverty as a result of the structure of society. It was agreed that the community had to take some responsibility for alleviating poverty, criminality, prostitution, poor housing, and intemperance. The expectation was that remedial work should be focused on the capacity of the individual for self-improvement but that society also could be altered. So, this first discovery of poverty also reflects a "can-do" attitude, the idea that government and the people can fix problems, even poverty.

It also was during these years that various insurance laws were enacted. These were mostly related to unemployment and disability protection, and their initiation was partly stimulated by the earlier German experience. During 1900–1914 (the Progressive Era), the federal government intervened for the first time since the Freedmen's Bureau, and much social legislation was passed, including antitrust laws, civil service reform, creation of the Children's Bureau, child labor laws, health and safety laws, the income tax, direct election of senators, and other laws with major social consequences but requiring limited federal expenditures.

The Fading of the First Discovery

With the onset of World War I, the progressive era of legislation faded and with it the focus on poverty. In the United States, disillusionment with and fear of left-wing philosophies, including socialism and anarchism, dampened the interest in initiating social legislation.

During the 1920s, there was a return to the philosophy of governmental nonintervention and the hope that the country could return to the "good old days." Thus the first discovery of poverty passed, leaving a wave of social welfare legislation in the states and on the federal level.

The one exception to the return to the laissez faire philosophy was the enactment of the Sheppard-Towner Act in 1921 (following the enfranchisement of women in 1920). This was the first federal program to provide grants to states to develop preventive health services for mothers and children. Despite common knowledge about high maternal and infant death rates, those opposing the act suggested the act threatened the basic values of the nation. Among those who opposed the bill were anti-suffragists, anti-feminists, and anti-communists. It was also opposed by states who feared a loss of power and by the American Medical Association, which feared state-sponsored medicine. By supporting federal intervention for a national social problem, the Sheppard-Towner Act was a conceptual link between the earlier progressive period and the New Deal to follow; despite the fact that it was proven effective, the act was eliminated just before the Great Depression.[6]

Second Discovery

A *second discovery* of the problem of poverty occurred during the Great Depression of the 1930s. So many people were unemployed and poor during the 1930s that the federal government was forced to act. It was no longer "they" who were poor; it was "us." President Herbert Hoover initially thought a return of confidence would correct the failing economy. He was also deeply committed to a conservative, free-enterprise philosophy based on a belief in individual and family responsibility. He was opposed to efforts to expand the federal role—for example, the provision of federal grants to states for direct relief, federally funded public works projects, or any federal-state employment role. Federal assistance was viewed negatively. At first,

Hoover limited himself to confidence-instilling statements, which failed to deter the continued deterioration of the economy. He attempted to expedite private relief efforts, to no advantage. Finally, the Reconstruction Finance Corporation was created to lend money to banks, railroads, and other institutions, and Hoover supported federal loans to states for their relief efforts.

The New Deal era initiated by President Franklin D. Roosevelt involved a very different strategy to counteract the Great Depression and was marked by an enormous variety of legislation designed to deal with the many human problems. Among these actions were federal protection for bank depositors and stock market investors, federal credit to ease the debt burdens of farmers and homeowners, programs such as the Civilian Conservation Corps and the National Youth Administration to put unemployed youth to work, fair labor standards, emergency relief and work-relief programs, public works programs such as the Tennessee Valley Authority, lending programs for middle-class homeowners to repair old houses or build new ones, and building low-income housing. Other interventions included rural electrification, legislation to support farm prices, a nationwide unemployment exchange system, and monetary, food subsidy, and banking laws.

Although there had been efforts to introduce various types of social security in the states and on the federal level, until the Great Depression, Congress had failed to enact social insurance. Then, in 1935, as part of a wave of New Deal legislation, the Social Security Act was passed. Based on contributions by employer and employee, the plan was federally administered and included unemployment compensation, public assistance, and services.

This second discovery of poverty faded during World War II, probably because of the focus on the war effort and the full employment it engendered. The decade of the 1950s was not unlike the decade of the 1920s in that social legislation in general played a low-key role in regard to social welfare.

Third Discovery

The first American discovery of poverty in the early twentieth century came at a time when poverty was viewed as a personal and moral fault of the poor. However, so many persons were poor during the second discovery period in the 1930s that the systematic and structural nature of poverty was clear, and invidious moralizing necessarily was limited. However, the *third discovery* of poverty began in an affluent period—the 1960s. Then, as we shall see, the key to poverty was thought to be a lack of "opportunity."

In the late 1950s, the general belief, exemplified by Kenneth Galbraith's *The Affluent Society*, was that poverty as a social problem in the United States was past. There was still residual poverty, in Appalachia and other isolated pockets, and case poverty among those with low level skills or with emotional problems. It was believed the personal characteristics of poor persons contributed greatly to their being poor. Therefore, it was believed that such poverty could be reduced by having more trained social workers in welfare departments rehabilitating the poor.

This latter perspective was the thrust of amendments to the Social Security Act in 1962, which sought more trained social workers in public welfare in order to rehabilitate those on "welfare." Although for the short run this was good for social workers, it involved ignoring the societal and structural aspects of poverty.

Into this atmosphere came Edgar May's book *The Wasted Americans* and Michael Harrington's *The Other America*. These books pointed out that, if in the depression of 1933 one of every three Americans was poor, in 1960 one in four was still poor. Furthermore, this 25 percent was essentially constant and had not decreased since World War II. Dwight MacDonald popularized these ideas, and the idea of a poverty "line" below which people should be considered poor, in a series of articles in *The New Yorker* magazine. These articles and books caught the attention of advisors to President Kennedy who were seeking programs to stimulate the economy. After the Kennedy assassination, these advisors brought their preliminary thinking to President Johnson. Johnson supported them, and thus was born the Economic Opportunity Act of 1964—the so-called "War on Poverty."

The strategies chosen to deal with poverty did not include transfers of money directly to the poor. Instead, like the 1962 amendments to the Social Security Act, the strategy focused on services and offered opportunities for self-advancement. This focus on services was—although subtly—victim-blaming. Implicit in the emphasis on services was the suggestion that one was poor because of personal shortcomings or because of a lack of equal opportunity, a structural approach. The problem of inadequate income was viewed as inseparable from these personal limitations and structural limitations, which in turn limited opportunities.

The nature of the poverty war was related to the values and philosophies of the period. The antipoverty agencies developed on the basis of strategies demonstrated earlier. The Ford Foundation in the 1950s and 1960s addressed itself to urban issues. Gradually its priorities shifted from study and research to direct action grants, particularly the "grey areas" programs that focused energy on deteriorating central city areas with the aim of transforming political and social life through community organization. Congress enacted the Juvenile Delinquency and Youth Offenses Control Act (1961) to provide multifaceted antidelinquency projects by providing a package of federal services to communities. Federal efforts were often implemented in tandem with efforts supported by the Ford Foundation.

At one time, delinquency was seen as related to certain genetic or physical characteristics of the delinquent. A more "modern" approach was to view the juvenile delinquent as psychologically disturbed. Sociologists then claimed that delinquent behavior represented normal participation in a separate delinquent subculture. But the theory current in the late 1950s was "opportunity theory" as developed by Lloyd Ohlin and Richard Cloward.[7] The delinquent gang did not operate in a separate culture with different values and aspirations. Instead, delinquents shared the same desires for a car and a house with a picket fence and the like. It was the gap between these aspirations and available opportunities that caused delinquent behavior. Opportunity needed to be opened. Therefore, it is no surprise that the War on Poverty was the Economic *Opportunity* Act and that its programs stressed access, opportunity, and participation for the poor. Out of these participatory efforts grew the later demand for income transfer itself.

The 1960s focused the most attention on the problems of poverty since the 1930s. The president, Congress, and the society at large agreed to attack poverty through the enactment of legislation. There was a federal, state, and local approach to the problem, one which brought some but not all resources to the task.

How did the third discovery of poverty develop? Two different points of view hold special interest because they reflect the realities of the 1960s and identify the development of a relatively new feature in society. Furthermore, they may be instructive in pointing out the directions from which future reforms will come.

The first view was suggested by Senator Daniel P. Moynihan, then assistant secretary of labor, that a new phenomenon had occurred: the professionalization of reform. The question of poverty was now being dealt with, planned for, and coped with by administrators, professional organizations, doctors, teachers, social workers, and others, and special initiatives were being taken by government-employed professionals and foundations. The Ford Foundation and others designed methods to help people move out of poverty and selected cities for funded experiments. It is noteworthy that North Carolina during Governor Terry Sanford's administration sought to apply techniques that formerly focused on urban centers to an entire state, including rural sections, and received funding from the Ford Foundation and the Babcock and Reynolds Foundations, matched by local funds and grants from Federal agencies. Within a year following the inception of the North Carolina program, Congress appropriated funds for a national war on poverty, unleashing experiments in every state.[8] Moynihan's argument was that the Office of Economic Opportunity (OEO) programs were the result of this "professionalization" of reform.[9] Based on social statistics, newly available for use, and expanded social science research, OEO included high-level planning by professionals and "maximum feasible participation" by the poor in the development of programs. Furthermore, Moynihan argued, these programs had the effect of re-creating ethnic politico-social organizations in the big cities. According to Moynihan, for the first time in history professionals took the lead in the search for reform. They had access to information, they had expertise, and they knew where the entry points to the gates of power were located. Thus, in a way, the search for reform had taken a new turn. Professionals, with whatever motives, took on the mission of reforming society as a part of their own job definitions and responsibilities. The War on Poverty had not resulted from marches, demonstrations, or popular demand but rather from ideas emanating from intellectual and professional circles.

Richard Cloward and Frances Fox Piven, on the other hand, claimed that the War on Poverty was a response to the Civil Rights movement, the beginnings of unrest in the cities, and political payoffs to poor urban constituencies to whom the Democratic party owed a debt.[10] According to this view, OEO was the continuation of a political process. The Cloward and Piven perspective contrasted with the Moynihan point of view that no one was specifically "banging on the door" for a War on Poverty. Where the two points of view apparently intersect is in the fact that maximum feasible participation, as a principle, was invented by the professional planners but was also inherent in political realities among the poor. Enhanced participation by the poor is found in their demand for greater recognition and involvement in the political process. Both theories are correct but incomplete. There would have been no War on Poverty without the unrest Cloward and Piven describe; yet it might not have developed when and in the way it did without the process described by Moynihan.

THE WAR ON POVERTY

During the ten-year period from the mid-1960s to the mid-1970s, the average annual growth rates in spending on social programs leaped ahead. In 1965, $77.2 billion (11.5 percent of the gross national product) was expended nationally on the social insurances, public assistance, health and medical programs, veterans' programs, education, and housing. By 1976, $332 billion was spent (19.5 percent of the gross national product). As a percentage of all government expenditures, total social welfare expenditures rose from 42.4 percent in 1965 to 60.3 percent in 1976. Much of these increases took place at the federal level, although there was also more limited growth in such expenditures at the state and local levels. The increases took place under both Democratic and Republican administrations of presidents Kennedy, Johnson, Nixon, and Ford.[11]

President Johnson achieved an impressive series of legislative successes in his "Great Society" program. In 1965 alone, the following laws and programs emerged: Medicare, Medicaid, general federal aid to local public schools, federal scholarships and loans for college students, the Voting Rights Act, the National Foundations for the Arts and Humanities, rent supplements for poor persons, highway beautification, grants, loans, training programs for physicians and other health professionals, and developmental assistance for Appalachia.

The Economic Opportunity Act (1964) was only one element in the call by President Johnson for the nation to conduct a War on Poverty, mainly a set of services. When we think of a War on Poverty, we think of a massive effort. However, the budget of the Office of Economic Opportunity, between 1965 and 1974, ranged from a low of $328.5 million to a high of $1.896 billion.[12] Although these may seem like large sums, in a nation such as ours they are quite modest.

The War on Poverty and its leaders in Community Action Programs around the country adopted many of the tactics and slogans of a radical tide in the United States at the time. There were confrontations, sit-ins, and demonstrations. However, if by "radical" we mean a fundamental restructuring of the social order and by "conservative" we mean staying with the status quo, then the War on Poverty was an essentially conservative program. It mandated no fundamental new income maintenance program. Our social welfare structure remains based on the Social Security Act rather than on the new developments of the 1960s. In fact, one may argue that, by focusing on local issues, the War on Poverty deflected true radical reform. It must be noted that in reality the major impact on poverty came from income transfer programs and health insurance, not from War on Poverty programs themselves. The biggest change in the social welfare system in the 1960s came through the adoption of Medicare and Medicaid, which were not a part of the War on Poverty.

Expectation and Delivery

If there is one criticism of the War on Poverty on which most analysts agree, it is that the expectations engendered by the promises were far beyond anything the program had the capacity to deliver. Success often was called "failure" when newer and higher goals implicitly replaced original program goals. Elimination of poverty was not enough. Expenditures for goods or services going to the poor must be effective, efficiently managed, and equitable. Participation of the poor in managing an antipoverty budget was replaced by assuring their participation in all matters that affect them. Some escalation of goals is evidence not of failure but of problems of success, perhaps intensified by failing to make goals more specific and limited.[13]

Some people see this as not all bad, because it created a sense of entitlement. Others criticize the War on Poverty precisely because it encouraged this sense of entitlement. There are those who believe that the gap between expectation and delivery may have been in part responsible, along with the Vietnam War, for some of the violence characteristic of U.S. society in the late 1960s. Perhaps Aaron Wildavsky put it best:

> A recipe for violence: promise a lot; deliver a little. Lead people to believe they will be much better off but let there be no dramatic improvement. Try a variety of small programs, each interesting but marginal in impact and severely under financed. Avoid any attempt at solution remotely comparable in size to the dimensions of the problem you are trying to solve. . . . Get some poor people involved in local decision making only to discover that there is not enough at stake to be worth bothering about.[14]

There were at least seven developments that resulted from the War on Poverty and governmental intervention:

1. The poverty rate was reduced from 22 percent in 1960 to 11.2 percent in 1974.

2. The community became involved in decision making. "Maximum feasible participation" was a phrase little understood by Congress when it voted for the Economic Opportunity Act, the basis for the War on Poverty, but it is a dramatic illustration of the power of guideline writers and bureaucrats. They were able to give meaning to this phrase by demanding the participation of the poor in the governance of Community Action programs. Out of this came a concept of community involvement that is so much a part of social welfare today that the younger student will find it hard to imagine the degree of change. Before the mid-1960s, it simply would not have occurred to social welfare planners to ask residents or local leaders if a new hospital or center should be placed in their community. Most people agree today that there should be community input and involvement. This general acceptance grew directly from the activities of the War on Poverty and its successor programs.

A latent consequence of the involvement of local people in community affairs during the War on Poverty was the training and emergence of indigenous leadership that moved beyond the local scenes. There are governmental leaders in Washington, D.C., and elsewhere whose training began on the local level during the Civil Rights movement and the War on Poverty of the 1960s.

3. Similarly, the client's right to know and to gain access to information grew dramatically with the War on Poverty. Before the War on Poverty, welfare rights organizations would have to have pages of welfare manuals surreptitiously photocopied so that clients could learn about regulations and processes. Today the right of access to information is legally supported (although sometimes not honored). In addition, client brokerage and advocacy are viewed as legitimate social service functions.

4. Evaluation of the Head Start program found that graduates as young adults performed better in school, were more interested in going to college, and were less likely to get into criminal difficulty than persons with similar backgrounds who were not in Head Start. Whatever the limitations of the Head Start program, it made the following contributions:

   a. It strengthened the legitimacy of early intervention;
   b. It supported the value of day care; and
   c. It improved nutrition and health care for young children and enhanced parental involvement in education.

5. There was a major change in the concept of legal services that grew out of one of the programs of the War on Poverty. Not only criminal but civil legal service for the poor is now an accepted fact. This has occurred even though legal services have been poorly funded and there have been executive and legislative efforts to limit or eliminate the role of such programs.

6. Through the Job Corps and other job-creation programs, the War on Poverty helped to develop a consciousness and, at that time, an acceptance of the potential role of public service employment. Later events placed much greater emphasis on private-sector employment. It remains to be seen whether the special employment and training needs of a number of groups can be accommodated within the private sector alone.

7. Through the Vista Corps, which followed up on the successful Peace Corps launched during the Kennedy administration, the War on Poverty established that there is a human reservoir of idealism and a willingness for voluntary action that can be mobilized on behalf of social issues. The "thousand points of light" concept promulgated by President Bush in some ways is an extension of this principle.

8. The New Careers movement encouraged the use of indigenous members of the community as paraprofessional workers in the human services. Career ladders in education, often through community colleges, were established.

THE "SKIRMISH" AGAINST POVERTY

Although there was certainly no acknowledged war on poverty in the 1970s, there was a scarcely noticed confluence of legislation that might best be viewed as a "skirmish" against poverty. Though seldom recognized, this series of legislative actions made important contributions to the antipoverty effort:

1. The Supplemental Security Income program (1972) replaced the former state-run old-age assistance, aid to the blind, and aid to the permanently disabled programs.
2. Title XX of the Social Security Act (1975) was enacted to give more flexibility to the states in designing their social service programs.
3. The Earned Income Tax Credit (1975), a form of negative income tax, provided cash supplements for working parents with relatively low incomes.
4. The Comprehensive Employment and Training Act (1974) and the Special Supplemental Food Program (Women, Infants and Children [WIC]) (1972) provided food assistance and nutritional screening to low-income pregnant and postpartum women and their infants, as well as to low-income children up to five years of age.

Although not precisely aimed at poverty, during these few years there was a flurry of other legislation with implications for social welfare: The Drug Abuse Office and Treatment Act (1972); the National Health Services Corps (1972); the Child Abuse Prevention and Treatment Act (1974); The Child Nutrition Act (1974); the Rehabilitation Act (1973); the Housing and Community Development Act (1974); the Developmentally Disabled Assistance and Bill of Rights Act (1975); the Education of All Handicapped Children Act (1975); the Revenue Sharing Act (1972); the School-Age Mother and Child Health Act (1975); and the Legal Services Corporation Act (1974). Among other creations were the Environmental Protection Agency (1970), the Occupational Safety and Health Administration (1970), and the Juvenile Justice and Delinquency Prevention Act (1974).

President Carter's administration, although not averse to governmental intervention, was not particularly active in regard to social welfare matters. Following the Carter administration, there occurred a reversal when President Reagan set out "to get government off the backs of people" to clear the way for the private sector to solve society's problems. Tax cuts initiated during President Reagan's first term, when combined with a large federal deficit, served as a major obstacle to attention to poverty and to antipoverty spending. Instead of closing the gap between the rich and the poor, there in fact developed greater income inequality. Fiscal and tax policies were implemented that redistributed income upward rather than down the economic ladder; those who had less channeled money to those who had more. Those who favored supply-side economics argued that investment by the wealthy would "sprinkle" dollars downward and thus help those who were not well off. Others argued that what really was needed was a "bubble up" strategy in which many people had more expendable income and their purchases would restimulate the total economy.

Comprehensive antipoverty programs require funding, an accepting political climate, and political leadership at the presidential and Congressional levels. Through the 1990s, none of these politically necessary ingredients were present, nor were they visible on the near horizon.

FAMILIES, CHILDREN, AND POVERTY

Earlier we saw how societal values influence the types and delivery of social welfare. U.S. society produces programs influenced by underlying values. This underlying structure of values results in opposing eligibility categories—the deserving and undeserving, the worthy and unworthy, those employed and unemployed. It is instructive to trace the evolution of two programs as exemplars of this two-track value system— Aid to Families with Dependent Children (AFDC), which is now entitled Temporary Assistance to Needy Families (TANF), and Old Age and Survivors Insurance (Social Security). Because so many values swirl about them, they are the nexus for major concerns in social welfare and in U.S. society. Observing how they have changed over time can highlight how they exemplify and reflect major values and trends in social welfare provision.

Aid to Families with Dependent Children ("Welfare")

Given impetus by the 1909 White House Conference called by President Theodore Roosevelt on the Care of Dependent Children, mothers' pensions to enable widows and deserted women to care for their children were first introduced statewide in 1911 by Illinois. Only two years later, these "pensions" had spread to 19 states.

By 1920, 40 states had enacted mothers' pensions. These provisions, although inadequately financed, provided numerous children more support than they would have had under earlier poor laws or private charity. But, the laws were not mandatory, and many counties did not follow them. Nevertheless, mothers' pensions did prevent many children from being placed in orphanages, poor farms, or institutions for delinquent children. In 1931, more than 80 percent of the recipients were widows; smaller percentages were deserted mothers or divorced. In that same year, only 55 beneficiaries in the entire United States were unmarried mothers.[15]

Although these programs multiplied rapidly, unanimity in regard to government-provided mothers' pensions was absent. Opposition came from business and economically conservative forces, as well as most charitable groups, including national associations such as the National Conference of Charities and Corrections. Most private charities defended their own voluntary measures for assisting widows and children and were critical of relief for the poor outside of institutions.[16]

The Report of the Committee on Economic Security (January 1935), which led to the Social Security Act, described mothers' pensions in this way:

> These are not primarily aids to mothers but defense measures for children. They are designed to release from the wage-earning role the person whose natural function is to give her children the physical and affectionate guardianship necessary not alone to keep them from falling into social misfortune, but more affirmatively to rear them into citizens capable of contributing to society.[17]

As one can observe, the intentions at that time were to maintain the family together, to keep mothers at home to raise their children out of institutions, and to prevent their children's inadequate supervision and potential delinquency. In 1935 *Aid to Dependent Children* (ADC), a federal-state cash grant program, became a part of the Social Security legislation to enable states to aid needy children without fathers. With the 1939 amendments to the Social Security Act, surviving wives and dependent children became eligible under certain criteria in 1940 for social security payments. It was thought at that time that ADC would fade away when the family survivorship benefits started. Viewed as a transitional program, ADC was considered necessary and helpful for deserving women and children. Between 1940 and 1955, the average number of families on ADC decreased.

At the end of the 1950s, the Social Security insurance program had grown but ADC also had increased numbers of recipients and costs, becoming the chief public assistance program of the United States for society's most vulnerable families. Divorce rates rose, and many persons migrated from rural farming communities to urban centers often unprepared for the demands of city life. Despite sustained economic growth and greater employment freedom for women, the ADC program kept expanding and became a worrisome social policy issue. Instead of aging widows, dependent children, and orphans, ADC began to serve unmarried, divorced, and deserted women. The name of the ADC program was changed in 1962 to *Aid to Families with Dependent Children* (AFDC), recognizing societal changes.

In the interim, there were various attempts to deal with the "welfare mess." In 1961, ADC was changed so that families with an unemployed parent could become eligible for assistance. However, coverage for families in which the primary wage earner was unemployed was not required of states, and half the states chose not to offer this provision. The 1962 amendments to this program mainly focused on rehabilitation and services to help people become economically self-sufficient. But social services proved to be unequal to the societal forces expanding the AFDC rolls.

AFDC, which began as a program to keep mothers at home to raise their children, now shifted its focus to encourage employment and work. The Work Incentive Program (WIN, 1967) was developed to provide opportunities for able-bodied adults to acquire vocational skills and work experience. However, prior to 1967, there was no "earnings disregard." If an AFDC parent earned $100 from working, she lost an equal amount from AFDC. After 1967, if working, she could retain a portion of the total earned. As a result, she would receive more than if she were not working.

The amendments of 1971 required all able-bodied AFDC recipients without children under 6 years of age to register for WIN services and states to provide training and work experiences. The promotion of opportunity was the theme of these changes, but their impact never met expectations and criticism continued.

During the early stages of the Richard Nixon presidency, the *family assistance plan* (FAP, 1969) was considered. This reorganization of the welfare system attempted to encourage AFDC recipients to work. The proposal called for a minimum cash payment for a family. If an AFDC recipient worked, the recipient could retain half of earnings above the minimum guaranteed annual income. The program also intended to shift the emphasis from services and rehabilitation to money and to make it possible for two-parent families to obtain AFDC. Food Stamps, a cash equivalent for AFDC families, were included in the package.

This plan was a radical departure from the traditional approach and was criticized by both conservatives and liberals. Some objected to a program that implied welfare assistance was a right. Others were concerned about the potential costs. Still others were concerned about the relationship of FAP to other benefits and work disincentives. Objections also were expressed about women being forced to go to work for low wages. One outcome of the debate was the 1972 creation of the Supplemental Security Income (SSI) program, which federalized benefits for the universally recognized deserving poor, aging, disabled, and blind.

In 1977, President Carter proposed the *Program for Better Jobs and Income*. The deserving poor would receive a guaranteed annual income. Those who were expected to work would be granted a lower sum and the possibility of raising their incomes through public-sector or government-subsidized private-sector employment. The proposal failed to win congressional approval because it required the creation of a huge number of jobs.

The thrust throughout the Reagan administration was toward tightened eligibility requirements and reduced benefits. The poor were viewed as responsible for their poverty, able to extricate themselves if they tried sufficiently, and better off with less governmental assistance.

In 1988, Congress passed the *Family Support Act*, which essentially defined AFDC until radical change was introduced in 1996. AFDC, a voluntary program, operated in all 50 states, the District of Columbia, the Virgin Islands, Guam, and Puerto Rico. The program assisted children in families in which need was brought on by the incapacity, death, continued absence, or unemployment of a parent.

The program was financed by uncapped federal funds and state matching funds based on formulas. The federal share of grants for benefits ranged from 50 percent to 78 percent (55 percent on average) and was inversely related to the per capita income of the state. Federal funds paid for 50 percent of the administrative costs in all states. Both state and federal funds came from general revenues. The total cost of benefits depended on the number of persons eligible and receiving benefits. Such an entitlement is usually associated with the individual applicant, but in reality, it was the states that were entitled to reimbursement from the federal government for all those for whom they paid benefits.

To qualify for funds, states complied with federal guidelines. Among these were the following: Anyone who wished to apply must be given the opportunity to do so; assistance could only be provided to those in need; both income and resources were to be considered when determining eligibility and payment levels; the program must be statewide and administered by a single state agency; and assistance must be provided promptly and an opportunity given for hearings if applications are denied or payments reduced or discontinued.

As of 1996, AFDC served more than 4.5 million families with 12.6 million recipients, including 8.6 million children. Because each state determined a need standard that it deemed necessary to maintain a minimum standard of living, eligibility criteria and benefit levels differed from state to state. The average family size was 2.8 persons and the average monthly benefit was $374; however, these monthly payments per family ranged from $148 (Alabama) to $731 (Alaska). Federal and state expenditures totalled $20.4 billion. The cost of administering this means tested program in 1996 was 14 percent of benefits expended. There were estimates that AFDC served only approximately half those who would have been eligible for benefits, if they applied. Furthermore, from 1970 to 1996, the maximum payment for a family of four in the median State declined (adjusted for inflation) by more than 50 percent, partly offset by Food Stamps indexed for price inflation. As of January 1997, no state provided cash and Food Stamps equal to 100 percent of the poverty level.[18] Other benefits included employment training and placement, assistance with establishing paternity and securing payments from absent parents, day care, and family planning.

Eligibility for AFDC ended on a child's 18th birthday; or states had the option of ending it on the 19th birthday if the child were a full-time student in a secondary or technical school and reasonably expected to complete the program before reaching age 19. Illegal aliens, strikers, recipients of SSI, and children for whom foster care payments were made were ineligible.

States had an option to provide assistance to a pregnant woman during the last four months of her pregnancy if she had no other eligible children. States were allowed to deny AFDC for the child of an unmarried parent under age 18 (and that parent) unless they lived in an adult-supervised supportive arrangement. However, states could treat minor mothers as "adult caretakers" of their own children and permit them to head their own AFDC household.

A condition of eligibility was that a parent was required to assign child support and spousal support rights to the state and to cooperate in establishing paternity of a child, obtaining child support payments, and identifying a third party who might be liable to pay for medical services for the child. Another condition for eligibility was the federal requirement that most able-bodied parents participate in the JOBS (Job Opportunities and Basic Skills Training) program unless their youngest child was under 3 years of age, and States were allowed to mandate JOBS participation of parents of a child as young as age 1. States were required to guarantee care for an AFDC child under age 13 years if it were needed to permit the parent to work, train, or attend school. Typically, states exempted those who were aged or ill, those who were needed to care for an ill person, and those under 16 years of age.

States were required to offer AFDC to children in two-parent families who were needy because of the unemployment of one of their parents (AFDC-UP). Eligibility was limited to families whose principal wage earner was unemployed but who had worked at least 6 of the last 13 quarters or engaged in schooling for 4 of those quarters.

States also were required to provide Medicaid to AFDC enrolled families and to provide transitional Medicaid benefits up to 12 months for those who lost AFDC eligibility as a result of increased employment earnings. Similarly, states were required to provide subsidized child care for up to one year to families that lost eligibility as a result of employment.

Before enactment of TANF—the successor program to AFDC—States could receive 50 percent matching federal funds for emergency assistance (EA) to families with children if the aid were needed to avoid destitution of a child or to provide living arrangements in a home. This aid could only be provided for up to 30 days in any

12-month period. Essentially, EA was provided to families affected by natural disasters such as floods, fires, storms, and other such crises threatening family or living arrangements such as eviction, homelessness, utility shutoff, and so on.

An Old-New Path

President Clinton promised during the 1992 election campaign to "end welfare as we know it." Following the Republicans' gaining control of Congress in 1994, they too promised as part of their "Contract with America" to reform public welfare. Thus, both the President and Congress were committed to changing public welfare.

Following intense debates and two prior vetos, in August 1996, Congress passed and President Clinton signed the radical Personal Responsibility and Work Opportunity Reconciliation Act (PRA) abolishing the AFDC program, thus reversing a federal guarantee of support for these families enacted in 1935 as part of the original Social Security Act.

The PRA resulted in momentous shifts in social policy. The new legislation gave states vast power to run their own welfare and work programs. In signing this legislation, President Clinton fulfilled his promise, and the Republicans also laid claim to having fulfilled their promise.

During the long debate, opposing ideologies played an important role, minimized somewhat by general agreement that public welfare needed to be reformed. Many forces coalesced to support changes. Among these factors were the following:

1. Many had distinct views of the proper distribution of governmental power, particularly Article X of the U.S. Constitution (the powers not delegated to the United States by the Constitution, nor prohibited by it to the states, are reserved to the states respectively, or to the people). Political devolution to the states was an important factor, a process whose efforts began with President Nixon's revenue-sharing program and accelerated during the Reagan administration. The claim was made that states, being closer to the people, could administer public welfare programs more efficiently, more flexibly, and with greater knowledge of what is needed. Forgotten was the fact that the program became federalized because states were not doing the job.

2. The legislation assumes the poor can best be motivated to compete successfully in a job market by being forced into it. This view dominated despite the existence of a job market that does not have a sufficient number of jobs reasonably available at a living wage for unskilled and semi-skilled persons.

3. Despite many positive achievements, genuine concern was expressed by all sides in the debate about the dysfunctions of the public assistance system, including intergenerational receipt of benefits, administrative complexity, and undermining self-reliance.

4. Both parties used reform efforts as a political strategy to gain votes during the upcoming presidential and congressional elections. The President's original intention was to create new and expanded training programs, expanded child care, universal health care, and—if necessary—government-supplied jobs as employer of last resort for those who would exhaust his proposed two-year time limit. However,

his early welfare plan would have added $10 billion more to the budget for spending on the poor, a proposal that was not acceptable politically.

5. The original public welfare system served widows and deserted mothers with children, not those who were divorced or never married, in the midst of the Great Depression. Those who favored radical change compared the nature of the poverty population today with those originally served and thought change was needed.

6. Policymakers expected that projected savings (approximately $55 billion over six years) would reduce substantially the federal deficit and/or make possible federal tax cuts or maintenance of middle-class entitlements.

Few people defended the system that many believed undermined values such as work, family, personal initiative, and independence. Although the new legislation was a revolutionary departure from the past, supporters of the legislation suggested that a new system could hardly do worse than the system then in place, viewed it as a magnificent new experiment, claimed it would free millions of people from dependence, restore them to self-reliance, and save billions of dollars. Opponents foresaw a grim future for approximately one million children who would be pushed further into poverty. Critics suggested the legislation was a retreat from a 61-year commitment that Republicans and Democrats, U.S. presidents, and Congresses of both major parties made on behalf of poor children. Still others thought this change was a precursor and the first step to dismantling the social contract that was in place since the mid-1930s, including Social Security and other social insurances.

A third group rejected radical change. This group pointed out that as a result of waivers approved by the Clinton administration, 45 states were engaged in public welfare experimentation at the time the new legislation was passed. Their suggestion was that the most prudent course was to examine the results of these experiments and choose among the most positive plans on the basis of real experience rather than a leap of faith. Proponents countered this view by suggesting the possibility of change deserves a leap of faith. Thus, AFDC had changed in many parts of the country and a quiet revolution was proceeding.[19]

Will the new legislation result in increases in the number of homeless persons and drive even more children into expensive and stressed foster-care systems? What will be the result of states competing to attract tax-paying families and corporations? Raising taxes to pay for child care, job placement, and other services would risk repelling these taxpayers and corporations.

Under block grants, AFDC payments would not increase rapidly—if at all—as the economy entered a recession. Instead, many persons believe that in such circumstances states would stay with preset spending limits either by raising eligibility standards or reducing benefits. To do so eliminates the antirecessional, counter-cyclical tool of placing dollars into the hands of poor consumers. The economic effects of these eventualities remain to be discovered.

Undoubtedly, there was a need for reform of the public welfare system. One cannot predict with assurance what will happen to people and how they will cope. No such risks have been taken in more than 60 years. Will misery be the great motivator? If it is the great stimulus, one could assume the poor would have reformed themselves. The crucial issue may be reflected in this question: Is public welfare needed because people lack self-reliance and because of personal characteristics or is it largely the result of structural forces at the societal level?

Temporary Assistance to Needy Families

Since Temporary Assistance to Needy Families (TANF) is the replacement program for AFDC, we will describe the program briefly here and continue our discussion and examination in chapter 9, where we also will present some preliminary answers to some of the questions raised earlier about this new/old program.

Temporary Assistance for Needy Families, created by the Personal Responsibility and Work Opportunity Reconciliation Act (1996), provides cash assistance and work opportunities to needy families. The development and administration of public assistance programs, including welfare and work programs, became the primary responsibility of states, partially funded by capped federal block grants that total $16.4 billion until the year 2002, with small sums appropriated for states with high population growth rates but no allowance for inflation. The law contains strong work requirements, a performance bonus to reward states for moving welfare recipients into jobs, state maintenance of effort requirements, comprehensive child support enforcement, and supports for families moving from welfare to work, including increased funding for child care and guaranteed medical coverage.

Almost all recipients must work after two years of assistance. Every state is required to have half the families off the rolls by 2002. Parents must work a prescribed number of hours per week: single parents, 20 hours the first year and 30 by 2000; couples, 35 hours. Work can be subsidized or unsubsidized employment, on-the-job training, work experience, community service, 12 months of vocational training, or child care provided to individuals participating in community service. Exceptions are allowed for six weeks of job search time, parents with a child under age 6 years who cannot find child care, and single parents with children under age one. States would have to deny cash assistance and food stamps to people convicted of drug felonies, unless they explicitly adopted different policies. Pregnant women and adults in drug treatment would not be denied assistance. States that did not meet their goals for employment of recipients would lose part of their public welfare block grants. The penalty would rise from 5 percent in the first year to 21 percent in the ninth year.

States must make an initial assessment of recipients' skills and develop personal responsibility plans that identify needed education, training, and job placement services. Various incentives are provided to encourage maintaining program spending levels.

Families cannot spend more than five years in total on TANF. States are free to specify fewer years, and can exempt up to 20 percent of the caseload from the time limit. After the time limit is exceeded, they can elect to provide noncash assistance and vouchers to families using Social Services Block Grant (see chapter 10) or state funds.

Child care funding is provided to help more mothers move into jobs. Women on welfare continue to receive health care coverage for their families, including a year or more of transitional Medicaid when they leave welfare for work.

To be eligible for TANF block grants, states must operate a child support enforcement program meeting federal requirements. The Federal Case Registry and National Directory of New Hires is used to track delinquent parents across state lines. Child support can be withheld directly from wages, and paternity establishment is streamlined; cash assistance is reduced by at least 25 percent in cases of failure to cooperate with paternity establishment. The legislation also established uniform interstate child support laws, central registries of child support orders and collections, and toughened enforcement of child support.

Unmarried minor parents are required to live with a responsible adult or in an adult-supervised setting and participate in educational and training activities in order to receive assistance. Efforts are to be undertaken to prevent nonmarital teen pregnancies.

The new legislation also imposed new verification procedures on all applicants for virtually all federal, state, and local programs in order to deny benefits to those not qualified or to illegal aliens. Exceptions were to be made for emergency medical services, short-term disasters, limited public health services for immunizations and treatment of communicable diseases; nonprofit, in-kind community services such as shelters and soup kitchens; certain housing programs; and school lunch and breakfast programs if the child is eligible for free public education.

Social Security

The historical path of Social Security has been quite different from that of AFDC. Instituted during the Great Depression as an old-age retirement program, Social Security was an omnibus legislative act that included a social insurance ("Social Security old age benefits") designed to provide monthly benefits to retired workers aged 65 years and over and a lump-sum death benefit to the worker's estate. The Act also contained provisions for old age assistance, unemployment compensation, aid to dependent children, and maternal and child welfare. Gradually the old age and survivor's program was broadened to include benefits for dependents and survivors (1939), followed by coverage for the permanently disabled and their dependents (1956) and health insurance for the aging (1965). However, when people refer to Social Security, by and large, they are referring to Old Age and Survivors' Insurance.

Social Security amendments provided that monthly cash benefits would be increased through automatic cost-of-living adjustments, which keep pace with inflation. One can observe that the Social Security program continued to expand the number of beneficiaries and the benefits. However, even this program, which is designed for "worthy" workers, was not received with open arms during the Great Depression. Resistance, for example, came from the U.S. Chamber of Commerce and the National Association of Manufacturers, among others. Some argued the program was a threat to the American way of life and would deprive citizens of their personal liberty. The compulsory nature of the payroll tax was objectionable to many who suggested the program should be voluntary.

Others argued the act did not go far enough. Initially, Social Security deliberately omitted inclusion of health insurance to avoid attacks by the medical lobby. A full-employment policy was dropped because it was too expensive and tainted by the temporary public works programs of the depression. Another inhibiting force was the fear that unless states and local governments significantly controlled eligibility, the expansion of federal activities would be found unconstitutional by the then-conservative Supreme Court.

Contrasting Values and Aims

In contrasting Social Security and Aid to Families with Dependent Children (replaced by TANF), we find they embody different American values. Despite some initial resistance, as described previously, Social Security has always received broad-based political support. Note the relative frequency of proposed and actual changes to the AFDC program compared with the relative infrequency of major changes to the Social Security program since its inception. This widespread consensus is derived from several features: Social Security is a national insurance program, one pays into the program prior to receipt of benefits when eligible, the benefits are standardized, and they are related to one's personal *employment*. One has earned the benefits. People of every social and economic class in all parts of the nation are served by the program. Today there are millions of recipients, many of whom have highly developed political skills.

Aid to Families with Dependent Children, on the other hand, has been a focus of controversy. The purpose of AFDC shifted over time. The original purpose was to encourage the care of needy children in their own homes, followed by strengthening family life and promoting family self-support (1956). There is no national consensus or standard rules and benefits supporting it. The program differs from state to state. There is no cost-of-living adjustment to offset inflation. The recipients are not viewed in terms of their work histories but are seen as dependent and unproductive beneficiaries of the general revenue taxes paid by those who are currently employed. They are perceived as unworthy, and the prevailing attitude is that benefits provided should be as short and as sparse as possible. Myths abound as to the race, age, duration of benefit receipt, and other characteristics of the beneficiary group.

THE POOR LAWS TODAY

Despite the passage of time and the many changes that have taken place in our society, the Poor Law mentality discussed in chapter 3 remains with us and recently has been reemphasized in TANF "welfare." The welfare system, broadly defined, is the nexus for conflicting values: humane and punitive.

The major trend toward secularism continues. Related to this is a blurring of the private and public sectors. In many respects, the private sector, including sectarian-sponsored social agencies, has become simply another vehicle for the delivery of services based upon the aims of government. This issue of private and public sectors will be examined in greater detail in chapter 11.

Risks and categories also remain with us. Poor persons are classified as either worthy or unworthy, disabled or able-bodied. During the 1980s, both physically and

mentally disabled persons were excluded from SSI benefits. In fact, the Reagan administration enforced severe eligibility requirements, forcing many disabled persons
off the rolls during the early and mid-1980s. These actions—later overruled by court
decisions—suggested that poor persons, including even the disabled, were viewed
as unworthy.

Public welfare categories have traditionally favored the aging, the blind, the disabled, and female-headed families. It was only the aged, blind, and disabled who
were included in the national SSI program. General assistance designed for single
adults and married persons without children continues to receive far fewer resources, to the point of not existing in some states. So categories remain, and it appears unlikely that in the foreseeable future the United States will design a welfare
system that abolishes categories and deals with people strictly on the basis of need.
Instead, the direction of social policy has veered more toward "blaming the victim."
It has become possible that entire programs will be abolished. Those people formerly served may have few places to turn, in which case, categories themselves become irrelevant.

There are few claims that indoor relief is cheaper or more productive than outdoor relief, although the desirability of indoor relief has been proposed again by conservatives. In general, we have learned that institutionalization is more expensive
than outdoor relief (except where costly technology and other intensive service are
required), for both the short and long term. A respect for independent functioning
also serves to support outdoor relief. However, deinstitutionalization, especially of
the mentally ill, has not worked out successfully in all areas. The funds required by
the system to implement the outdoor community services needed have not been
forthcoming. At the same time that there are significant problems with deinstitutionalization, there has also developed a clearer recognition that institutional care is absolutely necessary for some persons, and the dream that most—if not all—institutionalized persons could be served successfully in their communities cannot be fulfilled.

Residency laws are being eroded as the United States moves in certain respects
toward a national society. Greater mobility has been brought about by new modes of
transportation and the need for workers in various parts of the nation. The connections between what occurs in Mississippi, for example, and what happens in major
metropolitan areas of the northern or western states have increasingly become
clearer as the various regions become much more aware of their interconnections.
The erosion of residency laws also has been supported by court cases but recently
has been challenged.

Nevertheless, the local responsibility/local control argument is strong. In the
revolutionary TANF program (1996), to be discussed in chapter 9, the state rather
than the federal level is viewed as the most desirable arbiter of social welfare policy
and program priorities. Localities, it is argued, know better what their needs are.

The issue of less eligibility remains, even today, one of the most difficult and
intractable problems in social welfare. Benefits for social welfare payments are
typically computed on the basis of a percentage of the minimum level subsistence. Thus, those who receive "welfare" assistance are helped only at a subsistence level.

The treatment of poverty on a case-by-case basis has been changed primarily in the sense that our understanding has been broadened to appreciate structural components that contribute to poverty in individual cases. We understand better the relationship between public issues and private troubles. Even so, psychological counseling and moralizing are the treatments of choice for many of those with private troubles, as though the "fault lies in ourselves." Further, policy attention focuses on individual and family responsibility and avoids confronting how the structure affects lives.

Stigma remains a part of welfare today, and there is much victim-blaming. As the Poor Laws utilized stigma to control people's lives, creating a climate in which people would be punished for not working, it is reasonable to assume that today's remaining harsh attitudes also serve such purposes.

HUMAN NATURE AND THE AMERICAN DREAM

In every society people express their values about human nature and the image of the good society. We have seen that throughout history each society acts on its ideas through its social welfare system. In a sense, all modern societies are at the lead of long marches across time. Slowly, continuous historical processes have brought each society forward.

In the United States, according to the Constitution, we are to seek the "general welfare," but how should we seek it (with what means) and what is it? As in the beginning of our discussion in chapter 1, we arrive at values. If people are viewed as basically good, we open our hands to help them. If they are seen as evil, we will close our hands and turn from giving them a helping hand.

Besides our values, however, we have seen that other constraints enter the picture. Social welfare is intricately related to the view of humanity held by citizens, especially decision makers, but it also reflects our view of ourselves and the society we wish to create. Even on pragmatic grounds, it appears there is much to be said for an openhanded social welfare policy, because what is sown now will be reaped in a few years.

But American values are mixed. Along with the Protestant ethic and social Darwinism, there is an impetus toward egalitarianism, democracy, and a belief in mutual aid. The American dream also calls for equal opportunity. Although it does not make claims for all persons being equal, it does demand that American society strive to give all persons equal opportunity; which is to say that all persons, including those who need help from the society, have a right to equal opportunity to health, education, and the basic necessities of life. They, too, are building America.

The ideal of equal opportunity is as yet unfulfilled and today is being undermined. The degree to which the dream remains unfulfilled is dependent not only on the will of our society to fulfill it, but also on the inherent difficulties in achieving the dream. The fulfillment of the dream of equal opportunity for one individual may diminish that opportunity for other individuals; the enhancement of one group's, neighborhood's, or region's opportunity may have adverse effects on others. The complete resolution of such dilemmas about the American dream remains before us.

Finally, the American dream includes pluralism—many groups, many lifestyles, and many ethics—and this pluralism and differentiation must be respected by the law. Social welfare, as an important institution in our society, has to deal evenhandedly with all who need help, regardless of their values or their differences. The American dream is enacted in "minute particulars," in the way each person is dealt with under the law and by the professional social worker who makes decisions about a person's future.

SUMMARY

Turning now from values and the historical precursors and development of American social welfare, in chapter 6 we will introduce the major philosophical and sociopolitical assumptions and perspectives that influence the choices our society makes regarding the nature of the social welfare programs it chooses and does not choose to implement, along with a brief description of our federal and pluralist decision-making system. In addition, we will introduce economic concepts that can help one's understanding regarding the forces affecting social welfare.

QUESTIONS FOR CONSIDERATION

1. Do you believe Lester Ward's ideas make sense today? In what ways?
2. What are the positives and negatives of laissez faire philosophies for modern American life?
3. Is there any way around the idea of less eligibility?
4. If someone asked you to state *your* vision of the American dream, what would you say?

NOTES

1. Amy Gutmann, ed., *Democracy and the Welfare State*, Princeton, N.J.: Princeton University Press, 1988, p. 3.
2. Richard Hofstadter, *The Age of Reform*, New York: Vintage, 1955, p. 165.
3. Merle Curti, *The Growth of American Thought*, New York: Harper & Row, 1964, p. 165.
4. Henry Steele Commager, *Lester Ward and the Welfare State*, New York: Bobbs-Merrill, 1967, pp. xxxi, 223.
5. Ronald C. White and C. Howard Hopkins, *The Social Gospel: Religion and Reform in Changing America*, Philadelphia: Temple University Press, 1976, p. xi.
6. J. Stanley Lemons, "The Sheppard-Towner Act: Progressivism in the 1920s," *Journal of American History*, Vol. 55, December/March 1968, pp. 776–786; Kristine Siefert, "An Exemplar of Primary Prevention in Social Work: The Sheppard-Towner Act of 1921," *Social Work in Health Care*, Vol. 9, No. 1, Fall 1983, pp. 87–103.
7. Richard C. Cloward and Lloyd E. Ohlin, *Delinquency and Opportunity: A Theory of Delinquent Gangs*, Glencoe, Ill.: Free Press, 1960.
8. Terry Sanford, *Storm over the States*, New York: McGraw-Hill Book Company, 1967, pp. 174–175.
9. Daniel Patrick Moynihan, "The Professionalization of Reform," *The Public Interest*, Fall 1965, pp. 6–16.

10. Frances F. Piven and Richard A. Cloward, *Regulating the Poor*, New York: Vintage, 1993, pp. 256–263.

11. Ann K. Bixby, "Public Social Welfare Expenditures, Fiscal Years 1965–1987," *Social Security Bulletin*, Vol. 53, No. 2, February 1990, pp. 12–13.

12. Robert D. Plotnick and Felicity Skidmore, *Progress Against Poverty: A Review of the 1964–1974 Decade*, New York: Academic Press, 1975, pp. 8–9.

13. Aaron Wildavsky, "What Does It Do for the Poor?—A New Test for National Policy," *The Public Interest*, Vol. 34, Winter 1974, pp. 66–82.

14. Aaron Wildavsky, quoted in Daniel P. Moynihan, *Maximum Feasible Misunderstanding*, New York: Free Press, 1969, inside cover page.

15. Theda Skocpol, *Protecting Soldiers and Mothers: The Political Origins of Social Policy in the United States*, Cambridge, Mass.: Harvard University Press, 1992, pp. 424–426, 467.

16. Ibid., pp. 424–426.

17. *The Report of the Committee on Economic Security of 1935, 50th Anniversary Edition*, Washington, D.C.: National Conference on Social Welfare, 1985, p. 36.

18. *1998 Green Book, Background Material and Data on Programs within the Jurisdiction of the Committee on Ways and Means*, Washington, D.C.: U.S. Government Printing Office, May, 1998, pp. 410–411, 413, 416–417, and 435.

19. Center for Law and Social Policy, *The CLASP Guide to Welfare Waivers: 1992–1995*, Washington, D.C., 1995.

CHAPTER SIX

Concepts for Social Welfare

The definition of politics is this: In politics, there are no right answers, only a continuing flow of compromises between groups, resulting in a changing, cloudy and ambiguous series of public decisions, where appetite and ambition compete openly with knowledge and wisdom.
—Senator Alan K. Simpson[1]

There is a liberal myth that poverty is bad for kids.
—Robert Rector at privatization conference[2]

Politics is mostly about which part of the electorate gets the money. Saying so is usually said to be cynical, but this is one of those periodic times in American history when the question of who gets the money is too blatantly in the open to be ignored.
—Russell Baker[3]

OVERVIEW

In the previous chapters, we discussed the history of social welfare and the impact of social values on social welfare. In this chapter we will examine closely the concept "social welfare" and define important terms, including social policy, social services, and social work. We will discuss information about ideology, political decision making, and economics useful for understanding the context that influences social welfare policy.

WHAT IS SOCIAL WELFARE?

One can attempt to define social welfare in narrow or broad terms. In its narrowest sense, social welfare includes those nonprofit functions of society, public or voluntary, that are clearly aimed at alleviating distress and poverty. Just about everyone would include the Temporary Assistance to Needy Families program as part of the U.S. social welfare system. Similarly the Food Stamp program, hospital social service programs, social service departments in homes for the aged, and the like would be seen as part of the social welfare system. Perhaps a broader definition such as the following can be more helpful:

> . . . a nation's system of programs, benefits, and services that help people meet those social, economic, educational, and health needs that are fundamental to the maintenance of society.[4]

Such a broadened perspective that is not limited to the nonprofit sectors includes activities by voluntary (nonprofit), for-profit, and governmental programs, utilizing a wide variety of professional personnel such as social workers, physicians, nurses, lawyers, educators, ministers, and others, including family members.

This wider perspective reflects more nearly the contemporary reality in that no modern industrial state "permits natural or social contingencies fully to determine the life chances of its members. All have programs whose explicit purpose is to protect adults and children from the degradation and insecurity of ignorance, illness, disability, unemployment, and poverty."[5]

Some activities—collective goods—of society are primarily directed at the requisites of the society itself, such as national defense or flood control, and only indirectly and ultimately toward the fate of the individual. Other activities of society are those that provide direct services to meet immediate needs of individuals and families, such as subsidized housing, counseling, and medical and hospital services. It is in this last group that what we call social welfare tends to fall.

Neither the narrow nor the broad definition is perfect. Narrow definitions tend to exclude the most important and effective social welfare programs of society. They define social welfare in what will be defined later on as *residual* terms. Social welfare is seen as the activities directed toward helping people for whom the market failed. What links these definitions is the breadth of the activities included. Certainly, social welfare has a priority concern about those who are disadvantaged—the poor, ill, distressed, and vulnerable. But social welfare also has a broader aim. As President Franklin Roosevelt stated, "If, as our Constitution tells us, our Federal Government was established, among other things, 'to promote the general welfare,' then it is our plain duty to provide for that security upon which welfare depends."[6]

Programs of prevention or insurance—such as the Social Security system, which covers almost everyone today, social programs for the retired to meet a broad need for leisure and recreation, and Workers' Compensation for rich and poor alike—all evolved from the broad definition. Temporary Assistance for Needy Families, Food Stamps, and Medicaid, which focus on the needy, derive from the narrow definition.

Even the broad definitions of welfare are not fully inclusive, and at the same time, they suffer from being somewhat too inclusive. On the one hand, by distinguishing between the profit sector and the welfare sector, they appear to exclude the growing delivery of social services for profit in the context of the private sector. Private hospitals, nursing homes, day-care centers, and private practice by social

workers and other helping professionals all deliver services that are definable as social services and are part of the social welfare system, and yet they are not divorced
from the private sector. As we will see further on, the division between private and
public has become increasingly blurred in the United States.

Stated simply, even the broadest definitions may not cover everything that will
come to be recognized as social welfare. Furthermore, the broad definitions tend to focus on formal as opposed to informal social welfare institutions. But policymakers are
becoming increasingly aware that social welfare as an institution in the United States
needs to be cognizant of and more connected with the informal, natural helping systems that people use. For example, the neighbors in the garden apartment complex
who provide cooperative child care or who refer a person for counseling, the parish
priest, the police who intervene in family disputes, the bartender who encourages a
customer to go for help—all are, in a sense, part of the helping system and need to be
taken into account as part of a full appreciation of the scope of social welfare.

On the other hand, the broad definitions of social welfare are too all-encompassing when they claim to cover all collective interventions to meet needs. Such
broad definitions intrude on territory that has come to be defined institutionally as
belonging elsewhere. The non-market portion of society also covers police and fire
services, education, medical care, and the like, and we do not subsume all of these
under our definition of social welfare.

What then are we to do? Should we throw up our hands and admit defeat in an
attempt to define social welfare? To an extent, we must. The sophisticated student
must realize that social welfare is an ambiguous, changing, and blurred concept. Still,
we generally know what we are talking about when we discuss social welfare, and it
is possible to suggest a definition that will serve for working purposes. Our guiding
definitional principles will be the following:

1. Social interventions that are intended to enhance or maintain social functioning of human beings may be defined as social welfare in the largest and broadest
sense. Titmuss even goes so far as to try to break down all these interventions into
three basic categories of welfare: fiscal, occupational, and social.[7]

2. As social welfare programs enter the mainstream of society and become
more universally used and widely accepted, they tend to lose their identity as social
welfare services. This blurring will confuse the picture, but we need to understand
it. The best social welfare programs are those so accepted that they cease to be commonly defined as social welfare. The kindergarten movement started as a social welfare program in settlement houses. As it became accepted as an important part of the
U.S. educational system, it moved into the public school system, and now is seen as
part of the domain of education. There is no need for us to claim kindergarten or to
study it in a text on social welfare, although students should be aware that, in the
largest sense, kindergarten and the entire public school system is a welfare program.
Social Security, universally used and accepted, has become less identified as social
welfare than it once was. Recipients of Social Security do not think of themselves as
"welfare" cases in the same way that recipients of means-tested programs do.
Nonetheless, it is essential to study Social Security as part of the social welfare system of the United States. It is not part of any other domain.

3. Our definition will tend toward the broad rather than the narrow approach to what social welfare is. We will include interventions for the enhancement of social functioning, even where they are in the profit-making sector or where they are part of an informal, less clearly institutional structure. For the sake of practicality, however, we limit our consideration to those parts of the broad social welfare system that are not clearly the domain or territory of other fields or disciplines, such as education, medicine, and police and fire services. This, too, will pose problems, because the domains are not always clear. Health insurance and care can be said to be part of the domain of social welfare, whereas medical practice clearly is not. Similarly, there are social welfare programs and concerns related to corrections and public justice even though police science is not social welfare.

Our definitional guidelines are complex, but a student needs to understand this as the necessary concomitant of a society that is mixed in its functions between market and nonmarket activities and that is specialized and multidisciplinary in its provision of services. There is no easy answer or way out. But we think that the boundaries we have suggested will give us relative clarity in seeing what is part of our social welfare system and what is not. Briefly, everything for the enhancement of social functioning is encompassed, except those activities and functions clearly part of another domain or territory.

SOCIAL POLICY, SOCIAL SERVICES, AND SOCIAL WORK

Before proceeding, there are a few other terms that frequently come up in social welfare and need to be defined.

Social Policy

Social policy refers both to the social decision-making process by which a course of action is selected, defined, and promoted (policy making) and to the product or outcome of that process (the resulting policy). Although social policy may be made in both the public and private sectors, the preponderance of social policy is determined by what governments choose to do or not to do. They regulate certain behaviors, organize bureaucracies and programs, distribute benefits, and collect taxes. Our concern is with social policy and its relationship to social welfare.

Social Services

It is probably simplest to think of *social services* as those activities conducted by social welfare institutions. Occasionally, such services will be delivered by institutions that are not recognizable as social welfare institutions, and therefore, it is helpful to think in terms of services delivered rather than simply of social welfare institutions. To the extent that an institution delivers a social service, one could argue that it is, by definition, a social welfare institution. But the distinction is helpful, because often a largely nonwelfare institution will deliver a social service; for example, social services are provided by the Department of Defense, Corrections, and Industry but neither defense, corrections, nor industry as institutions can be considered social welfare institutions themselves.

Social services include both *personal services* (services to individuals based on relationships) and more *institutional services* (income programs, housing projects, and the like). Social services do not merely replace or seek to correct the family or earlier social forms; they are also new responses to new social situations. Alfred Kahn defines social services in terms of the functions they serve:

1. To strengthen and repair family and individual functioning with reference to ongoing roles.
2. To provide new institutional outlets for socialization, development, and assistance, roles that once were but are no longer discharged by the nuclear or extended family, neighbors, or the kin network.
3. To develop institutional forms for new activities essential to individuals, families, and groups in the complex urban society even though they are unknown in a simple society.[8]

Social Work

It is important that *social work* not be confused with social welfare or social services. Social work is a *professionalized occupation*. It operates largely in the delivery of social services and in social welfare institutions. Social welfare is the primary arena in which it operates. Social services are what it provides. Social work is the major professional provider in the social welfare arena. If an analogy might help, think of medical doctors as the professional group in the arena of health services. However, not everyone who provides social services is a social worker, just as not everyone providing medical services is a medical doctor.

The distinction can become very important. Headlines around the country, on occasion, proclaim that a "social worker" had failed to save a child from brutal abuse by a parent. Most times this person was not a professional social worker, but there is a tendency to use the term for anyone working in the social services.

IDEOLOGY, SOCIAL POLICY, AND GOVERNMENT INTERVENTION

Decisions regarding government action or inaction and regarding program design are predicated on particular views of the society and its functions. These basic beliefs reflect values strongly held by diverse groups, which have different assumptions about the nature of society, the role of government, and the path to attain the general welfare.

During the early 1960s, Daniel Bell and others introduced the idea that ideology had become tangential, a thing of the past, or only of value in developing nations.[9] According to the "end of ideology" thinkers, developed nations such as the

United States, those of western Europe, and even the former Soviet Union were confronted not by conflicts of values or ideology but instead by issues of strategy, bureaucracy, and expertise. From this perspective, all developed nations, regardless of economic system, faced one central issue: how to make the system work. The trend that Bell described in the 1960s seems to be confirmed by recent events in the former Soviet bloc. In addition to moves to democratize their societies, the former Soviet Union splintered into separate nations, and other eastern European states are moving from centrally planned economies and toward more or less free enterprise-driven economies. The outcomes of these efforts remain to be seen because there are also countervailing forces in eastern Europe and elsewhere.

However, Francis Fukuyama of the U.S. State Department's policy planning staff—stressing the power of ideas—concluded that the era of "post-history" had arrived. Liberal democracy had triumphed. Fukuyama suggested what we may be witnessing is not just the end of the Cold War, or the passing of a particular period of postwar history, but the end of history as such—that is, the endpoint of mankind's ideological evolution and the universalization of Western liberal democracy as the final form of human government.

According to this view, there is no viable alternative ideology; liberal democracy—politics and culture—will have the field to itself. Others thought the future would remain, as always, contingent, changing, unforeseeable, and replete with unanticipated events. As this is being written, Russia is in the midst of political flux, and the Communist Party has rebounded as a crucial decision maker. Others too suggest the globlization of national economies and cultures, as predicted by Marx, will have divisive and painful consequences, that global capitalism is a "false dawn."[10]

Samuel Mencher, in a prescient 1967 work, "Ideology and the Welfare Society," challenged the idea that social policy is chiefly determined by technical problems. In his view, ideological conflict is endemic to issues of expertise, governmental involvement in welfare, the balance of social and individual interests, and the goals of state policy. Ideology drives policy decisions critical to social welfare and social work. Ideology and values help to determine policies related to such questions as this: To what extent should the distribution of income resulting from the private economic market be permitted to be the final determinant of the distribution of income among the members of the society? And to what extent should the use of national income be dominated by private or public choices?[11]

The answers to these questions are based not only on ideological assumptions but also appear to be determined by the context in which they are asked. The Wall Street panic of October 1929 led to the Great Depression, and by early 1933 one in every four persons in the labor force was unemployed. Very few, if any families, were unaffected by a world that seemed to be crumbling. Within that context, President Franklin D. Roosevelt shifted ideological gears and instituted a New Deal, calling upon new governmental methods of intervention to meet unprecedented conditions. Pragmatically moving on many fronts, the New Deal attempted to shore up the economy, bring order and hope into a society experiencing conflict and pain, and restore as quickly as possible humane living conditions for as many people as possible.

The failure of the unlimited free market required counterbalances, so the New Deal created and utilized Social Security, unemployment insurance, home mortgage guarantees, rural electrification, farm price supports, bank deposit insurance, and other social programs to improve the general welfare.

When President Ronald Reagan stated in his first inaugural address that "government is not the solution to our problem; government is the problem," he sought to enhance a laissez faire attitude, reflective of a conservative philosophy. In general, the Reagan ideology promoted reduced taxes; deregulation of industry; return of powers to the state and local levels; less government, particularly at the federal level; "getting government off the backs of the people"; and encouragement of the business community while reducing the social welfare efforts of U.S. government—all intended to spur individual initiative. Minimal government with a spartan welfare state was the ideal Reagan sought.

Many persons saw these directions as an effort to return to social Darwinism. During the Reagan era, the focus on individualism and materialism were enhanced, while the thrust for public purposes, governmental responsibility, and mutual aid were blunted.

Social policy literature during this period supported this philosophy. Jude Wanniski, in *The Way the World Works: How Economics Fail—and Succeed*, wrote of the world that will ultimately reject all systems that do not revolve around the individual.[12] George Gilder championed an unbridled supply-side economics and capitalism of "high adventure and redemptive morality."[13] Charles Murray went a step further to claim in *Losing Ground* that social programs, including income transfers, were "disastrous for poor people of all races, but for poor blacks especially, and most emphatically for poor blacks in all-black communities." According to this view, "it is indeed possible that steps to relieve misery can create misery."[14] The theme of the destructiveness of social welfare continues, and Marvin Olasky's highly influential *The Tragedy of American Compassion* indicted all governmental social welfare, affecting the Personal Responsibility and Work Opportunity Reconciliation Act (1996). According to him, the War on Poverty was a disaster; an emphasis on entitlements displaced a focus on need; and the United States should return social services to compassionate private and religious institutions.[15] For some, these books were clarion calls for individualism and laissez faire.

Others saw a return to social Darwinism as the Reagan administration challenged social welfare programs, shifted expenditures from domestic and social concerns—especially those to help poor people—to defense, and called into question social welfare supports that had been won and accepted over many years. To some, the retrenchment of aid to the poor and vulnerable was understood as a social Darwinistic "blaming the victim" in the sense that spending for the poor was somehow responsible for the nation's problems and that—according to this view—the poor, regardless of general economic conditions, should be able to fend for themselves.

These examples reflect the expression of two major U.S. political ideologies, which can be roughly categorized as liberalism and conservatism. Liberals place an emphasis on equality before the law, equal treatment by the state, the protection of individual rights and freedoms, and government as a necessary protector of individuals from abuse by the market and other societal forces. The belief in the use of government as a corrective to foster justice and equality of opportunity is combined with a desire to preserve the rights of individuals and the right to own private property, including the means of production. Liberals support government intervention in the economy to offset the failures of capitalism and the market economy. On a more philosophical level, liberals generally believe in the possibility of improvement of the human condition and the possibility of progress. Things can be made to work; the future will bring improvements; barriers can be overcome. Liberals believe that the nature of modern society—technology, industrialization, internationalization—requires to one degree or another governmental programs to remedy the loss of liberties by those who are less well-to-do. The combination of affirmative governmental action with a politics of compassion is stressed in order to foster the development and well-being of each individual.[16] Further, liberals can be expected to disfavor legal enforcement of private morality; to favor greater sexual, political, and economic equality while attempting to reduce stark economic inequality through economic and welfare programs; and to favor neutralism—the government should take no side on moral issues and treat all citizens as equals. Finally, liberals do not insist on equality of result, only equality of access and opportunity.[17]

Conservatism emphasizes a defense of the status quo and resistance to major proposals for change in the economy and in the political sphere. Change should be moderated and the role of government limited, especially in regard to regulation of the economy, thus placing greater emphasis on economic free enterprise. Conservatives encourage individual achievement and favor the expansion of the private sector wherever possible, demonizing governmental action, idealizing the voluntary sector, and promoting entrepreneurialism, all as countervailing forces against government control. Major tenets of conservatism focus on private property rights and a belief in free enterprise. Conservatives believe that the private sector is capable of handling many societal problems and resist turning to the federal government for solutions to societal problems such as the amelioration of poverty, much preferring to turn to state and municipal action before federal action. Stability is a priority for conservatives in regard to the dollar, economics, politics, and international affairs. This emphasis on stability is also found among conservatives who believe that the traditional values of hard work, ambition, and self-reliance will lead to individual and family well-being. From a societal point of view, conservatives believe that individual effort, tax reductions, and a free economy will best achieve economic and social welfare. Their goal is equity. That is, if everyone is provided with an equal opportunity to compete, conservatives want to minimize policies that are designed to shape the final result.[18]

These descriptions of the traditional beliefs of conservatives provide an incomplete picture. Conservatives have both a social and an economic agenda. Although they may favor individual rights in regard to gun possession and property rights, or less regulation for businesses, they may concurrently argue against certain personal liberties such as abortion, family planning, sex out of marriage, homosexuality, and pornography. At the same time conservatives wish to conserve certain parts of the economy and society, they are more change oriented regarding deregulation, tariffs, immigration, and tax relief for the wealthy and reversing some values they find repugnant. They do, however, believe with some consistency that social injustice and inequality are best overcome through personal initiative and effort. Almost everyone, they believe, can improve his or her situation within an unregulated free-enterprise system.

The liberal-conservative conceptualization introduced here is generalized and is often encountered in discussions as social welfare decisions are contemplated. However, it is important to understand that these are ambiguous definitions and that each of the major camps include opposing perspectives. In addition, when it suits both the left and the right they can move from ostensibly ideologically pure positions. There are libertarian conservatives who defend individual private freedoms, want a sharply limited state and government, and advocate no governmental interference regarding private sexual activity. Libertarians emphasize both personal and economic liberty and believe that free markets in all aspects of life lead to free minds. Other conservatives favor governmental interference regarding such issues as abortion, "Baby Doe" cases, pornography, prayers in public schools, and private sexual behavior. Liberalism is also not monolithic. Some liberals may uphold the absolute right of free speech and assembly while others support censorship of movies, musical recordings, access to pornography, and seek limitations on harmful, "too free" speech.

From a political point of view, the United States has been relatively inhospitable to radical groups of either the left or right; democratic socialists and Marxists on the one hand and fascists or radical conservatives on the other have failed historically to win mass support. Although radicalism can emerge from either extreme, extreme radicalism never took hold as the dominant ideology. In the 1990s, in general, radicalism has arisen from the right. One of the reasons that the United States has been inhospitable to radical groups has been its relative success in providing for the needs of most people, more so than most other societies. While there are many individual exceptions and ambiguities, and although it is very difficult, if not impossible, to describe definitively the two main political streams in American life, we view liberalism and conservatism as general trends and descriptions that are incomplete shortcuts to understanding—but nevertheless convey political stances and directions.

As a further aid toward understanding the basic assumptions that influence our thinking about social policy and program choices, we examine briefly several major sociopolitical theories. The predominant perspectives are *structural-functional* theory (sometimes called "integrator theories") and *conflict* theory. The major assumptions of structural-functional theory include the following:

- *Stability*. Institutions serve positive purposes, contributing to the maintenance of society and the realization of its main goals;
- *Harmony*. The various parts of society cooperate for the good of the whole; and

- *Evolution*. Change occurs through adaptation to meet new needs and demands.

All of this occurs in general through consensus. From the perspective of structural-functional theory, an observer wants to know the nature of the social structure and what the consequences are of that structure. This theory supports a more static, conservative analysis of social systems which implies a preservation of the status quo.

Conflict theory views the world as continual conflict and change. Society is replete with competititon and conflict, and there are always winners and losers. There is an emphasis on stress and conflict and the ways in which they contribute to social change. The major assumptions of *conflict theory* include the following. *Competition* for scarce resources is at the heart of all relationships, and competition rather than consensus is characteristic of human relationships. There is *structured inequality* so that those who have power and get the rewards strive to maintain them. From the perspective of conflict theory, observers want to know who benefits from the social structures and how those who benefit maintain their advantage. Paradoxically, conflict theorists want to know how the society is functional for whom.[19] Despite the contradictory assumptions of the structural-functional and conflict theories, a synthesis of the two models involves perceiving society as having "two faces of equal reality—one of stability, harmony, and consensus, and one of change, conflict, and constraint." This combination of opposites suggests that a more realistic model has to combine both the order and and the conflict perspectives. A more complex understanding of society views both perspectives as concurrent and complementary.[20]

As we noted earlier, social policy is both the decision-making process and its outcomes concerned with social welfare, social services, and closely related spheres. Social policy thus refers both to the decision making by which a course of action is determined and to the resulting policy—which is a statement about the aims and planned activities in regard to a particular social problem. From our point of view, social policy can be positive governmental statements or can set direction through omission. To have no stance, or a "hands-off" policy, about a particular problem— that is, to relate to a problem in a laissez-faire manner—is also a policy position.

Formal social policies are determined in four basic ways, as indicated in the following paragraphs.

Legislation   When a legislative body enacts laws that establish the directions the society will take in regard to a particular social problem or issue, it establishes a formal social policy that expresses the aims and expected activities of the society. For example, in 1965 the Congress explicitly set forth several aims of the nation in regard to a growing aging population. The Older Americans Act created the Administration on Aging, and the Social Security Act provided for Medicare, a national system of health insurance for the aged. In 1972, the Supplemental Security Income program shifted aid for the aged, blind, and disabled to a national level from state administrative responsibility.

Governmental Guidelines for the Implementation of Legislation   Governmental bureaucracies influence social policy in many ways. The guidelines drawn up by the agency charged with implementing certain legislation may be vague or alter the original purposes of the legislative enactment; the staff may not be trained to fulfill the necessary tasks; or governmental agencies can skew the policy through reduced activity. As was noted earlier, the interpretation of the phrase "maximum feasible participation of the poor" made dramatic changes in the War on Poverty, beyond the intent of the original legislation. Passage of a law does not guarantee its implementation consistent with the intentions of the legislators. Writing regulations is a quasi-legislative function, in large part hidden from public view.[21]

Judicial Decisions   Decisions by courts at various governmental levels can also enunciate social policy and give direction to governmental and societal action. In *Shapiro v. Thompson* (1969) the courts struck down laws requiring a period of in-state residence as a condition of eligibility for public assistance. The Supreme Court decision in *Roe v. Wade* (1973) set forth the constitutional guarantee of the right to privacy and its application to a woman's decision to terminate her pregnancy. *Wyatt v. Stickney* (1972) established for the mentally ill confined in hospitals the right to adequate and effective treatment, a humane physical and psychological environment, adequate numbers of properly trained staff to provide treatment, and individual treatment plans. Similarly, *Youngberg v. Romeo* (1982) established a constitutional right to proper treatment for persons with mental retardation in state facilities.

Following the enactment of the Personal Responsibility and Work Opportunity Reconciliation Act (PRA, 1996), States began to challenge former court rulings related to public assistance such as *Shapiro v. Thompson*. At least eighteen states and the District of Columbia adopted some sort of restrictions on benefits to new residents in their Temporary Assistance for Needy Families programs. These changes are made despite evidence suggesting people do not move to gain public assistance benefits. A popular tactic is to pay new residents the benefit available in their former states for a period of six months or a year. One state adopted an across-the-board 30 percent reduction in benefits to all new residents for one year regardless of the state from which they came. Other states deny benefits for 30 or 60 days. All these variations are subject to constitutional challenges. Since TANF began at least three additional courts have joined those courts that ruled earlier that paying new residents the benefits available in their former states is unconstitutional. It is expected that litigation will continue and grow in number.[22]

Informal Processes   There is a fourth means for determining social policy; however, it is a matter of *informal* processes rather than formal. Public decision making and choices of societal direction also can be accomplished through a spontaneous understanding of a large-scale public will. Because of this, certain laws stop being enforced or are reversed, such as prohibition or speed limits on highways.

The Federal and Pluralist System

Legislation is a major determinant of social policy and is the result of a political process that involves political parties, special interest groups (for example, agriculture, business, organized labor, professional, religious, environmental, consumer groups), and the media (television, books, films, radio, magazines, and so on, which influence public opinion). In addition, the executive, legislative, and bureaucratic parts of the government also play parts in the process.

The United States is a federal governmental system in which power does not rest solely with the central government nor with the 50 states but, instead, depends upon a sharing of power between a strong central government and strong states. Further, the states share certain powers with local governmental units, which also play important roles, so that power is dispersed among the federal, state, and local governments.

Decision making and implementation in a federal system may involve actions at the federal, state, and local levels by executive, legislative, judicial, bureaucratic, and nongovernmental individuals and organizations within the context of the Constitution. Nongovernmental groups include both the proponents and opponents of particular policies or programs. Added to the complex of potential participants, there also exist regional quasi-governmental bodies. For example, in many metropolitan areas, there is significant decision making on issues such as metropolitan transportation, airport, water supply, ports, and solid and hazardous waste authorities formed by the adjoining governmental jurisdictions. Neither the directors nor their staffs are elected. They are responsible to governors or other elected officials but not accountable directly to the electorate. This type of quasi-governmental organization exists in a number of metropolitan and regional areas and exerts enormous influence on people's lives. It can determine the cost of bridge and tunnel tolls, transportation patterns, location of jobs, and so on. As a result, regional semi-governmental organizations are another important player in what is already a highly complex political configuration.

Federalism divides political power among the national government and the states and is a set of relationships in which there is no one source for leadership, which tends to result in compromise and piecemeal action. Through public and special interest opinion, certain problems come to the forefront. Many of the groups mentioned previously play a role in the formulation of policy alternatives. Several conflicting proposals are discussed. The potential policy is debated (for example, to change or not change the eligibility rules for a program), and ultimately, a policy is adopted. Successful implementation of the policy depends on the availability of sufficient knowledge for effective implementation, positive attitudes of the implementers, and adequate additional resources (people, dollars).

The Economic Sphere

Social policies are decided and implemented in the context of diverse values and ideologies and political and economic factors. The context and these policies affect every citizen's life and the life of the nation. At this point, we introduce selected *economic* concepts that can assist us in understanding the economic factors that affect social welfare decisions.

Economics is the study of income, production, and distribution of goods and services and is the study of social systems used to allocate scarce resources for different uses. In general, there are two major concerns of policymakers: growth and equality. *Growth* is the increase in total output; *equality* is concerned with how that output is divided among the population.

The economy of the United States is capitalist, by which we mean that the basic raw materials, means of production, and the goods produced are primarily privately owned. However, even in the United States state ownership can be found in electric power utilities, housing, transportation systems, public forests, and parks. In socialist societies, the productive assets are predominantly state owned. In regard to state and private ownership, nations can be found along a continuum. Over time, ownership patterns have in general been shifting toward the private sector, but all nations have a mixed pattern.

The United States utilizes a market system in which decisions are decentralized and made through the interaction of individuals, businesses, and other organizations. People are free to work where they wish but must compete for jobs. One is free to buy or sell whatever one possesses or has sufficient resources to purchase. It is often assumed that in capitalism free markets most effectively allocate goods and services to their best use. The way in which that allocation takes place in market systems is through prices. Prices act as signals to people to make their economic decisions and reflect their preferences, desires, and costs.

Conversely, other systems utilize centralized decision makers who decide what is to be done and issue directives to achieve certain desired ends. Individual choice is constrained by the expectations and regulations of the centralized system. In the decade following the collapse of the Soviet Union and following the problems of the debt crisis that strained the governmental budgets in developing countries, there has been a shift more toward market systems and away from planned economies.

The federal government (and state and local governments) exists within our capitalist society and may use fiscal and monetary policies for various purposes, deliberately or not: to increase employment and reduce unemployment or vice versa, achieve price stability, enhance productivity, and redistribute wealth or income.

Fiscal Policy   *Fiscal policy* is the use of government spending and tax policies. Government expenditures directly and government taxation indirectly through disposable income affect the demand for goods and services. The timing, size, and combination of these actions are important factors. When the federal budget is balanced, tax revenues and expenditures are exactly equal. If revenues are more than expenditures, the budget is in surplus. The reverse means the budget is in deficit. Deficits require an increase in borrowing by the government, obtained from the private sector or the central bank by selling treasury bills and bonds, a promise to repay a stated amount sometime in the future (both short term and long term). A government bond is to be paid in the more distant future.

The government can purchase goods and services or make infrastructure investments. In addition, the government transfers payments through social insurance programs, public assistance, and subsidies to agricultural, business, and industrial components of the nation.

Tax policy, the pattern by which individuals, families, and businesses are taxed, influences the amount of income/wealth available to individuals and businesses. There are three types of taxes. A tax is *progressive* if the average tax rate is higher for those with higher incomes: Those who are wealthier pay a higher percentage of their income. The tax rate percentage is larger as income rises. For example, a person whose income is $20,000 might not pay a tax or pay at a low percentage rate, while those who earn $300,000 pay at a 39 percent rate. A graduated income tax is an example of this type. *Regressive* taxes are those that take a larger percentage of income in taxes from poorer persons than from wealthier persons. Examples are sales taxes, the social security payroll tax, cigarette, gasoline, alcohol and beer, and airplane taxes. Thus, there is a larger relative burden on low-income persons than on those with higher incomes. A *proportional* tax is one in which all taxpayers pay exactly the same proportion of income, a constant percentage of their incomes. An example of this is the Medicare tax as part of the overall Social Security tax. The crucial differences are whether the tax takes from higher-income people the same fraction of income as from those with lower incomes (proportional), a larger fraction of income from wealthier people (progressive), or a smaller fraction of income from wealthier persons than it takes from lower income people (regressive). In Table 6.1 one can observe the differences/similarities of these three types of taxes.

A new form of taxation was introduced as a major issue during the 1996 presidential campaign—the *flat tax*. Although first introduced during the 1992 campaign by Edmund G. ("Jerry") Brown Jr., a former governor of California, it did not make headway but became a prominent issue. The flat tax would simplify an elaborate and complex tax system by eliminating a sliding scale of tax rates and make all taxpayers pay the same percentage of their income. Almost all deductions would be removed so that wealthier persons could not use deductions available only to them. Some persons argued that the elimination of "loopholes" would be fairer and reduce the size and cost of the internal revenue system.

Charitable deductions, income from interest and stocks, mortgage interest payments, and other deductions would be eliminated. The claim was made by proponents that people would support charities sufficiently without the ability to claim that deduction. Also it was suggested that people would not object to very wealthy persons avoiding taxes on interest and dividends because they would believe this income would already have been taxed at the corporation level.

Democrats and many Republicans argued against this type of tax, claiming it would have to be set at a level higher than claimed by proponents in order to gain sufficient tax income to balance the budget and reduce the federal debt, and the tax would favor the rich. Bankers and insurance and real estate companies were early opponents of the idea.

TABLE 6.1   Three Types of Taxes

Income	Regressive Tax Paid/Income%	Progressive Tax Paid/Income%	Proportional TaxPaid/Income%
$10,000	$1,000, 10%	$1,500, 15%	$150, .015%
$50,000	$1,000, 2%	$12,500, 25%	$750, .015%
$100,000	$1,000, 1%	$40,000, 40%	$1500, .015%

Another proposal is to tax consumption by instituting a national retail sales tax. A simple, single-rate sales tax would be paid on all new goods and services. Included would be a tax refund system so families would not pay taxes on the purchase of necessities. Called the Fair Tax, critics claimed the math supporting the plan was faulty and a third of the estimate of revenue was based on taxes the government would pay to itself. Furthermore, one fourth of the anticipated sales taxes would be paid on things like church services, free care at veteran's hospitals, and free checking accounts and other difficult-to-tax financial services.[23]

Monetary Policy   In the United States the central bank, the Federal Reserve Board, controls the banking system. It is through this mechanism that the government's monetary policy is executed. The Federal Reserve System ("the Fed") began operation in 1914 after passage of the Federal Reserve Act (1913). There is a board of governors appointed by the president. The seven members serve 14-year, staggered, nonrenewable terms of office, which overlap presidential administrations. The chairperson is appointed to a 4-year renewable term. (All appointments are confirmed by the Senate.) There are 12 Federal Reserve regional banks that serve various regions of the nation. The Federal Open Market Committee (FOMC) is composed of representatives of the board of governors and the regional Federal Reserve banks. The Federal Reserve Bank of New York (FRBNY) is the most important regional bank, executing much of monetary policy and acting in the international economy, in addition to other responsibilities. The board of governors is now relatively independent of both executive and congressional controls, but in the past from time to time has been more easily pressured by the administration or Congress.

One of the most important functions of the Federal Reserve is control of the supply of money. The Federal Reserve, through "open-market operations," can purchase or sell government securities on the open market, which contracts or expands the money supply. When the Federal Reserve buys a bond or bill from a household or firm, it pays money into the person's or firm's bank account, increasing the supply of money both for the individual or firm and for the bank. Conversely, when the Fed sells securities, it "soaks up" the money available for spending or loans. Dollars held by the Fed are not counted as part of the money supply. Dollars held by banks, individuals, and firms are counted as part of the money supply.

The Federal Reserve can also control the supply of available money by raising or lowering banks' deposit requirements—that is, the required reserves of banks. A bank's reserve is the amount of money it must set aside as an assurance toward its ability to pay out money owed to depositors. Money kept in reserve is unavailable for being lent out. It is the bank's money-lending ability that gives it its special role in the creation of money. The higher the required bank deposit reserve, the less money is available for banks to lend; the lower the requirement, the more money available for lending.

There are still other ways in which the Federal Reserve controls the supply of money. Banks may borrow from the Federal Reserve and from other banks. In the first case, the Fed sets a discount rate (the rate at which the Fed will lend money to banks). By increasing or decreasing the discount rate at which banks can borrow from it, the Fed influences the rate that banks can charge potential customers. Banks pass on the higher interest rates to their customers. The higher the rate, the lower the number of consumers who will borrow. The lower the rate, the easier it is to borrow. In the second case, the Fed sets the federal funds rate, which is the rate banks pay for interbank borrowing of money overnight.

There are additional governmental bodies that oversee bank regulations and activities. Among these are the Federal Deposit Insurance Corporation (FDIC), which guarantees funds on deposit for member banks and lends money or buys assets of those banks to facilitate mergers or prevent failures. The Office of Thrift Supervision, an agency of the Treasury Department, is responsible for savings and loan associations and savings banks through regulating, supervising, and chartering these institutions. The Comptroller of the Currency charters, examines, and supervises all banks with national charters. Banks can only be declared insolvent by the Comptroller, who is appointed by the President and confirmed by the Senate.

Money supply and money demand interact to determine the price level and interest rates. Interest rates are important because they provide an incentive for firms or individuals to make real decisions regarding investment, consumption, borrowing, and lending. The importance of money and hence monetary policy comes from the three roles money plays: (1) as a store of value—inflation eats away at this stored value; (2) as facilitator of transactions—unstable prices make economic transactions complex and difficult; and (3) as a unit of account—businesses and households need an accurate measurement of what they are worth.

THE IMPORTANCE OF FISCAL AND MONETARY POLICY

The importance of fiscal and monetary policy for social welfare is that the state of the economy—for example, how many and the types of jobs available, inflation (too many dollars chasing too few goods) and deflation (too many goods chasing too few dollars), and where jobs are located—is determined in part by these policy decisions. Fiscal policy is an important factor in managing the economy through alterations in government spending, borrowing, and tax rates.

One governmental role reflects the economic theories of John Maynard Keynes, a British economist. Keynes viewed economic depressions as a result of individuals and businesses decreasing substantially or stopping spending altogether and investing because interest rate changes or price changes were insufficient inducements to spend. These spending reductions cause a drop in output, usually with both job losses and wage decreases. Increased governmental spending or tax reductions can increase *the demand side of the economy*, which in turn leads to higher output and employment. High inflation, on the other hand, can be countered by raising tax rates or cutting government spending, unlikely events, to reduce demand. It is obvious how governmental expenditures or taxes (along with private decisions) influence the well-being of the citizenry. Monetarily, an increase in the money supply can offset a sluggish economy when unemployment is high. There is a belief that there is a "natural" rate of unemployment below which inflation will be accelerated. This rate is usually understood to be around 6 percent and it is referred to as the

NAIRU, the nonaccelerating inflation rate of unemployment. Or, the money supply can be decreased when inflation is high and "too many dollars are chasing too few goods."[24]

During the 1980s, the Reagan administration stressed quite a different economic theory known as *supply-side* theory (yet it was still "Keynesian" to the extent that output could be influenced by government tax and spending policies). This theory emphasized *tax cuts*, thought to *encourage saving, increase investment*, and thus *improve productivity*. To make the tax cuts more acceptable, some economists argued that with sustained growth in the economy, tax revenues would increase even with the tax break, offsetting any revenue lost through the initial tax cuts. However, the actual experience was that government deficits increased dramatically, and the substantial federal debt (the total of all previous deficits) created problems for the nation: high interest rates; overvalued dollars, which leads to increased imports and decreased exports; and future tax liabilities.

During the Reagan administration, in addition to a massive tax cut during his first term, spending in total dollars was increased. (In percentage terms, social spending for entitlements grew quickest.) The result of these actions was an increase in federal budget deficits and a tripling of the federal debt. An important factor that determines the ability of the nation to repay the debt is the *gross national product* (GNP), which includes all U.S.-owned production within the United States or at any other location and excludes production in the United States owned by foreigners. Another statistical summary is the *gross domestic product* (GDP), which counts all the production within the nation's borders regardless of whether the firm is owned by U.S. citizens.

Huge federal debts carry several problems. They may strain the ability of the nation to repay them in a timely manner. These debts shift tax burdens to future generations for the actions of current governmental services. The interest on an overlarge national debt is in itself a great burden on the budget and moves dollars away from private-sector productive investment by individuals and households ("crowding out"). To reduce deficits and the debt, the government has to either raise taxes, cut governmental spending, or use inflation to erode the value of the debt. These are not popular governmental actions.

In 1985, the government attempted, through passage of the Gramm-Rudman-Hollings Act, to gain control over the debt through a schedule of spending limits to control the deficits. This act provided for a schedule of reduced deficits so the budget would be balanced by 1993. However, the act only covered discretionary spending, while entitlements continued to grow quickly. Another technique for dealing with the debt was consideration of a balanced budget amendment to the Constitution. Such an amendment would have provided two escape clauses: waivers during wartime and decisions based on at least a two-thirds vote in both the House and Senate. After consideration and sponsorship by a Republican-controlled Congress in 1995, such an amendment was not passed.

There are several other economic concepts that students should become familiar with in order to think about social welfare within the socio-politico-economic context. The economy continually fluctuates in regard to the pace of economic activity. The economy is cyclical with "booms" as well as "busts." Eras of expansion and prosperity are followed by recessions (increased unemployment and lowered demand for goods and services with unused industrial productive capacity) or depressions (deep unemployment, loss of confidence in the future, few new investments). During the 1970s, the United States experienced "stagflation," which was inflation concurrent with unemployment. In the 1990s, during an economic boom some economic "truths" did not hold up. The Phillips Curve suggests that there can be low inflation or low unemployment but not at the same time. In the 1990s, this has not been the case because both unemployment (officially lowest since 1970, but many unemployed persons are not counted) and inflation both have been low. Growth has been stronger in the 1990s despite fiscal constraints and a reduced federal deficit. The money supply increased rapidly but this did not result in higher inflation. One would expect that oil prices would rise as the world economy grew. But that too has not occurred.[25]

Cycles are caused by fluctuations in "demand shocks," that is, shifts in consumption, and "supply shocks," for example, the oil crisis. The cyclical pattern derives from leaps and lags in the economy. Investment decisions typically are not made instantaneously; decision makers take time to react to "signals" in the economy, such as interest rates and prices, and the implementation of decisions also takes time. Factors that influence these decisions are changes in consumer preferences and expectations, interest rates, taxes, transfer payments, government expenditures, and technology changes. Another influence on economic fluctuations is change in investment expenditures. These expenditures are related to interest rates and include inventories, residential housing construction, plants and equipment, and infrastructure.

Spending has a *multiplier effect*; that is, the recipients of the payments engage in further spending of their own. New employment and incomes are created and—in turn—create further demand for goods and services. When the economy is in recession, certain social welfare programs (for example, unemployment insurance) provide counter-cyclical investments. They provide income to recipients that is spent, thereby offsetting the strength of the recession. During business cycle peaks, more social insurance taxes are paid. The effect of these counter-cyclical actions is to modify the sharpness of the business cycle.

AN INTERNATIONAL ECONOMY

Goods and services flow constantly among nations—food, raw materials, machinery, microchips, financial consultation, engineering, and so on. In almost every sphere of life, we can see the impact of imports and exports as international trade has expanded. Our nation exports goods such as Chevrolets, Coca Cola, teachers, banking and finance, construction, and movies, and imports goods and services such as Toyotas, Gucci, Absolut, Guinness, Volkswagen, software design, and Nestlé, Shell, and Heineken. In addition, U.S. firms own and produce goods in overseas locations, while other nations do the same in the United States. When U.S. industries as multinational corporations operate overseas subsidiaries, there are limits to the extent they can be controlled by the United States. A number of U.S. corporations depend to a significant extent on the profits of these overseas operations.

Production, marketing, and finance have become internationalized so that the decisions of boards of directors meeting in Germany can affect the economy of South Carolina and decisions made in Japan can affect the types of jobs in California and Ohio. Similarly, decisions made in Detroit or Dallas have an impact in many parts of the world.

The international economy is extremely complex but has importance for social welfare in several ways: (1) International trading influences the overall well-being of our society. Trade patterns and exchange rates influence the pattern and types of jobs in the economy. (2) The productivity and competitive ability of U.S. industries is forced to compete in this complex arena. (3) In general, the interdependent world economy has its greatest impacts in two ways: (a) capital mobility affects investment, inflation, interest rates, and the effectiveness of government policies across countries and (b) individual decisions affect micro-level consequences—where jobs are, what they pay, and what is traded. Our citizens, as well as the citizens of other nations, have to live with these decisions. (4) Decisions in one country—for example, the United States, Canada, or Mexico—can cause harm to other nations through "exporting" inflation, transferring capital, labor, or other resources, by the creation of pollution, acid rain, over-fishing, and other factors. (5) Groups of countries can join together to raise or lower the price of commodities through creating monopolies or otherwise controlling the market. Finally, (6) the ways other nations deal with their social welfare systems in relation to their contextual factors—unemployment, budget difficulties—give signals and form a climate of opinion about what is proper and permissible.

A Second Welfare System—Corporate Welfare

As we examine specific programs commonly identified as social welfare in chapters 9 and 10, one should keep in mind there is another welfare system, one that benefits individuals and corporations through tax breaks and subsidies.

Tax expenditures are revenue losses attributable to provisions of the federal tax laws that allow special exclusions, exemptions, or deductions from gross income or that provide special credits, preferential tax rates, or deferral of tax liabilities. They are, therefore, any reductions in individual and corporate tax liabilities that result from special tax provisions or regulations that provide tax benefits to particular taxpapers. These tax provisions are referred to as tax expenditures because they are analogous to direct spending programs, both of which may have similar budget policy objectives. Tax expenditures are most similar to direct spending programs that have no spending limits and are available as entitlements to those who meet the established statutory criteria.

To gain a sense of the dimensions of tax expenditures, estimates were prepared for the Joint (Congressional) Committee on taxation for the fiscal years 1998-2002, *but excluding those provisions which would result in less than $50* *million over the five years.* The anticipated total is slightly over $3 trillion. Among the larger expenditures are mortgage interest deductions, long-term capital gains, depreciation of equipment, charitable contributions, employer contributions for medical care, and health and long-term care insurance.[26]

Individual and corporate welfare costs taxpayers as much or more than means-tested assistance programs such as Temporary Assistance to Needy Families, Food Stamps, housing assistance, and child nutrition. Many expenditures are to encourage business, trade, development of natural resources, and other economic developments. One way in which government supports corporations is through research grants and subsidies. Even where no business will reap large profits, it may be necessary for the federal government to fund basic research in areas that have potential for enriching society. One never knows the potential of basic research or the possibilities of programs such as NASA, materials science, biotechnology, or other investigations. So one can assume there ought to be a federal role in which industry is subsidized, but questions can be raised about the aims, dimensions, and efficacy of such subsidies. Some subsidies provide housing or health care but others may be little more than political payoffs to constituents or business expense expenditures that businesses might be expected to pay themselves. It is interesting to note that the calls during the 1990s for reform and cutting of social programs were forceful and intense, but the call to reduce individual and corporate welfare through the tax system was muted.

A Changed World—New/Old Ideology, New Politics, New Economic Forces, New Social Policy, and New Social Services

Global issues that concern many nations and the broad spectrum of society have arisen and hold special importance for social welfare. The world has entered an age of intense international competition related to economic growth, employment, productivity, budget deficits, taxation, motivation, as well as ideologies deemed to be supportive of successful economic competition.

A backlash arose against social welfare provision in widely separated places, including western Europe, Canada, New Zealand, central and eastern Europe, and in the United States. In a number of South American and Caribbean nations social security pensions have been devalued and health services have deteriorated. Chile moved to privatize its social welfare system.

In the United States there has been a return to traditional anti-federalism, a focus on individual and family responsibility as social welfare strategies that do not cost tax dollars, and these along with voluntary efforts have once again become ascendent values. Many citizens and legislators turn away from governmental action and social welfare programs on the basis of political ideology. In their view, governmental action and social welfare programs are incompetent, untrustworthy, and cost-inefficient; undermine self-reliance by encouraging dependence; are tilted against freedom and autonomy; and undermine economic productivity. Such attitudes tap into deeply held beliefs by Americans. Only 34 percent of Americans basically trust the government, and there is a sense that politicians are corrupt. Nevertheless, two-thirds of Americans have positive views of federal workers and particular federal agencies, a view that contrasts with their negative view of Government as a whole.[27]

Among the factors that support these new directions are reevaluations of welfare financing, aging populations, technological innovations, and widespread aversion to taxes. Various groups have used the current situation to begin "rolling back" welfare programs. Major congressional figures have argued that people are not entitled to anything but opportunity. Calls for cost-containment and efficiency affect social welfare programs at every level and, undoubtedly, will continue to affect social welfare's future.

Until recent times, the creation of the modern world has brought with it the welfare state. However, as we approach the 21st century, the thrust of social welfare in the United States since the Great Depression was challenged by Republican and conservative forces, often joined by members of the Democratic party and by other former supporters of governmental action and services for people. This major challenge took place in a context that included a large federal debt, popular resistance to taxes, general discontent with government, shifts in federal funding expectations of the states, and a desire by conservatives to cut taxes and return federal functions to the state level. Critics charged that social welfare was too expensive, undermined the traditional family, encouraged the increase of single-parent families and children born out of wedlock, failed to reduce the number of poor persons, and fostered dependence.

Social welfare in U.S. society developed in a piecemeal and incremental fashion; it attacked one problem, relatively without regard to other problems that might contribute to the creation of the problem or that influence its dimensions. Although experience might teach that comprehensive and coordinated approaches could offer better solutions to problems and reduce the inadequacies of one program overburdening other programs, comprehensive approaches to social welfare have been impracticable in U.S. society.

Social workers and others may see the needs of people and the positive and negative effects of social welfare programs. But the individual observations of social workers are not made within a vacuum. On the contrary, they take place within the context of a national society at a particular time and state of development. Social welfare is in fact the collective supply of resources, a sharing of the burden or the risk. Two questions have to be asked: (1) What needs should be supplied by the collective action of the society and which left to individual effort? (2) What can the society afford?

What should and can be done to eliminate poverty or to deal with other social problems depends on the ideologies and values of those who make legislative decisions. A "backlash" has grown against social welfare provision in Western Europe. In the United States, a seismic shift is occurring in which individual responsibility is the ascendent philosophy. Many citizens and legislators turn away from governmental action and the programs designed to assist the poor.

Some attribute the successes of pro-market and anti-welfare governments to the fact that many welfare supports were in place minimizing the shock and burden of unemployment. Certainly, to a significant extent, such social welfare benefits minimized the shock and burdens of unemployment in the United States.

But various events have caused nations with highly developed social welfare systems to reevaluate their efforts. High unemployment rates in France, Italy, Spain, and Germany and other industrialized nations during the mid-1990s reached the highest levels those nations experienced since the recovery from World War II. The prospect of chronic joblessness led to examining assumptions about salaries, benefits, and tax policies. There was agreement that one important reason their economies are unable to create sufficient numbers of jobs is the high cost of occupational and social benefits. This led to revisions in the social welfare benefits provided. In addition to unemployment, other pressures reinforcing a need for this reexamination included aging populations, global economic competition, and widespread aversion to taxes.

A Changed Context

Is the modern welfare state self-limiting? To what extent can a viable economy tolerate a welfare state? On the other hand, to what extent can a modern industrial or post-industrial state do without social welfare programs and services? Mass production demands mass purchasing power. Social welfare programs, particularly income maintenance programs, serve the society as *economic stabilizers*. Nevertheless, they must be funded, and these funds are made available through taxation of current or future generations. The complexity of modern society becomes focused on the issue of whether social welfare will expand. The decision is not simply one of social justice or morality but is part and parcel of an economic scene in which taxation grows and is resented, in which the middle classes and middle-aged are burdened with the tax load, and in which purchasing power has been diminished by reduced incomes. Do these features of our modern society suggest there are inevitable limits to social welfare or do they indicate the context can change over time?

At the same time that tax policy alters the nature of social services because of the demands of various parts of the population for fiscal relief, another trend affects social welfare. The entire premise of progressive, liberal thought has become suspect, and questions of a serious nature are being asked about the limits of "doing good." The two-edged nature of social welfare has been recognized, that is, How does a greater emphasis on market exchange (exchanges between buyers and sellers that depend on their relative powers) affect social welfare? This focus on individuals and family responsibility defines the social good as the sum of individual desires and detracts from ideas of communal and societal responsibility. Efficiency is the overriding goal of social policy and results in market-based social policies.

Before we turn in the next chapter to the structural components, alternative characteristics, and evaluation of social welfare programs, we want to introduce here the major contextual factors that affect social welfare ideas, policy, planning, and program decisions in the United States. As one proceeds through the following chapters, be mindful of these background factors:

1. The United States is relatively secure from the threat of war and has no major rival around the world. However, potential global threats include recession/depression, poverty, pollution, disease, hunger, political disenfranchisement, terrorism, drug trafficking, cultural conflicts, and shortages of fresh water and arable land.

2. There has been a shift in power from governments to markets.

3. The national budget is balanced. Unemployment is down. But looming in the background is a significant federal debt that impedes attention being paid to social programs. At the same time, a budget surplus was achieved for the first time in 30 years and additional sizeable surpluses are estimated to reach $1.5 trillion over the next ten years.[28]

4. The chasm between the rich and the poor continues to increase.

5. There are strong forces that believe that government is ineffective and want to reduce further governmental action and service.

6. The shift from government to the market and voluntary efforts results in the following:

    A. *The privatization of public services*. There has been a shift from governmental provision of social services to provision by corporations. This often results in lower wages, fewer benefits such as health care, and more part-time employment.

    B. *There has been a shift to user charges rather than taxes to finance public services*. It is unclear whether this improves efficiency of services, but the substitution for taxes results in greater monetary burdens for the poor.

    C. *Universal services are replaced by services for those willing and able to pay*. Deregulation ends the requirement to serve low volume places or to price goods so as to ensure universal service.

    D. *Capital mobility has an impact on jobs, people, and communities*. Constraints on plant closings are loosened and jobs are transferred to lower tax or pay scale communities.

    E. *Welfare reform*. The terms of the social welfare debate are shifted from the level of benefits (Can a family live on this benefit?) to a focus on dependency and self-sufficiency. Attention is shifted from societal responsibility and the political and economic systems to individual and family behavior.

    F. *The New Federalism*. Society needs more market discipline, including federal, state, and local governments.[29]

7. Medicare has serious funding problems. Social Security has less serious problems that need to be addressed. There is a growing dominance of managed care plans.

As our society deals with these problems and makes decisions that limit and/or reduce social welfare, there will be positive outcomes but also negative consequences. The balance between positive and negative remains to be weighed. However,

> we can degrade people by caring for them; and we can degrade them by not caring for them. . . . All interventions have consequences, and one of the things we should learn to keep in the forefront of our consciousness is that the most important consequences of any intervention almost always turn out to be those consequences that were not intended or planned upon or could not have been calculated beforehand.[30]

Summary

In this chapter, we have looked closely at the concept of social welfare and defined and distinguished some essential terms such as social policy, social services, and social work. We have also given an overview of the ideological, political, and economic forces influencing how social policy is determined, social services delivered, and social work practiced. In the economic sphere, we've given a brief overview of monetary and fiscal policy and the types of taxes supporting social welfare.

Questions for Consideration

1. We have presented a broad definition of social welfare. Do you agree? How would you change it?
2. Suggest some ways in which ideology impacts on social welfare in your community.
3. Do you know the legislative process in your state regarding social welfare policy and legislation? What advocacy groups play parts in the process? Is it always the same groups?
4. (a) What kinds of taxes support social welfare in your state? Are they fair? (b) Has your state and social welfare been affected by the international economy? In what ways?
5. Does your state provide individual and corporate tax expenditures? To whom?

Notes

1. Adam Clymer, "Simpson Joins Ranks of Pragmatists Leaving Senate," *New York Times*, December 4, 1995, p. B5.
2. Ruth Conniff, "Welfare Profiteers," *The Progressive*, Vol. 61, No. 5, May 1997, p. 33.
3. Russell Baker, "Used to Talk, Now Shrieks," *New York Times*, June 29, 1996, p. 19.
4. Robert L. Barker, *The Social Work Dictionary*, 3rd Edition, Washington, D.C.: NASW, 1995, p. 357.
5. Amy Gutmann, *Democracy and the Welfare State*, Princeton, N.J.: Princeton University Press, 1988, p. 3.
6. Gutmann, p. 3.
7. Richard Titmuss, *Essays on the Welfare State*, "The Social Division of Welfare," Boston: Beacon Press, 1963, pp. 34–35.

8. Alfred J. Kahn, *Social Policy and Social Services*, New York: Random House, 1979, p. 16.

9. Daniel Bell, *The End of Ideology*, New York: Free Press, 1960.

10. Francis Fukuyama, *The End of History and the Last Man*, New York: Free Press, 1992, and Paul Lewis, "Marx's Stock Resurges on a 150-Year Tip," *New York Times*, June 27, 1998, pp. A17, A19.

11. Samuel Mencher, "Ideology and the Welfare Society," *Social Work*, Vol. 12, July 1967, pp. 3-11.

12. Jude Wanniski, *The Way the World Works: How Economics Fail—and Succeed*, New York: Basic Books, 1978.

13. George Gilder, *Wealth and Poverty*, New York: Basic Books, 1981, p. x.

14. Charles Murray, *Losing Ground: American Social Policy, 1950-1980*, New York: Basic Books, 1984, pp. 9, 223.

15. Marvin Olasky, *The Tragedy of American Compassion*, Washington, D.C.: Regnery Publishing, 1995.

16. James MacGregor Burns, J. W. Peltason, and Thomas E. Cronin, *Government by the People*, Englewood Cliffs, N.J.: Prentice Hall, 1987, pp. 435-436.

17. Ronald Dworkin, "Why Liberals Should Believe in Equality," *New York Review of Books*, Vol. XXX, No. 1, February 3, 1983, pp. 32-34.

18. J. M. Burns, J. W. Peltason, and T. E. Cronin, p. 437.

19. David B. Brinkerhoff, Lynn K. White, and Suzanne T. Ortega, *Essentials of Sociology*, 2d Edition, New York: West Publishing Co., 1992, pp. 10, 12-13; Neil J. Smelser, *Sociology*, Cambridge, MA.: Blackwell Publishers, 1994, pp. 26-27.

20. D. Stanley Eitzen, *In Conflict and Order: Understanding Society*, Boston: Allyn and Bacon, 1985, p. 45.

21. See John W. Kingdon, *Agendas, Alternatives, and Public Policies*, Boston: Little, Brown, 1984.

22. Mary R. Mannix, et al, "Welfare Litigation Developments Since the PRA," *Clearinghouse Review*, Vol. 31, January–February, 1998, pp. 435-453 and http://www.welfarelaw.org/artcommw.html; Donald L. Horowitz, *The Courts and Social Policy*, Washington, D.C.: The Brookings Institution, 1977, pp. 4, 14.

23. Robert S. McIntyre, "Kooky, the 23 Percent Solution," *New York Times*, January 23, 1998, p. A25.

24. Robert B. Ekelund Jr. and Robert D. Tollison, *Macroeconomics*, Boston: Little, Brown, 1986, pp. 145-148; Richard G. Lipsey, Peter O. Steiner, Douglas D. Purvis, *Macroeconomics*, New York: Harper & Row, 1988, pp. 318, 371-373.

25. Sylvia Nasar, "Unlearning the Lessons of Econ 101," *New York Times*, Week in Review, May 3, 1998, pp. 1, 4.

26. Joint Committee on Taxation, *Estimates of Federal Tax Expenditures for Fiscal Years 1998-2002*, Washington, D.C.: U.S. Government Printing Office, 1997.

27. Katharine Q. Seelye, "Americans Take a Dim View of the Government, Survey Finds," *New York Times*, March 10, 1998, p. A15.

28. David E. Rosenbaum, "Higher Surplus Estimate Stirs G.O.P. Tax Cutters," *New York Times*, July 16, 1998, p. A26.

29. Peter S. Fisher, "The Economic Context of Community-Centered Practice: Markets, Communities, and Social Policy," in *Reinventing Human Services*, Paul Adams and Kristine Nelson, eds., New York: Aldine DeGruyter, 1995, pp. 41-58.

30. Steven Marcus, "Their Brothers' Keepers: An Episode from English History," in *Doing Good: The Limits of Benevolence*, Willard Gaylin, ed., New York: Pantheon, 1978, pp. 65-66.

Examining a Social Welfare Program: Structural Components, Alternative Program Characteristics, and Evaluation

It is a hard thing to be a poor man in any culture, but hardest
to be a poor man in a rich culture.
—Max Lerner[1]

OVERVIEW

What tools does a student need in order to develop a coherent understanding of a social welfare program, some intelligent analysis of its characteristics, and some informed opinion as to its desirability? First, a student needs to know what basic components there are in any social welfare program. Second, he or she needs to know what some of the basic issues are about various ways of organizing social welfare programs and various characteristics that they may possess. Third, a student should have some beginning background in the political, social, and economic context that affects human need and social welfare decisions to meet those needs. Finally, the student needs to know what criteria he or she must apply to any social welfare program in order to evaluate it.

This chapter presents a rigorous schema for understanding and analyzing a given social welfare program. Prepared with this schema for examining the structure of a welfare program, a student can then apply it to a variety of social welfare programs in the United States, both economic security programs and programs that are generally termed the "personal social services." The schema for examining a social welfare program is summarized in Chart 7.1.[2]

CHART 7.1 A Schema for Examining Social Welfare Programs

I. Structural components
   A. What are the needs and goals to be met?
   B. What is the form of benefit that the program produces?
   C. Who is eligible for the program?
   D. How is the program financed?
   E. What is the level of administration?
II. Alternative program characteristics
   A. Residual, institutional, developmental, or socio-economic development
   B. Selective or universal
   C. Benefits in money, service, or utilities
   D. Public or private
   E. Central or local
   F. Lay or professional
III. Evaluating the program
   A. Adequacy
      1. Horizontal
      2. Vertical
   B. Financing
      1. Equitable
      2. Priority use of funds
      3. Efficient: cost and benefit
      4. Cost-benefit analysis
   C. Coherence
   D. Latent consequences

STRUCTURAL COMPONENTS

What Are the Needs and Goals to Be Met?

Social welfare programs, like all other governmental and private programs, are intended to meet certain needs, deal with specific problems, or enhance life. They are implemented to achieve particular goals in relation to needs such as economic security, child care, and health care; to ameliorate such problems as teen pregnancy, homelessness, and substance abuse; to enhance life through such means as education, socialization, and recreation. These goals may be stated or unstated in the legislation, but nevertheless, they are real and influential in determining the nature of the legislation and of the program. The Food Stamp Program, for example, has a stated objective to alleviate hunger and malnutrition by enabling low-income households to purchase a nutritionally adequate diet. It also seeks to expand the market for domestically produced food by supplementing the food-purchasing power of eligible low-income households. Similarly, the School Lunch Program is intended to safeguard the health and well-being of the nation's children and to encourage the consumption of domestic commodities.

Thus, these two programs have the stated goals of alleviating hunger and malnutrition but also of expanding the market for, and consumption of, domestically produced foods. But Food Stamps may not be used for the purchase of alcoholic beverages and tobacco, pet food, and cleaning and paper products, including toilet paper. Implicit in a portion of these restrictions is a moral objective to control the behavior of the recipients.

The stated or unstated goals for particular programs may differ from group to group: Farmers, warehouse workers, teamsters, wholesalers, retailers, salespersons, and those who do business with them all have their own sense of investment in the goals of the program and benefit in different ways as their own individual goals are met by the program.

What Is the Form of Benefit That the Program Produces?

This is simply another way of asking: What does the program produce? For instance, unemployment insurance produces a certain amount of cash income for a certain number of weeks. A family agency might "produce" individual or group counseling, or help in negotiating other social systems. A housing project might "produce" apartments at low cost. The concept is simple enough. Among the first things anyone who examines a social welfare program will want to know is what the benefits are and what form they take. It is important, to begin with, to get a good fix on precisely what the benefits of a given program are so that the program can be understood and evaluated on its own terms. We will see that the form the benefits take is a major issue. Should they be in the form of money such as rent, personal services such as tenant counseling, or the provision of a new social utility such as a housing development? The question of the level of benefit in programs is crucial. Is the level of cash benefit in an economic security program adequate? Is the kind of counseling available in a personal service agency adequate or underadequate or overadequate for the task?

Who Is Eligible for the Program?

Another way of saying this is: What risks of human existence are covered by the program? The concept of covering certain risks of living, or categorical programs, is basic to the Western social welfare system. At least since the English Poor Laws, and probably of necessity in any modern society, there are few agencies that simply provide "help." Even most generalized multiservice centers can offer services, provide information, and make referrals to others only for people within a given geographical area or a certain age range.

Criteria for eligibility are critical. In order to receive food stamps, for example, a person needs to meet federal poverty guidelines. To be eligible for service in a community mental health center, a person must live within a certain district; if not, the person is referred to another community mental health center. To be eligible for Medicare, a person must be above a certain age level, be disabled for a period of time, or have permanent kidney failure. To be eligible for Social Security, among other things, a person must be largely retired from working for wages. To be eligible for day care, a person must be below a certain age. So along with the question of what the benefits or output of a program are, one must ask the companion question: For whom are the benefits? How is eligibility determined? The choices in determining eligibility raise major issues in the characteristics of social welfare programs, as we will see. But if the student knows the answer to the questions of what the benefits are, and who is eligible for the benefits (what class or classes of people are eligible), he or she can get a good beginning understanding of the nature of the program.

Later in this chapter, the issue of *financial equity* will be introduced. Financial (economic) equity means that all individuals who have paid the same amount of money for some good (insurance, mortgage, or some other form of property) are entitled to receive the same amount of benefits. This is the principle of "you get what you pay for."

But equity also has a different meaning in social welfare. In social welfare, *equity* refers to similar cases being treated similarly. The use of criteria of similarity limits the discretion of those in authority and results in like decisions being made in like cases. Equity then in social welfare means that all individuals that are in the same circumstances (income, size of family, age, and so on) are entitled to receive the same social assistance irrespective of what they have contributed to the program or to society financially through taxes. In this case, you receive what you need—a form of social equity.[3]

How Is the Program Financed?

Financing is a crucial component of any social welfare program, and one that can be overlooked by those who are concerned only with the benefits of the program. The availability of the resources, where they come from, and in what proportion they are used are all crucial to what is produced. A social welfare program may be financed by any one or by a combination of sources including the following.

1. *General revenues*. At each level of government—local, state, and national— there are general tax funds collected from income taxes, sales taxes, and the like that go into a general purse. Out of this general purse the legislature allocates monies for various social functions—defense, highways, safety services, and social services. Some social welfare programs are financed completely or partially from such general revenue monies. In discussing financial equity as part of the evaluation of a social welfare program, we will see that whether monies come from general revenues or other sources can make a tremendous difference. The private or voluntary sector often has a rough equivalent of general revenues. In most communities there is a United Way branch that raises money for the social service needs of a whole variety of local agencies such as scouts and family service agencies. These funds become a kind of general revenue source for making allocations to the various member agencies for their own general operations.

2. *Earmarked taxes*. Sometimes the local, state, or national government will develop a special tax or revenue-collecting program, the money from which is earmarked in advance for a special purpose. A federal gasoline tax is an interesting example. Proceeds from this tax are kept in a special trust fund for purposes of transportation. A

state lottery may designate its proceeds for education or the aged. It sometimes makes taxes more palatable if the general public understands that the proceeds from a given tax are going to some agreed-on important purpose. This approach, however, provides for limited flexibility. For instance, there was much argument and litigation about using a transportation trust fund for public transportation as well as for the building of highways. Again, the umbrella funding agencies in the voluntary sector have a mechanism roughly equivalent to the earmarked tax when, in addition to the general fund-raising drive, they may have a special drive for a new building or for a specific local agency. Also, the option is offered to United Way donors to earmark their contributions for specific agencies.

3. *Employer/employee taxes.* A number of social programs are financed by taxes on employees or employers or both. Such programs tend to be for the social insurances. They connote, in some ways, an insurance concept: that a person pays for insurance out of his or her earnings and is thus getting back what was put in when a claim is filed. We will see in our discussion of Social Security that these are not really insurances in that the person who is contributing is not buying benefits with this contribution. But they do have the advantage of creating a sense of personal possession of the right to the benefit on the part of the payee. On the other hand, as we will discuss further under financial equity, these kinds of taxes to finance social programs tend to be regressive. We will be using the terms *progressive*, *regressive*, and *proportional* in describing taxes as introduced in chapter 6.

4. *Payment by the recipient of service.* Many social welfare programs derive at least a portion of their income from payments by the recipients of the services or "user fees." Payment is often on a sliding scale based on ability to pay; those who can do so, pay more. Those with lower incomes pay progressively less. Some services in social welfare are available only to those who can pay an additional fee for those services, such as Part B of Medicare, the supplementary medical insurance program.

5. *Third-party payments* and *purchase of services.* A growing phenomenon on the U.S. social welfare scene has been the financing of services through the purchase of services and third-party payments. This can mean different things. In its simplest form, a governmental unit is mandated or decides to provide a certain social welfare service. It may decide that, rather than create a new social service on its own, it may be more economical to purchase service from an existing institution or social agency or a new one created for that purpose. Thus the state agency that wishes to provide homemaker services may develop a homemaker division of its own or may purchase homemaker services for eligible clients from some voluntary or private for-profit organization. A public agency may pay the cost for placing children in day care or residential treatment rather than create a network of such centers of its own. This is what is generally meant by purchase of service. Although one can see where this might be economical, it is also easy to see where it could be wasteful. It can lead to a lack of accountability (or very expensive policing procedures so that there will be accountability) and opportunities for "sweetheart deals" between private contractors and the government.

Third-party payments usually refer to a more generalized form of this phenomenon. Here there is no plan, intent, or possibility of the social welfare program providing the service directly. The social welfare program itself consists entirely of payment to a "vendor," an external deliverer of services. Medicaid is an example of such a program. A Medicaid recipient goes to a medical facility, and payment may be made directly to the facility by the Medicaid program. There is a problem with such a system, particularly with regard to cost containment. This is because there is little motivation to keep prices down, and costs keep escalating. This escalation of health service system costs in the United States is one of the problems that accompanied the growth of third-party payments as a form of financing health and social welfare programs.

6. *Combinations*. Increasingly, social welfare programs are financed through a combination of some of the previously mentioned methods. A social welfare program or agency may be required to raise some of its own funds through fees. A voluntary agency may be receiving some money from insurance payments, the government, private foundations, the United Way, and individual contributions as well as other sources, some for general purposes and others earmarked. The complexity of financing may affect the efficiency of an agency operation. The time allotted to satisfying the accountability requirements of different grantors may be excessive. In the extreme and not uncommon case, an agency may recast its services, not in terms of the needs of its community, but in terms of the purposes for which funds are available.

To study a social welfare program, it is crucial to know just what the sources of funds are. We will see in examining specific social welfare programs that these questions affect the outcome.

What Is the Level of Administration?

Some programs such as Social Security or Medicare are completely federal or national programs. That is, although there may be offices in each locality, the program is a single one for the entire nation, consistent in its administration and its benefits. Local employees are employees of the national government, and policies are made in Washington, D.C. Other programs are under state, regional, or county auspices.

As with financing, there is a growing trend toward combinations of levels of administration and, particularly, greater emphasis on administration by states. There is a peculiar U.S. institution known as the grant-in-aid, which contributes to this complexity. In a grant-in-aid, one unit makes funds (a grant) available to another level of government or to a voluntary or private agency and allows that unit to administer the program itself, so long as it is in keeping with some general guidelines that are set by the granting agency. Some examples may help to clarify the grant-in-aid concept: The federal government provided 50 percent or more of the cost of public assistance to each state with a public assistance program. In order to receive that money, the state complied with certain regulations that are set down by the federal government when it gives its 50 percent. For example, it had to provide the opportunity for fair hearings or appeals by clients who are found ineligible. The public assistance program is administered on the state and local level, but to the extent that the administration must meet certain guidelines from the federal government, even administration could be viewed as also being federal. In the 1990s, there has been a decision to move away from this long-term format to one in which the states will receive money to operate these programs without federal interference.

And so in developing a basic understanding of a social welfare program, the student of such a program will want to know the following:

1. What are the needs or problems being addressed, and what are the goals of the program?
2. What are the benefits of the program?
3. What are the eligibility requirements for the program?
4. How is the program financed, at what level, or from what combination of sources?
5. How is the program administered, by whom, and at what level of government, or in what combination?

Alternative Program Characteristics

No matter what the basic structure of the social welfare program under study may be, the program may choose among alternative program characteristics. There are different ways in which the program may be organized and different philosophies that it may embody. We will examine some of the alternative program characteristics of social welfare programs.

Residual, Institutional, Developmental, or Socio-Economic Development

Over time social welfare programs tended in their approach to be more or less residual, institutional, or developmental. In recent years, another approach has been introduced and has gained recognition: socio-economic development. The *residual* or minimalist concept of social welfare is based on the premise that an individual's needs should be met through the market economy and through the family. Occasionally, however, individuals are unable to utilize the market system or the family; for example, there is some sort of disruption that hits the market system, such as a recession, or a family faces a crisis. In these cases, the social welfare system comes into play. It is seen as a kind of necessary evil, a backup system for the market and the family. Theoretically, the social welfare system is supposed to withdraw when these institutions of society—the family and the market—can once again function. We see this in the perspective that argues that if society were only properly organized, there would be no need for social work or that the goal of the public assistance system is to do away with itself—get everyone off welfare and into the job market. Few people seriously believe that this is a real possibility, and yet the whole public assistance program is structured as though it were only a necessary evil. Its success is evaluated on the basis of how many people leave the welfare rolls and its failure by how many come on. The residual concept in social welfare leads to the kind of programs in which eligibility is based on proving a need, that is, proving the breakdown of the other normative systems that should be working.

The *institutional* view of programs implies no such breakdown. From this perspective, it is accepted that we live in a complex, difficult environment and social welfare is a legitimate function of modern society. It is assumed, for instance, that when people become elderly they will cease working and may be faced with the problem of a lack of income. Therefore, an institutional structure such as Social Security meets a normal need. Similarly, it is assumed that there will be some industrial accidents. Therefore, Workers' Compensation is set up to meet the risks of working, so that people who are injured can get medical care and some income protection during the period of their absence from employment. The institutional point of view sees social welfare as regularized, permanent, necessary, and a desirable part of the social structure.[4]

What we are calling the *developmental* conception of social welfare moves one step beyond the institutional concept to focus on human development. The institutional view assumes some social problems that a social welfare institution is set up to prevent or correct. The developmental view, however, assumes that all citizens in a modern, complex society may need "a variety of socially provided goods and services to develop their capacity to participate in society and to achieve and maintain a desirable standard of living."[5] It is possible for society to set up a social welfare institution simply to make living better, to improve the quality of life, and to fulfill human development, not necessarily to solve a problem or to aid those in distress.

As an example, in social welfare if day-care services are instituted because certain parents are not yet properly trained or are incapable of taking care of their children as should be the norm, this is a residual concept of day care. If it is assumed that many parents in industrial society will need to work and will need the help of day-care services, this would be the institutional concept. If, on the other hand, a society simply said it would be better for the quality of life if parents in every neighborhood could have a nursery to drop their children off for an hour or two while they were shopping or taking courses or simply for a respite, and the society instituted a network of drop-in nurseries in neighborhoods, this would be a developmental approach to social welfare.

The *socio-economic development* perspective evolved through attempts to harmonize social welfare with efforts directed at economic development. Major interpreters of this perspective are Midgley and Sherraden, who focused on ways in which social welfare can contribute efficiently and effectively to economic development through social investment.

Midgley advocates the socio-economic developmental approach as an alternative to both residual and institutional welfare models because social welfare needs to be linked and contribute positively to economic development. Social development can generate returns on investment and contribute to economic growth by assisting in the mobilization of human capital, providing increased opportunities for productive employment and self-employment among low-income and special needs groups, and through investment in education, childhood nutrition, health care, and skills training.

Sherraden argues for investment that increases present and future productivity through asset development among low-income groups. Incentives and resources should be provided that encourage savings and asset development among the poor so they can accumulate the social investments needed to meet their needs and those of their children. Instead of an emphasis on subsistence income and consumption by poor persons, the focus should be on savings, investment, and accumulation in order to help them become "stakeholders" in society. When persons hold assets and have a stake in the system, they overcome their poverty economically, socially, and psychologically. Among these asset builders are Individual Developmental Accounts (similar to Individual Retirement Accounts) available to everyone in the United States, a universal program, connected to activities that promote individual and national development such as completion of schooling, high school graduation, post-secondary education, housing, self-employment, and retirement, and so on. Subsidized for poor persons and families, the accounts would be tax-favored (tax-deferred or tax-exempt) and could be used only for specified purposes.

The socio-economic development approach suggests that social welfare to one degree or another manages social problems, meets needs, and should provide opportunities for advancement to individuals, families, groups, communities, and even whole societies. Based on the work of the past half-century in developing nations, social development seeks ways that create human and social capital and foster peoples' welfare by simultaneous productive economic activities. Social welfare is thus linked to economic development and policies.[6]

The distinctions made here among the categories are not always that clear; there is no single on or off switch that can differentiate between residual and institutional programs, or institutional, developmental, or socio-economic developmental. It is more a question of the attitude toward the program, the way it was conceived, and what it is intended to do. Nonetheless, this is a rather fundamental issue in social welfare and affects the question of whether people are treated humanely or whether they are stigmatized, and whether a program is starved or encouraged.

There are alternative program characteristics in social welfare programs that are similar to the residual, institutional, and developmental ideas. The view of a social welfare program as a *right* versus a *charity* is one such alternative. The charity concept is very much like the residual concept. Because it is not a basic and permanent part of the system, it is something that society does for people, in a sense, out of the goodness of its heart. To the extent that social welfare is institutional or developmental, it is more like a basic social right of citizens in a given community. In the 1960s, we saw the development of welfare rights organizations, which tried to build on the assumption that entitlement to social welfare programs was as much a right of eligible citizens as the right to vote or to be treated without discrimination. On the other hand, the stigma and other concerns associated with many welfare programs, particularly the residual ones, continue to support the notion that social welfare is a charity.

Several decades ago, a number of Supreme Court decisions underscored public assistance as a right. *Shapiro v. Thompson* (1969) eliminated length-of-time residence requirements from public assistance programs. *Smith v. King* (1969) eliminated the man-in-the home rule and held that the presence of a man not their father living in their residence may not be considered a factor of children's eligibility for assistance because he has no legal responsibility for their support. The Court ruled in *Goldberg v. Kelly* (1969) and *Wheeler v. Montgomery* (1969) that aid cannot be discontinued prior to a hearing on a decision at issue until an evidentiary hearing is held. These Supreme Court rulings clarified the principle that citizens could not be deprived of welfare benefits without due process, at that time a revolutionary concept. Nevertheless, there is a sense of ambivalence around the issue of public assistance and rights.[7]

The history of seeing social welfare programs as a charity has led to evaluation of who is the worthy versus the unworthy poor—that is, who is deserving of the benefits of these special programs. When programs become more institutionalized or developmental, it is difficult to enforce this concept, and the very notion begins to change. For example, recipients of Social Security benefits feel that this is their right.

Another closely related conceptual design is the degree to which a social welfare program is seen as *minimal* or *optimal*. That is, does it seek to provide a basic floor below which no citizen should be expected to fall, or does it try to create an institutional structure that goes beyond the basics and adds to the quality of life? For instance, most income maintenance plans (public assistance or other kinds) attempt to be minimal at best. They establish a floor below which it is impossible to maintain any sort of living standard, and they may bring people up to that level. Beyond that level, it is expected that market mechanisms should take over and should provide for the other amenities of life. On the other hand, certain institutions, such as public libraries, are more institutional or developmental in concept and therefore more optimal than minimal in design. It is simply decided that the social system rather than the profit-making market system should be given responsibility for providing libraries to optimize the quality of life. It certainly goes beyond the minimal. It is also, in a sense, striving for equity in certain areas of life.

In income maintenance, it is not considered necessary or even desirable that everyone should have equal incomes. What is usually seen as desirable is that each person should have a certain minimum income in order to survive. To the extent, though, that tax laws are made more progressive, there is an attempt to provide more equity in society between rich and poor and not simply to provide minimum standards. To the extent that the same fire services are made available to everyone in society despite his or her contribution, such social welfare programs are organized to provide equity rather than minima. Any social welfare program may be designed essentially to provide a floor or minimum, or to provide more equity, or to optimize the quality of life in a given area. This, too, can be seen as another expression of the residual, institutional, and developmental concepts.

In examining or designing social welfare programs, residual, institutional, and developmental concepts need to be considered. They will affect how the program is structured, who is made eligible for it, the nature of the benefits, how it is financed, and so on.

Selective or Universal

A crucial question in any social welfare program is the degree to which that program is selective or universal. Here the definitions are a little more precise. A *selective* program is one in which eligibility is based on a determination of need and the individual financial means of the potential client. A *universal* program is one that is open as a right to anyone who meets certain class, category, or regional criteria. The benefit is provided to all who meet the criteria no matter how high the total cost to the public treasury. If a person has to prove eligibility based on individual financial status, that program is selective no matter how generous the provisions or how broad the coverage. For example, if anyone who is under 3 years of age or over 65 years of age, is a resident of Chicago, is a veteran, or has been laid off is eligible for a program without a test of individual financial means, that program is, by our definition, universal. The difference between the two concepts is crucial. Public assistance, Medicaid, and Food Stamps are all selective programs. Unemployment insurance, Workers' Compensation, Medicare, and Social Security are all universal programs. Somewhere between might be those programs, such as family services and some day-care services, that are open to everyone but on a sliding scale, based on an examination of individual ability to pay.

Universal programs normally provide benefits that are legally due one as a right. They are not based on a means test of one's income or assets. Programs that are residual in their concept, such as Temporary Assistance for Needy Families, will tend to be selective. Programs that are institutional or developmental, such as Social Security, are in concept more likely to be universal. If the program is more institutionally conceived—such as the Social Security system: anyone who is over 65 years of age, meets the criteria, and is not working and earning above a certain amount may receive Social Security no matter how wealthy that person is—the program is universal.

The student should be aware that residual concepts and selectivity go together and institutional concepts and universality go together, although not in perfect step. For instance, in disasters, floods, or earthquakes, programs may be set up that are residual in nature—that is, temporary and necessary because of the breakdown of a system that ordinarily meets people's needs—but may be operated universally—that is, anyone who needs help may avail him- or herself of disaster relief without proving eligibility based on financial need. Student loans and scholarships may be universally available but selective and provided on the basis of financial means tests.

Why should a program be selective or universal? What are the advantages and disadvantages of each? The most obvious advantage of the selective program is limitation on cost. Few programs or societies have all the resources or all the funds to do everything that might be desirable. Therefore, there is a natural tendency to try to limit a program to a specific target population—the one that is most in need. The simplest answer appears to be for a program to be limited to people who meet certain criteria of financial eligibility on an individual basis. This is the heart of the argument for selectivity.

It is also ideological in the feeling that society "should not" pay for services that can be afforded privately. Sometimes no real money difference is involved. For example, if I pay $5 in taxes to help support my poor neighbor for medical services and I pay $5 to my own doctor for my medical services, medical care is costing me $10. If I pay $10 in taxes for medical care that will cover both me and my neighbor, I am paying the same $10. The question becomes, Should only those who are unable to afford private services be subsidized by a state system and should others pay privately, or would it be better for society, for a variety of other reasons, to have one medical care system for all with my $10?

There are other reasons besides the basic financial one for preferring selective programs. For one, there is a fear on the part of some social planners that universal programs are "creamed" by the rich and middle class. That is, when a program is available to all, it is the wealthier and the more sophisticated who have better access to it, who hear about it, and who take advantage of it the best, leaving less for the poor. The public library that is kept quite busy by the middle class may not develop the kind of accessible services to provide reading opportunities for those without means of transportation. It is this fear of "creaming" that causes some people to favor services specifically targeted.

Why, then, might one prefer universal services over selective ones, if they do tend to cost more and if there is the danger of creaming, of not having the services go to the most needy population? There are several reasons many favor universal programs.

First, universal programs limit the sense of being demeaned that goes with an examination of one's income. The idea of being a welfare client still carries a stigma in society. A universal program eliminates this stigma. Anyone in a given category is eligible. There is no scrutinizing of one's individual savings or income.

Second, many have despaired of finding any fair formula by which one can administer a selective program. For instance, let us assume that you and I each earned $30,000 a year for 10 years. At the end of those 10 years, both of us found ourselves without employment or other insurance and turned to welfare. You had saved $1,500 a year of your salary and now had $15,000 in the bank. I had spent all my salary and had nothing but debts, including car loans, credit card debt, and a home. Should I be eligible for welfare and you ineligible because you had saved? Should you be penalized for your thrift? If you say no, what if you had $30,000 or $40,000 or $50,000 in the bank? How does one develop a fair system without trying to legislate public morals? The whole selective system lends itself to a continuation of judgments being made by others of who is the worthy and who is the unworthy poor, a distinction deeply embedded in the English Poor Law tradition.

Third, some persons argue that universal programs help poor persons without stressing that as their major aim. A universal program such as Social Security attracts major support, yet is able to target and assist those who have been lower earners during their lives.

Just as creaming may limit the availability of universal programs to the poor, there are other factors that limit the ability of selective programs to serve the poor. Selective programs have a limited constituency of those financially in need. Because these programs lack broad support from a large constituency, they also tend to lack the legislative power to improve programs and often find their budgets constrained or reduced. Yet universal programs, despite costs, tend to be improved and expanded. They are more difficult to change, and it is quite difficult to reduce their benefits. There are those who believe that programs for the poor tend to become poor programs.

Because of concerns about possible cheating, investigations and roadblocks are set up for recipients of selective programs. For example, recipients of public assistance are frequently recertified. This may lead many of the needy people who would be eligible to not apply. Because selective programs are not easily accessible, many of the poor never find their way onto their rolls. Under the former AFDC program it was estimated that there were as many people eligible for welfare who were not receiving welfare as those who were on the welfare rolls.[8]

Whenever the system is attacked, there are allegations of misuse of funds by ineligible recipients. However, there is also a certain amount of financial waste in selective programs. Although money is not "wasted" on the rich in these programs, there is a great deal of waste that is called *cost inefficiency*, the proportionate cost of a program used in its administration. Selective programs demand much more administrative budget than do universal programs because there need to be procedures for determining eligibility, investigators, checks, and double-checks. The vast universal Social Security retirement system is operated from a single computerized facility and serves its clientele with only a small percentage of the total funds used for administrative purposes (less than 1 percent). Public assistance, by contrast, uses a significant amount of funds (14 percent) in administering its own operation.

The waste in using the money allocated for a program in large measure on administration is called cost inefficiency. The so-called waste in having large amounts of the money go to people who are not needy or not the original targets of having such a program is called *benefit inefficiency*.

Even to the extent that universal programs generally serve those who are not poor, the benefits may go to those who are near poverty. Many social planners would not consider this wasted or benefit inefficient at all. People just above the poverty line may be in need as well as those below the line. This is another reason many planners favor a universal approach to social services.

Universal programs tend to be cohesive factors in U.S. society. Selective programs tend to pit recipients against nonrecipients. So long as I am getting some benefit from a program, I am willing to pay for it, even if you are getting a little bit more benefit from that same program. I am willing to see that program expand and improve. But as long as I am paying for a program for which I am ineligible, I will tend to be unenthusiastic and perhaps resentful of its recipients. Because of this, low- and middle-income persons often are hostile to the poor. Selectivity tends to perpetuate what is only a partial myth: that to get services in the United States one needs to be very rich or very poor.

It has been argued that with new technology the stigma associated with selective programs can be avoided. Each American would have a health credit card. A person would go to a health facility for care and have the card punched on the way out. The poor would get the service without cost and the rich would be billed for the same service. Thus you could have a selective program without the stigma normally attached to selectivity.

This argument does not eliminate the problems of how one determines in a fair way who is eligible and who is ineligible; neither does it deal with the complexity that has grown up in the U.S. welfare system as programs have been added. The more selectivity, the more problems associated with what has been called the *"notch" effect*: As people's incomes rise, they become ineligible for other kinds of selective programs so that their net positions may be worse than before. This is one of the disincentives to work that has been built into the current welfare system. For instance, if a person starts earning more than she had earned before, she might suddenly find herself ineligible for other benefits. Universal programs eliminate this notch disincentive.

Finally, even in terms of cost, if one keeps in mind that there is an input and an output side to the social welfare program equation, the problems of the cost of universal programs can be solved. Tax policies and tax rates can be designed to recover through "clawbacks" whatever portion is deemed desirable for a welfare program for which the rich are eligible. To the extent Social Security income is considered taxable income, those who are wealthy and have other income from stocks and dividends will return a portion of this so-called wasted money to the tax treasuries. Other income tax policies can be formed so that universal programs can be less benefit inefficient.

Theda Skocpol and others, mindful of the political forces that impose limitations on U.S. selective programs aimed specifically at the poverty population, have suggested an expanded use of universal programs to deliver services for the poor. Skocpol points out that from the beginning the Social Security system gave proportionately higher—although never absolutely higher—retirement benefits to formerly lower-income workers. Her argument is that universal policies support the development of coalitions that, in turn, support extension of benefits. Thus, in her view, some universal, cross-class programs may be viewed as having selective features and have the best chance of sustained assistance for the poor while helping families from all social classes. Others have argued that there are political problems with such programs because of their large costs and because the political power of universal programs can be overstated. Further, the political strength of the elderly—a potent group—does not apply to other groups who are not elderly, severely disabled, or do not work or work very little. There is an important distinction made between those who earned their benefits and those who are recipients of "welfare."[9]

There is probably no program characteristic more crucial to social welfare in our society than the question of selectivity and universality. The bias of the authors is toward a universal approach to social welfare. However, readers should be aware of the arguments for and against both types and utilize these concepts as they approach social welfare programs.

Benefits in Money, Services, or Utilities

Under the question of structural components, we have indicated that the nature of benefits is a crucial concern. The nature of a benefit, beside the question of amount, may take several forms. Benefits may come in the form of *money*—cash income or vouchers with which to purchase goods or services. Benefits also may come in the form of *services*—as a concrete service (such as an apartment or a medical exam) or as counseling. Services may take the form of *utilities*—sometimes called amenities. These are universal programs, serving people facing ordinary circumstances, not limited to those who pass a means test. The program—for example, day care, public health, a public library or a park—may charge fees that differ according to an individual's income, as long as the right to the service is not limited to those below a certain specific income level. The form that a social welfare program takes in its service delivery is quite important.

From time to time, there is a strong push away from the provision of services in favor of what has been called an income strategy. Services sometimes can be simply a sophisticated form of victim-blaming or of deciding who is the worthy or unworthy poor. Providing cash in place of services is a rather attractive philosophy in many respects. Social services do have a tradition of being judgmental. This has an appeal consonant with the free-enterprise and marketplace perspective. There is a straightforwardness to the idea of giving eligible people money and then letting them go out into the market and do what they wish with it. In fact, there was an interesting similarity of views on this question between conservatives who believe in a total free-enterprise society and liberals who believe in welfare rights. The former, since they had to accept some welfare program in a society that would not allow its casualties to starve, preferred to put that program in the form of cash (so that the recipients could function in the market) rather than to create governmental services and bureaucracies.

The poor themselves preferred the neatness of an income strategy. Earlier, a potential client for public assistance would meet a worker in the social service system who would become his or her worker, and that worker would determine eligibility, provide the monthly checks, offer counseling, and give whatever other help was supposedly needed to help that client do better budgeting and find a way to more independent living. The objections of the poor were that poverty did not imply any inability in social functioning and that a person should be able to establish eligibility independent of whether he or she needed other forms of assistance. There should, for example, be no presumption that being in poverty is the equivalent of a need for counseling. If they were eligible, they would get financial assistance. Applicants might separately request or be offered other public services, such as family planning and counseling, but one would have nothing to do with the other.

It is not necessarily true that whenever a choice is possible, an income or money strategy is better than a service strategy. It has been suggested that instead of public housing there should be vouchers (cash equivalent) that may be used for housing. Instead of aid to education, the poor should be given vouchers with which to help buy education. In some cases, vouchers may be desirable. In other cases, society as a whole may do a better job of creating a social institution rather than giving people money and sending them into the market.

One can give people money to buy medical services, or one may create a medical clinic. In some cases one may be desirable, in some cases the other, but we would be very cautious about abandoning the concept that social services, counseling or concrete, may be the best form for some social welfare programs. This is particularly true when the social services take the form of a utility or amenity to human life such as child and adult protective services, assistance for crime victims, disaster aid, and services for older persons. The same may be said of fire, park services, and other social services that are not strictly identified as social welfare. The same consideration should be applied to all social welfare services before we decide that an income strategy is the answer to all problems. Even people with adequate incomes may and often do need services.

Public or Private

The *private sector* can be divided into two parts: (1) the *private nonprofit sector* (often called voluntary), such as a philanthropic organization operating with a community board of directors (community members and leaders, philanthropists, and others in a cross-section of responsible people who are not members of its staff), which bears corporate responsibility for the enterprise, rather than by an arm of the government. These are the agencies that provide direct services, advocacy, fund-raising, and planning and coordination services in various communities; and (2) the *private proprietary* organization that is in the business of making a profit but in a social welfare-related area, for example, nursing homes or child care agencies. If the staff delivering services or their relatives serve as officers, it is most likely a proprietary agency. A proprietary agency may show no corporate profit; instead it may pay salaries and benefits to its staff and officers, who also are its owners. The difference between the two types of private agencies is usually in the form of accountability. Both the private nonprofit and the private proprietary sectors are important features of the U.S. social welfare scene. We have introduced this topic briefly here. In chapter 11 we will examine the private sector and its many issues in greater detail.

Central or Local

Another program characteristic is the degree to which any social welfare program is operated or administered on a local as opposed to a state or national level. What is the appropriate level of administration and control for various kinds of programs? Again the United States, because it is a federal society with a background of states' rights, has a peculiar history. In most countries of the world, policies are made much more centrally, even though local offices may exist to administer policy and may even have some discretion in administering policy. However, in the United States, one has a Social Security or Medicare or Veterans Affairs program, which is on a strictly national basis, and public assistance and Medicaid programs, which combine state and local benefits with national support and guidelines, and, for example, a correctional system, which can be local, state, or federal. In general there exists a crazy-quilt pattern for the administration of social welfare services. What are the trends and what is the appropriate level of control for each program?

    During the 1980s, the Reagan administration argued that the federal government was too intrusive and too large and that decision making and administration should devolve to the state level. In the 1990s, the rhetoric of community control is voiced mainly by conservatives who argue that politicians and bureaucrats in Washington are so far removed from the "people" that they do not know what is needed at the state and local levels. According to this view, the more layers of intervention between the people and the decision makers, the more decisions become confused, diluted, or sabotaged. Turning control over to states and localities and away from the federal government becomes a high-priority goal.

What is being overlooked, in fact, is that some of the best social welfare programs in the United States in terms of service to people and efficiency are national, such as the Social Security system. A direct federal program need not have many layers between it and the people it serves. However, the issue may not be efficiency or effectiveness but where power shall rest.

It is hard to see how giving states a blank check increases the responsibility or power of the people over their own decisions. Social workers need to understand community input and community control as vital elements of good social programs, whatever their source. But this is not the same as suggesting that state or local administration is better than federal administration of any given program.

As a result of the struggles of the 1960s, the principle that the recipients or a local community needed to be consulted on a social welfare program envisioned for that community found its way into legislation in all areas related to social welfare. This is a principle that all social workers need to accept. But community input is not community control. For example, community control has at times meant states' rights, white supremacy, and the ability of some groups to dictate what books would be permitted in local libraries and what a school's curriculum will be. Only federal constitutional amendments abolishing slavery and establishing equal protection principles could overcome local attitudes. The problem is how to maintain community participation and neighborhood vitality and activity without sacrificing the rights of minorities. The decision that is made on the local level cannot begin to take the entire public need into account.

Therefore, I elect legislators who represent me and who are supposed to be able to consider the larger picture in making decisions. I may recall or not reelect them if I am unhappy with their decisions. Similarly, in social welfare it is necessary to have a body that can make the overarching decisions about public policy, although, one hopes, without ignoring the input of local communities. How much local input and control are necessary in which kinds of programs are hard decisions that have to be made, issue by issue. Which social welfare program is best administered by the state or federal government or by the local community will also vary based on the nature of the community and program, but there are no pat answers.

In the 1990s, as noted before, there is much talk of shifting responsibility for social welfare from the federal to state levels. There are critical problems with this. First, poverty, recession, and social problems cut across state boundaries. The federal programs of the New Deal (Great Depression) were necessary to provide answers to problems that could not be solved at the level of the states. Second, there are great disparities between states in their fiscal and administrative capacities, in their costs of living, and in their benefits. For example, some states expend several times as much per capita on welfare benefits as do others. The major social problems in the United States of economic security, housing, employment, crime and corrections, and others are not going to be solved by states alone. What is needed are major legislative changes and adjustments in priorities and funding on the national level, in addition to the efforts of states and localities.[10]

Perhaps the greatest genius of the late Martin Luther King Jr. was his ability to merge local and national concerns. He operated on issues of community control and local significance such as voting in Selma, Alabama, and segregated seating on buses in Montgomery. Each of these issues was legitimate on the local level and in its own right, met people's needs, developed local leadership, and had all the assets of community control. But each of them was an orchestrated step toward changing national policies on segregation and voting, which was always kept in mind as the goal and target. It is that broad vision that all of us in social welfare need to maintain even while we work on the state and local level.

Lay or Professional

There are two major senses in which a social welfare program may have more of a lay or professional orientation. On the simplest level, there is the question of who delivers the services. There does not exist the general public acceptance of a body of hard skills that only the professional may apply, as there does with engineering or medical practice, for instance. In fact, social workers themselves believe that there are important roles for citizens to play in human services. Therefore, there is some confusion and often conflict over the appropriate division of labor between lay and professional involvement in social service programs. What kinds of tasks demand professional work skills, what kinds of tasks demand the skills of other allied disciplines, and what kinds of tasks can be performed by community leaders, volunteers, and untrained workers? How these questions are answered will affect the quality, cost, and legitimacy of a given program. There are times when for a specific purpose, such as maintaining contact with an indigenous community for a particular social service program, there may be more reliance placed on lay people, whereas in other situations more emphasis may be placed on professional skills.

In another sense, the question of lay versus professional is the question of control, policy, and decision making. What are the decisions that are legitimately the "people's" decisions in social welfare? What are the decisions that absolutely require professional judgment? For instance, no community board should tell a medical doctor what medicine to prescribe for a certain illness. However, medical doctors ought not make unilaterally the decisions about what kind of national health insurance plan the nation should have. Similarly in social welfare, there are professional judgments that social workers should make and other policy decisions that should be made by community advisory groups or boards of directors. How well a program confronts these issues will often determine its success or failure.

EVALUATING THE PROGRAM

Let us now assume that you have the basic tools for understanding any social welfare program. You understand the nature of the program in terms of the five basic struc-

tural components discussed previously. You also understand the program characteristics, whether it tends to be more residual and selective or more universal and institutional, the degree to which its services are seen as a right or as a charity, and all the
other characteristics that have been discussed thus far. You have also formulated an
opinion as to which characteristics would be most appropriate for a specific program in question. Finally, how will you evaluate whether the program is effective?
On the basis of an understanding of the preceding discussion, the following are some
of the questions that need to be asked about any program in its evaluation.

Adequacy

Is the program adequate to meet the problem for which it was set up? Adequacy has
to be judged on two axes, which we will call horizontal and vertical. On the *horizontal* axis we want to know whether the program reaches the target population.
Let us assume that we are setting up a teenage pregnancy prevention program for a
city of 300,000 people. The services that the program offers may be exemplary in
their quality, may even change people's lives dramatically. But if it is only geared to
serving 10,000 people, if information about its availability does not reach the rest of
the population, or if long waiting lists develop, then the program is horizontally inadequate. It cannot meet the problem for which it was set up. So one basic question
we must ask of any program is whether it has the coverage, capacity, will, resources,
and means of access to cover its target population. The allocations for many programs are based on the assumption that a major percentage of those who might be
eligible will not hear of it, apply for it, or actually participate.

One needs to ask how *vertically* adequate the program is. Is each recipient sufficiently covered? For example, an AIDS prevention program may "reach" in a sense
an entire city of 300,000, but its services may consist only of TV ads. In this case the
coverage for each person served is not adequate and is not of sufficient depth and
substance to effect major changes in people's lives. The program is horizontally adequate but vertically inadequate. Each program needs to be weighed in terms of its adequacy, horizontal and vertical, to see whether it is doing the job it was set up to do.
How many are served? How well is each served?

Financing

There are a number of questions about financing that need to be addressed in the
evaluation of every program.

1. *Is the program equitably financed?* The Social Security system may be a relatively excellent program in terms of the benefits it provides to people, the needs
and risks it covers, and the universality and neatness of its operation. But if it continues to be financed by a regressive tax that draws more heavily on the poor than on
the wealthy, this is a serious shortcoming in the program. One needs to look not
only at the output side but at the input side in order to evaluate a program. There is
little point in redistributing income to the poor on the output side of the program if

this is done by taking money from the poor on the input side of the program. And so the student needs to evaluate how a program is financed and how this needs to be changed to be made more fair, if necessary.

2. *Does this program represent a priority use of funds?* If resources were infinite, this question would not need to be asked. But because resources are finite, every time a dollar is spent on one program there is an *opportunity cost*: the loss of the opportunity to spend that dollar on some other program. Does the particular social welfare program have a high priority in terms of the needs of the community or nation? This is the kind of question about financing that the student needs to ask.

One can observe in Table 7.1 the sources of federal revenues and how they shifted between 1965 and 1995 so that revenues are derived from the same sources with different weightings.

3. *How cost or benefit efficient is the program?* In our earlier discussion we pointed out that all programs lose some resources one way or another. Administrative costs of operating a program will take away some portion of every dollar spent for the program. Money spent on service to those other than the target population can also

TABLE 7.1   Federal Revenues by Source for Selected Years in Nominal Dollars as a Percentage of Gross Domestic Product and Total Revenues. Selected Fiscal Years 1965–1996

	Percent of Revenues	
	1965	**1995**
Individual income	41.8	45.2
Corporate income	21.8	11.8
Social insurance	19.0	35.1
Excise	12.5	3.7
Estate and gift	2.3	1.2
Other	2.6	3.0
	Percent of GDP	
	1965	**1995**
Individual income	7.1	8.8
Corporate income	3.7	2.3
Social insurance	3.2	6.8
Excise	2.1	.7
Estate and gift	.4	.2
Other	.4	.6
Total	16.9	18.8

Note: An excise tax is an indirect tax collected by the federal government on a specific good—gasoline, alcohol, tobacco, and so on.
SOURCE: *Committee on Ways and Means, U.S. House of Representatives, Overview of Entitlement Programs, 1998 Green Book.* Table 1–11. "Federal Revenues by Source for Selected Years in Nominal Dollars, as a Percentage of GDP and Total Revenues, Selected Fiscal Years 1965–96," Washington D.C.: Government Printing Office, 1998, pp. 1365–1366.

be seen as a kind of waste or benefit inefficiency. If a program is set up to distribute funds, for example, but uses 30 percent of the funds for the staff needed to distribute them, this is severely cost inefficient. If a program is set up to do family counseling, but 30 percent of its funds goes for rental of facilities, this is cost inefficient. On the other hand, if a program is set up to serve a particular need of a particular group, and members of other groups use up 30 percent of the service, this is benefit inefficient.

Every program needs to be evaluated in terms of whether its dollar is being spent as well as possible in the delivery of the services to the target population for which the program was set up. It is almost impossible for any program to be 100 percent efficient, but the degree of inefficiency that can be tolerated needs to be part of the evaluation. Universal programs, as has been mentioned, tend to be much more cost efficient because they do not get involved in investigatory bureaucracy. Selective programs may be more benefit efficient in that they limit their eligible beneficiaries more stringently.

4. *Cost-benefit analysis.* A generally accepted mechanism for making evaluations of social programs is referred to as *cost-benefit analysis*, which differs from the cost and benefit efficiency discussed previously. Cost-benefit analysis is a frame of reference for relating costs to program results and attempts to identify the program effects produced by a particular program and the direct and indirect costs. These are then translated into monetary terms—dollars. The ratio of benefits to costs is then supposed to indicate the return society receives from its investment in the program.

Some examples of the kinds of questions one must deal with when considering costs and benefits are the following:

- What are the costs and benefits of inpatient therapy and community-based therapy for adults and children with emotional problems?
- If training or health care is provided for welfare recipients, what benefits and costs result from various approaches? What programs are most cost beneficial in regard to reducing poverty or improving health?
- What are the costs and benefits of returning people to communities from general or mental hospitals prematurely?
- What are the costs and benefits of different methods for dealing with child abuse or ensuring adequate childhood nutrition?

It is possible to overestimate the validity of cost-benefit analysis because many people are somewhat awed by its "economic" and "scientific" aura.[11] It is important to realize that such analyses have their limitations. Among the cautions one must be aware of is the fact that the method involves insisting that dollar costs and benefits must be assigned. However, some benefits are not easily translated into dollar terms. What monetary value should be assigned to enhanced self-esteem? Or, to participation in civic life when one formerly did not? Not everything can be converted into dollars. Both short- and long-term program achievements that depend on forecasting the future must be converted into present-time values. Future forecasting is always prey to uncertainties. Furthermore, it is very difficult to account for all costs or benefits; many can only be approximated.

Despite these limitations, in 1993 Congress enacted the Government Performance and Results Act (GPRA) that requires as of March 31, 2000 all agencies to set performance objectives expressed in *objective, quantifiable, and measurable* form for their programs and to compare and evaluate actual program results with the performance goals.

Coherence

In evaluating a program, a student needs to ask the question: Is this program coherent, that is compatible with other social policies and programs? Very often certain social policies may operate at cross purposes and undermine other social policies and programs. For example, when the government wanted to stimulate the economy in the face of a recession, certain taxes on automobiles were removed to encourage more purchases of cars. One might argue that this social policy to combat recession was not coherent with a social policy to combat pollution. Or, use of tobacco is dealt with as a health risk by one governmental department while it is subsidized through other governmental actions.

Latent Consequences

Programs never exist in a vacuum. As a result of one program, other things happen. Sometimes effects are anticipated and intended; sometimes they are unintentional and actually undermine the program itself, creating new problems.[12] We will see examples of this as we discuss the various social welfare programs. For instance, a jobs-creation program is often seen as a way of stimulating more jobs. As a certain number of people are put back on payrolls and earn incomes, they purchase more, creating the opportunity for still more jobs and a rising economic cycle. This is called a *multiplier effect*; a way in which a small investment in a social program can have consequences that will multiply its effects in the direction desired.

On the other hand, sometimes a latent consequence of a program undermines its very purpose. For example, in the unemployment insurance program, which will be discussed in chapter 9, an incentive was given to employers not to lay off workers. If they fired fewer workers, the insurance rates they paid for unemployment insurance would go down, thus saving them money. It was intended that this would keep employment higher. However, one of the latent consequences was that some employers were reluctant to hire new workers when they were not sure that these people could be kept on. Rather than take the chance of having to fire them later and have their insurance rates go up, the employers did not hire them in the first place. Thus the latent consequence of the program had the precise opposite effect to what was intended. Sometimes latent consequences are neither multipliers nor saboteurs of the program's intent but create new and different problems.

It is important to recognize that programs have both *anticipated* (expected and intended) and *unanticipated* (unpredicted and unintended) consequences. Both anticipated and unanticipated consequences may prove to have either positive or negative impacts. It is important that social programs have "feedback" mechanisms that provide information on their consequences. When dysfunctional (negative) consequences are identified, policy and program planners then have the option of corrective actions.

These are just some of the points to be considered in evaluating any social welfare program. Prepared with this schema of analysis for understanding and evaluation, it should be possible to examine a number of social welfare programs, to understand them much more clearly, and to identify their strengths and limitations.

In the next chapter, we will look at the question of who is a client of social welfare, examine several definitions of poverty, present a profile of those in poverty and the factors associated with poverty, as well as examine income and wealth disparities.

SUMMARY

This chapter has laid out a thoroughgoing schema for analyzing and understanding any social welfare program. It provides the student, or any citizen, with the tools to comprehend the structure and characteristics of the program, as well as to evaluate its effectiveness in delivering the services it claims to offer, in wisely using the funds that support the program, and in its coherence and latent consequences. Later, in chapters 9 and 10, we will apply this schema to a wide variety of social welfare programs currently in place in order to more fully understand their development, contexts, operation, and effectiveness.

QUESTIONS FOR CONSIDERATION

1. Take one social welfare program and identify its five major structural characteristics.
2. Ideally would you make all social welfare programs institutional, developmental, selective, or residual?
3. Since cost-benefit analysis translates the "bottom line" into dollars, do you think that is an acceptable way to evaluate all social welfare programs?
4. Can you identify some conflicting social policies and social programs in the United States?

NOTES

1. Max Lerner, *America as a Civilization*, New York: Simon & Schuster, 1957, p. 339.
2. The authors assume responsibility for the model that follows. It should be noted that it is, however, drawn from the schema developed by Eveline Burns in her writings and teaching.
3. John Rawls, *A Theory of Justice*, Cambridge, Mass.: Harvard University Press, 1971, pp. 237-238.
4. Harold L. Wilensky and Charles Lebeaux, *Industrial Society and Social Welfare*, New York: Russell Sage Foundation, 1958, pp. 139-140.
5. Alfred J. Kahn, "Therapy, Prevention and Developmental Provision: A Social Work Strategy," *Public Health Concepts in Social Work Education*, New York: CSWE in cooperation with the Public Health Service, Department of Health, Education, and Welfare, 1962, pp. 132-148.

6. James Midgley, *Social Development: The Developmental Perspective in Social Welfare*, Thousand Oaks: Sage Publications, 1995; James Midgley, "Toward a Developmental Model of Social Policy: Relevance of the Third World Experience," *Journal of Sociology and Social Welfare* 23, No. 1, 1996, pp. 59–74; Michael Sherraden, "Administrative Lessons from the Civilian Conservation Corps (1933-1942)," *Administration in Social Work*, 9 (2), 1985, pp. 85–97; Michael Sherraden, *Assets and the Poor*, Armonk, N.Y.: Sharpe, Inc., 1991.

7. Social workers and other citizens should know that professional social workers refused to make surprise "raids" on clients' homes, visits usually intended to see if a man was living in the home of a welfare mother. With the help of the profession, a social worker, Benny Parrish, was upheld by the courts in his right to refuse this unprofessional duty. *Benny Max Parrish v. The Civil Service Commission of the County of Alameda*, State of California, District Court of Appeal, 1 Civil No. 22556, San Francisco: Pernau-Walsh Printing Co., 1965.

8. See Committee on Ways and Means, U.S. House of Representatives, *Overview of Entitlement Programs, 1994 Green Book, Background Material and Data on Programs within the Jurisdiction of the Committee on Ways and Means*, Washington, D.C.: U.S. Government Printing Office, 1994, p. 399.

9. Theda Skocpol, "Targeting within Universalism," Christopher Jencks and Paul E. Peterson, eds., *The Urban Underclass*, Washington, D.C.: Brookings Institution, 1991, pp. 411–436.

10. Alan Brinkley, "Big Government Is a Check," *New York Times Magazine*, August 18, 1996, p. 37, and Kathleen Sullivan, "In Defense of Federal Power: The States Are Not Strong Enough," *New York Times Magazine*, August 18, 1996, p. 36.

11. Peter H. Rossi and Howard E. Freeman, *Evaluation: A Systematic Approach*, Newbury Park, Calif.: Sage Publications, 1993; Evert Vedung, *Public Policy and Program Evaluation*, New Brunswick: Transaction Publishers, 1997.

12. Nathan Glazer, "The Limits of Social Policy," *The Limits of Social Policy*, Cambridge, Mass.: Harvard University Press, 1988, pp. 51–58.

The Welfare Society and Its Clients

It's no shame to be poor, but it's no great honor either.
—Fiddler on the Roof

Wealth is well known to be a great comforter.
—Plato, The Republic

OVERVIEW

In this chapter, we will answer the question as to who is a client of social welfare, present various definitions of poverty, and then give primary attention to a profile of those in poverty and the factors associated with poverty. We also examine income and wealth inequality in the United States and suggest the major means for dealing with the problem of poverty. Finally, we will present the current dominant philosophy regarding social welfare as reflected in the United States during the late 1990s.

In chapters 9 and 10, we turn to an examination of the specifics of major programs, reflecting the relationship of values, ideology, political decision making, and social policy.

WHO IS A CLIENT OF SOCIAL WELFARE?

As discussed earlier, definitions of social welfare differ. Given a very narrow definition, one could conclude that only those who are public asssistance recipients are on "welfare." Given broader definitions of social welfare and looking at the many nonmarket functions that serve most citizens, we see that we are all clients of the welfare society.

For example, a U.S. senator offered the following scenario about one family illustrating the omnipresence of social welfare programs in people's lives. A veteran returning from service went to college on the GI Bill; bought his house with a Federal Housing Administration loan; saw his children born in a Veterans Administration hospital; started a business with a Small Business Administration loan; got electricity from the Tennessee Valley Authority; and, later, water from an Environmental Protection Agency project. His parents retired to a farm on Social Security; got electricity from the Rural Electrification Administration; and used soil testing from the U.S. Department of Agriculture. When the father became ill, the family was saved from financial ruin by Medicare and a life was saved with a drug developed through the National Institutes for Health. His children participated in the school lunch program, learned physics from teachers trained in the National Science Foundation program, and went through college with guaranteed student loans. He drove to work on the interstate and moored his boat in a channel dredged by army engineers. When floods hit, he took Amtrak to Washington to apply for disaster relief and then spent some time in the Smithsonian museums.[1]

Social welfare is pervasive throughout the breadth of the "welfare" society. According to Richard Titmuss, all collective interventions to meet certain needs of the individual and/or to serve the wider interests of society can be broadly grouped into three major categories of welfare: *social welfare*, *fiscal welfare*, and *occupational welfare*.[2] Welfare then may be found in diverse locations, including tax deductions or credits, employer-subsidized health programs, as well as Social Security and unemployment insurance.

The income tax system serves as one major *fiscal welfare* vehicle through which the government develops social welfare programs. Whether the government gives a person money (for example, the Temporary Assistance to Needy Families program [TANF]) or permits a particular tax deduction, the effect is the same: a transfer of funds to people for some socially determined good. Contributions to voluntary social agencies, for instance, are tax deductible. Such support is really another method for the government to support social welfare programs and voluntarism. But there are other ways in which the tax system functions as a welfare system. When a corporation or individual deducts given sums from taxes owed, these sums—because they are not to be paid and are retained by the taxpayer or corporation—are in reality "tax expenditures." That is, the retained monies are really payments to the persons or corporations.

Some observers have suggested that in the United States we have capitalism for the poor and socialism for the rich.[3] Just as social welfare guards against certain risks, there are those who believe that society has been more ready to share risks for large businesses than for individuals. The larger the business, the greater the protection afforded. Big businesses may be able to write off losses or be bailed out through government guarantees. Direct and indirect subsidies have helped large business. In this way, U.S. society has demonstrated greater generosity to the business enterprises than to salaried employees, who ultimately depend in many cases on their social insurances and public assistance.

Occupational welfare is generally associated with having employment. For example, if you are employed, you and your family may be the recipients of insurance benefits that cover health and hospital care, disability, retirement, dental work, and perhaps legal bills. In this way, to varying degrees, employment and occupations also serve as means for distributing welfare benefits, but only to those who are employed or their dependents.

We can see that social, fiscal, and occupational welfare systems are widespread throughout our society. Most people, if not all, are served by these different but functionally similar systems. All of the social welfare services described in this book, both economic security programs and personal social services, are forms of welfare. Many of these services (from social security to mental health programs) serve Americans of all classes. We are all "welfare clients" in one way or another. The issues are simply who benefits and to what degree from each program.

Still our concern here is primarily with the poor and the disadvantaged, and so we want to focus in large measure on the programs for alleviation of poverty in the United States, even while we recognize the universal nature of welfare in its several guises.

√ WHAT IS POVERTY?

There are different perspectives, complexities, and problems associated with the concept and definition of poverty. However, for our purposes, poverty is economic deprivation, a lack of economic resources by which to obtain the goods and services necessary for a minimally adequate standard of living. There are several ways in which poverty is defined. Basically, they fit into these three categories: (1) Poverty means a person or family has less than an objectively defined minimum; (2) They have less than others in society; or (3) They feel they do not have enough to get along.[4] Decisions about the choice of definition to be used are made on pragmatic grounds (What data is available?), political grounds (Which groups favor one definition or another?), and historical grounds (What has been our experience with particular definitions?).

Absolute Poverty

One way of defining poverty is to draw a clear poverty line, a dollar figure, and suggest that this absolute level represents an "objective" minimum. Below the established minimum, one is poor; above it, one is not poor. The poverty threshold is established for income and size of family. In 1997, the poverty line for a four-person family was $16,050 (except for Alaska and Hawaii). Such a line indicates that every four-person family below the line is in poverty, and every family of the same size whose income is greater is above the poverty level. For example, in 1996, using absolute thresholds, there were 36.5 million poor persons, representing 13.7 percent of the U.S. population.

The poverty standard most used is the index originated at the Social Security Administration by Mollie Orshansky, a Labor Department economist, in 1964. Now calculated by the Census Bureau, it became the official federal definition of poverty thresholds for statistical use. This index was based on earlier data that found that American families of three or more persons spent approximately one-third of their income on food and another survey that outlined the cost of a minimal subsistence budget (the economy food plan). The index used an estimate of the least costly economy food plan—a temporary, low-budget, nutritionally adequate diet—and multiplied the cost by three. A slightly different ratio was used for two-person families and for individuals. Originally, the thresholds were computed for households of different sizes, sex of the family head, ages of individuals, and whether the family lived on a farm. Adjustments for the sex of the family head and farm or nonfarm residence were abolished in 1981. Because it only involves considering money income, the index does not reflect noncash benefits such as Food Stamps, Medicaid, and public housing. It does include cash benefits such as Social Security and unemployment insurance. The threshold is adjusted for inflation every year in relation to the Consumer Price Index (CPI). In addition to the Census Bureau's threshold, a simplified version is derived by the Department of Health and Human Services and used for administrative purposes—for example, as an eligibility criterion for federal programs.

In addition to the impact these statistics have in regard to social welfare benefits directly, they affect many financial decisions, from monetary policy and the federal budget to buying a new house and expanding a business, from Social Security payments to union wage increases and individual tax brackets. The quality and accuracy of these critical governmental statistics have been criticized, just as government in general has been. A panel of economists appointed by the Senate reported that inflation as reflected in the CPI may be overstated by more than 1 percent. Much is at stake in defining the CPI, and a debate continues among legislators, administration officials, economists, and the Bureau of Labor Statistics to seek a consensus for action. Many experts counseled caution in considering revisions because of the value, technological, and political ramifications of decisions in this area. Projected changes could save $500 billion over ten years without forcing a single vote on spending hikes or tax hikes. Among the options are: legislation altering the CPI, leaving it unchanged, or leaving it unchanged but subtracting .5 percent from each published index figure and then using the lower figure to determine federal benefits and tax brackets.[5]

The efficiency of such standards lies in their ability to make possible comparisons over time. If we state that 22.4 percent of the population was in poverty in 1959 and 13.7 percent was in poverty in 1996, we have a basis for comparison over time. Even if we argue that the poverty line, as defined, is inadequate, there is a certain neatness in the concept of defining poverty as being anything below x dollars of income per year.

There are several limitations to this poverty line concept. The identification of progress in combating poverty can be deceptive. When there is dramatic change such as the reduction of the poverty population from 22 percent in 1959 to 12 percent in 1969, we know there has been progress. Such changes can make clearer whether there has been progress or retrogression. But even here, our estimate of the extent of poverty may be faulty. One has to place poverty into a context.

The poverty line excludes the near-poor and may give a deceptive picture of the population. Another limitation is that definitions do not include wealth or assets. There is a vast difference between two elderly people, each receiving $400 per month in Social Security benefits, if one owns a home free and clear while the other does not. Further, personal needs may differ according to such factors as disabilities, illnesses, and special dietary needs.

A further limitation of such an income-only–based poverty level, as noted before, is that it counts only cash received (including governmental cash benefits) but does not include in-kind assistance such as food or medical assistance. Government spending on noncash benefits has increased more rapidly than spending on means-tested cash benefits over the years. These omissions are serious, and as a result, questions can be raised as to the validity of the definition being used.

In considering definitions of poverty, one must ask questions such as: What are the new consumption patterns and what is "necessary" for people today? What goods and services are available today that were not available when the index was created? What proportions of income are needed for life's necessities? It is clear that in recent years, Americans have needed to spend much larger percentages of their income on housing and child care than on food.[6] Which is the fairest measurement of the number of poor persons? What should be included in the contemporary "market-basket"? What impact should a generally improving standard of living have on defining poverty? An accurate and fair count matters because our society needs to know realistically how many poor persons there are, who they are, and where they live. These facts tell us much about how our economy is performing and the nature of our society. Knowledge of the dimensions of poverty is one of the bases upon which arguments can be made either for or against governmental intervention.

In 1995, a panel of experts formed by the National Academy of Sciences at the behest of Congress recommended that the poverty threshold represent a budget based on disposable income (that is, the amount left after a family pays taxes and essential expenses such as for food, clothing, shelter, transportation to work, child care, and health care). The budget also includes a small additional amount to allow for other expenses such as household and personal care and transportation unrelated to work. According to the proposal, the family's cash income would be counted as well as noncash government benefits like Food Stamps, housing assistance, school lunches, and home energy assistance. Inclusion of these items would increase family income.

The panel recommended that the poverty threshold be based on actual consumer expenditures over the three previous years. Also, the poverty level would be adjusted to reflect the needs of different types of families and to reflect regional differences in living costs. Family resources, according to this proposal, would be the sum of money income from all sources together with the value of money equivalents, such as Food Stamps, that can be used to buy goods and services, minus expenses. These latter expenses include income and payroll taxes, child care and other work-related expenses, child-support payments to another household, and out-of-pocket medical care costs, including health insurance premiums. This new poverty threshold would be updated every year and would assume children need fewer resources than adults. The suggested new index would include families (including cohabiting couples) and unrelated individuals sharing a household.[7]

The Bureau of the Census and the Bureau of Labor Statistics "experimented" with the suggested new index by studying the years 1989–1994 using the recommended new poverty threshold. The poverty rates followed trends similar to the official poverty measure, differences among subgroups were stable over time, and the poverty population looked more like the total population in terms of demographic and socioeconomic characteristics. The poor were more likely to be white, to be married, and to have a family member in the workforce.[8]

Actually changing the measure of poverty is extremely complex and difficult. The poverty index is integral to both federal and state governmental activities (and in certain cases those of the private sector). In addition to the potential impact on various governmental agencies, there is uncertainty about the public reaction if it were found there are many more or many fewer poor persons. Further, resources distributed to states are often based on the number of poor people in the various states, individuals and families are deemed eligible or not for benefits based on how they are classified, and various societal groups will be affected differentially. All of this suggests the political difficulty of altering the poverty definition.

Some advocates for the poor postulate that the only problem of those in poverty is lack of money. They suggest that no theories or experts are needed, just an adequate annual income. But no matter what is established in any society as the income floor, there will still be relative inequality. The new floor becomes, in effect, the poverty line. Still, defining poverty as some amount under x dollars per year gives us a handle on poverty and suggests ways of combating it.

Relative Poverty

Some people have suggested the utilization of other thresholds that better indicate the standing of poor people in our society. In 1997, the poverty level for a family of four was $16,050. Would a better indicator of poverty be to define four-person families as poor if they had less than 50 percent of the median U.S. family income? In 1996, the median family household income was $43,082, 50 percent of which is $21,541. This figure is $5,941 more than the 1996 poverty level.

There are those who argue that such a relative threshold, by being tied to some average income level, would be a better indicator of who is poor in our society. Others suggest the costs of implementing such a threshold would prove too great. The value of a relative indicator is that it places the poor in relation to other members of our society and is more suggestive of where poor persons stand at a particular time in a certain context.

Peter Townsend proposed a "deprivation" index and argues that money is an inadequate measure of poverty and does not demonstrate what people need. Those who are poor lack certain commodities that are common in the society in which one lives. This definition is based on the concept of *relative deprivation*. His suggestion is that it is necessary to raise the poverty level to a point that allows people to live a basic civilized existence. Disabled people need more, as do families with children. This argument raises questions such as: Should poor children be able to have birthday parties? Should a poor family be able to afford a car or VCR? Should a poor parent be able to have a vacation? According to this view, the relationship of poor persons to their families and neighbors and the common experiences in their communities, and not money alone, is crucial. There is a point at which, without access to these basic existence activities, one is in a state of deprivation.[9]

Subjective Poverty

There is another way of defining poverty, which uses a subjective strategy. This measure does not provide a cutoff line prepared on the basis of the statistical data per se. Instead, the subjective measure uses the assessments of household members as to the "just sufficient" dollar amounts of income needed, in their estimation, by people like themselves to get along. If they have less than their estimate, they are said to be poor. Or, one can ask people what they consider to be their basic needs and let them specify how much they need to meet those basic necessities: What do they see as a minimally adequate or decent level of living? For example, a three-person family can be asked, "What is the smallest amount of money you believe necessary to get along in this community?" This approach suggests that instead of politicians or experts determining the needs of community members, the people likely to be affected should offer their views of what they consider to be a minimally adequate income level.[10]

A DESCRIPTION OF THE POOR

When you are poor in the United States, you are poor in one of the wealthiest nations on earth. Poverty in the United States is often hidden from the eyes of the middle and upper classes. But wealth and luxury are not hidden from the eyes of the poor, who see in movies and on television how the "good life" is lived. Moreover, no matter the odds, the societal expectation is that adequate people should be able to find adequate income. The following discussion uses the U.S. Bureau of the Census poverty threshold, an absolute measure, which is increased each year by the same percentage as the CPI.

As Table 8.1 illustrates, in 1996 there were 36.5 million poor persons in the United States. This represents 13.7 percent of all Americans, or almost one out of every seven persons. The poverty threshold for a four-person family in 1996 was $15,600, or 44 percent of the median income $43,082. Thus, the median family household income in the United States that same year was more than two and three fourths times the poverty level for a four-person family household.

In Table 8.2 we observe the numbers of poor people in various groupings. Of the 36.5 million poor in 1996, the majority lived in metropolitan areas, including more than 15 million who lived inside central cities. Although every group includes poor persons, one can observe that there were 14.5 million poor children under 18 years of age and 5.3 million children under 6 years of age (one in four) living in poor families, many of whom lived in families headed by the 4.2 million female householders with no spouses present.

We can focus directly on the well-being of people with lowest incomes by examining the poverty rate. Throughout the 1960s and the early 1970s, the poverty rate fell dramatically, from more than 22 percent to just over 11 percent in 1973. Re-

TABLE 8.1   Selected Median Household Income (1996)

1996	
36.5 million poor persons; 13.7 percent of the population	
Poverty threshold, family of four	$15,600
All households	$35,492
U.S. median family household income	$43,082
U.S. median nonfamily household income	$20,973
Married couple families	$49,858
Male householder, no wife present	$35,658
Female householder, no husband present	$21,564
75 years and older	$15,995
All white households	$37,161
All white married couple families	$50,302
White male householder, no wife	$36,938
White female householder, no husband	$24,375
White, 75 and older	$16,402
All African American households	$23,482
African American married couple families	$42,069
African American male householder, no wife	$30,995
African American female householder, no husband	$16,256
African American 75 and older	$12,102
*All Latino households**	$24,906
Latino family households	$27,152
Latino married couple families	$32,379
Latino male householder, no wife	$28,322
Latino female householder, no husband	$14,535
Latino 75 and older	$11,337
Asian and Pacific Islander family income	$46,356
Native American family income (1990)	$21,619

* Government studies use the term "Hispanics." We use the more contemporary term, "Latinos." Persons of Latino origin may be of any race. The Latino population in 1996 was estimated to be 28.3 million. Included are those with the following backgrounds: Mexican, Puerto Rican, Cuban, Central and South American, and others, including persons who are from Spain or describe themselves as Hispanic, Spanish, Latino, and so on.

SOURCE: U.S. Bureau of the Census, Current Population Reports, Series P-60–197, *Money Income in the United States: 1996*, U.S. Government Printing Office, Washington, D.C., 1997, pp. 1–4. U.S. Bureau of the Census, *Statistical Abstract of the United States: 1997* (117th Edition), "Social and Economic Characteristics of the Asian and Pacific Islander Population: 1990 and 1996," U.S. Government Printing Office, Washington, D.C., p. 50; Ibid., "Social and Economic Characteristics of the American Indian Population: 1990," p. 51.

maining low through the 1970s, the poverty rate fluctuated little during that decade. In the 1980s, the poverty rate rose dramatically, and only fell below 13 percent in 1989.

In Table 8.3, we observe that groups experience poverty at different rates. We note that all poor persons constituted 13.7 percent of the total population. But the differential rates among groups form a pattern: 8.6 percent (1 in 11) of all white persons; 20.5 percent of children under 18 years of age; more than 29 percent of Latinos

TABLE 8.2   The Number of Poor Persons, Families, and Unrelated Individuals (1996)

Population Group	U.S. Population (in Millions)
All persons	36.5
In metropolitan areas	28.2
White	24.6
Inside central cities	15.6
Children under 18 years	14.5
South	14.1
Outside central cities	12.6
African American	9.7
West	9.2
Latino	8.7
Unrelated individuals	8.5
Outside metropolitan areas	8.3
All families	7.8
Midwest	6.7
Northeast	6.6
Children under 6 years in families	5.3
Female householder, no spouse present	4.2
Persons 65 and over	3.4
Married-couple families	3.0
Asian and Pacific Islander persons	1.4
Native American persons	.6

SOURCE: Leatha Lamison-White, U.S. Bureau of the Census Current Population Reports, Series P60–198, *Poverty in the United States: 1996*, U.S. Government Printing Office, Washington, D.C., 1997; U.S. Bureau of the Census, "Social and Economic Characteristics of the American Indian Population: 1990," *Statistical Abstract of the United States: 1997 (117th Edition),* Washington, D.C., 1997, p. 51.

and 28.4 percent of African Americans (the poverty rate of Latinos surpassed that of African Americans for the first time in 1995); 43.7 percent of all African American female householders with no husband present. Similarly, more than 50 percent of Latino female householders without spouses are poor. However, almost 53 percent of children under 18 in female householder families are poor. It is important to note the various ratios among groups. For example, only 5.6 percent of married couples are poor, whereas 32.6 percent of female householders are poor. Latino and African American female householders are poor at respectively nine or ten times the poverty rate for married couples. One can observe other such relationships.

One can see in Tables 8.2 and 8.3 some of the important variables associated with poverty, and comparisons among groupings can be made. Taking the white poverty rate of 8.6 percent as the basis for comparison, one can see that almost 21 percent of all persons under 18 years of age were poor (one in five children). There are 14.5 million poor persons under 18 years, 4.2 million poor female householders without spouses, and 3.4 million poor persons 65 and older—just over 22 million poor persons. Thus, 60 percent of the poor can be found in those three categories.

TABLE 8.3   Poverty Rates for Selected Groups (1996)

Population Group	Poverty Rate (%)
All persons	13.7
In families	12.2
Related children under 18	19.8
Related children under 6	22.7
White	11.2
African American	28.4
Asian and Pacific Islander	14.6
Latino	29.4
Native American	31.2
Under 18	20.5
65 years and older	10.8
18 to 24 years	17.9
South	15.1
West	15.4
Inside central cities	19.6
Outside metropolitan areas	15.9
White families	11.0
African American families	26.1
Asian and Pacific Islander families	12.4
Latino families	26.4
Native American families	27.2
Female householder, no husband	32.6
White	27.3
African American	43.7
Latino	50.9
Children under 18 in female householder families, no spouse present,	52.9
Native Americans (1990)	31.2
All Latino persons	29.4
All African-American persons	28.4
Latino families	26.4
African-American families	26.1
No high school diploma (1995)	24.1
Children under 18 years	20.5
Inside central cities	19.6
South	15.1
West	15.4
Asian and Pacific Islanders	14.5
All persons	13.7
Asians and Pacific families	12.7
Northeast	12.7
All families	11.0
Persons 65 years and over	10.8

TABLE 8.3   Poverty Rates for Selected Groups (1996) *(cont.)*

Population Group	Poverty Rate (%)
Midwest	10.7
African-American married couples	9.1
Married couple	5.6
White married couple	5.1
BA or more (1995)	2.4

SOURCE: Leatha Lamison-White, U.S. Bureau of the Census, Current Population Reports, Series P60–198, *Poverty in the United States: 1996*, U.S. Government Printing Office, Washington, D.C., 1997; U.S. Bureau of the Census, "Social and Economic Characteristics of the American Indian Population: 1990," *Statistical Abstract of the United States: 1997* (117th Edition), Washington, D.C., 1997, p. 51; Bureau of the Census, *Statistical Abstract of the United States: 1995*, 115th edition, Washington, D.C., 1995, p. 484; Ibid., "Families Below Poverty Level, by Selected Characteristics: 1995," p. 479.

Until 1974, the poverty rate for the elderly exceeded that for children. However, since then, the poverty rate for children has been higher than for any other age group, particularly so for those younger than six. These configurations reflect how vulnerable women of any age and children are to poverty. There are strong suggestions that insecure employment and low earnings for fathers are important determinants of childhood poverty because of their direct effect on family income and because of their indirect effect through the rise of mother-only families. Mothers' employment, in turn, contributes to the poverty of children through the income mothers bring into the home and indirectly through facilitation of separation and divorce.[11] But this vulnerability is not limited to those children raised in single-parent families.

Most Americans experience significant fluctuations in their economic well-being on a regular basis. About three-fourths of the population experience their economic well-being go up or down by at least 5 percent from one year to the next. These fluctuations result from changes in living arrangements, program participation, work status, or other circumstances.[12]

Thus, your chances of being poor differ by personal characteristics (minority status, age, sex), family composition (married, female householder, single person), place of residence (central cities or rural areas, region in the United States), education (less than high school education completed), as well as employment and types of employment, among other factors. Some major groups overrepresented among the poor are persons in families with a female head of household, children under 18 years of age (and especially very young children), African Americans, and Latinos. Trends confirm earlier predictions that by the year 2000 the poverty population will be composed primarily of women and their children.

One serious misconception about the poor is the belief they do not work. In fact, the poor work more than is generally believed. Employment plays an important part in determining whether or not one is living at the poverty level, but employment does not explain everything. In 1996, 660,000 householders worked 50 weeks or more at full-time jobs and earned less than $10,000 (more than 25 percent earned less than $5,000).[13] The implication of these figures is that many jobs pay less than is needed to lift families out of poverty.

In 1996 some 15.8 million persons between the ages of 25 and 54 years neither worked nor looked for work at any time during the year. Of these, three out of four were women taking care of home or family (70 percent), ill or disabled (20 percent), or in school (5 percent). The reasons for unemployment for men contrasts with those of women. Of the 4 million men of those same ages who neither worked nor looked for work, 8 percent were taking care of family or home and 63 percent were either ill or disabled.[14]

For those who lack education and skills, employment opportunities are difficult to find. Manufacturing jobs have grown scarcer. Technology is used in place of people where possible. Where potential jobs exist in the service area, they are usually lower-paying and without benefits such as health insurance and pensions. Furthermore, technology has begun to affect the service sector as well. Another phenomenon affects employment opportunities: A "contingent workforce" has developed. These persons have no direct ties to a corporation. They are part-timers, temporary full-timers, and contract workers. Twenty-five percent of the nation's workforce is in this category.[15] But poverty is not simply a matter of unemployment or underemployment. In 1996, the median earnings for year-round, full-time employed males was $32,144, whereas the median income for year-round, full-time employed females was $23,710.[16] Thus, the average woman working full-time and year-round earned a median money income that was only three-fourths of that of a man working in the same pattern. This ratio, while up from 60 percent since 1980, indicates that there is still a significant gap between the earnings of men and women and, in fact, may be more related to slow earnings growth for men rather than advances by women.

Tables 8.2 and 8.3 indicate various factors associated with poverty. One's chances of being poor are compounded by the interplay and effects of multiple risk factors. When several factors are considered in combination, the risk of poverty soars. Consider that in 1996, 13.7 percent of all persons, more than 29 percent of Latinos, and 28.4 percent of African Americans were poor; but 43.7 percent of all African-American families with a female householder, no spouse present, were poor. Thus, race, age, single parenthood, and number of children, among other factors, compound the risk.

When poverty data were reported for 1997, they reflected three consecutive years of growth in income that restored household incomes and poverty to the pre-recession 1989 levels. Even with a booming economy and low unemployment, the poverty rate for the population decreased only .4 percent. This decline in the overall poverty rate was mainly due to decreased (but still high) poverty experienced by African Americans and Latinos. The poverty rate for African Americans was the lowest since the government began collecting such data in 1959. Income grew even for families headed by women. The poverty rate for children was under 20 percent for the first time since 1989. However, for households headed by persons from 35 to 54, income did not keep pace with inflation, so real income for them was lower than in 1989. The poverty threshold for a family of four was $16,400 ($12,802 for a family of three). Median household income, after adjusting for inflation, rose to $37,005.[17]

We turn now to how income and wealth are distributed in the United States. This will help us better understand the context in which one is poor in this nation.

INCOME AND WEALTH INEQUALITY

Poverty also can be approached from another perspective. Statisticians use two common methods to measure the degree of inequality. The *Gini coefficient* or *ratio* is expressed as a scale running from 0 to 1 on which 0 signifies perfect equality (everyone has the same income) and 1 indicates extreme inequality (one person or group has all income). In 1996, the Gini index was 0.455. The other method looks at the share of total income earned by various percentiles. In this case, one examines the total income of the nation to see how much of it went to the poorest 10 or 20 percent of the population and how much went to the richest 10 or 20 percent. Either method can indicate over time whether there is progress in sharing the wealth more equitably. We will look at the respective shares of income and wealth for groups.

Not income alone, but wealth is an important factor. In general, the term *income* refers to the amount of money received in any one year before taxes. *Wealth* usually means property and assets that have market value and can be exchanged for money or goods. Complex definitional issues abound about these two terms, depending on the purposes of the definitions. As many as seventeen alternative measures of income are being tested by the Bureau of the Census, and additional measures have been proposed in an attempt to gauge noncash government benefits such as medical and child care and taxes on income and poverty.[18] In regard to income, should in-kind income or services be included? Should a definition of income include money spent on taxes, home production of food or clothing, employee fringe benefits, or expenses required to earn income? Wealth may be in the form of assets of many kinds such as stocks, bonds, annuities, businesses and industries, housing, insurance, trust funds, personal or corporate properties, and so on. Should personal skills or personal contacts be considered forms of wealth? Licenses and credentials?

Income inequality in the United States remained fairly stable for several decades, but in 1996 the gap between rich and poor households reached the widest point recorded since the 1930s. One can observe in Table 8.4 that in 1972, the poorest one-fifth of U.S. households received 4.1 percent of national income; the top one-fifth received 43.9 percent. By 1996, the income received by the lowest one-fifth decreased to 3.7 percent; and the richest one-fifth received 49.0 percent of the country's total net income. The top 5 percent received 17 percent in 1972 and just over one-fifth of income in 1996. In 1996 the top 40% of households accounted for almost three fourths of all income.

Income and its distribution are intricately tied to structural factors and cannot be separated from social and economic trends, including those on the international level. Possible sources of income disparities are changes taking place in the nation's labor market, the slowdown in real earnings growth, a shift from goods production (where wages have also been reduced) to service production, and widespread low-wage, nonunionized jobs. Although higher wages have been available for highly

TABLE 8.4   Shares of Aggregate Income Received by Each Fifth and Top 5 Percent of Households, by Race and Latino Origin of Householder (1972 to 1996)

	Lowest Fifth	Second Fifth	Third Fifth	Fourth Fifth	Highest Fifth	Top 5%
All Races						
1972	4.1	10.5	17.1	24.5	43.9	17.0
1996	3.7	9.0	15.1	23.3	49.0	21.4
Whites						
1972	4.3	10.8	17.2	24.3	43.4	16.8
1996	3.9	9.2	15.2	23.2	48.4	21.1
African Americans						
1972	3.9	9.2	15.8	24.9	46.2	16.9
1996	3.1	8.0	14.5	23.7	50.7	21.7
Latinos						
1972	5.3	11.2	17.2	24.0	42.3	16.2
1996	3.8	9.0	14.7	23.1	49.5	21.5

SOURCE: U.S. Bureau of the Census, Current Population Reports, Series P60–197 *Money Income in the United States: 1996,* "Share of Aggregate Income Received by Each Fifth and Top 5 Percent of Households by Race and Hispanic Origin of Householder: 1967 to 1996," pp. B6–B8, Washington, D.C.: U.S. Government Printing Office, 1997.

skilled workers, wages for less-skilled workers have not kept pace, and there have been fewer job opportunities for the unskilled in manufacturing. Other potential contributing factors are the curtailment of public services and benefits, the divorce rate (women are major economic casualties of divorce), and the numbers of single-parent, female-headed households. Others have pointed to the effects of technology and the relocation of manufacturing industries out of central cities and overseas, and recent immigrants who are more poorly educated and who contribute to depressing wages.

Although these variables affect everyone, it is important to note that there are differential impacts by diverse and significant factors such as the nature of the job market, the nature of the job preparation people have received, and geographic factors (living in center-city or rural areas). Discrimination on racial, ethnic, gender, and other grounds, as we saw earlier, contributes to these differential effects.

Wealth in the United States has become extraordinarily concentrated. In 1979, the richest 1 percent of Americans held 22 percent of the nation's wealth. By 1992, their share had almost doubled to 42 percent. Between 1983 and 1989, the top 20 percent of wealth holders received 99 percent of the total gain in marketable wealth, while the bottom 80 percent of the population got only 1 percent. Middle-class families have more than two-thirds of their wealth invested in their own homes; however, home-ownership peaked in 1980 and has been falling ever since. The United

States has become the industrialized nation with the greatest disparity in terms of wealth.[19]

In 1993, 22.3 percent of white householders either had negative net worth or less than $5,000; Latinos, 49.6 percent; and African Americans, 48.7 percent. Only 15.4 percent of married couples were in similar straits, whereas both male (36.6 percent) and female householders (38 percent) held little wealth or had negative net worth. At the other end of the range of wealth, 11.5 percent of white householders held $250,000 or more; 1.7 percent of African Americans and 3.2 percent of Latinos enjoyed wealth at those levels.[20]

The social structure of the society determines the options available to people and affects almost every sphere of our lives, from where one lives to how one spends leisure time. When the United States is compared with other nations, it is consistently found to have a relatively high rate of upward mobility over time. Some of the findings of mobility studies follow: (1) There is a great deal of occupational inheritance; (2) Mobility rates among black men are substantially lower than those among white men; (3) There are regional differences in the rates of mobility; and (4) Geographic mobility is related to vertical mobility. Those who don't move have a higher rate of downward mobility. Some of the factors that influence mobility are industrialization, class differences in fertility rates, immigration rates, and institutionalized ethnic and gender discrimination.

Despite a long history of such upward mobility, a study of intergenerational mobility (the income status of fathers and sons) based on national longitudinal data found our society is less mobile than described in earlier research.[21]

THE EFFECT OF SOME GOVERNMENT PROGRAMS

One may ask: What part do governmental programs play in alleviating poverty, especially those programs aimed at economic security? What is the antipoverty effectiveness of governmental cash and noncash transfers (including federal income and payroll taxes)? Table 8.5 addresses these questions. The number of poor individuals in the United States in 1996 who were counted as poor prior to the receipt of any governmental transfer was 57.2 million. In Table 8.5, one can observe the economic effects on the 57.2 million persons. In the first section, we see that the total number of poor persons was reduced to 30.5 million, almost a one-half reduction. Social insurances such as social security, unemployment insurance and workers' compensation, and means-tested income transfer programs such as (at that time) Aid to Families with Dependent Children, Supplemental Security Income, General Assistance, and food and housing benefits, all contribute to this reduction. However, special note should be taken regarding the powerful contribution of social insurances to the reduction of the number of the poor.

Table 8.5 summarizes the effectiveness of governmental programs including valuation of in-kind benefits in reducing poverty. With this method one can determine their additional effect on household income through a series of definitions. *Income before taxes* equals money income excluding capital gains, less government

TABLE 8.5   The Antipoverty Effectiveness of Cash and Noncash Transfers (Including Federal Income and Payroll Taxes) for All Persons in Families or Living Alone (Selected Years–1996)

	Poor Individuals (in Thousands)
Cash income before transfers	57,228
Plus social insurance (Unemployment Insurance, Workers' Compensation, Social Security)	39,459
Plus means-tested cash transfers	36,529
Plus food and housing benefits	32,251
Plus EIC (Earned Income Credit) and less federal payroll and income taxes	30,538
Number of persons (in thousands) removed from poverty due to:	
Social insurance	17,769
Means-tested cash	2,930
Food and housing benefits	4,278
EIC and Federal payroll and income taxes	1,713
	Total: 26,690
Percentage of persons removed from poverty due to:	
Social insurance	31.0
Means-tested cash	5.1
Food and housing benefits	7.5
EIC and Federal payroll and income taxes	3.0
	Total: 46.6%

Before transfers and taxes, 21.5 percent were poor. After transfers and taxes, 11.5 percent remained poor. Total reduction in the poverty rate: 10 percent.
SOURCE: Committee on Ways and Means, U.S. House of Representatives, *Overview of Entitlement Programs: 1998 Green Book, Background Material and Data on Programs within the Jurisdiction of the Committee on Ways and Means*, Washington, D.C.: U.S. Government Printing Office, 1998, pp. 1341–1342.

cash transfers, plus capital gains, plus health insurance supplements to wage or salary income. *Income after taxes* equals less social security payroll taxes, less federal income taxes (excluding earned income credit), plus the earned income credit, less state income taxes, plus non–means-tested government cash transfers, plus the value of Medicaid, plus the value of other means-tested government noncash transfers, plus net imputed return on equity in own home. The effect of using fully adjusted income definitions (including taxes and noncash benefits) lowered income inequality by 11 percent when compared with pretax (official) money income. According to Bureau of the Census reports government transfers have a much more significant effect than taxes on redistributing income.[22]

Without accounting for the value of in-kind benefits, one can only have a partial understanding of poverty. However, there are numerous complex and perplexing problems associated with counting as income the value of in-kind benefits, not the least of which is the initial problem of what value one will place on a particular benefit. If one adds such benefits from one program to the "income" of poor persons, does that mean they will become ineligible for other programs? There are other quandaries in such valuations. If medical care is provided and a market value assigned to it, then while one is ill one's income rises. This can produce bizarre situations in which aging or other poor persons for whom large medical expenditures are made can be counted as rising above the poverty level. Further, if Medicaid benefits are to be treated as income for the poor, shall Medicare and employer-provided health care be counted as income for those who are not poor? There are political and other pressures to include in-kind benefits in poverty line calculations. The search for fair and objective measurements that include cash and noncash benefits as well as taxes has spurred the type of calculations reported in Table 8.5.

There are three ways of assigning values to in-kind benefits that have been used for measuring poverty: (1) market value, (2) recipient or cash-equivalent value, and (3) poverty budget-share value. The market value is equal to the purchase price in the private market of the goods received by the recipient. The recipient or cash-equivalent value is the amount of cash that would make the recipient just as well off as would the in-kind transfer. This reflects the value that would be set on the benefit by the recipient and is usually less but never more than the market value. This measure is difficult to estimate, particularly for medical care. The poverty budget-share value is tied to the current poverty definition and limits values assigned to food, housing, or medical transfers to the percentages spent on these items by persons at or near the poverty line in particular years. Valuations of in-kind benefits currently in use are those based on a market value technique that attempts to measure the private market cost of benefits provided in-kind.[23]

Transfer programs are powerful forces that can bring people out of poverty. However, as we have indicated previously, the working poor account for large numbers of those in poverty (one in six of the heads of poor families work full-time year-round). The interrelation of poverty, employment, wage levels, and income security programs is clear, and the reduction of poverty cannot be accomplished by income-transfer devices alone; obviously other interventions will be required.

THE NEAR-POOR AND EXPECTATIONS

The "near-poor" struggle with incomes that are only somewhat above the official poverty line. They too are in need of services, but overall, the near-poor are ineligible for many of the benefits for which those below the poverty line may be eligible. Some near-poor may, in certain instances, be eligible for means-tested programs because, implicitly, the government recognizes that the poverty line is too low. But they too have to pass a means test, which is considered demeaning, stigmatizing, and a situation many persons prefer to avoid. It is from this group, but not from it alone, that much of the backlash against selective programs arises.

The poverty line itself, as discussed previously, is an arbitrary division. Although it has been adjusted to account for inflation since the mid-1960s, it does not take into account the rising expectations or the norm of American living. Therefore, the gap between the official poverty line and comfortable living may be growing greater, and a large army of near-poor and nominally lower-middle-class people are really poor and feel discriminated against: women, children, racial minorities, and the working poor.

The poverty problems of women, children, the aging, and racial and ethnic minorities are clearly disproportionate, but it is important to note that the problem of poverty is endemic to our society and endured by many groups. The problem is widespread, and every group has a share in the burden, although some carry inordinate loads. But the problem of poverty cannot be understood or approached without also considering the groups whose income is slightly more than those in poverty.

At different times, different groups have been most discriminated against. Usually the latest wave of immigrants took the brunt of the oppression. For whites, the major force of such oppression may end, but for African Americans, Latinos, and Native Americans, there has been a continuity to the discrimination aimed at them, and their poverty has persisted even in the best of economic times. Although some Asian-American groups have made more rapid progress even while identified as "minorities of color," one in seven of them are poor.

Those who are in poverty are besieged by their difficulties. It is natural that one group or another should claim that the discrimination aimed at them is the most difficult, the most trying. Although programs aimed *selectively* at particular groups hold a certain fascination and promise easier success, they often have accompanying costs.

Counter to programs aimed only at particular groups is the need for *universal* services that offer equal access to opportunity for all groups. Universal coverage in a welfare society would meet basic needs and provide for the development of individuals, families, and communities. It is a truism that universal services are generally higher quality services and must meet overall community standards, not just those for the poor. However, universal services aimed at improving the conditions of all in society do not reduce the distance between those at the top and those at the bottom. This, too, can be questioned. More people are transferred out of poverty by the universalistic Social Security system than by selective public assistance programs.

OTHER VIEWS OF POVERTY

In spite of all the programs and progress, widespread poverty and near-poverty persist. If poverty is to be combated successfully, it must be understood and there must be a will to do so. But there are very different ideas about what poverty is. A common way of understanding poverty is as the result of individual failure, the traditional victim-blaming theory of causation. But if one adopts the idea that structural causes have the greatest impact on the incidence of poverty in our society, then more investigation and different interventions to deal with the problem are required.

The only convincing explanation of lagging health, education, and income associated with particular groups is that discrimination is structured into our society. But we are all losers in many ways because of such institutionalized discrimination.

We look next at the major definitions of poverty itself. This may seem overly simple at first. We all "know" what *poor* means. And yet there are significantly different explanations of what constitutes poverty, and the differences have profound implications for what should be done to minimize it. Automation, the need for higher level skills and knowledge, an international economy, discrimination, and other institutional factors need to be examined in order to understand poverty.

In the United States, for most purposes, *poverty* is defined as simply being income below an established dollar figure, a measurable cutoff minimum, and so we focused earlier primarily on the distribution of income and wealth. But there are other ways of understanding poverty, and we turn now to several of these perspectives.

RELATIVE INEQUALITY

According to some persons, the problem is basically one of rising expectations, which are in infinite acceleration. The standard of living has gone up, and so have expectations over time. An automobile was an unusual thing to own in the 1930s. As we enter the 21st century, it is practically impossible in many parts of the United States to work or live without one. Television, which was unusual in the early 1950s, is accepted as a typical, if not necessary, part of the home, as are VCRs. Similarly, the gap between the poverty line and median family income today is greater. Relative inequality is thus greater. It is this perception of relative inequality that is at bottom the most difficult problem of poverty, because relative poverty is an inescapable concomitant of poverty. When the government establishes a poverty line, it suggests it is responsible up to a point and has no responsibility beyond that minimum income, if that. It is stating that governmental responsibility is for the establishment of an income floor no one should fall below. But this still does not remedy the fact there always will be richer and poorer persons regardless of what the standard for poverty might become.

In addition, definitions of the expected services of a society alter over time. At one time in the United States, there was an expectation generally held that people might complete the eighth grade. Today it is widely accepted that almost everyone will complete high school and many will proceed to college. Health care was a privilege, and today it is coming to be judged as a right. Thus evolving rights also serve to alter the perception by those in poverty of what their situation means to them and change the definition of poverty.

Poverty may be defined as a standard of living less than the expectation of a society or as an unfair gap between one's resources and that of others. On one level this definition could become ludicrous. Is the ultimate goal the elimination of all difference, of all inequality? Obviously not. It is not necessary to be trapped into such absurd arguments. The answer to how much equality is wanted can be the same as American labor leader (1850-1924) Samuel Gompers's answer to the question of what the U.S. labor movement wanted: "more." The rich have the infinite capacity to invent new luxuries as yesterday's luxuries become today's necessities for many. Absolute equality is not achievable or even desirable. But the feeling that people live in a society that fairly allocates the necessities of life is one key definition of non-poverty. Titmuss pointed out that in wartime, when rich and poor lined up for rationed food, no one felt poor. It is the lack of something that others have and to which one feels entitled that defines poverty. Inequality is a less-exact definition of poverty than an absolute definition, but it may be more realistic. Accepting an equitable distribution of life's necessities as a solution to poverty suggests transfers of resources, through both income redistribution and amenities (utilities) equally available to all.

Lack of Power, Access, and Inclusion

Titmuss also suggested that "command over resources" is a measure of wealth and thus, by implication, poverty is the lack of command over resources. Paradoxically, as certain benefits become available to different categories of people, the "command" that controls access by some creates relative inequality for those who do not have such access.

Credentials and entitlements are a major form of wealth in our society. These entitlements vary. They include seniority and tenure, licenses and franchises, academic degrees and union membership, and many others. Each has a certain value translatable into tangible wealth, and some may be transferred or even inherited. The value of many credentials and entitlements is compounded to the degree that they serve as a form of capital rather than simply as a form of consumable wealth. An acre of land has an immediate market value or may produce a certain amount of grain. The same acre of land can also be used as collateral for additional purchases or can serve as the base for a high-rise apartment building. Similarly, a credential or an entitlement can be a building block for the development of additional wealth. A college graduate has the option not only of working and earning money as a result of having a degree, but of "investing" that degree in an advanced degree to bring still better returns in the future.

In the past, certain groups have been denied a fair share of, and access to, traditional forms of wealth. Now demands for greater equity are worldwide, and each society to some degree redistributes and transfers income. But as this "new property"—credentials or entitlements—grows more important, it becomes the focus of attempts to achieve greater equality. Without greater access to this form of wealth, the poor are doomed to continuing poverty or dependence. Not only do the economically deprived have less access to credentials, but there exist fewer safeguards for the protection of those credentials. In the long struggle for more economic opportunity and equality, certain gains have been made. If a person works for wages and does not receive them, he or she has access to the courts. But the credential system still exists largely in self-regulating and self-determining programs less subject to the legal safeguards that have developed around the marketplace. Diplomas and licenses are often awarded or withheld with broad discretionary powers. Individuals and governments are not allowed to walk into homes and steal a person's tangible property, but the state may strip a person of benefits or some other entitlement. Not all hearings of government regulatory agencies are subject to the same safeguards and restraints as are present in the legal tradition.

Privilege and aspects of an industrial and technological society combine so that the poor have less power and less access to resources. In large part, the poverty of many people is the result of the opportunity structure of our society.

To what extent is it possible for our society to create sufficient jobs for all potential workers on the basis of an unregulated labor market? Given a willingness to create jobs, to what extent can these jobs be productively targeted at those who are the least able and least trained and who are ill-equipped to do tasks that require high levels of skill? To what extent is the job market open to upward mobility for those who enter at very low levels of employment?

Racism, age discrimination, and sexism are all forms of denial of access. If a person is denied access to jobs, to entitlements, to respect, and to knowledge about where to go for service, that person may be defined as poor. Although few would argue that lack of power to affect the political system or discrimination is a complete definition of poverty, it can hardly be ignored as a factor. A whole variety of inclusionary strategies is needed if one sees this as a key factor in poverty.

The Underclass/Culture of Poverty Thesis

Poverty consists of economic inequality and also of noneconomic features. In a nation in which social honor, prestige, and self-respect as well as quality of life are important, poor persons are viewed as lacking in such honor and prestige and derive their self-image from society's view of them. To a degree, their sense of aspiration is battered and the gap between early aspirations and real opportunities grows large, resulting in behavior that assumes "making it" is impossible.

According to one point of view identified as the "culture of poverty" thesis, structural factors gave rise to poor persons who have particular behavioral characteristics, and these characteristics are transmitted from one generation to another because of their effects on children who cannot take full advantage of their opportunities.[24] Among the attributes suggested are inability to defer gratification, a present orientation with less emphasis on the future, lack of aspiration for upward mobility, female-centered families, alienation, a freer sexual code, and less investment in child rearing.

In recent years, the culture of poverty thesis has been replaced by the term *underclass*. The issue for both terms is the existence and persistence of poverty. There are two basic ways in which they explain poverty: the result of cultural or structural forces. According to the *cultural* view, poor persons have certain psychological and behavioral characteristics listed previously. These include motivational, cultural group, and lifestyle factors. The structural perspective emphasizes major economic and political systems which place various groups at risk. The importance one places on each of the perspectives differentiates explanations.

Exclusion from participation in paid employment and the general cash marketplace can lead to apathy, alienation, and family and community disruptions and disorganization. Cultural elements and discrimination do contribute to the extent of poverty (among other factors), but empirical evidence is lacking for the culture of poverty claim of intergenerational transmission. Family, social networks, and community provide buffers from some economic shocks and can serve as sources of strength.[25] Studies have found that the poor are not as distinctive in their values, attitudes, and aspirations as the culture of poverty thesis suggests.[26]

It would be foolish to ignore the fact that poverty influences behavior. What is crucial is that if the poverty is removed, the behavior tends to change, and social and economic mobility are frequent occurrences. For those who are tempted to believe that contemporary poverty groups are truly different in culture, the following excerpt written around the turn of the century may be instructive:

ITALIAN Americans

> The . . . race stock is inferior and degraded; . . . it will not assimilate naturally or readily with the prevailing "Anglo-Saxon" race stock of this country; that intermixture, will be detrimental; that servility, filthy habits of life, and hopelessly degraded standards of needs and ambitions have been ingrained . . . by centuries of oppression and abject poverty; . . . they are incapable of any adequate appreciation of our free institutions and the privileges and duties of citizenship; the greater part are illiterate and likely to remain so.[27]

The author was talking about immigrant Italians and assumes some intrinsic cultural failure among Italians similar to things said about other groups today. But generations later, Italians are generally believed to be among America's most achieving ethnic groups.

STRATEGIES FOR FIGHTING POVERTY

At least six major strategies for dealing with poverty have been identified: *social utilities, investment in human capital, transfers, rehabilitation, participation,* and *aggregative* and *selective economic measures.*[28] Each of these approaches has to be considered within the context of rationality, political feasibility, and value preferences. Each approach rests on particular assumptions about the definition or cause of poverty. Each has both positive and negative or functional and dysfunctional aspects. In short, social programs directed against poverty are usually mixed in the sense that they require trade-offs of certain gains against other losses.

Social Utilities

Social utilities are services that contribute to strengthening and enriching the quality of life. Access to birth control methods, family planning, or health services is in effect a transfer of money to the poor. Where our society makes available $1,000 worth of medical care for a poor family, we are providing, inside (health benefits as part of a job, including tax protected health spending accounts) or outside the market (means-tested health care), an equivalent of income for that family. Other examples are parks, free education, public libraries, police and fire services, employment

information, and subsidized housing. Some persons oppose social utilities and amenities because they require government planning and bureaucracy. One variation is to
provide poor persons with vouchers worth a certain amount of money that they
then can spend on food, education, or housing. In this latter case, vouchers support
the free market and may or may not give the poor person more options, depending
on the terms of the voucher and the realities of the marketplace. The great advantage
of amenities or social utilities is availability. Typically, social utilities are nonstigma-
tized services because the community recognizes the necessity for particular services in a complex and changing society, and they are available to all.

Vouchers run the danger of enriching purveyors of services without equalizing
services. Universal social utilities are a form of income transfer and a form of reducing inequality by offering opportunities. Those who see lack of access as a key to
poverty also may favor the development of utilities as a strategy.

Investment in Human Capital

This approach to poverty attempts to improve the capabilities of the poor by investing in them through education, health, job training, and the like. Just as investment
in capital goods such as machinery and new plants increases productivity, so does investment in the quality of the work force.

One of the important contributors to U.S. growth has been its world leadership
in universal, free public education, a form of investment in human capital. For example, literate farmers in the United States have read pamphlets and journals and utilized new methods; while farmers in some other countries, often illiterate, have
farmed traditionally, producing less. Public school education in the United States had
this effect on farmers and consequently on the agricultural production of the United
States. Essentially, this strategy is an indirect service strategy through education,
enhancement of workers' knowledge, health, and skills, social services, and other
services.

Perhaps the best example of investment in human capital occurred in the period that followed World War II. During the war, unemployment was almost entirely
erased. But economists feared a return of massive unemployment after the rapid de-
mobilization of millions of service persons. Two factors prevented this: First, people
had savings and money in their pockets as a result of the war effort, enjoyed high employment, and experienced a shortage of consumer goods. There was a backlog of
demand that created jobs. Second, millions of discharged veterans took advantage of
the educational opportunities made possible through the GI Bill, deferring entry into
the job market and eventually improving the quality of the labor force. One payoff
for the United States has been higher tax revenues from those who took advantage of
the opportunity. Several million people paying taxes through their lifetimes on incomes generated by a college education (rather than on income generated by a high
school education) have more than repaid the society for its investment in education.
Other payoffs have been less crime, higher morale, new inventions, social stability,
and a more productive society. Consider the alternative if 11 million returning veterans had not been either absorbed into the labor market or given other options.

Investment in human capital—training programs, low tuition community colleges and the like—is one way of bringing poor and disadvantaged groups into the system and therefore a way of combating poverty for specific target groups. These programs work best in an expanding economy where opportunities for moving up are more available. This type of investment is another approach to fighting poverty.

Income Transfers

Income transfer systems take money from one population group and redirect it to another. Such transfers can be made from middle-aged persons to the elderly, from the employed to the unemployed, and from the rich to the poor (or in some cases from those with less to those with more). There are two ways in which such redistributions can be made: Either money is redistributed vertically in the sense that those who have more channel their money through a tax system to those who have less; or redistribution can be made horizontally in that those who have, say, fewer dependents (including children) contribute through the tax system to those who have more dependents. The essential assumption of income transfers is that poverty is equivalent to a deficit of income. Although this is a main factor in poverty, as we saw earlier, it is not the complete definition of poverty.

However, a very strong taboo in American culture stands in the way of making such a commitment. There is something abhorrent in the American value system about giving money directly to both the "worthy" and the "unworthy" or able-bodied poor. Such an abhorrence seems ingrained in some Americans. Although programs such as public assistance, social insurance, family allowances, and earned income tax credits (negative income taxes) all have their potential uses in an attempt to minimize poverty, the essential issue is not one of technology (that is, the techniques by which poverty could be overcome most effectively or efficiently), but instead one of values. Specifically, to what extent do Americans want to redistribute income to do away with poverty? Who would support whom? What are the benefits in such a move? And what are the losses, such as higher tax rates, that supposedly would minimize investment in capital goods? However, such questions do not ask whether it could be done. They are all questions about aims and the trade-offs that would have to be made and the identification of who would pay at what price. None of these arguments denies that problems in social engineering exist in devising appropriate income transfer programs. But additional transfer in some form will need to be an essential part of any strategy to eliminate or minimize poverty.

Rehabilitation

Rehabilitation is aimed at changing people through psychological and sociopsychological methods to restore and enhance social functioning. The underlying assumption of some approaches to guidance, social casework, and psychotherapy is that the fault lies within the person or the family and not in the societal context. The assumption is made that people who are poor have problems for which they need help—that is, problems other than lack of money. Such programs are aimed at helping persons manage their emotional and interpersonal problems to a sufficient extent for them to be successfully employed. Such programs tend to be limited in scope and in their capacity to affect poverty.

However, this path has been a traditional major approach to the issue of poverty. The Social Security Act amendments of 1962 actually suggested that more trained labor power—social workers and others—would result in lower welfare rolls. If sufficient numbers of trained social workers, it was thought, were prepared, they could be expected to rehabilitate so many welfare recipients that this would serve as a means of eliminating poverty. However, the basic fallacy in such an approach is that it substitutes personal and familial causation for structural causation. The economic cycles of the nation are greater determinants of the rate of growth or decline of poverty than is the pool of trained social workers. This is illustrated by the fall in the numbers of persons on public assistance during periods of economic and employment expansion.

Nevertheless, rehabilitation has legitimacy because there are people who will have emotional and other problems and need support even in the best of worlds. Some people have special needs as situational crises occur, and they will be driven into poverty or be unable to drag themselves out of poverty without rehabilitation. Rehabilitation cannot be used as an effective, and certainly not as an efficient, means of eliminating poverty, but it is one of the legitimate ways of coping with some poor people as it is with helping some people of every class.

Aggregative and Selective Economic Measures

Aggregative economic measures are those that purport to help the poor at the bottom of the economic scale through economic growth that results from tax reductions, low interest rates, and incentives meant to increase hiring and production. A growth economy is required if we want to minimize poverty. An economy that is healthy and growing with high employment makes the greatest contribution to defeating poverty. A healthy economy in which labor is in demand and productivity and consumption are high may do more than specific programs to lessen the brunt of poverty.

The U.S. Congress in 1946 passed the Employment Act creating the Council of Economic Advisors. A commitment to stimulate high employment was reaffirmed in the passage of the Humphrey-Hawkins Full Employment and Balanced Growth Act in 1978. But a commitment to a full employment policy in which government provides jobs as the employer of last resort has never been seriously implemented. As a result, the coincidental phases of U.S. economic cycles have done more to create poverty or to do away with it than the employment policies of the government.

Selective economic measures are designed to create jobs, raise wages (the minimum wage, the "living wage"), and provide other opportunities to reduce poverty for those poor who could benefit. Although these strategies seem attractive, almost all those persons receiving public assistance are women and children. The redesign of jobs and the creation of jobs will not in themselves move all women and children off public assistance. However, where there is economic uncertainty because of unemployment, underemployment, or even the threat of unemployment, family instability often follows.

For this reason, job creation is of great importance for economic, psychological, and social reasons. The well-being of individuals and families, as well as the society, is tied to work and gainful full-time employment at a living wage. In general, recent efforts to create jobs focused increasingly upon the private sector and minimized the role of government. Nonetheless, serious employment problems exist, especially for men in the young adult range from 16 to 24 years old, particularly but not limited to minority males. Governmental efforts—which primarily utilize the private sector to deal with this problem, which is connected to other significant problems in our society—will be described in chapter 10.

There are dangers to a targeting approach. These special programs present several difficulties because, accompanied by high expectations, they are typically aimed at groups with complicated problems. These problems are not those of particular individuals but are related to societal and structural factors such as the shift from manufacturing and goods-producing to service employment; changes in the geographic location of industries, including what jobs are located where; and to international economic trends. Because of the complexities and difficulties presented by such factors, these programs do not seem to work sufficiently well and fall short of overly optimistic expectations, inviting criticism and political "backlash" directed at the program. Further, there is always the possibility of such selective programs contributing to the divisiveness that they can create in society as one group or another feels left out.

An intense debate focuses on the question as to whether a higher minimum wage reduces poverty. Some argue that raising the minimum wage leads to higher unemployment and more poverty because it reduces the number of jobs available for persons who are semi-skilled or without skill or work experience, while pushing other levels of wages higher. One study found that "despite its inefficiency in reaching the poor, a higher minimum wage would significantly reduce poverty among working families."[29] Another study found, contrary to expectations, that increases in the minimum wage resulted in an *increase* in wages accompanied by an increase in employment. It also was found that creation of businesses continued in the industries studied. Furthermore, it was found that workers earning the minimum wage were disproportionately drawn from families with lower earnings and the minimum wage had a modest effect on the standard of living of those families.[30] According to Robert M. Solow, a Nobel laureate in economics, the evidence of job loss due to raising the minimum wage is weak. This does not still the voices of opponents, some of whom resist any increase in the minimum wage and others who want to repeal the law. The consistent conclusion of a series of minimum wage studies found that no large disemployment effects would result from modest increases (10 percent) in the minimum wage.[31]

Growth in the gross domestic product (GDP)—that is, the total value of all goods and services produced—is a key ingredient in any program to reduce poverty. Growth is needed. As discussed, during World War II, there was practically no unemployment, and poverty was reduced through employment associated with the war effort. A bigger pie means potentially more for everyone, including those poor who may be recipients of redistributive efforts made possible by rising tax revenues, which result from an expanding economy. However, growth per se does not guarantee a reduction in poverty. Most people who seek to eliminate poverty are not satisfied that enough benefits will automatically trickle down to the poor. Other strategies are needed. But economic growth is a precondition for other efforts to succeed, or often, even to be tried.

Participation and Organization

Participation and organization programs are intended to promote *social inclusion* and *influence* and to reduce problems among the poor by providing them with a stake in society. Whether there are behavioral problems or problems of access or lack of power, or whether the key is discrimination, one strategy is to bring people into the mainstream through organizing efforts. Such programs are meant to raise the self-esteem of poor persons and to raise their honor and prestige in society by enhancing their political power. Such programs involve antidiscrimination laws, special programs for non–English-speaking children, zoning rules, access to municipal contracts and jobs, educational advancement programs for climbing the job ladder, access to the political process, voting, and direct engagement in political decision making. All these programs are devoted to the theory and policy of inclusion.

Ideology Revisited

In earlier chapters, we introduced the importance of values and ideology as key factors contributing to decisions about social welfare. The congressional elections of 1994 resulted in Republican majorities seizing control of both the House of Representatives and the Senate for the first time in 40 years. The essence of the Republican program was to return the society to one more reflective of laissez faire philosophy, to devolve programs from the federal level where possible to the control of states, to reduce taxes in the belief that tax reduction is needed to encourage greater risk-taking and expansion of the economy, to reduce the size of the federal government and the number of governmental employees at all levels, and to reduce governmental regulations for business and industry and in regard to the environment. Joined with tax reduction, they wanted to balance the budget while reducing federal deficits and overall debt. The ideological aim was to limit governmental responsibility. Concurrent with limiting governmental responsibility, individuals and families would be expected to be independent and governmental assistance for individuals and families would be reduced. On the basis of all these actions, it was expected productivity would increase and the GDP would rise sufficiently to generate higher living standards for the society.

As this edition is being written, there has been substantial reform of the welfare system since the 1996 (to be discussed in Chapter 9) repeal of the six-decade-old entitlement program for families with dependent children that resulted in the largest

devolution of power from the Federal government to the states since the end of Reconstruction. The economy of the United States was declared by Alan Greenspan,
the chairperson of the Federal Reserve Board, to be "in extraordinarily good shape . . .
as impressive as any I have witnessed in my near half-century of daily observation."[32] The economy combined strong growth and low inflation, low unemployment, and subdued price pressures. Huge investments in technology were helping
companies produce more for every hour worked, holding costs down even while
wages began to rise. Low inflation reduced interest rates and stimulated more investment and consumption. Not more than two months later, several background
factors threatened to bring the expansion to an end and/or threaten the international order. From an economic and political standpoint, an economic crisis in Asia,
including Japan, a turbulent Russian economy, along with problems in Europe combined with crises in Mexico, South America, and South Africa endangered the worldwide economic and political situation, perhaps leading to recessions, deflations, and
increased poverty. Threats to stability may also arise from international issues related to environmental pollution, disease, hunger, terrorism, political disenfranchisement, drug traffic, cultural conflicts, and shortages of fresh water and arable
land. The economy and social welfare cannot be separated from the context, both
nationally and internationally.

In the governmental sphere, President Clinton and the Congressional Budget
office predicted a record $39 billion budget surplus for the year, the first surplus
since 1969. The projected surplus was a result of strong economic growth, spending
restraint, tax increases, falling interest rates that reduced the Treasury's cost of borrowing, and a booming stock market, which resulted in a tax windfall for government. However, there were expectations smaller surpluses would be followed by
larger surpluses for at least ten years into the future, perhaps totalling $1.5 trillion.
Whatever surplus occurs, it will be followed by anticipated deficits associated with
the retirements of the "baby boomer" generation beginning in the first decade of the
21st century.

With the elimination of budget deficits, Democrats and Republicans began to
maneuver to use any surplus for their priorities. Republicans aimed to use any surplus for tax cuts. Democrats wanted to spend, for example, on education and health.
There was a third path: paying off the debt. To do so would reduce interest payments on the debt, 15.2 percent of federal expenditures in 1997.[33]

President Clinton's first priority was to deal with any anticipated problems in
the Social Security system (to be discussed in chapter 9). This stance placed him in
direct conflict with many Republicans who wanted to use part of the surplus on tax
cuts and part on paying down the $5.4 trillion national debt. Other suggestions
aimed at public investment in roads, bridges, railroads and bus service (the transportation infrastructure) or education, job training, and research.

Among the proposals in President Clinton's 1998 State of the Union message
with implications for social welfare were a balanced budget, Social Security reform, Medicare, child care, raising the minimum wage, education, job training,
health quality, housing, child support, public assistance rolls, crime, and low-income housing.

The great and historic battle was joined as a result of the Republicans gaining control of Congress in 1994 and is expected to continue over a number of issues. What should be the contract between an individual and society? Is society's purpose the "general welfare"? If so, how is that to be achieved? What are the responsibilities of individuals and families for themselves and for society?

Should society set a minimum standard and ensure that the oppressed and needy are raised to that level? Or, is society to ignore a minimum standard as individuals and families pursue their own well-being? What is and should be government's role? This question can be asked in almost every sphere of life. Further, what should be the respective roles of the federal, state, and local governments? What responsibilities should be maintained at what levels? Missing from the arguments were consideration of the economic features of the kind of government that developed in the United States. To what degree will cutting the costs of programs undermine purchasing power and the countercyclical effects of social spending? Is there some point at which reductions in the total budget, if made too quickly or too broadly, will lead to recessions and even major depression? These have not been considerations to date in the debates as two ideologies have faced off in regard to discrete programs without weighing the total impact of multitudes of program reductions and eliminations.

SUMMARY

In this chapter, we have seen how broadly based the beneficiaries of social welfare programs are, discussed several definitions of poverty, introduced a profile of the poor, examined the distribution of income and wealth, and described the chief strategies for ameliorating poverty. A number of structural factors contribute to the extent of poverty in the United States. Among these factors are the nature and performance of the economy, particularly in regard to productivity and the economic growth rate; the federal fiscal deficit and its implications for potential governmental interventions; trends in regard to marriage, divorce, and the increase in the number of female-headed families with children; the nature and location of employment opportunities; salaries and the fringe benefits associated or not associated with those jobs; discrimination; the employment of young people, especially minority young adults; and the pattern of taxation at the federal, state, and local levels as they affect the poor and the working poor.

Some outcomes of the ideological conflict and context described previously will be reflected in our discussion in this and the next two chapters. We will examine the major social welfare programs in the United States using the concepts and schema introduced in chapter 6. These programs were created in particular contexts and have evolved influenced by complex political, social, and economic values and factors. As you read about the programs, you might begin to formulate what you think would be the best set of programs both to deal with the problem of poverty in the United States and to deal more effectively with the general welfare of all citizens. At the end of chapter 15, we will suggest an approach to dealing with the problems of poverty and human need.

Questions for Consideration

1. We presented a broad characterization of social welfare clients. Do you think it is accurate? If you agree or disagree with the definition, why?
2. If the United States were to use a relative measure of poverty, what do you suggest it be?
3. When you review the tables in this chapter, what stands out?
4. In what ways have ideologies affected recent social welfare legislation in your state? in the nation?

Notes

1. Senator Ernest Hollings of South Carolina, quoted in "The South Carolina Hybrid," George F. Will, *Newsweek*, December 20, 1982, p. 92.
2. Richard M. Titmuss, *Essays on the Welfare State*, Boston: Beacon Press, 1969, p. 42.
3. This is a theme in Michael Harrington's *Toward a Democratic Left*, Baltimore: Penguin, 1969.
4. Aldi Hagenaars and Klaas de Vos, "The Definition and Measurement of Poverty," *The Journal of Human Resources*, Vol. XXIII, No. 2, Spring 1988, pp. 211-221.
5. Louis Uchitelle, "Balancing Quantity, Quality and Inflation," *New York Times*, December 18, 1996, pp. D1, D21.
6. Patricia Ruggles, *Drawing the Line: Alternative Poverty Measures and Their Implications for Public Policy*, Washington, D.C.: The Urban Institute Press, 1990, pp. 20-23.
7. Constance F. Citro and Robert T. Michael, *Measuring Poverty: A New Approach*, Panel on Poverty and Family Assistance, National Research Council, Washington, D.C.: Academy Press, 1995.
8. Thesia Garner et al., "Experimental Poverty Measurement for the 1990s," *Monthly Labor Review*, Vol. 121, No. 31, March 1998, pp. 39-61.
9. Peter Townsend, *Poverty in the United Kingdom: A Survey of Household Resources and Standards of Living*, Berkeley: University of California Press, 1979.
10. See Ruggles.
11. Tamar Lewin, "Study Finds That Youngest U.S. Children Are Poorest," *New York Times*, March 15, 1998, p. 19; Donald J. Hernandez, "Poverty Trends," in Greg J. Duncan and Jeanne Brooks-Gunn, eds., *Consequences of Growing Up Poor*, New York: Russell Sage Foundation, 1997, p. 33.
12. U.S. Department of Commerce, Census Bureau, *Current Population Reports*, P-70-56, Household Economic Studies, "Dynamics of Economic Well-Being: Income, 1992 to 1993, Moving Up and Down the Income Ladder," June 1996.
13. *Money Income in the United States, 1996* Table 2, p. 5.
14. U.S. Department of Labor, Bureau of Labor Statistics, *Issues in Labor Statistics*, Summary 98-4, May 1998.
15. Frank Swoboda, "How the Rules Have Changed," *The Washington Post Magazine*, April 23, 1995, p. 15.
16. *Money Income*, vii.
17. U.S. Census Bureau, "The Official Statistics," "Poverty Rate Down, Household Income Up—Both Return to 1989 Pre-Recession Levels, Census Bureau Reports,"; Also data specific to African Americans, Asians and Pacific Islanders, Hispanics, "1997 Highlights, Selected Characteristics, and Poverty Thresholds," September 25, 1998, http://www.census.gov/Press-Release/cb98-175.html; Robert Pear, "Black and Hispanic Poverty Falls, Reducing Overall Rate for Nation," *New York Times*, September 25, 1998, pp. 1 and A20.

18. *Economic Report of the President*, Washington: U.S. Government Printing Office, 1997, p. 177.

19. "Inequality: For Richer, For Poorer," *The Economist*, November 5–11, 1994, pp. 19–21; Edward N. Wolff, "How the Pie Is Sliced: America's Growing Concentration of Wealth," *The American Prospect*, No. 22, Summer 1995, p. 59; Keith Bradsher, "Gap in Wealth in U.S. Called Widest in West," *New York Times*, April 17, 1995, p. 1, D4.

20. U.S. Census Bureau, *Asset Ownership of Households: 1993*, Table 4. "Distribution of Household Net Worth, by Selected Characteristics: 1993," April 18, 1997, http://www.census.gov/hhes/www/wealth/wlth93t4.html).

21. Leonard Beeghley, *The Structure of Social Stratification in the United States*, Boston: Allyn & Bacon, 1989, pp. 57, 59, 60, 74; Edward N. Wolff, "Trends in Household Wealth in the United States, 1962–83 and 1983–89," *Review of Income and Wealth*, Series 40, No. 2, June 1994, pp. 143–174; Wolff, pp. 58–64; Gary Solon, "Intergenerational Income Mobility in the United States," *American Economic Review*, Vol. 82, No. 3, June 1992, p. 397.

22. Bureau of the Census, Current Population Reports, P60-197, *Money Income in the United States: 1996 (With Separate Data on Valuation of Noncash Benefits)*, Washington, D.C.: U.S. Government Printing Office, 1997, Highlights, pp. xii, xiv.

23. U.S. Bureau of the Census, 1995.

24. Oscar Lewis, *La Vida*, New York: Random House, 1966, p. xiv.

25. Rural Sociological Society, Task Force on Persistent Rural Poverty, *Persistent Poverty in Rural America*, San Francisco: Westview, 1993, p. 8.

26. Michael Morris, "Culture, Structure, and the Underclass," in *Myths about the Powerless*, ed. M. Brinton Lykes, et al., Philadelphia: Temple University Press, 1996, pp. 34–49.

27. Joe R. Feagin, *Racial and Ethnic Relations*, Englewood Cliffs, N.J.: Prentice Hall, 1989, p. 112, quoting Eliot Lord, et al., *The Italian Americans*, San Francisco: R and E Associates, 1970.

28. Martin Rein and S. M. Miller, "Poverty, Policy, and Purpose: The Dilemmas of Choice," *Economic Progress and Social Welfare*, Leonard Goodman, ed., New York: Columbia University Press, 1966, pp. 20–64.

29. Ronald B. Mincy, "Raising the Minimum Wage: Effects on Family Poverty," *Monthly Labor Review*, Vol. 113, No. 7, July 1990, p. 24.

30. David Card and Alan B. Kreuger, *Myth and Measurement: The New Economics of the Minimum Wage*, Princeton, N.J.: Princeton University Press, 1995, pp. 387, 391; Linda R. Martin and Demetrios Giannaros, "Would a Higher Minimum Wage Help Poor Families Headed by Women?" *Monthly Labor Review*, Vol. 113, No. 8, August 1990, p. 36.

31. Louis Uchitelle, "Minimum Wage and Jobs," *New York Times*, January 12, 1995, pp. D1, D19; "New Minimum Wage Research: A Symposium," *Industrial and Labor Relations Review*, Vol. 46, No. 1, October 1992, pp. 1–88.

32. Richard W. Stevenson, "Fed Chief Calls the Economy One of the Best He Has Seen," *New York Times*, June 11, 1998, pp. 1, D21.

33. Richard W. Stevenson, "Federal Deficit Will Fade Away in '98, Budget Office Predicts," *New York Times*, January 8, 1998, p. A19; Richard W. Stevenson, "Budget in the Black: A Dream Come True Proves to be Somewhat Hard to Cope With," *New York Times*, January 12, 1998, p. A16.

CHAPTER NINE

Current Social Welfare Programs— Economic Security

Security was attained in the earlier days through the interdependence of members of families upon each other, and the families within a small community upon each other. The complexities of great communities and of organized industry make less real these simple means of security. Therefore we are compelled to employ the active interest of the nation as a whole, through government, in order to encourage a greater security for each individual who composes it.
—Franklin D. Roosevelt[1]

OVERVIEW

As you read this and the next chapter, it will be obvious that there is no comprehensive and unified social welfare system in the United States. The U.S. "system" has developed incrementally in a crazy-quilt pattern. In reality, the U.S. social welfare institution is a series of systems, although they are sometimes more or less interrelated.

The scope of social welfare programs and services in the United States is so broad and complex that it is not possible to review all the social welfare programs in depth here. Each program is complicated, and the reader should be aware there are many details and intricacies that are not included in this discussion. In our discussion, we will introduce programs in general outline and try to indicate the nature of changes enacted or being considered.

Because these programs affect all our lives, it is important for social workers and all citizens to know about the various social welfare programs, their aims, for whom they are intended, benefits, funding, and administration. As we saw in chapter 1, emotional problems and family disturbances, stress, and income insecurity are intricately interwoven. Recessions, job loss, unemployment, and low incomes are all related to personal and family stress.

In this chapter, we review programs that provide for the income security—to varying degrees—of the citizenry, and in chapter 10 we will discuss programs designed to improve the quality of life by providing supports for health care, housing, nutrition, mental health, and other human needs.

In chapters 6 and 7, we presented concepts and a paradigm for the description and analysis of social welfare programs. This chapter is an exercise in the use of the analytical tools presented earlier. We will use the paradigm and analytical tools here and in chapter 15 when we consider alternative social welfare programs for several important areas of social concern.

As you read this chapter, it will be helpful to analyze in turn each of the programs as they are described so you can compare your own conclusions with the analysis provided. At the end of chapter 15, we will propose a program to minimize poverty.

SOCIAL INSURANCE PROGRAMS

Universal social insurance programs provide benefits to which recipients are entitled without reference to income or assets. Eligibility is a function of an individual's relationship to employment. The major income support insurance programs are Social Security, Unemployment Compensation, and Workers' Compensation.

Social Security (OASDI)

The Social Security Act of 1935 was a watershed piece of legislation establishing several assistance and insurance programs, but when people refer to Social Security, they usually mean Old-Age, Survivors, and Disability Insurance (OASDI). This program was originally enacted as old-age insurance designed to replace some income that is lost when a worker retires because of old age. The program as we know it today emerged through a series of legislated amendments. In 1939, even before the original program was fully operational, benefits were extended to workers' dependents and survivors and, in 1956, the disability insurance component was added. Over time, more categories of workers were added so that approximately 96 percent of jobs are now covered, in contrast to the 55 percent covered when the program was initiated. The full program is now referred to as OASDHI; the "H" is for hospital (that is, Medicare, which is discussed in chapter 10).

Details of the OASDI program regarding eligibility, benefits, and financing undergo numerous changes and continue to face changes. Therefore, it is necessary here to focus on the skeletal structure of OASDI rather than on specifics, which may be obsolete by the time they are read.

Who Is Eligible for the Program?   Coverage is generally compulsory but some of the 96 percent of the paid workforce is covered voluntarily. However, more than 6 million workers in 1996 were not covered by Social Security, the majority of whom were state and local government employees. As of 1983, state government entities may not terminate Social Security coverage, and all federal employees hired after 1983 are covered for OASDI. Beginning in 1984, all employees of nonprofit organizations became covered, and in 1991 state and local employees who were not members of a public retirement system were mandatorily covered under Social Security.

To be eligible for retirement benefits a worker must be 62 years old or over with the required number of quarters of covered employment (worked a requisite number of years). If one retires before age 65 years, reduced payments are received. For disability coverage, a worker must be assessed as unable to engage in substantial gainful activity by reason of a physical or mental impairment that is expected to last not less than 12 months or to result in death, be under age 65 years, and be fully insured under Social Security. There are special eligibility requirements for persons who are blind. From 2003 through 2008 the retirement age will gradually rise to 66 from 65 years, then from 2021 through 2027, it will gradually rise to 67, contrary to a decades-long trend toward earlier retirements. In 1995, the average age at retirement was 63.6 years.[2] Dependents' benefits are payable to the spouse of a retired or disabled worker if a currently married spouse is at least 62 years of age or is caring for one or more of the worker's entitled children who are disabled or are under 16; or a divorced spouse aged 62 years or older, not married, and the marriage to the worker lasted at least ten years before divorce became final. A divorced spouse may be entitled independently of the worker's retirement if both the worker and the divorced spouse are age 62, and the divorce has been final for at least two years.

Survivors must be dependents of deceased workers who were fully insured at the time of death. A monthly survivor benefit is paid to a widow (er) (aged 60 years or 50–59 years if disabled, with a waiting period) if he or she is unmarried or remarriage occurred after the widow(er)'s first eligibility for benefits. Dependent, unmarried, biological or adopted children, stepchildren, and grandchildren of a retired, disabled, or deceased worker receive a monthly benefit if under age 18 years, a full-time elementary or secondary student under age 19, or a disabled person age 18 or over whose disability began before age 22 years.

A monthly survivor benefit is payable to a mother (father) or surviving divorced mother (father) if the deceased was fully insured, if the beneficiary is not married and has one or more entitled children of the worker in his or her care. In the case of divorced persons, the child must be a natural or legally adopted child under the age of 16 years of age or disabled. A monthly survivor benefit is payable to the parent of a deceased fully insured worker who is 62 years of age or over, and has not married since the worker's death and was receiving at least one-half of her support from the worker at the time of the worker's death. Proof of support must be filed within two years after the worker's death or the month in which the worker filed for disability.

Eligibility for benefits is universal and not related to wealth, assets, or unearned income. But since OASDI is a benefit for those not working or those unable to work, there is a reduction or loss of benefits beyond a certain level of earned income.

What Is the Form of Benefit?   Benefits are in the form of a monthly check or funds transfer to a bank account. The amount ranges from a minimum to a maximum, depending mostly on the worker's covered earnings. The formula changes from time to time but has remained generally related to contributions. Beginning in July 1975, monthly payments were increased whenever the consumer price index (CPI) increased by 3 percent or more. In 1986, this cost-of-living benefit increase (COLA) was made contingent on any upward movement of the CPI in the past 12 months. The automatic benefit increase granted to all recipients is equal to the actual rise in the CPI.

The benefit amount may change if the beneficiary continues to work. In 1998, someone between the ages of 65 and 69 years could earn up to $14,500 and retain the full benefit. Those under 65 years could earn $9,120. For those beneficiaries under 65 years who exceed the earnings test, $1 was lost for every $2 of earnings. Those 65 years of age and older lost $1 for every $3 earned. Beneficiaries 70 years of age or older could earn any amount and still retain the full benefit. The exclusion of earnings without the loss of benefits is to climb to $30,000 by the year 2002. Earnings limits are hotly debated. Upper-income professionals are more likely to want to work than blue-collar workers. Those who regard Social Security as a pension believe benefits should only be received by those who are retired; others regard Social Security as an annuity owed to recipients whether they are working or retired.

Other recent changes created equity between husbands and wives if either spouse retires or dies and granted higher bonuses for delayed retirement. The amount of the bonus rises to 8 percent for those retiring workers attaining 65 years of age after 2007, and the retirement age rises gradually. Persons who opt for retirement from 62 to 67 years of age will do so with a penalty when their benefits are computed.

How Is the Program Financed?   The OASDI program is financed by an earmarked tax (Federal Employees Contribution Act [FICA]) by covered employees, by employers, and by the self-employed. This tax is a fixed percentage of the wage, up to a certain maximum. In 1998, the tax rate was 7.65 percent; the first $68,400 of earnings was taxable at this rate for OASDI. There was no limit on the maximum taxable payroll earnings for Medicare. Of the 7.65 percent tax, 6.2 percent is allocated for Social Security and Social Security Disability; 1.45 percent for Medicare. The self-employed paid 15.3 percent and were able to deduct for income tax purposes half of the tax to allow for the fact that employees do not pay income tax on the value of the employer's FICA tax.

Benefits are taxed at either 50 percent or 85 percent, depending on whether one files income taxes as an individual or a joint return and how much income one receives. This helps to finance the system more progressively, but also serves as a "backdoor" means test. Proceeds from those taxed 50 percent are credited to the OASDI Trust Funds and from those taxed 85 percent credited to the Medicare Hospital Insurance (HI) Trust fund.

What Is the Level of Administration?   The OASDI program is administered by the Social Security Administration with offices located in various parts of the United States. Because it has no up-front means test and is centrally administered, the Social Security system is among our most cost-efficient programs; costs typically constitute less than 1 percent of annual benefit payments.[3] Claims are reviewed in regional centers. The Treasury Department collects taxes, prepares checks, and maintains trust funds. Disability determinations are made by state agencies and reviewed by the Social Security Administration. The taxation or recoupment of benefits where incomes rise above particular levels is handled through the income tax system.

Discussion   The OASDI program is a national, universal, and institutional social welfare program. There is no means test, and everyone in the category is eligible for assistance. It is seen as a necessary and desirable element in society to provide some support for people who have retired or who have become totally disabled or for the dependent families of breadwinners who have retired or died. It is viewed as a right by those who receive it and does not bear the stigma attached to public assistance and some other social welfare programs. Central to this psychology of acceptance of Social Security has been its connection to employment and contributory nature—that is, those who ultimately are to receive benefits are those who have, to some degree, made contributions to the system. Thus it has a spirit very much akin to private insurance, and beneficiaries feel that they are entitled to receive the benefits—that they are in a sense being repaid their own money. All of this has contributed to making Social Security our largest income transfer program and the bedrock of social insurance in the United States.

When created Social Security included "insurance" in the title to indicate a social welfare program designed to ensure against a certain risk. However, Social Security is like insurance in that (1) in order to receive benefits one must contribute to the program and (2) people who pay very little get less in benefits than those who pay the maximum, and benefits are graduated along the scale from a very small minimum amount to the maximum contribution.

However, in at least three other ways Social Security is not like private insurance and should not be confused therewith:

1. Benefits are not exactly related to contributions. Although benefits will increase for those who contribute more, it is not in a direct relationship. Social Security benefits are skewed toward the bottom end; that is, the lowest earners receive replacement of approximately 58 percent of their preretirement income; average earners, 43 percent; and maximum earners, approximately 25 percent.[4] Thus, while benefits increase with contributions, they do not increase in a way that would be "fair" in private insurance. Social Security serves as a supplementary pension plan for those who contribute most, but also as a "welfare" program for those most in need.

2. Social Security is unlike private insurance in that the benefits are not due by contract at the time of entering the program. The benefits are based on whatever the current legislation is and not on any insurance "right." This can work to both the detriment and the benefit of the recipient. Thus one's benefits under Social Security are dependent on current legislation rather than on contributed funds. In order to make this possible, it is necessary for there to be the third and most important difference between Social Security and private insurance.

3. Benefits are paid essentially from current funds received rather than from reserves. In a private insurance system, the company may set aside a reserve fund to get started, but eventually the funds collected from contributors must be calculated to be sufficient to pay benefits as they are claimed by beneficiaries. Not so with Social Security. Funds contributed in the past by those now collecting Social Security would be insufficient to meet the current benefit levels. Although there is a reserve fund that helps to meet sudden emergencies and fluctuations, the benefits that are being paid to current recipients are for the most part the receipts from those who are now paying Social Security taxes. When those now paying Social Security taxes are eligible for Social Security, they will depend for their benefits on legislation that will be forcing those then working to contribute to the system. Thus, Social Security is an intergenerational transfer program. Even with a massive insurance reserve some people become concerned when they think of Social Security in terms of private insurance. The backing of the Social Security system, however, is not weak; it is the legislative power of the U.S. Congress—the power to tax—whether that tax is euphemistically called a contribution to an insurance system or one that goes to the general revenues.

Social Security is now running surpluses, and the program is not expected to begin spending more than it takes in until 2032. Meanwhile, the surplus, which amounted to approximately $731 billion in 1998,[5] is invested in Social Security trust funds, which invest in government securities that must be repaid with interest. The funds are not expected to be able to pay benefits in full (as now organized) by 2032. Even then, it would be able to pay 80–85 percent of the expected benefits.

When the problems confronting Social Security are considered, highlighted is its relationship to the "baby boom" generation, a large group of Americans born after World War II. Following this boom, there ensued a declining birth rate, producing fewer workers to support the huge baby boom generation retirees and those who follow. This ratio by itself, however, does not determine Social Security's future. Some experts argue that productivity matters more than the ratio of workers to beneficiaries: The total income that workers generate in relation to the costs of benefits is more important than the mere number of workers in relation to the number of retirees.[6] Two other factors also play a part: the lengthening of the average life span and periods of less than full employment when receipts diminish.

A continuing argument about Social Security has to do with the concept of minimal versus optimal levels. Social Security was never intended as a full-retirement system; it was seen as a way of supplementing people's savings, private insurance, and pension plans. Increasingly, current retirees do have other assets to draw on, but there remain many elderly who have no other insurance program, and the minimum level of Social Security benefits is too low to maintain adequate living standards for most people. To improve the minimum benefits to the point of adequacy would seem burdensome to taxpayers who resist having massive amounts of money spent for universal programs, because some of this would go to the rich who have other forms of income and do not need this higher minimum. However, not to improve it condemns many elderly to unrelieved poverty. (For those households of the elderly, aged 65 years and over, in 1990 Social Security payments were 80 percent of their incomes.[7]) The compromise has been to supplement Social Security minimums where there is no other income by using a means-tested program, formerly called Old-Age Assistance and since the 1970s known as Supplemental Security Income (SSI), which is discussed subsequently. Thus the problem of vertical adequacy, at least at the minimum level, is somewhat covered. With the improvements in Social Security coverage since its inception, horizontal adequacy is good, and almost all workers are covered today. It is the size and power of its constituency and broad inclusion that give the program its political strength, because it touches almost every family in the nation. This inclusivity also encourages societal cohesion rather than divisiveness, a mark of means-tested, selected programs. Beyond the immediate assistance Social Security provides recipients, there are indirect benefits for middle-aged families who have their parents cared for, thereby not forcing them to choose between supporting their parents and their own children.[8]

The most serious argument in recent years has been over Social Security's form of financing. Social Security, as we have pointed out, is not really an insurance program. The contributory form has been very valuable in affording beneficiaries dignity and giving people a sense of right of entitlement to benefits. It also has meant that the Social Security system is in reality a social welfare program financed by a most regressive tax somewhat offset for low-income workers by the Earned Income Tax Credit. Essentially, the policy choices are the following: lower benefits for future generations, add revenue to the system, have workers work longer, and invest some of the income in the stock market, performed either by individuals or as a part of the trust funds.

To recapitulate, the OASDI program is financed by a fixed-percentage tax on the wages of employees, employers, and the self-employed equal to the combined tax paid by employer and employees. All of this is up to a fixed maximum, which has been raised from time to time over the years. However, these two components—a fixed-percentage tax and a tax only up to a maximum—have added up to regressive taxation: So long as the person earning $25,000 a year and the person earning $68,400 a year are both paying, let us say, a 6 percent tax for Social Security contributions, this is regressive, because 6 percent of the poorer person's tax is much harder to afford than 6 percent of the higher-income worker's tax.

A progressive tax, as explained in chapter 6, is one in which the percentage of contribution goes up with income. However, the second feature of Social Security makes the tax even more regressive. If the maximum taxed income is, let us say, $68,400 per year, then someone earning $100,000 or more per year is paying the same total tax to Social Security as the person earning $68,400. This compounds the regressivity of the Social Security system. So long as the system is contributory and so long as benefits are related to contributions, some regressivity seems inevitable. To raise the level of contribution to an unlimited amount would make it necessary also to raise benefits exceedingly, beyond the intent of the Social Security system for the higher-income person. Numerous ways around this problem have been suggested, from raising the maximum base of amount taxed for the employer share only, so that benefits for the workers do not have to be raised, to infusing the Social Security system with some partial relief from general revenues that would make it more progressive, even while keeping the contributory system as a base. A partial solution legislated in 1983 was to tax benefits of those Social Security recipients who have other significant income, but the basic question of the equitable financing of the Social Security system is likely to continue to be an issue.[9]

Another problem with the Social Security system is its coherence with other social policies. If we are entering an age of automation, then we might want to push for earlier retirement benefits. On the other hand, if we need all the labor power we can get, then the availability of retirement at age 62 and at full funding even at age 67 years might be incompatible with this policy. Social Security policy has been related to our approach to employment. When laws are passed regarding the legality of mandatory retirement ages, this has an impact on the Social Security system.

The question of gender equity has confronted Social Security policymakers for many years. Legislative changes have eliminated distinctions based on gender. In 1950, husbands and widowers who were financially dependent on their wives became eligible for spousal benefits. In 1961, men were permitted to retire at age 62; women had been given this prerogative in 1956. In 1983, amendments to the Social Security Act further reduced inequities for men.

Notable gaps regarding women remain. Women who do not work outside their homes receive no benefits for work performed there. Women who divorce within ten years of marriage are not entitled to any benefits based on their former spouse's earnings. Older women who are divorced after a longer-term marriage and have never entered the workforce receive a generally inadequate benefit based on a percentage of their former spouses' primary insurance amount. Divorced older women receive an often deficient spousal benefit when their ex-husband retires.

Working married women are entitled to their benefit or one based on their husband's earnings, but not both. Because of the way benefits are currently determined, inequities may arise. The survivor of a two-earner couple, for example, often receives a lower benefit than the survivor of a one-earner family with the same total average indexed monthly earnings. Some of these issues are related to the fact that, as noted earlier, Social Security benefits are not directly linked to contributions. Others require consideration because of the high rate of divorce and the large numbers of women in the workforce, both factors not present when Social Security was designed in the 1930s.

Suggestions for enhancing benefit adequacy and equity in the Social Security system have been proposed. In the earnings sharing plan, the yearly income of both husband and wife are combined and divided evenly. In the double-decker system, each individual who is 65 years of age or disabled receives a guaranteed minimum monthly income. In addition, each can receive additional monthly monies related to prior earning. At this second level, the combined covered earnings of husbands and wives would be the basis for a married couple's benefits. Homemaker credits, in which homemakers earn Social Security credits for caregiving years out of the paid work force, also have been recommended. In view of current demographic trends, these problem-solving approaches may very well receive further attention in the next decade.[10] Another question regarding equity is raised by younger people who support the system but feel they will receive fewer benefits than the current retirees. While the Social Security tax burden generally falls on the employed, middle-aged population, careful computations would have to be done in order to compute exactly where the costs to society may rest. For example, the cost of retirement benefits may be offset by reduced benefits for smaller average-size families and increased numbers of women in the workforce.

Another unresolved issue regarding Social Security is the expanding monies in the OASDI trust funds. There have been several suggestions, from leaving it to collect interest to giving some back to using it for social welfare programs, to giving it all back and letting people provide for their retirement as they wish. This latter suggestion plays a part in proposals for altering Social Security as we shall see in later discussion. In any case, when the economy is expanding Social Security taxes increase and stave off future problems.

Reducing the regressive tax has been viewed by some persons as one way to increase the spendable income of low-paid workers. A related concern is that the surplus that by law can only be invested in government securities is included in the budget, thereby reducing—at least on paper—the size of the federal budget deficit and its rate of growth.

Social Security is one of those social welfare programs that have counter-cyclical consequences. That is, in times of high employment fewer people will be retiring so that less benefits will be pumped into the economy and more Social Security taxes will be taken out of the economy from working people. When unemployment is high more people will retire, and therefore, more benefits will be paid out while less money comes in. This is described further in discussing unemployment compensation, a classic counter-cyclical program.

The advent of Social Security also brought tremendous consequences for the development of leisure time activities: the culture of retirement. The fact that the benefits are national rather than local led to the possibility of retirement communities. If the benefits are mine wherever I go, then I can move to warmer states or to places where living costs are lower. This mobility is a consequence of the Social Security system. In fact, the availability of benefits no matter where the beneficiary goes has led a number of people to emigrate after retirement to countries where the cost of living is lower. Social Security has contributed to helping older people form perhaps the most powerful lobby in the nation and to establish a political system in which Social Security is almost sacrosanct in terms of the level of benefits. This is the most dramatic example we have of the degree to which universal social welfare systems tend to be improved even while selective ones may be cut.

Social Security is not the only federal retirement program. The United States Civil Service Commission, Bureau of Retirement, administers a federal civil service retirement system. This is funded by employer and employee contributions, and cash benefits are paid to retirees because of age or disability and to survivors under certain conditions. In 1934, the federal government mandated a similar system based on the Railroad Retirement Act for railroad employees. This program provides retirement, disability, and survivor annuities to workers whose employment was connected with the railroad industry for at least ten years. In 1974, some integration of this program with the Social Security program was developed by Congress, and Social Security credits earned during workers' employment careers are included in the benefit computation. Benefits are financed through a combination of employee, employer payroll taxes, income from a Social Security financial interchange, income from investments, federal general revenues, and a tax levied on railroad carriers. In 1997, there were 765,500 beneficiaries of the Railroad Retirement System at a cost of approximately $8 billion.[11] The Department of Defense administers a retirement, as do many local and state public employee systems.

The Future of Social Security   Retirement income rests on a four-tier system of arrangements: Social Security, employer-sponsored pensions, individual savings, and Supplemental Security Income (SSI). As it happens, the longer range picture for Social Security has become somewhat problematic. Problems include the long-term balance of funds, the ratio of contributions and benefits, and public confidence. Changes made in 1983 prevented insolvency of the program but expenditures are expected to exceed income by 2032 and to remain high thereafter. Long-range projections are complex and based on several assumptions, including the following: the gross domestic product will rise annually up to 2050, wages will rise at a particular rate, the cost of living will also rise at a particular rate, unemployment will be at a certain rate, and Social Security benefits will fall in relative terms as the age at which full benefits rises from 65 to 67 years of age over the first few decades of the next century. Those retiring under the higher age will get less than under previous age rules. The specific assumptions when taken by themselves seem to bode well for the system.

However, for a time, the baby boomers will be in their most productive years and the "baby trough" generation of the 1930s Depression will lead to a stable ratio of workers to recipients—that is, until approximately 2010. At that point, 76 million baby boomers begin to retire, and the ratio will erode rapidly. By 2025, most of the surviving baby boomers will be 65 years of age or older. Those over 65 years are expected to rise by 75 percent while the number of workers will rise by only 15 percent, reducing the ratio of workers to beneficiaries.

Under this forecast, the trust funds would be credited with a surplus of almost $3 trillion until 2020 and taxes will exceed expenses; trust fund balances will begin to decline thereafter and tax receipts would lag. Interest credited to the trust funds would provide for part of the needed benefits. However, at a point, the principal in the trust funds would have to begin to be drawn down. Unless economic and demographic assumptions are better than now forecast, the government would then have three options: raise other taxes, curtail other spending, or borrow money from financial markets.

The trustees' report projects Social Security will generate sufficient tax receipts for the short range, but questions must be raised about the long-range future. The projections depend on demographic factors that are known: the post–World War II baby boom, the subsequent birth dearth, and the general aging of society. To restore long-run solvency, income needs to be raised or expenditures cut. There are additional factors that must be taken into consideration: the fiscal situation of Medicare, the costs of medical care generally, and whether future technological advances will increase productivity beyond projections. Beyond these factors, there may be other contingencies that are not identifiable before they actually occur.

Proposals   An advisory council appointed by the Secretary of Health and Human Services (Social Security later became an independent agency) was charged with evaluating the long-term solvency of Social Security and reviewing other national retirement policies. When they reported in 1997, three proposals were presented; however, no one approach could be agreed upon to restore the long-term (75 years in the future) balance. They did agree on the following principles:

1. Means testing of benefits was rejected.
2. Employer and employee contributions through payroll taxes would be maintained.
3. Mandatory universal participation would continue.
4. Cost of living raises (COLAs) would be maintained as determined by the Bureau of Labor Statistics.
5. The amount of Social Security benefits that exceed what the worker paid into the system would be included in taxable income.

Three options were proposed, all of which satisfy the statutory requirement that the plan be in long-term, 75 year balance.

One group favored a *Maintenance of Benefits (MB)* plan, which retains the existing benefit structure but would invest approximately 40 percent of trust funds into common stocks indexed to the equities market. These investments would be guided by an investment policy board, which would invest funds on behalf of the trust fund and the government would bear the risk of the investments. The maximum years of wage history used to calculate benefits would be increased from 34 to 38 years. This plan requires no further increase in retirement age or reductions in disability/survivors' benefits, redirects the revenue from taxes currently going to the Medicare (HI) trust fund, covers all newly hired state and local government workers, and increases the payroll tax by 1.6 percent in 2045.

A second approach, labeled the *Individual Accounts (IA)* plan, creates a two-tier benefit structure. In the first tier, the benefits for primarily middle and high wage earners are reduced. In the second tier, a mandatory 1.6 percent of wages (an additional payroll tax) is contributed to an individual account and invested by the employee in a limited range of government-provided investment choices. Individuals bear the risk of these accounts. The plan also accelerates and extends scheduled increases in eligibility ages for benefits and suggests an automatic increase in the age tied to longevity. This plan calls for full taxation and a phaseout of minimum income thresholds, an increase in the maximum years of wage history considered, and coverage of newly hired state and local employees. This plan phases down the spouse's benefit to one-third of the worker's primary insurance amount and increases widows' benefits. Future benefit growth for middle and higher income workers would be reduced. There would be no redirection of tax revenues currently channeled to the HI trust fund.

The third group proposed the *Personal Security Accounts plan (PSA)*. This proposal is the most radical and also uses a two-tier system. The first tier provides a flat benefit roughly equal to slightly more than one half of the average benefit. In the second tier, the employee's current OASI payroll tax will be contributed to an account, invested in a range of financial instruments, and owned and managed by the individuals who bear the risk of their investments. An additional payroll tax of 1.52 percent (total split by employer and employee) is needed for 72 years to fund the transition to a new system. Acceleration and extension of already scheduled increases in ages of eligibility for benefits are needed. The balance of the payroll tax would fund a modified retirement program and modified disability and survivor benefits. There would be full taxation of reduced uniform benefits, derived from untaxed employer contributions, taxation of half of other social security benefits and a phaseout of minimum income thresholds for taxation. Other features would include state and local coverage, a reduction of benefits for future disabled workers, a reduction of benefits for women who never worked outside of the home, and an increase in benefits for many elderly widows. The basic benefit would increase to reflect increases in national average wages prior to retirement plus the proceeds of their PSAs. These latter two proposals would alter substantially the structure of Social Security as it has existed.

Among the technical changes suggested are the following: means testing the benefits, which would alter profoundly the nature of the program; raise payroll taxes, which would raise revenue but aggravate the regressivity of the tax; increase retirement age, which is being done; change the benefit formula, which provides cost of living adjustments (this too would most harm the poor); trim the benefits for new retirees; and subject more benefits to income taxation while protecting those with lower incomes.[12] What appears to be simple problem solving is greatly complex. For example, reducing the COLA by 1 percent below the Consumer Price Index compounds year after year. Thus, the longer a person lives, the greater the reduction they will experience in their Social Security benefits, the opposite of the compounding that occurs when you get an annual percentage raise in your wages. Furthermore, those who live many years after retirement are generally widows, whose financial situations may be poor.

There are other issues as well. If assumptions being used prove inaccurate, they could have produced overly pessimistic projections. Or, if the 40 percent of taxes is to be taken out of Treasury bonds, this will depress prices, and interest rates will have to rise. This action can result in greater costs for serving the federal debt, greater expenses for municipal and local jurisdictions competing for funds to borrow, and higher interest for mortgages and other personal and business needs.

Some persons argue that there is no serious crisis in regard to Social Security— after all the gap over the next 70 years is not great; others contend there are serious but manageable problems. Some persons suggest there is agreement among experts as to the technical requirements to solve problems, while others suggest that though there is agreement about some matters, there is also disagreement about which techniques should be used. Others argue that the major disagreements among proposals are based in ideologies.

In addition to the three plans introduced here, there are many others. As we have maintained throughout this book, choices in social welfare are influenced by ideology and values. One group wishes to maintain the system with relatively few changes and to continue a program that has been extremely successful. They believe the program needs adjustment but not radical change. Others suggest the program should be eliminated altogether. Everyone should be independent and responsible for themselves and their families and there should be no shared risks.

The group that contends there are manageable financing problems suggest the program needs prudent adjustment but not major revision. They argue that political ideologies are in contention and not technical adjustments. The questions raised by this group are whether Americans want a society in which all workers and their families are insured against risks of dying too young and outliving their retirement savings. This can only be done through collective insurance. Do Americans want a society that mandates savings and investments for retirement but leaves the ultimate security of workers and their families to be determined by the market and their successful investments?[13]

One group opposes governmental control, including the idea of investment by the government in the stock market. For this group, the critical problem is centralized control because they do not trust government, fear that a government board would over- or under-invest in particular sectors of the economy and, in their terms, generally fear government power and influence. They simply do not want government to have a major voice, as they see it, in the control of industry. Furthermore, these critics worry that investment decisions would be politically motivated.

The financial industry—insurance companies, mutual funds, "Wall Street," banks, various investment firms—all support privatization both on pragmatic and ideological grounds. Fees have to be charged for administering personal accounts, buying, and selling, and they favor "free market" solutions, believing them the better choice. Others favor privatization for other reasons. Every worker would become a shareholder, building retirement protection while securing the higher returns of private capital investment. Some proponents suggest privatization would also protect workers from political uncertainty about future benefits. At retirement, workers could withdraw their funds, whether working or not, and balances at death could be left to family members. Those who argue for privatization also suggest that more saving and investment will result, wages would be raised, and national income would increase in future decades.[14]

An option is to increase the earnings of the current system. One way this could be done is by privatizing the Social Security system in part or in total. But, there are gradations among even those plans that favor privatization. Some would limit the choices available for workers to invest some or all of Social Security's revenue in the stock market and give workers control over their own investment accounts. Others would have each worker manage his or her own account. Other planners suggest the existing system be retained but excess social security tax revenue be invested in the stock market by a government investment board, which, it is expected, in the long run would produce higher returns.

An argument supportive of individual private accounts is the fact that a growing number of Americans have had experience with Individual Retirement Accounts (IRAs) and 401(K) plans. The suggestion to use such accounts and stocks and bonds takes place in the context of a booming stock market for an extended period. Individual private accounts also have the palatable political implications of finding more money for the retirement system but without asking citizens to pay more taxes.

There are those who think that some who wish to privatize Social Security want to abolish it, opting for an enhanced sense of ownership by participants and individual responsibility for investment decisions and one's financial security in retirement and disability. Others wish to retain the shared responsibility of all working citizens. Paradoxically, some critics who opt for privatization view such a use of the market as a disguised move to nationalize and control the economy. Other criticisms expressed are that privatization will be less redistributive than Social Security and more likely to leave workers with low lifetime earnings in financial straits. Those who choose low-risk and low-return investments will be unable to offset the effects of inflation. More importantly, financial markets fluctuate. The 1990s may be good; but the 1930s were disastrous. Individual workers' decisions might contribute to greater market volatility. Individualized Social Security probably would have to have a lump-sum, cash-out option. What happens if recipients fall on hard times? Finally, what about the loss of inflation protection that now exists because of the cost-of-living adjustment?

Other criticisms have been identified related to women and privatization. Women earn on average less than men, so less money would go into their accounts. Women are viewed as typically more conservative investors, thus being protected when the market does poorly but falling behind when the market would do well. Women who amass as much as men would have to draw out less than men because they must anticipate living longer on average. None of the proposed plans provides monthly payments to a divorced spouse. When a worker dies today, a spouse can get the entire benefit. With private savings plans, the worker can take money as needed, so spouses get no income guarantees.[15]

Social Security has been a highly successful program. In chapter 8 we observed the important role it plays in raising people out of poverty. Benefits are currently kept up-to-date with wages before retirement and with prices following retirement. As one's standard of living rises, the Social Security benefit automatically rises with it. Thus, beneficiaries are guaranteed inflation proof. This inflation protection is particularly important for aging people as it offsets their personal savings' depletion over time. Other advantages include the opportunities created for younger workers when older workers make room for them and the multiplier effects of the economic activity generated by the recipients' expenditures. Finally, Social Security provides not just for retirement but also for family protection and disabilities, even relieving the burden of caring for aged parents by those who are raising families themselves.

At the time this is being written, a major debate is taking place, with discussions in many places. It is clear that a redesign of the Social Security system is impending. The question is to what extent changes will be made and the nature of those changes, moderate or more radical.

Unemployment Compensation

Goals   Unemployment compensation (UC) is a federal-state program designed (1) to provide temporary and partial wage replacement to involuntarily unemployed workers who were recently employed and (2) to help stabilize the economy during recessions. The first governmental unemployment compensation program was created in Wisconsin in 1932 and was the forerunner of the unemployment compensation program included in the Social Security Act of 1935. By 1937, all states, the then-territories of Alaska and Hawaii, and the District of Columbia enacted programs. Puerto Rico joined in the 1950s.

Who Is Eligible for the Program?   States developed diverse and complex methods for determining eligibility under federal and state laws. In 1995, about 98 percent of all wage and salaried employees, or 90 percent of all employed persons, were covered by UC. To receive benefits, persons must have worked recently for a covered employer for a specified period of time and earned a certain amount of wages. All states cover state and local government, certain agricultural labor, and certain domestic service. Special legislation provided coverage for federal civilian employees, ex-military personnel, and railroad workers. Among those excluded from federal coverage are self-employed workers, those employed by their families, members of the judiciary, elected officials, legislators, and those employed by a nonprofit agency that has fewer than four employees. States have the option of covering groups not included in federal legislation, and many do so. However, in general, states do not cover students, individuals unemployed because of family responsibilities, professional athletes between sport seasons, school personnel between academic years, and illegal aliens.

To be eligible, an individual worker must meet a state's specifications regarding the amount of wages earned and/or length of time worked during a "base period." The worker must be able to work, be available for work, and be registered for work at the state unemployment office. Some evidence of an active job-search effort is required by most states, and the person cannot refuse an offer of, or referral to, "suitable work" without good cause. In addition, the worker cannot be viewed as responsible for his or her unemployed status. Such circumstances as being fired because of misconduct, leaving a job without good cause, refusal of suitable work, and involvement in a labor dispute may lead to disqualification for all or part of the benefit year.

There is no assets test, and income from rents, dividends, or earnings of other family members is not used to determine eligibility. This is an insurance benefit available to anyone who qualifies, regardless of wealth; if you are laid off, seeking work, and unable to find it, you are probably eligible for UC. States' UC programs vary in how much proof they demand of unemployed workers regarding their weekly efforts to seek work.

In 1996, 36 percent of the unemployed population received benefits. Thus, approximately one-third of those unemployed actually received benefits, indicating horizontal inadequacy. This low percentage was attributed to several factors: changes in state program eligibility requirements such as increases in the base period earnings requirements in order to avoid raising taxes paid by employers; a decline in the proportion of unemployed from manufacturing industries; a shift in the workforce to service workers, many of whom are part-time or freelance, or, if covered for unemployment compensation, tend not to apply for benefits; geographic shifts in the composition of the unemployed. Other reasons for the decline include changes in federal policy such as partial taxation of UC benefits and changes in the number of unemployed measured.[16]

The Balanced Budget Act (1997) provided that age and claim information can be disclosed to the Department of the Treasury, the Social Security Administration, and State Child Support Enforcement agencies. Also, the Taxpayer Relief Act (1997) requires individuals filing new claims for UC to disclose whether they owe uncollected overpayments of Food Stamps. If so, repayment will be made through deductions from the individual's UC benefits based on an agreement by the individual and Food Stamp agency.[17] Administrative hearings are available to applicants who disagree with a denial of benefits or other issue, first appealing before an administrative law judge and later to the Unemployment Insurance Appeal Board. The case may ultimately be presented in the Appellate Division of the State Supreme Court. An employer who disagrees with a claims decision may use the same appeals procedure.

What Is the Form of Benefit?   Cash benefits are provided in varying amounts determined by wages earned during a "base period." States establish minimum and maximum benefits. The national average weekly benefit amount projected for 1996 was $189 for an average of 14 weeks.[18] The Tax Reform Act of 1986 made all unemployment compensation taxable when unemployment benefits plus other earnings exceeded certain levels. The additional revenue was to be used for offsetting the cost of supplementary benefits for persons unemployed for lengthy periods. Such tax plans serve to concentrate unemployment benefits at the lower income levels and away from middle- and upper-income families.

The regular state programs usually provide benefits up to 26 weeks. The federal-state extended benefits program provides up to 13 additional weeks of benefits when a state's unemployment rate is relatively high. An additional 7 weeks is available under an optional trigger, but only eight states have chosen to use this provision. In times of serious economic recession, temporary federal programs augment the permanent program extending the number of weeks covered. If a worker remains unemployed after the benefit period expires, he or she may be eligible for TANF or general assistance.

In 1994 Congress enacted the General Agreement on Tariffs and Trade (GATT), which requires each state to establish a system for withholding federal income tax from UC payments so that withholding can occur at the option of the claimant. This change became effective at the beginning of 1997. The Social Security Independence and Program Improvements Act (1994) gave states the option of excluding from coverage services performed by aliens admitted to the United States under temporary visas.

Several states added a small tax to cover temporary disability that is not work related. This has been one of the "cracks" between social insurances through which some people fall. Additional benefits are made available in the form of free placement and counseling services for use by employers, veterans, and employees. Work training and retraining programs may also be available.

How Is the Program Financed?   The unemployment compensation program is financed by a payroll tax paid by employers on their total payroll. The federal tax is 6.2 percent of the first $7,000 of each worker's covered wages. Employers in states with federally approved programs and with no delinquent federal loans may credit 5.4 percentage points against the 6.2 percent tax rate. This makes the generally applicable rate 0.8 percent. The federal share of the tax is earmarked for federal and state administrative expenses, the federal share of the federal-state extended unemployment compensation program, and a federal account for state loans. The funds returned to the states are supposed to finance the regular state programs and half of the federal-state extended benefits program. In 1994, 41 states had tax bases higher than the one established by the federal government. Any payments made to a state's unemployment compensation program are credited toward the federal tax. The actual tax paid depends on the stability of an employer's employment history. In almost all states, stability is measured by the amount of unemployment benefits paid to an employer's former workers. Generally, those who discharge fewer workers are granted lower tax rates on their payrolls. This system of "experience rating" was introduced to discourage layoffs. The tax is collected and deposited in the federal treasury in the U.S. Unemployment Trust Fund and then invested, and each state is credited with its share of the interest. States draw as necessary for payment of benefits.

What Is the Level of Administration?   The UC program is administered through the Employment Security Administration of the United States Department of Labor. The collection of taxes is the responsibility of the United States Department of the Treasury. But states each administer their own benefit programs. Programs vary by states, as do the governmental structures used to administer the program.

Discussion   Unemployment compensation is a classic example of the grant-in-aid described in chapter 7. The federal government never formally forced states to adopt UC programs. Instead, the federal government simply legislated a payroll tax on employers throughout the nation. If the state wanted to get the bulk of those taxes back into the state, it had to follow the guidelines for receiving that rebate; namely, setting up a state unemployment compensation system. State programs vary in maximum benefits, number of weeks covered, and so on, but all must meet certain basic guidelines of the federal legislation. This is the grant-in-aid principle:

Money and guidelines come from a higher level, and the administration and some local initiative remain at the lower level. The incentive was so great to get the grant-in-aid and not lose the money for the state that within two years of the establishment of the Social Security Act all states enacted programs.

Unemployment compensation is a universal and institutional program to meet the reality that in our society there will be temporary dislocations that result from shifting market needs, new job locations, and changes in the industrial system. Thus in the best of all economies, some businesses should close, change, and move locations, and some workers will be dislocated. Unemployment compensation is to give these workers breathing space so that the labor market is not degraded and they are not forced to take the first available job at a lower level of skill. It protects the worker, allowing time to seek employment at his or her level. The worker, in reporting to the unemployment compensation office, must demonstrate the fact that he or she has sought work but cannot be forced to accept work in another area from that of prior employment.

The UC reserves tend to build up in periods of high employment when there is little call on them by unemployed workers. This situation suggests that the benefits should be raised because the reserves are building up unnecessarily. However, during periods of a rise in unemployment or a recession, unemployment funds are drained, and the UC system is used as a quasi-public assistance system. The public assistance program is so degrading and stigmatized with its means test that there is great pressure on Congress to extend the benefits of UC for longer periods of time when many people need this kind of help. But the UC system was never set up to meet this massive need. All UC benefits are taxable, suggesting its being viewed as a public assistance program.

Not only is the UC program an income stabilizer, it is an economic stabilizer as well. The UC system is a classic example of a counter-cyclical program. Usually, in a capitalist or "free-enterprise" economy, the normal business cycle moves up and down like a wave every few years, through periods of high economic activity (high employment and the danger of inflation) to periods of low economic activity (high unemployment and the danger of recession). Government has viewed its role as trying to flatten these waves, to take steps that will counter the expected business cycle, deflating the economy in times of boom and pumping up the economy in times of recession. Programs that automatically have this effect are called counter-cyclical. Unemployment compensation is one such program. Some other social welfare programs also have the same effect. During a time of high employment, when there is an economic boom, little money is paid out of the UC system because there is less unemployment; more money is squirreled away in reserve funds because more people are working and there are more payroll taxes to be collected. This taking of money out of the economy is a deflating move, flattening out a tendency for economic boom. On the other hand, when unemployment is high in times of recession, the unemployment compensation system is collecting less funds because fewer people are employed and is pumping more funds back into the economy in the form of benefits because more people are collecting. This money added to the economy serves to generate more economic activity and is, thus, counter-cyclical.

Two principles are illustrated by the concept of experience rating, described previously. Experience rating is a way of rewarding the "good" employer who does not lay off workers. This is supposed to serve as an incentive to keep employees on the job. However, it shows the strains in every insurance program between the insurance principle and the incentive principle. The whole concept of insurance is to pool or share a risk. For example, if there are 40 people in a class and the odds are that one person will break a leg during the year, each of the 40 contributes something so that whoever breaks a leg will have adequate compensation. However, if an analysis is made of the likelihood of each person's breaking a leg and the amount each person contributes is based on that, we no longer have a true insurance system but a system in which each person is paying for his or her own care. Thus in health insurance, in auto insurance, and in the social insurances, experience ratings of specialized groups by age, sex, geographic location, prior experience, and the like, tend to break down the whole concept of pooled risk. On the other hand, some people feel that if one were not to reward safe drivers and good employers, for example, with financial benefits, one would take away the incentives. There is no "right" answer to this balance. The trade-offs are constantly argued by economists and social welfare experts.

But experience rating is also an example of how latent or unanticipated consequences may undo the purpose of a program. As explained, an experience rating was initiated to keep employers from laying off workers in order to maintain their lower insurance rates. However, it may also work in reverse. The concerned employer may not take on new employees or may lay them off before they have worked long enough to become eligible for unemployment compensation just to protect an experience rating. Thus the experience rating may produce just the opposite effect from that originally intended.

Some persons think that unemployed persons remain unemployed longer than they would if benefits were lower and that some unemployed persons end up with more money than some full-time, tax-paying workers. Those who take this point of view contend that benefits discourage aggressive searches for employment. Others suggest that unemployed persons do not obtain jobs because jobs are unavailable, especially during times of recession. The initiation of taxation of such benefits is viewed by some as a significant step toward the taxation of other governmental benefits paid by the federal government.

The relationship of UC to public assistance may become an issue. As welfare recipients are moved into employment, one can expect they will be at special risk of unemployment even in the best of times because of their limited education, work skills, and work experience. There are expectations that former welfare recipients are expected to have jobless rates twice the national average, but it is unlikely changes will be made to enhance or change benefits to deal with this group.[19]

Trade Adjustment Assistance   Trade Adjustment Assistance for Workers (TAA; Trade Act, 1974) consists of trade adjustment allowances, employment services, training and allowances while in training, and job search and relocation allowances for qualified workers. Administered by the Employment and Training

Administration of the Department of Labor through State agencies, the state agencies act as federal agents to provide program information, process applications, determine individual worker eligibility, issue payments, and provide reemployment services and training opportunities. Criteria are used for eligibility related to layoffs, decreased sales, and imports resulting from federal policies to reduce import restrictions that contributed to the layoffs and declining production.

The North American Free Trade Agreement (NAFTA, 1993) established transitional adjustment assistance as a new part of the Trade Act of 1974. The benefits provided are similar to those of the TAA program, but the imports must be from Canada or Mexico. These programs are funded from federal general revenues. Eligibility depends on the "impact" date and whether the worker was employed for at least 26 weeks in the preceding year at wages of $30 or more per week; was entitled to unemployment compensation; had exhausted all rights to any UC entitlement, including any extended benefits; and was enrolled in or had completed an approved training program.

Workers' Compensation

Goals   Workers' compensation (WC) is designed to provide cash and medical benefits to persons with job-related disabilities and survivors' benefits to dependents of those whose death resulted from work-related accidents or illnesses. This program protects workers from two of the problems of the industrial era. In a wage economy, workers are dependent on wages. "Out of work" means "out of wages." It is this risk that WC seeks to insure people against.

Workers' compensation was the first widespread form of social insurance in the United States. In 1902, Maryland enacted the first state compensation law in which benefits were paid without proof of fault, but the United States Supreme Court declared the law unconstitutional. In 1908, the federal government initiated a similar program for federal workers employed in hazardous work. By 1920, all states but six had WC laws; and by 1948, all states had such programs, but they differ greatly in extent of coverage, level of benefits, and insurance underwriting methods used. In addition, the federal government operates WC programs for government employees and for coal miners afflicted with pneumoconiosis ("black lung" disease). There are, therefore, not one, but many WC programs. In our discussion we will focus on their common features.

Prior to the enactment of these programs, the common law principle was well established that a worker had a right to recover damages only if it were proven that the employee's injury or death resulted from the employer's negligence. In such a system, workers were at a disadvantage because of the expense and other resources needed to challenge the employer.

It is easy to see why workers' compensation was the first system of social insurance not only in the United States, but also in England and Bismarck's Germany. Preceding it was an anarchic system in which the worker was never sure of compensation for work-related injury. Even if he or she did receive benefits, they only would come after long litigation. Thus the worker was not covered during the crisis period, and a good deal of the cost of the system went to pay attorneys. Even the employer had to live with uncertainty because eventually there could be a very large liability settlement that could be injurious to it as well. Therefore, both parties could see benefit in a no-fault insurance system, which is what WC is.

Who Is Eligible for the Program?   In 1993, 96.1 million workers (87 percent of wage and salary workers) were covered. Coverage is compulsory for most private employers except in South Carolina and Texas. If employers reject coverage in those states, they lose the use of common-law defenses against suits by employees. Many state programs exempt employees of nonprofit, charitable, or religious institutions, as well as very small employers, domestic and agricultural employment, and casual labor. Coverage for state and local public employees differs from state to state.

Although a worker is generally eligible regardless of fault or blame, most states do not cover injuries resulting from an employee's gross negligence, willful misconduct, or intoxication. Although claims for occupational disease account for small percentages of WC claims, amendments to and interpretation of state laws covering illnesses with long latency periods is expected to increase this percentage. In addition, medical advances have identified different types of disorders such as traumas caused by constant repetitive motion, pressure, or vibration. This type of disorder accounts for approximately half of all occupational illnesses.

Disputes regarding WC claims can be heard by a Workers' Compensation Law judge. The judge's decision in turn can be reviewed by the Workers' Compensation Board. Ultimately, participants in disputed claims can be heard by the Appellate Division of the State Supreme Court.

What Is the Form of Benefit?   Most WC benefits are paid by insurance companies through policies purchased by private employers and are tied to the requirements of state and federal workers' compensation laws covering the employers. Cash benefit levels are established by state formulas and are usually calculated as a percentage of weekly earnings at the time of the injury or death (typically two thirds) and are periodically paid during the time of disability. Each state (and the federal government for federal workers) sets a maximum benefit level, which they periodically adjust. Medical care and hospitalization costs are covered. In the case of death, payments, including burial expenses, are made to survivors.

A brief waiting period for eligibility is often used to eliminate short duration cases and serves to decrease the cost of the program. When the disability lasts longer than the period specified in law, payment of benefits is made retroactive to the date of injury. It is assumed that sick leave or savings can cover the average worker through time-limited crises.

Cash benefits are limited either by duration or amount. There are differences between benefits for permanent and temporary disabilities. Many states pay temporary total disability for as long as the worker is disabled. Some states have a maximum number of weeks for benefits for temporary disabilities. Some have maximum total payments. For permanent total disability, payments are made for life in a high proportion of the states. In other states, payments are limited to maximum amounts for a maximum number of weeks. Survivors' benefits are provided to spouses until remarriage and until the children reach a particular age. State provisions differ widely in regard to compensation and medical care for injured workers and death benefits and pensions for dependents of workers killed on the job.

Benefit amounts are based on the wage at the time of the accident or at the on-set of illness. Temporary total disability, permanent total disability, permanent partial disability, and death of a breadwinner are usually compensated at two-thirds of the wage, up to a limited maximum. For the black lung benefit program, there is an established federal rate, which is reduced if the state's WC program is also covering the disease. If a worker becomes permanently disabled, he or she may be eligible for cash benefits under both WC and the Social Security Disability Insurance program. However, total benefits under both programs cannot exceed the higher of 80 percent of the worker's former earnings or the total family benefit under Social Security.

Medical services, as needed, are also provided. However, some states have limits on such care, which can be extended under certain circumstances. Rehabilitation services are also provided in some states, as are maintenance payments during the rehabilitation period. Most states provide training in new jobs for workers who cannot continue in their old work because of injury. The federal government and almost all states have laws covering compensation for occupational diseases.

How Is the Program Financed? The funding of workers' compensation is almost entirely borne by employers. In a few states, employees contribute to medical care, and in some states contributions are made from general revenues to the WC fund. Several states have exclusive state WC insurance that employers fund. About a dozen states have state insurance funds and private insurance funds, and employers select their preference. In most states, there is no state fund, and employers are simply mandated to contribute to some private insurance fund. In most states, there is a penalty if an employer does not have insurance. In states where employers have the option, some large firms are self-insured. There is no federal government trust fund, and workers' compensation is dominated by commercial private and self-insurance. Premiums are based on the size of the firm and the nature of the risk involved in the work. Firms are assigned experience ratings on the basis of the use of insurance funds by their employees. This rating is an attempt to introduce a degree of equity into the programs.

The black lung benefit program is funded by general revenues and a federal trust fund supported by a tax on coal.

What Is the Level of Administration? Workers' compensation is enacted through state laws and is state administered through state departments of labor or independent WC boards, by insurance companies, or by state agencies and insurance companies together. The Office of Workers' Compensation Programs in the Department of Labor administers the federal program. As of 1988, the administrative expenses of private insurance carriers as a percentage of the premiums earned was 22.7 percent; the same feature for state-operated funds was 10.6 percent.[20]

Two major trends are reflected in the most recent legislation enacted by states. One focus is on dealing with fraud and the second is providing premium discounts for employers who maintain drug-free workplaces.[21]

Discussion   As one can see, the WC system is a universal form of social insurance. There is no means test based on the workers' income, and it is viewed as an insurance and as a right by the injured worker. Workers' compensation represents an institutional kind of social service program, recognizing that some degree of injury is inevitable in an industrial system, and seeks to provide a simple and equitable compensation for that eventuality. There are several principles that are illustrated by the WC system.

First, it is a basic no-fault system. The no-fault concept can be understood in comparison to its alternative: the liability concept. In the liability concept the person or institution that caused the injury or accident has to be determined. If there is fault or liability, then the faulty or liable party must pay damages to the injured party. In addition to paying for all the costs of the injury and making up for the loss, there may also be punitive damages for having been at fault. This is seen as an incentive for safety. In the no-fault system, there is no attempt made to assess liability. The insurance simply covers the injury and its related costs, and there are no punitive damages. The advantages of no-fault insurance are immense: It eliminates a waiting period and uncertainty; it reduces legal fees and litigation; and it avoids massive punitive damages that may destroy a somewhat innocent party who was responsible for the accident.

However, there are civil liberties purists and others who feel that the no-fault system and WC are unfair, that they deprive the citizen of a constitutional right to sue for damages. It is also argued that, since the original enactment of WC, there are now public assistance and other vehicles by which the injured party can get temporary relief while waiting to go through the courts. Finally, some see no-fault as injurious to incentives to maintain safety. However, the majority view seems to be that the current insurance system represents a dignified approach that serves the interests of the U.S. industrial system best, and there is no major movement to change its basic form.

Another principle that is illustrated by WC is that when a system is financed completely by the employer, as is the case in most states, rather than by employer-employee contributions or by general tax funds, the employers tend to have controlling interests in the regulatory boards and state commissions that govern WC. This has acted, according to workers' groups, to prevent the improvement of the WC system, has caused narrow definitions of what constitutes a work-related versus a non–work-related injury, and so on. It is easy to understand why unions often support employer-employee contributions to systems, even though it costs the worker money: It gives the workers "a piece of the action."

If one may borrow phraseology from community mental health, it is possible to see the evolution of systems for workers' safety in the following ways. The original system of suing for liability is a tertiary kind of care for the injured party, giving rehabilitative relief well after the fact. Workers' compensation represents a secondary level of care that is prompt, universal, and more adequate. The Occupational Safety and Health Administration (OSHA) attempts primary prevention by creating the kinds of conditions in the industrial society where accidents are less likely to occur. The concept of society's working to guarantee safe conditions has been challenged only by free-enterprise purists who believe that the government should stay out of this area completely.

The major criticism directed against the WC system is its still-incomplete horizontal adequacy. This gradually gets corrected as coverage broadens state by state. Whether a worker is declared partially or totally disabled makes a critical difference in the benefit received. The system is also criticized on the level of vertical adequacy. The maximums are seen as too low in some states—hence the calls for maximums up to average weekly wage levels or other such formulas. There is some cost inefficiency in the determination of whether an injury is work related or not. This would be eliminated in a national health insurance plan that covered all medical care regardless of cause. Apart from such a development, it is hard to see how this cost inefficiency can be eliminated. The total coverage of medical care makes it possible for doctors to prescribe whatever is necessary. On the whole, WC is one of the least criticized social insurance systems in American life and one that has found broad acceptance.

Workers' compensation is also a good example of a state welfare system as opposed to a federal one, with all the problems and benefits therein. The problems come from great variations among states, with workers sometimes being unaware of what benefits they actually have, particularly if they move, and the lack of a large federal insurance pool. On the other hand, the fact that there are state variations has allowed progressive states to move faster than the nation might have moved as a whole.

Cost increases for workers' compensation premiums are expected to moderate as the number of lower-risk service jobs grows much more rapidly than those in goods-producing industries. More hazardous employment tends to produce more serious injuries and higher benefit levels. The changing occupational mix in the United States should lead to smaller increases in the total premium amounts per worker paid by employers.

INCOME SUPPORT PROGRAMS

To this point, we have examined programs that are "insurances," but there are a number of means-tested economic security programs as well. In this section, we review three public assistance programs—Temporary Assistance for Needy Families, General Assistance (both commonly called "welfare"), and Supplemental Security Income. We also discuss the Earned Income Tax Credit, a negative income tax program that aids low-income working persons.

Temporary Assistance for Needy Families

Introduced in chapter 5, Temporary Assistance for Needy Families (TANF) is emblematic of a revolution in social welfare policy. Here we will review briefly its major outlines, report on early findings as a result of its implementation, and discuss the current situation.

Goals   Created by the Personal Responsibility and Work Opportunity Reconciliation Act (1996), TANF has four goals: (1) to provide assistance to needy families so that the children may be cared for in their homes or in the homes of relatives; (2) to end the dependency of needy parents on government benefits by promoting job preparation, work, and marriage; (3) to prevent and reduce the incidence of out-of-wedlock pregnancies and establish numerical goals for preventing and reducing the incidences of these pregnancies; and (4) to encourage the formation and maintenance of two-parent families.

What Is the Form of Benefit?   The program provides cash assistance based on need, income, resources, and family size. Nearly all recipients must work after two years in unsubsidized or subsidized employment, on-the-job training, work experience, community service, or 12 months of vocational training. Child care is to be provided for individuals participating in work or community service, child support is enforced, and medical coverage is made available. Exceptions are made for six weeks of job search time, parents with a child under 6 years who cannot find child care, and single parents with a child under age 1 year. A year or more of transitional health care is provided for those who leave welfare for work.

Who Is Eligible for the Program?   States make an initial assessment of a recipient's need, income, resources and skills and develop personal responsibility plans that identify needed education, training, and job placement services. Families cannot spend more than five cumulative years on TANF. States can specify fewer years and exempt up to 20 percent of the caseload from the time limit. After the time limit is exceeded, States can choose to provide noncash assistance and vouchers to families by using Social Services Block grants to state funds. States are expected to reduce rolls by 50 percent by 2002.

Unmarried minor parents are required to live with a responsible adult or in an adult-supervised setting and participate in educational and training activities in order to receive assistance. States are also undertaking efforts to prevent nonmarital teen pregnancy.

State eligibility for block grants depends on operating a child support program, participation in the Federal Case Registry and National Directory of New Hires. Child support can be withheld directly from wages, and paternity establishment is emphasized. Cash assistance will be reduced by at least 25 percent in cases of failure to cooperate with paternity establishment. Uniform interstate child support laws, central registries of child support orders and collections, and toughened enforcement of child support are all implemented.

How Is the Program Financed?   This program is financed by federal general revenues through a fixed basic federal grant of $16.5 billion annually through 2002, plus expanded child care funding. These grants are based on prior federal expenditures for AFDC and a supplemental fund for certain States with low TANF grants relative to poverty and high population growth; a bonus fund for states that reduce out-of-wedlock birth rates without increasing abortion rates; a bonus fund for "high performance" states; a contingency fund for states that experience high unemployment and/or increased Food Stamp caseloads; and welfare-to-work grants. All these grants are capped.

What Is the Level of Administration?   States are largely responsible for administering TANF within certain federal conditions. In addition, the law authorizes states to administer and provide TANF services through contracts with charitable, religious, or private organizations. Beneficiaries who object to the religious nature of organizations must be provided an alternative provider. Federally recognized Native American tribes have the option of designing and operating their own cash welfare programs with funds subtracted from their state's TANF block grant.

Initial Findings   The following description of early TANF results is based on the First Annual Report to Congress by the Administration for Children and Families of the Department of Health and Human Services. The first public assistance caseloads declined dramatically since their peak in 1994. Between January 1993 and March 1998, there was a 37 percent decline, or 5.2 million fewer recipients. Along with the enrollment decline, states expended 18 percent less in December 1997 than they did in March 1994. The percentage of the U.S. population receiving assistance during 1998 was the lowest since 1969. Even before the Personal Responsibility Act became law, 43 states changed their programs from "public assistance" to jobs programs and had declining enrollment because of work requirements, time limited assistance, making work pay, improved child support enforcement, and encouraging parental responsibility.

Under the block grant to states, the federal funds received do not decline with the caseloads. The block grant is based on peak enrollment funding. Early data suggest states are reducing overall spending for the population as caseloads decline but are not reducing their spending per case. Several states are actually increasing their own expenditures for child care, diversion before enrollment, "rainy day" funds, cash- and work-based assistance, and state-earned income tax credit provisions.

Reports indicate there is increased employment among TANF recipients, as well as increased employment among low-income women with children. The strong economy was undoubtedly an important factor in this increase, as had been true in other economic expansion periods. The available evidence included the following:

1. The Current Population Survey calculated for national unemployemt rates found a dramatic increase between 1996 and 1997 in the number of AFDC

recipients who were employed in the following year. In addition, the CPS found larger annual increases in employment by single mothers whose income was under 200 percent of the poverty level. There was also a large increase in the proportion of single mothers with younger children (those under age 6).

2. Evaluations of state reform efforts that began as waiver demonstrations suggest increases of employment of 8–15 percentage points in several states. These evaluations were limited in number and state focused.

3. State surveys of people who left welfare generally find that 50–60 percent were working in the period following public assistance receipt. The remainder were unemployed. Early national data showed that one in three families who received public assistance in 1996 (1.7 million people) were working in March 1997.

All three sources of information point in the same direction, suggesting that the goal of employment was occurring at a dramatic rate. These studies were suggestive but did not isolate the extent increased employment resulted from a strong economy rather than policy shifts.

Child support cases rose and more dollars were collected. The number of paternities established increased two and a half times from 1992 to 1997. Much of this increase was attributed to encouraging fathers to acknowledge paternity at the time of the child's birth. The new National Directory of New Hires through automated technology located 1 million delinquent parents since it began in October 1997. Approximately one third of child support cases involve parents living in different states, and the new technological approach matches wage records throughout the nation. Although a decreasing trend continued in the birth rate for teenagers, it is unclear how the decline relates to the TANF program changes.

Some Characteristics of TANF Families and State Programs   At the outset of TANF, the median length of time on assistance was two years following the opening of the case. One in three families had been in the program for one year or less; one in four had been on the rolls for five years or more. Since 1994 there had been an increasing percentage of long-term recipients on state caseloads. The monthly average TANF payment was $362 in 1997, twelve dollars *less* than the average AFDC monthly payment in 1996. The percentage of families with earned income increased but at low levels. The average number of persons in TANF families remained at 2.8 and a majority of TANF families lived alone. Seventy-five percent of the families had two recipient children. Only 7 percent of the families included two or more adult recipients.

Sixty percent of TANF families were members of minority or ethnic groups. The average age of TANF children was 7.7 years. Almost half of the children were under 6 years of age. The 201,000 TANF teenage mothers represented 5 percent of the total number of TANF families. One in five families had countable assets averaging $489, and the average monthly cash income of all TANF households was $594. Almost all states have moved to "Work First" models requiring recipients to move quickly into available jobs. Almost all states have instituted "social contracts" or other personal responsibility agreements in which recipients agree to specific steps toward self-sufficiency. States are enforcing these agreements and sanctioning people who fail to sign or live up to their agreements. Among these sanctions are the removal of entire families from assistance where a parent refuses to cooperate with work requirements. Forty-two states changed their policies to make work pay, generally by increasing the amount of earnings disregarded in calculating benefits, and raising the level of resources and/or the maximum value of an allowed vehicle.

There is a great variety of state policies regarding time limits. Slightly more than half the states chose the federal limit of 60 months; but others chose to limit the consecutive months of recipiency with a longer period of time, for example, 24 months within any 60-month period. Others chose limits of less than five years but with exceptions or exemptions. Several states, including New York and California, which have the largest caseloads, are devolving key policy and program decisions to counties. Families losing TANF benefits due to increased earnings from work will receive one year of Transitional Medicaid Assistance (TMA). If benefits are lost due to collection of spousal or child support, TMA will be made available for four months. These policies are the same as before under AFDC, but several states chose to provide TMA for longer than the required 12- and 4-month periods. States have to guarantee child care to the extent it is necessary for an individual's employment in any case in which a family ceased to receive assistance as a result of increased hours of or increased income from employment, or as a result of disregarded earnings. This assistance was available for 12 months; the family had to contribute to the cost of care in accordance with a sliding scale based on ability to pay.

Twenty-five states offer up-front diversion programs, in which support is provided as an alternative to TANF assistance. Short-term financial assistance is provided to meet critical family needs in order to secure or retain employment. When such assistance is provided, generally the family agrees not to reapply for cash assistance for a specified period of time.

Exemptions to the time limit are in the following categories: age of parent or caretaker; mentally or physically disabled parent or caretaker; caring for a disabled dependent; victim of domestic violence; actively seeking employment; and high unemployment in the state. Extensions are given in some states to allow nonexempt families that have reached the time limit to continue receiving assistance for an extended period of time, ranging from 3 to 60 months. The most common reasons for extensions are to allow individuals to complete a training program or because the family is unable to find work and is making a good faith effort to find employment.

States are given the option of whether to provide TANF assistance to "qualified aliens." States may not deny assistance to refugees in the United States for less than five years, to asylees and aliens whose deportation is withheld for five years from the date such status was received, to legal permanent residents who have earned 40 qualifying quarters of coverage, or to aliens who served in the armed forces (and their spouses and unmarried, dependent children). Funds may not be used to provide assistance to an alien entering the United States on or after August 22, 1996, for a period of five years beginning with the date of the alien's entry into the country as a qualified alien with the exceptions listed previously. All states except Alabama, Mississippi, and South Carolina chose to continue providing benefits to qualified aliens. Twenty-six states certified they will assist victims of domestic violence and another three states are developing screening and counseling standards.

Discussion   Temporary Assistance for Needy Families, the nation's largest public assistance program, is at the heart of what is commonly referred to as the "welfare problem." Society is often depicted as needing to protect itself against a horde of unwed mothers and other "cheats" striving to live off the public dole. This image is inevitable given the kind of program that public assistance is and persisting negative perceptions of those in need. Interestingly enough, AFDC started in 1935 as a method of keeping mothers in the home to prevent family breakup and to spare mothers from the necessity of having to work. Today, a major objective of the program is to encourage mothers, except for those with very young children, to go to work outside the home. Thus the same program has been altered to meet changing values and priorities in society.

There is probably no way in which the stigma and the ugliness can be completely removed from a massive means-tested program such as TANF. If there were more social insurances, such as childrens' or family allowances or less unemployment or other means by which the rolls could be reduced dramatically, it might be possible to develop a more responsive system, but this is not an immediate prospect.

The question of whether and at what point welfare destroys the incentive to work has been with us since the Poor Laws introduced the principle of less eligibility—that a person on public assistance should not do as well as or better than the lowest-paid working person. This idea is related to the view that the individual requires motivation to work and if given a choice, would not.

Critical Issues   Under the provisions of TANF states are allowed to treat families moving into the state from another state differently than state residents with respect to eligibility rules and benefits levels. Crucial issues for future and current recipients revolve around this feature. As discussed in chapter 6, schemes to treat citizens from other states differently have been found to be unconstitutional. Nevertheless, states continue to advocate for such discriminatory treatment. When one recognizes that the average monthly family income has already been reduced, although slightly, there are indications that states may wish to reduce such expenditures as part of their overall strategies and thus benefits may be further depressed.[22] In fact, in 1998 the Supreme Court accepted an appeal filed by the State of California to decide whether states can constitutionally place special limits on the welfare benefits they make available to new residents. Two-tiered benefit levels were authorized by Congress in PRA (1996), and California was a leader in challenging the original Supreme Court ruling. Previously the U.S. Court of Appeals in San Francisco held there was "persuasive authority" for finding it unconstitutional under Supreme Court precedents holding that the constitutional right to travel protects people from being discriminated against on the basis of their state of origin. The State argued that people remain free to travel or move to California but the State is not obliged to fund the exercise of a constitutional right.[23]

A second major issue is the effect of sanctions. When sanctions and restrictions are imposed on parents that drop cash benefits even as low as to zero, the results can prove injurious to the very children to be protected. Families with very young children are vulnerable to the effects of sanctions because they are the most at risk because of poverty and mothers with very young children are least able to support themselves through the labor market. Some families will be able through one means or another to replace part or all of the payments, but many others will see their incomes fall well below low poverty levels.[24]

Widely publicized reporting of initial successes with regard to jobs and training led some people to believe that TANF is well on its way to solving the many problems encountered. But, the initial employment successes came from the same groups that earlier moved into and out of welfare relatively quickly. This is the group of motivated people with previous work experience who lack physical, mental, and substance abuse problems. Furthermore, as this is being written, available data as to work participation requirements under TANF were incomplete, and definitions of countable work activity were unclear. In addition, different rules apply to different groups such as single and two-parent families, making counting difficult.[25]

The beginning TANF efforts took place at the end of a prolonged economic boom. Press releases trumpeted the dramatic and unprecedented decline. Yet to be confronted is what will happen to recipients whose time limits are reached when the nation is faced with a serious recession and a loss of jobs and training slots. States will then be faced with employers who are not so eager to help, citizens who do not wish to have their taxes raised, and more citizens themselves seeking work. This latter competition reared its head early on. In New York TANF recipients competed for the jobs held by the working poor. There were claims wages were depressed by these new entrants into the job market and that they were being used to replace government employees. A similar problem cropped up when working and TANF parents competed for limited day care places.[26]

Furthermore, some public assistance recipients have undiagnosed learning disabilities which hinder their education, training, and work success. Several studies have found that 25–35 percent of welfare-to-work participants had learning disabilities.[27] Others also have limited educations and lack work skills and experience. This group is at special risk of unemployment. Yet to be determined is whether states will invest in the expensive efforts to raise work participation rates by those who are hardest to place.

For those who qualify for jobs, they are eligible for low-paying jobs without health benefits. At minimum-wage levels and full-time employment, people shift from welfare to the ranks of the working poor, remaining dependent on food stamps and housing subsidies. Those employed part-time have even more difficult circumstances. Marriage is less and less a promising refuge. Men with low educational levels, even if employed, find their wages unequal to inflation. One part of the TANF effort focused on absent fathers, a group that is undereducated and underemployed, and who have distant relationships to their children. Young women turned in some cases to public assistance because this group's earnings were insufficient even when they were motivated to support a family. A large number of efforts have developed to increase their earnings and the amount they pay for child support. A closely watched effort to reach these goals—Parents Fair Share—failed to increase the earnings or employment of noncustodial fathers, although it showed a small increase in the average amount of child support the fathers paid. The study conducted by the Manpower Demonstration Research Corporation was viewed as disappointing by those who were hopeful of greater success.[28]

Similarly, Hispanic mothers in New York City found their efforts to leave public assistance hampered by English language difficulties, training programs that cannot accomodate students with limited English skills, cultural values that favor stay-at-home mothers, husbands who think mothers should stay at home, and distrust of day-care centers and baby sitters.[29]

The Center on Hunger and Poverty of Tufts University developed a scale to document and analyze state welfare program inputs and to evaluate their likely investments in the economic security of low-income families. Among the findings were: (1) the majority of states created TANF programs that ultimately will worsen the economic circumstances of the poor; (2) more than two thirds of the states implemented welfare policies that will make the economic situations of families worse than under the former system; (3) less than a third of the states created policies that are likely to improve poor families' economic conditions.[30]

For how many will TANF improve their lives and for how many make life more unbearable? Will TANF result eventually in an increase in homelessness and drive children into expensive foster care systems? Will states compete to attract tax paying families and corporations by reducing taxes and expenditures for TANF? What happens to children whose families lose benefits, even partially? Some members of Congress expressed major concerns when first reports were made. The point was made that caseload decline has become the measure of success and little was known about what actually happened to families and their children.[31] The true testing of TANF will come when the economy moves into more turbulent waters. Then states will be faced with fewer jobs and more children in need, and Congress will have to decide the extent to which it will attempt to bail out states and localities. In any event, TANF benefits are often inadequate both horizontally and vertically, and yet in the states where TANF is very low there is little inclination by society to raise benefits. On the horizontal side, there are large numbers of potentially eligible people who will never reach TANF because of shame, ignorance, or roadblocks put in the way of their applying. It will take some time before the TANF experience will be completely understood, and that requires a period when the program is not undergirded by a prosperous economy.

TANF is the classic example of cost inefficiency because of the massive problems of means testing and the administrative cost and effort that this entails. It is financed as equitably as possible under our tax system and is a highly necessary program, with all its faults. But the consequences of this form of welfare are stigma, cheating, indignities, and wasted money.

That these income support programs are viewed as something more than a product of government largesse is suggested by the fact that they, as the social insurance programs, have procedures for client appeals of agency decisions. All states, in order to receive federal funding for these programs, must administer hearings that incorporate certain due process mechanisms. Among these are the right to timely and adequate prior notice of an agency action, to cross-examine witnesses, to representation, to a prehearing examination of evidence, and to aid continuing until a hearing decision. The 1970 *Goldberg v. Kelly* Supreme Court decision recognized the constitutional bases for procedural due process in welfare hearings.[32]

Supplemental Security Income

Goals   The Supplemental Security Income (SSI) program is a means-tested, federally administered, income assistance program to provide monthly cash payments in accordance with uniform, nationwide eligibility requirements to needy aged, blind, and disabled persons. As originally envisioned, it was hoped the program would assure those eligible they would not have to subsist on below poverty-level incomes.[33]

The SSI program—implemented in 1974—instituted a national assistance program and replaced three state-administered federally reimbursed programs: Old Age Assistance (OAA); Aid to the Permanently and Totally Disabled (APTD); and Aid to the Blind (AB). These had been part of the grant-in-aid public assistance program established by the Social Security Act. SSI is available in all states.

Who Is Eligible for the Program?   To qualify a person must meet the program criteria for age, blindness, and disability as well as income and assets criteria. Recipients must be U.S. citizens or lawfully admitted aliens living in the United States with limited income and resources or a child of a military person or family stationed overseas, or a student temporarily abroad. A recipient must be 65 years of age or over, or legally blind, or unable to engage in any substantial gainful activity by reason of a medically determined physical or mental impairment expected to result in death or that has lasted, or can be expected to last, for a continuous period of at least 12 months. Generally, the person must be unable to do any kind of work that exists in the United States, taking into account age, education, and work experience. If disabled, the person must accept vocational rehabilitation services if they are offered.

Children may qualify for SSI if they are under age 18 years (or under 22 years if a full time student), unmarried, and meet the applicable SSI disability, blindness, income, and resource requirements. Infants born at less than 37 weeks of gestation and weighing less than 1200 grams meet the disability requirement. Those infants weighing more but with additional problems may also meet the disability requirement. The Personal Responsibility and Work Opportunity Reconciliation Act established a new disability definition for children under age 18 years that requires a child to have a medically determinable physical or mental impairment that results in marked and severe functional limitations, and that can be expected to result in death or has lasted or can be expected to last for a continuous period of not less than 12 months. Previous criteria based on a Supreme Court ruling (*Sullivan v. Zebley*, 1990) were generally considered less stringent. New eligibility criteria took effect August 1997. Many children whose eligibility was based on earlier criteria had their benefits terminated, and it was projected approximately 100,000 will ultimately be removed from the program.[34] Payments may not be made to individuals who are fleeing prosecution for a felony crime or fleeing to avoid custody or confinement after conviction for a crime that is a felony, or violating a condition of probation or parole imposed under either federal or state law.

The SSI law permits six months' benefits to be paid to applicants before a formal decision is made when available information indicates a high probability that the person will be eligible. Among other disabilities, Social Security field offices may find that an individual with HIV whose disease manifestations are of listing-level severity is presumed to be disabled. This ruling has been challenged in at least one state on the grounds it discriminates against women because the course of the disease differs for them.

In 1996, Congress passed legislation that ended drug and alcohol addictions as conditions that qualify individuals for SSI benefits. Substance abusers, thus, became ineligible. However, where a person has more than one disability, it is possible for the benefit to be retained.

What Is the Form of Benefit?   Cash benefits are paid on a monthly basis. As of January 1997, the maximum SSI payment from the federal government for an individual was $484 and $726 for a couple living in their own household. For those living in another's household, the amounts were respectively $322 and $484. Persons residing in Medicaid institutions (where more than half of the bill is paid by Medicaid) receive $30 per month, and those who live with an eligible person and who are considered necessary to provide essential care and services for the person receive $242, provided they meet criteria related to relationship and history.

If an SSI recipient works, there is a dollar for dollar reduction against the maximum amount. Not all income is counted for SSI purposes. A major exclusion is the first $20 of monthly income from almost any source (Social Security but not means-tested veterans' pensions) and the first $65 per month of earned income is excluded. For every $2 earned over $65, the SSI payment is reduced by $1. These policies provide a work incentive. Benefits automatically increase whenever there is a Social Security cost-of-living increase. Many states supplement the federal grant. To prevent reduction of income when persons were transferred to the new national program, states were required to supplement the federal payment to bring it up to what the state level had been. Many states have continued to supplement federal SSI payments, but the total grant is combined administratively into one check for the recipient. In 1998, all but eight States and jurisdictions provide some form of state supplementation.

States provide Medicaid for SSI recipients under three options: (1) A state makes all SSI recipients automatically eligible for Medicaid, (2) the recipient must complete a separate application for Medicaid, or (3) the state may make eligibility criteria more restrictive than SSI criteria, as long as the criteria are no more restrictive than those for the state's Medicaid plan as of a certain date. Except in California, which converted Food Stamp benefits to cash included in the state supplemental payment, SSI recipients may be eligible to receive Food Stamps. Children who lose SSI will continue to receive Medicaid only if they are eligible on other grounds.

Related to an increase in Social Security coverage, there has been a steady decline in the number of persons receiving SSI benefits on the basis of old age. As of 1996, other trends included a slight increase in the number of blind children under 18, a very large increase for children with disabilities, and a sharp increase in the number of adults receiving benefits on the basis of disability.

How Is the Program Financed?   All costs of the benefits and administration of the federal SSI programs are funded through monies from federal general revenues and from states providing supplementation. The administrative costs of federally administered state supplements also are funded in this way.

What Is the Level of Administration?   The Social Security Administration manages the SSI program through regional and district offices located in many parts of the nation. The Social Security Administration may contract for state or local agencies to administer SSI operations. Some states administer the state supplement portion of SSI themselves, but most states that offer this additional benefit have the federal government administer the entire program. There is continuing "outreach" to notify two groups of Social Security beneficiaries: those about to reach age 65 and those disabled persons who have been receiving Social Security for 21 consecutive months and will soon be eligible for Medicare. Outreach efforts to elderly single females particularly can make a great difference.

Discussion   Supplemental Security Income is an interesting potential predecessor of what many thought might become a federalized public assistance program. As we saw in chapter 5, in the early 1970s, there was a move toward a national assistance plan, a little bit like a negative income tax. When this proposal failed, Congress was able to take the less controversial parts of public assistance— the categorical sections of aid to the aged, disabled, and blind—and to federalize them. This occurred because there was not at the time the same pejorative picture of these categories as there was of other welfare recipients, nor are those categories so large. With the blind and the aged, society seems to be more willing to accept the fact that continued public support at some level will be necessary. However, this is not true for those who are substance abusers.

In any event, SSI is a good forerunner of what welfare would be like if TANF were federalized as well. The level of aid is higher than it was in the average state, although not as high as the most generous states were paying. SSI's more humane and reasonable approach permits people to have some minimal assets before becoming eligible, but fundamentally it is simply public assistance on a federal level rather than on a state one. This makes little difference to the client and to the benefit of society but relieves states of a major burden and transfers this burden to the federal government.

The point has been made by some that SSI could be removed from public assistance altogether instead of simply being federalized if (1) the money spent on this program was contributed from general revenues to the Social Security system and (2) the Social Security minimum simply became the SSI minimum. The problem with this is that Social Security, being universal, would also give this minimum to people who had other income. However, most of the people on the minimum level of Social Security are people who are generally poor and who do not have other sources of income—the same people who are applying for SSI.

Reports of substance abusers using SSI payments to purchase drugs led to a representative payee for each substance abuser, mandatory treatment and expected progress in addiction treatment, and the limitation of benefits to a three-year period.

Key Eligibility Provisions Related to Immigrant Status   The Personal Responsibility and Work Opportunity Act (PRA, 1996) cut disabled elderly legal immigrants from the SSI program, fearing the attraction of additional immigrants. The Balanced Budget Act (1997) restored eligibility, affecting approximately 350,000 persons. As this is being written, the following rules applied. Legal immigrants who were receiving SSI on August 22, 1996, may retain SSI and Medicaid benefits. Certain legal immigrants who were residing in the United States on August 22, 1996 and who are blind or disabled are eligible for SSI, regardless of age or the date their disability or blindness began. Immigrant residents as of August 22, 1996 who reach 65 but are not disabled and new immigrants arriving after August 22, 1996 are ineligible for benefits. Most non-citizens are ineligible for Food Stamp benefits.

New immigrants are barred from *federal means-tested benefits* (TANF, Medicaid, and Social Service Block Grant [SSBG] programs) for five years. After the five years, new immigrants who have sponsors must include their sponsor's income when applying for federal means-tested benefits until the immigrant attains citizenship or ten years of work. States have the option to determine immigrants' eligibility for TANF, Medicaid, and SSBG for those resident as of August 22, 1996 and for new immigrants after the five year bar. States may bar or provide state-funded programs to current residents and newly arriving immigrants. Undocumented immigrants are ineligible for federal, state, and local public benefits. All state and local agencies must verify that immigrant applicants are qualified aliens and eligible for such benefits. Refugees, asylees, and individuals whose deportation has been withheld can be eligible for SSI up to seven years. In 1999 closing benefit gaps were being considered for legal immigrants.

General Assistance

Goals   The goal of general assistance (GA) is to provide benefits to low-income persons ineligible for federal assistance. Based on the concept of local responsibility for the destitute, 42 states (including the District of Columbia) have GA programs. Of these 33 have programs throughout the state and the remainder provide GA only in a portion of the state. These are programs of "last resort."

Who Is Eligible for the Program?   In 1996, of the 42 states with GA programs, only 12 provided assistance to all financially needy persons ineligible for federally funded cash programs. The eligible categories differ among states, including disabled, elderly, or otherwise unemployable persons, low-income children or families with children, including pregnant women with their first child. Only four states provided assistance to employable adults or able-bodied adults with barriers to employment. Persons must be financially needy, and asset limits differ by state. Most states limit assistance to citizens and legal aliens. A number of states require drug and alcohol treatment where needed. A number of states require registration with the employment service, and employable adults to enter work or training programs to maintain eligibility. These programs are means tested, and there is no income that is disregarded. In addition to the usual relative-responsibility rules (husbands for wives or vice versa and parents for minors), some states' GA programs also consider adult children responsible for their parents and make siblings, grandparents, and grandchildren responsible for other family members.

What Is the Form of Benefit?   Benefits range from extremely low cash payments, usually insufficient to cover basic necessities, to free groceries and shelter in emergency situations. Most GA recipients are also eligible for Food Stamps and commodities. Medical care may also be provided. Transportation may be offered to return a person to his or her place of residence; burial is provided for deceased indigents.

How Is the Program Financed?   No federal funds support these programs. Using general tax revenues, the GA programs are financed by state funds, combinations of local and state funds, and, in some cases, solely by local funds.

What Is the Level of Administration?   General assistance programs are administered by state public assistance departments on a local level, by local government jurisdictions supervised by the state, or by local governments alone. Most common is administration on a county basis. There are also combinations of state, county, and local administrative organizations.

Discussion   General assistance to some degree and in some form probably will be necessary in the best of societies. No matter how tightly one tries to develop a social insurance system, there are likely to be emergency situations and people needing assistance who fall between the cracks of the system. The categorical eligibility requirements in the current federal public assistance programs eliminate many financially eligible persons, for example, nondisabled adults without children or the physically and mentally disabled who do not meet SSI's criteria.

General assistance is both horizontally and vertically inadequate, rarely providing enough to cover basic necessities. When several states terminated or limited their GA programs in recent years, relatively few former recipients found employment after their benefits were terminated. When they found jobs, they were usually part-time or temporary. Some supported themselves working at odd jobs; others depended on friends and relatives or panhandled on streets. Many able-bodied GA recipients need assistance to overcome serious barriers to employment, including lack of job skills, poor health, and inadequate transportation. Several studies found that almost half of GA recipients did not have a high school diploma or GED (general education development) certificate. When GA was eliminated in Michigan, a study two years later found that in Detroit the cancellation placed even greater financial burdens on the federal government because of disability payments and on Michigan, which was forced to spend more for emergency shelters.[35]

Among suggestions for reform are facilitating the movement of disabled GA recipients onto SSI; providing a more adequate level of benefit for recipients; providing for those with temporary physical or mental disabilities ineligible for SSI, including persons who are unemployable because they care at home for a disabled relative; supporting the able-bodied person's attainment of job skills and education; and, in addition to providing job search and unpaid work experience, offering educational and training services to those who are employable.[36]

GA is contracting. Between 1992 and 1996, it was found that benefit levels remained stagnant or fell; eligibility tightened; and services provided previously were eliminated. The federal safety net has shrunk, heightening the need for GA programs. With the poor law mentality persisting in the major public assistance programs' categorical approach to eligibility, a national response in the near future is unlikely, despite the need.[37]

Earned Income Tax Credit

Goals The Earned Income Tax Credit (EITC) was added to the Internal Revenue Code in 1975 to give cash income supplements to working parents with dependent children and other working adults with low incomes who pay taxes.

Who Is Eligible for the Program? The basic EITC in 1997 was available to taxpayers who met the following criteria:

1. There is a qualifying child living in the home in the United States for more than six months.
2. The taxpayer has earned money during the year.
3. The earned income and adjusted gross income is less than $29,290 when the family includes two children.
4. The employee, a spouse, and those children included must have assigned Social Security numbers.
5. Eligibility is denied for ten years if a fraudulent claim is submitted; two years if the claim is a result of reckless or intentional disregard of rules.

Those eligible are families with dependent children in which a family member works and the family income is below a specific amount and low-income workers over age 24 to 64 years without qualifying children. The maximum eligible income is indexed to inflation. A person must file an income tax return; couples must file a joint return. Eligibility is restricted for those persons with investment income (interest, dividends, rent, royalties, capital gains) that exceeds $2,200, a threshold which is indexed. Military families, including those posted overseas and those in which a family is overseas unaccompanied by their families, may also be eligible. In 1998, the projection is that 18.8 million families will receive benefits amounting to $27.6 billion for an average credit of $1,557 per family.

What Is the Form of Benefit?   More than 80 percent of payments are received as a lump-sum refund following the filing of an income tax return, or the EITC can be used to reduce the amount owed. The benefit also can be given in increments as part of a worker's paycheck after furnishing a certificate of eligibility to the employer. The credit amount rises with earned income as a percentage of annual earnings up to a specific earnings level and then is phased out. In 1997, the maximum credit for families with two or more children who qualify was $3,656. The maximum for taxpayers with no qualifying children was $332. The amount of the benefit is indexed to inflation on an annual basis.

EITC benefits are not counted as income or assets and do not jeopardize a family's eligibility for and benefits from these programs: TANF, Medicaid, SSI, Food Stamps, and low-income housing programs.

How Is the Program Financed?   The program is financed entirely by the federal government out of general revenue.

What Is the Level of Administration?   This is a federal program administered through the Internal Revenue Service. Information is shared between the Treasury Department, State and local governments regarding child support orders and Social Security Administration records may be used to enforce the tax laws, including the EITC.

Discussion   The EITC traditionally has been supported by persons across ideologies. The program was designed originally to give low-income employed families with children who had been excluded from income transfer programs incentive to stay in the job market and off public assistance. Part of the motivation for the creation of EITC resulted from complaints about the regressivity of the Social Security payroll tax for low-income employed households and the rising cost of living. Although EITC offsets social security taxes for the employee and does provide money and is a supplement to earnings, it also allows employers potentially to pay lower wages when they consider the credit.

EITC is a negative income tax program, a refundable credit as a cash grant, which serves to offset the Social Security payroll tax. All paperwork for this credit is done through the federal income tax system, so there is no public stigma. The amount of money provided is, of course, helpful to a family with dependents.

This program is an example of a residual, means-tested program that has minimized stigma and is aimed precisely at those families needing economic assistance and avoids work disincentives by adding to the wages of low income workers. Attacking poverty, the EITC enables single parents to stay off welfare and underscores the value of work. This program has been supported by legislators and presidents from both major parties because it offsets the Social Security tax, adds to the minimum wage, and makes work more profitable than public assistance.

This program has special importance because it provides incentives for TANF families to work by subsidizing *earned* income. This incentive is enhanced because the program is not stigmatized yet it makes a crucial difference for families. Although EITC is valuable for those employed and their children, the extent to which it is used by employers to subsidize wages is unclear.

Some criticize the fact that benefits are increased only up to two children when additional children also cost money to raise. Some of those who complain about the regressivity of the Social Security tax suggest the exemption of dollars of wage income from that tax, an idea rejected mainly because it would complicate employers' implementation of the payroll tax and perhaps undermine the claim of workers to Social Security benefits.

When we consider this type of program, however, implicit in our review are several other questions: How can the society be helpful to low-earner families without undermining work incentives? What should be the limits of such help? These families have low earnings but are playing by the rules. What should be the role of universal family support programs such as family or children's allowances? After all, it is only one step to making such a program universal for all parents with children. The same mechanism of the tax system could be used to "claw back" the funds provided for families over particular income levels. In this way, an effective and efficient income support for families becomes possible.

Social Security, Medicare, and SSI applicants and recipients are also entitled to appeal an action regarding their benefits. This appeals process begins with a reconsideration review or conference held at the local Social Security office. If the decision at the reconsideration level is in the agency's favor, the individual can appeal to the Appeals Council in Washington, D.C., which reviews written records. If the Appeals Council upholds the original agency determination, the last stage of appeal is to federal court.

Summary

In this chapter, we have reviewed the major income support programs currently available in the United States. These programs are both universal (Social Security, unemployment insurance, WC) and selective (TANF, GA, SSI, EITC). Some were initiated with the New Deal or shortly thereafter; others are the product of more recent efforts to provide income security. Incrementally developed, the programs are flawed by insufficient benefit levels and gaps in populations covered. Other programs, however, help address the issue of adequacy as they attempt to enhance the quality of life for those in need. Some of these programs are examined in chapter 10.

Questions for Consideration

1. Why does Social Security have such a high degree of acceptance in the United States? Interview someone who knows what life was like for people before Social Security was created. On balance, what do you think the benefits of this social insurance are?

2.   What is your state's current program designed to assist poor families with children? What income security program would you suggest to bring poor families with dependent children, particularly those headed by female householders, up to some minimum income level?

3.   How many people in your state receive benefits from the EITC? Why do you think both liberals and conservatives favor this program?

4.   Do you agree with the statement made by President Franklin D. Roosevelt with which this chapter began? If yes, why; if no, why not?

NOTES

1.   Franklin D. Roosevelt, *Message to Congress*, June 8, 1938, *The Public Papers and Addresses of Franklin D. Roosevelt*, Vol. 3, New York: Random House, 1938, p. 288.

2.   Committee on Ways and Means, U.S. House of Representatives, *Overview of Entitlement Programs: 1998 Green Book, Background Material and Data on Programs within the Jurisdiction of the Committee on Ways and Means*, Washington, D.C.: U.S. Government Printing Office, 1998, p. 21; Richard W. Stevenson, "Sides Are Squaring Off on Raising Retirement Age," *New York Times*, July 12, 1998, p. 12.

3.   *1998 Green Book*, p. 81.

4.   *1998 Green Book*, p. 27.

5.   Ibid., p. 62.

6.   James Gollin, "Everybody's Nest Egg," *New York Times*, February 1, 1995, p. A21; Dean Baker, "Nine Misconceptions about Social Security," *Atlantic Monthly*, Vol. 282, No. 1, July 1998, pp. 34-39.

7.   Steven A. Sass and Robert K. Triest, "Social Security: How Social and Secure Should It Be?" *Social Security Reform*, Boston: Federal Reserve Bank of Boston, 1997, p. 31.

8.   Robert Kuttner, *The American Prospect*, No. 39, July–August 1998, pp. 30–36.

9.   *1998 Green Book*, p. 1366. Largely as a result of the 1983 revisions in the Social Security program, the proportion of total federal revenues coming from the regressive payroll taxes rose from 30.5 percent in 1980 to 35.1 percent in 1995—a 15 percent increase.

10. Robert Lewis, "Women vs. Social Security," National Retired Teachers Association, Division of American Association of Retired Persons, May 1992, Vol. 33, No. 5, pp. 1, 12.

11. *1998 Green Book*, pp. 363 and 366.

12. William A. Cox, *Social Security Reform Proposals: Economic and Budget Issues*, Washington, D.C.: Congressional Research Service, The Library of Congress, August 14, 1997.

13. Jerry L. Mashaw and Theodore R. Marmor, "The Great Social Security Scare," *The American Prospect*, November–December 1996, pp. 30–37.

14. Carolyn L. Weaver, "Creating a New Kind of Social Security," *The American Enterprise*, Vol. 8, No. 1, January/February 1997, pp. 45–48.

15. Jane B. Quinn, "Some Social Security Changes Would Be Costly for Women," *The Baltimore Sun*, February 16, 1998, p. 15C.

16. *1998 Green Book*, p. 331.

17. Diana Runner, "Changes in Unemployment Insurance in 1997," *Monthly Labor Review*, Vol. 121, No. 1, January 1998, pp. 29-36.

18. Ibid., p. 275.

19. Wayne Vroman, "Effects of Welfare Reform on Unemployment Insurance," http://newfederalism.urban.org, October 1, 1998.

20. William J. Nelson Jr., "Workers' Compensation: 1984-1988, Benchmark Revisions," *Social Security Bulletin*, Vol. 55, No. 3, Fall 1992, pp. 41-58.

21. Glenn Whittington, "Workers' Compensation Legislation Enacted in 1997," *Monthly Labor Review*, Vol. 121, No. 1, January 1998, pp. 22–28.
22. Mary R. Mannix, et al., "Welfare Litigation Developments Since the PRA," October 1997, http://www.welfarelaw.org, September 25, 1998, pp. 2–3.
23. Linda Greenhouse, "High Court Will Add to Sex Harassment Rulings, Taking Up Offense by Student," *New York Times*, September 30, 1998, p. A13.
24. Greg J. Duncan and Jeanne Brooks-Gunn, "Making Welfare Reform Work for Our Youngest Children," *News and Issues*, National Center for Children in Poverty, Vol. 8, No. 1, Spring 1998, pp. 4–5.
25. Department of Health and Human Services, Administration for Children and Families, *First Annual Report to Congress*, August 1998, http://www.acf.dhhs.gov.
26. Joe Sexton, "Working and Welfare Parents Compete for Day Care Slots," *New York Times*, March 24, 1997, p. A17; Louis Uchitelle, "Welfare Recipients Taking Jobs Often Held by the Working Poor," *New York Times*, April 1, 1997, pp. 1, A16.
27. Jodie Levin-Epstein, *CLASP UPDATE*, January 28, 1998, p. 9.
28. Jason DeParle, "Report on Effort to Aid Poor Fathers Offers Discouraging News," *New York Times*, September 29, 1998, p. A16.
29. Rachel L. Swarns, "Hispanic Mothers Lagging as Others Escape Welfare," *New York Times*, September 15, 1998, pp. 1, A29.
30. Tufts University, Center on Hunger and Poverty, *Are States Improving the Lives of Poor Families? A Scale Measure of State Welfare Policies*, Medford, MA, February 1998.
31. Jodie Levin-Epstein, *CLASP Update*, Washington, D.C., April 16, 1998, p. 2.
32. *Goldberg v. Kelly*, 397 U.S. 254 (1976).
33. *The Green Book*, 1998, p. 262.
34. "4 of 10 Poor Children Have Disability Benefits Restored," *The Baltimore Sun*, July 8, 1998, p. 2A.
35. Joyce Purnick, "When Welfare Is Gone: A Cautionary Message," *New York Times*, February 27, 1995, p. B3.
36. Marion Nichols and Kathryn Porter, *General Assistance Programs: Gaps in the Safety Net*, Washington, D.C.: Center on Budget and Policy Priorities, 1995.
37. Cori E. Uccello and L. Jerome Gallagher, "General Assistance Programs: The State-Based Part of the Safety Net," Washington, D.C.: The Urban Institute, http://newfederalism.urban.org/html/anf_a4.htm, August 27, 1998.

Social Welfare Programs: Sustaining the Quality of Life

We the people of the United States in order to . . . establish justice . . .
promote the general Welfare, and secure the Blessings of Liberty to
ourselves and our Posterity. . . .
—The Constitution of the United States

OVERVIEW

In the previous chapter, we reviewed the major social insurance and public assistance programs. These focused on income for the aged, disabled, unemployed, and parents or guardians with dependent children. In this chapter, we will study an array of programs whose purpose is to sustain the quality of life, either by providing in-kind benefits to meet a person's basic needs for food, housing, and medical care or by improving the physical and psychological well-being of the individual. We also discuss two social welfare programs designed for targeted groups—veterans' benefits and corrections.

Over the past two decades the programs reviewed in this chapter were the foci of intense political maneuvering as budget considerations and ideologies clashed. A major factor influencing health and mental health care with implications for social welfare and social work is managed care, which created a new environment for the delivery of services. In order to understand more completely the environment in which health and mental health services—as well as other services—operate, we present information about managed care and follow it with a discussion of the various programs.

Managed Care: A Radical Change

Traditionally, most people who had health insurance were covered for most health expenses through indemnity or fee-for-service plans but had to find their own practitioners and arrange for their own care. In these cases, the insurance company paid

232

for all or part of the bill for any doctor, hospital, or other health care provider a person chose. *Managed care* was propelled by rapidly rising health care costs well beyond the rate of inflation resulting from a number of factors: a growing aged population, technology and costly new treatments, the frequent ability to keep people alive at a cost, an emphasis on acute care rather than preventive services, varying standards of treatment according to geographic locations, among others.

The disturbing expense of health care is illustrated by several statistics. In 1995 the United States spent more than 14 percent (1 in 7 dollars) of its gross domestic product (GDP) on health care and 1 in 6 dollars of total public expenditures. More than $3,700 dollars were expended per capita. There were estimates health care expenditures would continue to skyrocket. These concerns plus others, including privatization and profit-seeking, led to the proliferation of managed care organizations. Although managed care has not won popularity contests and was designed to restrain costs, the percentage of employees enrolled rose from 48 percent in 1993 to 85 percent in 1997.[1]

The ostensible focus of all managed care organizations is the control of costs while assuring access and quality of service. Yet, more employees are paying more for their health insurance than ever before, and the proportion of those required to pay more has been rising for almost two decades. Workers enrolled in health maintenance organizations (HMOs) were more likely to pay toward the cost of their coverage than were those enrolled in other types of plans. Furthermore, in 1995, the average employee contributions were three or four times what they were in 1983. During that same time period, the medical care costs component of the Consumer Price Index (CPI) doubled.[2]

There is no standard, all inclusive definition of *managed care*. Suffice it to say that managed care attempts to lower costs by providing care at predetermined or discounted fees by specifying which health care providers and hospitals a person can use and overseeing treatments and referrals. Managed care evolved through at least three generations: (1) Placing some limits on benefits through deductibles, cost sharing, utilization review, second opinions, and other means; (2) different types of benefits in and out of the system; and (3) advanced provider selection, patient care monitoring, and the utilization of quality measures.[3]

Managed care organizations try to balance access, quality, flexibility, control, and accountability while remaining fiscally viable. An enrollee or subscriber receives health care from a group of approved health professionals and hospitals. Typically, the provider network assigns a primary care doctor who provides routine health care and decides if the enrollee needs to see a specialist. Managed care contracts directly with health care providers to set payment for services and restrict the use of costly services. Providers discount their standard fees. Out-of-pocket costs are lower for those enrollees who use providers in the network. If at the end of the year, money paid by employers and employees is left over, the HMO keeps it. If there is a loss, the HMO is responsible.

A growing number of physicians provide health care through capitation, in which HMOs pay groups of primary care and specialist physicians a lump sum for each enrollee. If at the end of the year, money is left, the physicians, not the HMO, keep it. If no money is left, the physicians absorb the loss. In this way, the physicians have a stake in holding down costs.[4]

Major Organizational Types

Managed care is implemented through a variety of mechanisms. The major types are described in the following sections.

Health Maintenance Organizations Health maintenance organizations provide a wide range of health services to covered members for a fee or premium paid by an employer, a government, or a person or family. A member chooses a "gatekeeper" physician who provides care and makes treatment recommendations and referrals to specialists. Premiums are usually lower than traditional plans, and there are no deductibles or co-insurance payments; however, there are low co-payments. Members are limited to using the HMO's personnel and hospitals and must get approval for treatment and referrals. One type of HMO is a *closed panel* or *staff* model, which employs its own health personnel (e.g., physicians, social workers, psychologists, technicians) and operates its own clinics and hospitals. A second type is a *group or network* model, in which the HMO contracts with one or several groups of multi-speciality health practitioners to provide services to the members for a fixed amount per plan member. A third type is an *independent practice* association (IPA): The HMO contracts with an association of private practice health providers to provide services to its members. Health providers may maintain their individual practices, and health practitioners generally work in their own offices.

Point-of-Service Plans With the point-of-service (POS) plan, members make a decision about the care they need at the point of service when the service is required. These plans allow members to go to health care providers outside of their HMOs for care, provided the member pays the extra cost.

Preferred Provider Organizations A preferred provider organization (PPO) is a network of independent health care professionals that contract to provide care at discounted rates. Providers must agree to utilization management and fixed reimbursement rates. A member may use health services *in* or *outside* of the network but must pay a higher co-payment for going outside the network of providers.

Physician Sponsored Networks With the physician sponsored network (PSN), large groups of health professionals join together and accept the financial risks of covering their patients' health care needs. This arrangement substitutes for the traditional role played by insurers and maintains health provider autonomy while reducing administrative and other costs.

Managed care contains conflicting purposes. Health services are delivered but benefits are reviewed, controlled, and managed. Reviews can focus on whether services can be provided, what the type and scope of the benefits will be, access to providers, and control of costs. Patients may be preauthorized to receive particular treatment or denied access; the treatment can be reviewed and continued or terminated. The treatment of choice can be determined by the managed care organization rather than the practitioner.

Impact on Services and Practitioners

Managed care is an industrialization of the delivery of health care. There are those who believe the emphasis is more on controlling costs and increasing profits than on access or quality of care. In fact, there can be adversarial priorities. Altruistic professionals are trained to be helpers, but they must operate within a context of cost-consciousness and profit seeking. These conflicting purposes have a heavy impact on social workers and others involved with health and mental health care.

These radical changes in social services, health, and mental health have strongly affected mental health systems and practitioner roles. The traditional mental health care system has been largely dismantled. In-patient psychiatric care has been reduced; there are limits on long stays. Health care practitioners are forced to find places on mental health panels (from which practitioners are assigned cases) to which they may or may not be accepted. The practitioner must agree to a case manager determining who and how to treat persons referred. There are protocols for the length and nature of care on the basis of diagnostic related groups (DRGs). Further, there is an emphasis on biological and cognitive-behavioral treatments.

Proponents

The proponents of managed care claim that the short-term consequences will be uncomfortable but the escalating costs of health care must be controlled, especially since the baby boom generation is approaching retirement age. According to these proponents, more people will be provided with cost-effective health care. Treatment decisions will be based on what is considered "best practice," which in turn rests on outcome research.

Criticisms

Critics, however, point out that the for-profit motivation has replaced long-tested professional standards, treatment procedures, and ethical standards. Profit making becomes the major goal, especially where earnings and shareholders are concerned. Quality has suffered. Professionals have been disempowered as their professional judgments may be overruled by case managers whose training may be less than that of the practitioner, and costs continue to rise. One fallout from these activities is the demise of high quality traditional agencies that contributed for long periods to communities. Collateral interventions are not allowed (school visits, family members, legal representatives, public assistance, landlords, employers) or not reimbursed, and the emphasis is on face-to-face contacts. All these factors result in rationing services for all but the wealthy.[5]

Few federal standards apply to private or employer-provided managed care, and this is viewed critically by many persons. States apply and enforce standards in different ways while people are mobile. What happens if one becomes ill while away from home? Do people receive the services they contracted and paid for? Are good practice standards enforced universally? Such standards will require a combination of state and federal legislation and means for enforcement.

Munson and Shapiro identified several negative impacts of managed care on social work practitioners.[6] There are effects of "speeding up" practice when it is clear more time and sessions are needed for clients to be helped sufficiently. As one can imagine, the relationships between clients and practitioners also are being altered by the managed care policies described previously. There are administrative costs to managed care, particularly as necessary to control costs. A lack of privacy for clients and patients is enhanced by the number of organizations and people who have access to personal files and case information. Little is known about the effects of the discontinuation of services. Clients (as well as practitioners) must constantly be concerned with whether their request for benefits will be honored. Managed care establishes an environment in which clients cannot be certain they should place trust in the relationship because the treatment can be discontinued by decision makers outside their relationship with the practitioner, decision makers whose goals may not be quality treatment but cost savings.

There also are implications of managed care that shift social work practice far from its historic two-track methods—casework (clinical) and macro (organizations, neighborhoods, and communities)—and diminish attempts to achieve goals in the external environment. Managed care focuses almost entirely on the presenting problems of individuals, and there is little if any reimbursement for collateral interventions. This fact can serve to isolate the individual client and restrain practitioners from attempting to influence larger systems.

Research on Quality of Care

One study compared the performance of HMOs with that of fee-for-service plans by analyzing 37 peer-reviewed studies of managed care plans. The study found there were an equal number of significantly better or worse results for HMOs. In several instances, Medicare HMO enrollees with chronic conditions showed worse quality of care. Fears that HMOs uniformly would lead to worse quality of care were not supported by the evidence.

The author identified three factors that make for unfavorable results: payment incentives, disincentives, and inadequate information. In many cases, financial payments do little to reward quality on the part of plans and providers. There are disincentives to care for the sickest and most expensive patients. Consumers and purchasers (employers, the government, and individuals) lack sufficient information on access to care and quality of care. Further, improved quality of care requires new processes, but practitioners change clinical processes only slowly.[7]

Strategies to Achieve Profits

Schamess identified the strategies by which HMOs generate their profits from standard business practices applied to problems that are not amenable to business solutions:

- Denying coverage to people with preexisting conditions or those who seem likely to use services extensively;
- Limiting and/or denying treatment to people whose difficulties do not respond to standardized treatment protocols;
- Replacing professional judgment with multiple levels of organizational decision making;
- Increasing requirements for record keeping and report writing;
- Removing case managers responsible for utilization review from direct contact with both patients/clients and practitioners and providing them access only through overloaded telephone lines;
- Requiring clinicians to comply with insurer policies and protocols or risk their employment;
- Instituting difficult appeal procedures;
- Using economic power to drive down payment rates to treatment institutions and practitioners; and
- Promoting managed care as the most efficient, if not the only approach to cost containment.[8]

Public Criticism and Legislation

There has been much public criticism of managed care. The responsibility for responding to these criticisms rested mainly at the state level until late in the 1990s. Among the regulations states implemented are fiscal requirements to ensure the solvency of insurance plans, mandates as to services that must be covered, and the prevention of misrepresentation to enrollees. Many states regulated the process of utilization review by insurance companies, providers, or external review agents.

Other regulations were intended to expand the information that health plans must provide to enrollees and new requirements for grievance and appeal procedures. Some state legislation has been enacted, but there are expectations that legal appeals will be made that state regulations are preempted by the federal Employee Retirement Income Security Act (ERISA). This act governs pensions and welfare benefits, exempting employee health plans from state regulation. Included among these state regulations are limiting financial incentives to manage utilization and the cost of care and banning "gag rules" that barred physicians from discussing treatment options not covered by the plan, disclosure of plan limitations, disparaging comments about the plan, and undermining member confidence in the plan. Other legislation encouraged continuity of care so that health provider familiarity with the person's health condition will be maintained, thus improving the quality of care and satisfaction of both providers and members. Still other legislation established "due process" rights for health practitioners in their relationship with managed care plans, including access to information about the standards for application to a network, termination decisions, and economic profiles of their practice patterns.[9]

In 1998 public anger over managed care elevated citizen concerns to a major national issue, and legislation was introduced in Congress to define and protect the rights of patients and to regulate managed care companies. There appeared to be agreement that legislation was needed to guarantee payments for emergency room visits in any situation that a "prudent lay person" would regard as an emergency; provision of an affordable and timely appeals process for patients denied coverage to an independent, impartial reviewer outside their health plan; and assurance that patients have access to detailed information about health plans, including physician freedom to discuss all treatment options with their patients, regardless of whether the health plan covers such services. Further, health plans should disclose data and information so consumers can compare their performance and determine whether patients are satisfied. Two bills in Congress failed to move forward because of lobbying by the insurance industry and the personal difficulties confronting President Clinton. The defeat of The Patient Protection Act and the Patient's Bill of Rights Act underlined again the difficulty of passing health care legislation affecting physicians, patients, lawyers, insurers, and employers of all sizes.[10] However, in 1997, Congress set similar standards for health plans serving people under Medicare.[11]

There were expectations that legislation would be reintroduced in the next session. Meanwhile, the federal appeals court in San Francisco ruled unanimously on a nationwide class action suit that Medicare patients are entitled to immediate hearings and other protections when they are denied care by HMOs.[12] Also, states began to enact a wide range of laws to define patients' rights and regulate HMOs. These efforts received broad bipartisan support in many states, perhaps because they are seen as a form of constituent service rather than political and ideological conflict.[13]

On the national level, lobbyists and legislators resisted the enactment of patients' rights, particularly the right of patients to sue insurers that refuse to approve medical treatment. Some argue such rights would lead to businesses dropping health care coverage. Proponents argue it is the fair thing to do. The State of Texas became a laboratory for the expense of litigation where such suits were allowed: Although nationwide estimates of the increase in health plan premiums nationwide if patients were free to sue insurers for denial of care were 1.2 percent, the actual costs in Texas were a .1 percent increase in total spending per member per month of full-service HMOs.[14]

Social Work Roles

Many voices supported federal and state legislation (A Patient's "Bill of Rights") to force HMOs to provide more care, expand patient choice, and require health plans to document their treatment of patients, thus making insurance companies and other parts of the system accountable for their quality of care. But other voices predicted the "Bill of Rights" would prove counterproductive. Some experts expected that such provisions, instead of expanding consumer options, would drive patients into more restrictive HMOs with smaller rosters of providers. In addition, fee-for-service health insurance could be eliminated, minimizing those health choices that are primarily in the hands of providers and patients. Further, public accountability clashes with choice. Accountability requires, according to this critical group, complex record keeping and reduced choice of providers, because the more providers, the more difficult and expensive the accountability procedures. Plans would restrict panels to those they know will provide the types of services they expect. These outcomes would probably be a result for fee-for-service plans as well. Thus, it is suggested that accountability will limit choice, the opposite of what American consumers value.[15]

Social workers provide services in inpatient, outpatient, medical, rehabilitation, psychiatric, private practice and other health care settings, all of which are affected by managed care. Although there are fewer opportunities for autonomous decision making by practitioners, social workers must deal with case managers and help clients to avoid the loss of options, including type, duration, and place of service. When clients lose their service options, professionals lose autonomy about such decisions as well.

In practice, social workers advocate for their clients or patients with case managers and managed care organizations, work to improve the delivery of services, and participate in efforts to change health and social service policy for the better. A growing number of social workers are involved in managed care organizations directly in many roles, from owners to case managers. The degree to which social workers will be advocates for clients and families from within these organizations remains to be seen. Social workers also have roles in trying to influence managed care systems so they provide quality services for beneficiaries.

Health Care Programs

In the mid-1960s, two health programs were introduced under the Social Security Act: Medicare and Medicaid. Medicare is insurance based, whereas Medicaid is a means-tested program. Approximately one third of dollars expended for health care in the United States are used for these two programs.

Medicare

Goals The Medicare program is a national insurance program to provide health care for the aged and certain disabled persons. Hospital insurance is provided through Part A and supplementary medical insurance through Part B.

Who Is Eligible for the Program? Most Americans 65 years of age or older are automatically entitled to protection under Part A (the hospital insurance program) by either themselves or their spouses having paid the Hospital Insurance (HI) tax on earnings covered by Social Security or the Railroad Retirement Systems. Part A also provides coverage after a 24-month waiting period for persons under 65 years of age who are receiving Social Security disability cash benefits but their dependents do not. Most persons, regardless of age, who need a kidney transplant or renal dialysis may also be covered. Persons aged 65 years or older who are not automatically entitled to Part A may obtain coverage by paying the full actuarial cost, which was $309 in 1998 or $170 for persons who had at least 30 quarters of covered employment. In fiscal year 1997 Part A covered an estimated 38.1 million aged and disabled persons, including those with chronic kidney disease, at a cost of $136 billion.

Part B is voluntary. All persons 65 years of age or older (even those not entitled to Part A) and all persons enrolled in Part A may enroll in Part B by paying a monthly premium ($43.80 in 1998). In fiscal year 1997, Part B covered an estimated 36.5 million aged and disabled persons at a cost of $72.7 billion. Voluntary enrollees in Part A must enroll in Part B.

What Is the Form of the Benefit?   Part A provides coverage for inpatient hospital services, up to 100 days of post-hospital skilled nursing facility care, home health services (examined in chapter 15), and hospice care. The first 60 days of *inpatient hospital services* in a benefit period are subject to a deductible ($764 in 1998). A benefit period commences upon entry and ends when the person has not been in a hospital or skilled nursing facility for 60 days. For days 61–90 in a benefit period, a coinsurance amount ($191 in 1998) is imposed. If more than 90 days are needed in a benefit period, a patient can choose to draw upon a 60-day lifetime reserve. There is a coinsurance charge for each reserve day ($382 in 1998).

Skilled nursing facility care is provided up to 100 days following hospitalization for those who need continued daily skilled nursing care and/or rehabilitation services. After the first 20 days, there is a daily coinsurance ($95.50 in 1998).

Home health care services are described subsequently and discussed in chapter 15. *Hospice care* is provided to terminally ill beneficiaries with a life expectancy of 6 months or less for two 90-day periods, followed by an unlimited number of 60-day periods. Ill persons must be recertified as terminally ill at the beginning of 60-day periods.

Part B generally pays 80 percent of the approved amount (fee schedule, reasonable charge, or reasonable cost) for covered services in excess of an annual deductible ($100). Coverage includes *physician's services* (surgery, consultation, and home, office, and institutional visits; limitations apply to services provided by dentists, podiatrists, chiropractors, and treatment of mental illness); *other medical and health services* (laboratory and other diagnostic tests, x-ray and other radiation therapy, outpatient hospital services, rural health clinic services, durable medical equipment, home dialysis supplies and equipment, artificial devices other than dental, physical and speech therapy, and ambulance services as required); *specified preventive services*, as of January 1, 1998, mammography screening annually for all women over 40 years of age, and at specified intervals for the disabled, a screening pap smear and pelvic exam (including clinical breast exam) once every three years, except for women who are at high risk of developing cervical cancer, and specified colorectal screening. Beginning July 1998 coverage was authorized for diabetes self-management training services and bone mass measurements for high-risk persons. Prostate cancer screenings are covered beginning January 1, 2000.

Medicare in general does not provide for outpatient *prescription drugs or biologicals*. Part B pays for immunosuppressive drugs for 36 months following an organ transplant, drugs for treatment of anemia for persons with chronic kidney failure, and certain specified oral cancer drugs. The program does cover flu shots, pneumococcal pneumonia vaccines, and hepatitis vaccines for those at risk. *Home health services* include an unlimited number of medically necessary home health visits for persons covered under Part A. The 20 percent coinsurance and $100 deductible do not apply to such benefits. The Balanced Budget Act of 1997 gradually transfers some home health costs from Part A to Part B beginning in 1998. There is no income or assets test for Medicare eligibility.

Medicare beneficiaries have the option of enrollling in a private health plan, typically an HMO. As discussed under managed care, such a program receives a predetermined per capita payment from Medicare for each enrolled beneficiary. Most services are provided by *Medicare-Choice* (a new Part C of Medicare). Under the Balanced Budget Act (1997) every individual entitled to Medicare Part A and enrolled in Part B will be able to elect the existing Medicare benefits through either Medicare fee-for-service (traditional Medicare) or a Medicare-Choice plan. But the same Act will reduce Medicare spending by $115 billion over the next five years.

Only 15.6 percent of Medicare's 37.5 million members are enrolled in Medicare HMOs. In order to attract members, HMOs agree to provide more benefits than traditional Medicare does. The odds seem to favor the HMO because 90 percent of Medicare enrollees are healthy and require few services, with costs averaging below the stipends provided by Medicare.[16] The focus of the HMOs, however, appeared to be less on improving health care than in reducing the cost of doing business for large corporations. As a result, HMOs, which were expected to be the hope for the future in health care, began to retreat because of high costs from certain types of Medicare HMOs and beneficiaries began to be attracted to one particular model.[17] This situation left those dropped enrollees with two choices: use the traditional fee-for-service Medicare program with or without supplementary insurance or enroll in another HMO, perhaps at a higher cost. Preparations were being made to expedite HMO operations in those counties from which services had been withdrawn to enable recoverage.[18]

The fastest growing HMOs are those that are least managed. These plans try to keep costs in check by persuading physicians and hospitals to agree to reduced fees. Preferred provider organizations (PPOs) have found their popularity surging. Members can go to any physician without asking permission, but costs are increased for them to go to physicians or hospitals outside the PPO network. The popularity of this type of service is related to improved recruitment and retention of employees, keeping track of the costs of beneficiaries seeking help outside the system, administrative costs, expense of some HMOs, experience with "hassles," and perhaps Americans simply seeking more choices and to be less controlled.[19]

The Balanced Budget Act also authorized a demonstration to test the feasibility of *Medical Savings Accounts* (MSAs; see additional discussion in the section "New Health Insurance Legislation"). This authorization, the first for Medicare, followed the Health Insurance Portability and Accountability Act (1996), which established an MSA demonstration for employed individuals not yet eligible for Medicare. The Medicare-Choice option is a combination of an MSA plan providing health insurance with an annual deductible limited to $6,000 and a Medicare+Choice MSA. New enrollments will not be allowed after 2002 or after the number of enrollees reaches

390,000. MSA plans are not available to certain low-income or disabled persons. While enrolled in these plans, individuals cannot enroll in other health insurance plans (including Medigap plans) and must reside in the United States for at least half the year.

Reimbursement will be provided for items and services under Parts A and B. However, such reimbursement will only be paid after the enrollee incurred expenses equal to the annual deductible ($6,000) indexed for inflation. Countable expenses include expenses under Parts A and B and deductibles, coinsurance, and copayments. At the plan's option, other expenses may also be counted. After the deductible is met, the plan would reimburse 100 percent of Parts A and B expenses or 100 percent of what Medicare would have paid.

Contributions to Medicare+Choice MSA are made annually after the premium has been paid. Contributions to accounts are exempt from taxes, as are account earnings. Withdrawals are also not taxed if used to pay unreimbursed enrollee medical expenses that are deductible under the tax code. Unqualified withdrawals will be included in the individual's income for tax purposes.

In 1988, the Catastrophic Coverage Act was passed by Congress. The bill was designed to assist with a very expensive, lengthy illness and to prevent severe depletion of resources. Its provisions included unlimited inpatient hospital care with only one annual deductible, 150 days of skilled nursing care without a preadmission hospitalization, respite care for caretakers of the elderly or disabled, a limit on doctor's bills, and payment for prescription drugs. However, in a very unusual action, Congress repealed this act one year later largely because of lobbying efforts by seniors, who opposed the bill because it was funded through a tax levied only on them.

How Is the Program Financed?   Medicare Part A is financed by an earmarked payroll tax paid by the employer, employee, and those who are self-employed. Additional sources of income include transfers from the Railroad Retirement account, reimbursements from general revenues for certain persons, premiums from voluntary enrollees, payments for military wage credits, taxes on Social Security benefits, and interest. Employers and employees each pay a tax of 1.45 percent on all earnings. Self-employed persons pay 2.9 percent, and there is no limit on earnings subject to this tax. Medicare Part B is financed by monthly premiums paid by the aged, disabled, and chronic renal disease enrollees (25 percent of costs) adjusted yearly and by federal general revenues (75 percent). In 1998 the premium was $43.80. These premiums and federal contributions are kept in the federal Supplementary Medical Insurance Trust Fund (SMI). The monthly premium is deducted from the enrollee's Social Security, Railroad Retirement, or federal Civil Service Retirement annuity. All states must pay Part A and B premiums and other expenses for certain aged and disabled Medicaid beneficiaries eligible for Medicare.

The Medicare Hospital Insurance Trust Fund (HI) finances services provided under Part A. The SMI finances services covered under Part B. Additional income sources include premiums paid by voluntary enrollees, Railroad Retirement Account transfers, government credits, interest on federal securities, payments for military wage credits, and taxation of a portion of Social Security benefits.

Part B is financed from premiums paid by the aged, disabled, and chronic renal disease enrollees and from general revenues. The premium rate is computed annually based on the projected costs of the program for the coming year. In 1998 the cost was $43.80 per month.

In 1983 a system of DRGs was established by the federal government. Under DRG, Medicare's reimbursement rates to hospitals are set according to illness category. If a patient remains in the hospital beyond Medicare's predetermined discharge date, Medicare ceases payment. The DRG system, despite an appeal process and mandated discharge planning, is said to cause premature discharge and other difficulties for some Medicare recipients.

What Is the Level of Administration?   The Health Care Financing Administration (HCFA) of the Department of Health and Human Services has the overall responsibility for the administration of Medicare. The daily work of reviewing claims and making payments is done by intermediaries for Part A and carriers for Part B. These are usually commercial insurers or Blue Cross/ Blue Shield plans.

Discussion   Medicare disbursements began to exceed income in 1995, and it is projected that Part A (the HI program) will be insolvent in 2010.[20] The future size and shape of this extremely popular health care program has to be decided in the near future. The program faces the increased numbers of the baby boom generation, the shift in the ratio of covered workers supporting each HI beneficiary, costs rising faster than income, and the increasing size of the program relative to other parts of the economy. Over the long haul, it is expected that Medicare could account for as much as 5 percent of the GDP.[21]

Costs, consumer choice, the range of available services, the roles of prevention and cure, greater efficiency and effectiveness, and ideological issues focusing on the role of government and the roles of the marketplace all are important considerations. Medicare has been horizontally adequate, efficiently reaching all persons 65 years of age or older (most of the recipients). Questions have been raised about its vertical adequacy in relation to preventive services, prescription coverage, and long-term health care costs, but recent changes have implemented some new preventive services. Medicare is a cost efficient program, with administrative costs between 1 and 2 percent of program outlays in 1996, and virtually all of its funds are used for services; but guarding against waste, fraud, and abuse is very important.[22]

Some people believe that Medicare is benefit inefficient because many persons who could afford to pay for their health care receive services. Others think that a major strength of the program is its universality. All proposals for change shift costs to the elderly, either directly or indirectly, which raises questions about fairness, especially for those with low incomes.

Some proposals for change include increasing monthly premiums, raising deductibles for Part B, increasing the eligibility age to 67 by the year 2003, setting annual limits on the growth of Medicare spending, relaxing antitrust laws so that doctors and hospitals could more easily form health networks to serve Medicare benficiaries (doctors would be able to set their prices in consultation with other doctors), and setting limits for noneconomic legal damages such as pain and suffering at $250,000 or three times the economic damages, whichever is greater. Finally, included in suggested revisions are means testing for participants so that subsidies for Part B (out of general revenues) would be phased out at a set income level, thus ending the universal nature of the program and shifting it incrementally toward selectivity.

Critics also suggest that budget cuts result in too few dollars to deliver quality health care because they do not keep up with health care costs. Limits on the annual growth of per capita payments to HMOs in some parts of the country have proven to be insufficient to attract HMOs. Furthermore, because there would be no limit on the growth of private health care premiums, low-income persons might have to choose low-cost plans while higher income persons could purchase more extensive services, creating a more inequitable system. Concern is also expressed that retirees could choose the tax-free accounts when they are well and choose the traditional Medicare program when they become ill. Other critics suggest that cuts in Medicare and Medicaid could be used to balance the budget and pay for tax cuts for the middle class and wealthy.

Aside from the financial and ideological issues, there are several underlying issues which are seldom discussed but are implied in the debates: What is basic health care? Should health care be provided only in the marketplace? Are those who have not cared for their health (e.g., by smoking or substance abuse) entitled to the same treatment as those who have?

Medicaid

Goals   Medicaid, authorized under the Social Security Act in 1965, is a federal-state matching entitlement program to provide means-tested medical and health-related services to low-income individuals and families. Participation is optional, but all states and the District of Columbia have programs.

Who Is Eligible for the Program?   In 1995 there were 36.2 million Medicaid recipients. Within federal guidelines, each state designs and administers its own program. This results in much variation among the states: different eligibility standards; different types, amounts, duration, and scope of services; and rates for payments of services. Low income is one test for eligibility, but assets and resources are also measured against thresholds determined by each state. Each state has broad discretion as to the groups Medicaid will cover; however, states must cover "categorically needy" individuals such as recipients of Supplemental Security Income (SSI), Temporary Assistance for Needy Families (TANF), low-income pregnant women, infants, and children, and certain low-income Medicare beneficiaries.

The historic automatic connection between cash assistance and Medicaid was severed by the Personal Responsibility and Work Opportunities Act (PRA; 1996). The PRA preserves Medicaid entitlement for individuals who meet the requirements for the Aid to Families with Dependent Children (AFDC) as of July 16, 1996 even if they do not qualify for TANF. States are required to use the eligibility determination process already in place for AFDC and Medicaid, including the same income and re-source standards and other rules. States must continue Medicaid assistance for re-ceipients of adoption assistance and foster care. As under prior law, if a family be-comes ineligible for Medicaid because of earnings or child or spousal support income and received Medicaid in three of the prior six months, the family is eligible for a period of transitional Medicaid assistance. States may also continue Medicaid to children up to age 21 years who meet what were the AFDC income and resource re-quirements in effect mid-1996 but do not meet the definition of dependent child. States are permitted to deny Medicaid benefits to nonpregnant adults and heads of households who lose their TANF benefits because of refusal to work but must con-tinue Medicaid coverage of their children.

States are required to cover pregnant women and children under age 6 years with incomes below 133 percent of the federal poverty guidelines. All children un-der the age of 19 years and whose family income is below 100 percent of the federal poverty level are expected to be covered by fiscal year 2002.

States are permitted but not required to cover pregnant women and infants un-der one year not covered under the mandatory rules whose family income is not more than 185 percent of the federal poverty level. The Balanced Budget Act (1997) gave states the option to provide health care coverage to low-income children under age 19 years if their families earn less than 200 percent of the federal poverty level. Sliding scales may be implemented for families whose income is more than 150 per-cent of the poverty level. Also, states are to presume eligibility for low income chil-dren, thus providing services during the time that eligibility is determined.

States are generally required to cover recipients of SSI. States may, however, use more restrictive eligibility standards for Medicaid than those for SSI if they were using those standards on January 1, 1972 (before the implementation of SSI). States using more restrictive income standards must allow applicants to deduct medical ex-penses from income (exclusive of SSI or State Supplemental payments) in determin-ing eligibility. States must continue coverage for several groups, including those who lost SSI or State Supplemntal Payments eligibility. Qualified severely impaired per-sons are those disabled who have returned to work and have lost eligibility as a result of employment earnings but still have the condition that rendered them disabled and meet all SSI criteria except income. States must also continue coverage for persons who were once eligible for both SSI and Social Security and who lose SSI because of a cost-of-living adjustment in their Social Security benefits or veterans benefits. Also, states must continue Medicaid for certain SSI-related groups who received benefits in 1973, including essential persons who care for a disabled person. States are permit-ted to provide Medicaid to those individuals who are not recipients of SSI but do re-ceive state-only supplementary cash payments.

Limited Medicaid coverage must be provided for aged and disabled persons who are receiving Medicare whose income is below 100 percent of the federal poverty level and whose resources do not exceed twice the allowable amount under SSI. States must pay Medicare Part B premiums (and, if applicable, Part A premiums) for qualified Medicare beneficiaries, along with required Medicare coinsurance and deductible amounts.

In addition, states may provide Medicaid to certain otherwise ineligible persons who are in nursing facilities or other institutions or who would require institutional care if they were not receiving alternative services at home or in the community. Home and community-based services may be provided to individuals who otherwise would require institutional care. Services may also be provided for persons who would be eligible if they were in an institution. These include children being cared for at home, persons of any age who are ventilator dependent, and persons receiving hospice benefits in place of institutional services.

Legal immigrants arriving in the United States after August 22, 1996, are ineligible for Medicaid benefits for five years. Coverage after the five years is a state option. States are required to provide Medicaid coverage to legal immigrants who resided in the country and were receiving benefits as of August 1996, and for those who were residents then and became disabled at a later time. States must provide Medicaid for refugees for their first seven years in the United States after asylum is granted; asylees for the first seven years after asylum is granted; those whose deportation is being withheld by the Immigration and Naturalization Service for the first seven years after grant of deportation holding; lawful permanent aliens after they have been credited with 40 quarters of coverage under Social Security; and honorably discharged U.S. military veterans, active duty military personnel, and their spouses and unmarried dependent children. Qualified aliens and nonqualified aliens who meet the financial and categorical eligibility requirements for Medicaid may receive emergency Medicaid services. In 1999 benefits for legal immigrants were reconsidered.

Finally, a large number of States and other jurisdictions provide Medicaid to some groups of "medically needy" persons. These are persons who meet the nonfinancial standards for inclusion but who do not meet the applicable income or resource requirements for eligibility. The state may establish higher income or resource standards, or individuals may spend down to the medically needy standard by incurring medical expenses. The state may set its standard for a family up to 133 percent of the maximum payment for a similar family under the State's AFDC program as of mid-July 1996.

What Is the Form of Benefit?   The benefits are in-kind medical care services. There are no cash benefits for beneficiaries; payments are made directly to the providers of services. Basic Medicaid services include inpatient and outpatient hospital services; prenatal care; vaccines for children; physician services; nursing facility services for those 21 years of age or older; home health services for those eligible for skilled nursing care; family planning services and supplies; rural health clinic services; laboratory and x-ray services; pediatric and family nurse-practitioner services; qualified health center services, including ambulatory services; nurse-midwife services; and early and periodic health screening, diagnosis, and treatment for those under 21 years of age.

States may also provide approved optional services such as diagnostic services, drugs and prosthetic devices, clinic services, nursing facility services for the aged and disabled, intermediate care facilities for persons with mental retardation, optometrist services and eyeglasses, rehabilitation and physical therapy services, and transportation.

How Is the Program Financed?

There is no preset limit (cap) on the total federal expenditures for Medicaid. The federal government assists states with the cost of Medicaid services through a variable matching formula, which is adjusted annually. The federal matching rate is inversely related to a state's per capita income, ranging from 50 to 83 percent, although in 1997 the highest rate was 77.22 percent. The federal share of administrative costs is 50 percent for all states, except for certain items for which the match is higher. All funds are obtained from general revenues both on the state and federal levels. Total U.S. expenditures in 1996 were $162 billion.

What Is the Level of Administration?   Medicaid is a state-administered program. At the federal level, HCFA of the Department of Health and Human Services is responsible for overseeing state operations. There must be one state agency that administers Medicaid, and it is typically the state Department of Social Services, the state health agency, or an umbrella human resources agency. The one responsible agency may contract with other state organizations to conduct some program functions. States may process claims for reimbursement themselves or contract with other organizations or health insuring agencies to process claims. An increasing number of states are requiring Medicaid receipients to receive their services from HMOs. President Clinton announced new protections for recipients, among these were access to obstetricians and gynecologists, emergency services whenever a "prudent person" would think them necessary, and the right to challenge decisions denying, limiting, or terminating coverage of services.

Discussion   Table 10.1 illustrates the differences between Medicare and Medicaid. The problems with Medicare and Medicaid regarding their adequacy are the classic problems of selective and universal programs. Medicare, which is universal, has excellent horizontal adequacy for the aged, at least in the automatic hospital insurance portion, but its benefits are limited and often run out for the elderly, forcing them to use up their limited assets until they become eligible for Medicaid. Medicaid serves as the long-term care safety net. Many Americans quickly deplete their savings and qualify for Medicaid. Cuts and restrictions in Medicaid spending for nursing home care mean greater burdens can be expected to fall on informal caregivers, and given such restrictions by states, there would be little recourse for those in need. One option is to reduce the number of people served, many of whom are severely ill. Another option is to cut reimbursement. This latter choice leaves decisions to cut up to the nursing homes themselves. Further, there is little optimism about states raising taxes to provide broader coverage. There is an additional issue related to potential reductions in Medicaid funding for nursing home care: The families of nursing home residents—spouses, adult children—could find themselves responsible for the burden by either the state or their own sense of

TABLE 10.1   Differences between Medicare and Medicaid

	Medicare	Medicaid
Who is eligible	All aged recipients of Social Security for hospital insurance; all aged recipients of Social Security who contributed for medical insurance; disabled after 2 years; and those with end-stage renal disease	All needy, as per means test
Form of benefit	Partial hospital and medical service	All medical services
Funding	Payroll tax on employers, employees, and self-employed for hospital coverage; general revenues match voluntary insurance	General revenues from the federal government with a share of the contribution for medical cost from the general revenues of the states
Administration	National, using various insurers to process claims	Grant-in-aid; federal guidelines, state variations, and administration

obligation. If Medicaid were not available for them, adult children could be forced to choose between their parent's need for nursing home care and providing their own children an education.

Medicaid is vertically more adequate, at least technically, because just about all kinds of medical care and services are covered, but it is not as adequate horizontally because it is means tested, and one has to prove poverty to be eligible. Even the vertical adequacy of Medicaid is affected by the degree to which all programs for the indigent become "poor programs" and in the degree to which the poor are provided "mass-produced" medical care. Moreover, because Medicaid is not an insurance program and because states can expand or contract covered services, Medicaid cannot be said to provide a national health system for the poor.

The unprecedented congressional repeal of the Catastrophic Care Bill one year after its passage raised some crucial questions. Why, in contrast to Social Security and the rest of Medicare, was catastrophic care to be funded only by beneficiaries? Why would Congress not alter the controversial financing format instead of abolishing the program? How will the growing aging population pay for lengthy, costly, serious illnesses? What will happen to the millions of elderly persons who are ineligible for Medicaid but cannot afford private insurance (Medigap) to cover costs not currently assumed by Medicare?

Coverage for catastrophic illness is not the only problem in the current health care system. Perhaps the most critical issue is the estimated 41 million Americans totally without health insurance. Many of these persons are ineligible for Medicare and Medicaid but cannot afford private insurance. In addition, persons with disabilities must wait two years before being eligible for Medicare. There are estimates that more than 40 million persons are without health insurance coverage, among these 10 million children. The Balanced Budget Act (1997) gave states the option to provide Medicaid coverage for about half those children regardless of whether they continue to meet income eligibility tests and to presume eligibility for low-income children while that eligibility is being determined.

The latent consequences of this system are many and were not all anticipated. The emphasis in Medicare on hospitalization tends to encourage physicians to treat those who are ill according to the way they are insured, thus causing a run on the most expensive services of all and increasing health costs. Another latent consequence that led to the escalation of health costs is the third-party payment system described in chapter 7. For all of these reasons, Medicare and Medicaid are critical stopgaps in meeting health needs, but they are inadequate for a comprehensive rational system of health insurance for the nation.

To contain escalating health care costs and improve access to Medicaid, states have increased their use of managed care, discussed earlier in this chapter. Between 1991 and 1996, enrollment in Medicaid managed care increased by nearly 400 percent. In the latter year, more than 13 million Medicaid beneficiaries were served in this fashion (40 percent of the total Medicaid population).

Because states have to fund the program, Medicaid competes for general revenue funds with other state budget items such as education and transportation. State governors have complained about the costs of Medicaid, many of which have been mandated by congressional action; the paperwork required to comply with federal regulations; and bureaucratic rules that limit state flexibility.

New Health Insurance Legislation   The Health Insurance Portability and Accountability Act (HIPAA; 1996) included provisions for MSAs. MSAs are a four-year, market-driven experiment for 750,000 employed persons under age 65 years. Individuals can make tax-free deposits to cover expenses, deductibles for insurance policies, and insurance copayments. Within certain limits, contributions to an MSA are deductible when made by an eligible individual and are excludable from income and employment taxes if made by the employer (other than contributions made by a cafeteria plan). Earnings on an MSA are not currently taxable. Withdrawals for medical expenses would be nontaxable; those for nonmedical, personal use would be taxed.

MSAs became available in 1997 to employees covered under an employer-sponsored, high-deductible health plan (at least $1,500 and no more than $2,500 for an individual, $3,000 and no more than $4,500 for family coverage) of a small employer (50 employess or fewer) and to self-employed individuals covered under a high-deductible health plan, regardless of size of the entity.

After December 31, 2000, no new contributions may be made to MSAs except by or on behalf of an individual who previously made MSA contributions and employees employed by a participating employer. Those self-employed persons who contributed to an MSA during 1997–2000 also may continue contributions after 2000.

Because individuals would benefit financially if they keep their medical expenses down, there are expectations this program will reduce overutilization of health care services. After four years, the effects of the MSA experiment will be reviewed, perhaps to consider including Medicare recipients. The HIPAA authorized an MSA demonstration for employed individuals who are not yet eligible for Medicare to test the feasibility of MSAs for Medicare. Initial enrollment was scheduled for late 1998.

The HIPAA legislation also required that insurers cover mental health problems the same as physical problems (same aggregate and annual payment limits) for certain-size employers.

Enacted to protect people from losing coverage because of job loss, illness, or a change of jobs, the law is helpful to those who have health insurance but does nothing for the approximately 41 million persons who are without coverage because they are unable to pay insurance premiums. The high cost of family coverage for most people requires an employer's contribution. The legislation restricts the denial of insurance because of preexisting health problems and credits new employees for each month of coverage they had under a previous plan: If previously covered for 12 months or more, a person would have uninterrupted coverage upon taking a new job or with individual coverage. Self-employed persons who can pay the premiums would also be protected.

Nutrition Programs

Nutrition programs help low-income persons meet their nutritional needs. The Food Stamp Program is a means-tested entitlement program, and the Supplemental Food Program for Women, Infants, and Children has a budget cap, and is not only means tested but targets a very specific category of recipient.

The Food Stamp Program

Goals   The Food Stamp Program is designed primarily to increase the food purchasing power of eligible low-income households so they can buy a nutritionally adequate low-cost diet.

Who Is Eligible for the Program?   Eligibility is based on financial, employment/training, and categorical tests. A means test requires that those eligible have monthly income and assets below limits set by Food Stamp law. Certain household members must register for work, accept suitable job offers, and fulfill work or training requirements such as looking or training for a job. A 1996 law limits Food Stamp eligibility for able-bodied adults without dependents to 3–6 months in any 36-month period unless they are working half time or in a work or training activity. Eligibility rules make some persons automatically eligible (many TANF, SSI, and general assistance recipients) or others ineligible (strikers and most noncitizens, post-secondary students, and people living in an institutional setting). Applications cannot be denied because of the length of time the household lived in the welfare agency's jurisdiction or because the household has no fixed mailing address or does not reside in a permanent dwelling. The program reaches many people—there were

25.5 million recipients in 1996 (9.6 percent of the total population, 69.8 percent of the poor population).

What Is the Form of the Benefit?

Benefits are related to a household's size, net monthly income, and maximum monthly benefit levels (in some places adjusted for geographic location). An eligible household's net income is calculated, a maximum benefit level established, and the benefit calculated by subtracting an expected contribution (30 percent of net income) from the maximum allotment.

Low-income persons receive Food Stamp booklets of coupons of specified amounts. They then can use the coupons like cash to purchase most foods for consumption from participating stores. A growing number of states are utilizing electronic benefit transfer (EBT) systems, which replace coupons with an automatic teller machine–like card and with which purchases are deducted at the point of sale from the recipient's account. Food Stamp allotments are not taxable, and Food Stamp purchases may not be charged sales taxes. Receipt of Food Stamps does not affect eligibility for benefits provided by other assistance programs, although it may influence the level of a benefit. Purchases are made in approved grocery stores and include food for home preparation and consumption (not alcohol, tobacco products, or hot foods intended for immediate consumption); seeds and plants for gardens to produce food for personal consumption; for the elderly and SSI recipients and their spouses, meals prepared and served through approved communal dining programs; and meals prepared and served to residents of drug addiction and alcoholic treatment programs, small group homes for the disabled, shelters for battered women and children, and shelters or other establishments serving the homeless. Homebound aged and disabled persons who cannot prepare their meals may use Food Stamps for Meals-on-Wheels. In certain remote parts of Alaska, equipment for procuring food by hunting and fishing may be obtained. Some other products are not eligible: For example pet food and cleaning and paper products may not be purchased with food stamps. In 1996, the average monthly benefit per person was $73.30, and the four-person maximum monthly allotment was $397.

How Is the Program Financed?   The entire cost of benefit payments is covered by the federal government from general revenues, except where states pay for issuing Food Stamp benefits to ineligible noncitizens or those made ineligible by the new work rule for able-bodied adults without dependents. The federal government is also responsible for its own administrative costs: overseeing program operations, printing and distribution of coupons to welfare agencies, redeeming stamps through the Federal Reserve, and payments to the Social Security Administration for certain intake services. In most cases, the federal government provides half the cost of state public assistance departments, including their outreach activities. The federal share can be increased 10 percent if the state has a very low rate of erroneous benefit determinations. The federal government shares the cost of employment and training programs as well as support services for food stamp recipients involved in employment and training. States are allowed to retain a portion of improperly issued benefits (other than agency errors) that are recovered, fraud cases, and other circumstances.

What Is the Level of Administration?

At the federal level, the Food Stamp program is administered by the U.S. Department of Agriculture's Food and Consumer Service, which gives direction to welfare agencies through federal regulations that define eligibility requirements, benefit levels, and administrative rules. It is responsible for arranging for printing Food Stamp coupons and distributing them to welfare agencies, overseeing state programs for EBT and approving and overseeing participation by retail food stores and other outlets that accept Food Stamps. Administrative roles of other federal agencies are as follows: the federal system redeems stamps and has some jurisdiction over EBT methods; the Social Security Administration is responsible for the social security numbers that recipients must have, providing limited intake services, and verification of recipients' income; the Internal Revenue Service provides assistance in verifying recipients' income and assets; the Immigration and Naturalization service helps welfare offices confirm alien applicants' status; and the Secret Service and the Agriculture Department's Inspector General are responsible regarding counterfeiting and trafficking investigations.

States and other jurisdictions implement administrative responsibilities through their local welfare offices, determining eligibility, calculating benefits, and issuing Food Stamp allotments following federal rules. They also carry out employment and training programs in cooperation with the Employment Service of the U.S. Department of Labor through state employment offices that administer the Food Stamp Program's work registration requirements.

Discussion Funding for the Food Stamp Program was reduced in 1996 by $23 billion over six years (not including cuts to legal immigrants). Food Stamp assistance was reduced for poor families with children that pay more than 50 percent of their income for housing by capping the Food Stamp deduction for shelter costs. Other adjustments such as those of the Thrifty Food Plan, a low-cost food budget used to calculate the amount of food stamps for a family, were meant to reduce Food Stamp aid. Childless, nondisabled individuals from 18 to 50 years of age can only receive three months of food stamp assistance in a three-year period unless they are working or participating in a workfare program at least 20 hours per week. They can get up to six months of Food Stamps if they go to work and lose their job in the three-year period.

Special Supplemental Food Program for Women, Infants, and Children

Goals The Special Supplemental Food Program for Women, Infants, and Children, commonly referred to as WIC, provides food assistance, nutrition risk screening, and related services such as nutrition education and breast feeding support to low-income pregnant and post-partum women and their infants, as well as to low-income children up to age 5 years.

Who Is Eligible for the Program? Participants in the program must have family income at or below 185 percent of poverty and must be judged to be nutritionally at risk, defined as detectable abnormal nutritional conditions, documented nutritionally related medical conditions, health-impairing dietary deficiencies, or conditions that predispose people to inadequate nutrition or nutritionally related medical problems. Only pregnant and postpartum women, infants, and children under age 5 years may participate. State WIC agencies may set lower income standards but seldom do so. Receipt of TANF, Food Stamps, or Medicaid assistance also can satisfy the WIC program's income test.

What Is the Form of the Benefit? Recipients receive supplemental foods monthly in the form of actual food items or, more generally, vouchers for purchases of specific items in retail stores. The law requires that the WIC program provide foods containing protein, iron, calcium, vitamin A, and vitamin C. Among the items that may be included in a food package are milk, cheese, eggs, infant formula, cereals, and fruit or vegetable juices. These food packages are tailored for age level, special dietary needs, and pregnant, nursing, and postpartum women and are prescribed by a WIC health care professional. Recipients must also receive nutritional education. In 1996 the national average federal cost of a WIC food package after rebates from infant formula manufacturers was $31 per month, and the average monthly administrative cost for each participant was about $11.

Benefits are received for a specified period of time and sometimes are recertified if there is continuing need. Pregnant women may continue to receive benefits throughout their pregnancy and for up to six months after childbirth without recertification. Nursing mothers are certified at six-month intervals, ending with their child's first birthday.

How Is the Program Financed?

The WIC program is federally funded from general revenues. It is not an entitlement program, and participation is limited by the amount of federal funding appropriated, whatever state supplementary funding is made available, and the extent of manufacturers' infant formula rebates.

What Is the Level of Administration?

Federally funded, the WIC program is administered by state and local health agencies. This program was authorized by the Child Nutrition Act of 1966, In 1993, there were on average 5.9 million recipients, including 1.7 million infants and 2.8 million children. Because of insufficient funding, many of those who are income-eligible and at nutritional risk do not receive WIC.

School Lunch and Breakfast Programs

Goals   The School Lunch and School Breakfast programs provide federal cash and commodity support for meals served by public and private nonprofit elementary and secondary schools and residential child care institutions that enroll and guarantee to offer free or reduced-price meals to eligible low-income children.

Who Is Eligible for the Program?   Both the Breakfast and Lunch programs have a three-tiered system that allows children from families with incomes below 130 percent of the poverty line to receive free meals; children from families from 130 to 185 percent of the poverty level to receive meals at a reduced price; and provides a small subsidy for children whose family income does not qualify them for free or reduced price meals or whose families do not apply. Children in TANF and Food Stamp households may automatically qualify for free school meals without an income application.

What Is the Form of the Benefit?   The programs provide breakfasts and lunches to children.

How Is the Program Financed?   Both programs are funded from federal general revenues through the budget of the Food and Consumer Service, Department of Agriculture.

What Is the Level of Administration?   These programs are administered on the federal level by the Food and Consumer Service and administered locally by school districts, individual schools, and certain nonprofit residences. Other federal child nutrition programs include the Child and Adult Care Food Program and the Summer Food Service, which provides subsidies for meals served during the summer months to children participating in recreational and other programs in low-income areas. The National School Lunch Program (NSLP) and the School Breakfast Program (SBP) provide cash and commodity support to participating public and private schools and nonprofit residential institutions that serve meals to children.

Discussion   The Food Stamp Program is a good example of a program initially not particularly favored by social welfare experts, but that has come to be viewed as highly valuable. To begin with, almost all social welfare planners would have preferred to use the money involved in financing the Food Stamp Program to increase general welfare benefits. This was seen as more dignified and would have eliminated the administrative expenses involved in setting up a Food Stamp operation. However, as the program grew each year and as more poor people came to depend on it, it became harder for people concerned with the poor to oppose it.

Among the objections to the program was that it forced the recipient to parade dependency in stores whenever a purchase was made. The program also lent itself to the abuses inherent in a selective program. Although the issue of stigma remains, and although some may still advocate replacing Food Stamps with cash benefits, the

Food Stamp Program has notable strengths. It helps the poor meet basic nutritional needs, providing federal assistance in all states including those in which additional state allocations for the poor would be highly unlikely. It is therefore an income supplement program.

Moreover, benefits are entirely federally funded, and there are uniform national benefit levels. Unlike TANF, then, inequities in benefit levels are eliminated. The Food Stamp Program also requires funds outreach to potential recipients, and recent legislation has sought to assist vulnerable populations such as the homeless.

The WIC program is another selective in-kind food program but, in contrast to the Food Stamp Program, is lauded precisely because of its selective, in-kind characteristics. By providing nutritious food and medical care to pregnant and nursing mothers and young children, it has been shown to prevent costly conditions such as premature and low-birthweight babies. Despite demonstrated effectiveness and efficiency, WIC enrollment is limited by the amount of federal funding appropriated, state supplementation where it exists, and the extent of manufacturers' rebates. Because it is not an entitlement program, there are limits to funding allocations and to the numbers of eligible applicants who receive benefits.

Low-Income Home Energy Assistance

Goals

The Low-Income Home Energy Assistance Program (LIHEAP) is aimed at helping eligible households pay their home heating or cooling bills, providing assistance for low-cost weatherization, and providing assistance during energy-related emergencies.

Who Is Eligible for the Program?

States have considerable discretion to determine eligibility criteria and the types of assistance to be provided. Recipients of SSI, TANF, Food Stamps, or means-tested veterans' benefits may receive benefits. States can also opt to make payments to households with up to 150 percent of federal poverty guidelines or 60 percent of the state's median income, whichever is greater. States cannot establish an income ceiling below 110 percent of the poverty level. Priority for assistance may be given to households that meet criteria based on home energy burden in relation to household income; and households with younger children, frail elderly, or persons with disabilities and those energy needs that arise from a natural disaster or other emergency.

States are required to have an outreach plan so that eligible households, in particular those with a disabled or elderly member, are informed about the program. In 1995, LIHEAP served 5.1 million households.

What Is the Form of the Benefit?

States may provide three types of services: (1) help eligible households pay their home heating or cooling bills; (2) use up to 15 percent of their LIHEAP allotment for low-cost weatherization; and (3) provide assistance to households during energy-related emergencies. States may provide cash or vendor payments, two-party checks, vouchers/coupons, and payments directly to landlords.

How Is the Program Financed?

The LIHEAP is a block-grant program funded entirely by the federal government. Funding reached a high of $2.1 billion in 1985 and a low of about $1 billion in 1996, when it survived an attempt in Congress to eliminate the program, perhaps because of a storm of protests and negative publicity.

What Is the Level of Administration?

At the federal level, the program is administered by the Administration for Children and Families of the Department of Health and Human Services. States, Native American tribes, and territories administer LIHEAP programs through the state welfare agency or at the local level and must provide for hearings for those denied benefits, public participation, and public hearings in the development of the plan.

Discussion

This program illustrates the problems that occur when a needed service is not an entitlement. Because funding for this program is capped, once the available dollars are spent, those who come for heating and cooling assistance are turned away. The program is horizontally inadequate; it is vertically inadequate as well because, especially in severe weather, the available dollars are not equal for many persons in relation to their needs.

Housing

Goals

Several federal programs attempt to address housing needs by improving housing quality and reducing housing costs for lower income households, promoting residential construction, expanding housing opportunities for disadvantaged groups and groups with special housing needs, promoting neighborhood preservation and revitalization, increasing home ownership, and empowering the poor to become self-sufficient.

Who Is Eligible for the Program?

Most federal housing aid is now targeted to very low-income renters through rental assistance programs, including new construction or rehabilitation of projects. Rental assistance generally reduces tenant's rent payments to a fixed percentage (currently 30 percent) of their income after defined deductions. Currently, new funding commitments are directed through mortgage interest subsidies and a new construction program for elderly and disabled persons. President Clinton in 1996 changed the rules so that public housing authorities could evict tenants arrested for drug-related and violent crimes. Debates have also occurred between those who assign priority in public housing to those who are the neediest and those who are the working poor.

In 1998, Republicans and Democrats enacted a compromise bill responding to the needy/working poor issue. The bill created 90,000 vouchers that will disperse re-ceipients throughout the housing market; three-fourths are to go to the neediest poor. Efforts, including some community service, are required to maintain eligibility. The bill also attempts to deter racial or economic segregation.

The federal government assists some low and moderate income households in becoming homeowners by making long-term commitments to reduce their mort-gage interest. New housing assistance directions were authorized in 1990: the Home Investment Partnerships Block Grant program, the Home Ownership and Op-portunity for People Everywhere (HOPE) program, and the National Home Owner-ship Trust demonstration. Since 1996, funds have only been appropriated for the Home program.

The Home program is intended to increase the supply of housing affordable to low-income families through the provision of federal grants to states and local gov-ernments. Funds may be used for either tenant-based rental assistance or for acquisi-tion, rehabilitation, or, in limited circumstances, construction of both rental and ownership housing. Participating jurisdictions must match federal grants with contri-butions of at least 25 percent.

What Is the Form of Benefit?

Among the benefits of the various housing programs are the following: rental subsi-dies through reduced rents and certificates for reduced rental rates and vouchers; in-sured and reduced mortgages, property taxes, and insurance costs; interest subsidies to the mortgage lender on behalf of lower-income families; rent supplement pay-ments equal to the difference between fair market value rental for particular housing and a percentage of the family income. There are also efforts to increase the supply of affordable housing for low-income families through the provision of federal grants to state and local governments to be used for rental assistance or for the acquisition, rehabilitation, or, in limited circumstances, construction of both rental and owner-ship housing. Counseling and technical assistance are sometimes available. The McK-inney Act provides for some support services for residents in shelters and housing they fund. In addition, the Fair Housing Program is administered through this depart-ment to eliminate discrimination in housing on the basis of race, color, religion, sex, and national origin.

Section 8 housing provides several forms of benefits. Households may rent an apartment in a Section 8 project or rehabilitated building. Rent will be low and based on the household's income, size, and expenses. Under the voucher-certification pro-gram, a family rents a unit of its choice from a private landlord who agrees to partici-pate in the Section 8 program. In most cases, the family pays no more than 30 per-cent of its adjusted family income for rent, and the government pays the landlord the difference up to an approved rent level. The voucher-certification program is an ongoing benefit. If a recipient household moves out of one apartment, it can use the benefit in another rental unit. If the family has a voucher, it can carry its Section 8 benefit anywhere in the United States. Under the certification program, the family can transfer the benefit only in its local area. In addition to affordable rents, all Section 8 recipients benefit from the fact that rental units must meet established standards, and the Section 8 lease must offer certain protections.

There has been a marked shift away from the production of housing to the uses of existing housing. The oldest existing program is low-rent public housing, which was enacted under the U.S. Housing Act of 1937. The Section 8 rental assistance programs are currently among the major housing supports for low-income families.

Funds are also provided to county and city governments for housing-related activities such as the rehabilitation of properties and the improvement of public facilities. In addition, there is housing assistance for veterans, which is not means tested, and guaranteed mortgage loans, which have made it possible for millions of people to purchase homes.

How Are the Programs Financed?

These housing programs are financed by federal general revenues, state and local monies, special insurance funds, closed-end appropriations, rental excesses over costs deposited to special funds, loans, a revolving rural housing insurance fund, and the like. Because federal legislative commitments run from 1 to 40 years, the appropriations are actually spent gradually over many years, thus expanding the pool of available aid and increasing the number of households served.

What Is the Level of Administration?

The major housing programs are administered by the U.S. Department of Housing and Urban Development (HUD) through area offices and local public housing authorities and the U.S. Department of Agriculture's Farm Service Agency (FSA), which administers housing programs for rural families and domestic farm laborers through state and county governments and with county committees appointed by the secretary of agriculture. The Office of Indian Housing of HUD administers the Indian Housing Program. The Veterans Administration housing program is administered through regional offices of the Department of Veterans Benefits.

Homelessness has continued as a national problem. The major federal response is the Stewart B. McKinney Homeless Assistance Act of 1987, which provides funds for emergency, transitional, and permanent housing for the homeless.

Discussion

Even as the economy was robustly growing, low-income families faced record-level problems trying to pay the rent. Two studies found that despite the booming economy, the housing problems of the poor continued. Affordable apartments are at a premium in all parts of the nation. In 1995, the typical poor family of renters spent about 60 percent of its income on shelter, twice the figure the government considers affordable.[23] So the current programs are not equal to the task.

There is a continuing debate between those who favor vouchers or other systems to make private housing and the open market available to the poor and those who believe in public housing, housing developments, and similar projects. The former argue that major housing developments have tended to re-create slums and re-segregate people and are expensive to maintain. In their opinion, it is a lot simpler to provide cash assistance with enough dollars for the poor to give them the opportunity to live in decent housing in the community. Actually, the record of housing developments in "projects" is mixed. Some have been quite successful, but most publicity goes to the major big-city, high-rise public housing projects that re-create slum conditions. It is important to remember that the major effort in social welfare housing has been to help the middle class move into private housing through mortgage guarantees and loans. The federal government has expended much more on this over the past years than it has on public housing. There are growing efforts to replicate "middle-class-type housing" programs for the poor by helping them move from impoverished areas and center cities to residences in suburban middle-class and mixed-income neighborhoods. These efforts are viewed as incentives for those moved to maintain their new domiciles and as supports for improved education and financial betterment.

Affordable housing is a pressing national problem. Rising housing costs have put home ownership out of the reach of many young families. Rentals have escalated to the point that low- and moderate-income persons are often unable to afford even inadequate housing. Some have joined the swelling ranks of the homeless. Many existing old units were abandoned, demolished, or converted into higher-cost housing. The issue of housing provides a graphic example of how governmental, economic, and social forces can complement each other and contribute to the rapid development of a major social problem. Large numbers of homeless persons in every part of the country are evidence of the consequences of such a confluence of forces. Efforts have focused on increasing allocations for and designing new approaches to meeting the nation's housing needs. Among these were the aforementioned home ownership for low-income persons, more funding for the nonprofit sector, and housing and related social services targeted to special needs populations.

VETERANS' BENEFITS

Goals

Veterans' benefit programs are provided as recognition of service to the nation.

Who Is Eligible for the Program?

Eligibility for most veterans' benefits is based on discharge from active military service under other than dishonorable conditions for a minimum period specified by law; family members or survivors of deceased veterans are also eligible. "Active service" generally means full-time service as a member of the Army, Navy, Air Force, Marines, or Coast Guard or as a commissioned officer of the Public Health Service, the Environmental Services Administration, or the National Oceanic and Atmospheric Administration. Completion of at least six years of honorable service in the Selected Reserves also provides for home-loan benefits for those not otherwise eligible. Certain veteran's benefits require wartime service.

What Is the Form of Benefit?

The Department of Veterans Affairs (VA) programs include veterans' compensation and pensions, readjustment benefits, medical care, and housing and loan guaranty programs. Also provided are life insurance, burial benefits, and special counseling and outreach programs.

"Service-connected" compensation is paid to veterans who have disabilities from injuries or illnesses sustained while in service. The amounts of monthly payments are determined by disability ratings based on presumed average reductions in earning capacity caused by the disabilities, ranging from 10 to 100 percent. Death compensation, or dependency and indemnity compensation, is paid to survivors of veterans who died as a result of service-connected causes. In fiscal year 1996, about 2.2 million disabled veterans and 306,241 survivors received compensation payments.

Veterans' pensions are means-tested cash benefits to war veterans who have become permanently and totally disabled from "non–service-connected" causes, and to survivors of war veterans. Under current law, benefits are based on family size, and the pensions provide a floor of income (In 1997 an eligible veteran living alone received $8,486.) Less generous benefits are available to survivors.

Several VA programs support readjustment, education, and job training for veterans and military personnel who meet certain eligibility criteria. The largest of these programs was the Montgomery GI Bill (MGIB). The MGIB provides educational assistance to persons, who as members of the Armed Forces or Selected Reserves, elect to participate in the program. Active duty personnel contribute monthly for the first year of enlistment. This program provides an entitlement to basic educational assistance and provides educational assistance to help in readjustment to civilian life, to aid in recruitment and retention of qualified personnel in the armed forces, and to develop a more highly educated and productive work force. Benefits are contingent upon length of service: The maximum benefit of three years requires three years of continuous service. Vocational rehabilitation is provided for disabled veterans, and the Department of Labor provides employment counseling and job training for veterans.

The VA provides an array of inpatient and outpatient medical services through medical centers, nursing homes, domiciliaries, ambulatory clinics, and readjustment counseling centers. Free medical care, both inpatient and outpatient, is provided for service-connected conditions and to low-income veterans for non–service-connected conditions. (The latter program is means-tested.) As facilities and resources permit, the VA provides care to veterans with non–service-connected conditions with incomes that exceed the income conditions but co-payments are required. Nursing home care is provided, with priority given to those with service-connected disabilities. The VA can contract with private facilities when it is determined to be in the best interest of the veteran and cost effective for the VA. VA nursing home care is augmented through contracts with community nursing homes and with per diem payments to state-run homes for veterans.

The VA also provides programs to improve health care services for veterans, including priority counseling and treatment for sexual trauma for eligible veterans. The trauma may result from a physical assault or battery of a sexual nature or sexual harassment that occurred while on active military duty. Sexual harassment is defined as repeated, unsolicited verbal or physical contact of a sexual nature that is threatening in character. This service was scheduled to continue to the end of 1998.

Former prisoners of war; those suffering from medical problems that may be related to exposure to Agent Orange (a herbicide used extensively during the Vietnam Conflict that is linked to cancer, miscarriages, and birth defects in laboratory animals), or radiation from nuclear testing; those eligible for Medicaid; and those 65 years of age or older are among those who receive free care regardless of their income or assets. Gulf War veterans are being reached out to in order to determine and assist those who can help to identify the causes of Persian Gulf War veterans illnesses.

The VA also provides educational benefits to eligible dependents of certain veterans under the Survivors' and Dependents' Educational Assistance Program. Dependent children and spouses of veterans who died or are permanently and totally disabled as a result of a service disability are eligible, as well as the dependents of veterans who died from any cause while such service-connected disability was in existence; service persons missing in action or captured in line of duty by a hostile force; and service persons forcibly detained or interned in the line of duty by a foreign government or power. These persons may be eligible for up to 45 months of education benefits.

The VA also provides educational benefits under the Post-Vietnam Veterans' Educational Assistance program (VEAP). This program provides educational and training opportunities to eligible persons who contributed to VEAP while on active duty. If veterans (or in some cases, active-duty personnel) meet certain criteria (dates of service, contributions to VEAP, duration of service, release from service other than dishonorable), they may be eligible for up to 36 months of educational benefits. There are also several employment and training programs for veterans, including transition assistance for persons scheduled for separation from active duty and programs for veterans who have been unable to find employment following military service.

How Are the Programs Financed?

The VA is funded from federal general revenue, except where military personnel contribute or copayments are required. In 1996, a total of $36.9 billion was expended.

What Is the Level of Administration?

The VA is a federal program administered nationally by the Department of Veterans Affairs in coordination with other agencies where appropriate to the service to be provided, including—among others—the Department of Labor, the Farm Service Agency of the Department of Agriculture, Department of Housing and Urban Development for mortgage insurance, and the Small Business Administration.

As discussed earlier in this book, after World War II the GI Bill was one of the major factors in upgrading the U.S. workforce and in preventing a disruptive depression when millions of veterans were discharged in 1945 and 1946. In recent years, veterans' benefits have become less adequate compared with the cost of tuition and maintenance, and some have argued for an increase in benefits. Others have said that there is no reason this educational program should be limited to veterans if, as seems to be the case, it has enhanced the U.S. economy so greatly.

Veterans are also eligible for a variety of other benefits. For example, they may receive money from a limited income maintenance program based on need, free burial, prosthetic appliances, and home modifications to accommodate a disability. The astute social worker will always want to know if the client needing help or a member of the family is a veteran because, depending on the period during which the person served, the benefits might be worth looking into and might prove helpful.

Veterans of the Vietnam War experienced special problems, largely because of the ambivalence of the American public about the war. To serve this group, the U.S. Department of Veterans' Affairs makes special efforts to provide services for them, including some help for those exposed to Agent Orange and referrals to Vet Centers designed to give help "without hassles" to Vietnam-era veterans. These centers provide counseling, career guidance, help for emotional problems, family treatment programs, and linkages to federal, state, and local organizations that could help veterans secure special benefits, drug and alcohol treatment, medical care, legal aid, and emergency services.

Discussion

It is interesting that, in contrast to the rest of the U.S. health care system, the veterans' medical program is a true form of nationalized medicine. There are no third-party payments or the like. Doctors and other staff are salaried, and all medical care is available for the eligible veteran. Evaluations of this system differ. Although veterans' facilities have been criticized for a variety of defects, on the whole the hospitals are not considered to be less adequate or less well funded than other medical systems in the United States, and the system has been of great benefit to many thousands of people. If the United States ever moves to national health insurance, the question of how veterans' medical care would be integrated in such a plan is a major one.

Services for veterans mingle selective and universal programs. Some programs are means tested and others are not. Veterans who are not eligible for some programs may be eligible for other services. Criticisms have been voiced about changing eligibility rules as well as problems of access. However, these services play very important roles. Poor veterans are the predominant users of VA health care services.[24] The VA reorganized in 1997 when it cut 40 percent of its hospital beds and shifted services to clinics, consolidated services, and trimmed services. By 1998, veterans testified in Congress that they cannot get needed health care at VA centers. In addition to the fundamental service shift, the VA budget for health services has not kept up with rising costs. A spokesperson for the VA reported that surveys find that most veterans are satisfied with the services they receive.[25]

From time to time suggestions have been made to "fold" VA health services into universal health care programs, but to date none of these suggestions have been accepted. Services for veterans and their families have been staunchly defended. No group is considered more deserving than veterans disabled while on active duty. In addition to other support, veterans and their families comprise a large number of voters.

EMPLOYMENT PROGRAMS

The Workforce Investment Act (WIA, 1998) rewrote federal statutes governing job training, adult education and literacy, and vocational rehabilitation, replacing them with a new system designed for a "work first" approach that uses the labor market to evaluate the pool of workers seeking employment and training assistance. A second emphasis of the legislation strengthens links between the workforce investment system and the reauthorized adult education, literacy, and vocational rehabilitation programs. Individual programs are maintained, but summer and year-round youth programs are to be operated under the Job Training Partnership Act (JTPA, 1982).

Linkages are established through state workforce boards with authority to guide the development of the system, local area workforce boards, One-Stop systems, unified state plans, and accountability. Eligibility is expanded for core employment services (job search, assessment, information and referral) to all adults, not just disadvantaged or dislocated workers. Core services must be provided through one-stop employment and training centers. Job training providers are to be screened according to their performance on key outcomes. The use of individual vouchers is promoted rather than contracts for obtaining job training and services. The legislation also restricts training to adults who are not employable after receiving core services or who are employed but need training to become self-sufficient.

Among the programs are the Job Corps; Youth Opportunity grants; Native American programs; Migrant and Seasonal Farmworker programs; Veterans; and demonstration, pilot, multiservice, research, and multistate projects and evaluations. In addition, there are National Emergency grants. Other programs are Adult Education and Literacy and Workforce Investment-Related activities, including employment services and collection of employment statistics. A 21st Century Workforce Commission was also created to conduct a study of the information technology workforce in the United States. The Rehabilitation Act was amended; it now requires an annual report on vocational rehabilitation that expands the performance and accountability information collected. Research and training is also provided for in the legislation. The bill also expanded The National Council on Disability. The bill requires federal agencies to procure, maintain, and use electronic and information technology that provides individuals with disabilities with comparable access to what is available to individuals without disabilities.

Among the programs are the JTPA; the Job Corps; the Employment and Training Administration of the Department of Labor; the Senior Community Services Employment Program; Employment and Training Assistance for Dislocated Workers; the Veteran's Employment Program; the Native American Employment and Training Program; the Women's Special Employment Assistance Program; and the Federal Work-Study Program. The President's Committee on Employment of People with Disabilities is designed to enhance the employment of persons with disabilities. Unemployment Insurance, Food Stamps, and TANF utilize employment services for recipients.

In addition, the Carl Perkins Vocational Applied Technology and Education Act of 1990, administered by the U.S. Department of Education, provides much of the funding for displaced homemakers' programs. A little-publicized but important employment-related program, which is operated through the states with federal funding, is vocational rehabilitation. Under this program, people with various disabilities are eligible for support and educational benefits for education and training programs that are calculated to make them more likely to be self-supporting and to develop careers. Vocational rehabilitation is still an important welfare program of which social workers should be aware. All these programs are now subsumed under the WIA (1998).[26]

Personal Social Services

Historically, five major social welfare systems have been identified: education, income maintenance, health, housing, and employment. Comparative international studies led to the identification of a sixth system with a long tradition—the personal social services. These services are intended to meet the normal anticipated social needs that arise in modern industrial nations.[27]

As we now look at the personal social services, the point must be made that some of them are integrated into other systems; that is, counseling or employment programs may be tied to public assistance. We also will discuss mental health, although in another sense it is part of the health system.

The functions of personal social services are the following:

- Contributing to socialization and development;
- Offering daily living and growth supports for average people (not just problem groups);
- Disseminating information about and facilitating access to services and entitlements anywhere in the social sector, inclusive of all six social welfare fields;
- Securing for the frail and aged, the handicapped, those with mental retardation, and the incapacitated a basic level of social care and aid necessary to support functioning in the community or in substitute living arrangements;

- Arranging substitute home or residential care or creating new, permanent family relationships for children whose parents are not able to fulfill their roles;
- Providing help, counseling, and guidance to assist individuals and families facing problems, crises, or sickness to reestablish functional capacities and overcome their difficulties;
- Supporting mutual aid, self-help, and activities aimed at prevention;
- Overcoming problems in community living;
- Advocating changes in policies, programs, and service planning;
- Integrating the variety of appropriate programs or services as they influence individuals and families, to assure coordination for maximum effect; and
- Controlling or supervising deviant individuals who may harm themselves or others, while offering care or opportunity for assistance, guidance, growth, or change.

We can look somewhat more closely at services provided for families and at those focused on child welfare as exemplars of the personal social services. We want to look particularly at those services in which social work is the profession that provides leadership.

Services to Families

In the best of times, all families need services that enrich their lives and the general nature of community living. As we have grown interdependent as a society, not everyone can be an expert at everything, and it is normal for families to call on experts and services in many ways. Some families will be unable to cope with harsh economic situations, loss of jobs, and financial, interpersonal, and intrafamilial difficulties. Divorce and separation, family and domestic violence, parent–child conflict, strained relationships between husband and wife or domestic partners, as well as the difficulties of combining families all are among the types of family problems for which people seek help.

It is important to keep in mind that not everyone who seeks help is experiencing problems out of the ordinary and that seeking help cannot be equated with mental disturbance. For example, family services are provided for those individuals and families experiencing special stresses such as single-parent families, families with children or parents with disabilities, and families experiencing various traumas. Family services are also provided for prevention and for life-enhancement purposes. Social groups, respite centers for parents and guardians, parent education, family life and sex education, stress management workshops, seminars on improving family communications, preparations for retirement, and household management and budgeting are among the many life-enhancing services available. Greater attention has been paid in recent years to the impact of ethnic, racial, socioeconomic, religious, gay and lesbian, and group-living arrangement factors among others as these patterns have more often replaced traditional domestic relationships.

The impact of home care services, which is discussed in chapter 15 illustrates the important contributions made by the personal social services. These services reduce the time some persons are institutionalized or required to be in hospitals, can in some instances prevent hospitalization, can enable wage earners to continue working when illness or other crises strike, and can assist others to cope with the world when it is beyond their strength to cope alone.

Assistance in family matters also is provided in the public welfare sector. Public welfare personnel provide information and advice; referrals for jobs, housing, employment, and health care; and adult and child protective services to families in need. Intensive social work with families is provided in cities across the nation by nonprofit nonsectarian and sectarian family service agencies affiliated with the national Family Service America, Inc. These local agencies in larger and smaller cities provide psychosocial help and certain concrete services for families, particularly in relation to marital and domestic problems, parent–child difficulties, and problems specific to children and adults. There has also been a movement among these agencies to expand their educational, preventive, and life-enhancement efforts through programs offering family life education and parent education. Many provide a broad range of services to meet contemporary family problems, such as domestic violence, teenage pregnancy, care of the elderly, employee assistance programs, and substance abuse. In addition, these family agencies may offer case advocacy services for individuals and may engage in cause advocacy activities such as coalition-building and legislative lobbying.

Other organizations also provide some family services. The VA, National Travelers Aid, and local mental health agencies provide counseling for individuals and families. In addition, many Americans purchase help for personal, familial, and interpersonal problems in the marketplace by paying fees to social workers, psychiatrists, psychologists, and family therapists.

Services to Children

Child welfare services have two broad emphases: (1) the enhancement of the functioning of all families and all children and (2) services provided for families and children with special needs. All families and children face developmental stresses and problems. The social health of families determines to a large extent the welfare needs of children. There are basic services in our society that are supportive of family life and the lives of children. Income security and employment opportunities are fundamental to the social health of families and their children. Housing; nutritional aid; maternal, child, and family health care; child care programs; education; recreation; mental health; and a host of personal social services assist families to deal with issues and needs that arise as they deal with the various life-cycle developments and socialization (e.g., pregnancy and birth, early years, school entry, major milestones, divorce, separations, death). Counseling and rehabilitation services are helpful where needed. Mutual aid groups have arisen in recent years, and information and referral services enable families and children to find the proper service for particular needs.

Services are also provided for children and families at risk of separation and with special needs. Children may experience neglect, physical and sexual abuse, and severe interpersonal conflict and need family-based services to prevent out-of-home placements; parents may be persons with mental illnesses, have physical or mental disabilities that interfere with parenting, or may be substance abusers. Children may be involved in delinquent behavior, or parents may become incarcerated or institutionalized. Children or parents may experience severe emotional problems. Extremely young parents and others may be unable to cope with their responsibilities.

In addition to the broad-based programs that provide general supports for families and children, child welfare services include parent and child counseling, advocacy, and brokerage to enable children and their families, where possible, to obtain required resources. Such services also include those aimed at children and families at risk of separation or those with special needs such as the provision of substitute care and adoption for children whose homes or parents are not available or are unsuitable. Services for children at risk have emphasized family preservation through such preventive services as homemaker services, family counseling, and intensive case management. These are all parts of protective services for children. When these services fail to protect children or when children are in imminent danger, protective services provide foster care placement until the family is ready for unification.

Under legal mandate in each state, a child welfare department is responsible for child welfare and provides services directly and through other mechanisms, such as purchase of services. With Congress's passage of the Adoption Assistance and Child Welfare Act (1980), there are some federal funds for adoption subsidies. Efforts are made to facilitate the return of children placed in foster care, and to promote subsidized adoptions of children with "special needs." At the same time, there has been recognition of the necessity for quality foster care for the increasing numbers of children requiring this service, including those with AIDS and babies born addicted to crack cocaine. Social workers in schools, mental health agencies, hospitals, and other settings increasingly recognize the special problems experienced by gay and lesbian young people. Many social workers are seeking to upgrade their training so as to be helpful to this group of persons.

There are recent creative developments designed to provide homes for children who might otherwise not be adoptable such as older children, those with disabilities, and those with minority backgrounds. Among the new approaches are broadened eligibility rules for adoptive parents. For example, people who are single, older, less wealthy, gay or lesbian are all more readily accepted as adoptive parents today.

Several forms of residential treatment are also provided for children. Some of these serve juvenile psychiatric inpatients and some serve those with developmental disabilities. Furthermore, children who have been adjudicated in juvenile or family court often are treated in rehabilitation institutions.

Day care and child development are essential services to support families and children. Among the types of services provided are group day care, Head Start programs, infant group care, nursery schools, day schools, drop-in centers, after-school programs, public school centers, and family day care. Services such as these enrich children's lives and also make possible work or a respite from family responsibilities for parents who may also use the time for personal education and training that can advance their own vocational opportunities and sense of life enrichment and fulfillment.

Special care is needed for children who are restricted to their homes because of disabilities and for their parents or guardians, whose responsibilities are never ending. Home health care, home tutors, homemakers, life skills development, housing resources for those with serious physical problems, and other services make life possible, enrich it, or help to rehabilitate children whose needs are special.

In 1996, important legislation affecting adoptions was enacted. The Small Business Job Protection Act (1996) contained a number of matters unrelated to the minimum wage or other business issues. The act provided a $5,000 tax credit—a subtraction from tax liability—for the expenses of adopting a child both in the United States and from foreign countries. A $6,000 credit was provided for adoptions of U.S.-born special-needs children with mental or physical disabilities. The $5,000 credit ends after the year 2001, but the special-needs credit is permanent. Neither applies to the adoption of stepchildren. The credit or deduction where employers pay the costs is phased out for families with annual incomes between $75,000 and $115,000.

The PRA changed the context for children and families. Fundamental issues concerning child welfare and child protection will continue to be raised and intensified. Although there will be successes, there will also be families whose situations become more vulnerable. It is unclear how a much criticized system with inadequate funds and staffing resources will cope with the child welfare needs created by the TANF programs. Will one result of TANF be the creation of increased need for foster care? This will become more crucial when the nation inevitably experiences a recession. The voluntary sector, as we note in chapter 11, simply cannot take up the load resulting from a lightened federal role.[28]

Essential to services for families and children are the enforcement of necessary regulations and standards so that children and families will receive services of high quality. This requires licensing, enforcement, sufficient funds, and other resources. These in turn suggest the importance of advocacy for children and their families during a time when the attention of the nation is turned mainly to financing Social Security and Medicare.

The personal social services respond to needs of all citizens, not the poor alone: the aged in need of community support systems, parents choosing day care for their children, people who need help with "normal" life contingencies, the ill/young/old and those with disabilities requiring community protection, and victims of the addictions. In the public sector, many of these services are provided through categorical programs. At one time, public attention shifts to the needs of children; at another time, the aged, those with mental illness, those with mental retardation, the physically disabled, and others. Constant competition occurs among various groups for available public funds.

From a cursory look at the many programs available, one can see that boundary questions exist as there is overlap between programs. Does one ask for child welfare or family welfare, family welfare or mental health care, mental health care or drug and alcohol rehabilitation? Undoubtedly, greater coordination among services is needed. Under what circumstances is it possible to provide integrated personal or social services in the public sector? What should be the relationship between personal social services delivered by the public sector and those offered by nonprofit and for-profit agencies? Furthermore, which personal services should be provided universally as social utilities available on demand? Which should require means or diagnostic testing?

In both public and nonprofit family and child welfare services in recent years, there has been a growing emphasis on the prevention of family disruption, child abuse and neglect, and domestic violence. Counseling and homemaker services as well as family treatment and education have helped in many cases to prevent family breakdown and diminished the need for placing children in foster care with families or in institutions. Family planning and parent education programs are there to lessen family stress and to enable parents to deal better with the stresses that affect them and their children. Single-parent groups, mutual aid groups of various types, intergenerational supports, and consumer education all play a part in helping families live together. What emphasis (funds) should be placed on services that feature prevention and enhancement of individual and family life? And what emphasis should be focused on rehabilitation and treatment after the fact?

Who Is Eligible for the Programs?   Eligibility for public social services varies by state and, for nonprofit services, by agency. Some persons purchase services in the marketplace. Some personal social services such as child guidance and psychiatric treatment require a diagnostic assessment or other determination of need and eligibility. Fees may be charged to consumers on the basis of income or may be available free to all who have a particular status—for example, use of a public library or an information and referral service by a town's residents.

Title XX

Goals   The purpose of the Title XX (of the Social Security Act) Social Services Block Grant program is to assist states in furnishing services aimed at one or more these goals: (1) achieve or maintain economic self-support to prevent, reduce, or eliminate dependency; (2) achieve or maintain self-sufficiency, including reduction or prevention of dependency; (3) prevent or remedy neglect, abuse, or exploitation of children and adults unable to protect their own interests, or preserving, rehabilitating or reuniting families; (4) prevent or reduce inappropriate institutional care by providing for community-based or home-based care, or other forms of less intensive care; and (5) securing referral or admission for institutional care when other forms of care are inappropriate, or providing services to individuals in institutions.

Who Is Eligible for the Programs?   States are given wide discretion to determine the services to be provided and the groups that may be eligible for services, usually low-income families and individuals.

What Is the Form of the Benefit?   In 1995 the services provided by the largest number of states in descending order were day care for children; home-based services (homemaker, chore, home health, companionship, and home maintenance);

preventive and interventive services such as assessments, family centered early intervention, home evaluation and supervision, preventive and restorative services; foster care for children; and child protective services. This group is followed by other jurisdictions that provide adoptions, protective services for adults, and special services for those with disabilities.

Title XX also permits a few universal and free services—for example, information and referral and adult and child protective services.

How Is the Program Financed?   This program is a capped multiple program. Block grant funds are given to states. The period from 1977 to 1997 saw a funding reduction of two thirds in real dollars (accounting for inflation) for this grant. The financial ceiling in 1997 and subsequent years was supposed to be $2.38 billion, but Congress only provided $2.5 billion in fiscal year 1997.

The two largest categories of spending are child day care (15 percent) and child-welfare related services (22 percent), which occur in several categories. Home-based services account for more than 10 percent of funds, as do administrative costs, which are 13 percent of expenditures.

The law that created Title XX gave states authority to transfer up to 10 percent of their annual allotment to several health care block grants and to LIHEAP. In 1997 states were allowed to transfer up to 10 percent of their TANF allotment to Title XX, regardless of how much they transfer to their Child Care and Development Grant. However, TANF funds transferred to Title XX must be used for families with incomes no higher than 200 percent of the federal poverty guidelines and may be used to provide vouchers for families ineligible for cash assistance under TANF because of time limits, or for children denied cash assistance under TANF because they were born into families already receiving benefits for another child.

The Omnibus Budget Reconciliation Act (1993) made $1 billion available grants-in-aid funds under Title XX for states to provide social services in qualified empowerment zones and enterprise communities. In 1994 President Clinton selected 105 areas to participate in the program, which requires that criteria in the Internal Revenue Code be met and that a strategic plan be formulated. Social services provided must be directed at three goals of the basic Title XX grant funds.

The act allows states to transfer up to 10 percent of the welfare block grant into the social services grant, but such a transfer can only be accomplished by reducing cash aid for children and families. Different means of funding support the personal social services. In the public sphere, services are supported by tax funds—depending on the particular program level—with money provided by the federal, state, or local government, or in combination from two or more levels, in the form of grants. In the private sector, sources of income include membership and user fees, grants, bequests, purchases of service, third-party payments, and donations, which are tax deductible. Title XX of the Social Security Act, Title III of the Older American Act, and various titles under mental health provide most federal funding. The overwhelming majority of social welfare funds, even in personal social services, comes from the public sector. Such transferred funds can only be used for children and families under 200 percent of the poverty level. The implication of these funding cuts is fewer services for low-income families with children and homeless and disabled individuals.

What Is the Level of Administration?   There is no central coordinating organization to give direction to the personal social services. There is overlap among types of services; among public, nonprofit, and private auspices; in various funding patterns; and the like. Services may be administered locally and relatively autonomously, or by the state, or in combinations of national, state, regional, and local authorities through umbrella organizations. Increasingly, states and localities purchase services from voluntary social agencies or private vendors.

Title XX social services block-grant funds are allocated to the states on the basis of population. Over the years the funding has declined significantly in real terms. The federal funds are available to the states without a state matching requirement. In 1994, the Title XX entitlement ceiling was $2.8 billion, more than in 1997.

The consolidation block-grant tactic and reduced allocations forced states to choose among programs and the levels of their funding. For example, should they give less to the aged or more to the disabled? Provide services for children or assist needy adults? Block grants for the social services distributed in this way meant that bargaining for funds had to be accomplished at the state level, a divisive situation in which very difficult decisions had to be made. Questions also have been raised about the competence of the states to deliver necessary services with less money, with fewer resources available, and with conflict in the relationship between states and localities, as well as special interest groups within the states.

Discussion   Public monies, until recently, increasingly supported private services. Budget cuts and accompanying tightened eligibility requirements have compromised widespread utilization of some personal social services. The United States does not have a coordinated network of personal social services. As with income security programs, the personal social services are diversified, decentralized, and incrementally developed.

MENTAL HEALTH SERVICES

Who Is Eligible for the Program?

The intensified need for mental health services during World War II, especially in the military, led to the passage of the National Mental Health Act (1946), which focused attention on the mental health needs of the populace and emphasized treatment and prevention services. This initial step was followed by the establishment of the National Institute of Mental Health in 1959. In 1963, the Mental Retardation Facilities and Community Mental Health Centers and Construction Act provided funds for the construction of community mental health centers, and subsequent amendments funded personnel. Medicaid and Medicare also provide psychiatric services for eligible persons.

Mental health services are designed to promote and maintain mental health, prevent mental illness, and treat and rehabilitate mentally ill persons. Mental health problems involve a range of behaviors—severe impairments requiring hospitaliza-tion, behavior that is mildly impairing, as well as the promotion of maximum mental health. Mental health services have not been restricted to treatment of mental illness but also provide supports during life transitions and difficult stresses. However, there has been a shift toward aiming services more toward those with seriously disabling conditions and away from aims such as personal self-fulfillment. This trend has been intensified by managed care and other funding mechanisms. The interrelationship of biological and psychosocial factors has received more emphasis in recent years.

Mental health facilities include both public (state and county) and private psy-chiatric hospitals. One can either voluntarily commit oneself or be involuntarily com-mitted for treatment on the basis of a court order or following certification by two physicians. When discharged from a hospital, aftercare is often provided for dis-charged patients in a local community facility. Some psychiatric hospitals also pro-vide ambulatory care. There has been an increase in the number of general hospitals that provide emergency and acute psychiatric services. The VA also provides inpa-tient, outpatient, and supportive psychiatric services for veterans, as does the federal government for Native Americans.

Community mental health centers provide a variety of services, including emer-gency services, diagnosis, treatment, referral, and community education and coordi-nation. Community residences and other outpatient services are provided for those who are reentering the community or need less than total hospitalization. Other ser-vice providers are self-help groups and nursing homes.

What Is the Form of Benefit?

The benefits received in mental health programs are diagnosis, treatment in the hos-pital or community, long-term or emergency consultation, professional care, case management, and educational services in the community. Recent years have seen the development of community-based services for the chronically mentally ill, with spe-cial focus on those who are multiply disabled—for example, mentally ill substance abusers and persons with developmental disabilities who are mentally ill. The home-less who are mentally ill and the minority patient population also have been targets of new initiatives. Community support programs designed to promote functioning in the community and prevent reinstitutionalization have been developed. Under these programs, a case manager coordinates services and advocates for the client. There also has been a growing emphasis on consumer participation. The client gives input into the treatment and medication plan and has access to records.

In addition, there has been increasing interest at the federal level in mental health services for children. To receive federal funding, each state is required to de-velop a comprehensive service plan for children as well as adults.

How Is the Program Financed?

Using monies from federal block grants, state mental health departments or state health departments operate statewide networks of mental health services. Mental health services are sometimes financed by state departments of education through special education programs. User fees also provide some funds, often on a means-test basis and with sliding scales for clients based on income. Recently, more health insurance plans have become restrictive in their coverage for mental health services, including those provided by social workers. Indigent patients are served by the public mental health system.

What Is the Level of Administration?

The Substance Abuse and Mental Health Services Administration of the U.S. Department of Health and Human Services administers the federal block grant. The National Institute of Mental Health is responsible for the Community Support Program. Other mental health programs are supported by the U.S. Department of Veterans Affairs, the Office of Vocational Rehabilitation, and the Department of Defense. The federal government also provides mental health services to Native Americans. In addition, state and local governments administer mental health systems in every state. A large number of professional associations are involved in mental health services on the national, state, and local levels, as well as organizations such as the National Mental Health Association, a voluntary organization. There is an active consumer movement, including the National Alliance for the Mentally Ill, which supports research and inclusion of family members in treatment planning.

A number of issues confront those concerned with mental health care. What will the future role of state hospitals be? How can additional community resources be found? Will sufficient attention be paid to the need for psychosocial rehabilitation as well as preventive services? What will be the effects of privatization? How can appropriate and sufficient services be provided for minority groups, women, children and adolescents, older adults, the homeless, and those with AIDs? Solutions for these issues depend on financing, civil rights questions, advocacy, as well as planning and coordination.[29]

CORRECTIONS

The Massachusetts Bay Colony built a jail in Boston in 1632, adding a correctional alternative to fines, lashing, branding, and mutilation. By 1655, every county in the colony was ordered to erect a correction house for drunkards and petty offenders. Correctional facilities have a long history in the United States.

Who Is Eligible for the Program?

Today youth and adults become "eligible" for correctional services by being convicted of violating federal, state, or city laws, being detained in a correctional facility on a pretrial basis, or being found to be in need of supervision.

What Is the Form of Benefit?

The number of Americans in local jails and state and federal prisons reached 1.7 million in 1997 even while the crime rate dropped. Many states adopted tougher sentencing laws; some states abolished parole, and other states' parole boards have less discretion than formerly. Also an increasing number of prisoners are incarcerated for parole violations. As one can imagine, a number of additional problems beset prisoners, including those with AIDs and mental illness. There are estimates that more than one in ten people behind bars are suffering from the most severe mental illnesses.[30] Ostensibly, correctional services have as a goal the rehabilitation of the offender. However, in reality, rehabilitation is not the major thrust of the correctional system today so much as are incarceration and punishment. Some say rehabilitation as a goal has proven to be an illusion and should be discarded in favor of crime deterrence. Others claim that rehabilitation has never really been given an adequate trial. Nevertheless, there are correctional services that aim at rehabilitation. Probation departments conduct pretrial investigations of defendants, which enable the court to make a disposition of the case on an informed, individualized basis. Probation is used by the courts as an alternative to incarceration and often includes a mandate for treatment as a condition of release. The offender remains in the community under conditions imposed by the court, under the supervision of a probation officer. Probation officers use the resources of the community to assist the offender to become rehabilitated.

Parole is for offenders who have served some time in a state or federal correctional facility but who are released into the community under supervision and treatment by a parole officer. Jails are city or county custodial institutions in which detainees are held for pretrial determinations and sentences less than a year for a misdemeanor. Prisons are correctional institutions where persons are incarcerated for longer than a year and are state or federal institutions.

Community correctional services include release programs, treatment centers to reintegrate offenders into the community, work-release programs, halfway houses, therapy, counseling, and assistance with training, employment, housing, and other life problems. Probation departments offer diagnostic assessments in order to judge an offender's eligibility for community placement as part of the presentence investigation process. In addition, voluntary community agencies often provide diagnostic and treatment services for pretrial detainees. Both assessment processes are part of a growing movement toward community-based alternatives to incarceration.

Some jails and prisons offer services such as basic adult education, vocational training, alcohol and drug programs, group and individual counseling, job development, and placement services. In recent years, criticisms arose against "coddling" prisoners with recreation, television, and other programs. Most state and federal prisons have mental health programs that offer counseling and psychiatric care.

Certain juvenile delinquency programs sponsored by various subdepartments of the Department of Health and Human Services provide diagnosis, treatment, rehabilitation, and prevention services to delinquent and predelinquent youth, and develop community-based alternatives to imprisonment.

Among new trends in corrections are the expansion of drug treatment programs within the prison system, privately owned and operated prisons, and attention to the needs of special populations—for instance, women caring for young children in prison, the elderly, and persons with AIDS. Shock incarceration programs are a new and expanding alternative approach for young adult offenders. In these programs, offenders spend several months in a highly structured experience similar to military boot camps and then may be supervised in the community. On the other hand, there is also a trend toward more client-oriented, flexible approaches in juvenile detention, including minimum security detention, in which a more positive, supportive environment is developed.

Although some persons have lately despaired of rehabilitation as a goal of corrections, most people agree that jails and prisons tend to reinforce criminal attitudes. Therefore, the tendency is to support the idea of incarceration only for the "hardened" criminal as both a deterrent to crime and as a protection to society, and to use various community-based programs for the "nonhardened" criminal. Therefore, the social welfare system is likely to increase its interaction with corrections in the coming years.

How Is the Program Financed?

The Violent Crime Control and Law Enforcement Act (1994) emphasized the construction of new prisons, boot camps, and other facilities, funding for additional police officers, and prevention programs. The Bureau of Prisons and Board of Parole, funded by general federal revenues, is part of the U.S. Department of Justice. State and local correctional programs are funded by state and local jurisdictions from general revenues.

The federal role in the criminal justice system has several facets. Within the Department of Justice, the Bureau of Prisons is responsible for federal prisons and community-based facilities. The National Institute of Corrections provides technical assistance and training for state and local correctional agencies throughout the country and provides grants for research, evaluation, and program development. The Community Corrections and Detention Division is responsible for the Bureau's community corrections and detention programs. The Bureau of Justice Statistics is responsible for collecting, analyzing, publishing, and disseminating statistical information on the criminal justice system, crime, its perpetrators and victims, probation, and parole at all levels of government. The National Institute of Justice is the primary research and development agency to provide the knowledge needed to prevent and reduce crime and improve the criminal justice system.

The Office of Juvenile Justice and Delinquency Prevention oversees grants to states, and provides funds to public and private nonprofit agencies and individuals to foster new approaches to delinquency prevention and control and to the improvement of the juvenile justice system. The Research and Program Development Division sponsors research about national trends in juvenile delinquency, drug use, serious juvenile crime, the causes of delinquency, prevention strategies, program evaluation, and improvement of the juvenile justice system. The division also sponsors training for juvenile justice practitioners and technical assistance in planning, funding, establishing, operating, and evaluating juvenile deliquency programs. Data on adults and juveniles are collected by the Federal Bureau of Investigation for its Uniform Crime Reports, including violent crimes, property crimes, and status offenses. Although not precisely part of the correctional system, the Social Security Act through Title XX makes funds available at the discretion of the states for programs for Persons in Need of Supervision (PINS) and Children in Need of Supervision (CHINS). These youths have not broken the law or committed an offense. They are, however, seen as being in need of supervision because of incorrigible behavior. Many of these children are treated through the voluntary child welfare system in either group homes or residential treatment settings often funded by the school districts under their Committees for Special Education.

What Is the Level of Administration?

The offices mentioned previously administer research and program demonstration grants on a federal level and assist state and local authorities in the correctional field. As noted, the Bureau of Prisons, National Institute of Corrections, Community Corrections and Detention Division, the Bureau of Justice Statistics, the National Institute of Justice, and the various units in the Office of Juvenile Justice and Delinquency Prevention all administer various parts of the correctional system. The Department of Defense also administers a correctional facility program. State and local governments operate their own facilities and programs, but there has been an increase in contracting jail services to private corporations. There is no overall coordination of the several levels of correctional programs, and facilities and combinations of state and local correctional programs take many forms.

Summary

In chapters 9 and 10, we examined public programs that provide the major income security and life-sustaining services. In chapter 11, we will describe and examine social welfare in the private sector, including the roles of voluntary, nonprofit organizations and of profit-making enterprises. We will discuss their interrelationships with each other as well as with the predominant public, governmental sector.

Questions for Consideration

1. Aside from Medicare's contribution to health care for the elderly, what economic and social roles does it play for the children and other family members of beneficiaries?
2. Can you locate any research findings that relate school lunch and breakfast programs to student learning?
3. What are the arguments for and against the federal and/or state governments' serving as "employers of last resort" for those who cannot obtain employment?
4. Identify and make a list of the personal social services, both public and private, in your community. Can you categorize them in some way?

Notes

1. Milt Freudenheim, "Study Shows Dominance of Managed Care Plans in '97," *New York Times*, January 20, 1998, p. D8.
2. US Department of Labor, Bureau of Labor Statistics, "Issues in Labor Statistics," Summary 98-3, April 1998.

3. Gary Rosenberg, "Challenges of Managed Care for Health Professionals: Implications for Social Work Practice," in *Critical Social Welfare Issues*, Arthur J. Katz, Abraham Lurie, Carlos Vidal, eds., New York: The Haworth Press, 1997, p. 149.
4. Milt Freudenheim, "Risky Business," *New York Times*, May 30, 1998, p. B1.
5. Gerald Schamess, "Who Profits and Who Benefits from Managed Mental Health Care?" *Smith College Studies in Social Work*, Vol. 66, No. 3, June 1996, pp. 209-220.
6. Carlton E. Munson, "Autonomy and Managed Care in Clinical Social Work Practice," *Smith College Studies in Social Work*, Vol. 66, No. 3, June 1996, pp. 241-260; Joan Shapiro, "The Downside of Managed Mental Health Care," *Clinical Social Work* Journal, Vol. 23, No. 4, Winter 1995, pp. 441-451.
7. Tracy E. Miller, "Managed Care Regulation in the Laboratory of the States," *Journal of the American Medical Association*, Vol. 278, No. 13, October 1, 1997, pp. 1102-1109.
8. Gerald Schamess, "Who Profits and Who Benefits from Managed Mental Health Care?" *Smith College Studies in Social Work*, Vol. 66, No. 3, June 1996, pp. 217-218.
9. Tracy E, Miller, "Managed Care Regulation in the Laboratory of the States," *Journal of the American Medical Association*, Vol. 278, No. 13, October 1, 1997, pp. 1102-1109.
10. Robert Pear, "Senators Reject Bill to Regulate Care By HMO's," *New York Times*, October 10, 1998, pp. A1 and A8.
11. Peter T. Kilborn, "Voters' Anger at H.M.O.'s Plays as Hot Political Issue," *New York Times*, May 17, 1998, pp. 1, 22.
12. Robert Pear, "Rights Expanded in Medicare Case," *New York Times*, August 14, 1998, pp. A1, A18.
13. Robert Pear, "States Take Lead in Health Legislation," *New York Times*, September 14, 1998, p. A10.
14. Carol Marie Cropper, "In Texas, a Laboratory Test on the Effects of Suing H.M.O.'s," *New York Times*, Money & Business, September 13, 1998, pp. 1, 9.
15. Michael M. Weinstein, "In Health Care, Be Careful What You Wish For," *New York Times*, Week in Review, May 31, 1998, p. 1.
16. David J. Morrow, "Medicare Panacea Turns Patient," *New York Times*, September 9, 1998.
17. Robert Pear, "HMO's Are Retreating from Medicare, Citing High Costs," *New York Times*, October 2, 1998, p. A17.
18. Robert Pear, "Clinton to Announce Help As HMO's Leave Medicare," October 8, 1998, p. A20.
19. Milt Freudenheim, "(Loosely) Managed Care Is In Demand," *New York Times*, September 29, 1998, pp. C1, C3.
20. Green Book 1998, p. 117.
21. Green Book, 1998, p. 123.
22. Green Book, 1998, pp. 120-121.
23. Jason DeParle, "In Booming Economy, Poor Still Struggle to Pay the Rent," *New York Times*, June 16, 1998, p. A14.
24. Elliott S. Fisher and H. Gilbert Welch, "The Future of the Department of Veterans' Affairs Health Care System," *Journal of the American Medical Association*, Vol. 273, February 22, 1995, pp. 651-655; James A. Pittman, "The Future of Veterans' Affairs: Utilization, Costs, Politics, and Presentism," *Journal of the American Medical Association*, Vol. 273, Editorial, February 22, 1995, pp. 667-668.
25. "Veterans Testify They Cannot Get Care They Need at Under-Funded VA Centers," *Baltimore Sun*, September 26, 1998, p. 4A.
26. The Workforce Investment Act of 1998, http://www.reg10.doleta.gov/wia_nga.htm, October 11, 1998.

27. Robert Morris and Delwin Anderson, "Personal Care Services: An Identity for Social Work," *Social Service Review*, Vol. 49, No. 2, June 1975, pp. 157–174.
28. Sheila B. Kamerman and Alfred J. Kahn, *Child Welfare in the Context of Welfare Reform*, New York: Cross-National Studies Research program, Columbia University School of Social Work, 1997.
29. Phillip Fellin, *Mental Health and Mental Illness*, Itasca, Ill.: F.E. Peacock Publishers, Inc., 1996.
30. Fox Butterfield, "Prison Population Growing Although Crime Rate Drops," *New York Times*, August 9, 1998, p. 18 and "Prisons Replace Hospitals for the Nation's Mentally Ill," *New York Times*, March 5, 1998, pp. A1, A26.

CHAPTER ELEVEN

Nonprofit and Private Social Welfare

As soon as several of the inhabitants of the United States have taken up an opinion or a feeling which they wish to promote in the world, they look out for mutual assistance; and as soon as they have found each other out, they combine.
—Alexis de Tocqueville[1]

OVERVIEW

For centuries, the efforts of nonprofit or voluntary social welfare agencies enriched the social welfare offerings and capabilities of U.S. society, unleashed the energies of millions of persons in creative helping efforts, and developed a diversity of mutual aid and nonprofit social welfare organizations. In recent decades, the nonprofit or voluntary sector has been joined by a growing phenomenon: social welfare services provided for profit. In this chapter, we examine the contemporary situation and issues of the nonprofit and private sectors within the context of U.S. society. To do so, we must understand the complexity of the U.S. economy, including the *nonprofit* (voluntary), *private for-profit*, and *governmental* (public) sectors. The nonprofit sector has been identified in several ways, including the charitable, independent, voluntary, and tax-exempt sector.[2] We will refer to profit-seeking organizations as *private*, although historically nonprofits also have been referred to as voluntary private agencies.

EARLY PATTERNS

During the colonial period in America, the line between public and nonprofit responsibilities in the area of social welfare was less sharply drawn than in later times.

279

In fact, there was a cooperative approach. The overseers of the poor called on churches for special collections when funds were needed, and the bequeathing of property to public authorities was a favored form of charity.[3]

Both nonprofit and public social welfare tended to be small-scale, local efforts provided for neighbors in relatively small settlements. At later stages, as we saw earlier, nonprofit social welfare became more varied and expansive and, still later in the 1930s, public welfare burgeoned in response to massive human need.

The Nonprofit Sector

There are several types of nonprofit and private social welfare. Because of the changing nature of this social welfare sector, certain characteristics of nonprofit organizations and for-profit businesses have become ambiguous and confusing.

Both *nonprofit* and *private* organizations fulfill ideological roles. Those who favor limited government wish to enhance both the nonprofit and private sectors in order to minimize what is perceived as governmental growth. Others who fear governmental intrusion in personal and communal life also wish to encourage these approaches. There are still others who wish to encourage nonprofit social welfare because to do so promotes a sense of mutual aid and community participation.

Several theories have been suggested for the existence of the modern nonprofit sector:

1. This sector exists to supply goods and services that are needed as a result of market and governmental failures or that are not yet offered through public policy. These goods and services are not desired or needed by society as universal commodities; therefore the nonprofit sector exists to provide services needed by only a segment of the community. As such, they are vehicles for the expression of diverse opinions and new ideas. The more pluralistic and diverse the population, the greater the expected size of the nonprofit sector.

2. Because nonprofit agencies are not in business to make money, it is assumed that their primary motivation is the delivery of services of quality. They can protect those who are most vulnerable, such as the frail elderly or those who are disabled. They may be the most appropriate or best vehicle to provide an advocacy and ombudsperson function for the sake of clients, sometimes in an adversarial position with the government. Such a function will always remain needed in the best of societies, and it is only the nonprofit agency that can devote itself to such causes.

3. Nonprofits are a first-line series of services, not just secondary supports. They can specialize in a problem or a method of intervention. They can advocate on behalf of people with special needs. And they can help organize peer self-help and other consumer-sponsored organizations.

4. Nonprofit agencies are thought by some to have greater potential than governmental agencies to minimize bureaucratization, rigidity, and impersonality. This is because it is difficult to mobilize governmental action in relation to many social problems.

5. The nonprofit, voluntary agency is the only one that appropriately should deliver sectarian services or services for any special ethnic or interest group. Public ser-

vices are and should be open equally to all citizens and should not be geared toward a specific position or point of view. On the other hand, it is quite legitimate in a plural society for Catholics, for example, to want to instill values of Catholicism among Catholic youth and to do this in the context of recreational or leisure-time activities. It is quite legitimate for African Americans to appreciate their common heritage and seek their empowerment. Ethnicity and cultural pluralism are hallmarks of the United States scene and should be nurtured and continued. And it is only the nonprofit agency that can devote itself to such causes.

6. There is a growing recognition of the importance of self-help groups from Alcoholics Anonymous to postmastectomy groups. These groups harness volunteer energies of citizens, save money, and provide a unique form of help, which is impossible in a more bureaucratized or public system.

Nonprofit services also have certain limitations. Among these are the following: (1) They focus on particular problems, groups, or individuals. By focusing in this way, gaps are created, and nonprofit aid may be uneven and constantly changing. (2) Nonprofit resources are often insufficient.[4]

Types of Nonprofit Agencies

Classic Nonprofit Board-Directed Agency   Historically in the United States, nonprofit social welfare agencies served myriad social welfare aims. These nonprofit agencies initially were staffed by volunteers and only later turned to employed staff. They were incorporated by the state under specific legislation. They have boards of directors, which are accountable for the policy and implementation of all facets of the organization. Members of the board may come from the population to be served or from other backgrounds useful to the maintenance and advancement of the nonprofit organization.

Federated Local or National Service Agency   The United Way is an example of a federated local or national service agency. It was founded by and is sponsored by a group of agencies and serves to coordinate, raise funds, do research and planning, and generally support the efforts of other nonprofit agencies. Such a federated organization may be formed at local, state, regional, or national levels. A wide range of national service agencies exist to support the efforts of local and state agencies such as the Girl Scouts, Family Service associations, and Catholic Charities, among others.

Indigenous Self-Help Mutual Aid Group   Alcoholics Anonymous, Nar-Anon, Recovery Inc., and Parents Anonymous are examples of indigenous self-help mutual aid groups. Many groups of this type begin as informal mutual aid efforts by those who are faced with a problem. Later, as the programs develop, there often evolves a need for paid staff members, as there are service constraints that arise with a totally volunteer-run organization. The Association for Help for Retarded Children is an example of an organization begun by volunteers as a mutual aid effort that developed into a highly complex and broad-based organization designed to serve the needs of persons with developmental disabilities and their families. As these organizations evolve, they become more formal and must meet certain legal requirements; they incorporate, elect a board of directors, and in other ways take on the trappings of a formal social welfare agency.

The Conduit or Vendor Agency   A conduit or vendor agency can serve as the deliverer of public funds and grants or grants from nonprofit foundations, or as the vendor and provider of public services through a nonprofit or for-profit mechanism. Nonprofit and private agencies may deliver services where the public sector chooses not to do so because of cost, a lack of human or other resources, or a philosophical commitment to the nonprofit or private sector. Public agencies may purchase a service for a group of consumers or may provide grants to particular agencies so that they can deliver the service on behalf of the public agency.

Quasi-Governmental Organization   One hybrid type of agency is the quasi-governmental organization, which is largely or completely dependent on governmental funds, although its structure is like the classic board-directed agency. The RAND Corporation, the Hudson Institute, as well as some institutes for the study of poverty, welfare, law and other "thinktanks" are examples of the quasi-governmental, quasi-nonprofit type of organization. Other examples of quasi-governmental agencies are regional transportation agencies such as BART, SEPTA, or the Port Authority in the San Francisco Bay area, Philadelphia, and New York, respectively. These agencies and others like them are neither governmental nor nonprofit/private. They are run by boards and administrators who are not elected but have been appointed by elected officials.

THE PROPRIETARY PRIVATE FOR-PROFIT ORGANIZATION

Traditionally, most students of social welfare did not include profit-making organizations as part of the social welfare system. From our perspective in today's world, there is every reason to consider such organizations to be a part of social welfare. Child care agencies, nursing homes, homemaker services, mental health and substance abuse treatment centers, camps, and many other forms of human services are provided through the for-profit sector. Employee assistance programs provide services to workers and sometimes to their families as part of their overall business effort.

In addition, the boundaries between public and nonprofit/private sectors have become more ambiguous as funding for both nonprofit and for-profit agencies often derives from the public sector. In order to grasp the totality of social welfare, it is necessary to account for those services provided under public auspices, those services that are in the nonprofit sector, and those services that are provided by for-profit organizations in the marketplace at large.

A major source of economic security today is private pensions, supplementing income from Social Security and personal savings. These pensions are a part of fringe benefits provided by industry sometimes with worker contributions and sometimes administered by labor unions. Pensions, also, may be based on individual investments subject to government regulation.

SERVICES OF THE NONPROFIT AND PRIVATE SECTORS

One can find a rich array of social welfare and health agencies and services in major metropolitan areas with more limited services available in rural locations. If we look at these agencies more closely, we find that the nonprofit sector emphasizes personal and rehabilitative services, as well as services specifically for ethnic, racial, religious, lifestyle, sexual orientation, and disability groups. In contrast, the public sector provides the primary services for income security, medical and health services, housing, education, human resource development, corrections, and child welfare. The nonprofits may contribute to each of these latter areas to a degree, but the paramount contributions are made by the public sector. For-profit agencies are often found in health care, nursing homes, counseling services, substance abuse rehabilitation, and services for children and aging persons.

People may make use of a number of services and, depending upon their particular circumstances and needs, may not limit their use to public, for-profit, or nonprofit services. For example, in some communities, one can find a number of services for aging persons, including clubs, centers, nutrition programs, counseling, residential facilities, telephone reassurance and emergency services, as well as vacation facilities. Aging persons may utilize concurrently homemaker services, health services, financial assistance, housing services, a senior citizens center, and public transportation to reach the needed services. But it is often the case that persons with particular personal or family needs are unfamiliar with the available resources that could be of assistance. Information and referral services have developed that can enable persons in need to find their way to the appropriate services.

Many local agencies are participants in national coordinating organizations. Membership of local organizations in national bodies—such as the YMCA; YWCA; Alliance for Children and Families; Child Welfare League of America; and Jewish Community Centers Association—provides the local organization with services, which range from referral of potential employees to providing consultation and publications. The degree of national control varies; some are organized as loose federations, leaving the ultimate authority to the local agency. Others set standards, priorities, and program policy at the national level.

GETTING AND SPENDING

Total spending for social welfare purposes in 1930 consisted of $1.474 billion expended in the nonprofit sector (1.6% of the gross national product [GNP]) and $4.085 billions spent in the public sector (4.5% of GNP) for a total expenditure of $5.5 billion. By 1993, even with retrenchments in social welfare, *public* (federal, state, and local) social welfare expenditures amounted to $1.36 trillion (21.1 percent of gross domestic product [GDP]) and 66.7 percent of total government outlays. The larger shares of these expenditures were made on health, income maintenance, education, and a much smaller share on welfare services.[5]

Private-sector social welfare expenditures (health and medical care, income maintenance, education, and welfare services) almost doubled from 7.7 percent of GDP in 1972 to 13.3 percent in 1994. Included in these private expenditures are health and medical care expenditures, education, income maintenance (group life insurance, supplemental unemployment benefits, sickness and disability benefits, long-term disability, and employment-related pension plans), and welfare services, including individual and family counseling and referral services, adoption services, emergency and disaster services, child day care, senior citizen services, residential care (group foster homes, halfway homes, care and shelters for the homeless, recreation and group work, job training, sheltered workshops, vocational and skill training workshops). In 1994, health care alone accounted for more than 57 percent of total private-sector expenditures.[6]

The magnitude of public expenditures far outweighed spending by the private and nonprofit social welfare sectors. Nonetheless, in 1994 expenditures by the private and nonprofit social welfare sectors were sizable. One can observe in Table 11.1 that in 1994 $.9 trillion, including health spending, was expended (13.3% of GDP). Although these private expenditures were large, they were much smaller than those made in the public sector. Together the public, private, and nonprofit social welfare sectors are major economic forces.

In 1996, Americans contributed $150.7 billion to nonprofit organizations. Approximately 87 percent of this amount was given by individual donors, and the remainder was given by companies, corporate foundations, and noncorporate foundations. These contributions have remained relatively stable at 2 percent of the GDP with some minor fluctuation since 1966.[7] All charitable contributions in 1996 amounted to only 11 percent of public social welfare expenditures in 1993. It should be clear from these figures that calls for the nonprofit and private sector to replace any major government programs are simply political rhetoric. The nonprofit and private sector and the public sector operate on totally different scales. In fact, in 1995 funding public assistance and Supplemental Security Income (SSI) alone would have cost more than $50 billion.[8]

TABLE 11.1 Private Social Welfare Spending by Category: 1972–1994 and Percent of Gross Domestic Product (in millions)

Total	Health	Income Maintenance	Education	Welfare Services	%GDP
1972					
$96.3	$55.8	$17.1	$14.8	$7.57	7.7%
1994					
$921.4	$528.6	$204.7	$101.8	$86.2	13.3%

SOURCE: Wilmer L. Kerns, "Private Social Welfare Expenditures, 1972–94," *Social Security Bulletin*, Vol. 60, No. 1, 1997, p. 55.

Contributions generally are allocated by donors in descending order to religion; education; health; human services; art, culture, and humanities; public/society benefit (civil rights, community development, public affairs, and scientific research); and environment/wildlife and international affairs. Historically, approximately one half of all philanthropic funding has gone to religious associations.[9]

In addition to the large size of nonprofit social welfare expenditures, another indicator suggesting the complexity of the nonprofit sector is that of the almost 23 million national nonprofit associations in 1997 there were 1.9 million such organizations devoted to social welfare.[10]

As noted earlier, occupational benefits also account for large social welfare expenditures. The dimensions of the pension and health plan coverage for employees reflect the substantial amount of social welfare services provided by private-enterprise, profit-seeking businesses.

In addition to those services provided by business and industry for their employees, in recent years there has been a push to "privatize" many governmental services—for example, mass transit, garbage disposal, and the operation of prisons. In 1998, there are ongoing attempts to privatize public assistance, job training, placement, and support; child support enforcement; and management, computerization, and child welfare services such as foster care and adoptions. These privatization efforts have not always been successful in efficiency, goal attainment, cost savings, and profitability.

Privatization efforts are a result of ideological, budgetary, and political forces. Olasky in *The Tragedy of American Compassion* indicted all governmental social welfare and argued that all social welfare efforts should be returned to the private and religious institutions. Various arguments are put forward to make a case for privatization. Among these are that privatization means competition and choice. Prices and profits as motivators will do a better job at helping people. Privatized services will become more efficient and therefore less costly; they will serve as a competitive spur to the public sector; and they will prod the public sector on to greater efficiency.[11]

In 1998, 1 in 20 federal prison inmates was in a for-profit prison. More than one in every eight hospital beds was in investor-owned hospitals.[12] Some want to privatize as one strategy to roll back governmentally provided services. Others, opposing privatization, point out that it sometimes results in a "creaming" of clients. They argue that the difficult and costly clients are avoided and, in fact, referred or channeled to the public sector, which must then pick up the greater per capita cost. There is also no guarantee that privatized services will not suffer from precisely the shortcomings sometimes identified in public sector programs. As pointed out in chapter 10, there are early stirrings of a backlash against complete market philosophies in profit-minded managed care and hospitals. Where the line should be drawn is an important question as our society seeks a balance between market forces and humane concern. Does the public interest coincide with private interests, and if it doesn't, how can private for-profit companies adequately be regulated?

Recent studies found that the privatization movement of the late 1980s and early 1990s lost some momentum during the 1990s. This may be due to several factors, including the political power of public employees and the improving fiscal situation of local governments. Some local governments turned to contracting out (privatization), while others simply dropped the service, which left residents to seek services from other providers.[13]

Few challenge the right of nonprofit social welfare agencies to receive tax-deductible donations. During the early 1990s, however, several United Way scandals occurred concerning the theft of charity funds, excessive salaries, and misuse of funds by high-level administrators. These incidents led to increased mistrust by potential givers and years of declining fund-raising support. Donations began to rise in 1997, reversing a trend in which donations fell from 1991 to 1995 and remained low in several large cities. Nonetheless, 1997 receipts remained below those in 1991.[14]

As a result of the United Way scandal, attention began to focus also on some nonprofit organizations' legal but easily abused use of for-profit subsidiaries. Among the types of abuse discovered have been concurrent pay for employment in the non-profit and for-profit affiliates, nepotism, concealed employee identities, and shifting revenue to the nonprofit and expenses to the for-profit side for tax purposes. Although most experts agree that most charities and foundations operate within the law, detecting which are legitimate and which abusive is sometimes difficult because of the ability of these organizations to operate with high degrees of privacy. On the state level, states have focused mainly on full compensation disclosure, including transactions between an organization and its board members. The Internal Revenue Service (IRS) steps in where there are large sums to be recovered and/or there is blatant fraud. There is some concern that these events diminish donations.[15]

Finally, in 1998, the IRS implemented the Taxpayer Bill of Rights (1996), which requires tax-exempt groups to mail copies of their tax returns to anyone who submits a written request, thus making them more available than previously was the case.[16]

Another major challenge to the operation of nonprofit social agencies concerned forays into for-profit territory. Because of reduced government funding, constrained government services, and inflation, some nonprofit organizations entered the competitive marketplace to sell various items and services, from calendars to health club memberships to insurance. Businesses were threatened by such competition, and complaints were registered that nonprofits in certain cases were taking unfair advantage of their tax-deductible status to compete in areas impinging on the potential of the private for-profit sector.

There are those who recommend that nonprofit organizations be far more restricted from engaging in unrelated business activities that are outside their tax-exempt activities. Generating revenues and making profit, it was argued, is unfair competition, because nonprofit organizations operate under different rules and regulations than private, profit-seeking firms. They have special advantages such as exemption from taxation.[17] Other critics argued that profit-making actions divert the organization from its primary social aims and place strains on management. The ability to define client needs and to shape services may shift to the marketplace, undermining the authority of the staff and board of directors.

There is still another economic dimension to the nonprofit sector, the monetary value of volunteering. There are estimates that in 1995 almost 50 percent of the population over 18 years of age volunteered an average of 4.2 hours per week. Assigning a value of $12.84 per hour, the annual value of volunteer time was the equivalent of $201.5 billion to tax-exempt nonprofit organizations.[18]

PRIVATE AND NONPROFIT AGENCIES AS SOCIAL WELFARE PROGRAMS

Who Is Eligible for the Programs?

Private and nonprofit social welfare agencies provide services for people who have experienced almost every human risk: job loss, poor mental or physical health, low income, and inadequate housing, and so on. They provide preventive, rehabilitative, and personal- and family-fulfillment services. Agencies are sponsored under both sectarian (religious) and nonsectarian auspices. They offer services based on the needs of the local community and neighborhood services directed at particular groups (such as African Americans, Catholics, Latinos, West Indians, women, and persons with disabilities). Services are dependent on the context and history of the community and the agency itself. Programs in the nonprofit sector often are offered on a fee-for-service basis, on a sliding scale according to income, or on membership or user fees. For-profit programs require payment either by the consumer or by a third party. Some nonprofit services, such as American Red Cross disaster relief, are offered on demand without fee. Increasingly, as nonprofit and private agencies administer public programs, the public regulations for eligibility apply. In business and industrial settings, social welfare services are available for the employees and sometimes for spouses and children.

What Is the Form of Benefit?

Almost the total range of social welfare services is present in private and nonprofit agencies, and a significant number and type of benefits are distributed in relation to the workplace. Pensions of varying types are provided by many business and industrial concerns so that long-term economic security is provided in the work arena as well as in the public sphere. Private and union pensions are a significant economic force, and the federal government has established rules to protect the rights of contributors. In addition, benefits found in workplaces include health, medical, and hospital insurance; food, recreation, library, and other facilities; counseling, referral, and mental health services; drug abuse and alcohol treatment; day care; and physical health services.

Nonprofit agencies emphasize, to a greater extent than public agencies, services for social development such as youth services and recreation. These agencies also serve as "guardians." For example, there are consumer organizations that police and critique the government or help clients understand their rights. However, non-profit agencies since the Great Depression have been involved to a much lesser de-gree than public agencies in economic security, being limited generally to short-term emergencies or supplementing public funds in special situations.

Nonprofit agencies directly or as vendors of publicly mandated services pro-vide food (hot lunches), housing (nursing homes and residences for the well el-derly), homemaker and home help services, rehabilitation, mental health services, child welfare services, and a host of other benefits such as services for military per-sonnel and their families (Red Cross), rehabilitation (Good Will Industries), skills training (Lighthouse for the Blind), family planning (Planned Parenthood), general services to merchant marines (United Seaman's Service), and emergency aid (Salva-tion Army).

Community centers and settlement houses provide many services including community development, adult education, socialization, and recreation. Hospitals and ancillary organizations provide a range of medical and health care services. Health and welfare councils coordinate nonprofit agencies and their services in a community. The United Way or similar organizations raise money for distribution to the social agencies in a city or region.

Family and Friends

There are yet other voluntary social services that should be highlighted. There are more than 22 million English-speaking households in the United States who provide informal care to a relative or a friend. Most caregivers provide care for one person, but almost one in three provide care for two or more persons. Among the major ill-nesses or problems for which care is provided are mobility, dementia, heart disease or condition, cancer, stroke, arthritis, and diabetes.[19]

Along with volunteering and providing informal assistance to others, families also give gifts and bequests. The predominant pattern is parents giving to adult chil-dren. When asked if they ever gave large gifts or major financial assistance to their children, 48 percent of the respondents reported they did so at some time. These gifts are concentrated within families and flow mainly from older to younger family members.[20] The dollars dedicated to such low-visibility connections between gener-ations are not trivial. In 1990, the aggregate amount attributed to private transfers to-talled *$1.6 trillion*, largely between age groups. That same year, government transfer payments amounted to just under $700 billion, less than half the total of the private transfers.[21]

How Are the Programs Financed?

Funding for private and nonprofit agencies is derived in varying patterns from a num-ber of sources: private contributions, fees (membership or users' fees), payment for services by individuals or third parties, donations, governmental purchase of services and contracts, funds from communal fund-raising agencies (such as the United Way or a local Federation of Social Agencies), endowment funds, and payments from governmental sources in the form of subsidies, goods, third-party payments, and governmental and private foundation grants.

Contributions to nonprofit welfare agencies are tax deductible, provided the agency is recognized by the Internal Revenue Service as a qualified organization. This policy supports the voluntary factor in society and diversity of nonprofit agencies and services. Local affiliates of national organizations help through dues or other fees to support their national umbrella organizations such as the YMCA; Boy Scouts; Girl Scouts; Jewish Community Centers; Catholic Charities; Alliance for Children and Families; and the Child Welfare League.

Fund-raising organizations have proliferated in every imaginable direction. Approximately 500,000 organizations are registered as tax-exempt charities. In addition to competing with more organizations, communitywide fund-raising such as that of the United Way has been influenced by "designated giving," in which contributors specify the particular agencies or programs to which they want their contributions directed. This results in a multitude of donors deciding where dollars will be spent. One consequence of these factors is that communitywide fund-raising efforts originally formed for reasons of efficiency become less so, and efforts at coordinated planning also may be diminished.

Several concerns have arisen because of the purchase of services strategy used by governments. Nonprofit agencies fear their potential loss of independence. In some cases, agencies sell their services to the government for negotiated payments, typically on a unit-cost basis. If the agency does not receive adequate reimbursement, it must make up the deficit by seeking additional funds. In this case, there are hidden costs to the agency related to uses of staff time to offset the losses. If, on the other hand, it is reimbursed fully, the reimbursement rate may be sufficient to entice competitive profit-making organizations into the situation. Furthermore, if there is no cost advantage, the government may decide to operate the program itself. The chase of single, narrow, time-limited grants may shift an agency into fragmentation and veer it away from its original mission. In addition, the pursuit of governmental grants is conducted in an uncertain and anxiety-producing environment where there are frequent policy, legislative, and guideline shifts, constant uncertainty about budgets, and many resources needed for grant seeking.[22]

Research findings about the effects of governmental purchase of services on social agencies are scarce. In the 1990s, purchase of service decision making has been dominated by funding and fiscal considerations consistent with early governmental motivations for such purchases. The original intention was to maximize public and private resources for human services by combining public funds in order to leverage nonprofit agency funds.

What Are the Levels of Administration?

There is no overall organization that administers or coordinates private and nonprofit social welfare agencies, although the national nonprofit agencies do act in concert to protect their interests. Organizations can be established on the local, state, regional, and national levels. There are various degrees of autonomy for social agencies, ranging from independence (with the exception of responsibility and accountability to the state through incorporation and guidelines) to control by a council or national organization. Private and voluntary social welfare agencies are legally responsible to a governmental body and, therefore, are never entirely free agents. The use of non-profit and for-profit agencies to deliver and manage services is based on the belief that the private sector will provide better care more efficiently because it is open to market pressures to control costs and prices.

There are mixed findings regarding comparative costs; however, one national study uncovered significant information. Utilizing data from a national survey of the Drug Abuse System, public and private (nonprofit and for-profit) outpatient sub-stance abuse treatment units were studied. For-profit units reported that smaller pro-portions of their clients leave treatment involuntarily or because they are incarcer-ated. A higher proportion of clients are reported as meeting their treatment goals at the time of discharge. It was also found that for-profit units charge more for their ser-vices and generated proportionately more surplus revenues for the services they pro-vide. Other findings included that for-profit units serve a smaller proportion of clients who are under age 20, are unemployed, are unable to pay for treatment, or who have multiple drug problems. It was found that for-profit units serve a less dis-abled, less vulnerable, and more resourceful pool of clients. The implication of these findings is that for-profit units occupy and operate within a distinct organizational niche or segment of the market. They specialize, and the niche makes it possible for them to be protected from market forces, ironically, the very forces that privatization was intended to draw upon.[23]

These findings indicate that the for-profit units "creamed" the potential clients. This undermines the capacity of the nonprofits and public programs, which lose po-tential income from clients able to pay for the services and are left to serve those with the fewest resources.

A Point of View

From our perspective, the choice is not governmental services versus private- and nonprofit-sponsored services. Governmental services are neither a totally "good" or-ganizational and philosophical approach, nor are governmentally sponsored social welfare services an "evil" to be shunned at all costs and minimized. But this is also true of the nonprofit and private sectors as well. Instead, there is need for govern-mental, private, and nonprofit services. The important question is whether a *particu-lar* service can be better performed under governmental, private, or nonprofit aus-pices. For ourselves, we do not view these different types of approaches as completely trichotomous. Furthermore, it is our belief that governmental, nonprofit, and private efforts have the ability to "free up" citizen creativity. They have grown in tandem, although governmental services are much larger in scope and funding. The private and nonprofit sectors cannot replace governmental social welfare in its en-tirety. The proper balance and most effective use of various auspices, consistent with American political and economic ideals and realities, is required for a healthy

American social welfare system. Further, although nonprofit and private organizations may compete, there is much to be learned about how they most effectively can collaborate with each other and governmental agencies.

Leadership, Class, and Gender

Nonprofit associations are voluntary, mutual aid efforts to provide services. There is no economic profit to be gained by participants in these organizations other than salaries and the perquisites that accompany some high-level positions. In addition to paid staff, many persons participate as volunteers; that is, they receive no remuneration for their services. Some volunteers provide the direct services of the agency while others serve in policy-making and fund-raising roles as members of boards of directors, trustees, committees, or special task forces.

Certain characteristics have been found among persons who serve as volunteers in the nonprofit sector. One is more likely to volunteer if one's background includes higher income, educational levels, and occupational and family status; if one owns property; and if one volunteers for multiple organizations. Socioeconomic status is also associated with the kinds of organizations for which one volunteers. Blue-collar volunteers tend to volunteer for churches, unions, fraternal societies, and recreational centers. Middle- and upper-class persons tend to volunteer in general interest organizations, business and professional organizations, and service, cultural, educational, and political pressure groups.[24]

The vast majority of board membership today consists of persons from higher socioeconomic groups. These people may be more attractive recruits for many nonprofit agencies because of their access to money, community leaders, and other resources. Volunteers, through their participation, typically value the mission and goals of the organization and gain feelings of security and usefulness. Volunteering also is a social act through which participants enjoy sharing common experiences as well as social contacts and social prestige.

Service to the community is often cited as a major reason for becoming involved. Some persons volunteer for "business" reasons and the visibility that participation provides for increasing their personal or employer's business. Contacts are made through such social networks, and prominence in nonprofit agencies often serves as a powerful business influence. Others become involved so they can express themselves. Some people find after a time that their work or business does not call upon all their potential skills and abilities. Participation in nonprofit agencies for these persons becomes a mechanism for further skill development and opportunities for self-expression. Others use such participation as a form of career exploration to test themselves and to examine how congruent their personalities and needs are within a particular field or type of activity prior to their making serious commitments to job changes, more education, and so forth. Volunteering also plays an important part for people during periods of transitions. They establish social contacts and develop new interpersonal networks and skills, for example, during the entry phase in a new community, after a separation or divorce, or after the death of a spouse.

Although this discussion has focused on volunteering in the nonprofit sector, it should be noted that similar participation occurs in the public sector but to a lesser extent. For example, volunteers serve on advisory boards for public departments and also may offer their services in public hospitals, nursing homes, day-care programs, and so on. There is no limiting principle restricting where people will volunteer, but traditionally volunteers have been most active in the nonprofit sector.

Two thirds of the employees in the nonprofit sector are female; more than half of the volunteers are women. A traditional view is that women find in the nonprofit arena opportunities for leadership, power, and influence not available to them in business and government. More recently, it has been thought that power in the non-profit sector is not nearly as influential as in business and government. So even when women gain power in the nonprofit sector, they are leading in a societal arena that—with some exceptions—is not a powerful player in the overall political structure.[25]

Private and Public Spheres

Today the relationships among public, nonprofit, and private spheres are more ambiguous than at any time since colonial days. These relationships raise a number of issues: (1) uses of public funds, (2) tax laws and policy, (3) programmatic links, (4) accountability, and (5) national policy.

Uses of Public Funds and Power

Public funds, from federal, state, and local governments, are provided for both the private and nonprofit sectors through purchase of service contracts and through third-party payments. In the 1960s, the federal government through the Economic Opportunity Act (1964) encouraged the use of nonprofit community agencies to develop services. Later, Title XX of the Social Security Act (1975) authorized grants to states for social services to be directed toward achieving or maintaining economic self-sufficiency and preventing dependence. Welfare reform (Temporary Assistance to Needy Families, 1996) encouraged states to involve nonprofit and for profit organizations in the delivery of social services. States have wide discretion as to which services will be provided and how they will be organized and delivered.

As a result, over the past generation, a mixed economy has evolved in the field of social welfare, in which the conventional differences between sectors have become blurred as nongovernmental organizations have increasingly been used to implement public policy. In the personal social services, purchase of service contracting has become the primary financing method and method of service delivery, often severing funding (governmental) from administration (nonprofit or private) of the delivery of personal social services. Practically, this blurring of auspices led to greater interdependence among government, private, and nonprofit social welfare efforts. This trend is a result of a historical American ambivalence toward and distrust of government as well as budgetary constraints. Such development enables the creation of desired public services without necessarily resulting in the growth of government.

In fact, some view these moves as leading to more limited government, apparently stemming governmental growth and extending services without increasing the number of governmental employees.[26] The drive to use private organizations to deliver public services is intensified when governmental budgets are squeezed. It is then that the "less government is better government" ideology joins with fiscal imperatives to retrench public services in order to slow or halt the expansion of the welfare sector, or to shift services so they are privately delivered, as governments try to maintain stability and services. Even where there are some savings, in many cases privatization may produce savings that are largely the result of private companies paying low wages and providing limited benefits. The net result may be that one arm of government saved money while another arm—public assistance and health facilities—may spend more because of the layoffs of governmental employees.

Public money is provided in order to implement a public purpose. However, public purposes and those of the private sector may not always be entirely compatible. Those who pay the bill cannot be viewed as equals in the relationship, and contractual power tends to move in only one direction—toward the public sphere. Use of public funds can also inhibit the ability of the nonprofit and private sectors to question and advocate. There are those who argue that nonprofit agencies that receive public funds are in reality constrained from participating in social action or advocacy. Others argue that such losses of autonomy are exaggerated and that the critical and advocacy roles of the nonprofit sector remain influential.

According to one point of view, when the public uses private agencies to fulfill its own purposes, those private agencies should be viewed as being in reality governmental entities: Because there is guidance and restrictions on how such payments should be used, these agencies are agents of the government. In essence, state power is given over in part to private and nonprofit providers. Paradoxically, contracting results in unprecedented governmental involvement in the affairs of nonprofit organizations. From this point of view, child-care institutions that receive the great preponderance of their funds from governmental sources and are the means by which the government discharges its responsibilities cannot be considered private agencies. Such agencies are essentially other governmental institutions, although it is unclear at what point this happens.

Tax Laws and Policy

Public funds are provided for nonprofit social welfare through the tax system as well as through direct public funding. The federal government encourages charitable donations by individuals and corporations and makes provision in law for these contributions to be used as tax deductions, which reduce individual or corporate taxes. This tax policy appears to be solidly entrenched in American values. Only a limited number of persons challenge the use of such charitable donations as deductions. They typically do so not as a challenge to the principle of nonprofit efforts but on the basis of the separation of church and state, arguing that deductible contributions confer a benefit on religious organizations. Because charitable giving is related to the provisions of the tax code, efforts to create new tax systems (e.g., flat tax, sales tax) may not be aimed specifically at social welfare organizations but may have the inadvertent effect of eliminating charitable tax deductions, including social welfare.

Accountability

The expenditure of funds calls for accountability. Grant-providing agencies need to have some proof of the proper use of the funds provided, and the demand for accountability causes certain dilemmas. Social welfare services are "soft" services when compared to, let us say, engineering. In engineering, the bridge is either built or not; it supports the predicted weights under particular conditions. In the human services area, outcomes and appropriate measurement instruments may be in short supply. What is the optimum expectation in the case of an abused or mentally ill child in a problematic family? Short-term outcomes may be measured in some way, but they would only supply a limited knowledge of real progress. In such a case, it may be necessary to examine long-term benefits to the individuals, the family, neighborhood, and society to gain a proper perspective on the investment being made. Measurements of outcomes are difficult and can only be made over long periods of time, time that is often unavailable to the granting agency.

Furthermore, in an attempt to provide data for proof of effectiveness, it is possible that prized organizational values may be compromised. Fair value must be given, but freedom for performance is also needed. Thus, there is a tension between independence, the kinds of help needed by persons with particular human difficulties, and accountability. Central control by governmental agencies is required in order to ensure accountability, but the degree and nature of the control are issues that remain to be worked out over time.

National Policy

An important issue in regard to the relationship of the public and private spheres is that of the church–state relationship. Church-sponsored social welfare is a significant portion of all social welfare efforts. Indeed, much of social welfare in the United States developed originally out of a religious motivation, and social welfare sponsored by various religions continues to occupy an important role in the totality of such services. Organizations such as Jewish and Protestant Welfare Federations, Catholic Charities, a myriad of hospitals under religious sponsorship, as well as a host of other social welfare efforts are delivered under religious auspices.

Notable social welfare programs are sponsored by churches, synagogues, mosques, and other religious organizations. As an example, African American churches serve their members but also serve the African American community as a whole as they respond to current issues. Among the sponsored programs are housing, anti-drug efforts, family life centers, child care, health services, AIDS education, community and senior centers, home health care, parenting programs, adult education, tutorials, food and clothing, counseling, community-owned businesses, prison ministries, scouts, and so on.[27]

The case of *Wilder v. Sugarman* (1974) drew attention to complex constitutional issues concerning fundamental questions in social welfare and foster care regarding the First Amendment establishment clause and the role of the state in rearing children. In 1974, the U.S. District Court upheld the right of New York City's private foster-care institutions (nearly half of them sponsored by Roman Catholic organizations) to get state support despite the constitutional prohibition of state aid to religion.

After a long period of litigation and legal review, a federal appeals court approved in *Wilder v. Bernstein* (1988) a settlement reached by the parties that religious-sponsored agencies should place children in foster care on a first-come, first-served basis, except that a preference for religious matching requested by parents will be honored when it does not give a child greater access to a program appropriate for his or her needs over children who have been waiting longer for the program. It also prohibited the display of "excessive religious symbols" in common areas open to children. Furthermore, family planning services for foster children must be made available in their placement regardless of the agency's religious affiliation.[28]

Questions arise from time to time in regard to public monies being used by religion-sponsored social welfare agencies. On one hand, religion-sponsored agencies often wrestle with the notion of accepting public funds because they are fearful acceptance will constrain in some way their own particular goals. Others fear that religious auspices translate automatically into social welfare services that necessarily must be religiously imbued. The relevant constitutional principle is based on the First Amendment of the U.S. Constitution and states that the government cannot utilize religion as a standard for action or inaction, either to confer a benefit or impose a burden.[29]

Governmental action cannot establish religion or interfere with its free exercise. Governmental aid to religious institutions, tax exemptions for religious organizations, purchase of services from religious organizations, adoption criteria, the ambiance of social agencies and institutions, camps, and other organizations, religious garb, and religious dietary requirements—all are issues for social welfare within the perspective of the church-state tension.

MARKETPLACE AND THE NONMARKET DOMAIN

One major dilemma that arises when public agencies use private institutions for public purposes is the specific problem of the profit motive. We have seen in this chapter that proprietary organizations play important roles in the delivery of social welfare services. A major criticism of profit-making social welfare services is that encouraging efficiency and profit-making implies risks to the quality of services.

But just as there are reasons to believe that private, profit-oriented institutions will fail to allocate resources efficiently (or equitably) under specified conditions, so too there are reasons to believe that governmental institutions sometimes fail to accomplish their aims and are inefficient and inequitable. There are limits to what both private and governmental institutions can accomplish.

Those who question the independence of the nonprofit sector sometimes categorize it simply as another part of the social control mechanism in a capitalist society. For these persons, it is assumed that a social and economic elite controls social welfare in the private sector (private and nonprofit). Some persons are opposed in principle to the private sector per se; others simply wish the private and public sectors were more decentralized in their decision making and that greater democratic participation across class and other lines were an accomplished fact.

Historically, social services have been viewed as being provided outside the marketplace in a separate domain. The world of social welfare has grown more complex over time. Today, as we have seen here, the line between nonprofit and public agencies is blurred, and it is clear that in order to understand fully the institution of social welfare and the delivery of social welfare services the private profit-making sector must be included in the domain of social welfare. Others who oppose the inclusion of profit-making services within the domain of social welfare find private, for-profit social services insufficiently humane, discriminatory, and not social. The service recipient is a customer who is to provide income, and priority rests with producing a profit for the investors.

The Family

Although rarely stressed, help provided by relatives and friends for persons who are no longer able to manage all aspects of their daily life is a very important, albeit informal, part of social welfare. A study found the average of the caregiving was 4.5 years for an average of almost 18 hours per week, largely provided by females to female relatives. The problems encountered by persons needing care ranged from mobility problems to life-threatening illnesses. Help is provided with transportation, grocery shopping, housework, meal preparation, managing finances, arranging/supervising outside services, and giving medications.[30]

TOWARD THE FUTURE

There is a worldwide increase in the number of nonprofit organizations as people organize to improve their living conditions and to attain their rights.[31] Decisions supportive of this major trend develop out of ideological, political, economic, and social factors. Recent Congresses and presidents emphasized the nonprofit sector as part of a strategy to cut back on governmental social spending and interventions. Some legislators advocate the dismantling of the welfare state and turning over many governmental functions to the nonprofit and private sectors, suggesting that helping the needy requires shifting assistance from bureaucracies to neighborly help. Those familiar with social welfare in the United States point out the discrepancy between the scale of efforts required by all levels of government and those of the nonprofit sector. They suggest the implausibility that the nonprofit sector can compensate sufficiently for governmental cutbacks.

These debates occur within a context in which the welfare state is sharply criticized; government has too much to do and cannot do it well. The United States has an enormous debt (mostly built up in the 1980s), which colors all decisions about social welfare and has stimulated organized resistance to increased taxes. Thus, the relationship between government and the nonprofit as well as the private sector changes as various pressures combine to force a shift in their respective responsibilities, minimizing government's role, seeking maximum efficiency, and utilizing partnerships that may leverage resources for the greatest possible effectiveness.

Certainly, it is unthinkable that the United States will nationalize the personal social services. Federal control of these services is not a real choice. The devolution strategy expects that local government will provide some services and the nonprofit sector will fill identified gaps. This strategy is consistent with a control of services at the state and local jurisdictions. An emphasis on the use of the profit-making sector to the greatest extent possible has been in effect for a generation. Reliance on competition in the marketplace is viewed as a good in itself. Also valued is faith in and empowerment of the nonprofit sector along with encouragement and greater utilization of nonprofit associations, religious institutions, neighborhood groups, and the primary social systems. This view perceives the nonprofit sector as one means in an attempt to recover the lost sense of community and of defending against the involvement of the state in the private affairs of citizens. The degree to which this strategy can be successful, however, really depends on funding and the feasibility of the assignments thrust on the nonprofit sector.

Thus, shifting away from federal responsibilities, reducing the overload on government, especially lessening the power of the federal government, and utilizing the private and nonprofit sector to provide decentralized services at reduced costs is a major strategy being pursued. Whether the changes that take place will be radical or more incremental remains to be seen.

Pragmatism is also an American value, and the interdependence of government and the nonprofit and private sectors will continue with increased emphasis on accountability, efficiency, and bottom-line effectiveness where governmental funds are used. This pragmatic view of the future seems most consistent with U.S. society and its emphasis on pluralism, incremental change, and its increasingly strenuous commitment in ideology to the private and nonprofit sectors.

Government is not the enemy some see. Government can provide freedom *to do* as well as freedom *from*. There are limits on the intrusion of government into our lives; our constitutional rights are protected in this society. But the efforts of government to create opportunity through health care, educational benefits, housing, child care, and nutrition, support the freedom of those who could not possibly attain self-fulfillment without the assistance of government. Governmental efforts such as those of the Food and Drug Administration and the GI Bill opened up freedom, options, and creativity for many individuals and for our society. The ultimate questions should not revolve around the issue of whether government should intervene but, instead, should be focused on when, where, and how governmental interventions will be most helpful for the individual and for society.

It is clear that the private and nonprofit sectors simply cannot do all the required tasks of a social welfare system in a complex and interdependent society such as ours. Lester Ward, an early American critic of social Darwinism, strongly suggested that governmental intervention was necessary precisely in order to protect freedom. The predatory behavior of unbridled competition works to destroy free-dom. According to Ward, such matters as sanitation, health, unemployment, the rights of employees to organize, and many other matters require governmental inter-vention to protect the freedom of individuals and the community. The proper bal-ance of the public and the private and nonprofit sectors in regard to the delivery of social welfare services remains to be worked out over a long period of time.[32]

The attainment of access to services, adequacy, accountability, effectiveness, and efficiency in social welfare will require the combined efforts of government and the private and nonprofit sectors. Their respective roles in regard to the scope of in-terventions, costs, benefits, and the mechanisms for the delivery of services remain to be balanced as our society, its problems, and its resources change.

SUMMARY

In this chapter, we examined the place of private and nonprofit social welfare in the overall picture. We can readily see the important and prominent part this sector plays in the delivery of social welfare services. The complete list of role players in the social welfare institution has to include the state, the market, the nonprofit and private sectors, and the household.

In chapters 12 and 13, we will deal with the emergence and development of social work as a profession, a major but not the only professional group that serves in social welfare. Following that discussion, we will examine the functions of social work as a profession, the context within which it operates, and some issues con-fronting the profession.

QUESTIONS FOR CONSIDERATION

1. What nonprofit and for-profit social welfare organizations are there in your community?
2. Suggestions have been made that the nonprofit sector can handle many of our society's social welfare needs. Do you think that could be done in your community? What's your opinion and what facts do you base it on?
3. Can you identify women in your state who occupy significant social welfare leadership roles?
4. For what social welfare services should families be responsible? Why?

NOTES

1. Alexis de Tocqueville, *Democracy in America*, Richard D. Heffner, ed., New York: Men-tor Books, 1956, p. 201.
2. Lester M. Salamon and Helmut K. Anheier, *Defining the Nonprofit Sector*, New York: Manchester University Press, 1997, p.12.
3. Robert H. Bremner, "Private Philanthropy and Public Needs: Historical Perspective," *Re-search Papers: The Commission on Private Philanthropy and Public Needs*, Vol. 1, *His-tory, Trends, and Current Magnitudes*, Washington, D.C.: Department of the Treasury, 1977, p. 103.

4. Lester M. Salamon, "The Non-Profit Sector and Government: The American Experience in Theory and Practice," *The Third Sector: Comparative Studies of Nonprofit Organizations*, Helmut K. Anheier and Wolfgang Seibel, eds., New York: Walter de Gruyter, pp. 219–240.

5. Although the 1930 data and later figures are not absolutely comparable, they do indicate the gross weighting and directions of expenditures. See U.S. Bureau of the Census, *Statistical Abstract of the United States: 1997*, 117th edition, Table 576, "Social Welfare Expenditures under Public Programs: 1980 to 1993," p. 372, and Table 577, "Social Welfare Expenditures under Public Programs as Percent of GDP and Total Government Outlays: 1980 to 1993," p. 372, Washington, D.C., 1997. GDP is the economic measure now used most equivalent to the measure (GNP) used in 1930. See chapter 6 for GDP and GNP definitions.

6. Wilmer L. Kerns, "Private Social Welfare Expenditures, 1972–94," *Social Security Bulletin*, Vol. 60, No. 1, 1997, p. 55.

7. Ann E. Kaplan, *Giving USA: The Annual Report on Philanthropy for the Year 1996*, New York: American Association of Fund Raising Counsel Trust, 1997, pp. 17–19, 29.

8. *Statistical Abstract, 1997*, Table 580, "Public Income-Maintenance Programs—Cash Benefit Payments: 1980 to 1995," p. 374.

9. Ann E. Kaplan, *Giving USA: The Annual Report on Philanthropy for the Year 1996*, New York: American Association of Fund Raising Counsel Trust, 1997, p. 19.

10. U.S. Bureau of the Census, *Statistical Abstract of the United States: 1997*, Table 1286, "National Nonprofit Associations—Number, by Type: 1980 to 1997," p. 780.

11. Marvin Olasky, *The Tragedy of American Compassion*, Washington, D.C.: Regnery Publishing, 1995.

12. David Wessel and John Harwood, "Capitalism Is Giddy with Triumph; Is It Possible to Overdo It?" *The Wall Street Journal*, May 14, 1998, pp. A1, A10.

13. Yolanda K. Kodrzycki, "Fiscal Pressures and the Privatization of Local Services," *New England Economic Review*, January/February 1998, pp. 39–50.

14. David C. Johnston, "United Way Reports Gifts Are Up 4.7%," *New York Times*, August 16, 1998, p. 20.

15. Reed Abelson, "Charities Use For-Profit Units to Avoid Disclosing Finances," *New York Times*, January 9, 1998, pp. A1, A12.

16. Kit Lively, 'Treasury Department Proposes Rules on Tax Returns of Non-Profit Groups," *The Chronicle of Higher Education*, October 10, 1997, p. A33.

17. James T. Bennett and Thomas J. DiLorenzo, *Unfair Competition: The Profits and Nonprofits*, New York: Hamilton Press, 1989, p. 1.

18. Ann E. Kaplan, *Giving USA: The Annual Report on Philanthropy for the Year 1996*, New York: American Association of Fund Raising Counsel Trust, 1997, p. 65.

19. *Family Caregiving in the U.S.: Findings from a National Survey*, Bethesda, Md.: National Alliance for Caregiving and the American Association of Retired Persons, June 1997, pp. 8, 14.

20. Robert A. Harootyan and Robert E. Vorek, "Volunteering, Helping, and Gift Giving in Families and Communities," in *Intergenerational Linkages*, Vern l. Bengston and Robert A. Harootyan, eds., New York: Springer Publishing Co., 1994, pp. 105, 108.

21. Karl Kronebusch and Mark Schlesinger, "Intergenerational Transfers," in *Intergenerational Linkages*, p. 137.

22. Ralph M. Kramer, "Voluntary Agencies and the Contract Culture: "Dream or Nightmare," *Social Service Review*, Vol. 68, No. 1, March 1994, pp. 33–60; Peter M. Kettner and Lawrence L. Martin, "Purchase of Service Contracting in the 1990s: Have Expectations

Been Met?" *Journal of Sociology and Social Welfare*, Vol. XX, No. 2, June 1993, pp. 89–103.

23. Anna C. Burke and Jane A. Rafferty, "Ownership Differences in the Provision of Outpatient Substance Abuse Services," *Administration in Social Work*, Vol. 18, No. 3, 1994, pp. 59–91.

24. Jone L. Pearce, *Volunteers: The Organizational Behavior of Unpaid Workers*, New York: Routledge, 1993, pp. 64, 66, 70, 78.

25. Michael O'Neill, "The Paradox of Women and Power in the Nonprofit Sector," in Teresa Odendahl and Michael O'Neill, eds., *Women and Power in the Nonprofit Sector*, San Francisco: Jossey-Bass, 1994, p. 2.

26. Steven R. Smith and Michael Lipsky, *Nonprofits for Hire: The Welfare State in the Age of Contracting*, Cambridge, Mass.: Harvard University Press, 1993, p. 193.

27. Andrew Billingsley, *Climbing Jacob's Ladder*, New York: Simon & Schuster, 1992, pp. 349–378.

28. Martin Guggenheim, "State-Supported Foster Care: The Interplay Between the Prohibition of Establishing Religion and the Free Exercise Rights of Parents and Children: Wilder v. Bernstein," *Brooklyn Law Review*, Brooklyn, N.Y.: Brooklyn Law School, 1990, Vol. 56, No. 2, pp. 603–655.

29. Philip B. Kurland, *Religion and the Law of the Church and State and the Supreme Court*, Chicago: Aldine, 1962; Frank J. Sorauf, *The Wall of Separation: The Constitutional Policies of Church and State*, Princeton, N.J.: Princeton University Press, 1976.

30. National Alliance for Caregiving and the American Association of Retired Persons, *Family Caregiving in the U.S.: Findings from a National Survey*, Bethesda, Md., June 1997.

31. Lester M. Salamon, *The Global Associational Revolution: The Rise in the Third Sector on the World Scene*, Paper No. 15, Johns Hopkins University, Baltimore, Md.: Institute for Policy Studies, April 1993, p. 6.

32. Henry Steele Commager, *Lester Ward and the Welfare State*, New York: Bobbs-Merrill, 1967, p. 223.

Social Work: The Emergence of a Profession

. . . the good we secure for ourselves is precarious and uncertain,
is floating in mid-air, until it is is secured for all of us and incorporated into
our common life.
—Jane Addams[1]

OVERVIEW

Depending on who is doing the "name-calling," social workers are referred to as "do-gooders," "bleeding hearts," "radicals," captives of and apologists for "the establishment," organizers of the poor, and servers of the middle class. All these are ways in which people stereotype social workers and the functions they perform in society.

As we have seen, social welfare has evolved through a lengthy process, but social work as a professionalized occupation started its evolution at a much later stage, gaining momentum as a result of the Industrial Revolution.

In this chapter and the next, we explore the profession of social work within the context of social welfare. We review historical antecedents of modern social workers and the creation of the profession, describe the functions of social work and the arenas in which social workers perform their functions, and examine a number of current issues that confront the profession.

Social work is a professionalized occupation that delivers social services largely in social welfare institutions. Although social work is the major professional group in social welfare, social workers are by no means limited to delivering services in the social welfare area, nor are all services in social welfare delivered by social workers.

THE WORKERS OF "GOOD WORKS"

Antecedents of professional social workers are found among people who have helped others through the ages. Services have been provided in many forms by religious institutions and charities, public and voluntary services, and by little-known "good Samaritans." Among these predecessors, it has been suggested that Father Vincent de Paul, a seventeenth-century Roman Catholic clergyman—later canonized—initiated the training of social workers. When he founded the Daughters of Charity in 1633, young peasant women who wanted to devote themselves to charitable work were trained especially for nursing the poor. Others pointed out that a century earlier Juan Luis Vives developed a plan of organized relief (1537) at the request of the mayor of Bruges in Flanders that required that good persons "remember that the burden of their neighbor's calamities must be relieved not only with alms but also with their presence in visiting, comforting, helping, and in executing the deeds of pity." Along these lines, in the American colonies as early as 1626 *siecken troosters* (comforters of the sick), after passing an exam, were appointed to visit ill persons at their homes in New Amsterdam (later New York) to offer counsel in relation to spiritual and other matters.[2]

People have always reached out to help other people. Family, church, and other groups often tried to institutionalize this helping function. It was particularly during the nineteenth century that more definitive forerunners of social work as a profession were established. The coming of industrialization and an accelerated movement from rural to urban locations produced social needs and social problems that were beyond the coping capacities of individual families. Along with modernization, functions that traditionally would have been performed by family members soon became the tasks of specialists. For example, rather than milking one's own cows, one obtained milk provided by dairy farmers, dairies, distributors, truckers, and grocers. And today the child with developmental disabilities, who was once cared for entirely at home, is transported to a child-development center for education and training by specialists.

Specialization developed in many facets of American life, including one dealing with pauperism and poverty. Following the War of 1812, a short harvest occurred in 1816 because of weather conditions. Shortly after, there followed the 1817–1821 postwar depression. John Griscom in New York organized the Society for the Prevention of Pauperism. The society aimed to investigate the circumstances and habits of the poor, to devise means of improving the situation of the poor both morally and physically, to suggest plans by which the poor could help themselves, and to encourage economy and saving. Among the remedies utilized were house-to-house visitation of the poor and the flow of charities into one distribution channel in order to prevent cheating.[3]

Around the same time, Thomas Chalmers, a minister and philosopher, believed that his parishioners (the poor included) could provide for themselves through their own resources, the kindness of relatives, and the sympathy of the wealthier members of the community. Taking over a Glasgow parish, he implemented a new plan from 1819 to 1823. All local parish church collections would be left with the parish rather than transferred to a central fund. These funds could be used at Chalmer's discretion to provide for the people of the parish, but would not be used for new families moving into the area.

The parish of 8,000 people was divided into 25 districts. The office of deacon was responsible for providing for all new applications for public assistance. Deacons were given general instructions and individual supervision and advice. For approximately four years, Chalmers supervised the program for relief in St. John's parish. The parish took over the care of individuals previously under the care of the town hospital, and some money was left for the parish school.

At a time when workhouses were used cruelly and indiscriminately, Chalmers created a system of personal influence and individualization outside the framework of the Poor Laws. Investigation and district assignments were systematic techniques. Although Chalmers believed in an ethic of "noblesse oblige" by the wealthy for the poor, he, nevertheless, created an administrative plan and trained persons to implement it, based on the belief that personal factors cause poverty and that the effort of "helping" people could bring them out of poverty. The investigation of individual situations was a factor in the creation of the concept of *casework*, by which we mean that each person or case is unique. Thus benefits were related to the individual assessment.[4]

Among other social work precursors were the volunteers of the New York Society for the Prevention of Pauperism formed as a result of the 1819 depression. Similarly, the New York Association for Improving the Condition of the Poor (NYAICP) was organized in 1843 to relieve pauperism and aid the worthy poor through the use of volunteers. It, however, was not staffed only by volunteers. Instead, employed staff members, primarily missionaries, were used to do administrative work for districts and to train and supervise the volunteer visitors. Families were investigated by the volunteer visitors who provided health, housing, and child welfare services. The family conditions found by the visitors were reviewed by the paid agents serving as district secretaries. By 1866, the district secretaries were dismissed and the NYAICP returned to an almost entirely volunteer effort. However, in the 1870s, paid visitors were once again employed. These paid district secretaries were forerunners of the later social workers. The AICP structure served as a model for succeeding private agencies and the agency later merged with the New York Charity Organization Society to form the eminent Community Service Society of New York.[5]

Still other predecessors of social workers emerged from the Civil War. Members of the U.S. Sanitary Commission, a federation of voluntary organizations, helped to serve the needs of Union troops during the Civil War by supplying bandages, clothing, and food and by establishing lodging places for soldiers on leave, meals while in transit, and assistance with pay claims.[6] The workers in the Freedmen's Bureau for former enslaved persons, created in March 1865, implemented a comprehensive program including temporary relief, food, clothing, hospitals, schools, orphan asylums, homes for the aged and the infirm, lease of lands, job finding, supervising labor contracts, housing and transportation for job seekers, courts, and legal counsel as to rights.

The Freedmen's Bureau was family centered. Designed to minimize the social upheaval of the war and the stressful emancipation of enslaved persons, the Freedmen's Bureau offered—in contemporary terms—child welfare services, income maintenance, medical care, work projects, government housing, provision for the aged and infirm, employment counseling, family location, marriage counseling, legal aid, assistance with resettlement, protective services, and education.[7]

Philosophies and techniques continued to evolve. Franklin B. Sanborn, a New England intellectual associated with John Brown, after becoming the executive secretary of the Massachusetts State Board of Charities in 1863, encouraged the use of homes for delinquent and nondelinquent children. He initiated the use of foster homes for the emotionally disturbed on the basis of observations made in Scotland, Belgium, and France. He also recruited local volunteers, for the most part women, to serve as visitors. These "*friendly visitors*" were middle- and upper-class women who had time and wanted to do good. They would visit the poor and try to teach them to be better citizens and parents, to budget, and to practice sobriety in all matters. The expectation was that through moral instruction one could learn how not to be poor.[8]

A major economic depression in 1873, one of many during the nineteenth century, created severe unemployment problems. It became clear that agencies, programs, and resources were not equal to the tasks they were called on to perform. As a result, during this period an English invention—the Charity Organization Society (COS)—caught the imagination of a number of U.S. communities.

A first attempt to form a citywide Bureau of Charities was initiated in New York in 1873 but was abandoned when several influential institutions refused to cooperate. Boston also instituted a charity organization that year, but it was operative only in the North End. The first operational citywide COS originated in Buffalo, New York, in 1877, and similar societies then developed rapidly in a series of cities, including New Haven, Philadelphia, Boston, Brooklyn, Cincinnati, and New York.[9]

It was hoped that charity organizations could meet the pressing social problems of the cities—unemployment, orphans, beggars, the ill, and others—and clarify the interrelations of private and public relief agencies that had overlapping functions and different policies. These new organizations were to assume two different roles: (1) direct service to individuals and families; in this respect they were the immediate forerunners of social casework and of family service agencies, and (2) planning and coordinating efforts, which preceded the development of community organization and social planning. Thus, implicit in the creation of these new agencies were two different functions, reflecting the two tracks of cause and function, a theme to be discussed further in chapter 13.

The general principles on which the charity organizations operated were

1. detailed investigation of the applicant,
2. a central system of registration to avoid duplication,
3. cooperation among the various relief agencies, and
4. extensive use of friendly volunteer visitors.

Investigative and administrative responsibilities belonged to the paid staff. The major treatment and helping roles belonged to the friendly visitors who as volunteers had the task of directly helping those in difficulty.

Roy Lubove reports that work was viewed at this time as the solution for all problem families. When persons came for assistance, the Conference of the Boston Associated Charities, for example, "boasted that when the poor first called for assistance, they requested 'clothing, money, etc., etc.,' but were refused anything except work."[10] Thus there is an amazing consistency in attitude and approach to the poor in England and America from the fourteenth century until the latter part of the nineteenth century, and although diminished for a time the same theme of individual responsibility continues to this day, unmindful of the altered economic and societal context.

To further illustrate the incipient social work roles and tasks about the same time, a *Manual for Visitors Among the Poor* was developed by the Philadelphia Society for Organizing Charitable Relief and Repressing Mendicancy. The suggestions for friendly visitors are instructive: sympathy and encouragement are more important than money; women are the best friendly visitors; help, if urgently needed, may be obtained from neighbors; personal assistance should take the form of employment; cultivate the habit of looking below the surface of things; poverty is associated with disease and a consequent lack of vitality; know the sanitary laws; the poor have not learned thrift; and so on. The thrust of these instructions places the responsibility on the person or family involved. The effort to make change is marked by "moral suasion."[11]

At this point in the development of social work, volunteers were primarily motivated to change people as "doers of good works." It was through social investigation and attempts to understand family situations that social work began to gestate as a profession. The time and effort required to deal with many cases led to making comparisons among situations and searches for underlying causation. Although there was a strong sense of moral judgment involved, friendly visitors and charity organizations moved toward understanding and took a major step on the road to professionalization.

To the contemporary mind, these forerunners of casework stand out for their judgmental and patronizing qualities and the tendency to place total responsibility for a person's or family's problems solely on them. Although these attitudes were present, it is important to note that these movements set down one of the basic principles of all contemporary social work practice: that each person is unique and has to be understood in individual terms.

Concurrently, settlement houses were being instituted in the United States following the establishment of Toynbee Hall in 1884 in London. A group of people from the middle and upper classes would live in a poor neighborhood so they could experience firsthand the realities of neighborhood life and search simultaneously for ways to improve conditions in cooperation with the residents of the neighborhood. Many of the early U.S. settlement house workers were daughters of ministers. No doubt they tried to do away with any airs of superiority and supplant such feelings with neighborliness. By assisting their neighbors, they hoped their experiences would make them more effective social reformers. By 1910, 400 settlement houses had been formed, three fourths founded by women. The settlement house movement was a creative and influential force in American life. Among its creations were new communal organizations such as the National Association for the Advancement of Colored

People, which grew out of the Henry Street Settlement (New York, 1909), and the U.S. Children's Bureau (1912), among many other accomplishments.

It is important to place these developments in the context of the times. These women were part of the first generation of women graduating from college in significant numbers, and their career possibilities were limited, mainly marriage or teaching. Life in the settlements was viewed as moral and unselfish. It was semi-protected, and offered a social life as well. Settlement houses and social work offered public roles of potential influence at a time when women were still unable to vote, thus providing an alternative route to influencing policy.[12]

Women's voluntarism preceded the settlement house movement. Beginning in the 1820s Protestant women formed lay organizations. One such organization created before 1870 was the American Female Moral Reform Society (AFMRS). By 1839 this organization had 500 local chapters in New England and New York. During the depression winter of 1873–1874, another Protestant organization—the Women's Christian Temperance Union (WCTU)—began and supplanted the AFMRS. By 1883 there was a branch of WCTU in almost every American county. Their work was not limited to temperance matters. In Chicago, the site of the WCTU headquarters, the organization maintained two day nurseries, two Sunday schools, an industrial school, a mission that sheltered 4,000 homeless or destitute women in a 12-month period, a free medical dispensary that treated more than 1,600 patients a year, a lodging house for men that had by 1889 provided temporary housing for more than 50,000 men, and a low-cost restaurant. Among the ideas they advocated were prison reform, special facilities for women offenders, the eight-hour working day, model facilities for dependent and neglected children, the kindergarten movement, shelters for the care of children of working mothers, social "rooms" other than saloons for the urban poor, mothers' education, and vocational training for women.[13]

Thorstein Veblen, however, commenting on the roles of leisure class women in charity work and social amelioration efforts, did not accept the "philosophy" of settlement house workers quite as benignly as offered and suggested:

> The solicitude of "settlements," for example, is in part directed to enhance the industrial efficiency of the poor and to teach them the more adequate utilization of the means at hand; but it is also no less consistently directed to the inculcation, by precept and example, of certain punctilios of upper-class propriety in manners and customs.[14]

Settlement houses played important roles in cities, especially in immigrant communities. Their focus was on improving housing, health, and general living conditions; finding jobs; teaching English, occupational skills, and hygiene; and attempting to change the environmental surroundings through cooperative efforts. Social casework started in charity organization work. Social group work, community organization, and social action were developed by settlement houses and workers.

In addition to dealing with local problems by taking local action, settlement houses played important roles in gathering facts, promulgating them, preparing legislation, and collecting forces to influence social policy and legislation. Many of the key legislative enactments of the reform era had their inception in the work of the settlement houses. The settlements learned what the realities of life in slum communities were and included staff members who were nationally influential, not only through their social work efforts but also through personal and familial connections. Settlement houses emphasized reform through environmental changes, but "they continued to struggle to teach the poor the prevailing middle-class values of work, thrift, and abstinence as the keys to success."[15]

Jane Addams of Hull House in Chicago thought that settlement house residents could eventually help slum-dwellers to "express themselves and make articulate their desires."[16] By changing neighborhoods, together they would change communities; and through changing communities, they would alter the nation.

According to Mary McDowell, settlements in 1896 worked from within the neighborhood and among the people, sharing the fate of the slum-dwellers, whereas the charity organization's visitors came from without and returned to the outside after the visit. The two approaches differed in methodology but complemented each other's efforts, doing together what neither could do entirely as separate agencies.[17]

By the end of the nineteenth century, two major tracks emerged along which professional social work evolved. Future developments would be dramatically influenced by the different natures of the two tracks and by their confluence within social work.

THE PROCESS OF PROFESSIONALIZATION

Harold Wilensky traced the growth of 18 professions, and all follow the same pattern:

1. A substantial number of people begin doing full-time some activity that needs doing.
2. A training school is established.
3. A professional association is formed.
4. The association engages in political agitation to win the support of law for the protection of the group.
5. A code of ethics is developed.[18]

The developmental pattern and professionalization process for social work follows a typical pattern. When charity organizations or societies received contracts to administer relief funds, they began to hire people as executive secretaries to organize volunteers properly and established procedures to show accountability for the money received from the city. These executive secretaries can be considered among the first paid social workers. They began meeting in conferences, and—reflective of the professionalization process—they established standards and training courses.

In the summer of 1898, the New York Charity Organization Society offered the first course in practical philanthropic work to charity workers. By 1904, a one-year program was offered by the newly formed New York School of Philanthropy, and by the end of World War I, 17 programs were members of the Association of Training Schools for Professional Social Work. The American Association of Social Workers (AASW) was formed as a professional association in 1921 following a vain effort to form an association several years earlier. It was not until 1951 that an official code of ethics was prepared by the AASW, followed by the code developed by the National Association of Social Workers (NASW) in 1960.

Social work is a profession whose development in the modern era has been supported by general professionalization trends and the growth of services resulting from industrialization, urbanization, and specialization. The evolution of many new professions in our society supported the rapid strides social work made as a profession, condensing into several decades evolutionary processes that took centuries for other professions. This trend is reflected in the American experience. By 1996, 18.7 million persons were employed in professional specialty occupations (almost 15 percent of total employment). Managerial and professional speciality employment combined accounted for almost 29 percent of total civilian employment.[19] Professional occupations are expected to continue these growth trends.[20]

A BRIEF HISTORY OF PRACTICE AND METHODS

Mary Richmond, one of the outstanding founders of social work and active in charity organization efforts, could say in 1890 that "only two things are necessary in order to do good work amongst the poor; one is much good will, and the other is a little tact."[21] However, 12 years later, she was defining social casework more precisely as "those processes which develop personality through adjustments consciously effected, individual by individual, between men and their social environment."[22]

Physician Richard C. Cabot introduced medical social work to Massachusetts General Hospital in 1905. Soon social workers were employed in schools, child-guidance clinics, courts, and other settings. Building on the investigatory and friendly visiting functions by charity organization volunteers and paid staff, social casework methodologies continued to develop. Initially based on moral categories, the work of the caseworker was to help through persuasion and example. As knowledge developed based on practical experience and as new knowledge became available from psychology, sociology, and psychiatry, the efforts of social caseworkers led to greater understanding of the interaction of individuals and their environment. A "diagnosis" could be formulated and strengths and limitations identified for use in the helping process. Typically, early efforts to make changes were educational and persuasive.

However, it was recognized that there are limits beyond which the individual is not responsible for his or her situation and that society has a reciprocal responsibility for collective action that influences the lives of individuals. The experience of the settlement house confirmed this view. Addams reported:

> We early found ourselves spending many hours in efforts to secure support for deserted women, insurance for bewildered widows, damages for injured operators, furniture from the clutches of the installment store. The Settlement is valuable as an information and interpretation bureau. It constantly acts between the various institutions of the city and the people for whose benefit these institutions were erected.[23]

Not only were early social workers brokers, but they were also advocates, interested not only in techniques for individual and family change, but also in altering society. This perspective of societal change was cogently stated by Florence Kelley, a consumer advocate, in 1905:

> A government which finds it possible, for instance, to take care of the health of young lobsters on the coast of Maine, would seem to have ingenuity enough at a pinch to enable it to make some sort of provision for the orphan children of skilled and unskilled workmen. It may take a long time. It has taken a long time to learn to take care of the lobsters.[24]

An important event took place in 1915 when Abraham Flexner, a significant critic of medical education, turned his attention to social work in a presentation at the National Conference of Charities and Corrections. Training and creation of a scientific method for social work had been advanced, and yet Flexner raised a question as to whether social work was a profession or not. His answer was equivocal and suggested that "if social work fails to conform to some professional criteria, it very readily satisfies others. . . . In the long run, the first, main, and indispensable criterion of a profession will be the possession of professional spirit, and that test social work may, if it will, fully satisfy." Flexner was strenuous in his criticism, stating that social work lacked a specific skill for a specific function and, insofar as this was true, could not become a profession.[25]

Despite this criticism of social work, several events followed shortly after that energized the continued professionalization of social work. Training schools were formed, a professional association was created, and a formative book was published. Within two years after Flexner's presentation, Richmond published *Social Diagnosis* (1917), a work that organized a theory and methodology for social work. She formulated a common body of knowledge for casework based on collecting information and understanding the meaning of the information. The book was important for the development of the profession because it expounded an orderly professional process consisting of study, diagnosis, prognosis, and treatment planning. Reflective of Richmond's charity organization background, the focus was on the individual or family—the case—in determining what was wrong, what could be done, and how the worker should intervene.

With the advent of medical social work, psychiatric social work, the mental hygiene movement, and psychoanalytic psychology, social work searched for a defined professional methodology and professional status.[26] From the latter years of the nineteenth century until approximately 1915, casework changed from a movement on a one-by-one basis to a method with nascent scientific underpinnings. The "cause" mission of the profession, which had set out to change the world, was changed to focus more on the functions of the social worker and the skills and knowledge that support those functions.

Social workers were employed in a broad diversity of specialized settings. Each social worker identified to a significant extent with particular settings so that professional roles, identities, and functions experienced a centrifugal expansion as social workers identified themselves with the fields in which they practiced. Beyond the development of social work in psychiatric settings, including child-guidance clinics, much of social work became infused with psychiatric knowledge and was especially influenced by psychoanalytic thought, both Freudian and Rankian. Approximately two years following the publication of *Social Diagnosis*, Mary Jarrett, a psychiatric caseworker, rediagnosed the cases presented by Richmond and concluded that at least 50 percent included psychiatric problems.[27] Addams helps to place this influx of psychoanalytic thought and emphasis on individual psyche, technique, and method in perspective. She pointed out that the veering away from social reform can be viewed within the context of the times:

> Throughout the decade (the Twenties) this fear of change, this tendency to play safe was registered most conspicuously in the field of politics, but it spread over into other fields as well. There is little doubt that social workers exhibited many symptoms of this panic and with a kind of protective instinct carefully avoided any identification with the phraseology of social reform.[28]

During the 1920s, many social workers thought of themselves as therapists, or at least believed that there were therapeutic emphases within their social work practice.[29] Social work continued to proliferate in health, school, family, and psychiatric settings. As the proliferation of practice fields continued, concern increased about the specialized nature of social work in many settings, and a systematic study was undertaken to determine what the generic elements of the profession were. A series of meetings was held from 1923 to 1929 to identify the general knowledge shared by all social workers regardless of setting. This work group became known as "The Milford Conference." In 1929, the work group, consisting of executives and board members, reported that generic social casework, that is, casework applicable in all potential settings, was viewed as having these common aspects:

1. Knowledge of typical deviations from accepted standards of social life;
2. The use of norms of human life and human relationships;
3. The significance of social history as the basis of particularizing the human being in need;
4. Established methods of study and treatment of human beings in need;
5. The use of established community resources in social treatment;
6. The adaptation of scientific knowledge and formulations of experience to the requirements of social casework;
7. The consciousness of a philosophy that determines the purpose, ethics, and obligations of social casework; and
8. The blending of the foregoing into social treatment.[30]

The Great Depression began soon after the Milford Conference Report on a generic social casework predicated on individual change. Despite the fact that the depression refocused attention on social change, the social casework stream in the social work profession clung to an individual-centered and personality-focused approach.

Meanwhile the overwhelming nature and scope of human need created by the Great Depression caused social policy shifts, which affected social welfare and social work. Everyone was affected; many were unemployed. It clearly was not the result of personal responsibility: Systemic and structural factors were at work. The society and government searched for new security, and new roles for government were accompanied by new social planning trends. These new trends were supported by the general agreement that government should help people—a new assumption in American life.

A myriad of New Deal programs responded to the need for national governmental entry into comprehensive social welfare provision. Concurrently, there was a call for prepared personnel to expand public social services. Because of new public assistance programs, the number of social workers increased rapidly in the 1930s. Numbering 31,000 in 1930, by the 1940 census there were at least 70,000 social and welfare workers. The American Association of Social Workers, the largest professional organization, doubled its size. Seventeen new schools of social work opened, and established schools increased in size.

There was a shift during the 1930s in the relative importance of the public and private sectors of social welfare, the greater weight by far now moving to the public sector. Many social workers were active in starting new programs, including Social Security, and also were employed in public assistance and child welfare. Others continued to work in voluntary agencies and in public institutions such as hospitals. One significant result of the Depression was the introduction of unions into the field of social work.[31]

A major issue arose during the years of the Great Depression centering on the role of social work in an expanding welfare state. Integral to this issue were questions about theories of causation, both personal and societal, and about the roles of social workers in institutional services for normal but disadvantaged persons.

A second issue was an intense struggle, which over the decades faded: the vying between two schools of thought, diagnostic and functional social work. The two schools share the vocation of social casework but differ on underpinning theories of personality. The diagnostic school, also known as the psychosocial (the "person-in-situation") school, was based on Freudian thought and stressed the importance of diagnosis and of the powerful role of a person's past interpersonal and intrapsychic experience in the treatment process. The functional school, based on a psychology of growth, stressed the impact of the agency's function on the ability to help in the process of casework and emphasized the relationship between the social worker and the client in the here-and-now helping process.

Paradoxically, a psychologically based casework preoccupied with individuals remained the major trend in social casework while the economy was crumbling. Perhaps there is an explanation for this curious persistence. Psychological casework had become the professional tool, developed over decades, of social workers. A therapeutic emphasis also was supported by the Great Depression itself. Social welfare agencies, especially private social welfare ones, sought new roles as public welfare assumed the responsibility for income maintenance, a task completely beyond the resources of private philanthropy. An emphasis on psychologically oriented case-work then was an answer to the quest for a professional knowledge base and helped to define the changing functions of private social welfare agencies.

At the same time, social workers affected social legislation and social planning as they developed as part of the New Deal. Among the social workers playing impor-tant parts in the "cause" efforts of the 1930s were Harry Hopkins, Frances Perkins, and Bertha Reynolds. They were active and influential in determining governmental policy and the administration of expanded social welfare.

World War II was a time when social work continued to emphasize the thera-peutic aspects of treatment as it dealt with family disruption, problems of relocation, and the needs of military personnel at home and abroad. Following the war, social work continued to be mainly influenced by psychodynamic psychiatry, but the social sciences began to be introduced to a greater extent in schools of social work. There was an emphasis on seeking out the hard to reach, working with delinquent youth and multiproblem families, and initiating private social work practice. The common-alities and differences between social casework and psychotherapy were debated.

In the 1960s, the emphasis on the therapeutic function diminished somewhat as social workers became active in community action and advocacy as part of the civil rights struggle and in regard to housing and racial discrimination, juvenile delin-quency control programs, neighborhood organization and multiservice centers, draft resistance and anti-Vietnam War efforts, the National Welfare Rights Organization, the efforts for economic security programs such as a negative income tax and guar-anteed annual income, and the flowering of minority group organizations of many kinds.

Since the 1960s, social problems and developments in schools of social work contributed to social workers engaging in a broad variety of practice efforts. Among these efforts were social work with HIV positive persons and those with AIDS; prac-tice in industrial and business settings, with immigrants and refugees, substance abuse, domestic violence, the needs of women, the homeless, managed care, gangs, and teen pregnancy; social work and technology; chronic mental illness; suicide pre-vention; and private solo and group practice, among many others.

In social work education, both graduate and undergraduate, a diversity of prac-tice models were developed, including a focus on social problems (such as sub-stance abuse, women's issues, severe mental illness, and poverty), methods (clinical social work, policy, planning and community organization, political social work, gen-eralist practice), populations at risk (impoverished communities, age, ethnicity, cul-ture, class, physical or mental ability), and fields of practice (aging, children, families, youth, disabilities, health, mental health, and rural).

DEVELOPMENT OF THE PROFESSIONAL ASSOCIATION

Beginning in 1874, the National Conference of Charities and Correction provided an opportunity for social agency employees to meet together on a national basis. Lo-cally, various clubs and social work organizations were formed. The National Social

Workers Exchange began operations in 1917 for job placement in social work positions.

By 1918, there was an attempt to organize a national association of social workers, but the effort failed partly because of lack of agreement on membership qualifications. In 1921, the American Association of Social Workers was formed. In addition, social workers from specialized settings formed national organizations, including the American Association of Medical Social Workers (1918), the National Association of School Social Workers (1919), the AASW (1921), the American Association of Psychiatric Social Workers (1926), the American Association of Group Workers (Study Group, 1936; Association, 1946), the Association for the Study of Community Organization (1946), and the Social Work Research Group (1949). In 1955, those associations then in existence combined to form the NASW—the national professional association that now represents the full range of professional social workers.[32]

The professional association provides a variety of services including insurance benefits, regulation and credentialing, standards for several types of practice and services, publications, a register of clinical social workers, continuing education, and practice sections for aging, child welfare, community organizing, criminal/juvenile justice, employee assistance programs, gay and lesbian issues, HIV/AIDS, hospital social work, macro social work, management, and women's issues. There are two affiliate organizations, the National Center for Social Policy and Practice and the NASW Communications Network, as well as four subsidiaries: the Research and Education fund, Insurance Trust, the Legal Defense Service, and PACE (Political Action and Candidate Election), which plays an active political action role. The NASW also promotes sound public policies in regard to welfare reform, AIDS, comprehensive national health care policy, protection of civil rights, prevention of violence, and other timely and important social welfare matters.

Several smaller groups have developed—for example, national associations of African American, Latino, Native American, and industrial social workers; social workers with groups, community organization and social administration; oncology and clinical social work; social work managers; hospital social work administrators; Commission on Gay Men/Lesbian Women of the Council on Social Work Education, the North American Association of Christians in Social Work, and others. This burgeoning of splinter groups reflects the pluralism in our society, the multiplicity of functions and fields in social work, the creation of new specializations, the difficulty of having one organization satisfy all segments of the profession, and efforts by particular groups to enhance their legitimate goals. In addition, the American Association of State Social Work Boards was organized in 1979 and oversees national credentialing licensing examinations, which can serve to further develop national standards of social work practice.

The membership of NASW multiplied more than sevenfold from 22,027 in 1957 to 155,000 in 1998.[33] Membership is open to baccalaureate and master's graduates from accredited schools and holders of doctorates in social work or social welfare. By comparison, the memberships of some other professional organizations in 1996 were American Medical Association, 297,000; American Nurses Association,

210,000; American Bar Association, 375,000; and American Psychological Association, 134,000.[34]

Social Work with Groups

Social work with groups developed from several sources different from those of social casework. Settlement houses, influenced by the social reform movements of the early twentieth century, focused in part on group services, including cultural and art groups, recreational groups, education, and physical health. They emphasized social participation and association, mutual aid and cooperative problem solving, democratic processes, learning and growth, the encouragement of interaction among persons of different backgrounds, the impact of the environment on persons, and the potential impact of persons on the environment.

In group service agencies such as community centers, camping, and youth service organizations, there was a belief that the road to democracy was through democratic participation. Group service agencies would foster such participation at every level—from children to adults—and from the group itself to the greater society. Support for the evolving methodology came from sociology and progressive education as expounded by John Dewey.

The first course on group work in a school of social work was taught by Clara Kaiser in 1923 at Western Reserve University in Cleveland. The University of Pittsburgh and the New York School (later to become the Columbia University School of Social Work) instituted programs in the 1930s, with other schools soon also offering group work courses.

By 1936, the American Association for Study of Group Work was formed. Noteworthy was a great increase in the use of groups in psychiatric settings during World War II, in part created by the need for the few available trained persons to work with large numbers of persons affected by the war experience. In 1946, the National Conference of Social Work recognized social group work as a part of the social work profession.[35]

Early social group work had several goals:

1. Democratic experiences,
2. Cooperative problem solving and mutual support,
3. Improvement of society, and
4. Character development.

Although there was hesitancy about the place of social group work in the social work profession as early as the Milford Conference Report in 1929, the fundamental methods of social work were "recognized as social case work, community organization, group work, social research, and since social work is almost invariably carried on through the medium of organizations, we may add the technique of administration."[36] Thus the elite group that prepared the Milford Conference Report concluded that group work was an intrinsic part of social work.

Three major models of social group work—social goals, remedial, and reciprocal—were defined during the 1960s and 1970s by Beulah Rothman and Catherine

Papell. In brief, the social goals model was concerned with social consciousness and social responsibility, the creation of an informed and able democratic citizenry, and socially oriented tasks. The remedial model reflected treatment goals focusing on the enhancement of functioning and individual change within the group process. The reciprocal model had a dual focus: society and the individual, which meet in the group as a mutual aid system. The reciprocal model focuses on group process aimed at serving both individuals and society. The focus is on interdependence: mediating the interdependent actors and nourishing social functioning of both individuals and society.[37]

A large number of theoretical perspectives expanded earlier models. Among these perspectives are the interactionist, humanistic, socioeducational, mainstream, empowerment and social action, cognitive behavioral, and developmental models. Much experimentation took place during the 1970s when social workers were involved with sensitivity, encounter, transactional analysis, gestalt, behavior modification, and psychodrama groups.

Illustrative of the diversity of group workers current service is their work with people with HIV/AIDS, single-parent families, substance abusers, sexual abuse and incest survivors, violent men, inner-city youth, immigrant groups, bereaved persons, cross-cultural and cross-gender groups, holocaust survivors, multifamily groups, persons with Alzheimer's disease, the homebound, and a host of other populations.

Despite the multitude of perspectives, technologies, contexts, and populations served, a core set of values and concepts has been identified as belonging to the social work method with groups. These unifying concepts include the following:

- A systemic perspective—that is, groups are social systems. This view underscores a dynamic view of group development and operation, stresses the reciprocal nature of relationships, and highlights the relationship of the group to its context.
- Group dynamics, including group climate and processes, influences on members, goals, maintenance, and task functions, decision making, developmental stages, norms, conflict, cohesion, and power structures.
- Concepts of intervention, including planning and analysis, worker's engagement, power of the group as the medium of service, individual, group, and environmental interventions.[38]

In recent years, social work with groups has involved exploring the implications of feminist thought for social group work and efforts have been ongoing to define a feminist group work.[39] Social group work, which began with a focus on work with children and youth in settlement houses and in adult education and social action, now is practiced in a great variety of settings. From groups in administration to treatment groups, from informal education to social action groups, and from consciousness-raising to socialization, social work with groups is used for many purposes in many different settings. Today there appears to be a growing utilization of groups by social workers for various purposes, including treatment, support, education, personal, organizational and community development, administration, advocacy, and social action.

Community Organization and Social Planning

Community organization and social planning have their roots in the reform efforts of the latter part of the nineteenth century. The Charity Organization Society originally sought to develop cooperative planning and coordination among local charities and worked for reforms in housing codes, antituberculosis associations, legislation in support of juvenile courts and probation, programs for the care of dependent children, cooperation with the police in regard to beggars and vagrants, and legislation to require absent fathers to support their children. As time went on, and as we saw earlier, settlement houses played major roles in organizing neighborhoods, studying social problems, making policy and program proposals, forming pressure groups, and conducting campaigns. Their efforts eventuated in changes that affected localities, states, and the nation.

Social workers such as Jane Addams and Lillian Wald were much involved in efforts to improve the quality of life in the United States. Following Addams's election as president of the National Conference of Charities and Corrections in 1909, a committee was appointed to undertake a study of the minimum requirements for well-being in an industrial society. In 1911, Florence Kelley, activist and general secretary of the National Consumers League, chaired the committee, followed, in 1912, by Owen Lovejoy, secretary of the National Child Labor Committee.

One outcome of this study was the minimum platform that was created in "Social Standards for Industry": the eight-hour workday, the six-day work week, abolition of tenement manufacture, improvement of housing conditions, prohibition of child labor under 16 years, regulation of employment for women, and a federal system of accident, old age, and unemployment insurance.[40] Social workers were in the forefront demanding new child labor laws, health and safety legislation, and social insurance, and on many issues were in the vanguard, helping to move the nation toward new social welfare ideas.

From these early beginnings to contemporary times, community organization efforts were conducted in many ways, including voluntary organizing efforts focused on the creation and implementation of health and welfare councils and community chests for communal fund-raising, planning, and coordination of services. Other efforts included grassroots organizing to improve the quality of life in neighborhoods through political power and the redress of problems; self-help and community-change organizations of African Americans, Latinos, and Asian Americans; Native American survival and community and tribal development; rural community organization related to electrification, access to water and other resources, mutual aid and cooperatives among rural residents, and the development of basic services such as schools and fire brigades, as well as unionization. Recent years have seen a growing emphasis on organizing by and for women, gays, and lesbians.

In 1939, the Lane Report emphasized community organization as a social work method and suggested that local welfare councils and other coordinating bodies all shared the purposes of local planning and coordination in order to seek the congruence of community social welfare resources and needs. During World War II, community organization was one part of the massive war effort, especially through the

U.S. Office of Civilian Defense and the Office of Defense, Health, and Welfare Services to coordinate health and welfare services, public and private, for defense-affected localities. Following World War II, community organization emphasized integrative efforts, consensus, and process-oriented models to increase the capacity for cooperation within society.[41]

Generally, community organization was a method that for a long time focused on cooperative efforts to organize efficiently the social services in a community. The basic methodology was consensual. Conflict was minimized and the attempt was made—as in intergroup work—to utilize a process that led to understanding and co-operation. The process was intended to be enabling in that rival entities could be helped to identify common goals and through cooperative efforts attain their respective goals and a better society.

By 1947, the Association for the Study of Community Organization published *Community Organization: Its Nature and Setting* to clarify issues, terms, roles, and methods.[42] In 1962, the Council on Social Work Education issued a curriculum policy statement identifying community organization as a major social work method.

During the 1960s, our society underwent great change in an atmosphere of participatory democracy. Community organization was an important contributor to efforts to overcome juvenile delinquency, to attain civil rights, and to develop communities through the War on Poverty and model cities programs. A major emphasis during this decade was on grassroots organizing and community participation and action.

Current community organizing efforts include the following models:

1. Neighborhood and community organizing, designed to develop the capacity of the members to organize and to improve the quality of life in the geographic area;
2. Organizing functional communities of like-minded people in a community, region, nation, or internationally to advocate for a particular issue or population;
3. Community social and economic development for improved income, resources, and social supports;
4. Social planning for citywide or regional proposals for governmental or human services;
5. Program and service development and community liaison for a specific population by improving service effectiveness and/or organizing new services;
6. Political and social action, building political power toward institutional change in order to change policy or policymakers;
7. Coalitions to influence program directions or to gain resources related to a specific issue, social need, or concern; and
8. Social movements, action toward social justice for a particular population group or issue.[43]

Among recent organizing efforts are community organizing for neighborhood and economic development, safe and drug-free schools and communities, anti-hunger, increased housing for persons of modest means, health promotion, violence and homicide, "living wage" campaigns, assuring bank loans in low-income neighborhoods, people with HIV/AIDS, development of small businesses, teen pregnancy, the homeless, and the environment and hazardous wastes in poor neighborhoods. Some groups focus on the creation of low-income housing and elections. Other efforts include ACORN (Association of Community Organizations for Reform Now), which developed out of the 1960s welfare rights movement and now organizes low-income neighborhood residents around housing and other issues with a direct action approach. Citizen Action places an emphasis on health questions and tenant organizing. Other groups organize around particular identities and focus on the civil rights of various groups: Latinos, women, gays and lesbians, disabled persons, and others. Self-help and mutual aid groups also organize related to addictions and other problems—Mothers Against Drunk Driving, Alcoholics Anonymous, and advocates for the homeless. There is a new ethnic politics and organization both within and between groups, some of which formerly were in conflict. Community organization efforts raise political consciousness, are training grounds for democracy, and focus on local issues, but organizing necessarily reaches beyond the local to regional, state, and national interventions.[44]

TOWARD A UNIFIED PROFESSION

Modern social work with individuals and families are the predominant social work methods and have remained in the practice mainstream of the profession, along with group work and community organization. But practitioners have evolved in all methods a plethora of continually expanding models for and approaches to working with people. Theories range from aboriginal theory to ego psychology, from feminist theory to neurolinguistic programming and transpersonal social work.[45]

The need to define a common core and common methodologies continues unabated in social work. Concern about the effect of forces that move away from a common core in the profession is often expressed as there continue to develop diverse types of social work practice. Graduate social work education prepares students for work in direct practice (individual, family, group), community organization and planning, administration or management, and combinations of direct practice and community organization and planning (or administration or management). The largest numbers of students are being prepared for work in mental health, family services, child welfare, school social work, and aging.[46] The types of concentrations increase, but simultaneously, there is a strong sense of concern that a generic core should be maintained for all social workers.

In the professionalization process, social work has created training programs, a professional association, and a code of ethics; is licensed or certified in all 50 states, the District of Columbia, Puerto Rico, and the Virgin Islands[47]; and has created a knowledge base. Notwithstanding these accomplishments and its rapid development and growth, social work is an insecure profession because of its status. This internally and externally generated status insecurity is in part related to social work's association with poor and problematic groups and to its championing unpopular causes, among other factors.

Social work continues to grow. In 1982, there were 88,000 members of the professional association and more than 384,000 social workers employed in the United States. By 1996, more than 745,000 persons were employed in social work positions, just short of doubling since 1982; and, as we have seen, the professional association in 1998 had 155,000 members.[48] The overwhelming majority of social workers are women. In chapter 13, we will examine their numbers and the role and status of women in the profession.

So social work as a profession in most respects seems to have very much completed the professionalization process with one important exception: that it does not control its varied "turf." Although some, even within the profession itself, may disagree with this assessment, society, through regulating sanctions, is moving forward in its recognition of social work as a profession. But there remain limits to the ability of the social work profession to control use of its name; and there are two streams of personnel, one professionally qualified and the other consisting of persons who are employed in social work positions but lacking professional education and credentials. Differentiating these two types of persons who occupy positions with social work titles remains problematic for the profession, and this ambiguity often is misunderstood by those not familiar with the profession.

Summary

In this chapter, we have examined the emergence and evolution of the social work profession. We turn next in chapter 13 to a discussion of the functions of the profession, the contexts in which it operates, and several major issues with which social work must deal.

Questions for Consideration

1. What do you think Jane Addams meant by the quotation with which this chapter opens?
2. How many kinds of social workers can you identify in your community?
3. Which would you choose as the better social work approach—charity organization society or settlement house?
4. What social work professional organizations are there in your community?

Notes

1. Jane Addams, *Twenty Years at Hull House*, New York: Macmillan, 1961, p. 92.
2. Karl de Schweinitz, *England's Road to Social Security*, New York: A. S. Barnes, 1975, pp. 30, 35–36; David M. Schneider, *The History of Public Welfare in New York State: 1609–1866*, Chicago: University of Chicago Press, 1938, p. 10.
3. Robert H. Bremner, "The Rediscovery of Pauperism," *Current Issues in Social Work Seen in Historical Perspective*, New York: Council on Social Work Education, 1962, p. 13.

4. de Schweinitz, pp. 100–113.
5. Dorothy G. Becker, "The Visitor to the New York City Poor, 1843–1920," *Social Service Review*, Vol. 35, No. 4, December 1961, pp. 382–396. Also see Brian Gratton, "The Invention of Social Work: Welfare Reform in the Antebellum City," *The Urban and Social Change Review*, Vol. 18, No. 1, Winter 1985, pp. 3–8.
6. Robert H. Bremner, *From the Depths*, New York: New York University Press, 1967, p. 43.
7. Victoria Olds, "The Freedmen's Bureau: A Nineteenth-Century Federal Welfare Agency," *Social Casework*, Vol. 44, No. 5, May 1963, pp. 247–254.
8. Frank J. Bruno, *Trends in Social Work*, New York: Columbia University Press, 1948, p. 11.
9. Frank D. Watson, *The Charity Organization Movement in the United States*, New York: Macmillan, 1922, pp. 178–179.
10. Roy Lubove, *The Professional Altruist*, New York: Atheneum, 1971, p. 8.
11. Ralph E. Pumphrey and Muriel W. Pumphrey, eds., *The Heritage of American Social Work*, New York: Columbia University Press, 1965, p. 170.
12. Judith A. Trolander, *Professionalism and Social Change: From the Settlement House Movement to Neighborhood Centers 1886 to the Present*, New York: Columbia University Press, 1987, pp. 12–13.
13. Ruth Bordin, *Woman and Temperance: The Quest for Power and Liberty, 1873–1900*, Philadelphia: Temple University Press, pp. 13, 98; Kathryn K. Sklar, "The "Quickened Conscience": Women's Voluntarism and the State, 1890–1920," *Philosophy & Public Policy*, Vol. 18, No. 3, Summer 1998, pp. 27–33.
14. Trolander, pp. 176–181; Thorstein Veblen, *The Theory of the Leisure Class*, New York: Modern Library, 1934 (Original, 1899), pp. 339, 344.
15. Dorothy G. Becker, "Social Welfare Leaders as Spokesmen for the Poor," *Social Casework*, Vol. 49, No. 2, February 1968, p. 85.
16. Clarke A. Chambers, *Seedtime of Reform*, Minneapolis, Minn.: University of Minnesota Press, 1963, p. 15.
17. Nathan Cohen, *Social Work in the American Tradition*, New York: Holt, Rinehart, and Winston, 1958, p. 71.
18. Donald Feldstein, "Do We Need Professions in Our Society? Professionalization Versus Consumerism," *Social Work*, Vol. 16, No. 4, October 1971, pp. 5–11, and Ronald M. Pavalko, *Sociology of Occupations and Professions*, Itasca, Ill.: F. E. Peacock, 1971, p. 277.
19. U.S. Bureau of the Census, *Statistical Abstract of the United States: 1997*, 117th edition, Table 645, "Employed Civilians, by Occupation, Sex, Race, and Hispanic Origin," Washington, D.C., 1997, p. 410.
20. George Silvestri and John Lukasiewicz, "Projections of Occupational Employment, 1988–2000," *Monthly Labor Review*, Bureau of Labor Statistics, November 1989, p. 43.
21. Lubove, p. 46.
22. Ibid., p. 48.
23. Addams, p. 167.
24. *Proceedings of the National Conference of Charities and Corrections*, Press of Fred J. Heer, 1905, p. 577.
25. Abraham Flexner, "Is Social Work a Profession?" in *Proceedings of the National Conference of Charities and Corrections*, 1915, pp. 576–590.
26. Pumphrey and Pumphrey, p. 306. Nathan Cohen suggested the search for method came at a time when the profession was eagerly trying to rebut the criticisms of Flexner and at

the same time that psychoanalytic thought was making inroads into American culture. Cohen, pp. 120–121.

27. Scott Briar, "Social Casework and Social Group Work: Historical Foundations," *Encyclopedia of Social Work*, Vol. 2, New York: National Association of Social Workers, 1971, p. 1239.

28. Jane Addams, *The Second Twenty Years at Hull House*, New York: Macmillan, 1930, p. 155.

29. The rise of psychoanalytically oriented casework parallels a movement away from social reform. The climate of the times militated against such efforts. But psychoanalytic thought helped veer social work's understanding of people in difficulty, moving it away from the idea that people with difficulties simply lacked character to an understanding of psychological stress and disability. See Herman Borenzweig, "Social Work and Psychoanalytic Theory: An Historical Analysis," *Social Work*, Vol. 16, No. 1, January 1971, pp. 7–16. However, Leslie Alexander suggested that Freudian theory was little known to social workers and had an influence limited to the professional elite rather than the major part of the profession. Alexander suggests social workers used a more sociological than psychoanalytical approach during the 1920s and also that social reform debates and demands continued in relation to women's rights, child welfare, unemployment, housing reform, and the need for federal action on public assistance and social insurance. Because of the nature of the times, major social reforms had to await the 1930s. Leslie B. Alexander, "Social Work's Freudian Deluge: Myth or Reality?" *Social Service Review*, Vol. 46, No. 4, December 1972, pp. 517–538.

30. *Social Casework: Generic and Specific*, New York: American Association of Social Workers, 1929, Classic Series, Washington, D.C.: National Association of Social Workers, 1974, p. 15.

31. Jacob Fisher, *The Response of Social Work to the Depression*, Cambridge, Mass.: Schenkman, 1980, pp. 233–241.

32. Donald Brieland, "History and Evolution of Social Work Practice," *Encyclopedia of Social Work*, Vol. I, 18th Edition, Anne Minahan, ed., Silver Spring, Md.: National Association of Social Workers, p. 747.

33. *Encyclopedia of Social Work*, Vol. 2, Washington, D.C.: National Association of Social Workers, 1977, p. 1670, and personal communication from Josephine Nieves, Executive Director, NASW, July, 1998.

34. Sandra Jasczak, ed., *Encyclopedia of Associations 1996*, Vol. 1, Detroit: Gale Research Inc., 1996.

35. Scott Briar, "Social Casework and Social Group Work: Historical and Social Science Foundations," *Encyclopedia of Social Work*, Vol. 2, New York: National Association of Social Workers, 1971, pp. 1237–1245.

36. *Social Case Work: Generic and Specific*, p. 78.

37. Beulah Rothman and Catherine Papell, "Social Group Work Models: Possession and Heritage," *Journal of Education for Social Work*, Vol. 2, No. 2, Fall 1966, pp. 66–77.

38. Janice H. Schopler and Maeda J. Galinsky "Group Practice Overview," *Encyclopedia of Social Work*, Vol. 2, Washington, D.C.: National Association of Social Workers, 1995, pp. 1129–1142.

39. Charles D. Garvin and Beth Glover Reed, "Sources and Visions for Feminist Group Work," in *Feminist Practice in the 21st Century*, Nan Van Den Bergh, ed., Washington, D.C.: NASW Press, 1995, pp. 41–69.

40. Allen F. Davis, *Spearheads for Reform: The Social Settlements and the Progressive Movement: 1890–1914*, New York: Oxford University Press, 1967, p. 196.

41. Donald S. Howard, ed., *Community Organization: Its Nature and Setting*, New York: American Association of Social Workers, 1947.

42. Ibid.

43. Si Kahn, "Community Organization," *Encyclopedia of Social Work*, Vol. I, Washington, D.C.: National Association of Social Workers, 1995, pp. 569–576; Marie Overby Weil and Dorothy N. Gamble, "Community Practice Models," *Community Organization: Its Nature and Setting*, Donald S. Howard, ed., New York: American Association of Social Workers, pp. 577–594.

44. Robert Fisher, *Let the People Decide*: *Neighborhood Organizing in America*, New York: Twayne Publishers, 1994; S.M. Miller, Martin Rein, and Peggy Levitt, "Community Action in the United States," *Community Empowerment*, Gary Craig, ed., Atlantic Highlands, N.J.: Zed Books, 1995, pp. 112–126.

45. Francis J. Turner, *Social Work Treatment*, 4th Edition, New York: The Free Press, 1996.

46. Todd M. Lennon, *Statistics on Social Work Education in the United States: 1997*, Alexandria, Va.: Council on Social Work Education, pp. 80, 83.

47. American Association of State Social Work Boards, *Social Work Laws and Board Regulations: A State Comparison Study, 1995 Edition*, Culpeper, Va., 1995.

48. U.S. Bureau of the Census, *Statistical Abstract of the United States: 1997*, 117th Edition, "Employed Civilians, by Occupation, Sex, Race, and Hispanic Origin: 1983 and 1996," Washington, D.C., 1997, p. 410.

CHAPTER THIRTEEN

Social Work: Functions, Context, and Issues

*But it is perfectly alright to say that in Darwin's world individuals always act
in their own interests and the bald principle holds but it is no longer quite
clear what an individual is. Groups and societies are individuals too. And I
think therefore the growing ties among us, that universal brother- and
sisterhood to which we aspire, is perfectly good biology, and
the enlarged notion of individuality is not just outdated liberal
hope or mushy romanticism.*
—Stephen J. Gould[1]

OVERVIEW

In this chapter we examine the functions of social work, the context within which
social work is practiced, and issues arising from their interaction. Among the topics
explored are the purposes of social work and the relationship between professionals
and the organizations in which they practice, including issues related to authority
and professional autonomy. Private practice as an alternative to organization-based
practice is considered, as well as social work's relationship to its assigned societal
functions. The evolution of the "cause" (social reform) track and the "function" (case
services) track and the historical tensions between the generic and specialized
thrusts of social work are explored. The profession is also reviewed in the context of
racism, sexism, and a pluralistic society.

THE PURPOSES OF SOCIAL WORK

Social work as a profession is committed to the enhancement of human well-being,
to the alleviation of poverty and oppression, and to "raising life to its highest
value."[2] The profession receives its sanction from public and private auspices and

323

implements its purposes through a broad variety of interventions in practice. The purposes of social work are as follows:

1. The promotion, restoration, maintenance, and enhancement of the social functioning of individuals, families, groups, organizations, and communities by helping them to accomplish goals, prevent and alleviate distress, and use resources;
2. The planning, formulation, and implementation of social policies, services, resources, and programs needed to meet basic human needs and support the development of human capacities;
3. The pursuit of policies, services, resources, and programs through organizational or administrative advocacy and social or political action, to empower groups at risk and to promote social and economic justice; and
4. The development and testing of professional knowledge and skills related to these purposes.[3]

There is practically no institution (e.g., education, defense, health, justice, religion) in our society that is without social workers, because social and human problems affect every institution and, in turn, these same institutions affect individuals, families, groups, and communities. Social workers are employed under public and private auspices on the local, state, regional, national, as well as international level. Some social workers are self-employed private practitioners.

Social workers assist persons, groups, and communities to cope with a multiplicity of issues, covering most of the social problems people experience. The tasks needed to implement the aims of social work include an array of activities ranging from counseling to research, from organizing to administering, and from planning to legislative advocacy.

Several brief examples can give a sense of social workers in action. Suppose a person encountered a series of social and psychological setbacks, including loss of job, serious illness in the family, depleted funds, and conflicts within the family that seem to derive from stress. A social worker would attempt with the client to select from all the client's problems which to focus on and to work on them in order of priority with the person(s) involved. This could mean assistance in finding work, in dealing with hospital or medical personnel, and in assisting the family with its interpersonal problems through social work counseling.

A social worker employed by a community development agency may discover a large number of young adult men and women in the neighborhood who do not have jobs. Because of much time on their hands, frustration, and resultant anger, they are involved in a series of destructive acts, against both themselves and society. Social workers may work with employers, city or county agencies, and other organizations to create jobs, training programs, reentry into schools, and other needed resources. A social worker also may help to form groups of such young people to help them work on personal and family difficulties and in other ways to help them reach their legitimate goals.

Social workers in a family service agency may organize services for aging persons who live isolated and lonely lives, have difficulty shopping, and eat poorly. They may help by arranging homemaker services, organizing a volunteer group that visits with isolated persons and renders simple assistance, organizing shopping assistance, or establishing a Meals-on-Wheels program for those unable to prepare hot meals for themselves.

THE PROFESSIONAL WITHIN THE ORGANIZATIONAL CONTEXT

The goals, roles, and actions of a social worker are in major part determined by his or her position in the organization, and the functions that he or she can carry out are heavily influenced by the policies and structure of the organization, whether governmental, nonprofit, or private. There are limitations on the worker's actions that result from working within a complex organization, and there are strengths for social service that derive from the organizational setting for social work practice.

Social workers typically work in organizations that frequently encounter problems that are not well understood, are unpredictable and of uncertain quality, cannot be treated as routine, and are nonrepetitive. Rue Bucher and Joan Stelling report on the contradictions between hierarchical, "top-down," chain-of-command systems and the delivery of services by professionals. They make the point that professionals derive their aims and methods from professional bodies. Their work requires a certain independence, and there is often a conflict between the requirements of the organizational system and the values of the professional. As a result, in professional organizations, these types of employees need to exert considerable measures of control and influence over their own sectors of the organization and over the goals and policy making of the organization. However, there simply are no ideal models of professional organizations by which to balance these differing values.[4]

Social work practice deals with diverse social situations, each human situation being different from all others. There simply cannot be universal rules established by which all or most situations are treated the same, for each situation requires individualized service. When faced with unique situations that have unpredictable qualities, quality service requires professional judgment and an organization that is flexible enough in its use of resources to serve persons whose problems cannot be pigeonholed.

THE PROFESSIONAL WITHIN COMPLEX ORGANIZATIONS

As our society becomes more complex and interdependent, as business and other organizations grow in size, there has been more employment within complex organizations, even by professions that in the past have been noted for their "free" stances. Sociologists studying the professions point out this increased organizational employment by professionals: Physicians are now affiliated in larger numbers with hospitals and health maintenance organizations; attorneys with law firms and, in increasing numbers, with industrial corporations; scientists and engineers with industry, government, large independent research organizations, and a collection of institutes and departments in academic institutions.[5]

Professions and complex organizations are intricately tied, but there are real problems for social workers as professionals as they function within these complicated human networks. Essentially these problems can be categorized into two areas: (1) the relationship between organizational structure and professional culture and (2) the structure of authority.

Complex Organizations and Professional Culture

Alfred Kahn suggested that organizational factors and realities may supersede professional ethics. Overall professional and organizational perspectives affect the ways in which a problem is perceived and structured, the values that are held supreme, the priorities given to components of and the sequences in a solution to a person's or family's difficulties, and the "costs" to be tolerated for given outcomes or benefits.[6]

The effects of professional identity within a complex organization include subtle issues. For example, Robert Vinter makes the point that when professionals are present in large numbers and assume elite positions, the organization's dependence on them brings with it limiting commitment to particular ideologies and strategies of change. Alternative approaches are thus denied the organization except as these are mediated through the profession. The risk is that the approaches defined by one or another profession may not be sufficient for achievement of treatment goals, yet the organization is no longer as free to pursue alternative means.[7]

Complex Organizations and Authority

Professional identity and perspectives cause the selection of particular intervention strategies. Generalized professional knowledge and identity, however, are expressed in the individual case. It is here that individual professions may enter areas of potential conflict with their superiors in the hierarchical arrangements in the bureaucracy. Amitai Etzioni suggested that a basic administrative principle is thus put in jeopardy because knowledge is largely an individual property, not the property of the organization; unlike other organizational resources, it cannot be transferred from one person to another by decree. Creativity is basically individual and can only to a very limited degree be ordered and coordinated by the superior in rank. Even the application of knowledge is basically an individual act, at least in the sense that individual professionals have the ultimate responsibility for their professional decisions. Only if immune from ordinary social pressures and free to innovate, to experiment, to take risks without the usual social repercussions of failure, can a professional carry out his or her work effectively.[8]

But these are requirements that are difficult for a complex organization to accept, not only because of internal accountability but because of accountability to the wider community. Peer support for professional experimentation or decision making is one thing, but administrative responsibility and accountability run counter to such freedoms.

The longer the training and the more intense the professional orientation, the greater the tendency to take as one's reference group the profession rather than the employer.[9] This, too, runs counter to a demand of complex organizations. In social agencies or other organizations one method of standardizing the discretionary component in the work is to make rules. Another method is to reduce the number of written rules by employing personnel who have complex rules *built into them*. We generally call these people "professionals."[10] Thus social agencies, when possible, hire professionals to ensure high standards and the delivery of high-quality service. But, paradoxically, being professional in itself runs counter to organizational demands while it meets the need for narrowing the outer limits of discretion through professional training. Perhaps the critical issue is who controls which aspects of daily professional practice.

The Profession and Professional Autonomy

The problem as posed in the preceding section is to reconcile professional autonomy with bureaucratic demands. Willard Richan pondered this question and placed the dilemma in a different context: The individual worker must be viewed within the context not only of the agency and the profession, but the agency *and* worker must be viewed within the context of the profession within the social welfare or other societal institution. The power of the social work profession depends on the cohesion of the profession. Richan suggests "the issues of professional autonomy and professional cohesion are closely related. To achieve the former, the organized social work profession must demonstrate the latter; that is, its ability to speak for the social work community. And both of these depend, in turn, on effective control over social work practice and the social work education process."[11]

Paradoxically, the attainment of greater autonomy for social workers is tied to greater controls. The regulation of practice, control over who practices and the conditions for practice, and licensing and "enforceable expectations"—that is, greater regulation of social workers—is the means for achieving greater autonomy.

An issue that highlights the question of autonomy is social reform and social work's role in it. Social reform is one part of the social work tradition. However, as Kathleen Woodroofe asserted, the struggle to gain professional acceptance in the community accentuated some of the stresses within social work itself. Some of these stresses spring from attempts to fix rightful boundaries to its domain; others from efforts to define its function to new areas and settings. Some spring from limitations of its knowledge and experience; others arise from the nature of its own activity. But perhaps the most serious source of stress has been the attempt to reconcile the caution of professionalism with social work's traditional commitment to reform.[12]

There are other more pedestrian problems and dysfunctions of complex organizations. For example, the specialization of social workers within an organization means task specialization. Such specialization increases the quality and quantity of work, but it also may lead to discrete responsibilities and areas of service. When this occurs, it is often accompanied by disjunctions among the several services available, and people who need service may fall through the cracks.

Work within organizations is accompanied by frustration, lack of congruence between individual and organizational needs, skewed time perspectives, rivalry, and conflict. To the extent that these attitudinal effects carry over into work with clients, members, and others who come for service, they may be dysfunctional in regard to services.

Supervision as frequently conducted in social agencies also plays a part in the professional's self-image, and not entirely as a negative factor. Close supervision may allow "caseworkers to maintain their conception of themselves as professionals in a manner not possible under the more direct control attempts associated with the bureaucratic approach."[13]

Alternative Roles and Settings

A growing literature has developed aimed at understanding organizational settings and developing ways of operating successfully within them.[14] The range of options available runs from less active and dramatic roles for the social workers to conscious and planned efforts to alter the agencies in order to improve services. Others suggest the need for organizations that decentralize decision making, practice participative management, and are more adaptable and responsive to their members.

According to some social workers, the trend toward private practice is a key lever to offset the forces of bureaucracy that act on social workers. The private practice of social work and employment in private profit making organizations are, indeed, important components of contemporary professional practice. However, when those directions are selected by many, a question can be raised about the social commitment and philosophy of the profession.

To the extent that social workers become private practitioners, they delimit the communal (societal) sanction they receive through social welfare and other sponsoring organizations. Social sponsorship and commitment have been important factors in the development of social work's professional identity. According to some observers, tendencies away from the social commitment of the profession lead to a deemphasis on social action, acceptance of the role of technician-implementer in contrast to policy changer, and an increase in the congruence between social workers' ideas and those of the dominant groups in society.[15] Thus, complex organizations, although subject to criticism, may be better settings for social workers to engage in social change and social action than some of the alternatives offered.

SOCIETY, THE FUNCTIONS OF SOCIAL WORK, AND SERVICES FOR PEOPLE

Society sets certain demands and limits on the profession. Nevertheless, the parameters of social work have been vigorously debated within the social work community. Essentially, the question is, how many functions of social work should there be: rehabilitation, prevention, provision of resources, enhancing human rights, or social justice? The major functions expected of social work determine how social workers must be prepared to implement them.

From one perspective, all roles performed by social work can be viewed as deriving from two basic societal functions: social control and social change. Society assigns the functions of social welfare, and therefore of social work, in formal and informal ways. Various sanctioning bodies provide that social welfare agencies and social workers will perform specific functions, and these bodies typically determine how these functions will be implemented. These sanctions derive not only from consumer demand but also from legislation, funding, and other formal and informal sources. Thus, the roles and functions of social workers are dependent on the priorities set by society through various control mechanisms. In addition, social agencies themselves exert control over the work of social workers in several ways, including identifying populations to be served, services to be provided, and methods of service. Thus, not only are social control mechanisms manifested through social agencies that wish to socialize clients to dominant societal values, but more subtle controls are expressed through the choice of methods and technologies to be used.

Finally, both on philosophical and empirical grounds, there are social workers who suggest that any profession that focuses primarily on individual change cannot be truly focused on social change. According to this view, individual change is simply inconsistent with the demands of social change and, in reality, such an approach is more consistent with social control. To this group, the fact that social work maintains its clinical, individual, and family focus suggests not social change but social control as the higher professional value.

The "Bottom Line"

Social workers are not "free agents" who can choose whether they wish to be part of a profession of social control or of social change. Regardless of whether the profession operates within organizational settings or as an entrepreneurial service, it is dependent on the sanctions of society. In addition to whatever limitations exist as to knowledge needed for social change or the choices of interventions, social work can only make choices within certain limits. Societies do not hire "social change" agents; rather they hire persons who can perform important functions that serve the society.

THE TWO TRACKS OF SOCIAL WORK: CAUSE AND FUNCTION

In regard to the roles of social workers, a historical tension exists between two tracks of social work that have survived in an uneasy alliance. These two streams have been described variously as *cause* and *function* and, respectively, as the social reform and case service tracks. Almost from the inception of social work, the two tracks came to be associated with particular persons and institutions. The function or *case service* track, which developed from the work of Thomas Chalmers as translated to the United States, is ordinarily associated with the friendly visitors of charity organization societies. The cause or *social reform* track is associated with the settlement houses and social workers involved in seeking better environmental conditions through legislation and other means. The function track is best represented in the United States by Mary Richmond, who developed early casework theory and techniques, and the cause track by Jane Addams, who, as a settlement house founder and director, was active in social reform.

These two tracks reflect separate and different conceptions, and yet the social work profession remains intact. Why this is the case is an important question. Historically the dichotomy—the two tracks—arises in different forms and under different names. During the 1890s, there was hostility toward settlement houses and their workers at the National Conference on Charities and Corrections. Originally formed by volunteers who created neighborhood service centers in the midst of poor neighborhoods, the settlement houses and their leadership focused not only on services to individuals, families, and neighborhoods, but also on changing society and the world in which the poor existed. They were not confident of their acceptance by others in the field of social welfare. In 1897, Addams apologized for being at the national conference because "settlements are accused of doing their charity work very badly."[16]

Through her writings and work, Addams represented the social reform track. On the basis of her experiences, she recognized a multicausation for social ills, a fact that suggested multifocused action was needed to change life conditions. In regard to this multicausation in life she stated:

> The settlements have often been accused of scattering their forces; as institutions they are both philanthropic and educational; in their approach to social problems they call now upon the sociologists, now upon the psychiatrist; they seek the services of artists, economists, gymnasts, caseworkers, dramatists, trained nurses. . . . [in order to deal with] bewildering legal requirements, ill health and conflicting cultures which the settlements find so baffling.[17]

Representative of the case service track in social work, Mary Richmond was employed in charity organization societies in Baltimore and Philadelphia, formulated the first global statements of the principles of social casework, taught at the New York School of Philanthropy, and was the author of *Social Diagnosis* (1917), the first formulation of the theory and method of social casework.[18] From the start, the social workers at charity organizations were investigating each needy person and family in detail, attempting to avoid duplication of benefits of any kind, seeking cooperation among agencies, and fostering the use of friendly visitors.

Very early in its development the case service track had an individual and family focus, based on the character of the individual, the relationship with the people to be helped, and a search for technique. On the other hand, the social reform track, while serving individuals, families, and neighborhoods, also stressed more global change through political action, publicity of social problems, legislation, and a greater emphasis on the surroundings in which people lived. This stream of social workers was doing the preliminary work to attain workers' compensation, health insurances, and mothers' pensions, and generally worked to prepare for the financial and other protection of workers and their families.[19]

Thus, in its early stages, social work contained several different kinds of social workers. They were employed or served as volunteers in a wide variety of situations. They were based in settlement houses and focused on societal changes. They were employed as administrators and friendly visitors in charity organization societies, constructing a method for helping individuals and families. They were crafting and lobbying for the preliminary social insurances and for other social legislation.

Despite the differences in emphasis, spokespersons for the two tracks (social reform and case services) agreed there were commonalities between the two tracks, and each had need for the complementary actions of the other. In *Social Diagnosis*, Richmond concluded that the majority of social workers were in casework: "in work, that is, which has for its immediate aim the betterment of individuals or families, one by one, as distinguished from their betterment in the mass. Mass betterment and individual betterment are interdependent, however, social reform and social case work of necessity progressing together."[20]

Various people struggled with this conundrum. In 1929, Porter R. Lee, director of the New York School of Philanthropy, in his presidential address to the National Conference of Social Work, provided a perspective on the tensions that existed between the social reform and the case service aspects of the profession and suggested that social work was both *cause* and *function*. He defined cause as a "movement directed toward the elimination of an entrenched evil"; a function he viewed as an "organized effort incorporated into the machinery of community life in the discharge of which the acquiescence at least, and ultimately the support, of the entire community is assumed."[21]

Thus, Lee defined these two aspects of social work as overlapping and symbiotic; they also were parts of an historical process through which society and social work both change.

> Social work . . . is cause as well as function. Much of what we do in social work we do because, on the whole, we prefer a civilization in which such things are done to one in which they are not. Some values are beyond measurement. . . . Efficient social work everywhere means the constant discovery of new evils, of ancient evils in new forms which are taking their toll of men. Good social work creates the necessity for more social work.[22]

In a catchy phrase, Clarke Chambers offered another way of viewing these two social work tracks: He called them the *"retail"* and the *"wholesale"* services; not only do the two tracks differ in regard to cause or function, but they also differ in regard to the size of the population unit to which they give emphasis and in regard to the roles their professionals play. He suggested that

> the two overlapping phases of social work continue to exist, not always harmoniously, but certainly in interdependence—the one focused on the individual and his or her welfare, strongly influenced by the psychological disciplines, introspective, dealing in personalized retail services; the other concerned with reform, with reconstruction, informed primarily by the social sciences, extroverted, dealing in group or community or wholesale services.[23]

Chambers went further and suggested the two tracks of social work require two different major roles: *priest* and *prophet*. The priest is a "shepherd, he serves, he counsels, he comforts, he reconciles, he listens, he accepts, he judges not, he plays out a ritualistic role, he bears witness to a transcendent concern." The prophet, on the other hand, "holds up absolute standards against which the sins of man and the shortcomings of the world may be measured and judged; his cry is less for charity and compassion than for justice; he is not content merely to stand and serve; repentance and reform or doom is his prophecy."[24]

But the argument as to cause and function, case services or social reform, is dismissed by those who suggest that the different methodologies of social work are all conservative, social control forces, the only differentiation being which level of society is addressed for intervention. Some suggest that casework operates on a sociopsychological view insufficiently related to the societal roots of people's dilemmas and therefore cannot develop strategies equal to making social change. Furthermore, community organization—even through the more radical of its historical interventions—also serves as a conservative force in that whatever changes it accomplishes do not lead to change in the basic structures of society. Others argue that specialization, elitism, and career structures result in professionalism, which serves the dominant class of society.

In recent years, feminist practice emerged to challenge the assumptions and roles of social work based on five principles: eliminating false dichotomies and artificial separations, reconceptualizing power, valuing process equally with product, the validity of renaming, and making the personal political.[25] Feminist practice requires understanding women's lives and experiences, the nature of inequality between the sexes, and the structuring of gender. This type of practice centers on the connections among gender, privilege, social class, culture, sexuality, and the concept of self, thus close attention must be paid to the effects of the social context on the difficulties of the client. Included in feminist practice is a revaluing of behaviors often performed by women, recognizing differences in male and female experiences, rebalancing perceptions of normality and deviance, an inclusive stance, attention to power dynamics, recognizing the personal is political, and empowerment practice.[26] Such a practice focuses on personal and political transformation because personal problems arise from the failures of society. Feminist social work is concerned not just with the problems of patriarchy but "with *all* institutionalized systems and ideologies of domination/subordination, exploitation, and oppression that are inimical to individual and collective self-actualization."[27]

These arguments call for the politicization of social work as a profession. The early social workers of the progressive era took political stands and affected party platforms and legislation to significant extents. Still later, other social workers influenced decision makers and legislation. Over the years, however, as Daniel Moynihan suggested, there arose the "professionalization of reform."[28] This implies a certain objectivity and attention to professional expertise rather than investment in the movement aspects of the professional aims and their achievement. Ideology can be a resource and lead social workers toward the achievement of social reform or help to veer social work onto new professional paths. It is possible that more radical professional stances, including alliances with particular political parties, could serve to create new roles for social workers as their functions change. This might be one method of combining the cause and function dichotomies into unique, new professional configurations. However, the alliance with particular political parties or ideologies is a two-edged sword, which also can cause losses. Given the existence of a democratic United States in which parties move in and out of power, it appears more likely that on balance social work will not choose to become overly identified with one party or to cut off its links with any party or ideology that has the potential of helping create better services for people.

Some social workers have attempted to create pathways out of the two-track dilemma through new methods and new types of professionalism. Others have attempted to reconcile the differences through redefining traditional methods, so that the connections between the two tracks stand out.

William Schwartz, in attempting to reconcile the two tracks, reminds us that certain human dichotomies seem always with us: mass or individual betterment, process or goals, individual or state, freedom or discipline. The emphasis is always on the choice—either one or the other. But, as he suggests, the choices once made seem incomplete. Schwartz joins private troubles and public issues through the mediating role of the social worker. The mediating process between individuals and society—the engagements of people with their systems—are real struggles in which both can change. The professional role of social workers is to help change the nature of individuals and of the society through these engagements, thus tying societal and individual change (cause and function) together.[29]

Another effort to resolve the dilemma revolves around the issue of generalist practice. In generalist practice, the social worker maintains a focus on the interaction among systems—the person/family, their environment, and their transactions. The situation determines the particular practice approach to be used by the social worker. This requires that social workers have a broad knowledge and skill base from which to serve clients or client systems.[30] Through generalist practice, an eclectic knowledge base, professional values, and a wide range of skills social workers are enabled to target any size system.[31] In this way, generalist practice combines the element of cause with the element of function.

Roy Lubove suggested another possible explanation as to why the disparate elements within the profession hold together. Casework, that is, case services, was a key to "a knowledge base and helping technique more 'scientific' and hence more professional." However, "if social work could claim any distinctive function in an atomized urban society with serious problems of group communication and mass deprivation, it was not individual therapy but liaison between groups and the stimulation of social legislation and institutional change" which offers that unique function. Agreeing with Abraham Flexner that social work's unique feature is its "traffic cop" function, Lubove suggests that the clinical case services offer social work a baseline for practice while reform gives the profession its uniqueness, and the two—cause and function, social reform and case services—together form a team that provides the profession with a territory, the arena of social welfare. The functional specialty is needed to give social work a professional image and base, and the cause element is needed to give it distinction from the other therapeutic or helping professions.[32]

But using what is known about cases to move to causes is not simply a matter of differentiating social work from other professions. Advocacy offers a way for agencies and staffs to bridge the gap between the many cases of individual and family need and grievances against social institutions and the broader-scale actions needed to bring about institutional change. The social worker's intimate knowledge of individual families provides a grassroots basis for social action improving the social environment of families.[33]

Generic-Specific Social Work

Even within the relatively homogeneous case services stream of social work, there were and are questions of generic skills, knowledge, and attitudes applicable to a broad variety of practice settings. Simultaneously there were counterforces demanding specific training for specific agencies and fields of practice.

Social work historically juggled tensions between generic and specific qualities just as it has between cause and function. The price of being able to practice in a wide variety of settings (functional diffusion) and the required generic qualities was the workers' limited sense of identity as social workers and a limited sense of the totality of the profession as social work. The more practice settings there are, the more difficult it is to achieve a common professional identity. Constant, in addition, was the early-identified problem of educating workers equally prepared for work in several fields.

In the 1929 monograph *Social Casework: Generic and Specific*, these issues moved to the fore. A work group (the Milford Conference) struggled with the generic and specific aspects and the issues that underlay the concepts. Their work commenced from

> a recognition of the importance of the problems of division of labor among case work agencies. This, again, was not a new question. It furnished material for discussion for a generation. After a generation's discussion, however, it seemed to the group that dividing lines between the specific fields of social case work were still lacking, as well as the fundamental principles underlying the practical working divisions among the case work agencies of the community.[34]

But it was not simply a question of division of labor. The different philosophies (for example, cause or function) and different methodologies (specialized or generic) raised bothersome but important questions. In 1936, Sophonisba Breckenridge, a professor at the University of Chicago, reported the problem and drew attention to its importance. In an article on professional education for social work, she remarked:

> Another subject on which agreement has been slowly developing is the generalized, as over against the specialized, nature of the desirable curriculum. Some schools, possibly because of the nature of their origin, provided instruction in family welfare, in child welfare, and in group work, organizing the instruction in fields quite distinct from the others. On the other hand, some schools have taken the position from the beginning that their responsibility was the education of persons who should enter a field of social work, thus recognizing the probability of a worker's passing from one area in the field to another.[35]

With a social worker's passage from one field of service to another or entry into new settings, the profession became *functionally diffuse* (social workers function in many settings with many different sets of skills to meet many different kinds of needs). This fact, on the one hand, creates problems for the profession, mainly relating to issues of education and professional identification: What are the commonalities of social workers trained in diverse ways who practice in even more diverse settings?

On the other hand, the fact that the profession is functionally diffuse and of a generalized nature allows for the entry of social workers into many different types of employment and service settings. The functionally generalized nature of the profession also makes it possible for it to bring knowledge and skills when the society alters its major concerns or new problems arise. Social work has been quite successful at entering new fields and making contributions. This flexibility is the positive side of the functionally diffuse nature of the profession.

While some view the diversity of social work as a drawback, it can be viewed as an important strength or, even more, as an unplanned strategy related to the achievement of widespread social services. The fact that the profession plays an important intermediary role among different institutions makes it possible for the profession to help people meet varying needs.

Another positive attribute derives from functional diffusion. It has been suggested that specialized roles in organizations allow professionals to carry out their activities with a greater degree of freedom than would be the case where substructures and roles are more generalized. The autonomy of a professional in an organization is supported by the differentiation of roles and consequent specialization.[36] By analogy, the social work profession also may function in this manner. Specialization tends to support the autonomy of separate divisions of the profession. However, problems of communication, influence, and cooperation may be created because of a lack of a common language and the resistance of different camps to accept the views of others.

Despite the difficulties of diverse preparation and functional diffusion and despite the problems related to professional identity, it is clear that the development of the profession and services for people have been encouraged by this diffuse/diverse feature of the profession. Although difficulties arise, they seem on balance to be outweighed by the gains for society and for the profession.

Ambiguity, complexity, fluidity, and differing assumptions along with multiple and varying visions of the nature of social work practice lead to a plurality of practice modes and theories. In an attempt to prepare social workers with common knowledge and skills, the Council on Social Work Education has required educational programs to implement a generic foundation. The generic foundation includes a liberal arts base, specific social work knowledge such as social work's purpose, the focus of social work on the person in the environment, professionalism, sanction to practice, values and philosophy, basic communication and helping skills, ethnic and diversity sensitivity, the change process, and understanding of human relationships. These core (generic) elements serve as the base for generalist practice—the ability to assess situations, choose the appropriate means of intervening, and to intervene as a worker who possesses a wide variety of skills and/or for specialty practice organized around fields of service, population groups, problem areas, or practice roles and interventive modes.[37]

PROFESSIONALS AND VOLUNTEERS

Social work is organized formally with two academic entry points to the profession: baccalaureate and graduate. As of 1995, the Council on Social Work Education (CSWE) put into effect a new *Curriculum Policy Statement* (CPS, 1992) and *Accreditation Standards and Procedures* (1994) for baccalaureate degree and master's degree programs. The purposes of social work as described in the CPS earlier were introduced in this chapter in the section "The Purposes of Social Work."

The baccalaureate level prepares graduates for generalist social work practice. Master's-level social work education equips graduates with advanced practice skills together with concentrations organized along various lines: fields of service, population groups, problem areas, professional roles, interventive modes, and advanced generalist practice. All social work practice is expected to take place within a configuration of social work values and ethics. Among the values practitioners are expected to understand and utilize are as follows:

- Respect for individual worth and dignity, mutual participation, acceptance, confidentiality, honesty, and responsible handling of conflict;
- Respect for each individual's right to make independent decisions and to participate actively in the helping process;
- Assist client systems to obtain needed resources;
- Strive to make social institutions more humane and responsive to human needs; and
- Demonstrate respect for and acceptance of the unique characteristics of diverse populations.

It is expected that social workers will be responsible for their own ethical conduct (based on the Code of Ethics of the National Association of Social Workers), the quality of their practice, and to seek continuous growth in the knowledge and skills of their profession.

In addition to content on human behavior and the social environment, social welfare policy and services, social work practice, and research, the CPS places important emphases on the following:

- The preparation of students to understand and appreciate human *diversity*, including groups distinguished by race, ethnicity, culture, class, gender, sexual orientation, religion, physical or mental ability, age, and national origin;
- Understanding the dynamics, consequences, and potential means to achieve *individual and collective social and economic justice*; and
- The presentation of theoretical and practice content about patterns, dynamics, and consequences of discrimination, economic deprivation, and oppression.

The curriculum must provide content about people of color, women, and gay and lesbian persons, as well as additional *populations at risk.*[38]

Despite efforts over several decades to retrench social services and social workers, by 1997, 781,000 persons were employed as social workers, 69.3 percent of them women, 21.7 percent African American, and 8.7 percent Latino. At least 40 percent of social workers are employed by state, county, and local governments in a host of settings. A small number of social workers are employed by the federal government. Others are employed by voluntary, nonprofit agencies, with a number involved in international service as consultants, administrators, and direct service practitioners. There is a growing number of social workers employed by private for-profit businesses, and an increasing number of social workers who conduct private practices.[39]

Volunteers occupy an extremely important position in the social welfare arena. Volunteers are involved in direct service programs, fund-raising, and policy making through boards and committees. Surveys have estimated that almost 50 percent (93 million) of American adults served as volunteers in 1995, contributing billions of hours of their time to nonprofit organizations, including religious organizations, education, recreation, social services and welfare, arts and culture, and national, state, and local governmental organizations, as well as helping neighbors. These volunteers represent the equivalent of over 8 million full-time employees. The estimated dollar value of formal volunteer services in 1995 was $201.5 billion.[40]

Task differentiation among professional social workers (bachelor's and master's), paraprofessionals, untrained persons employed in social work positions, and volunteers is a relatively undefined but important area of concern in social welfare. The entire issue of who may do what is somewhat ambiguous and unsettled. Even the value of volunteerism itself is subject to objections from those who want to enhance employment opportunities and who view volunteerism in some situations as undermining the goal of paid work. And yet the development of citizen leadership and involvement are also basic goals of social work.

Questions about the areas of competency of professionals and of laypersons confound many professions. Which social policy decisions should be decided by laypersons and which only by professional social workers (or by physicians, engineers, and so on)? Some questions about health insurance or public assistance programs may rest in the broader citizen sphere, whereas questions requiring specialized competency (such as whether or not to operate, or whether to place a child in a foster home) belong in the professional sphere. Yet other social welfare policy questions are ambiguous so that it is difficult to differentiate the dividing line between professional and layperson or citizen decision making.[41]

The Number of Social Workers

As one can see by the discrepancy between the number of members in the professional association (153,000) and the number of persons employed in social work positions (781,000, 1997), many persons employed in social work positions as defined by employers are untrained in social work prior to their employment. The implication is that the profession has not been in a position as yet to control sufficiently the use of the professional title or to prepare sufficient numbers of trained personnel. At the same time, social work by 1995 was licensed or regulated in all 50 states, the District of Columbia, Puerto Rico, and the Virgin Islands.[42]

The Impact of Managed Care

There are a number of factors external to the profession heavily affecting agency practice as well as those who are in private practice and profit making organizations. One of these, managed care, is a strategy developed to gain control over health and mental health costs, which have escalated beyond the rate of inflation. Managed care attempts to control costs by monitoring access to and the type of health/mental health care a patient will receive from professionals and/or health maintenance organizations. The goal is to reduce costs by controlling the services practitioners can provide and fostering competition among human service organizations. Managed care plans attempt to reduce costs through controlling the types of providers utilized, limiting access to service, and prescribing the type and length of service provided. An emphasis on brief therapy is part of this movement. Managed care is having a profound impact on social work practice, the financing of agencies, and on private practices. An extensive discussion of managed care and its impact is found in chapter 10.

RACISM, SEXISM, AND A PLURALISTIC SOCIETY

The profession of social work has made efforts to deal constructively with racism and sexism within its professional ranks and in society. Social work as a profession has done well compared with other groups. Nonetheless, problems remain, and the efforts need to be continued.

The membership of NASW in 1998 was 80 percent female, and almost 84 percent of the full-time students enrolled in master's programs in 1997 were female. Fourteen percent of the professional association members are minority-group members,[43] and 25 percent of full-time master's degree students are members of minority groups. In graduate schools of social work and joint programs (graduate and baccalaureate), almost 62 percent of the faculty is female; 22.3 percent of the faculty are minority-group members.

Of the full-time students enrolled in undergraduate social work education in 1997, 86.5 percent were female and 31.3 percent were members of ethnic minorities. Of those faculty members teaching in baccalaureate only programs, 63.6 percent were female and 24.2 percent were members of minority groups.[44]

Estimates of the proportion of females in administrative positions in general social work practice are far below their percentage of professionally trained social workers. In 1997 46 percent of the deans or directors of accredited graduate and joint degree programs were females and more than 57 percent of baccalaureate directors were female.[45]

Leadership positions in social welfare organizations associated with higher pay scales go disproportionately to men. Social service employment, generally, is underpaid for both women and men. Recent studies of social workers' pay found that incomes for male social workers continue to be higher than those of females, and this gap exists at all income levels—perhaps reflecting the income gender gap in society at large, and at direct service, supervisory, and management levels. The predominance of women in performing direct service work (lower paid roles) contrasts with the predominance of males in social welfare administration (higher paid roles) and produces differences in compensation and rewards. These findings generally are supported by salary studies of the members of NASW. For master's degree holders, social workers' median annual salary (primary income) in 1995 was $34,215. Private practice (solo or group) is the predominant source of secondary income.[46]

At one level, all people are the same and have "common human needs," but at another level, we are all different. One way we deal with differences in our society is by discrimination. As a result, there is a need for affirmative action programs in social work and social welfare, at least for the foreseeable future. One major reason for affirmative action is the need that all groups have for role models to identify with in terms of gender, race, and ethnicity. But this rationale must not be taken too far; we are not arguing that only African Americans can work with African Americans, or that the blind can only work with those similarly disabled, or those who have been addicted with those who are addicted. Social work is struggling with this problem. It is legitimate that a social service in a Latino neighborhood ask that most workers speak Spanish and be familiar with Latino cultures, but to ask that all workers also be Latinos may be going to an extreme.

Race and ethnicity are factors in American culture, and social work's recognition of this has influenced recruitment, admissions, hiring, and promotion patterns. Similar decisions regarding women are being made relative to promotion to leadership positions. These trends are not just personal, professional career decisions affecting individuals; they have an impact on the delivery of social services, resource allocation, and community conflict and consensus. Race, ethnicity, and gender are important areas for social work and social welfare in which significant strides have been made. Continued efforts are needed to attain equitable methods of dealing with people in a pluralistic society.

For all its limitations and ambiguities, the profession of social work is strong, growing, and a fundamental part of contemporary society. However, both internal and external pressures are exerted on the profession. Emblematic of internal criticism are those who suggest that social work has abandoned its mission to help the poor and oppressed and now devote their energies to psychotherapy and private practice. These critics, harkening back to earlier social work times, believe social work's mission should be to build a "meaning, a purpose, and a sense of obligation, and social support" for all. The external pressures derive from the global context in which social work is practiced. The context has dictated leaner budgets, increased paperwork and documentation, briefer treatment, and greater accountability. These affect the quality of services, reduce interventive choices, reduce follow-up efforts, and can lead to alienation between clients and services unable to meet basic needs. All of which may tend toward the devaluation of social workers.[47]

Summary

In this chapter, we examined the functions of social workers and the organizational contexts in which they practice, as well as issues that arise from their interactions. We also examined the roles of social work as a profession in our society as a cause and/or function and the history and tensions between generic and specific social work practice methods. Also discussed were the social work profession today and the contributions and roles of volunteers. Finally, information regarding racism, sexism, gender and the profession were set forth. In chapter 14, we will discuss major societal trends that affect the needs of people and the social welfare responses of society. We will examine growth, demography, and resources; productivity and the service economy; individual and shared goals; ethnicity and pluralism; gender; gays and lesbians; the new property; technological change; crime; and the economy.

Questions for Consideration

1.   What do you see in social work that suggests either a dominant social control or social change role for the profession?
2.   If it could, should social work better combine the two streams—cause and function? What suggestions would you make to do so?
3.   What does feminist social work suggest are the ways the profession should seek to integrate personal and societal transformation?
4.   Can you identify the ways in which volunteers and professionals cooperate in the delivery of social services? In what ways might they have conflicting purposes?

Notes

1.   Stephen J. Gould, *The Individual in Darwin's World*, Edinburgh: Edinburgh University Press, 1990, p. 33.
2.   Jane Addams, *Jane Addams: A Centennial Reader*, New York: Macmillan, 1960, p. 85.
3.   Council on Social Work Education, *Handbook of Accreditation Standards and Procedures*, "Curriculum Policy Statement," Alexandria, Va., 1994.
4.   Rue Bucher and Joan Stelling, "Four Characteristics of Professional Organizations," *Colleagues in Organization: The Social Construction of Professional Work*, Ralph L. Blankenship, ed., New York: John Wiley & Sons, 1977, p. 137.
5.   Howard M. Vollmer and Donald M. Mills, *Professionalization*, Englewood Cliffs, N.J.: Prentice Hall, 1966, p. 264.
6.   Alfred J. Kahn, "Perspectives on Access to Social Services," *Social Work*, Vol. 15, No. 2, April 1970, pp. 95–101.
7.   Robert D. Vinter, "Analysis of Treatment Organizations," *Social Work*, Vol. 8, No. 3, July 1963, p. 9.

8. Amitai Etzioni, *Modern Organizations*, Englewood Cliffs, N.J.: Prentice Hall, 1964, p. 76.

9. Ibid., p. 88.

10. Charles Perrow, *Complex Organizations: A Critical Essay*, 3rd Edition, New York: Random House, 1986, p. 22.

11. Willard C. Richan, "The Social Work Profession and Organized Social Welfare," *Shaping the New Social Work*, Alfred J. Kahn, ed., New York: Columbia University Press, 1973, pp. 147-148.

12. Kathleen Woodroofe, *From Charity to Social Work in England and the United States*, Toronto, Canada: University of Toronto Press, 1974, pp. 224-225.

13. W. Richard Scott, "Professional Employees in a Bureaucratic Structure," *The Semi-Professions and Their Organization*, Amitai Etzioni, ed., New York: Free Press, 1969, p. 110.

14. See, for example, George Brager and Stephen Holloway, *Changing Human Service Organizations: Politics and Practice*, New York: Free Press, 1978; Ralph Dolgoff, "Clinicians as Social Policymakers," *Social Casework*, Vol. 62, No. 5, May 1981, pp. 284-292; Marie Weil, "Creating an Alternative Work Culture in a Public Service Setting," *Administration in Social Work*, Vol. 12, No. 2, 1988, pp. 69-82; Herman Resnick and Rino J. Patti, eds., *Change from Within: Humanizing Social Welfare Organizations*, Philadelphia: Temple University Press, 1980.

15. Herbert Bisno, "How Social Will Social Work Be?" *Social Work*, Vol. 2, No. 2, April 1956, pp. 12-18.

16. Allen F. Davis, *Spearheads for Reform: The Social Settlement and the Progressive Movement 1890-1914*, New York: Oxford University Press, 1967, p. 195.

17. Christopher Lasch, ed., *The Social Thought of Jane Addams*, New York: Bobbs-Merrill, 1965, p. 216.

18. D.G. Becker, "Mary Ellen Richmond," *Encyclopedia of Social Work*, Vol. 2, Robert Morris, ed., New York: National Association of Social Workers, 1971, pp. 1135-1136.

19. Roy Lubove, *The Struggle for Social Security 1900-1935*, Cambridge, Mass.: Harvard University Press, 1968.

20. Mary E. Richmond, *Social Diagnosis*, New York: Russell Sage Foundation, 1917, p. 25.

21. Porter R. Lee, *Social Work as Cause and Function*, New York: Columbia University Press, 1937, pp. 3, 5.

22. Ibid., pp. 19, 21.

23. Clarke A. Chambers, "An Historical Perspective in Political Action vs. Individualized Treatment," *Current Issues in Social Work Seen in Historical Perspective*, New York: Council on Social Work Education, 1962, p. 53.

24. Ibid., p. 63.

25. Nan Van Den Bergh, *Feminist Practice in the 21st Century*, Nan Van Den Bergh, ed., Washington, D.C.: NASW Press, 1995, p. viii.

26. Helen Land, "Feminist Clinical Social Work in the 21st Century," in *Feminist Practice in the 21st Century*, Nan Van Den Bergh, ed., Washington, D.C.: NASW Press, 1995, pp. 5-6.

27. Mary Bricker-Jenkins, "The Propositions and Assumptions of Feminist Social Work Practice," *Feminist Social Work Practice in Clinical Settings*, Mary Bricker-Jenkins, Nancy R. Hooyman, and Naomi Gottlieb, eds., Newbury Park, Calif.: Sage, 1991, pp. 271-303; Jeffrey H. Galper, *The Politics of Social Services*, Englewood Cliffs, N.J.: Prentice Hall, 1975, pp. 11-13; David Wagner, *The Quest for a Radical Profession*, New York: University Press of America, 1990, p. 7.

28. Daniel P. Moynihan, "The Professionalization of Reform," *The Public Interest*, Fall 1965, pp. 6-16.

29. William Schwartz, "Private Troubles and Public Issues: One Social Work Job or Two?" *Perspectives on Social Welfare*, Paul Weinberger, ed., New York: Macmillan, 1974, pp. 346–362.
30. Armando Morales and Bradford W. Sheafor, *Social Work: A Profession of Many Faces*, 6th Edition, Boston: Allyn and Bacon, 1992, p. 19.
31. Karen K. Kirst-Ashman and H. Hull Grafton, Jr., *Generalist Practice with Organizations and Communities*, Chicago: Nelson-Hall Publishers, 1997, pp. 7–8.
32. Roy Lubove, *The Professional Altruist: The Emergence of Social Work as a Career, 1880–1930*, New York: Atheneum, 1969, pp. 210–211.
33. Jack Rothman and Jon S. Sager, "Advocacy," *Case Management: Integrating Individual and Community Practice*, Boston: Allyn and Bacon, 1998, pp. 176–192.
34. *Social Casework: Generic and Specific*, New York: American Association of Social Workers, 1929; Classic Series, Washington, D.C.: National Association of Social Workers, 1974, p. 4.
35. Sophonisba P. Breckenridge, "The New Horizons of Professional Education for Social Work," *Social Service Review*, Vol. 10, No. 3, September 1936, pp. 434–444.
36. Bernard Barber, "Some Problems in the Sociology of the Professions," *Daedelus*, Vol. 92, Fall 1963, pp. 669–688.
37. Mona S. Schatz, Lowell E. Jenkins, and Bradford W. Sheafor, "Milford Redefined: A Model of Generalist and Advanced Generalist Social Work," *Journal of Social Work Education*, Vol. 26, No. 3, Fall 1990, pp. 217–230.
38. Council on Social Work Education, *Handbook of Accreditation Standards and Procedures*, Alexandria, Va., 1994.
39. U.S. Department of Labor, Bureau of Labor Statistics, *Employment and Earnings*, "Employed Persons by Detailed Occupation, Sex, Race, and Hispanic Origin, 1997," January 1998, p. 176; U.S. Department of Labor, *Occupational Outlook Handbook*, 1996–97 edition, Washington, D.C.: U.S. Government Printing Office, 1996, pp. 132–134.
40. Anne E. Kaplan, ed., *Giving USA: The Annual Report on Philanthropy for the Year 1996*, New York: American Association of Fundraising Counsel Trust for Philanthropy, 1997, p. 65.
41. Donald Feldstein, "Do We Need Professions in Our Society? Professionalization Versus Consumerism," *Social Work*, Vol. 16, No. 4, October 1971, pp. 5–11.
42. American Association of State Social Work Boards, *Social Work Laws and Board Regulations: A State Comparison Study*, Culpeper, Va., 1995.
43. Personal communication from Josephine Nieves, Executive Director, NASW, July 1998.
44. Student and faculty data is from Todd M. Lennon, *Statistics on Social Work Education in the United States: 1997*, Tables 43 and 44, Alexandria, Va.: Council on Social Work Education, 1998, pp. 44–45.
45. Ibid., Table 17, p. 17.
46. Margaret Gibelman and Philip H. Schervish, *Who We Are: A Second Look*, Washington, D.C.: NASW, 1997, pp. 149–150; Ruth Huber and Betty P. Orlando, "Persisting Gender Differences in Social Workers' Incomes: Does the Profession Really Care?" *Social Work*, Vol. 40, No. 5, September 1995, pp. 585–591; Patricia Y. Martin and Roslyn H. Chernesky, "Women's Prospects for Leadership in Social Welfare: A Political Economy Perspective," *Administration in Social Work*, Vol. 13, Nos. 3/4, 1989, pp. 117–143.
47. Harry Specht and Mark E. Courtney, *Unfaithful Angels: How Social Work Has Abandoned Its Mission*, New York: Free Press, 1994, pp. 4, 27; Michael B. Fabricant and Steve Burghardt, *The Welfare State Crisis and the Transformation of Social Service Work*, Armonk, N.Y.: M. E. Sharpe, 1992, p. 118.

CHAPTER FOURTEEN

Social Trends Affecting Social Welfare

*Is it possible to make sense of what is going on in the world, to set oneself
for the future? Of course we cannot predict the sudden storms
of history. But history is more than storms; it is also a great Gulf Stream,
carrying us along on its broad currents.*
—Robert L. Heilbroner[1]

OVERVIEW

In this chapter, we will examine contextual social trends: growth, demography, and
resources; the family; productivity and the service economy; individual and shared
goals; ethnicity and pluralism; gender; gays and lesbians; the new property; technological change; crime; and the place of welfare in a changing context.

GROWTH, DEMOGRAPHY, AND RESOURCES: INTERNATIONAL PERSPECTIVES

Within a global context, projections of the future are essentially optimistic or pessimistic. The neo-Malthusians (catastrophists) are those convinced that continued
population growth and economic development will lead to starvation, exhaustion
of resources, and the "collapse" of the world system. Paul Ehrlich, in his widely
read book *The Population Bomb* (1968), reflecting the neo-Malthusian view, suggested that "the battle to feed all of humanity is over. In the 1970s the world will
undergo famine—hundreds of millions of people are going to starve to death. . . .
At this late date nothing can prevent a substantial increase in the world death
rate."[2]

Obviously this did not happen. In 1990, Paul and Anne Ehrlich revised their projections:

> So even though birthrates have declined somewhat, *Homo sapiens* is a long way from ending its population explosion or avoiding its consequences. . . . Global warming, acid rain, depletion of the ozone layer, vulnerability to epidemics, and exhaustion of soils and groundwater are all . . . related to population size. They are also clear and present dangers to the persistence of civilization. . . . The population explosion will come to an end before very long. The only remaining question is whether it will be halted through the humane method of birth control, or by nature wiping out the surplus.[3]

When others pointed out their projections were unfounded, they suggested the "green revolution" increased food production for poor nations, but major problems continued. However, even this positive food development was viewed as a mixed blessing, producing new strains to meet new conditions and raising questions about "how familiar will the Four Horsemen of the Apocalypse—famine, pestilence, war, and death—become as resource scarcities intensify?"[4]

In addition to concerns about population growth, food, and fuel, there is another neo-Malthusian theory: The generation of carbon dioxide associated with economic growth and atmospheric warming, along with ozone depletion and destruction of rain forests, suggest to some people the possibility of ecological instability with worldwide implications, particularly for the poor. The warnings about population growth and depletion of resources continue. Recently, some observers pointed out that after almost half a century of unprecedented expansion in both land-based and oceanic food supplies, the world has begun to experience a loss of momentum. From 1950 to the 1980s, expanded food production reduced hunger and malnutrition. In recent years, according to these observers, these trends have slowed or been reversed. Growth in grain production slowed; ocean fisheries are being fished at or over capacity, and some fisheries are in a state of decline. According to this view, there is a shortage of unused agricultural technology, the growth of human demands is pressing against the limits of fisheries and farmlands, the demands for water are reaching their limits, and densely populated countries run the risk of losing their crop lands at a rate exceeding the rise in land productivity. Social problems undermine some national governments in their attempts to expand food production. Further, the population increases are nearly all projected for developing nations where life-sustaining resources are already deteriorating.[5]

Those who are more optimistic (cornucopians) point out that Malthus's prediction that world population would outstrip food supply has proven false. The rate of the world's population growth peaked in the early 1960s and has been declining ever since. Birth rates are falling even in nations too poor for economic development to stabilize rapid population growth. The United Nations found that the population growth has begun to fall sooner than expected and is stabilizing; it is estimated it will level off at 10.7 billion shortly after 2200.[6] The optimists suggest that by changing the ways we use and distribute access to the world's resources an additional 9 billion people can be accomodated in good health and reasonable comfort. This will require the regeneration of the soil's fertility; protection of limited water resources; production of crops in ecologically benign and sustainable ways; diets based on grains instead of animals; and technologies utilizing renewable resources; broad economic growth accompanied by distributive equity.[7]

Those are complex and demanding tasks. A United Nations Food and Agriculture study (1995) reported that the failure to alleviate poverty is the main reason undernutrition persists. The overall evidence shows that the world as a whole faces no major constraints in increasing food production by as much as is required to meet the growth of demand. Long-term food prices have not risen in real terms and have—on balance—declined. The report's preparers too are concerned about the degradation of some resources: soil erosion, overuse of chemicals, and effluents from livestock operations. But, the rate of world population growth is on the decline. Although it is expected the *rate* of grain production will be lower in the next 20 years compared with the recent past, it is expected that total production will continue to grow. Sub-Saharan Africa (worse off today than 20 to 30 years ago) is where food supply prospects are low.[8]

Ominous and gloomy predictions caused some persons to believe that as people use more of the earth's limited resources, there would inevitably be less for those who come later. Stephen Moore reports that contradictory evidence exists:

> . . . whatever the dangers the planet may face . . . , on one score the 1980s demonstrated that our fears were overblown. The predicted scarcity of material resources as a result of increasing population and increased industrial activity did not occur. Indeed, by every objective measure natural resources became more, not less, plentiful in the 1980s. Since 1980 the price of virtually every source of energy, every agricultural commodity, every one of the earth's minerals, and every forest product has declined.[9]

As children survive, the birth rate is expected to decrease. The United Nations International Children's Emergency Fund (UNICEF) found that the death rate among small children and infants is declining in much of the developing world. Based on past experience, this trend suggests that parents will voluntarily begin to limit the size of their families because they will not fear the premature death of many of their children.[10]

The population estimate experience of the United States following World War II underscores the tentative and precarious nature of population projections. During the late 1950s and early 1960s, demographers envisioned a U.S. population between 300 million and 320 million by the year 2000. This projection was based on the post–World War II baby boom. But, unlike physical factors, the variables that affect social changes cannot be predicted with great accuracy, and nations cannot know with assurance what events will affect their future.[11]

Today, experts suggest that hunger persists because of political and distribution problems. Economist Amartya Sen influenced the way governments deal with the problem of hunger. His work demonstrated that famine is not just a consequence of nature but also a human-made disaster, an avoidable catastrophe. Declines in food production rarely account for mass starvation. Typically, there is even in the midst of starvation sufficient food to go around or enough money to import it. In fact, there are cases in which food is being exported from an area because of market demands at the same time there is famine and starvation. Sen found that disaster strikes when the poorest people can no longer afford to buy food because of unemployment or increases in the price of food. The strategy of choice is now the creation of public works that create jobs to replace the lost incomes of the poor.[12]

Julian Simon, representative of the optimists, approached these issues from the standpoint of an economist and argued that scarcity will be defeated by inventiveness. According to Simon,

1. The per capita food situation has been improving since World War II and famine has progressively diminished;
2. The amount of agricultural land has been increasing, and in the United States the amount of land used for forests, recreation, and wildlife has been increasing;
3. Natural resources have become progressively less scarce and less costly;
4. The long-term future of energy supplies is as bright as that for other natural resources; and
5. All population growth estimates are being lowered.

Simon's argument is the following. Consumption increases as population and incomes grow; these in turn heighten scarcity and increase prices. Higher prices present opportunities that steer inventors and entrepreneurs to seek ways to satisfy the shortages. Some fail, others succeed. The final result is that we end up better off than if the original shortage had never arisen. The growth of the population brings with it an increase in useful knowledge.[13]

Which is the correct vision? Have we reached beyond the limits of our finite resources and absolute limits to sustainable expansion? Or, are people a resource rather than a burden? The power of innovation will counter scarcity, and creativity will produce enough to sustain the world.[14] There is no necessity of believing either the optimistic or pessimistic projections. A third school of thought believes it is difficult, if not impossible, to choose between the two future scenarios. But, the history of population growth is that constraints develop out of hostile environments and populations seek equilibrium. The best projections of the United Nations are that the world population will reach 8 billion in 2022. But, the rate of increase (1985–1990 = 1.7%) will decline to 1 percent in 2020–2025. Population reacts and adapts to the possibilities for expansion that are encountered. Many variables, including the development of technology, the elasticity of the concept of quality of life, and the ability to adapt in a complex and dynamic system, all play a part in determining the future. If we do not know with any certainty what will develop as a result of continued population growth, it is certainly wiser to be cautious. Therefore, the future must be prepared for, and that has implications for everyone, rich and poor. Only continuous growth can begin to deliver, in modest degree, what the coming world will require health, welfare, and human dignity.[15]

Such long-term considerations serve as assumptions for actions in the present. One group strongly favors limitations on population and economic growth, but such limitations will have future effects on everyone. Eduard Pestel in *Beyond the Limits to Growth: A Report to the Club of Rome* underscores the argument that "intentional economic zero growth would be not only utopian, but also disastrous, if it were tried in earnest on a worldwide scale." It would mean an increase in poverty and in unemployment and "lead to conflicts regarding the distribution of the wealth of nations."[16]

The line of reasoning of the neo-Malthusians, those who take the pessimistic approach, is congenial to those who are already prosperous; by the same token, the "have-nots" essentially have to opt for the "bigger pie" with more for everyone. If we believe the economy and world growth are to reach a stage of stasis, of steady state, then wealth will be static as well. In this case, redistribution can only be resisted by those who are the "haves." Philosopher John Rawls, in *A Theory of Justice*, argued that equity should be based on a reparations approach.[17] However, reparations (redistribution) depend on taking from the rich and giving to the poor. To the extent the "pie" is bigger and expanding, it seems more probable redistribution can be accomplished when the wealthy continue to gain wealth, albeit at a diminished rate. Thus growth versus no growth is the fundamental issue that confronts the world's population, our society, and, in turn, social welfare provisions. Continued economic growth, we hope in nonpolluting directions, seems to us a prerequisite to improvements in social welfare.

Growth and Demography: The United States

Population Growth

On a national level, the issue of growth and shifts in the composition of the U.S. population are of immediate concern to social welfare. The 1930s was a period of low fertility. However, following World War II, the United States experienced a dramatic period of high fertility, often referred to as the "baby boom." As a result, from 1950 to 1960, the number of young persons aged 14 to 24 was almost constant, rising only slightly. But in the 1960s, reflecting the postwar baby boom, the cohort jumped 44 percent.[18]

The "bulge effect" of the baby boom created a need for more elementary classrooms, high schools, and college facilities and produced more marriages and the need for more housing. For many years in the future, this "bulging generation" will be a dominant factor in American life. For example, competition for better jobs and better pay are intense among those of the baby boom generation. Furthermore, the population projections for persons 65 years of age and over are expected to remain level until 2005 as the relatively small birth cohorts of the 1920s and 1930s reach age 65. With the entry of the baby boom cohorts into the 65-plus age group, this population will increase rapidly.

If one traces this bulge from birth to death, it has been possible to predict the extent of many of the social welfare needs that must be met. Beginning with social services related to childhood, the pattern of services needed by this large group of people shifts as they enter different periods of life: school, marriage, forming and raising families, and now extending to retirement, Social Security, and Medicare.

The Family

Changes in the general environment—including technological changes such as birth control methods, the women's movement, a questioning of traditional family patterns, and a search for personal fulfillment—have led to changes in the family. American families have become smaller; more are led by one parent, mainly female; and more have mothers who work outside the home. Americans continue to marry, but they marry on average 3.5 years later than they did a generation earlier.[19] From 1980 to 1996, there was a 21 percent absolute increase in the number of married persons, but their percentage of the total population fell almost 5 percent. The number of divorced persons doubled from 1980 to 1996. Although the rate of divorce decreased by 15 percent, divorced persons as a percentage of the total population increased slightly more than 50 percent. Within five years of the dissolution of their first marriages, slightly fewer than 50 percent of women have remarried. Marriage has become less important as more women achieve economic independence, more remain in the labor market, and the legal line between marriage and cohabitation is blurred.[20]

Other changes also are occurring that further alter the traditional forms of marriage and family life. The number and percentage of persons 18 years of age and older who have never married increased substantially, indicating both a delay of marriage and decisions not to marry.[21] Between 1970 and 1996, the number of families headed by a female family householder rose two and one fourth times, and these families are much more likely to be poor. Female-headed nonfamily households experienced a similar increase.[22]

The number of births for unwed women 19 years of age and younger doubled between 1980 and 1994 but decreased by a fourth as a percentage of total live births.[23] The number of births by teenagers in 1980 (552,161) declined to 494,272 by 1996 and the birthrate (or fertility rate) for all women in the United States continued a long decline, remaining generally below the replacement rate through 1994.[24]

Marriage remains an important norm, and most Americans marry at least once. In 1996, 54 percent of households were married couple families, a continuing percentage decline, and those with their own children under 18 showed a miniscule absolute loss compared with 1980 but were only 25 percent of family households.[25]

The number of "nontraditional" households has increased. Many Americans now live with extended family, roommates, partners, grandchildren, boarders, health-care providers, or other group caregivers. There are reports that one of every eight Americans aged 45 and over lives in such a household. Unmarried couples, fewer than half a million in 1960, exceeded 4 million in 1997. There were 1.25 million interracial married couples. Another family phenomenon is that 10 million children live in families in which there is a stepparent or siblings who are less than full brothers and sisters.[26]

First marriages occur about 3.5 years later on average now than they did a generation ago; families are having one less child; more women, married and unmarried, are employed (including women with very young children); and more couples are surviving jointly for longer periods after their children marry. All these appear to be crucial changes that are significantly altering family life patterns. Although there is disruption of family life and new household and family configurations, social welfare sees as a special concern those families under stress in our society.

Three other developments of the past several decades must be taken into account to better understand and assess the American family in the 1990s:

1. Poverty is the greatest nemesis for children. (Introduced in chapter 8, it will be further examined in chapter 15 in relation to single-parent households.)
2. The participation of women in the workforce is a continuing phenomenon with implications for themselves as individuals and for families.
3. With divorce and remarriage, the number of blended or reconstituted families has become significant. This development poses new issues for family life and for social welfare services.
4. Sexual activity among teens is no greater in the United States than in a number of Western nations even while pregnancy and abortion are. This poses issues for family planning and must be a factor in debates on abortion and the availability of birth control information. One result is that teenage pregnancy and family dependency are major concerns expressed in the Temporary Assistance to Needy Families (TANF) discussed in earlier chapters.
5. There also is the emergence of a "sandwich" generation—adults caring for both their children and their aged parents. It has been estimated that many families spend more years as caregivers for their parents than for their children. This outgrowth of longevity and an aging society will be ever more prominent in the next decades.

The future and existence of the American family does not appear to be in doubt. What does appear to be changing are the dimensions of the family of the future: How shall families adjust to poverty, an increasing number of women working, shifting roles within the family, and more leisure time together after the children are gone?

The glorification of the individual, self-fulfillment, and self-gratification are not values that enhance families; rather family life requires loyalty, self-denial, and sharing. It remains to be seen to what extent personal self-fulfillment will supersede or be made compatible with the importance of family life. What effects on children will the changes in family life bring? Social welfare, through its services to families and individuals, will play a role in helping people sort out their options and make choices as to the dimensions of their lives.

Aging

A major trend of great significance is the growth of the number of aging persons in the population. We examined this issue in chapters 9 and 10 and will do so again in chapter 15 in relation to the need for home health care.

Fertility Rate

Since 1960, the U.S. fertility rate generally has dropped through 1994. Average family size decreased from 3.58 in 1970 to 3.2 in 1996, a 16 percent difference.[27] Smaller families have effects on child-rearing patterns; the middle-aged will have to bear the brunt of supporting the society as taxpayers; and mandatory retirement ages may have to be postponed.

Whichever way the birthrate moves—continuing downward, leveling off, or increasing—there are social welfare implications: size of tax force, family patterns, proportions of age groups within the overall population, resources available for distribution, and other concerns such as living space and number of retirees. Predictions regarding birth trends remain complex. It is unknown what effects the economy, immigration, the "surfacing" of illegal immigrants, and unforeseeable national and international events will produce. Prediction is difficult, but social welfare decisions need to be made nonetheless. What provisions need to be made for those yet to be born and for the life stages of those already born?

PRODUCTIVITY AND THE SERVICE ECONOMY

Issues affecting social welfare also derive from the nature of *productivity* in U.S. society. A rise in output per employed person is a rise in productivity, which is a major source of economic growth. Productivity creates the "pie" to be divided among the various demands within society. In 1853, an American writer predicted the day would arrive when "machinery will perform all work, automata will direct them. The only task of the human race will be to make love, study, and be happy."[28] So far, the automation revolution has not yet reached that millennium. Quite the reverse. In 1853, almost 33 percent of the total U.S. population was employed.[29] By 1998, the figure doubled to 67 percent of the civilian noninstitutional population.[30] To the extent that wealth is created through technological and other advances, the social welfare programs of the nation are potential recipients of the "bigger pie." Nevertheless, social welfare has to compete with other "goods" within the society, and such competition has been weakened by a political focus on the federal debt and the requirements of a large and soon-to-be-retired generation of aging persons. Increasing productivity in itself does not mean greater emphasis on social welfare concerns. Society has to be concerned about how many workers are unemployed or underemployed. Recessions raise questions about structural unemployment and the growth of the gross domestic product. During recessions, however, when productivity is at lower levels, society has to be much more concerned about how many workers are unemployed or underemployed.

In response to such questions, issues are raised about *structural unemployment* and how to deal with it. Certain sectors of the economy, because of technological changes and competition from other nations, among other reasons, fail to maintain their shares of the world markets. Which industries will be the wave of the future—microelectronics, basic industries such as steel and automobiles, or service industries? If we can identify which industries hold out the most optimism for the nation, what should be the role of government in planning, human resource development, resource allocation, funding supports, and so on? The ultimate issue is whether improved productivity and the necessary industrial emphases can efficiently and effectively be made without radical changes in the political and economic system. If need be, how will we adjust to a society in which a growing number of persons could be unemployed? How shall the governmental and private sectors minimize unemployment and maximize productivity, all the while balancing inflation and employment?

Other issues related to productivity affect social welfare, including the shift from production of goods to the production of services. Our society has become postindustrial, in the sense that the majority of workers are no longer engaged in manufacturing or the production of goods. We have reached a high level of productivity so that it takes much less than half of the workforce to produce all the goods to supply the population. In 1996 in the United States, more than 80 percent (excluding agriculture) of the workforce was employed in services and the remainder in goods-producing employment.[31] The United States is the pioneer in such an economy. This trend has continued to such an extent that the 1995 *Fortune* 500 list—an annual compilation of the 500 largest industrial corporations in the United States—included for the first time service corporations such as J.P. Morgan, Metropolitan Life, AT&T, Viacom, and American Express.[32] The downside of a service economy is the problem created for those who lack the skills, education, and health needed for higher paid positions. This group does not have the "living wage" opportunities of the past in manufacturing jobs. There are real limits for them in attaining a living wage and benefits equal to supporting a family.

Some argue that a service-dominated economy is problematic and associated with a productivity decline. For example, if a factory manufactures 100 shirts per hour, a new invention may make it possible to create 200 shirts an hour, so then any one worker can be more productive. But there are natural limits to how many persons can be served by a social worker during any one day. This is an illustration of *labor-intensive* industry.

It is an open question as to how productive services can become. To what extent can social workers, teachers, or other workers be made more productive? Paraprofessionals and technology can be used to increase the productivity of some professionals. Ultimately, however, we are dealing with labor-intensive industries in which it is difficult to raise production. During the 1990s, the service sector actually became transformed through deregulation, global competition, utilization of information technologies, and various other cost-control efficiencies. Productivity in the service sector rose significantly, contributing to low inflation.[33] Just as "optimists" have shown that population increase and immigration need not damage the economy but can help it, they have also argued that society has an infinite capacity through invention and innovation to increase productivity further. Surprises do occur and dramatic increases in productivity still develop from time to time. The ultimate upper limit remains unknown.

Social welfare has to compete with other parts of the society for resources; this competition is minimized in an era of expanding productivity and made more difficult in an economy in which taxpayers and legislators become very concerned with costs and priorities. All of these factors suggest that social welfare goals can be met only if (1) productivity continues to be increased in manufacturing, farming, and in service areas where productive possibilities need to be exploited and (2) social welfare services themselves can be delivered more efficiently.

A NATIONAL SOCIETY

The United States is a national society, one in which events in one part of the society can have immediate repercussions in every other part. A national economy, transportation system, and media of communication have served to develop an interdependent society. In regard to mass media, people receive more and more information from central sources; information is gotten from national—even international—television, national news weeklies, and nationally distributed papers.

In some respects, as a nation we are developing a mass culture; we attend the same movies, see the same television shows, and in general are developing a culture of a single society. Yet, as we shall see later, there are countertrends away from a single set of values toward a multiplicity of values.

Mobility has helped to create this national society. Typically, 17 percent of the population change residence each year. Most people move within the same county or between counties in the same state. Relocation peaks in the 20s and then declines with age. Among those 65 years of age and older there is almost no movement. Demographers attribute the mobility pattern to an aging population, the growth of two-income families, and the decline in family size; perhaps some stay put because they feel there is no place left to seek a better life.[34]

Individual and Shared Goals

For many years, there was a tide of rising expectations. A nation involved in mass production also has to ensure mass purchasing power. The way in which expectations are met, at least minimally, is through pooling the risks so that those who are less able to produce nevertheless are entitled to and provided with certain goods. A major theme of the Reagan administration of the 1980s was the firm belief that Americans could "have it all"—lower taxes, stronger defense, and no sacrifice. However, this claim was accompanied by a diminished sense of interdependence and shared responsibility.

As we approach the 21st century, more and more people are rejecting the idea of providing for those in need. A great shift occurred, which fostered individual rather than shared aims: The market became the arbiter of decisions. At the same time, there has been a concern about individual and group rights. Freedom is no longer defined as freedom for the individual citizen alone, but as freedom for diverse groups to have equality of rights. Thus two separate trends are occurring: a national ethos of commonality on one level, and individual and group competitiveness, which seeks inclusion as well as a greater share of the "pie."

In "The Cultural Contradictions of Capitalism," Daniel Bell discussed the development of hedonism (the pursuit of pleasure) in our capitalist society. Capitalism was generated by and accompanied by the Protestant ethic (delay gratification, put money in the bank, invest it, make it work for you, don't be profligate, spend little, idleness is the worst sin, be productive, work hard, and if you are successful you are blessed by God, but if not you have not received grace). The contradiction, according to Bell, is that when capitalism works, as it has in the United States, the reverse situation is produced. The hedonistic ethic arises in which self-fulfillment, "do your own thing," becomes the result and the keynote of an economy of abundance.[35]

The emphasis on immediate gratification becomes more the American norm. The idea of delayed gratification, the traditional capitalist ethic, is less the common ideal of the American scene. If it feels good, it is right. Bell suggests this changed ethic is the result of the affluent, postindustrial society, but it is a change that may undo society because the common glue for a society may become weaker.

ETHNICITY AND PLURALISM

Ethnicity, a growing and visible phenomenon in U.S. society, is an important ingredient in the formation of identity, for both families and individuals. It is possible that ethnic group identity can serve as a counterforce against the encroaching national forces that make for a certain degree of homogenization. It is also possible that identification with an ethnic group serves to counterbalance feelings of alienation brought on in a technological and enlarged society. The growing phenomenon of group identity and its emphasis in American culture as a political and social force also may serve as a means of expression and as a means for achieving meaning in people's lives. But what serves as a primary support of social cooperation and order, simultaneously, also is a major source of conflict and division in our society.

The United States is a nation built on immigration from many lands by many different groups of people. Between 1830 and 1930, almost 40 million Europeans crossed the Atlantic Ocean to try to make lives for themselves in America.[36] African Americans were brought first as indentured workers and then as enslaved persons. Mexicans inhabited the Southwest for centuries. Chinese persons were in California as early as 1815.[37] Native Americans were here already.

Ethnic clashes are a part of U.S. history, sometimes based on ideological conflicts but more often based on economic competition, especially for jobs. One reaction to growing diversity is an effort by some persons to defend the status quo. These concerns are expressed in various ways, including support for a more restrictive immigration policy. Another result is California's Proposition 187, which seeks to prohibit state and local governmental agencies from providing publicly funded education, health, public assistance benefits, and social services to noncitizens or persons illegally admitted to the United States. Governmental employees were expected to report those suspected of illegal immigration to the Immigration and Naturalization service.

Notwithstanding a history of intergroup conflict, there was much cooperation as well. Two group philosophies arose to point the way to the future. The *melting pot* theory held that Americans of whatever background would become "Americanized" into a happy amalgam. As late as the end of World War II, there were predictions that "the future of American ethnic groups seems to be limited; it is likely that they will be quickly absorbed."[38] This has not happened—quite the reverse. There has been an acceleration of *cultural pluralism*, the concept that group identity should be maintained and that the United States can provide a supportive setting for group continuity and group expression within a diverse but democratic society.

Immigration has contributed in an additional way to the growing diversity of American society. Immigration fueled the growth of American Muslims, Buddhists, and Hindus; enlarged the number of Roman Catholics; increased the diversity of local congregations; and led to the expansion of some churches overseas. There are 2,000 distinct religious groups in the United States. Amazingly, Los Angeles is the only place in the world that you can find all forms of Buddhism; not even Asian countries have all forms of that religion.[39] Although there may be a degree of truth to the melting pot theory (there is acculturation to a general American culture), the civil rights revolution of the 1960s, particularly the phenomenon of black pride, joined with new immigration patterns initiated a reemergence of cultural pluralism. Groups became more aware of their heritages and more sensitive to what they were losing as they ceded their traditions, language, and cultures to some mythical American ideal type.

It is clear that distinct ethnic identities and cultures exist in our diverse society. Assimilationist and anti-assimilation biases coexist in the modern United States. New responses to ethnicity and new methods of accommodation will be necessary during the next decades. African Americans have been the principal minority group in the United States. This is changing as Latinos now outnumber African Americans in Los Angeles, Houston, and will soon do so in New York and Dallas. Latinos are expected to become the nation's largest minority group by the year 2005 and one fourth of the population by 2050, as Latinos birth rates continue and African American fertility has diminished.[40] There are predictions that by the middle of the next century, 40 percent of the population will be non-white. Greater diversity is expected, which will bring many economic and social issues. The fact is that even in a time of a robust economy, means will have to be found to solve issues of distribution of resources such as jobs, government contracts, political power, and others.

However, pluralism is not limited to ethnicity or racial groups. There are groups that organize to advocate their rights, including those based on disability, religion, income levels, and sexual orientation. These ethnic and other special interest groups occupy important positions in U.S. society.

We have a national society, and we have pluralist groupings. Cultural pluralism, in fact, seems embedded in U.S. society. The libertarian values of the United States support pluralism, and pluralism suggests trade-offs and compromises. Compromises between groups suggest political incrementalism, a strategy that operates to preserve the autonomy of multiple interest groups. Thus one value supports another, pluralism reinforcing political trade-offs, which in turn support ethnic pluralism.

On a personal level, there are psychological implications of living in a diverse society. A pluralistic society requires the ability to live with differences. One result of not fully comprehending the thinking of people with whom one works with or lives near is anxiety. Handling such anxiety requires new skills and even new attitudes. For social workers, the delivery of social services for different cultural groups requires knowledge, skills, and flexibility.

This latter point is not simply one of personal psychology. Social services for ethnic groups is a matter of the distribution of resources. Which neighborhoods and people will be served by what means are issues directly connected to questions of intergroup conflict and accommodation. Questions of poverty and inequality similarly have political implications. Which ethnic groups will control a school district? Which neighborhoods will have greatest access to housing or job-training funds? Given such powerful questions, the answers profoundly influence people's lives. With the perspective that ethnic identity is an important reality in relation to decision making about services and control, U.S. society has so far proven to be remarkable for its ability to manage these intergroup balancing acts.

One example of the way in which this conflict between groups is played out is seen in the issue of quotas, goals, and affirmative action. The preferential treatment of one group can usually be offered only at expense to other groups and their members. As a result, group interests and individual rights clash in, for example, admission to colleges and professional schools and preferential hiring. Such issues remain to be worked out within an accommodation that enables our society to balance two "goods" simultaneously—the protection of individual rights and individual merit in contrast with group rights and justice for groups that have been discriminated against.

Caught within this strain among groups in a pluralist society, the human psyche demands a sense of community. The development of ethnic, women's, gay, and other groups may be indications that either humankind or the nation is too vague an entity with which to identify oneself. A person must invent a community if it does not exist. In this way, people become part of groups with a sense of social responsibility. The future will reveal whether ethnic and other groupings in our society are a result of a search for community, a way in which people can express themselves and gain "their" share in this productive society, or, as is likely, both.

GENDER

Over the past century, there has been a rapid evolution of the roles of women, family structures, and sexual mores. More women are employed, even while they have young children. As we saw earlier, more women are single-parent heads of households than ever before. Women are choosing to have children even though unmarried. They enter the professions in growing numbers.

These developments challenge male dominance and change the definition of female and male roles. Increasingly, women have been elected to political offices, including the House of Representatives and the U.S. Senate; run for the vice presidency; and have become cabinet secretaries at the federal level and Supreme Court justices, as well as governors and other state officers. Among the women who have achieved stature in numerous fields are Madelaine Albright, Maya Angelou, Carol Browner, Elizabeth Dole, Marian Wright Edelman, Jodie Foster, Betty Friedan, Bernadine Healy, Anita Hill, Mae Jemison, Audre Lorde, Wilma Mankiller, Martina Navratilova, Angela Oh, Janet Reno, Donna Shalala, Linda Chavez Thompson, Christine Todd Whitman, and Oprah Winfrey.

Although there has been progress, women continue to face restrictions, discrimination, and "glass ceilings." Sexual discrimination and harassment, although less open than they used to be, remain serious problems. Women still earn considerably less on average than men. In addition to "old boys' networks" and role models that favor men, many women have the stress of balancing work, family, and caregiving, which makes life as well as career advancement difficult. A recent study of women's perceptions found women believe they are mostly given low- or mid-level jobs, are held to higher standards than men, are discriminated against in life and business, and that young girls are not encouraged to aim for management positions.[41]

The Equal Rights Amendment to the U.S. Constitution was not approved by the number of needed states within the required time. Discrimination continues, including that against poor women, especially those receiving TANF and the prevalence of rape, domestic violence, and sexual harassment, all of which take a heavy toll on women's lives. In chapter 8 we saw how many women are oppressed by poverty, and in chapter 15, we will examine more closely female-headed households, children, and poverty. In addition, most poor aging persons are women.

In the past several decades, women have made political gains:

- The Equal Pay Act (1963) requires that women be paid the same salary as men for doing substantially the same work.
- Title VII of the Civil Rights Act (1964) bans discrimination against women and is the basis for claims of sexual harassment.
- Title IX of the Education Amendments Act (1972) prohibits sex discrimination in educational programs that receive federal funds.
- The *Roe v. Wade* (1973) Supreme Court decision ensures women the right to have an abortion within certain time limitations.
- The Pregnancy Discrimination Act (1978) states that pregnant women must have the same rights as other workers on the job.
- The Family and Medical Leave Act (1993) provides reasonable job leaves for medical reasons or for the care of a child, spouse, or parent.
- *U.S. v. Virgina re Virginia Military Institute* (1966) and *Faulkner v. Jones re The Citadel* gained the right for women to attend the last two state supported schools to prohibit women from admission.

From the perspective of social welfare, there are critical unresolved issues concerning gender in regard to poverty, discrimination, equal pay and comparable worth, equal access to and opportunities for education, health care, mental health care, and other resources, violence, changing roles and needs of single and married women, as well as women in other household relationships, including lesbian and "melded" families, and various group living arrangements. Social work has increasingly recognized the effects of sexism. Social work, particularly feminist practice, seeks to empower women and remove discriminatory attitudes and policies.

Gays and Lesbians

Homosexuality has always been present in human societies. John Boswell found that, in ancient and medieval Europe, gays were not persecuted and were often accepted, influential, and respected. The importance of Boswell's work is that it illustrates the reality that homophobia (an irrational hatred, fear, or dislike of homosexuals) has not always been the norm in Western history.[42] There is evidence of the acceptance of homosexuality in Asia and ancient China as well.[43]

Many historians date the beginning of the "gay" movement to the mid-nineteenth century. The rise of industrialization created new employment opportunities when persons living in rural areas and dependent upon their families could move to the expanding cities. It was there that personal freedom grew and individuals who felt oppressed in rural areas could gain a new sense of security. It was possible to live alone and survive, meet people like yourself, and also experience privacy. Few people knew who you were in cities and fewer still cared.

It was in the cities that communities of gays and lesbians developed as they began to find one another. Same-sex relationships were often viewed by the larger community as immoral, sinful, or later as a sign of psychiatric illness.[44] It is probable that these stigmatizing terms and mistreatment helped to build gay and lesbian communities as they had need for mutual support in stressful environments.

For gay Americans, World War II was a turning point as the conscription of millions of persons enabled people to travel and to meet in an ever-wider sphere persons who shared their own interests and concerns. The Chicago-based Society for Human Rights, founded in 1924, was the only gay rights organization in existence prior to World War II.

Some identify the appearance of the first stirrings of movement activity among recently demobilized men—following World War II—in the Veteran's Benevolent Association in New York and among working women in Los Angeles. Both groups formed out of existing friendship networks and made no attempt to gain public recognition. It was not until 1950–1951 that the Mattachine Society was formed, where gays could meet and share with each other in a nonsexual environment. This group, named for the medieval Italian court jester who expressed popular truths from behind a mask, took as its mission to unify, to educate, and to lead. The recruitment of members was slow; however, a first convention was held in 1953.

Homosexuality became caught up in McCarthyism and political "witch hunts" during the late 1940s and early 1950s. Issues of loyalty were fought on the federal level, but repression extended to state and local governments. Many gays were fearful during this era of losing their jobs. Also the Mattachine Society's leadership focused

on the "adjustment" of gays to society. This low-profile, accomodationist stance, however, was not an acceptable perspective for those who did not see themselves as having the problem. The first postwar lesbian organization—the Daughters of Bilitis—
was formed in 1955 in San Francisco.

In the 1950s and 1960s, making a life as a gay person took considerable
courage and problem solving. Gays and lesbians faced discrimination and ostracism.
Openly choosing a gay life meant in many cases the loss of family, friends, career,
and community. Nevertheless, many persons made such choices. The early 1960s
witnessed a new militance. For instance, the East Coast Homophile Organizations
(ECHO) conducted public demonstrations at the U.S. Civil Service Commission,
Department of State, Pentagon, and White House, and at Independence Hall in
Philadelphia.[45]

Influenced by the civil rights, student and anti–Vietnam War movements, the
event that galvanized the gay community to advocate gay liberation were the
Stonewall Riots of June 27–28, 1969. Patrons of the Stonewall Inn in Greenwich Village in New York City—angry because of continual police raids, harassment, and sur-
veillance—responded to a raid by throwing beer cans and bottles. The riots lasted
two nights and involved 2,000 persons battling 400 police. But this event was not an
isolated occurrence as rallies were held in Los Angeles against police harrassment
and radical student caucuses developed.

Stonewall served as a symbolic end to stigmatization and the resulting fear of
exposure, which previously restrained gays' and lesbians' behavior. Where gays had
previously acquiesced to police brutality, they now fought back. Following
Stonewall, "gay power" graffiti began to appear in Greenwich Village—public statements indicating a new phase. The Gay Liberation Front and the Gay Activists Alliance were formed, and similar groups were organized across the nation. Groups
were now focused on fighting back rather than "fitting in" to society.[46]

There are a number of issues affecting homosexuals and lesbians. At the federal
level, Congress failed to enact the Employment Non-Discrimination Act, which
would have created federal civil rights protections for homosexuals in the workplace. Tax laws do not provide for "domestic partners," and discrimination exists in
the military, despite the "don't ask, don't tell" policy. The policy has proven less than
successful, and a federal appeals court upheld the military's policy.[47] On the other
hand, a California judge ruled against the Defense Department policy and ordered
the California National Guard to admit openly gay members.[48]

At the state level, discrimination continues regarding jobs, housing, and public accomodation, domestic partner benefits, and laws regarding sexuality. Discrimination also exists in areas of family law: marriage, custody cases, foster care,
adoption (New Hampshire and Florida specifically bar adoptions by gay couples),
inheritance rights, and spousal benefits for insurance and pensions. Discrimination
also takes a destructive turn when police or others harass homosexuals and lesbians, when violence is perpetrated against gays and lesbians, and in HIV/AIDS-
related discrimination.[49]

As of 1998, gay rights laws protecting gay men and lesbians from discrimination exist only in California, Connecticut, Hawaii, Massachusetts, Minnesota, New

Hampshire, New Jersey, Rhode Island, Vermont, and Wisconsin. Maine in 1998 was the first state to repeal its law barring discrimination against gay men and lesbians in employment, housing, credit, and public accomodations.[50]

In regard to employment discrimination, the Supreme Court rejected without comment a case being appealed from Georgia. The dispute involved a woman who had been offered a job in the state law department in 1991; however, the offer was withdrawn when officials learned she planned a wedding-like religious ritual with her lesbian companion. The woman stressed in her appeal that she was not claiming a right to be married in a legal sense but sought protection against being punished by the government through denial of a public job solely because of her private relationship with her partner.[51]

In Hawaii the Supreme Court ruled in 1993 that it is unconstitutional to ban same-sex marriages and to do so violated the due process clause in the state constitution, unless the state could prove a compelling public interest in doing so. The case was returned to the trial court for the state to justify itself. This led to the State Legislature passing a bill to grant gay couples many rights and benefits and also put on the ballot for 1998 a measure that could lead to denying legality to gay marriages.

The issue of marriage for gays and lesbians became an important and widespread political conflict during 1996, a presidential and congressional election year. Concern that the U.S. Constitution's "full faith and credit" clause will require other states to honor whatever Hawaii does led to the Congress passing the preemptive Defense of Marriage Act. The Act defined a marriage as a legal union of one man and one woman as husband and wife. Although the act does not specifically forbid same-sex unions, it withholds federal tax and other benefits, which would deny gay couples many of the civil advantages of marriage. The Act was signed by President Clinton. The legislation would also allow all states to ignore same-sex marriages performed elsewhere. A major argument proffered was that the law confirms the right of each state to determine its own policy. In part because of the Hawaiian developments 25 states and Congress passed laws against homosexual marriage. It is likely that—as this is being written—same sex unions will become a constitutional right in Hawaii. Whatever the legal situation, clergypersons conducting same-sex union rituals have become more common.[52]

Sometimes events in one arena affect other issues. This may prove to be the case in regard to same-sex unions. The Supreme Court curbed the power of major companies to control corporate whistle-blowers. If a company gets a "gag" order against a whistle-blower in one state, that cannot be used to stop that witness from testifying in other states. Although the decision focused on consumer products, it may affect other disputes and the duties of states to respect the actions of other states, clarifying the "full faith and credit" clause that makes court orders in one state valid in others. If gay couples gain the right to marry in Hawaii, that clause will be directly at issue in the future as gay couples married in Hawaii will undoubtedly seek recognition of their marriages in other states.[53]

Laws do not in themselves protect people from attack. State and city laws protecting gays and lesbians from being fired from jobs, evicted from housing, or denied meeting spaces because of their sexual orientations do not ensure fair treatment. Although they give people the right to sue, much depends on peoples' attitudes.

Discrimination against gays and lesbians persists in many parts of the United States. Citizens—gay and heterosexual—from many types of groups organize to seek civil rights legislation and protection. Others counterorganize. The Supreme Court, in *Bowers v. Hardwick* (1986), upheld the constitutionality of sodomy laws by a vote of 5–4. The decision held that consensual sex between consenting adults is not protected by the Constitution even in a person's own bedroom. The majority opinion cited proscriptions against homosexuality and referred to religious rationales. The minority opinion held that private, consensual gay conduct should not be condemned because it does not interfere with the rights of others.[54]

The agenda of policy issues concerning gays includes workplace and life space security, domestic partner benefits, same-sex marriage, anti-discrimination rules, violence, divorce, custody, adoptions, and foster care issues.[55] Harassment in regard to sexual orientation, hate crimes against lesbians and gay men and lesbian and gay youth, and discrimination against gays and lesbians continue. Social work has important roles to play in direct services for gays and lesbians, educating toward attitudinal change for professionals and laypersons, assuring nondiscriminatory work environments, and working for macro-change, including legislative changes.

THE NEW PROPERTY

Land, food, clothing, housing, automobiles, and other tangible goods have long been the sign of wealth. One of the effects of a postindustrial society is the creation of a new kind of property.[56] In a service economy, there is a new property of credentials, licenses, and franchises so that now wealth is not measured just by a house or car, or even a savings account, but also by how many diplomas one has, whether one has the right credentials, and so forth. In addition to the tangible "goods" of society the importance of access to pensions, to training or education; subsidies to farmers or corporations; health; and other "properties" have grown in this postindustrial society.

The right to these new properties holds special importance for social welfare. Social welfare must be concerned with helping people gain the rights to which they are entitled. All this is complicated for social welfare because in some instances social welfare personnel serve as the advocates for citizens to obtain their rights and entitlements; at other times, social welfare personnel are the controllers of the new property itself. In 1990s, a historic debate about this issue continued in the nation. Questions were raised as to the rights to which people are entitled. There are many persons who believe that society owes no responsibility to anyone other than those who cannot possibly care for themselves. Others are expected to take complete responsibility for themselves and their families. Longstanding entitlements such as the welfare "safety net" were being challenged. "Welfare" was attacked and the concept that it is a right and an entitlement for those families in need became a critical issue in the debate.

How our society will balance such issues as the division of new property, especially where the property had been envisioned as an inheritance of real wealth, is a moot question. Needless to say, such conflicts are powerful. But, ultimately, the conflicts that surround the new property relate to the issue of the "size of the pie." Only with an expanding economy can we ensure that our society is able to meet all the expectations to which citizens are legally and legitimately entitled.

Additional Societal Issues Affecting Social Welfare

Specific societal issues change year to year, some directly, others indirectly, linked to social welfare. Although we cannot examine all of them, there are several we want to present briefly in addition to those we have presented earlier in this chapter.

Technological Change

The United States has shifted from a predominantly industrial to a service and informational society. More people work with information and services than work producing goods. In an age of computers and the Internet, cable TV, satellites, and microelectronics, many workers, including those in service and goods-producing industries, are involved in the creation, processing, and distribution of information.

Given today's electronic devices, more and more people use them to gain access to information, including stock listings and news. There are obvious implications for education in the information revolution, but also for social welfare. The place of work shifts from office to home, if not entirely then perhaps partially.

The information industry has implications for socialization, work styles, family life, and the kinds of personal problems individuals and families will experience. Special problems of privacy and confidentiality arise in such systems. The nature of social services in such an environment is today as yet unpredictable. Just as chronically ill persons who are shut in can participate "by remote" in classes, groups, and projects, the use of electronic devices—e-mail, videophones, and so on—for counseling and therapy may also be possible under certain circumstances. These changes undoubtedly have implications for social work practice, the delivery of social services, and the organization, resources, staffing, and methods of social welfare agencies.

There is another trend, which is derived from technological change. Technology has raised the output of the average skilled worker relative to that of the unskilled. The demand for skilled workers grows compared with that of the unskilled, thus raising the relative earnings of the skilled. During the past decade the economy appears to have been "skill-biased." The relative earnings of the skilled rose even while the relative supply of these workers grew. This rise in the relative earnings of the skilled occurred in virtually every industry. Technological innovation appears to have diminished the demand for unskilled labor by many millions of person-years. Thus, unemployment, especially for the unskilled, is a growing problem.

Crime

A second contextual factor of great importance is the pervasive fear of crime that affects people of all ages in rural as well as urban settings. Random acts of violence such as car-jackings, drive-by shootings, and muggings and murders undermine faith in other people. This feature of our society lessens trust and diminishes the possibility of cooperation among groups, strangers, agencies, and those in need. The true extent to which fear of crime isolates people is unknown. Does it keep them from using services such as attending senior centers or getting out for recreation in the evenings? Nevertheless, it is believed to be widespread. Such a lack of trust has implications for social needs, social services to meet these needs, and the organizing efforts required to deliver services to people who are isolated through fear. Perhaps social services will need to organize these people against crime.

The Place of Social Welfare in a Changing Context

As the United States moves toward a new century, there is great fear of intensified economic dislocations. For a time, the peaceful ending of the Cold War, so long the nation's greatest threat and cost, provided hope that in the long term more resources—a peace dividend—would be made available to meet social needs. However, because the federal debt is immense, no peace dividend appeared. It remains to be seen what future roles and what priority will be placed on social welfare.

Until recent times, the creation of the modern world has brought with it the welfare state. However, the entire thrust of social welfare in the United States since the Great Depression has been challenged. This major challenge took place in a context that included a large federal debt, popular resistance to taxes, general discontent with government, shifts in federal funding expectations of the states, and a desire by conservatives to cut taxes and return federal functions to the state level. Critics charged that social welfare is too expensive, undermines the traditional family, encouraged the increase of single-parent families and children born out of wedlock, failed to reduce the number of poor persons, and fostered dependence. Conservatives rejected anti-poverty efforts supported by governmental interventions, other than personal and familial efforts; and those in favor of even small degrees of governmental intervention found themselves stymied by the national debt and the reach for budget surpluses.

Social welfare in U.S. society developed in a piecemeal and incremental fashion; it attacked one problem, relatively without regard to other problems that might contribute to the creation of the problem or that influence its dimensions. Although experience might teach that comprehensive and coordinated approaches could offer better solutions to problems and reduce the inadequacies of one program overburdening other programs, comprehensive approaches to social welfare have been impracticable in U.S. society.

Social workers and others may see the needs of people and the positive effects of social welfare programs. But the individual observations of social workers are not made within a vacuum. On the contrary, they take place within the context of a national society at a particular time and state of development. Social welfare is in fact the collective supply of resources, a sharing of the burden or the risk. Two questions have to be asked: (1) What needs should be supplied by the collective action of the society and which left to individual effort? (2) What can the society afford to do and to not do?

The two-edged nature of social welfare has been recognized, that is:

> We can degrade people by caring for them; and we can degrade them by not caring for them; . . . All interventions have consequences, and one of the things we should learn to keep in the forefront of our consciousness is that the most important consequences of any intervention almost always turn out to be those consequences that were not intended or planned upon or could not have been calculated beforehand.[57]

SUMMARY

In this chapter, we have examined major trends that impact on the needs of people and on the social welfare response of society. Among the factors we looked at were growth, demography, and resources; productivity and the service economy; individual and shared goals; the family; ethnicity and pluralism; gender; gays and lesbians; the new property; technological change; crime; and the place of social welfare in a changing context.

In chapter 15, we will discuss alternative programs to meet the needs of female heads of household and their children, immigration, the aging and long-term health care, persons with disabilities, and technology and social action. We will also explore alternatives facing practitioners, where we are, and two scenarios affecting social welfare's future. We conclude with our proposal for the amelioration of poverty.

QUESTIONS FOR CONSIDERATION

1. Can you locate trend data that suggest future social needs in your community in relation to a specific problem: teenage pregnancy, child abuse, depression among the elderly, and so on?
2. What effects of the baby boom generation do you foresee for your community in the coming decades?
3. In what ways do you think technological changes affect social welfare?
4. What human needs do you believe should be supplied through collective action and which left to individual effort?

NOTES

1. Robert L. Heilbroner, "Trying to Make Sense of It," *New York Times*, October 10, 1977, p. 29.
2. Quoted by Jeff Jacoby, "Dr. Doom," *The Baltimore Sun*, February 7, 1995, p. 15A; "The Population Bomb, Reconsidered," *New York Times*, Editorial, November 30, 1978, p. A22.
3. Paul R. Ehrlich and Anne H. Ehrlich, *Population Explosion*, New York: Simon & Schuster, 1990.

4. Paul R. Ehrlich and Anne H. Ehrlich, *Healing the Planet*, Reading, Mass.: Addison-Wesley Publishing Co., 1991, and Paul R. Ehrlich, Anne H. Ehrlich, and Gretchen C. Daily, *The Stork and the Plow*, New York: G.P. Putnam's Sons, 1995, p. 3.

5. Lester R. Brown and Hal Kane, *Full House: Reassessing the Earth's Population Carrying Capacity*, London: Earthscan, 1995, pp. 21–24, 31.

6. Barbara Crossette, "World Is Less Crowded Than Expected, the U.N. Reports," *New York Times*, November 17, 1996, p. 3.

7. Patricia L. Kutzner, *World Hunger*, Santa Barbara, Calif.: ABC-CLIO, Inc., 1991, pp. ix, 34, 25–26, 50.

8. Nikos Alexandratos, ed., *World Agriculture: Towards an FAO Study*, New York: John Wiley & Sons, 1995, pp. 1–2, 4–7.

9. Stephen Moore, "So Much for 'Scarce Resources'," *The Public Interest*, No. 106, Winter 1992, p. 97.

10. Paul Lewis, "UNICEF Sees Death of Infants Ebbing," *New York Times*, December 19, 1990, p. A8.

11. Daniel Bell, "The World and the United States in 2013," *Daedelus*, Vol. 116, No. 3, Summer 1987, p. 4.

12. Sylvia Nasar, "The Conscience of the Dismal Science," *New York Times*, January 9, 1994, p. 8F; Amartya Sen, *Poverty and Families*, Oxford: Clarendon Press, 1981.

13. Julian L. Simon, *The Ultimate Resource*, Princeton: Princeton University Press, 1996, pp. 5, 6, 12.

14. William B. Meyer, *Human Impact on the Earth*, New York: Cambridge University Press, 1996, p. 33.

15. Massimo Livi-Bacci, *A Concise History of World Population*, 2nd Edition, Malden, Mass.: Blackwell Publishers, Inc., 1997, pp. 218, 223.

16. Eduard Pestel, *Beyond the Limits to Growth: A Report to the Club of Rome*, New York: Universe Books, 1989, p. 41.

17. John Rawls, *A Theory of Justice*, Cambridge, Mass.: Harvard University Press, 1971.

18. Eleanor Bernert forecast in *America's Children* (New York: John Wiley & Sons, 1958) the need for services generated by this "bulge" cohort.

19. U.S. Bureau of the Census, *Statistical Abstract of the United States: 1997*, 117th edition, Table 148, "Marriage Rates and Median Age of Bride and Groom, by Previous Marital Status: 1970 to 1990," Washington, D.C.: U.S. Government Printing Office, 1997, p. 106.

20. U.S. Bureau of the Census, Table 58, "Marital Status of the Population by Sex, Race, and Hispanic Origin: 1980 to 1996," p. 55; U.S. Bureau of the Census, Table 152, "Marriages and Divorces—Number and Rate, by State: 1980 to 1995," p. 108; U.S. Bureau of the Census, Table 150, "First Marriage Dissolution and Years Until Remarriage for Women, by Race and Hispanic Origin: 1988," p. 107.

21. U.S. Bureau of the Census, Table 58, "Marital Status of the Population by Sex, Race, and Hispanic Origin: 1970 to 1994," p. 54.

22. U.S. Bureau of the Census, Table 66, "Households, Families, Subfamilies, Married Couples, and Unrelated Individuals: 1970 to 1996," p. 59.

23. U.S. Bureau of the Census, Table 97, "Births to Unmarried Women, by Race of Child and Age of Mother: 1980 to 1994," p. 79.

24. Stephanie J. Ventura, et al., "Teenage Births in the United States: National and State Trends, 1990-96," National Vital Statistics System, Hyattsville, Md.: National Center for Health Statistics, 1998, p.6; U.S. Bureau of the Census, Table 93, "Total Fertility Rate and Intrinsic Rate of Natural Increase: 1960 to 1994," p. 77.

25. U.S. Bureau of the Census, *Statistical Abstract of the United States: 1997*, 117th edition, Table No. 68, "Households, 1980 to 1996, and Persons in Households, 1996, by Type of Household and Presence of Children," Washington, D.C.: U.S. Government Printing Office, 1997, p. 60.

26. U.S. Bureau of the Census, Table 58, "Marital Status of the Population, by Sex, Race, and Hispanic Origin: 1980 to 1996," p. 55; "Unmarried Couples in the U.S. Exceed 4 Million," *Baltimore Sun*, July 27, 1998, p. 3A; Randolph E. Schmid, "More People over 45 Are Setting up 'Nontraditional' Households," *The Baltimore Sun*, September 7, 1995, p. 9E; U.S. Bureau of the Census, Table 66, "Households, Families, Subfamilies, Married Couples, and Unrelated Individuals: 1970 to 1996," p. 59.

27. U.S. Bureau of the Census, Table 66, "Households, Families, Subfamilies, Married Couples, and Unrelated Individuals: 1970 to 1996," p. 59.

28. Richard A. Peterson, *The Dynamics of Industrial Society*, New York: Bobbs-Merrill, 1973, p. 48.

29. Ibid.

30. U.S. Department of Labor, Bureau of Labor Statistics, "Employment Status of the Civilian Noninstitutional Population by Sex and Age, Seasonally Adjusted," *Employment and Earnings*, Vol. 45, No. 6, June 1998, p. 34.

31. *Statistical Abstract 1997*, Table 660, "Nonfarm Establishments, Employees, Hours, and Earnings, by Industry: 1960 to 1996," p. 422. The shift to service-producing economies is international in scope among nations with advanced economies. See Tom Elfring, *Service Sector Employment in Advanced Economies*, Brookfield,Vt.: Avebury Publishers, 1988, p. 27.

32. Deidre Carmody, "Fortune Adds Service Sector to Its '500' List of Corporations," *New York Times*, April 24, 1995, p. D1.

33. Stephen S. Roach, "Good News on Inflation!" *New York Times*, July 18, 1994, p. A15.

34. U.S. Bureau of the Census, "Geographical Mobility of People 1 Year Old and Older by Sex, Between March 1996 and March 1997," www.bls.census/gov/cps/pub/1997//mobility.htm, July 30, 1998, and *Statistical Abstract, 1997*, "Table 32, "Mobility Status of the Population, by Selected Characteristics: 1980 to 1996," p. 32.

35. Daniel Bell, "The Cultural Contradictions of Capitalism," *Capitalism Today*, Daniel Bell and Irving Kristol, eds., New York: New American Library, 1971, pp. 27-57.

36. Stanley Feldstein and Lawrence Costello, eds., *The Ordeal of Assimilation*, Garden City, N.J.: Anchor Books, 1974, p. 1.

37. H. M. Lai, "Chinese," *Harvard Encyclopedia of American Ethnic Groups*, Stephan Thernstrom, ed., Cambridge, Mass.: Harvard University Press, 1980, p. 21.

38. Rudolph J. Vecoli, "Ethnicity: A Neglected Dimension of American History," *Overcoming Middle Class Rage*, Murray Friedman, ed., Philadelphia: Westminster Press, 1971, p. 160.

39. Gustav Niebuhr, "Land of Religious Freedom Has Universe of Spirituality," *New York Times*, March 30, 1997, pp. 1, 16.

40. William H. Frey and Jonathan Tilove, "Immigrants In, Native Whites Out," *New York Times Magazine*, August 20, 1995, pp. 44-45; Steven A. Holmes, "Hispanic Population Moves Closer to Surpassing That of Blacks," *New York Times*, August 7, 1998, p. A15; U.S. Bureau of the Census, *Statistical Abstract of the United States: 1997*, 117th edition, Table 13, "Resident Population—Selected Characteristics, 1790 to 1996 and Projections, 2000 to 2050," Washington, D.C.: U.S. Government Printing Office, 1997, p. 14.

41. Judith H. Dobrzynski, "Women Less Optimistic About Work, Poll Says," *New York Times*, September 12, 1995, p. D5.

42. John Boswell, *Christianity, Social Tolerance, and Homosexuality*, Chicago: University of Chicago Press, 1980.

43. Kevin Jennings, *Becoming Visible*, Boston: Alyson Publications, 1994, pp. 52–63.

44. Warren Johansson, "Psychiatry," *Encyclopedia of Homosexuality*, Vol. 2, Wayne R. Dynes, ed., New York: Garland Publishing, 1990, pp. 1072–1074.

45. Barry D. Adam, *The Rise of a Gay and Lesbian Movement*, Boston: Twayne Publishers, 1987, pp. 58, 62–63; Cynthia C. Poindexter, "Sociopolitical Antecedents to Stonewall: Analysis of the Origins of the Gay Rights Movement in the United States," *Social Work*, Vol. 42, No. 6, November 1997, pp. 607–615.

46. Margaret Cruikshank, *The Gay and Lesbian Liberation Movement*, New York: Routledge, 1992, p. 69.

47. Andrew Sullivan, "Undone by 'Don't Ask, Don't Tell'," *New York Times*, April 2, 1998, p. A31; Alan Finder, "Court Backs the Pentagon on Gay Rights," *New York Times*, September 24, 1998, p. A14.

48. "National Guard Is Told to Admit Homosexuals," *New York Times*, July 1, 1998, p. A18.

49. Wallace Swan, ed., *Gay/Lesbian/Transgender Public Policy Issues*, New York: Haworth Press, 1997.

50. Carey Goldberg, "Maine Voters Repeal a Law On Gay Rights," *New York Times*, February 12, 1998, pp. 1, A33.

51. Lyle Denniston, "Supreme Court Rejects Plea to Hear Ga. Gay-Rights Case," *The Baltimore Sun*, January 13, 1998, p. 4A.

52. Carey Goldberg, "For Couple Who Stirred Issue of Same-Sex Marriage, Surprise Mixes with Hope," *New York Times*, July 28, 1996, p. 12.

53. Lyle Denniston, "Supreme Court Loosens Muzzles on Corporate Whistle-Blowers," *The Baltimore Sun*, January 14, 1998, p. 3A.

54. Cruikshank, p. 53.

55. Wallace Swan, ed., *Gay/Lesbian/Transgender Public Policy Issues*, New York: Haworth Press, 1997.

56. Charles Reich, "The New Property," *The Public Interest*, Vol. 1, No. 3, 1966, pp. 57–89.

57. Steven Marcus, "Their Brothers' Keepers: An Episode from English History," *Doing Good: The Limits of Benevolence*, Willard Gaylin, ed., New York: Pantheon, 1981, pp. 65–66.

Alternative Programs to Meet Social Welfare Needs

No choice is a choice.
—Yiddish Proverb

Life's business being just the terrible choice.
—Robert Browning

OVERVIEW

At any given moment, there are debates over alternatives in social welfare programs. Old programs evolve; new programs are introduced. All citizens, and certainly social workers, need to have informed and intelligent opinions on alternatives. In this chapter, we want to help the reader not just to understand what currently exists but to develop opinions and to see which of several directions are preferable. We will accompany the reader through an analysis of several programs, studying alternatives and developing a point of view.

The structures of social welfare programs and not just specific benefit levels or provisions are extremely important; in part because these programs, once in place, with few exceptions have tended to maintain their skeletal structures. Since 1935, the Social Security system has been changed and improved many times. Still, the changes have been incremental, and the Social Security system continues to operate within the general outlines of the 1935 enactments, with the basic inequities that have been pointed out almost since the system's inception.

There are so many social welfare programs that it is impossible here to analyze alternatives suggested for them all. For that reason, we focus on program examples in several areas that exemplify the general issues and choices: (1) female heads of household, children, and poverty; (2) immigration; (3) the aging and long-term home

367

health care; (4) persons with disabilities; (5) technology and social action; (6) where we are; (7) two scenarios; and (8) our proposal.

FEMALE HEADS OF HOUSEHOLD, CHILDREN, AND POVERTY

A classic election campaign photo opportunity is one in which a campaigner is seen holding and kissing a baby, indicating the campaigner's concern for children. Americans, including our politicians, exude warmth and caring about our children. We are often told children are our future. But when we look closely at what laws are passed and what budget priorities actually are chosen, we are faced with the differences between our societal rhetoric about the importance of children and the reality of childrens' lives.

In the United States, diversity and inequality among American families have grown for several decades. Over time there has been an increase in marital instability, a reduction in remarriage rates following divorce, a decline of births among married couples accompanied by continued out-of-wedlock births. As a result, there has been an increase in the numbers of single-parent families. These changes are taking place in the context of growing racial and ethnic diversity with minority populations increasing in number more rapidly than the white population.[1] Women earn on average only 74 percent of the earnings of men; many women feel they do not get the pay, benefits, or recognition they deserve. During 1995, 28.9 million persons lived in mother-only families (never married, separated, divorced, and widowed). Of these, 12.8 million were poor (44.5 percent). Whereas only 18 percent of all families in the United States had a female householder with no spouse present, 54 percent of all poor families had such a householder.[2]

The poverty rate for U.S. children is about twice that of most other industrialized nations, and it has increased in the United States from the early 1970s. Several causes are suggested for this poverty rise: (1) economic changes have eliminated many blue-collar jobs that paid well; (2) the percentage of children living in single-parent families has increased; and (3) the real value of governmental benefits has declined because of inflation. In addition, policy changes have reduced the dollar amount of benefits and the number of children eligible for them. In addition, (4) the results for this population of the rigorous reform of public assistance begun in 1997 cannot be predicted at this time. The effects of a recession joined with implementation of sanctions for some families may prove to be harmful for children, the most vulnerable group, whose parents are least prepared to support themselves and family through employment.[3]

In 1996, the AFDC program served on average 5 million families, mainly female-headed households and two-thirds children, even while some recipients were employed either full- or part-time. The average monthly benefit was $374 per family, or $109 per recipient. Average family size was 2.7 persons. Even with Food Stamps, combined benefits were only slightly above 60 percent of the poverty guidelines. It is unlikely that benefits will rise to more reasonable levels.

As indicated here, growing up in a single-parent household is one of the less se-cure living arrangements for children. There are many mother-headed families whose financial security is undermined by fathers who do not pay child support. Af-ter parents divorce or separate, children have been found to be almost twice as likely to be living in poverty than they were before the breakup. These findings underscore the relationship between family structure and economic well-being. A family breakup can cause poverty, but poverty can also cause families to break up.[4] What-ever the reason for a family's being poor, money can buy good food, a safe and de-cent shelter, opportunities to learn, and good health care, and can reduce family stress and conflict.

As we saw in chapter 1, there are both social and economic costs to poverty for these women and their children. Low-income children are at higher risk for the following:

- death during infancy
- low birthweight
- being abused or neglected
- being partly or completely blind
- physical or mental disabilities
- overall injuries
- hospitalization
- iron deficiency in preschool years
- asthma
- school days missed due to acute learning disabilities and chronic health conditions

- being below grade in school
- death during childhood
- stunted growth
- being partly or completely deaf
- mild mental retardation
- more days in bed because of injuries
- fair or poor health
- pneumonia
- decayed, missing, or filled teeth
- being a dropout at age 16 to 24.[5]

Providing adequate nutrition on a below-poverty-level budget is by definition an extremely difficult or impossible task. Nutritional difficulties can lead to other dif-ficulties, and poor housing can contribute to lead poisoning and risks such as living in fire-prone mobile homes. Poverty reduces the number of opportunities to learn at all educational levels. Money reduces family stress and conflict and can provide the opportunity to live in decent neighborhoods and receive health care. Money buys transportation, communication, and economic opportunities. Thus, to be poor is to suffer the impact of many adverse forces. Furthermore, the many effects of poverty on families and their children all interact and are cumulative. Childhood poverty re-duces the lifetime productivity output of workers, reduces employment opportuni-ties, and increases ill health and mortality. These adverse conditions have societal economic costs, ranging into the many billions. They result in reduced worker out-put measured by lower lifetime earnings, and it is clear that the social and economic costs of children in poverty are substantial not just to them personally but also to the entire society.

Studies show that poor children in the United States are poorer than the chil-dren in most other Western industrialized nations. There are proportionately more children in poverty in the United States than in other affluent societies. One contributing factor is the shortage of child care in the United States. When inexpensive, high-quality child care is available, it is easier for mothers to return to the workforce. Because these studies excluded in-kind benefits such as free medical and child care services, some claim that the situation for poor children in the United States would compare even less well to these other industrialized nations. Furthermore, the income gap between poor households with children in the United States and affluent households with children is larger in the United States than in any of the other developed nations. Also, welfare programs in the United States are less generous than in these other countries. Finally, households with children in the United States tend to have lower incomes than the national average, a pattern not shared by many other nations.[6]

Social policy and the resulting programs meant to deal with the problem of poverty among single-parent women and their children have never been sufficient to the task. Programs do not focus on preventing a fall into poverty. They provide benefits and services only after families are unable to meet their own needs.

Limitations of Current Programs

What are some of the limitations of programs that have been designed to assist these parents and their children?

1. The residual nature of the programs and their accompanying means tests cause many people to be declared ineligible because they do not fall completely within specified guidelines, although their need may be real. The stigma associated with means-tested programs leads many persons not to apply because they do not want to be seen as dependent and failing.

2. Benefits are inadequate to the task. Public assistance, the mainstay of many female-headed families and their children, has never provided in any state—other than Alaska and Hawaii—cash and the value of Food Stamps equal to the official poverty level. Few states provide a maximum grant equal to what they define as 100 percent of the "need standard"—the income the state decides is essential for basic consumption items.

3. Poor children tend to live in school districts in rural and inner-city areas which are inequitably financed through property taxes. These school districts are less able to provide a quality education than those in suburban areas.

4. As noted previously, poor children and their families experience difficulty gaining access to medical and dental care for a variety of reasons. They receive poorer quality care and are hospitalized more frequently than persons with private health insurance.

5. They tend to live in unsafe and unhealthy housing.

6. The several programs designed to serve this group are uncoordinated. They are administered at several levels of government, by different agencies and personnel, and with differing eligibility criteria. It is the task of the recipient to ascertain eligibility criteria, meet deadlines, and negotiate varying requirements expected by

agencies unmindful of the requirements of other agencies that affect the family's needs.

Improved Social Policy

What should U.S. social policy be? The basic question is to what degree should the society support female-headed households and their children? There are those whose position is clear: Support women and families to the greatest extent possible for their individual sakes and the sake of the society now and in the future. Others argue that if you improve the conditions for single parents and their families, you undermine the traditional family. The latter argument expresses traditional values that challenge much of what is going on in modern life. The former argument suggests there is no moral alternative and that it is more practical and a higher value for the society to attempt to assist such families with income, educational opportunity, and health care, among other supports. Various industrialized societies react to these questions in different ways.

Sheila Kamerman identified four clusters of policies and programs that are used as strategies in industrialized nations for mother-headed families:

1. *A targeted focus on poor families*. This approach provides public assistance to all poor families and assumes that mothers, whether in one- or two-parent families, will remain at home to rear their children.

2. *Categorical targeting of lone mothers with modest incomes*. These programs assume that most mothers prefer to stay home with their children if financially possible and that women who parent alone have special needs.

3. *Universal support for young children*. Whether married or single, mothers with very young children are covered by these programs. This type of program assumes that financial support and job-protected leaves for parents with children under 3 years of age would find they want to stay home and that children are better off if parents who prefer this choice can do so.

4. *Combining labor market and family policies*. This policy provides cash benefits, services, and other policy supports for working families with children. The goal is to enable parents to enter and remain in the workforce without undue hardship during the child-rearing years.[7]

A Set of Ideal Services

We suggest a combination of strategies (3) and (4): A universal, economic support program for young children and methods that enable parents to enter and remain in the workforce without undue hardship during the child-rearing years. In place of the current scattered efforts for poor single mothers and their children, the United States should seek the welfare of all families and their children. The philosophy we choose to guide social policy for families and their children, not just single-parent mothers and their children, ought to be institutional and universal. Universal, non-means-tested programs should replace selective and means-tested approaches. A focus on poor families that utilizes residual and selective programs intensifies a sense of stigma for those who need assistance. The means-tested approach also excludes those who fall slightly above what is a relatively arbitrary eligibility level.

Some persons advocate changes in public policy such as more stringent divorce laws, holding parents responsible for their childrens' actions, holding fathers responsible for child support, and finding ways for citizens to return to more traditional family values and structures. Others emphasize the provision of material resources such as money, education, health and child care. The provision of additional resources will certainly require reallocation of resources from other sources—the aging, other governmental programs, and families and individuals without children. Certainly, the implementation of Temporary Assistance for Needy Families (TANF) has made the situation of many women and their families more problematic. One way to achieve such a reallocation is through the requirement that employers provide benefits such as paid leave and subsidized child care. The costs of these benefits could be shared among all workers and among consumers. To choose the employer route will avoid certain public budget conflicts. But that strategy will usually be less efficient and less equitable than direct government programs. An alternative way to approach the problem is through government action such as tax credits, subsidies, and child allowances. Choosing this path requires raising taxes, reducing spending, changing priorities, or all three actions.[8]

Raising a family is a normal, legitimate, and necessary function in our society, and our society benefits from healthy, educated, and productive citizens. The needs of families are not abnormal, nor should they be stigmatized. Families should not have to prove their needs in order to be eligible for programs that make it possible for all children and their parents to have a reasonable quality of life. Programs that make this possible should be universal and open to all families and their children below a certain age limit. Such an approach would provide a basic standard of living for all families and the creation of a healthy, appropriately housed, educated, and productive citizenry. Such an approach is preventive, mitigates the structural antecedents of poverty, and supports the morale enhancing idea that our society cares for all its families and their children.

The United States should provide a basic guaranteed annual income and a family allowance to all families with children younger than 18 years of age. The amount provided should be sufficient for the expense of raising children. The cost of these two income security programs can be recouped from those who are well off through the income tax system, which will avoid stigma and create a cost-efficient program. In addition, the minimum wage, whose value has seriously been eroded, should be raised to a level that would allow a working adult to provide at least for a three-person family at the poverty level. (The average public assistance family is slightly fewer than three persons.) The minimum wage should be indexed to inflation to protect its purchasing power. As part of this income security approach, job opportunities—including public work employment and the government's serving as employer of last resort—should be made available for all those able and wishing to work.

Among the other services and benefits that should accompany these economic aspects, our society should strive to provide high-quality public education for all children; safe, affordable, and uncrowded housing for all families; comprehensive and accessible medical and dental care; public and inexpensive transportation; child care for all on a sliding scale; universal application forms, procedures, and eligibility requirements for all services. In addition, agencies serving families and children should be expected to coordinate their services to assist families applying for and receiving the services they need.

One strategy suggested as a complement to these services is "the women's economic agenda." Women and other disadvantaged groups are affected differentially by low and inequitable wages and lack of access to capital. A single mother in a minimum-wage job has to pay from half to three-quarters of her salary for licensed day care. Over one-half of those women starting new businesses have to pay high interest for credit to begin their businesses. Many women workers are also part-time and temporary and so receive few, if any, benefits.

The Women's Voices for the Economy Commission proposed the following agenda:

- Capital to start and expand businesses;
- Job training, continuing education, and skill development;
- Equitable pay and benefits for contingent, temporary workers;
- Flexible schedules; and
- Adequate care for children and the elderly.

This agenda seeks to encourage public-private partnerships in the development of child care centers; support training programs for women who want to work in nontraditional jobs; establish the government as a broker between contractors and service providers; and encourage businesses to offer incentives for investing in their communities. The agenda features partnerships, incentives, individual contributions, and the leveraging of available resources.[9]

Later in this chapter, we will examine a problem concerning aging persons who need home health care. By juxtaposing the needs of these two groups, we emphasize the nature of the social policy trade-offs that must be considered. Demographic changes indicate a growing percentage of the population who are aging with their special needs. As a greater priority is placed on resources and services for the aging, the difficulty grows of finding funds for the reforms and social programs needed for poor women and children. In the next section, we turn to one important need for aging persons.

THE AGING AND LONG-TERM HOME HEALTH CARE

The "graying" of the United States continues as the elderly population increases both numerically and as a percentage of the total population. Improved nutrition and preventive and acute health care services have increased the longevity of the population. In 1996, the number of persons 65 years of age and older reached 33.8 million (one in eight persons)—the highest level in history—and is expected to continue increasing as the baby boom generation ages.[10] In 1996, there were 14.2 million persons 75 years of age and older, including 57,000 persons *100* years of age and older.[11]

The successes attained over the past decades bring with them new problems. An aging population, despite the good health of many, is at high risk for age-related chronic illness and disability. As those 75 years and older age, the number of persons with disabilities, chronic illnesses, and other special needs increases.[12] Poor elderly persons are at higher risk than the rest of the population for experiencing chronic illness and disability.[13]

To date we have chosen to devote most of society's resources to acute medical care rather than relatively less technologically sophisticated services. A number of trends support the continuation of this pattern. National policy seeks to minimize the number of those who must depend on institutions for personal assistance. For-profit medical care has grown. The refusal to provide long-term care benefits forces women to provide unpaid informal care. The nonprofit sector has experienced a decline in its ability to provide social support services for those who cannot pay privately.

Social policy—in general—has been focused on increasing family responsibility and dependence, on women working, on the "informalization" of care, along with early discharge from hospitals. All this is done to minimize corporate and state costs, as well as restrain taxes.[14] Although we refer here to home health care and the aging, a student should know that this is an issue for children and their families as well.

The United States faces a serious problem: how to organize and pay for long-term care for elderly disabled people. In addition to acute illnesses that require hospital care, many aging persons require long-term care either at home or in nursing homes. Because of technological advances, those who have what were not long ago fatal illnesses now have prolonged lives and increased duration of chronic disabling conditions.[15] Heart disease, strokes, arthritis, and Alzheimer's disease are among the many diseases and disabilities that create a need for long-term care. Choices include nursing homes for those most frail, but also home care, assisted living, and adult day care.

Most long-term care services are provided by family members and friends, often at considerable financial, energy, and emotional cost. Family caregiving for older persons usually falls to adult daughters who in many cases will devote more years to caring for aging parents than doing so for their own children. A 1996 study found more than 22 million persons served as caregivers for relatives or friends over 50 years of age, including many who provide constant care.[16] However, the expectation is that the problem of care will worsen because fewer offspring will be available to provide informal care for future elderly persons.

Medicare, the primary health insurance for the elderly, emphasizes comprehensive coverage for *acute care* services rather than services for chronic disabling conditions. Long-term care was excluded from Medicare in 1965 for fear the program would become too expensive. Limited Medicare nursing home benefits are designed for convalescence from an episode in a hospital, not for chronic disabilities. Medicaid includes provision for long-term benefits for the poor, but few expected it to be an important service for the middle class.[17] In 1995 home health care represented only 8.7 percent of overall Medicare costs.[18]

In 1988 legislation was introduced funding long-term care in the home. Unfortunately, this attempt was caught up in the battle regarding the Catastrophic Care Act (1988). In 1990 the U.S. Bipartisan Commission on Comprehensive Health Care recommended legislation intended to ensure that all Americans have coverage for health care and long-term care.[19]

Legislation for long-term care (Long Term Care Family Security Act, 1992) again was introduced, and President William Clinton called during his first presidential campaign for public funding of long-term care without means tests. Despite efforts by advocates for the elderly, these national efforts to expand governmental funding of home care have not succeeded. On the state level, nursing and home health care were approximately 14 percent of state and local health care spending. Nevertheless, some states are attempting to expand home and community-based services for older persons. Medicaid pays only the costs that the elderly themselves cannot. Institutional care is largely available only for those with the most severe disabilities who do not have family supports. Because the need is expected to grow dramatically, there is little expectation that there will be an infusion of funds equal to the demand.[20]

Several new demonstration projects sponsored by the federal government are being tested to control costs. They capitate payments (set a dollar limit for a given time period) for enrollees and combine in some cases money from Medicare, Medicaid, and premiums paid by enrollees: (1) The Partnership for All-Inclusive Care for the Elderly (PACE) serves frail older persons who are certified as needing a nursing home level of care. The goal is to help the individual continue living in the community by funding all necessary medical, restorative, social, and supportive services. A multidisciplinary team assesses and ensures needed services, utilizing a day health center as the primary setting. (2) Social Health Maintenance Organizations (S/HMOs) are testing whether comprehensive health services for primarily functionally independent older adults and some functionally impaired or frail elderly can prevent or delay nursing home placement. Integrating acute and certain extended care services for older persons under the Medicare program, the aim is to prevent nursing home placement. Coordinating acute and some chronic care within a managed care setting, individuals are referred to appropriate services based on an evaluation of needs. A case management system coordinates and authorizes long-term care services for those who meet certain disability criteria. Funding is on a capitation basis using Medicare and Medicaid dollars as well as enrollee premiums. Voluntarily enrolled Medicare recipients pay a monthly premium and assign their Medicare benefits to the S/HMO. By coordinating acute and chronic care, the attempt is to hold costs at or below public costs of Medicare and Medicaid while reducing nursing home placement.

When elderly citizens were asked to pay for expanded coverage under the Medicare Catastrophic Care Act (1988), they rejected the legislation, and Congress was forced to repeal the law, the first major expansion of Medicare since its inception. The changes would have provided substantial improvements for those with serious disabilities and acute illnesses. The issue was a surtax on middle- and upper-income elderly persons and the introduction of differential payments according to income, thus making visible redistributive funding. This program was beneficial for many persons, but those elderly persons with higher incomes were asked to pay and they reacted negatively to the idea. Some persons thought only low-income elderly persons would benefit and only high-income elderly persons would pay. Ironically, long-term care is the major reason aging persons incur catastrophic health expenses.[21]

The result of these decisions is that Medicare covers acute care expenses and long-term expenditures are paid by a means-tested program—Medicaid—intended for the poor but also used by middle-class persons who must "spend down" their assets during long illnesses in order to access the service. Much is spent on long-term care. Are there better ways to do so? What are the implications of a public system for the poor and those who gain access by becoming poor and those with higher incomes who utilize a private system through long-term care insurance? As more persons need home care, who will define eligibility and for what services?

The expenditures for care are not trivial, as shown in Table 15.1.

Some persons argue for government insurance for long-term care. These proponents suggest that a majority of the elderly cannot afford private long-term care insurance and a universal government entitlement would avoid the stigma associated with Medicaid. Further, Medicaid financing is insecure, subject to state budget constraints, and coverage and access are not uniform across states. Since most citizens would be enrolled, adverse selection would be prevented and those with preexisting and high-risk conditions would be covered. Such a program would be inflation proof through the government taxing power and not viewed as "welfare" because every-

TABLE 15.1   Total Expenditures for Nursing Home Care, by Type of Facility: 1990 and 1996

	Amounts in Billions Hospital-Based Nursing Home Facilities	Freestanding Nursing Home Facilities
1990	3.7	50.9
1996	9.0	78.5

SOURCE: Health Care Financing Administration, *Health Care Financing Review,* Washington, D.C.: U.S. Government Printing Office, 1997, p. 168.

Total Expenditures for Home Health Care, by Type of Facility: 1990 and 1996

	Amounts in Billions Hospital-Based Home Health Facilities	Freestanding Home Health Facilities
1990	1.6	13.1
1996	7.8	30.2

SOURCE: Health Care Financing Administration, *Health Care Financing Review,* Washington, D.C.: U.S. Government Printing Office, 1997, p. 169.

TABLE 15.2   Medicare Home Health Care Utilization, 1983–1996

| | People Served | Visits | |
	No. Per 1,000 Enrolled	No. (in millions)	Per 1,000 Enrolled
1983			
1,318,000	45	36.9	1,234
1996			
3,735,000	99	285.7	7,578

SOURCE: Committee on Ways and Means, U.S. House of Representatives, *1998 Green Book, Background Mater-ial and Data on Programs within the Jurisdiction of the Committee on Ways and Means,* Washington, D.C.: U.S. Government Printing Office, 1998, "Medicare Home Health Care Utilization and Payments Per Visit, 1983–96," p.139.

Medicaid Payments for Home Health Care with Percentage of Total Attributed to Health Care and Number of Recipients

1981	$729 million	1.6%	402,000
1995	$9,406 million	7.8%	1,639,000

SOURCE: "Medicaid Payments by Service Category, Fiscal Years 1975, 1981, 1990, and 1995," and "Medicaid Recipients by Service Category, Selected Fiscal Years 1975–1995," *The Green Book,* pp. 981–982.

one 65 or older would be covered. Cost containment would be built into the system from its inception.[22] Since 1988, the home health benefit has been Medicare's fastest growing benefit, as shown in Table 15.2. There have been increased numbers of users and an increased number of visits per beneficiary. Some portion of the growth may be a result of increased need for skilled home care resulting from incentives to discharge patients more quickly to their homes, more liberal criteria for those with medical problems that require personal care assistance, aging of the population, technological advances that make care in the home more equal to that previously found only in hospitals, and an expansion of the number of agencies participating in Medicare.

The ability of those needing long-term care to gain access and afford services is problematic, influenced by price, family preferences, ability to pay, and availability of the service. But chronic conditions limit one's access to private insurance and force many persons to rely on governmental provision. Many experts believe that private long-term care insurance cannot be relied upon for financing necessary care.

Family members are primary caregivers for those with chronic conditions; therefore, as community care becomes more prevalent, the demands on these care-givers will intensify. Opportunities for respite for caregivers are essential because of the draining physical and emotional demands placed on caregivers. Respite workers can provide services in the home when appropriate. Respite can also be provided for the homebound person in adult day care programs as well as freestanding respite fa-cilities. Respite for the elderly according to functional levels may also be provided in skilled nursing facilities, intermediate care facilities, adult homes, senior housing, and hospitals. These services assure continual care, provide support for caregivers, can provide a break for caregiver and homebound person, provide an opportunity for rechecking drug and diet, and provide new information or suggestions to care-givers.[23]

As the United States continues to wrestle with issues related to allocation of scarce resources and funding of health services in general for the growing elderly population, questions may increasingly be raised as to how much should go toward persons with disabilities and in need of chronic care.

The effort to control health care costs contributes to the growth of the home health care industry. Such care reduces the number of hospital days for both termi-nally ill and non-terminally ill patients. The increased use of home care reflects the decreased use of nursing homes and the decreased average length of stay in nursing homes. The cost of home care is much less than a hospital stay or in a skilled long-term care facility.[24] Despite this fact, home care services were denied to many frail elderly persons, and Congress has reduced funding for these services. Federal judges restored the benefits to thousands of cases and Congress was considering raising the funds allocated to these services.[25]

We need both institutional and community care. The question is how much of our social welfare resources should be invested in each. This complicates the prob-lem for the social welfare student. In each situation, there needs to be an analysis ac-cording to the program paradigm of horizontal and vertical adequacy, financial costs, coherence with other social programs, and latent consequences—a complex reckon-ing but nonetheless necessary. In such calculations, alternative living and/or care arrangements also should be considered, including nursing homes, congregate liv-ing, supportive services, apartment complexes for the elderly, and day hospitals. What decision would you make?

IMMIGRATION

To understand immigration to the United States, it must be placed within the global context in which great movements of people arise from the accelerating process of global integration. Movements of commodities and capital are followed by move-ments of people. In addition, cultural interchanges, improved transportation, and the electronic media also lead to migrations. A part of history from earliest times, world-wide migrations have grown in volume since 1945, particularly after the mid-1980s. Growing inequalities of wealth between earth's northern and southern hemispheres impel a search for better living standards. The end of the Cold War and economic upheavals also led to massive movements in Europe and may do so as well in Asia. Furthermore, ethnic conflicts and the creation of new free trade zones contributed to the pace of migrations.

The International Organization for Migration estimated in 1990 that more than 80 million persons were migrants in that year alone, out of which 15 million were refugees and asylum seekers. For perspective, this number is equal to the entire pop-ulation of United Germany. The general tendencies of migration are globalization, ac-celeration, different types simultaneously, and greater participation by women.[26]

American immigration takes place within the context of these great global movements. During the first decade of the twentieth century, immigrants arrived in the United States at the rate of 10.4 persons per 1,000 U.S. population. From 1991 through 1995, this ratio diminished from 7.2 to 2.7, a substantial decrease.[27] Following the Immigration Act (1924), sometimes referred to as the Quota Act, the sparse immigration that did exist was based on nationality quotas that favored western Europeans and restricted Asian, Pacific, eastern and southern Europeans, and practically excluded Africans. After 40 years, political pressures led to revision of immigration policy. The 1965 amendments to the Immigration and Nationality Act were related to the civil rights thrust of the 1960s and abolished the discriminatory national origins quota system. As a result, the nature of the immigrating populations changed, although the reason for their coming had not altered: They came seeking better opportunities for themselves and their families.

The immigration flow was not simply a result of individual decisons and actions. As a receiving country, the United States was not passive, and the international activities of businesses and government encouraged immigration. In a way, the 1965 liberalization was impelled by the civil rights revolution taking place internally and was a continuation of this pattern externally. From 1951 to 1960, 92 percent of legal immigrants arrived from the Americas and Europe. In contrast, almost 86 percent of legal immigrants who arrived from 1981 to 1986 came from Asia and the Americas, and only 11 percent came from Europe.

The renewal of mass migration to the United States occurred during a period of expanded U.S. economic and military activity in Asia, Central America, and the Caribbean basin. Furthermore, the United States is at the heart of worldwide investment linkages, all of which encouraged immigration.[28] Surging immigration from Mexico, Central and South America, the Caribbean, and Asia stimulated intense feelings and debates. According to some observers, the only comparable intercontinental migration, heretofore, was the migration of enslaved Africans to the Americas and the Caribbean. Even so, the contemporary numbers are relatively small when compared with the mass migrations of the nineteenth century.[29]

The relative rate of immigration is much lower now since the population is almost three times larger than it was then. With the exception of two years in the 1990s (6.1 and 7.2 per 1,000), the rate hovered around 3 per 1,000. These rates are far short of the rate from 1901–1910.[30]

In 1986 the Immigration Reform and Control Act implemented an amnesty program for undocumented immigrants who lived continuously in the United States since 1982, provided access to permanent legal resident status for Cuban and Haitian entrants who lived in the United States before 1982, provided for a special agricultural workers registry, and an update for undocumented persons living in the United States before 1972. The Act was aimed at controlling illegal immigration, a great concern of many citizens.

More than three-quarters of the immigrants in the 1980s settled in six states, and more than half settled in just eight metropolitan areas. Unlike past immigrants, more than 80 percent now are from Latin America and Asia. Minority immigrants are now settling in coastal ports of entry such as San Francisco, Boston, and Miami, while whites disperse to other regions.

The arrival of these new immigrants brought diverse cultural, racial, social, and economic backgrounds. It also brought controversies about the cultural and political impact of immigration and raised the question of whether immigration is a problem for the society. There are both proponents and critics of immigration. Critics argue that there was no shortage of labor when the liberalization took effect in 1960s. Furthermore, the increase in immigration took place when the baby boomers were entering the job market in growing numbers. The new immigrants were disproportionately poor, uneducated, unskilled, members of racial and ethnic groups, settling in central cities and lacking reading, writing, and English speaking skills. In fact, they had lower educational qualifications and poorer job skills than earlier immigrants. Concurrently, new jobs being created were knowledge based in a service economy. The jobs being created demanded communication skills and were geographically scattered. Simultaneously, the labor market was challenged to purge itself of past discrimination and integrate previously excluded groups, including the accommodation of an unprecedented labor force participation by women. Finally, all this was taking place when the economy was opened to foreign competition for the first time and productivity was needed to remain competitive, for real wages to increase, and for jobs to stay within the country's borders. According to this point of view, mass immigration was in direct conflict with the nation's economic objectives.[31] Other critics suggested that important values were at stake, including the standard of living of the existing American population, equity, preservation or modification of the existing American culture, ethnic and class conflict, and the power of the United States in international affairs.

Those who seek a reduction in legal immigration view such cuts as a tool also to cut illegal immigration. They argue that whole industries exploit compliant immigrant labor, deteriorating working conditions for all workers in those industries. Also, they claim some results of mass immigration were the reversal of the long trend of rising wages, real wages for workers were depressed, and poverty increased. An aggressive civil rights program for Americans was modified, and community cultures were changed against the wishes of the inhabitants. Population growth affected the environment. Further, immigration has contributed to an increasing disparity between the rich and the poor, and increasing poverty fueled crime and social disintegration.[32]

Proponents suggested that as a result of a declining U.S. fertility rate, the legal immigration accounts for a substantial number of new and needed additions to the population. Some point to the creation of additional jobs, infusion of capital, and the increased ability of United States businesses to compete internationally. Immigrants pay taxes and contribute to social insurance funds. Also, they contribute to the cultural diversity of American society. Others point out that the military power of the United States is linked to immigration and the size of the population. Further, immigrants enhance foreign relations with particular nations, and their welcome in America is viewed as a moral force in the perceptions of those in other nations who observe U.S. actions.

Proponents also argue that the aggregate impact of immigration on the United States economy is not large. Immigration may be large in absolute terms but small relative to the United States labor force. Immigrants substitute for less skilled workers but may also bring wealth and new needed skills. The effects of their immigration become distributed and smoothed quickly in the U.S. economy as both labor and capital are highly mobile and the effect of new immigrants is quickly dissipated.[33] There are many critics of immigration, some of whom wish to remove all illegal immigrants and stop or substantially reduce the number of legal immigrants. Others wish to encourage immigration based on the belief that immigration is good for the United States, traditionally has enriched the nation, and is needed. Some radicals argue impractically there ought to be completely free and open borders and that people throughout the world should have the right to migrate to any nation of their choice.

However, other forces argue for particular changes. The Immigration Act of 1990 continued the emphasis on family relationships as the dominant criterion for immigration but tilted and increased the emphasis on employment-based entry—priority workers, professionals with advanced degrees, skilled workers, special categories such as foreign medical school graduates, and investors with large sums. These new emphases are consistent with a view that immigration policy should be a human resource development policy.

Some cities and regions are heavily affected by immigration, including California, Florida, Illinois, New Jersey, New York, and Texas. Studies in Los Angeles County found that the influx of Mexican immigrants had no adverse effect on unemployment but the reason was that there was a mass net out-migration of non-Hispanic whites. However, some wage depression was attributed to immigrants.[34]

Opposition flares up in particular locations as happened with Proposition 187 in California. California, beset by a recession, passed a proposition that sought to stem the flow of illegal aliens into the state, to encourage illegal residents to go home, and to bar anyone not a citizen, legal permanent resident, or legal temporary visitor from receiving public social services, health care, and education. Parenthetically, the law imposed three duties on service providers—to verify the immigration status of all who seek services, promptly inform state officials and the Immigration and Naturalization Service about whoever is "determined or reasonably suspected to be" violating immigration law, and notify them of their illegal status (or parent/guardian). There have been legal challenges to this proposition at both the state and federal levels.[35] Congress in the mid-1990s also moved to deprive not only illegal but also legal immigrants of some income maintenance and medical benefits. For the nation as a whole, the immigration of unskilled workers may have a negative effect on the wages of native unskilled workers. However, the reduction in the average wage for unskilled workers may preserve or expand certain industries in the United States that otherwise would not be able to survive international competition. Also, native workers may get new jobs as forepersons, managers, professionals, and government workers that would not have existed otherwise. There is no consensus on the total, both direct and indirect, of the net fiscal impact of immigration to the United States. However, there is agreement that the total net fiscal impact for the federal government is more positive than the impact on state and local governments.[36] There is a question as to whether immigration policy should be more restrictive or more liberal and what the criteria for selection should be. The bipartisan Commission on Immigration Reform authorized by the Immigration Act of 1990 recommended in 1995 reducing legal immigration by a third and shifting visa priorities. The major aims should continue to reunify families, to provide employers an opportunity to recruit foreign workers to meet labor needs, and to respond to humanitarian crises around the world. Priority should be given to nuclear family members—spouses and minor children of U.S. citizens, parents of U.S. citizens, and spouses and minor children of lawful permanent residents. Immigrants should be chosen on the basis of the skills they contribute to the U.S. economy (except for nuclear family reunifications or humanitarian admissions). Those who are without a high school degree are to be discouraged. Steps should be taken to curb unlawful immigration and management of the system improved.[37]

There are those who propose the emphasis on family relations continue as the major criterion. Others favor a skills-based admission policy and suggest that immigration ought to be directly contributive to the economy. There is an ongoing contest among states, agribusiness, manufacturing, humanitarian groups, unions, ethnic organizations, zero-population growth advocates, and others, each with their own agendas. U.S. policy attempts to balance economic, political, and humanitarian trade-offs. The result of immigration, however, is a greater pluralism with all that it connotes, both positive and divisive.

Implications

Immigration and its surrounding issues raise a number of issues for social workers and social welfare. At one policy level, education is needed to clarify the choices before the nation and before individual practitioners. This requires becoming familiar with the terminology and status of immigrants because benefits and services depend on their status. We have focused here on *immigrants*, those individuals lawfully granted permission to reside permanently in the United States. Many immigrants have sponsors—persons or organizations guaranteeing economic support for the first three years of residence in the United States. A *temporary resident* has legal permission to live and work temporarily in the United States. An *undocumented person* is a person who has no current legal authorization to be in the United States. A *refugee* is a person who is outside of and unwilling to avail himself or herself of the protection of the home country because of persecution or fear of persecution on account of race, religion, nationality, membership in a particular social group, or political opinion. An *asylee* is a refugee who applies for this status from U.S. territory, whereas a refugee applies for asylum from another country. A *parolee* is a person who is admitted to the United States under emergency conditions or is admitted because the person's entry is considered in the public interest.[38]

A second policy level focuses on those services assisting immigrants to adjust and integrate themselves into the United States. This requires that institutional supports are available that make it possible for social workers to orientate immigrants to local customs, services, and resources. In general, immigration is a time of crisis, and immigrants need help in system negotiation. These require language, job skills, housing, and accessible services.

To the extent possible, programs are needed that familiarize immigrants with naturalization processes, tenant organizing, legal services, information and referral, and job training and development. Culturally sensitive programs can assist immigrants with parenting, prevention of domestic violence, family conflict management, after-school programs for children and adolescents, intergenerational communication, health care, home health care, and day care. All these services need to be provided in a sensitive and congruent manner by personnel prepared to "tune in."[39]

Regarding cultural awareness in policy, program design, and service delivery, social work and social welfare have made great strides in preparing programs for ethnically diverse populations. However, in addition to the culture immigrants bring with them, those designing and delivering services need greater understanding of the context of immigrants' former lives and their immigrant experiences. Such knowledge enables those working with immigrants to be more effective in their work with people whose life experiences have involved crossing international borders. Knowledge about the decision to migrate, settlement experiences, and social, economic, and political links to the country of origin all can assist helpers to understand the immigrant experience and provide appropriate and timely services.

To gain such knowledge requires becoming familiar with the informal and formal social welfare services of their home country. Knowledge of the informal resources enables service providers (1) to promote informal caregiving as an alternative to some formal services where appropriate, (2) to link or integrate formal and informal caregiving, and (3) to employ community caregivers to deliver services.

In regard to formal services, immigrants based on their experiences in their countries of origin may lack familiarity, view such services as stigmatized, be confused by the disconnected "patchwork" of services. Furthermore, the identification of services used in the country of origin may help to target ways to connect immigrants in the United States to both formal and informal service providers. Finally, understanding how immigrants seek help and react to services may suggest alternative service models for the United States.[40]

Although there are major cultural differences among those who arrive from different societies, there is an important caveat about individual groups as well. A student of Filipino culture suggested it is difficult to offer generalizations that apply to the Filipino community as a whole. They are a diverse population as to the time of their personal or family arrival, differ in socio-economic background, educational level, language, factors surrounding immigration, dialect, geographic origin, social class, and levels of acculturation. It is helpful to keep in mind that the diversity within the group is true as well for all immigrant groups.[41]

Finally, as suggested by Yolanda Padilla, social workers should adopt a national political stance on social welfare legislation that threatens to adversely affect vulnerable immigrant populations, become involved in the legislative process, and organize for community-based services as well as form coalitions to respond to relevant social welfare legislation.[42]

Persons with Disabilities

For many persons in American society, "people with severe or multiple disabilities are invisible,"[43] and their daily frustrations and struggles with everyday activities go unremarked. Nevertheless, the number of persons with disabilities is large. In 1994, there were 29.4 million disabled persons, almost half with severe disabilities.[44] The following year, there were 16.8 million Americans from 16 to 64 years of age with work disabilities, slightly more than 10 percent of the population.[45] Furthermore, in 1995, 4.2 million disabled workers and their dependents were recipients of Social Security disability payments.[46] In 1995, 2.2 million disabled veterans received compensation payments as a result of service-connected disabilities.[47] In that same year, there were almost 5 million disabled persons receiving Supplemental Security Income (SSI) and others receiving General Assistance. So those with disabilities may not be on the public's radar screen, but there are many of them, as well as their dependents.

When we speak of persons with disabilities, we include a vast array of people with differing abilities, types of disabilities, and different numbers and degrees of disability, ranging from minor to severe impairments. Among those with disabilities, there are a variety of physically functional limitations such as hearing, seeing, and speaking, as well as developmental and mental problems.

There are definitional problems regarding disabilities. What is viewed as a physical or health condition by many persons may not be understood as a limitation by others. Nevertheless, definitions are important in many ways. Definitions and assessments are used to make decisions about health care, eligibility for educational and training services, Social Security disability, SSI, and other programs and services. In general, a disability refers to any long- or short-term reduction of a person's activity that results from an acute or chronic condition that interferes with the ability to perform the activity in the manner and range considered normal.

It is not possible here to review all disabling limitations, nor the specific histories of the ways in which our society has dealt with each of them. Although there have been improvements, in general, community members are uncomfortable with and about persons with disabilities. This discomfort ranges from mild reactions to stigmatization, stereotyping, and avoidance. Several social policies have been enacted as legislation and have moved our society toward the goal of normalization for the greatest number possible of those with disabilities. Many of those concerned with the disabled have an additional goal their empowerment to obtain their rights, access, and services as needed.

Civil Rights

During the past 30 years, the United States gradually reduced legal barriers based on race, religion, sex, and national origin. The Americans with Disabilities Act (ADA) removed barriers that deny equal opportunities to individuals with disabilities. Sponsored by Senator Lowell Weicker (R-Conn.) and Representative Tony Coelho (D-Calif.), the legislation became law in July 1990.

The act, amalgamating the Civil Rights Act (1964) and the Rehabilitation Act (1973), provides civil rights protections for persons with disabilities parallel to those established by the federal government for women and minorities. One provision of the act prohibits discrimination against individuals with disabilities in public- and private-sector employment. This part of the act requires employers to make reasonable accommodations to the known physical or mental limitations of a qualified applicant or employee, unless the accomodation would impose an undue hardship on the employer.

A second provision of the act seeks to ensure that individuals with disabilities have access to transportation. Still another provision provides that public accommodations ensure access and includes business establishments, educational institutions, recreational facilities, and social service centers. The act, however, exempts religious organizations from the public accommodations requirements.

The act amended the Communications Act (1934) to require that telephone companies provide telecommunications relay services to permit speech- or hearing-impaired persons to have opportunities for communication equivalent to those provided by other customers.

Malinda Orlin reviewed the ADA in order to identify the act's implications for providers of social services. Agencies are required to make reasonable modifications of their policies and procedures in order to attain the act's aims. These aims include making architectural and communication changes that remove barriers to the service for persons with disabilities. Also, the goal is full participation by people with disabilities, so agencies need to examine their operations to identify barriers that reduce the participation of those with disabilities. Those who serve persons with disabilities need to be certain they review all facets of their agencies to best achieve the aims of the act and also empower them to the highest extent possible.[48]

The largest group of persons in poverty are those with disabilities. More than one in six (17.8 percent) of persons 15 to 69 years of age with a work disability is poor.[49] There are several income security programs that assist persons with disabilities. Social Security Disability Insurance and Supplemental Security Income were discussed in chapter 9. Their importance is reflected in the total number of their beneficiaries, including disabled workers, spouses, children, the aging, and those who may be ineligible for Social Security, including those who are blind and otherwise disabled.

Family and Medical Leave Act

The Family and Medical Leave Act (1993) is designed to balance the demands of the workplace with the needs of families through entitling employees to take reasonable leave for medical reasons or for the care of a child, spouse, or parent. This program is only available for workers in businesses with 50 or more employees.

The poverty of some persons with disabilities is a result of difficulties finding employment because of discrimination and other barriers. Sandra Kopels pointed out the potential power of the ADA for alleviating the problems of some persons with disabilities and specifically identifies Title I as an advocacy tool to help reduce poverty and discrimination for this group. Title I prohibits employers with 15 or more employees from discriminating against qualified individuals with disabilities—just because they have disabilities—in job application procedures, hiring, advancement, compensation, job training, and other conditions of employment.[50] In fact, the Supreme Court found unanimously that disabled state prisoners are covered against discrimination by the ADA.[51]

The ADA was passed by a Democratic Congress and signed into law by a Republican President, George Bush. There are people who see the law as positive and those who find fault with it. As a result of the act, persons with disabilities have attained a greater ability to find employment, travel, enjoy recreation with their children, and participate in life more fully. Some point to the benefits to businesses that hire those with disabilities, seek to sell goods or services to them, and to the utility for the general population of technologies intended originally to help the disabled such as computer speech-recognition programs. Others complain about unnecessary expenses attributable to a national building code that requires building access even where sparsely used. Some national legislators have called for rewriting the law to more narrowly define what is considered a disability.

Children, Learning, and Social Participation

Federal laws require that every student has a right to free and appropriate public education. The landmark Education for All Handicapped Children Act (1975) first opened the doors for children with disabilities to free and appropriate education in the public schools by providing funds to enable local school districts to provide such education without cost to the students' parents and regardless of the severity or type of disability. No child was to be denied an education because of perceived educability. Prior to this legislation, many students with disabilities were either excluded from public schools or, if in the public system, were educated in segregated and separate facilities. Educational programs, where they existed, were viewed as custodial rather than educational.

The Rehabilitation Act (1973) required that all children—those with and without disabilities—be treated equally whether in regular or special education settings. Also, the ADA (1990) required state and local governments to make their programs and services accessible to qualified persons with disabilities.

The Individuals with Disabilities Education Act (1990) requires that children with disabilities be mainstreamed in educational institutions unless the severity of their disability or the need for special services and supports precludes satisfactory progress in regular classrooms. Among the children considered disabled are those with mental retardation; hearing, visual, orthopedic, and other chronic or acute health impairments; the speech-impaired; seriously emotionally disturbed; as well as those with specific learning disabilities. This type of legislation is based on the assumption that children with disabilities will benefit both educationally and in social interaction when they are included in the ordinary educational classroom setting and not placed in what many consider to be isolating and stigmatizing settings.

The services to be provided to a particular child are determined on a case-by-case basis following a school evaluation process, which must be consented to in writing by the parents. Within 30 days of the completion of the evaluation process, an individualized education program (IEP) must be prepared and presented in a meeting that includes one or both parents and the team of professional educators.

The results of several studies suggest that mainstreaming has not improved the social relations and interactions of children with disabilities. These studies have shown that nondisabled children are less accepting and direct more negative behaviors toward children with disabilities. In addition, children with disabilities are frequently ignored or excluded from activities. Furthermore, the nondisabled children often assume adult roles in relation to children with developmental disabilities, in this way undermining the potential of child-to-child interactions. These findings suggest that mainstreaming children with disabilities requires support systems and social skills programs as part of the provision of opportunities for the development of friendships.[52]

General Social Services for Persons with Disabilities

The chief goals of social services for this varied group of persons are normalization and empowerment so they can participate as fully as possible in society—educationally, vocationally, as well as socially. Basic to all services is the concept of empowerment so that persons with disabilities will know the rights to which they are entitled and have access to assistance when needed for advocacy of their rights. There is a special role for social workers to advance understanding of ADA rights by individuals with disabilities and/or other significant persons, while recognizing the difference between social work advocacy and legal advocacy. One result of education and advocacy for the pursuit of legal rights should be greater employment and other rewards, greater financial and pyschological resources, and more options regarding lifestyles.[53] Associated services are efforts aimed at overcoming community rejection and stereotyping of those with disabilities, a major force that supports resistance to mainstreaming and other normalization efforts. During the 1980s, attempts were made to remove Social Security benefits from persons with disabilities. During the 1990s, efforts were made to deny SSI to children with disabilities and to deny benefits to *legal* immigrants with disabilities. Efforts such as these are influenced by the cultural representation of persons with disabilities and suggest social workers have an important role in overcoming such cultural representations.[54]

Among other social services provided are, as appropriate, education, employment, and a variety of work opportunities, including sheltered workshops. Vocational rehabilitation is of assistance for those who are in need of this service. Other services include group homes, nursing homes, residential treatment facilities, day-care centers, hospitals and health care, Meals-on-Wheels, home health services, homemaker services, transportation, improved access to buildings and other resources, and counseling for both individuals and families.

ALTERNATIVES FACING THE PRACTITIONER

Policy choices are not just made at the macro level, although as one reads about social programs the policy choices are most often discussed at this high level. But social workers at the "line" level and in supervisory positions also influence policy choices that affect services.

For example, the staff at a community center meets to set fees for a day camp service. There are serious policy decisions to be weighed. If no fee is charged, there will be insufficient funds to fully support the program and fewer children will be served. Also, the day camp may take on a "charity" flavor in the locality, and those children who do attend may be stigmatized. If a high fee is charged, perhaps based on the full cost of the program, only 20 or 30 percent of the families can pay this full fee. As a result, there will have to be a means test for the other 70 or 80 percent of families to use the service. Stigma usually accompanies such tests, and some people will probably pay less than they should; others will forego the service rather than submit to a test.

Thus do problems of universal versus selective service touch every level. In the case cited, the staff may decide on a low fee for all. This gives clients the dignity of contributing to a service, brings in some income, and minimizes the number who cannot pay and need a means test. Or the decision may be for a higher fee to maximize income, with a low fee available on a simple declaration of need. But the choices are not simple. If the service is made universally available, this decision will reduce the question of stigma but also will reduce the possibility of aiming the program specifically at a group of children who may need the program and its services most. On the other hand, if the day camp is aimed at those children who are most needy, one sacrifices inclusivity for serving the needs of a special group, thus running the risk of demeaning the quality of the service and perhaps fostering divisive feelings in the community. Serving the poor, the middle class, or the wealthy in such situations may be a question of balance, not a question of either/or. But this too depends on the goals that one has in a community for the service provided. The population served and the needs to be met determine, finally, what the choices and the shadings of choices will be.

Suppose a staff member of a community mental health center is seeking apartments for people who have been hospitalized for mental illness. Because of community resistance to this kind of program, in spite of all the community education that has been attempted, she is having great difficulty in locating apartments for people waiting to be discharged from hospitals. An urban university has space in its dormitories for a few groups of three or four mental patients. For a variety of reasons the worker is reluctant. The dormitory community is less of a natural community than the surrounding neighborhood. It will be harder for the patients to integrate. There will be times when the dormitories are vacant, and the patients will be living in a kind of a ghost town. Here the worker is struggling with the dilemma of vertical versus horizontal adequacy. If she maintains her principles about getting the best possible service, she will have fewer group homes available; or the ones she finds will be closer to the desirable pattern but more people will be left behind in the mental institution. If she sacrifices vertical adequacy for horizontal adequacy, more patients can be discharged to halfway houses and can have a chance at integration, but in a less-desirable setting. One has to weigh the gains and losses in each case in making this kind of decision.

As another example, suppose the parents who use a day-care center are dismayed by the cost. The worker attempts to move them toward social action to pressure the state office to provide more adequate funding for the day-care center. However, the parents, in part despairing of that kind of change, volunteer to do supplementary fund-raising and to provide all the amenities missing in the day-care center. Is this step to be encouraged? It could provide the improvement in services needed, but it is not equitably financed. What should be done?

All these cases are attempts to illustrate that the "line" worker in day-to-day practice is faced with social welfare decisions not unlike those described on the macro level throughout this book. This is not a text on practice methodology, and therefore we will not get into a description of how a worker effects social change and social policy. But it is important to know that workers are involved in social policy on the micro level at least and that they need to be armed with analytic tools to help them decide on the directions in which they will press, using the skills learned in other courses and from other texts. How important this can be is perhaps best illustrated in the earlier example of how guideline writers in the War on Poverty may have shaped the whole "maximum feasible participation" component of the effort in ways never anticipated by the legislators. It is clear from this that what each social worker does in each situation makes a difference. Perhaps the point of this entire book has been that what each citizen and what each social worker knows can make a difference, and what that citizen or social worker does can contribute to the general welfare. In the following section, we introduce how technological tools can be used in social action to attain important goals.

Technology and Social Action

The United States has a rich history of community organizing, social action, lobbying, and community development as individuals, groups, and communities work to improve their world.[55] Jack Rothman and John E. Tropman identified methods for changing systems above the level of the individual, group, and family, that is organizations, neighborhoods and communities, regions and states, and national systems. A major model for community organization practice is *social action* that attempts to shift power relationships and resources and seeks basic institutional change to improve conditions for disadvantaged populations, enhance social justice, minimize deprivations, and reduce inequities.[56]

Community organization involves active, voluntary engagement of citizens as individuals and groups to change problematic conditions and to influence policies and programs that affect the quality of their lives or the lives of others.[57]

For generations, community organizers used meetings, phones, mailings, telegrams, and other means to organize and affect problematic conditions, using various strategies. Recently technologies have expanded and powerful new tools are available to serve community and political groups.

Although basic organizing methods and strategies do not differ from those used in the past, the significant difference today is speed and efficiency. On a local level, new means of organizing can enhance organizing efforts of working people, women, ethnic and cultural minorities, the poor, and the disadvantaged.[58] Today, there is almost no group that does not have access themselves or through others to new technologies for communication, organization, and influence. Similarly, political action at regional, state, and federal levels may follow the same organizing principles as earlier, but the speed and ability to target decision makers have been enhanced.

New technologies can play a part in every stage of community organization and social action. Here is an abbreviated outline of such methods:

1. Problem identification and data/information gathering;
2. Identifying relevant persons and institutions by interest and/or involvement in the problem at local, state, region, national, and international level;
3. Selecting appropriate strategies and objectives to resolve or at least reduce the problem;
4. Targets to achieve change;
5. Involving persons, groups, and organizations in the organizing and advocacy effort;
6. Implementing the strategy; and
7. Monitoring and evaluating the results, identifying additional problems, and making on-course corrections.

New technologies that can be used at each of the preceding stages are computers (email, the Internet, World Wide Web, conferencing and message disks), teleconferencing, faxes, videoconferencing, and videotapes. In addition, it is possible to use the mass media as aids to organizing efforts. Use of the media requires skill at reaching them and getting them to enhance in appropriate ways the community organization and social action efforts. Organizers can obtain information: governmental statistics and reports, input from organizations concerned with the problem area, and finding and obtaining reports from persons with the same concerns. They can track problems though community bulletin boards, teleconferencing, and email.

Technology can be used, for example, to obtain demographic and census data, for voter registration; voter targeting; analysis of voter turnout; voting patterns; lobbying efforts; tenant, environmental, and other organizing; identifying "swing" election districts; obtaining profiles of voters; testing messages; and making personal appeals. Evidence supportive of the organizing effort can be obtained from relevant sources, including official documents, legislation, court rulings, administrative regulations, statistical data. One can obtain information as to who would be an active ally, an opponent, or be uninvolved, or who sits "on the fence" and might be open to involvement. As with all organizing, the message can be individualized and the delivery of the message can be specifically aimed and delivered as needed. Furthermore, technology can enhance "getting one's message across," an organizing campaign's fund-raising ability, and the way an organizing effort markets its program.

These technologies can be used for coalition building and also as a means for targeting influentials, contacting local, state, and national legislatures, government officials, courts, and those who administer policy and programs. Not only can one send messages, but the fact that the message was received can be confirmed. Use of the computer and other technologies does not rule out the use of traditional means to organize and advocate, such as one-on-one meeting with influentials; establishing a power base through individuals, groups, and coalitions; group visits; letters; telephone drives; debates; community meetings; written and oral testimony; and *amicus* briefs for courts. Preparation of computer disks or videotapes also hold promise as being useful at various stages of an organizing effort.[59]

Mass media can also play a part in community organizing and social action. Among the potential tools are network television, national and local newspapers, journals, and cable television. Among the organizing aims are educating the public and influential segments regarding the needs and/or problem; providing accurate information; interpreting the organizing effort's goals, characteristics, and activities; and educating regarding the desirability of change. Use of the media requires the skillful development of contacts, including reporters; obtaining opportunities for interviews; news releases; letters to editors; radio and TV appearances.[60]

WHERE WE ARE

As the United States approaches the end of the century, the nation is going through a period of intense social, political, and economic change. For a brief time, the peaceful ending of the Cold War—so long the nation's greatest threat and cost—provided hope that in the long term a peace dividend (more resources) would be made available to meet the nation's needs. In fact, for the first time since 1969, the federal budget had a surplus and a debate began as to how to use it. There were three positions: pay off the debt, cut taxes, and spend more on social needs and repairing the physical infrastructure. President Clinton insisted the surplus should be used to protect Social Security and, by implication, to secure adequate financing for Medicare.

During June 1998, the Federal Reserve described the performance of the U.S. economy as excellent with brisk production, ample jobs, and low inflation and continued growth since the last recession in 1990–1991.[61] By August, the stock market had experienced major losses, purchases slowed, earnings and expected profits were down, the rate of growth decreased, exports were off, real interest rates were rising, personal debts were high, and many parts of the world were going through economic crises with rising unemployment.

Until recent years, the creation of the modern world brought with it the welfare state. The evolution of modern society is accompanied by problems that seek solutions. Whatever their economic or political system, whatever the ideologies of elites or masses, the more economically developed countries over the past century have converged in types of health and welfare programs, in increasingly comprehensive coverage, and, to a lesser extent, in methods of financing. The fraction of national resources devoted to these programs climbed, eventually at a decelerating rate.

However, the entire thrust of social welfare in the United States since the Great Depression is being challenged. One agenda focuses on private, personal solutions to problems. Many persons doubt the efficacy of government intervention and, in some instances, view such actions as destructive of individual and family values. This individualistic philosophy is based on the "can-do" American myth, which suggests that those who work hard enough can succeed, regardless of the nature of the job market and the economy. Others argue that governmental intervention is necessary to shore up the economy of the United States and other nations whose economies influence that of the United States.

Joel Blau places this debate in the context of rights and suggests the right to an entitlement is not a right accepted by all persons. The issue is the conflict between property rights and personal rights and between two political traditions. In one tradition, property serves as an economic and political counter to the state's power. Those who have a financial stake in the society can be expected to behave responsibly. This leads to civil liberties. The second tradition—the radical democratic tradition—holds that people need protection from the power of both government and private property. According to this latter tradition, such resources as medical care and affordable housing are natural rights. Conservatives support the rights of property over the rights of persons; social welfare is a form of charity delivered by the state but not a right or an absolute entitlement.[62]

There is a continuing shift in national involvement between public purpose and private interest, an oscillation between the maximization of profit, the cult of the free market, the survival of the fittest, and equality, freedom, social responsibility, and general welfare. Furthermore, as Daniel Bell suggested, the state increasingly has the double problem of aiding capital formation and growth and meeting the rising claims of citizens for income security, social services, social amenities, and the like.[63] Both liberals and conservatives intend to balance the budget but differ in their priorities and the rate of changes. Conservatives desire cuts in domestic programs and seek to diminish the size of the federal government by reducing taxes and devolving federal functions to the state level. Conservative critics charge that social welfare is too expensive, undermines the traditional family, encourages the growth of single-parent families and children born out of wedlock, has failed to reduce the number of poor persons, and encourages dependence. This conservative agenda was spelled out earlier when David Stockman, budget director for President Ronald Reagan, suggested the federal debt and annual deficits that exploded during that administration could be used as leverage to roll back federal and other governmental services, thus starving Congress of revenue.[64]

As a result of these cross currents, the administration of President Clinton and the Congress were unable to make any comprehensive changes except in the case of public assistance. The accomplishments of the Clinton presidency were incremental: more police on the streets, school uniforms becoming common, reading tutors from colleges, improved child support, standards for TV ratings, development of a national registry of sex offenders, more health care for children, 48-hour hospital stays for new mothers, Americorps, restricting tobacco sales, V chips to monitor children's TV. These accomplishments were not earth-shaking but enriched the lives of ordinary people. Also, they were congruent with the conservative tenor of the times, which opted for less government, not more.

To what extent can a capitalist society provide for a cooperative morality *and* for individualism, the enhancement of all individuals as opposed to the autonomy of some individuals? How can we achieve a proper relationship between individuals and society, freedom and planning, pluralism and shared values? What should and can be done to eliminate poverty or to deal with other social problems depends on the ideologies and values of those who make legislative decisions. A backlash has grown against social welfare provision in quite different societies. Individual responsibility is touted as the answer to economic and social problems. The advocacy of individual responsibility is emphasized in a society in which the Federal Reserve system uses unemployment to offset possible inflation, and there is a shortage of jobs at a living wage for those who are unskilled.

Some persons attribute the successes of the pro-market and anti-social welfare position to the fact that many social welfare supports are in place buffering the shock and burden of unemployment. A number of social insurance and public assistance programs are counter-cyclical in nature and come into play when recession forces begin to appear. Even so, various events have caused nations with highly developed social welfare systems to reevaluate their efforts.

These issues grow out of ideological and political values and perspectives on the nature of social welfare in a capitalist society. From one point of view, social welfare serves to repair, contain, and suppress the negative effects of the capitalist system. There are always casualties of this kind of economy as businesses enlarge, move, and lay off workers. Furthermore, the culture of capitalism leads to and depends on an individualistic ideology and morality. These then call forth the need for a second set of social welfare measures to restore social morale and a sense of community. The worldwide collapse of communism encouraged a turn to capitalist solutions to social problems. No viable political or economic alternative to democratic capitalism appears on the horizon.

The strength of the U.S. economy is critically influenced by its relationship to other nations. We live in an interdependent world in which U.S. social welfare is closely interrelated with other parts of U.S. society and, in turn, U.S. society and social welfare are influenced by developments in other nations. Perhaps we have reached a stage of recognized interdependence in which the nations of the world need to share the risks through cooperative efforts to provide for the welfare of all people.

The market and a "thousand points of light" cannot rectify injustices in a modern state or allow socially more or less unfettered forces to determine the life chances and quality of life of its members. Aside from altruistic ideas, a society such as ours requires healthy persons involved in the life of the society with high morale. Robert Heilbroner and Lester Thurow argue that when problems arise from the market process itself there is no way of coping with those problems other than by government. ". . . Therefore, all market economies must have public sectors. It is impossible to have an economic system in which government would play no role whatever in the allocation of resources, where the dollar would decide everything and the voting rights of individuals would decide nothing. What is at stake is where to draw the line, not whether to draw the line."[65]

Where the state is unable for whatever reasons to adequately confront the social problems of the day, the path leads to policy failure and is perceived as unfairness. One result is a loss of popular support for social programs. The suggestion has been made that:

> from the point of view of progressive reform, the failure of a too-small welfare state to meet people's needs has created the worst of worlds

because it has convinced many that government cannot work for them and paved the way for a symbolic politics of blame rather than a sustained effort to restructure government to make it more effective.[66]

Two Scenarios

As suggested earlier, future developments hold the key to the nature of social welfare. Essentially, there are two scenarios, both developed on the basis of technological innovations, one pessimistic and the other optimistic. The *pessimistic* perspective describes today's global unemployment as having reached a level higher than any time since the Great Depression. Computer and communication technologies are replacing humans with machines. Their impact is being felt more and more on workplaces and communities as the world traverses a great revolution. Even fewer workers will be needed to produce goods and services. In the past, when employment needs were reduced in one area of the economy, another area took up the slack. In turn, manufacturing took up the slack from agriculture, and services took up the slack from a drop in manufacturing employment. Today, all three sectors are experiencing the same technological displacement. The results of these factors are both liberating for some and destabilizing for many others.[67]

The more *optimistic* view predicts an American renaissance, a long-term economic resurgence. According to this view, the United States reinvented its economy at the end of the Cold War with new technologies. The United States has ample room for expansion, favorable demographics, and a dynamic labor market. Information technology and information will grow cheaper, to the benefit of all those who have access to them. The United States with available capital will be able to control networks and high-tech information systems. With a large and diverse population, the United States is poised to take advantage of the electronic cultural revolution, and it will be both a market and a source for new cultural ideas—music, video, and writing. With technological advantages and the ability to create and use new technologies, optimists expect the United States for the foreseeable future to lead the world into the next millenium.[68]

Our Proposal

In our view, the amelioration of poverty cannot be left to the vagaries of the marketplace. The current situation requires governmental intervention. Basic to the general welfare is the growth of the economy and improved economic conditions for individuals and families. Economic growth along with a reduction of the federal debt and deficits are essential prerequisites for combating poverty. Governmental actions are needed to redistribute wealth through income transfers, education and training, and job creation. Our aim is not equality of incomes but equal access for all Americans to basic necessities such as food, education, appropriate housing, and health care to sustain life at a decent level as well as fair opportunities to pursue a range of opportunities in a healthy environment. Continual encouragement of employment in the private sector is needed along with the public sector's serving as the employer of last resort. This is necessary so that as many people as possible can work, especially low-skilled workers and those who have sought work but have been unable to find employment. This requires enlarged labor markets, both private and public, forming a work-based safety net. In addition, the minimum wage needs to be adjusted upward to keep pace with inflation.

The use of a family or children's allowance and enhanced use of the Earned Income Tax Credit and the enhancement of TANF, child support assurance, and an increased use of "living wages" will better protect poor children and their employed parents. Income security, training and education, housing, food, health care, social services, day care, and family planning are basic programs. These fundamental programs—joined with inclusion, antidiscrimination laws, and investment in human capital—add up to a strategy that could enable the United States to move toward the minimization of poverty.

SUMMARY

Throughout this book, we have examined the impact of values and of social and economic structures on social welfare and on peoples' lives. We recognized the importance of both social and economic structures *and* individual responsibility. We believe people are responsible for their actions and behavior, if not their fates, within the boundaries of opportunity available to them. We have seen that private troubles and public issues are interrelated and people with unequal capacities encounter different obstacles (including for many people oppressive social forces) and opportunities. Illustrative of this is the finding that greater inequality in the distribution of income contributes to higher overall mortality rates and deaths from heart disease, cancer, and homicide.[69]

The elimination and diminishment of life-sustaining basic guarantees for food, housing, and other necessities is regressive and injurious to many children and adults. Such regressive actions are not consonant with the American dream of "general welfare" and will decrease the quality of life of those who need help but also diminish the rest of us as well.

QUESTIONS FOR CONSIDERATION

1. Select one social problem that interests you (and is not discussed in this chapter). Why is it a problem?
2. How has the United States (your state or community) dealt historically with the problem?
3. Can you identify any theories about the causation of the problem? Can you identify the social and economic costs of the problem? Can you identify the relevant policies, legislation, and services currently provided?
4. If the necessary resources were available, what would you suggest an ideal set of services to deal with the problem would include?

Notes

1. Sara McLanahan and Lynne Casper, "Growing Diversity and Inequality in the American Family," *State of the Union, America in the 1990s*, Vol. 2, *Social Trends*, Reynolds Farley, ed., New York: Russell Sage Foundation, 1995, pp. 1–45.

2. *1998 Green Book*, Table G-11, "Persons Living in Mother-Only Families by Mother's Marital Status, Family Living Arrangement, and Family Poverty Status: 1995," p. 1256; Leatha Lamison-White, U.S. Bureau of the Census, Current Population Reports, Series P-60-198, *Poverty in the United States: 1996*, Washington, D.C.: U.S. Government Printing Office, 1997, p. viii.

3. Aletha C. Huston, Vonnie C. McLoyd, and Cynthia G. Coll, "Children and Poverty: Issues in Contemporary Research," *Child Development*, Vol. 65, 1994, pp. 275–282.

4. Jason DeParle, "Child Poverty Twice as Likely After Family Split, Study Says," *New York Times*, March 2, 1991, p. 8.

5. Arloc Sherman, *Wasting America's Future: The Children's Defense Fund Report on the Costs of Child Poverty*, Boston: Beacon Press, 1994, pp. 13–15.

6. Keith Bradsher, "Low Ranking for Poor American Children," *New York Times*, August 14, 1995, p. A9.

7. Sheila B. Kamerman, "Gender Role and Family Structure Changes in the Advanced Industrialized West: Implications for Social Policy," in *Poverty, Inequality, and the Future of Social Policy*, Katharine McFate, Roger Lawson, and William J. Wilson, eds., New York: Russell Sage Foundation, 1995, pp. 244–245.

8. Victor R. Fuchs and Diane M. Reklis, "America's Children: Economic Perspectives and Policy Options," *Science*, Vol. 255, January 3, 1992, pp. 41–46.

9. Barbara P. Noble, "Women Seeking a Working Agenda," *New York Times*, February 5, 1995, p. F23.

10. U.S. Bureau of the Census, *Statistical Abstract of the United States: 1997*, 115th Edition, Table 14, "Resident Population, by Age and Sex: 1980 to 1996," Washington, D.C., 1997, p. 15; Ibid., Table 13, "Resident Population Characteristics—Percent Distribution and Median Age, 1850 to 1996, and Projections, 2000 to 2050," p. 14.

11. Ibid., Table 16, "Resident Population, by Sex and Age: 1996," p. 16; Ibid., Table 17, "Resident Population Projections, by Age and Sex: 1995 to 2050," p. 17.

12. Nancy S. Jecker, "Caring for the Disabled Elderly," in *Choosing Who's to Live*, James W. Walters, ed., Urbana, Ill.: University of Illinois Press, 1996, p. 77.

13. George H.S. Singer, "Trends Affecting Home and Community Care for People with Chronic Conditions in the United States," *Redefining Family Support*, George H.S. Singer, Laurie E. Powers, and Ardis L. Olsen, eds., Baltimore: Paul H. Brooke Publishing Co., 1996, p. 12.

14. Vida Y. Jones and Carroll L. Estes, "Older Women: Income, Retirement, and Health," in *Women's Health*, Sheryl B. Ruzek, Virgina L. Olesen, and Adele E. Clarke, eds., Columbus: Ohio State University Press, 1997, pp. 183–230.

15. Nancy S. Jecker, "Caring for the Disabled Elderly," in *Choosing Who's to Live*, James W. Walters, ed., Urbana, Ill.: University of Illinois Press, 1996, p. 75.

16. *Family Caregiving in the U.S: Findings from a National Survey*, Bethesda, Md.: National Alliance for Caregiving and American Association of Retired Persons, 1997.

17. Alice M. Rivlin and Joshua M. Wiener, *Caring for the Disabled Elderly*, Washington, D.C.: The Brookings Institution, 1988, p. 156.

18. *The Green Book*, 1998, p. 247.

19. U.S. Bipartisan Commission on Comprehensive Health Care, *A Call for Action*, Washington, D.C.: U.S. Government Printing Office, 1990.

20. Joshua M. Wiener and David G. Stevenson, "Long-Term Care for the Elderly: Profiles of Thirteen States," August 1998, http://newfedralism.urban.org/html/occal2.html.

21. Linda Boise, "The Demise of the Catastrophic Coverage Act: A Reflection of the Inability of Congress to Respond to Changing Needs of the Elderly and Their Families," *Journal of Sociology and Social Welfare*, Vol. XVII, No. 2, June 1990, pp. 107-123.

22. Claudia R. Campbell, "The Economics of Insurance for Long-Term Care: Can We Afford Another Entitlement?" in *Applying Health Services Research to Long-Term Care*, James C. Romeis, et al., eds., New York: Springer Publishing Co., 1996, pp. 3-22.

23. Carol Hegeman, "Models of Institutional and Community-Based Respite Care," in *Respite Care: Programs, Problems, and Solutions*, Lynn M. Tepper and John A. Toner, eds., Philadelphia: The Charles Press, Publishers, 1993, pp. 3-29.

24. Barbara J. Haupt, "An Overview of Home Health and Hospice Care Patients: 1996 National Home Care and Hospice Care Survey," *Advance Data*, U.S. Department of Health and Human Services, National Center for Health Statistics, p. 6.

25. Robert Pear, "Home-Care Denial in Medicare Cases Is Ruled Improper," *New York Times*, February 15, 1998, pp. 1, 32.

26. Stephen Castles and Mark J. Miller, *The Age of Migration*, New York: Guilford Press, 1993, pp. 3-4, 8.

27. U.S. Bureau of the Census, *Statistical Abstract of the United States: 1953*, 74th Edition, Table 101, "Immigration: 1820 to 1952," Washington, D.C., 1953, p. 97, and U.S. Bureau of the Census, *Statistical Abstract of the United States: 1997*, Table 5, "Immigration: 1901 to 1995," Washington, D.C., 1997, p. 10.

28. Saskia Sassen, *Losing Control?*, New York: Columbia University Press, 1996, pp. 59, 84.

29. Timothy J. Hatton and Jeffrey G. Williamson, *The Age of Mass Migration*, New York: Oxford University Press, 1998, pp. 3-4, 7.

30. U.S. Bureau of the Census, *Statistical Abstract of the United States: 1997*, 115th Edition, Table 5, "Immigration: 1901 to 1995," Washington, D.C., 1997, p. 10.

31. Vernon M. Briggs, Jr., "Immigration Policy and the United States Economy: An Institutional Perspective," *Journal of Economic Issues*, Vol. 30, No. 2, June 1996, pp. 376, 387-386.

32. Roy Beck, *The Case Against Immigration*, New York: W.W. Norton, 1996, pp. 10, 16, 243.

33. Barry Edmonston, ed., *Statistics of U.S. Immigration: An Assessment of Data Needs for Future Research*, Washington, D.C.: National Academy Press, 1996, p. 11.

34. David M. Heer, *Immigration in America's Future*, Boulder, Co.: Westview Press, 1996, p. 186.

35. Peter H. Schuck, "The Message of 187," *The American Prospect*, No. 21, Spring 1995, pp. 85-92.

36. David M. Heer, *Immigration in America's Future*, Boulder, Co.: Westview Press, 1996, p. 194.

37. U.S. Commission on Immigration Reform, *Report to Congress, Executive Summary*, March 7, 1998, http://www.utexas.edu/lbj/uscir.

38. Diane Drachman, "Immigration, Statuses, and Their Influence on the Service Provision, Access, and Use," *Social Work*, Vol. 40, No. 2, March 1995, pp. 188-197.

39. Ana Paulino, "Dominicans in the United States: Implications for Practice and Policies in the Human Services," *Journal of Multicultural Social Work*, Vol. 3, No. 2, 1994, pp. 53-65.

40. Margaret S. Sherraden and Judith J. Martin, "Social Work with Immigrants: International Issues in Service Delivery," *International Social Work*, Vol. 37, 1994, pp. 369–384.
41. Pauline Agbayani-Siewert, "Filipino American Culture and Family: Guidelines for Practitioners," *Families in Society*, 75, No. 7, September 1994, pp. 429–438.
42. Yolanda C. Padilla, "Immigrant Policy: Issues for Social Work Practice," *Social Work*, Vol. 42, No. 6, November 1997, pp. 595–606.
43. Stanley L. Witkin, "Chronicity and Invisibility," Editorial, *Social Work*, Vol. 43, No. 4, July 1998, p. 293.
44. *Statistical Abstract 1997*, #210, "Disability Status of Persons 21 to 64 Years Old: 1991 to 1994," p. 140.
45. *Statistical Abstract 1997*, #599, "Persons with Work Disability, by Selected Characteristics: 1995," p. 384.
46. *Statistical Abstract 1997*, #587, "Social Security (OASDI)—Benefits, by Type of Beneficiary: 1980 to 1995," p. 378.
47. *Statistical Abstract 1997*, #571, "Disabled Veterans Receiving Compensation: 1980 to 1995," p. 366.
48. Malinda Orlin, "The Americans with Disabilities Act: Implications for Social Services," *Social Work*, Vol. 40, No. 2, March 1995, pp. 233–239.
49. U.S. Bureau of the Census, *Statistical Abstract of the United States: 1995*, Table 751, "Monthly Measures of Poverty Status, by Selected Characteristics: 1990-91 Period," p. 483.
50. Sandra Kopels, "The Americans with Disabilities Act: A Tool to Combat Poverty," *Journal of Social Work Education*, Vol. 31, No. 3, Fall 1995, pp. 337–346.
51. Linda Greenhouse, "Disabled State Inmates Protected by U.S. Law Barring Discrimination," *New York Times*, June 16, 1998, p. A18.
52. Juanita B. Hepler, "Mainstreaming Children with Learning Disabilities: Have We Improved Their Social Environment?" *Social Work in Education*, Vol. 16, No. 3, July 1994, pp. 143–154.
53. Robert H. Woody, "Americans with Disabilities Act: Implications for Family Therapy," *American Journal of Family Therapy*, Vol. 21, No. 1, 1993, pp. 71–78.
54. Michael Berube, "The Cultural Representation of People with Disabilities Affects Us All," *The Chronicle of Higher Education*, May 30, 1997, pp. B4–5.
55. Charles D. Garvin and Fred M. Cox, "A History of Community Organizing Since the Civil War with Special Reference to Oppressed Communities," *Strategies of Community Organization*, 4th Edition, Fred M. Cox, John L. Ehrlich, Jack Rothman, and John E. Tropman, eds., Itasca, Ill.: F.E. Peacock Publishers, Inc., 1987, pp. 26–63.
56. Jack Rothman and John E. Tropman, "Models of Community Organization and Macro Practice Perspectives: Their Mixing and Phasing," *Strategies of Community Organization*, 4th Edition, Fred M. Cox, John L. Ehrlich, Jack Rothman, and John E. Tropman, eds., Itasca, Ill.: F.E. Peacock Publishers, Inc., 1987, pp. 3–26.
57. Dorothy N. Gamble and Marie O. Weil," "Citizen Participation," *Encyclopedia of Social Work*, 19th Edition, Richard L. Edwards, ed., Washington, D.C.: National Association of Social Workers, 1995, pp. 483–494.
58. Gary Chapman and Lodis Rhodes, "Nurturing Neighborhood Nets," *Technology Review*, October 1997, http://www.techreview.com, October 1, 1998.
59. Willard C. Richan, *Lobbying for Social Change*, New York: Haworth Press, 1996; John Downing, et al, eds., *Computers for Social Change*, New York: Haworth Press, 1991.
60. Edward A. Brawley, *Human Services and the Media*, Newbury Park, Calif.: Harwood Academic Publishers, 1995.

61. "High Praise from Fed," *The Baltimore Sun*, June 18, 1998, pp. 1D and 8D.

62. Joel Blau, "Theories of the Welfare State," *Social Service Review*, Vol. 63, No. 1, March 1989, pp. 35–36.

63. Daniel Bell, "The Future World Disorder," *The Winding Passage*, Cambridge, Mass.: Abt Books, 1980, p. 215.

64. David A. Stockman, *The Triumph of Politics*, New York: Harper & Row, 1986.

65. Robert L. Heilbroner and Lester C. Thurow, *Five Economic Challenges*, Englewood Cliffs, N.J.: Prentice Hall, 1981, pp. 55, 77.

66. Charles Noble, *Welfare As We Knew It*, New York: Oxford University Press, 1997, p. 156.

67. Jeremy Rifkin, *The End of Work: The Decline of the Global Labor Force and the Dawn of the Post-Market Era*, New York: G.P. Putnam's Sons, 1995, pp. xv–xviii.

68. Michael Moynihan, *The Coming American Renaissance*, New York: Simon & Schuster, 1996, *passim* and pp. 285–289.

69. Robert Pear, "Researchers Link Income Inequality to Higher Mortality Rates," *New York Times*, April 19, 1996, p. A26.

A P P E N D I X

Sources of Information

The following are some leads for beginning research. The first task is to be as clear as possible as to the subject you want to study, the key words (for example, employment, minimum wage) associated with the subject or other words or concepts that define the same subject (voluntarism, volunteerism, volunteers, and so on). The more specific your search, the greater the possibility the search can be useful. Bibliographical searches can be done by computer in most libraries, which lead you to books and journals, magazines, newspapers, and so on. In many cases, governmental documents will also be listed. Remember too as you read publications that their bibliographies also can supply you with additional leads.

Electronic information sources are becoming a dominant mode of exchanging information. Here are several leads. Some access is through universities and colleges. Other access is through commercial ventures.

WEB SITES ON THE INTERNET

For a comprehensive review of governmental sites, see Bruce Maxwell, *How to Access the Federal Government on the Internet, 1998,* Washington: Congressional Quarterly, 1997.

To connect directly to sites for specific *government* agencies, go to these sites:

Bureau of Labor Statistics   http://stats.bls.gov/blshome.html

U.S. Census Bureau   http://www.census.gov/

Catalog of Federal Domestic Assistance   http://www.gsa.gov/fdac/default.htm

Census State Data Centers   http://www.census.gov/ftp/pub/sdc/www/

Centers for Disease Control   www.cdcnac.org

Congressional Budget Office Studies & Reports   http://www.cbo.gov/reports.cfm

Department of Health and Human Services, Administration for Children and Families http://www.acf.dhhs.gov

Department of Health and Human Services, Research, Policy and Administration http://www.os.dhhs.gov:80/policy/index.html

Department of Health and Human Services: Childhood and Youth Policy http://aspe.os.dhhs.gov/hsp/cyphome.htm

Department of Housing and Urban Development   www.hud.gov

Department of Veterans Affairs   www.va.gov

Federal Budget   http://www.access.gpo.gov/su_docs/budget98/maindown.html

FEDSTATS   http://www.fedstats.gov

Fedworld Information Network   http://www.fedworld.gov

Health Care Financing Administration (HCFA)   http://www.hcfa.gov/

Library of Congress   http://lcweb.loc.gov/

Medicare   www.medicare.gov

National Data Archive on Child Abuse and Neglect   www.ndacan.cornell.edu/

National Institutes of Health   http://www.nih.gov

National Institute on Alcohol Abuse and Alcoholism   www.niaaa.nih.gov/

National Institute of Mental Health   http://www.nimh.nih.gov/
Nonprofit Gateway   http://www.nonprofit.gov/
Social Security Online   http://www.ssa.gov/
State and Local Government on the Net
http://www.piperinfo.com/state/states.html
Statistical Abstract of the U.S.   http://www.census. gov/statab/www/
THOMAS: Legislative Information   http://thomas.loc.gov/
U.S. House of Representatives   http://www.house.gov/
U.S. Senate   http://www.senate.gov/
White House   http://www.whitehouse.gov/

Nongovernment Sites

AIDS   www.hopkins-aids.edu
American Association of Retired Persons   www.aarp.org
American Public Welfare Association   www.apwa.org
Center on Budget and Policy Priorities   www.cbpp.org
Center for Law and Social Policy   www.clasp.org
Center for the Study of Issues in Public Mental Health   www.rfmah.org/csipmh/
Center for Substance Abuse Prevention   www.covesoft.com/csap.html
Children Now   www.childrennow.org
Child Welfare League of America   http://cwla.org/
Child Welfare Resource Center   http://www.child welfare.ca
Children's Defense Fund   cdfupdate@childrensdefense.org
Citizens Budget Committee   www.epn.org/cbc/
Citizens for Tax Justice   www.ctj.org
Council on State Governments   www.csg.org
The Electronic Policy Network   www.epn.org
Mental Health Net   http://cmhc.com/   http://cmhc.com??
National Aging Information Center   http://www.aoa.dhhs.gov/naic/
National Alliance for the Mentally Ill   www.nami.org.
National Association of Developmental Disabilities Councils
www.igc.apc.org/NADDC/
National Association of Social Workers   http://www.naswdc.org
National Clearinghouse for Alcohol and Drug Information   www.health.org/
index.htm
National Federation of the Blind   www.nfb.org
Social Work and Social Services Web Sites   http://gwbweb.wustl.edu/websites.html
The National Governors' Association   www.nga.org
The Society for Prevention Research   http://www.oslc.org/spr/sprhome.html
The Urban Institute   www.urban.org
The Welfare Information Network   www.welfareinfo.org
Welfare Law Center   http://www.welfarelaw.org

ENCYCLOPEDIA/HANDBOOKS

Encyclopedia of Social Work
Statistical Abstract of the United States
Social Work Dictionary
Social Work Almanac

INDEXES/ABSTRACTS

The following sources are available in both computerized and print formats:

Social Work Research and Abstracts
PAIS International
Psychological Abstracts
Monthly Catalog of U.S. Government Publications
New York Times Index
Washington Post Index

SERIAL PUBLICATIONS

Brookings Review
Child Welfare
Congressional Quarterly Weekly Report
Journal of Health and Social Policy
Journal of Policy Analysis and Management
Journal of Sociology and Social Welfare
Monthly Labor Review
New York Times
OECD in Figures: Statistics on the Member Countries (Organization for Economic Co-Operation and Development)
Policy Studies Journal
Policy Studies Review
Population Bulletin
Public Welfare
Social Security Bulletin
Social Security Bulletin, Annual Statistical Supplement
Social Service Review
Social Work
Social Security Throughout the World
Washington Post

OTHER SOURCES OF INFORMATION

Federal Information Center (800-688-9889) for information about taxes, Social Security benefits, governmental publications, federal programs, agencies, and services, and so on.

GOVERNMENT DOCUMENTS

Here are the Superintendent of Documents classification codes of some useful sources in a Government Documents section. (Note some libraries may classify these materials with their regular collection.)

Bureau of the Census: C3.612:IN 2/5/994

Joint Economic Committee of the Congress: Y4.EC 7:D 36/14

Joint Committee on Taxation: Y4.T 1914-10:995-99

House of Representatives Committee on Education and Labor: Y4.ED 8/1:103-77

Senate Committee on Labor and Human Resources: Y4.L 11/4:S.HRG

House of Representatives Committee on Ways and Means: Y4.W 36:10-7/994

Department of Health and Human Services: HE 1.1/2:993-94

Department of Labor: L1.1:993

Bureau of Labor Statistics: L2.2:OC1/53

National Center for Health Statistics: HE 20.6202:H 34/15

National Institute of Mental Health: HE 20.8102:AN 9

National Institute on Aging: HE 20.3852:AL 9/5

National Institute on Drug Abuse: HE 20.8202:EP 4/3/992

President of the United States: PR 42.2:   P 31

Social Security Administration: HE 3.1:994

Substance Abuse and Mental Health Services Administration: HE 20.8008:AL 1/11

Women's Bureau: L36.114/3:94-1

INDEX

famine, 38
welfare benefits, 38
Middle Ages, late
beggars, 44, 47
Bubonic Plague, 43–44
cities, 42
contracts, 40
famines, 38
foundations, 41
free laborers, 43
guilds, 41, 44
hospitals, 41
laborers, 43–44
law and order, 43
landowners, 41
new freedom, 43
religious orders, 41
Statute of Laborers (1349), 43
status, 40
tithing, 42
trade, 42
urbanization, 42
vagrants, 40
wages, 43
Middle Ages, middle
economic activity, 39
relation to landowners, 39–40
treatment of the poor, 40
village revolts, 40
Midgley, James, 143
Milford Conference, 310, 314, 334
Mills, C. Wright, 2, 9
Minimum wage, 187, 395
Monasteries, 29, 32, 39, 41, 47, 51, 56, 65
Monetary policy, 125–126
Montagu, Ashley, 11
Moore, Stephen, 345
Mothers' Pensions, 98
Moynihan, Daniel Patrick, 93, 332
Muckrakers, 89
Multiplier effect, 128
Murray, Charles, 117
Mutual Aid, 2, 20–22
Mutual aid societies, 71–73
Myths
frontier, 7, 71
hero, 5
idealized, 6
immigrants, 71

individualism, 5, 72
loner, 5

National Association of Social Workers,
313–314, 337–338
National Conference of Charities and Correc-
tion, 312
National Institute of Mental Health, 273
National society, 352
National Youth Administration, 91
Native Americans, 8, 73–76
General Allotment Act (1887), 75
Indian Reorganization Act (1934), 75
Northwest Ordinance (1787), 74
Self-Determination and Education Assis-
tance Act (1974,1988), 75
Neanderthals, 20
Near poor, 176–177
Neo-Malthusians, 343–344
New Deal, 91, 116, 311
New Federalism, 133
New property, 360–361
New York Association for Improving the
Condition of the Poor, 69, 303
New York Charity Organization Society, 303
New York Society for the Prevention of
Pauperism, 69, 303
Nixon, Richard, 94, 99, 102
Non-profit sector, 280–282
Agency types, 281–282
Notch effect, 149
Nutrition programs 250–255
Food Stamps, 250–252
School Lunch and Breakfast, 254–255
Supplemental Food for Women, (WIC),
252–253

Ohlin, Lloyd, 92
Olasky, Marvin, 117
Older Americans Act, 120
Opportunity theory, 92
Origin of Species, The, 80
Other America, The, 92

Paine, Thomas, 88
Papell, Catherine, 315
Parents Anonymous, 281
Pauper, 26
Pensions, private, 285

A B O U T   T H E
A U T H O R S

Dr. Ralph Dolgoff
is a professor at the School of Social Work at the University of Maryland, Baltimore, where he also served as Dean. Previously, he served as acting Dean and associate Dean at the Adelphi University School of Social Work, and as senior program specialist at the Council on Social Work Education. Dr. Dolgoff is coauthor (with Frank Loewenberg) of *Ethical Decisions for Social Work Practice* (5th Edition). He has published widely on social and welfare services, ethics, social policy, and social work education.

Dr. Donald Feldstein
has had a distinguished career in Jewish Communal Service and in Social Work Education. He is the author of numerous monographs and articles in the previously mentioned fields.